Teaching Students with Severe Disabilities

DAVID L. WESTLING
The Florida State University

LISE FOX
University of South Florida

Merrill,
an imprint of Prentice Hall
Englewood Cliffs, New Jersey Columbus, Ohio

Library of Congress Cataloging-in-Publication Data
Westling, David L.
Teaching students with severe disabilities/David L. Westling and Lise Fox.
p. cm.
Includes bibliographical references and indexes.
ISBN 0-02-426581-0
1. Handicapped children—Education—United States. 2. Handicapped youth—Education—United States. 3. Handicapped—Services for—United States. 4. Special education—Vocational guidance—United States. I. Fox, Lise. II. Title.
LC4031.W47 1995 94-41684
CIP

Cover art: © Debbie McGraw, Courtesy of Southeast School, Columbus, Ohio
Editor: Ann Castel Davis
Production Editor: Linda Hillis Bayma
Photo Editor: Anne Vega
Production Buyer: Patricia A. Tonneman
Electronic Text Management: Marilyn Wilson Phelps, Matthew Williams, Jane Lopez, Karen L. Bretz

This book was set in Bitstream Zapf Calligraphic by Prentice Hall and was printed and bound by R. R. Donnelley & Sons Company. The cover was printed by Phoenix Color Corp.

Photo credits: pp. 20, 56, 84, 110, 140, 149, 185, 354, 482, 568, Scott Cunningham/Merrill and Prentice Hall; pp. 66, 170, 235, 276, 359, 427, 503, 542, 590, Lise Fox; pp. 2, 30, 129, 296, 418, 442, 516, Barbara Schwartz/Merrill and Prentice Hall; p. 552, Anne Vega/Merrill and Prentice Hall; pp. 196, 222, Tom Watson/Merrill and Prentice Hall; p. 384, Todd Yarrington; pp. 264, 324, Todd Yarrington/Merrill and Prentice Hall.

Printed in the United States of America

10 9 8 7 6 5 4 3 2 1

ISBN: 0-02-426581-0

Prentice-Hall International (UK) Limited, *London*
Prentice-Hall of Australia Pty. Limited, *Sydney*
Prentice-Hall of Canada, Inc., *Toronto*
Prentice-Hall Hispanoamericana, S. A., *Mexico*
Prentice-Hall of India Private Limited, *New Delhi*
Prentice-Hall of Japan, Inc., *Tokyo*
Simon & Schuster Asia Pte. Ltd., *Singapore*
Editora Prentice-Hall do Brasil, Ltda., *Rio de Janeiro*

PREFACE

There are many exciting career choices that individuals may make today and certainly one at the top of the list is teaching. Being a teacher allows one to influence lives in meaningful, sometimes long-lasting, ways. Certainly there are challenges and difficulties, but the accomplishments often outweigh the shortcomings in the teaching profession.

Teaching students with severe disabilities is somewhat different from teaching students without disabilities or those with mild disabilities, but it also has its many rewards—maybe even more. When college students come into teacher-preparation programs to become special educators, they often have already realized through volunteer work the satisfaction that comes with working with individuals whose needs are beyond those that most of us experience. It is that satisfaction that leads them into their career choice. But where does it come from? It's difficult to say and, most likely, it is different for different people. But one source of influence that is frequently mentioned is that there was often such a great discrepancy between what the teacher-to-be anticipated the person with the disability could do and what the person actually was capable of accomplishing. When it becomes apparent that one's effort can have a notable and significant impact, the reinforcement is apparently often strong enough to lead to a career decision.

What is interesting about this realization, a realization that perhaps occurred in the span of a few weeks or months, is that it is exactly the same conclusion that can be reached by examining the history of what has happened to people with severe disabilities in about the past 200 years. Essentially, we as a society never fully realized the potential of people with severe disabilities because our focus has been more on the disability and less on the person and his or her life among us. So often we have thought more in terms of what the person cannot do instead of what can be done through inclusive life opportunities and appropriate learning experiences.

But not all in our society have come to fully realize this and thus the person who would become a professional in this field also needs to realize that political agendas differ over various issues related to the lives, living conditions, and schooling of people who have severe disabilities. You will encounter people who believe that some persons should not be given the opportunity to learn since they cannot learn all that others can. You will meet others who believe that those who have severe developmental delays should be warehoused in institutions and set aside from the rest of society. And you will meet those who say that persons with severe disabilities are "special" and that only "special" people can teach them and that they belong only in "special" programs, schools, classes, homes, activities, and so on.

Future teachers and others who will provide services to individuals with severe disabilities should approach their career with the understanding that not all in society have come to a sufficient level of maturation to realize that all individuals are of value, have the potential to learn and, yes, to contribute in some way to society, and are deserving of a quality of life like others' in society.

A good teacher of students with severe disabilities will do two things. First, this person will teach her or his students skills to the full capacity of their ability. Second, this person will help to educate society to the full capacity of its ability about the nature of disabilities and the rights and needs of those who have them to live and learn among us. These two major teacher actions will reinforce each other. The more students with disabilities learn, the more they will be accepted; the more they are accepted, the more they will learn.

What we have tried to do in this book is provide information to teachers and future teachers about what they must do to realize both of these goals. The teaching strategies and tactics that are presented are intended both to lead to student learning and to increase the acceptance of students with severe disabilities by others. Throughout the book we have tried to present very practical information and also to display the positive potential of people with severe disabilities. We believe that both the skills and the attitudes of teachers are key to their success and therefore we have attempted to affect each.

No book can do everything that its authors would like it to do, and this one is no exception. Although there are many good books today on the nature and needs of persons with severe disabilities and appropriate services for them, we felt there was a need for a relatively comprehensive text for preservice and in-service teachers that contained practical information presented in a straightforward, reader-friendly manner. We tried to write such a text and include in it the principles and practices that many today agree are the most appropriate. Certainly our biases will show. We believe that those with severe disabilities should be included in school and society, that they should learn skills and behaviors that will help them to be included and have a good quality of life, and that learning processes should be as natural and pleasant as possible. To us, none of this seems to be unreasonable.

The text has been laid out in a manner that seemed logical to us and that could be followed during one semester of an undergraduate or graduate course. In Part I (Chapters 1–3), we set the stage and orient the reader to key issues that should be understood about educating students with severe disabilities. We address the complex, multidimensional nature of persons categorized in different ways who fall under the rubric of severe disabilities (Chapter 1); the philosophy and best practices that we believe should permeate instructional practices and related service (Chapter 2); and the interrelated roles of parents of individuals with severe disabilities and the professionals and paraprofessionals who provide services (Chapter 3).

Part II (Chapters 4 and 5) contains information about actions that must be undertaken prior to initiating instruction: planning instructional programs (Chapter 4) and conducting assessments to determine instructional needs for individual students (Chapter 5). In Part III (Chapters 6–9) we present information that we consider to be generic to instruction for all students with severe disabilities regardless of the age of the student, the degree of severity of the disability, or the content of instruction. This content includes methods for teaching students how to acquire new skills (Chapter 6), teaching skills in a way that would promote maintenance and generalization (Chapter 7), monitoring the progress of students as skills are being learned (Chapter 8), and developing inclusive environments for students and ways to teach them in those environments (Chapter 9).

In Part IV (Chapter 10–17) we present content about teaching and assisting students in particular areas. These include teaching communication skills (Chapter 10); providing positive supports to improve challenging behaviors (Chapter 11); working with students who have sensory and motor disabilities (Chapter 12); providing support for special health and medical needs (Chapter 13); and teaching self-care and daily living skills (Chapter 14), leisure and recreational skills (Chapter 15), appropriate academic skills (Chapter 16), and community and domestic skills (Chapter 17).

Part V contains two chapters devoted to working with special age groups. Chapter 18 offers information for designing programs for preschool-age children and Chapter 19 addresses the needs of adolescents and young adults and planning for their future beyond the school years. In Part VI, the final part of the book, there is only one chapter, Chapter 20. Here we discuss what we see to be continuing trends and issues related to teaching students with severe disabilities.

The information presented in this text is based on our experience teaching students with severe disabilities and working with their families, teaching preservice and in-service teachers, writing and research contained in the professional literature, observations in classrooms, and discussions with teachers and other professionals. We have tried to take these sources of information and influence, synthesize them, and present them in a way that is meaningful and comprehensible. As we said, no text can do everything but we hope that this book, along with material presented through class lectures and learning activities, and the experience one will acquire through direct work with individuals with disabilities will lead to the production of competent teachers.

We would like to thank those who provided support and assistance to us as we worked on this text for what seemed to be a never ending period of our lives. Foremost are our spouses and children: Wendy, Jennifer, Jessica, and Meredith Westling; and Robert and Patrick Brady. We also appreciate the colleagues who supported us during the writing in different ways: Mary Frances Hanline, Bruce Menchetti, Mark Koorland, Donna Williams, Greg Valcante, and Vivian Correa. We must also acknowledge our appreciation to the many families who let us into their lives and expanded our understanding of disability. The reviewers who provided much useful feedback were of great assistance in helping us to shape the final version of the text. These individuals were Susan Bashinski, University of Texas at Tyler; Margaret (Meg) Cooper, West Georgia College; Edwin Helmstetter, Washington State University; Merri Jamieson, Ashland University; M. Eric Kruger, East Stroudsburg University; Ann L. Lee, Bloomsburg University; and Anjali Misra, SUNY–Potsdam. We would also like to thank Ann Castel Davis at Merrill who brought us into this project, monitored our activity throughout the process, and wouldn't let us give up. The production editor for Merrill, Linda Bayma, has also been of great assistance as we came to the final stages of the project.

There is much to be accomplished to make this world a better place and we all hope that we can do a little to help in the struggle. We hope this textbook will be seen as a small contribution by us and that those who read it will multiply our effort many times.

D.L.W. & L.F.

CONTENTS

PART I
Important Considerations Prior to Teaching Persons with Severe Disabilities 1

CHAPTER 1

Persons with Severe Disabilities: Definitions, Descriptions, Characteristics, and Potential 2

Traditional Categories of Severe Disabilities 4
- Mental Disabilities 4
- Autism 6
- Dual Sensory Impairments and Multiple Disabilities 11

Characteristics of Persons with Severe Disabilities 12
- Learning Characteristics 12
- Personal-Social Characteristics 14
- Physical Characteristics 15

Learning Potential of Persons with Severe Disabilities 10
- Language Skills 20
- Social Skills 21
- Domestic and Daily Living Skills 22
- Recreational and Leisure Skills 23
- Community Skills 23
- Vocational Skills 24

Conclusion 25
- Questions for Reflection 25
- References 26

CHAPTER 2

Philosophy and Best Practices for Educating Persons with Severe Disabilities 30

The Evolution of Philosophies and Practices for Teaching Students with Severe Disabilities 32

Contemporary Best Practices for Students with Severe Disabilities 33

The Meaning of Special Education 35

Best Practices Within Educational Programs for Students with Severe Disabilities 36
- Collaborating with Other Professionals and Parents 36
- Assessment and Planning 36
- Early Intervention and Preschool Programs 37
- School Placement 38
- Curriculum and Instruction 39
- Community-Based Instruction 39
- Related Services 40
- Social Integration 41

Improving Challenging Behavior 42
The Bases of Best Practices 42
Social Values 43
Legal Mandates 45
Professional Consensus 48
Conclusion 51
Questions for Reflection 52
References 52

CHAPTER 3

Collaborative Teaming with Parents, Professionals, and Paraprofessionals 56

The Meaning of Collaboration 57
The Multidisciplinary Team 58
The Interdisciplinary Team 59
The Transdisciplinary Team 60
Assessment and Planning 60
Providing Integrated Therapy 62
Role Release by Professionals 62
Functioning as a Transdisciplinary Team 63
Benefits of Collaboration 64
Building Effective Teams 65
Collaborating with Parents 65
What Parents Often Need 67
What Teachers Should Know and Do 68
Collaborating with Other Professionals 72
Special Educators 72
General Educators 73
Physical and Occupational Therapists 73
Communication Disorders Specialists 74
Social Workers 74
School Psychologists 75
School Nurses 75
Vision Specialists 75
Audiologists 76
School Administrators 76
Physicians 76
Others 77
Collaborating with Paraprofessionals 77
Delineating the Roles of Professionals and Paraprofessionals 77
Directing and Supervising Paraprofessionals 78
Assignment of Duties 79
Supervision and Evaluation 79
Personal Interactions 80
Conclusion 80
Questions for Reflection 81
References 81

PART II
Preparing to Teach: Planning and Assessment Procedures 83

CHAPTER 4

Planning Instructional Programs for Students with Severe Disabilities 84

Types of Plans 85
The Importance of Planning 86
Individual Educational Plans 87
Current Performance Levels 88
Annual Goals and Short-Term Objectives 88
Special Education, Placement in the Regular Classroom, and Related Services 90
Projected Date for the Initiation of Services and the Duration of the Services 91
Annual Evaluation Procedures 92
Individual Transition Plans 93
Individual Family Service Plans 95
Alternative Approaches to Planning 97
Personal Futures Planning 99
The McGill Action Planning System (MAPS) 103
Choosing Options and Accommodations for Children (COACH) 104
Conclusion 107
Questions for Reflection 108
References 108

CHAPTER 5

Conducting Assessments to Determine Instructional Needs 110

Reviewing Existing Records 112
Interviewing Parents to Determine Educational Goals 112
Adaptive Behavior Scales 113
Curriculum/Activity Guides 118
Conducting Ecological Inventories 125
Direct Observation of the Student in Natural Environments 128
Observation of the Student During Structured Activities 129
  Simple-Discrete Behaviors 131
  Continuous-Ongoing Behaviors 131
  Complex-Chained Skills 131
  Functional Routines 131
  Recording and Charting Performance During Structured Assessment Activities 132
Assessing Related Skills 132
  Communication Skills 133
  Motor Skills 133
Assessing Traditional Academic Skills 134
Conclusion 137
  Questions for Reflection 137
  References 137

PART III General Instructional Procedures 139

CHAPTER 6

Teaching Students to Acquire New Skills 140

Types of Objectives to Teach 141
  Function over Form 142
  Extending the Objective 143
  Partial Participation 143
Good General Teaching Practices 144
How Behaviors and Skills Are Learned 145
Instructional Tactics for Teaching New Skills to Students with Severe Disabilities 147
  Instructional Prompts 147
  Applying Prompts During Skill Acquisition Training 150
  Modifying Stimulus Materials 158
  Use of Natural Cues 160
  Reinforcing Correct Responses 161
  Correcting Errors 163
  Writing an Instructional Program 164
Conclusion 165
  Questions for Reflection 167
  References 167

CHAPTER 7

Teaching Skills for Maintenance and Generalization 170

Defining Generalization 172
Strategies That Have Been Used to Achieve Skill Generalization 172
  Train and Hope 172
  Sequential Modification 173
  Introduce to Natural Maintaining Contingencies 173
  Train Sufficient Exemplars 173
  Train Loosely 173
  Use Indiscriminable Contingencies 173
  Program Common Stimuli 173
  Mediate Generalization 174
  Train to Generalize 174
  Teach Functional Target Behaviors 174
  Specify a Fluency Criterion 174
  Train in the Natural Setting 174
  Use General Case Programming 174
Effectiveness of Generalization Strategies 175
  Train and Hope 175

Arranging Consequences During Initial Training to Improve Generalization 176
Arranging Antecedents During Initial Training to Improve Generalization 176
Mediation During Generalization Training 178
Summary of the Effectiveness of Generalization Strategies 178
Applying Generalization Strategies 179
Tactics of Generalization Programming 180
Applying Decision Rules About Generalization Strategies 181
Using the General Case Method 184
Maintenance 189
Defining Maintenance 189
Strategies for Teaching Skill Maintenance 189
Skill Overlearning 189
Learning Through Distributed Practice 190
Intermittent Reinforcement 190
Building on Learned Skills 190
Using a Maintenance Schedule 191
Using the Skill at Home and Elsewhere 191
Writing Instructional Programs to Include Generalization Training and Promote Maintenance 191
Conclusion 193
Questions for Reflection 193
References 194

CHAPTER 8

Monitoring and Evaluating Student Progress 196

Direct Measures of Student Performance 198
Types of Behaviors and Units of Measure 198
Defining the Behavior 198
Observation of the Behavior 199
Recording the Data 199
Data Collection During Baseline 208
Data Collection During Instruction 208
Data Collection During Generalization 209
Graphing the Data 210
Interpreting the Graphs 212
Indirect Measures of Student Performance 214
Schedule of Student Activities 214
Daily Log 215
Incident Record 215
Portfolio Assessment of Student Performance 217
Conclusion 219
Questions for Reflection 219
References 219

CHAPTER 9

Creating Inclusive Educational Environments 222

The Importance of School Inclusion 223
Legal Rationale 224
Philosophical Rationale 225
Educational Rationale 225
The Benefits of Inclusion 225
Instructional Benefits 225
Friendship Formation 226
Impact on Nondisabled Peers 226
The Inclusive Education Model 228
Facilitating School Acceptance 229
Classroom Placement 229
Awareness Training 229
Teacher Modeling 231
Curriculum Infusion 231
Collaborative Teaming 231

Community and Family Involvement 233
Peer Programs 233
Facilitating Interactions 233
Peer Support Networks 237
Meaningful Instructional Arrangements 238
Basic Principles of Instructional Arrangements 239
Providing Individualized Instruction 241
Instructional Arrangements in the Regular Classroom 242
Peer Interaction During Instruction 248
Implementing Inclusive Instruction 250
Organizing Individualized Support 252
The Role of the Special Educator 253
Scheduling Support Personnel 253
Case Study One: Sarah 254
Case Study Two: Ray 256
Conclusion 257
Questions for Reflection 257
References 257

PART IV
Specific Instructional and Management Procedures 263

CHAPTER 10

Teaching Communication Skills 264

Communication Skill Development 265
Early Communication Development 266
Intentionality 266
Communicative Means and Functions 267
Assessment Issues 268
Communication Skill Assessment 269
Ecological Assessment 271
Selecting a Communication Mode 272
Augmentative and Alternative Communication 272
Gestural Communication 273
Aided Systems 274
Selecting an Alternative or Augmentative Communication Mode 278
Facilitated Communication 280
Instructional Strategies 281
Interaction Style 281
Interacting with Learners Who Are Nonsymbolic 282
Designing Instructional Strategies 284
Naturalistic Teaching Procedures 284
Interrupted Chains 288
Conversational Skill Training 289
Van Dijk Method 290
Generalization Issues 291
Conclusion 293
Questions for Reflection 293
References 293

CHAPTER 11

Providing Behavioral Supports to Improve Challenging Behavior 296

Defining Problem Behavior 298
Stereotypic Behaviors 298
Self-Injurious Behaviors 298
Aggression 299
Inappropriate Social Behavior 299
A Functional Approach to Changing Behavior 300
Eliminative Approach 300
Functional Approach 301
Conducting a Functional Assessment 303
Lifestyle Understanding 303
Indirect Assessment 304
Direct Observation Assessment 305
Hypotheses Development 308
Hypotheses Testing 311
Intervention Strategies 313
Ecological and Setting Event Strategies 313

Antecedent Strategies 313
Consequence Strategies 314
Teaching Functionally Equivalent Communication Skills 317
Developing Intervention Plans 318
Conclusion 320
Questions for Reflection 320
References 321

CHAPTER 12

Managing Sensory and Motor Disabilities 324

The Sensory Systems 326
Atypical Sensorimotor Responses 327
The Motor System 328
Muscle Tone 328
Primitive Reflexes 328
Posture and Movement 329
Positioning and Handling 330
Body Mechanics 331
Facilitating Posture and Movement 332
Positioning 333
Instructional Programming 337
Sensory Integration 337
Neurodevelopmental Treatment 337
Behavioral Programming Intervention 338
Integrated Programming 338
Sensory Impairments 338
Hearing Impairments 339
Adaptive Devices 340
Vision Impairments 341
Vision Assessment 341
Vision Correction 344
Functional Vision Training 345
Orientation and Mobility Skills 346
Dual Sensory Impairments 350
Conclusion 350
Questions for Reflection 351
References 351

CHAPTER 13

Providing Support for Health and Medical Needs 354

Therapeutic Management 356
Universal Precautions 356
Hand-Washing 357
Incontinence and Toileting 357
Dental Care 358
Seizure Management 359
Skin Conditions 363
Postural Drainage 364
Passive Range of Motion 364
Medication 367
Nutrition and Feeding 368
Nutrition 368
Eating Skills 370
Tube Feeding 372
Special Concerns 374
Tracheostomy 374
Ileostomy and Colostomy 376
Catheterization 377
Infectious Disease 378
HIV/AIDS 378
Conclusion 381
Questions for Reflection 381
References 382

CHAPTER 14

Teaching Self-Care and Daily Living Skills 384

General Considerations 385
Appropriate Instructional Procedures 386
Skill Generalization 386
When and Where to Teach Personal Skills 386

Eating, Self-Feeding and Other Mealtime Skills 387
Finger-Feeding 388
Drinking from a Cup 388
Learning to Eat with a Spoon 390
Learning to Use Other Utensils 391
Decreasing Inappropriate Mealtime Behaviors 391
Teaching Other Appropriate Mealtime Behaviors 393
General Suggestions for Improving Eating 393
Learning to Use the Toilet 394
Determining Readiness for Toileting 394
Teaching Independent Toilet Use 395
General Suggestions for Improving Toileting 400
Learning to Dress 401
Selecting Skills to Teach 401
Assessing Dressing Ability 402
Instructional Strategies for Teaching Dressing 404
Dressing and Students with More Severe Disabilities 406
Teaching Skills Related to Dressing 407
General Suggestions for Improving Dressing 407
Learning Personal Grooming Skills 409
Personal Dental Care 409
Menstrual Care 413
General Suggestions for Improving Personal Grooming 414
Questions for Reflection 415
References 415

CHAPTER 15

Teaching Leisure and Recreation Skills 418

Recreation Skill Instruction 419
Selecting Recreation Activities 420
Assessing Student Preference 422
Leisure Activity Goals 425
Choice-Making Issues 427
Social Interaction 428
Instructional Methods 428
Partial Participation 431
Adapting Activities 433
Community Recreation Opportunities 434
Developing Friendships 435
Friendship Skills 436
Friendships with Disabled Peers 437
Conclusion 438
Questions for Reflection 438
References 438

CHAPTER 16

Teaching Appropriate Academic Skills 442

Issues Related to Academic Instruction 443
Who Can Learn Academic Skills? 443
Levels of Academic Curricula 444
Defining Functional Academic Instruction 445
Beyond Functional Instruction 445
Location of Academic Instruction 446
Summary of Issues Related to Teaching Academic Skills 446
Teaching Reading 446
Reading Targets 446
Teaching Individual Sight Words 447
Teaching Word Analysis (Phonics) Skills 451
Teaching Oral Reading from Books 455
Using Commercial Programs to Teach Reading 458
Teaching Comprehension Skills and Reading in Applied Settings 458
Summary of Approaches to Teaching Reading Skills 460
Teaching Writing 460

Writing Targets 460
Expanding Writing Content 461
Teaching Writing Mechanics 462
Summary of Strategies for Teaching Writing 464
Whole Language 464
Defining and Describing Whole Language 464
Elements of Whole-Language Instruction 465
Use of Whole Language with Students with Disabilities 466
Teaching Arithmetic 467
Acquiring Basic Concepts and Skills 467
Applying Skills to Handling Money 470
Applying Skills to Time Management 473
Summary of Strategies for Teaching Arithmetic 476
Teaching Academics in the Regular Classroom 476
Cooperative Learning 476
Parallel Learning Activities 477
Multilevel Curriculum 477
Curriculum Overlapping 477
Adaptive Instruction 477
Individual Tutoring 477
Considerations for Delivering Instruction in the Regular Classroom 477
Conclusion 478
Questions for Reflection 478
References 479

CHAPTER 17

Teaching Community and Domestic Skills 482

Why Teach Community and Domestic Skills? 483
General Procedures Related to Teaching Community and Domestic Skills 484
Who Should Participate in Community and Domestic Instruction? 484
Partial Participation 484
Where to Teach Community and Domestic Skills 485
Determining Target Sites and Skills 486
Determining Operational Skills to Be Taught 486
Determining Associated Skills to Be Taught 487
Developing Instructional Plans 487
Planning for Skill Generalization 488
Implementing Instruction in Community Settings 488
Using Simulated Community Settings in Schools 490
Providing Concurrent Instruction in School 491
Evaluating Community Skills 491
Securing Adequate Funds for Community Instruction 492
Teaching Community and Domestic Skills in the Most Meaningful Way 492
Community Settings and Activities 493
Grocery Stores 494
Restaurants 495
Vending Machines 497
Public Transportation and Pedestrian Skills 499
Domestic Activities 501
Preparing Snacks and Meals 501
Performing Household Chores 504
Using a Telephone 505
Issues Related to Community-Based Instruction 508
School Administrative Policies 509
Separating Students With and Without Disabilities 509
Relation of Other Instruction to Community Instruction 510
Conclusion 510
Questions for Reflection 511
References 511

PART V
Instructional Considerations for Younger and Older Students 515

CHAPTER 18

Meeting the Needs of Young Children 516

- Historical Development 517
- Efficacy Research 519
- Goals of Early Intervention 519

Teaching Young Children 520
- Transactional Approach 520
- Instructional Activities 521
- Instructional Content 521
- Family Support 521

Family-Centered Approach 524
- Individualized Family Service Plan 525

The Intervention Context 529
- Interagency Collaboration and Teaming 531

Assessment in Early Intervention 533
- Curriculum-Based Assessment 533
- Judgment-Based Assessment 533
- Interactive Assessment 534
- Norm-Based Assessment 534
- Systematic Observation 534

Instructional Programs for Young Children 534
- Developmentally Appropriate Practice 535
- Activity-Based Instruction 535
- Naturalistic Teaching Procedures 536
- Environmental Arrangements 539
- Infant Intervention 543

Inclusion and Young Children 543

Transition Issues 545
- Preparing for Transition 545
- Transition from the NICU 546
- Transition from the Early Intervention Program to Preschool 546
- Transition to Kindergarten 547

Conclusion 548
- Questions for Reflection 548
- References 548

CHAPTER 19

Teaching Employment Skills and Planning for Transition 552

Developing an Individualized Transition Plan 555
- Identifying Transition Goals 555
- Conducting the Transition Planning Meeting 556

Vocational Preparation 557
- Vocational Instruction 557
- Community Work Experience 560
- Instructional Strategies 561

Supported Employment 564
- The Importance of Supported Employment 564
- Supported Work Models 567
- Natural Supports 569
- Job Development 570
- Situational Assessment 574
- Social Interaction 575

Evaluating Employment Outcomes 585

Conclusion 585
- Questions for Reflection 586
- References 586

PART VI
Trends and Issues 589

CHAPTER 20

Trends and Issues in the Education of Students with Severe Disabilities 590

Societal Issues 591

Educational Reform 593

Effective Schools 594
Effective Instruction 595
Special Education and the Reform Movement 598
Changes for Persons with Severe Disabilities 604
Self-Determination 604
Self-Advocacy 605
Quality of Life 606
Implications for Teachers 608
World Changes and Individual Differences 608
Educational Change and Special Education 608
Choice-Making and Self-Determination 609
Self-Management 609
Self-Advocacy Movements 610
Quality of Life 610
Conclusion 610
Questions for Reflection 611
References 611

Appendix A Individualized Education Plan 615

Appendix B Individualized Transition Program 621

Appendix C Individualized Family Service Plan 631

Name Index 647

Subject Index 657

PART I

Important Considerations Prior to Teaching Persons with Severe Disabilities

CHAPTER 1 Persons with Severe Disabilities: Definitions, Descriptions, Characteristics, and Potential

CHAPTER 2 Philosophy and Best Practices for Educating Persons with Severe Disabilities

CHAPTER 3 Collaborative Teaming with Parents, Professionals, and Paraprofessionals

CHAPTER 1

Persons with Severe Disabilities: Definitions, Descriptions, Characteristics, and Potential

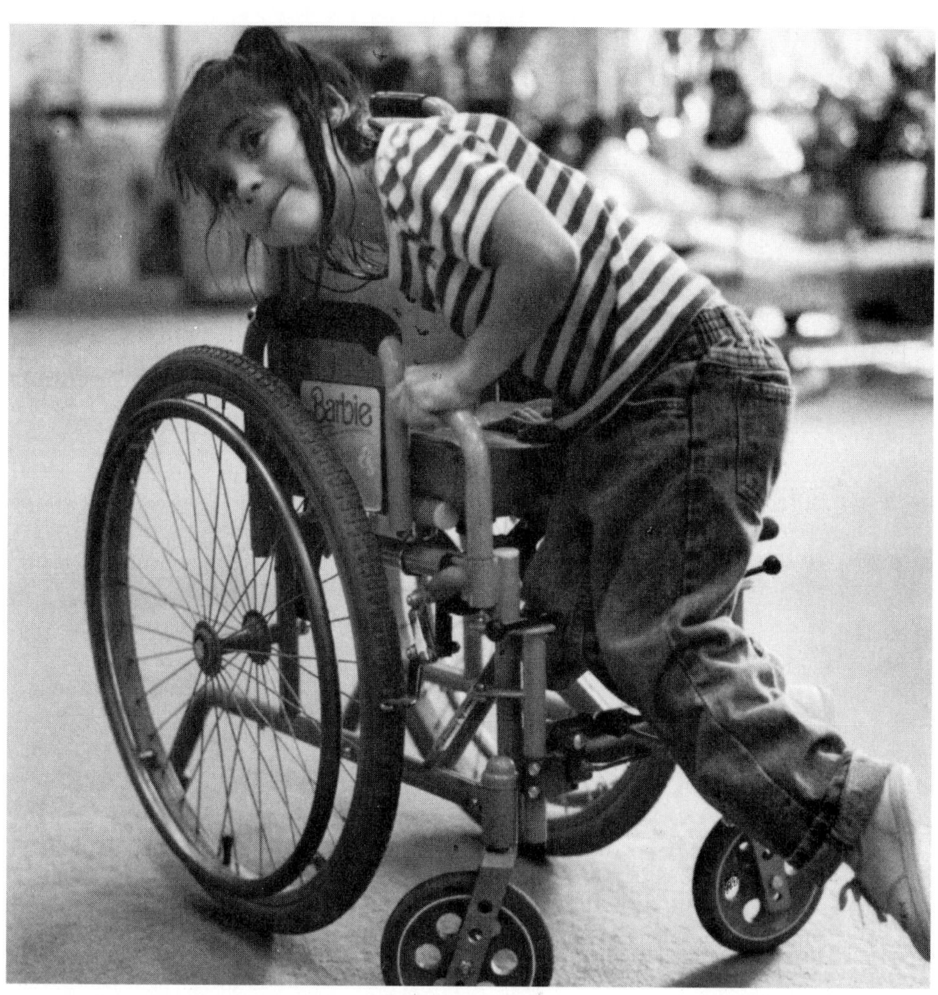

Chapter Overview

In this chapter definitions and concepts of "severe disabilities" and traditional categories covered by this term are discussed. In addition, there are descriptions of learning characteristics, personal-social characteristics, and physical conditions often associated with severe disabilities. The chapter concludes with a discussion of the potential of persons with severe disabilities given appropriate forms of instruction.

The term *severe disabilities* has been defined by various authorities in several ways. It implies a condition in which typical abilities are in some way adversely affected, with the degree of this condition being relatively more debilitating in comparison to a person without disabilities or one who has "mild" disabilities (Abt Associates, 1974; Baker, 1979; Brimer, 1990; Justen, 1976; Sailor & Haring, 1977). A person who has a severe disability, like other people, has many positive traits. Unlike most others, however, this individual is challenged by significant deficits in learning abilities, personal and social skills, and/or sensory and physical abilities. The general ability to demonstrate behaviors and skills necessary to maintain oneself independently in typical life environments is reduced for persons with severe disabilities and often requires assistance and support from individuals without disabilities.

The Association for Persons with Severe Handicaps (TASH) defined the condition in this way: "These people include individuals of all ages who require extensive ongoing support in more than one major life activity in order to participate in integrated community settings and to enjoy a quality of life that is available to citizens with fewer or no disabilities. Support may be required for life activities such as mobility, communication, self-care, and learning as necessary for independent living, employment and self-sufficiency" (Adopted by TASH, December, 1985, revised November, 1986; reprinted in Meyer, Peck, & Brown, 1991).

Traditional categories of persons usually referred to as having a severe disability include those who have been classified as moderately, severely, or profoundly mentally disabled; those who are autistic (or demonstrate autistic-like behaviors); and those who have dual sensory disabilities associated with cognitive disabilities. Persons with severe disabilities have also been described as exhibiting uncommon behavioral characteristics such as self-stimulatory behavior or as lacking in typical abilities such as self-care or verbal communication skills (Abt Associates, 1974). In other words, these individuals are lacking in the abilities and skills necessary to achieve complete independence (Baker, 1979; Brimer, 1990). Others have defined the condition of severe disabilities as one in which more extensive services are required for the person to achieve maximum potential (Justen, 1976; Sailor & Haring, 1977).

It is most important to note that there is not a homogeneous population of persons with severe disabilities. Instead there are many individuals who may be characterized as having severe disabilities but who are, in fact, quite different from each other. The common bond among the members of this population is that their general functioning is below that exhibited by about 99% of the rest of the population.

In the following sections of this chapter, more detail about the nature of severe disabilities is provided by looking at the traditional categories of persons with severe disabilities and by examining significant characteristics—including learning, personal, and physical characteristics—that are displayed by many members of this population. While there is some danger of negative stereotypes being derived from these descriptions, it is important for you to acquire information pertinent to the population. We hope that these descriptions will not be interpreted as being demeaning or derogatory, nor as suggesting that people with severe disabilities are without many positive qualities. In fact, it is more important to know that even with the various conditions often affecting persons with severe disabilities, they generally maintain much potential for achievement. Therefore, in the final section of this first chapter, recent findings about the learning abilities of persons with severe disabilities are discussed.

Traditional Categories of Severe Disabilities

In many parts of society, including community agencies and school systems, several different categories may be used to refer to persons with severe disabilities. These include mental disabilities (or mental retardation or handicap), autism, and multiple disabilities. Descriptions of individuals within these traditional categories are presented below.

Mental Disabilities

Historically, persons diagnosed as being mentally retarded or mentally disabled have been placed in subcategories based primarily on their level of intelligence (Heber, 1959, 1961; Grossman, 1973, 1977, 1983). More recently, the American Association on Mental Retardation (AAMR) created a new multidimensional classification system that eliminated the subcategories and instead requires an evaluation of individuals in multiple areas to determine strengths, weaknesses, and optimal levels of support. Because the traditional system will likely be used for many years to come, it will be considered first as it relates to the concept of severe disabilities. Then the new system will be discussed.

Moderate and Severe Mental Disabilities

According to the traditional diagnostic and classification system of the AAMR (Grossman, 1983), persons with *moderate mental disabilities* score above 35 to 40 and below 50 to 55 on traditional intelligence tests. Generally, individuals who fall within this classification are quite capable of learning many basic skills in the areas of communication, self-help, functional academics (or in some cases more advanced academics), domestic skills, community functioning skills, and vocational skills. For example, many adults with a moderate mental disability are able to manage all of their own daily self-care needs; prepare some foods for themselves and others; demonstrate adequate body control, including good gross and fine motor development; participate in common conversations; have some basic functional reading skills; interact cooperatively or competitively with others; make purchases in a grocery store, using money with fair accuracy; and carry out many occupational routines. An individual classified as moderately mentally disabled might also be capable of self-initiation and show an ability to assume a degree of responsibility (Grossman, 1983). Based on some concepts of severe disabilities, not all persons who have a moderate mental disability would also be considered to have a severe disability.

Historically, individuals have been classified as having a *severe mental disability* if their level of adaptive behavior is relatively lower than that described for persons with moderate mental disabilities and if their measured IQ is between 20 to 25 and 35 to 40 (Grossman, 1983). Ability examples of adults with severe mental disabilities include being able to eat adequately with a fork or spoon (but may need help with cutting); dressing and bathing with some supervision; using the toilet independently; and washing hands and face without help (but may have to be told or reminded to do so).

The individual's physical ability is generally good and he or she is probably able to walk, run, hop, skip, and dance, and maybe skate or sled or jump rope. The ability to communicate should also be adequate in that speech is relatively clear and understandable, and complex sentences may be used and understood. The person with a severe mental disability probably does not possess many academic skills, such as reading, but may be able to recognize some words and common signs. He or she may know that money is of value, but may not be able to state the specific value of coins.

Profound Mental Disabilities According to the traditional AAMR definitions, an individual diagnosed as being *profoundly mentally disabled* falls within the most severe subcategory of the classification system. Often these individuals are referred to as having "the most severe" disabilities and have IQs below 20 to 25 points on a standardized test of intelligence, if such a test is administered to them. Individuals in this group often have multiple disabilities.

It is difficult to provide a typical profile of an individual with a profound mental disability because there is such an extreme degree of variability among the individuals so classified. Some persons are capable of relatively independent functioning in common self-care activities such as eating and toileting and also possess functional skills in other domains of development such as vocational and domestic skills. Others, however, may have much more restricted abilities, including severe sensory and/or physical disabilities, and they may be nonambulatory and have extremely limited communicative ability or exhibit communication patterns that are not easy to detect. Many of these persons, however, demonstrate the ability to learn and are capable of at least "partial participation" in normal daily activities.

The 1992 AAMR Diagnostic and Classification System Under the most recent AAMR system, there are no longer distinctions made using the traditional subclasses (e.g., mild, moderate, severe, or profound). Instead, an individual who is diagnosed as being mentally disabled must be described using a multidimensional approach that provides a comprehensive description of the person (AAMR, 1992). The dimensions include the following:

Dimension I: Intellectual functioning and adaptive skills.

Dimension II: Psychological/emotional considerations.

Dimension III: Physical/health/etiology considerations.

Dimension IV: Environmental considerations.

The first dimension is considered when making the initial diagnosis. All dimensions are then used to identify strengths, needs, and types and degrees of support. The types of support possible are listed in Figure 1–1. As can be seen, the degrees of support include intermittent, limited, extensive, and pervasive. These types of support not only vary across individuals, but may also vary across skill areas (e.g., communication skills, self-care skills) and from one time in life to another.

It may be expected that most individuals considered to have severe disabilities would require at least "limited" support in most areas and "extensive" to "pervasive" support in many areas.

Figure 1–2 provides a matrix for identifying support functions and activities for individuals classified as having mental disabilities and for showing the level of intensity required in each area.

Autism

Individuals who are diagnosed as autistic are often considered to have a severe disability, but the range of ability within this syndrome is broad. Some individuals with autism might function at or near a level of independence. Although their physical features often do not suggest that they have a severe disability, their disability is manifested in the nature of their language and personal and social behavior. While there is a range of "autistic" characteristics, generally individuals who are diagnosed as autistic behave in a manner that shows little emotion and excludes much of the rest of the social world.

A notable aspect of most persons with autism is their lack of social reciprocity. They often do not interact with others with the type and degree of emotionalism that typically occurs between two people. They appear to lack an awareness of the existence or the feelings of others and do not look to others for comfort during times of distress or discomfort. They do

Intermittent

Support on an "as needed basis." Characterized by episodic nature, person not always needing the support(s), or short-term supports needed during life-span transitions (e.g., job loss or an acute medical crisis). Intermittent supports may be high or low intensity when provided.

Limited

An intensity of supports characterized by consistency over time, time-limited but not of an intermittent nature, may require fewer staff members and less cost than more intense levels of support (e.g., time-limited employment training or transitional supports during the school to adult provided period).

Extensive

Supports characterized by regular involvement (e.g., daily) in at least some environments (such as work or home) and not time-limited (e.g., long-term support and long-term home living support).

Pervasive

Supports characterized by their constancy, high intensity; provided across environments; potential life-sustaining nature. Pervasive supports typically involve more staff members and intrusiveness than do extensive or time-limited supports.

Figure 1–1

Definition and Examples of Intensities of Supports

From *Mental Retardation: Definition, Classification, and Systems of Supports* (9th ed.) by the American Association on Mental Retardation, 1992, Washington, DC: Author. Copyright 1992 by the American Association on Mental Retardation. Reprinted by permission.

Name ______________________________ Date ________________

List the support function, the specific activity, and the level of intensities needed in each of the areas and/or dimensions.

Levels of intensity are: I- Intermittent; L- Limited; E- Extensive; P- Pervasive

Dimension I: Intellectual Functioning & Adaptive Skills

Dimension/Area	Support Function	Activity	Level of Intensity I L E P
Communication			
Self-Care			
Social Skills			
Home Living			
Community Use			
Self-Direction			
Health & Safety			

Figure 1–2

Profile and Intensities of Needed Supports

From *Mental Retardation: Definition, Classification, and Systems of Supports* (9th ed.) by the American Association on Mental Retardation, 1992, Washington, DC: Author. Copyright 1992 by the American Association on Mental Retardation. Reprinted by permission.

not learn many social skills, such as waving bye-bye, through imitation. Often children with autism do not engage in social play with other children and have difficulty forming close peer relationships or friendships (American Psychiatric Association, 1987; Volkmar, 1987).

Some persons who are diagnosed as autistic demonstrate behavioral characteristics that

Dimension I: Intellectual Functioning & Adaptive Skills *(continued)*

Dimension/Area	Support Function	Activity	Level I L E P
Functional Academics			
Leisure			
Work			

Dimension II: Psychological/Emotional Considerations

Dimension/Area	Support Function	Activity	Level I L E P

Dimension III: Physical/Health Considerations

Dimension/Area	Support Function	Activity	Level I L E P

Dimension IV: Environmental Considerations

Dimension/Area	Support Function	Activity	Level I L E P

Figure 1–2, *continued*

functionally increase the severity of their disability. For example, some display stereotyped movements such as hand flicking, spinning, or complex body movements. Or they may show an uncommon preoccupation with some particular item or items (or parts of items) for which there does not seem to be any reason. They may, for example, insist on carrying

Dimension IV: Environmental Considerations

Describe the extent to which the individual's living, work and educational environments facilitate or restrict opportunities for community integration, social supports (family and friends), and material well-being (income, housing, possessions).

• Living Situations

Strengths	Source
Weaknesses	Source

• Work

Strengths	Source
Weaknesses	Source

• Educational

Strengths	Source
Weaknesses	Source

Optimal Environment

Describe the optimal environment that would facilitate the individual's independence/interdependence, productivity, and community integration.

Figure 1–2, *continued*

around a blanket or a particular book, or they may show unusual fascination with items by continuously touching them, feeling them, spinning them, or smelling them. There is apparently no limit to the types of items that may be of interest.

Following strict routines or being rigid in many daily activities may also be important to individuals who are autistic. They tend to want aspects of their environment to be arranged in a certain order and daily events to proceed in a predictable manner. In their regular activities their interests and attention do not vary. For example, they may insist on eating a certain food or watching a certain television show at a set time. If there is some variation in this routine, the person may become very upset—even to the point, sometimes, of having a temper tantrum.

Persons with autism often show a severe lack of language development. Those with the most severe degree of the disability may not communicate at all, although this is the minority. However, even those who do communicate do so in a limited or abbreviated fashion, usually showing various abnormal speech and language characteristics. For example, their body language does not express the typical features that appear when people normally communicate with each other. They may not make or sustain eye contact, vary their facial features, use gestures, or change their body posture when conversing. These unique communicative characteristics can often be traced back to the individual's infancy. Very early in life the child may have begun to show a lack of responsiveness when held and talked to by parents or others (Paul, 1987).

Persons with autism also usually show atypical characteristics in the production, form, and content of their speech. Speech sounds may have inappropriate volume, pitch, rate, rhythm, or tone, be monotonous, have a melodylike quality, or be high pitched. The speech that is produced may be stereotyped or repetitive and the individual may use inappropriate parts of speech, saying, for example, "you want to go to the store?" when he means "I want to go to the store." In other cases the meaning of the speech that is produced may be difficult to interpret, especially for someone who does not know the individual. Sometimes these individuals say particular sentences or phrases over and over when the context of the statements does not appear to warrant them. Usually persons with autism will not participate in conversations of normal length and quality. They seem to be incapable of "reading" the social situation or participating actively in it.

There is no consistent, identifiable cause of autism. Early theories attributed autistic characteristics to emotional distress that occurred between mothers and infants during early infancy, but these theories were never substantiated. It is more likely that this social-language disability is the result of some form of brain dysfunction that occurs before or around the time of birth. Although brain injury is not detectable through medical examination, it has been noted that the incidence of autism is higher among the population of persons with known brain injuries; occurs more often in children born with rubella; occurs more often with children who have identifiable chromosomal anomalies; and occurs at a higher rate among siblings of children with autism (Schor, 1990). Because of these and similar findings, an organic etiology appears to be most likely (Rutter, 1985).

The majority of persons with autism are also mentally disabled. Rutter (1985) stated that several studies have demonstrated that the characteristics of autism are associated with a "basic cognitive deficit." He also pointed out that not only do autistic children lag in their cognitive development as do children with mental disabilities, but also that the course of their development tends to be unordinary with greatest deficits in symbolization, abstraction, conceptual meaning, and skills in memory and visual spatial tasks such as puzzles.

Dual Sensory Impairments and Multiple Disabilities

The least common form of disability is dual sensory impairment, or the inadequate functioning of both the visual and the auditory systems. Nationally, only 1,516 deaf-blind students between the ages of 6 and 21 were reported to the federal government as being served in the public schools during the 1988–89 school year (U.S. Department of Education, 1990). This low prevalence rate translates to only 3 of every 1,000 children with disabilities being classified as deaf-blind.

It is important to understand that although this type of disability sounds most onerous and isolating, and that even though its seriousness should not be underestimated, not all persons so classified are considered to have a "severe disability." Over 90% of persons who are deaf-blind have some functional vision and/or hearing and many are of average or above average intelligence, as was Helen Keller (Fredericks & Baldwin, 1987). Our concern, then, will be directed more toward persons who have dual sensory impairments that are relatively more severe and who simultaneously function at a level of moderate, severe, or profound mental disability. In this most severe form, the person has very limited social and communicative abilities and needs many structured learning opportunities to acquire various daily living skills.

A significant characteristic of persons with severe deaf-blindness is that they often attempt to create a degree of self-stimulation because normal sources of environmental stimulation are lost or diminished due to the nature of the disability. To create the stimulation there is a turning inward or to oneself and the production of self-stimulatory behavior. It may appear that the individual is passive, noncompliant, or unresponsive to overtures from people or the environment in general. There may be a lack of interaction with others and often inappropriate repetitive or stereotyped behavior, such as hand flapping, finger flicking, or head rocking, will occur. It is important to realize that this behavior is probably occurring to satisfy the need for sensory-physical stimulation, which is a basic need of all persons (Smithdas, 1981; Van Dijk, 1985).

There are several causes of multiple sensory impairments. One of the most well known is rubella, or German measles. If a pregnant woman contracts the disease when she is in the early stages of pregnancy, particularly in the first 8 weeks, there may result some degree of hearing and visual loss as well as other disabilities, including mental disabilities, congenital heart lesions, neurological disorders, and seizure disorders (Bleck, 1982b; Carter, 1975). During the mid-1960s, prior to the development of immunization against rubella, a large number of children were born with multiple disabling conditions some months after a rubella epidemic. Today, because people are usually immunized against this disease when they are children, it is a less common source of multiple disabilities. During the last several years, there have been fewer than 20 new cases of congenital rubella per year in the United States (Blackman, 1990b).

More common today than rubella as a cause of deaf-blindness is Usher's syndrome. This syndrome is due to an autosomal recessive genetic disorder, which means that both parents must be carriers of the condition but will not manifest it themselves. The child with Usher's syndrome will be born deaf and will gradually acquire other disabilities, including blindness and mental disability.

It is not adequate to treat a student with a dual sensory impairment as a blind person who also has a hearing loss or as a deaf person who also has a visual loss. The unique condition of this disability requires that the individual be considered holistically and that a transdisciplinary model of intervention be developed (Downing & Eichinger, 1990). Consideration needs to be given to the degree of residual vision and hearing that exists in order to maximize the functional use of these abilities.

Besides dual sensory impairments, persons with severe disabilities often have multiple disabilities. For example, a person with a profound mental disability is likely to have cerebral palsy and epilepsy associated with his or her cognitive disability as well as having single or dual sensory impairments. When an individual has multiple impairments it is essential that a holistic approach be used to develop an appropriate educational program. In order to better understand the different conditions that contribute to multiple disabilities, they are discussed separately later in this chapter under "Physical Characteristics."

Characteristics of Persons with Severe Disabilities

The descriptions presented in the previous sections should clearly indicate that persons with severe disabilities are very diverse in their characteristics, their abilities, and their needs. This is true both within and between different traditional categories. There are, however, some traits that occur with such frequency that they warrant consideration. Understanding these traits will help us better understand the needs of individuals with severe disabilities and how to address these needs. Key characteristics of persons with disabilities are discussed in the following sections. We will examine learning, personal-social, and physical characteristics that bear on the lives of these individuals.

Learning Characteristics

Persons who are classified as having a severe disability have significantly more difficulty learning than do most other individuals. Although many persons with very challenging disabilities such as dual sensory impairments or multiple physical disabilities may have normal or above average intelligence, our concern here is primarily with those who have limited cognitive ability. Quantitative measures (i.e., IQ scores) as well as qualitative indicators (such as their ability to demonstrate independent adaptive behavior) indicate that they are functioning below average in intelligence. In practical terms this means that they are weak in certain learning characteristics, resulting in greater amounts of time being required to learn skills, greater difficulty in learning more complex skills, and overall fewer skills being learned as compared to others (Brown et al., 1983). While it must be stressed that it is possible for many skills to be learned, the number and type of skills will not be comparable to those learned by most individuals. This fact has implications for the necessary relevance of skills that teachers and others teach. Some of the reasons that fewer skills are acquired are explained below. These characteristics have been explained in more detail in various references (Brown et al., 1983; Ellis, 1963, 1979; Mercer & Snell, 1977; Westling, 1986).

Attention to Stimuli, Dimensions, and Cues A significant learning difficulty experienced by many persons with severe disabilities is determining what particular part of the environment, or what particular stimulus or aspect of the stimulus, should be attended to. In other words, they may have difficulty in learning what feature of an item or situation gives the information necessary for correct action. An example of this would be looking at a set of keys and learning which key to select to open a particular door. In a period of time before the selection becomes automatic (i.e., is learned), the learner must decide first which dimension of the keys should be considered (size? color? shape? position?) and then which cue within the selected dimension indicates the correct choice (large or small? bronze or silver? jagged or smooth? middle, right, or left?). Learning this two-step system takes longer for persons with cognitive disabilities.

Observational and Incidental Learning Observational learning is learning through watching and imitating a model, that is, another person. Incidental learning is learning something that was not taught directly. People with severe disabilities benefit from these forms of learning less well than do people who do not have disabilities. Part of the reason for this may be their weakness in attending, as described above. Another reason may be the environment and the instructional programs they have been in. In other words, there may have been little opportunity for observing and imitating others or experiencing many interesting situations.

Memory Remembering skills and information that have been learned previously also presents a challenge to persons with severe disabilities. The major problems in this area appear to be related to being adequately exposed to the learning condition initially, having insufficient opportunity to practice or use the information or skill after it is initially learned, and then not using strategies adequately to pull the information from long-term memory for use when needed. As a result of this learning characteristic, important skills that are not adequately practiced over an extended period of time usually need to be taught again.

Skill Synthesis Most individuals who do not have intellectual disabilities may learn separate skills such as reading, writing, and arithmetic and then pull these skills together in an organized, useful way to undertake a particular activity such as grocery shopping. For persons who have cognitive disabilities, however, the ability to synthesize information and skills is very limited. They often fail to see the relation of one bit of information to another. Therefore one cannot teach isolated skills and expect them to be cohesively organized for application. Instead, more specific instruction is necessary and relevant skills must be taught in clusters to better ensure meaningfulness.

Generalization One of the most significant learning weaknesses of persons with severe cognitive disabilities is their weak ability to generalize acquired skills—to apply what was learned in one situation to another situation (Haring, 1988). Generalization is usually considered the demonstration of skills among different people, using different objects or materials, in different settings, and at different times. It is not usually sufficient to learn how to do something in one isolated location and nowhere else if the skill is expected to be demonstrated in a new situation. Because the ability to generalize is often very important, specific instructional strategies must usually be undertaken to get it to occur (Fox, 1989; Horner, Sprague, & Wilcox, 1982).

Self-Regulation Because persons with severe cognitive disabilities often do not apply what they have learned to other environments or situations, it may be concluded that they have difficulty in self-regulation, or identifying the appropriate action that should be taken under a certain condition (Whitman, 1990). In order to self-regulate, an individual must monitor his or her own behavior, evaluate it as being correct or incorrect, and then self-reinforce or withhold reinforcement. This obviously represents a sophisticated task, and research on how to improve this process for persons with mental disabilities has just recently begun (Agran, Fodor-Davis, Moore, & Deer, 1989; Hughes & Petersen, 1989; Hughes & Rusch, 1989; Salend, Ellis, & Reynolds, 1989). One important suggestion that has been made is that persons with mental disabilities may be weak in this ability because of the degree of external regulation that has typically been provided for them. With more opportunity and with specific training efforts they may be able to improve in the ability to regulate or manage their own behavior.

Personal-Social Characteristics

It is important to stress again the individuality of persons with severe disabilities when we consider issues related to their personal behavior and their relations with other people. There are many who have relatively normal lives, replete with friends and social activities, while others may have fewer social relations and more personal difficulties. Some of the personal problems experienced by persons with severe disabilities may be closely related to their intellectual or physical development, but many may also be explained by their learning history, environmental influences, and the attitudes of others in society.

Friendships and Personal Relations The quality of life of persons with disabilities is related to the network of friends and acquaintances they develop in their schools, workplaces, and communities. Some studies have shown that persons with disabilities have relatively little in the way of social relations with other individuals, both with and without disabilities (Crapps, Langone, & Swain, 1985; Davis & Rogers, 1985; Sullivan, Vitello, & Foster, 1988). In contrast, others have reported more favorable social behavior patterns, including the development of acquaintances, friends, and best friends (Kennedy, Horner, & Newton, 1989; Strully & Strully, 1985). The best predictor for the development of relations with others by persons with severe disabilities may be the same as for those who are not disabled: opportunity, understanding, and common interests.

Studies of the social interactions between people with severe disabilities and nondisabled persons have shown that individuals with disabilities are generally isolated until they or the persons without disabilities have been taught or prompted to interact (Gaylord-Ross & Peck, 1984). However, the opportunity for social interaction is certainly important. In an observational study of national scope, Brinker (1985) found that students with and without severe disabilities had more positive social interactions than did homogeneous groups of students with severe disabilities. The persons without disabilities provided more positive social responses for the social bids of the students with disabilities.

Sexual Relations The existence of a severe disability, per se, does not necessarily affect the sexual tendencies of an individual in one way or another. There is no evidence to indicate that sexual desires are reduced or heightened as a result of a disability. However, because of relatively lower rates of social interactions and increased rates of physical disabilities, many persons with severe disabilities have less opportunity for engaging in sexual activity. There are, of course, many exceptions, and there are certainly a number of persons with severe disabilities who engage in sexual activity.

Challenging Behaviors Some individuals with severe disabilities, particularly those with the most severe disabilities, exhibit challenging behaviors, including stereotyped behaviors (repetitive behaviors such as hand flapping), self-injurious behaviors (such as head banging), or aggressive behaviors (such as hitting other people). The cause of these behaviors is often difficult to interpret, and several theories have been developed in an attempt to explain them.

The most recent theories and research have considered the context in which inappropriate behavior occurs and the possible motivation for the behavior. In some cases, it may occur as a basic form of communication, that is, expressing discontent or dislike, the need for help, and so forth. In others, it may occur in order to escape from a demanding situation, one in which the individual does not want to participate. Other possibilities also exist, leading several authors to suggest the need to functionally analyze the environment to determine factors that may be causing or maintaining the unusual behavior (Demchak & Halle, 1985; Lennox & Miltenberger, 1989).

Mental Illness Having a severe disability, even a severe or profound degree of mental disability, does not mean that an individual is mentally ill. However, it is possible for some individuals to have a *dual diagnosis*—to have both a cognitive disability and some form of mental illness. The latter may include relatively mild forms of mental illness, such as personality disorders, or more severe forms, such as psychosis.

One difficulty with the determination of mental illness among persons with intellectual disabilities is differentiating whether the problem observed is a function of the mental disability or the mental illness. There are often discrepancies in estimations of the prevalence of persons with dual diagnosis, which range from about 10 to 40% of the persons with mental disabilities (Borthwick-Duffy & Eyman, 1990; Reiss, 1990). It should be noted that the majority of persons who are dually diagnosed fall into the range of mild to moderate mental disabilities (Jacobson, 1990).

Physical Characteristics

Individuals with severe disabilities may have physical disabilities or health disorders associated with their cognitive disabilities. Jacobson and Janicki (1985) examined the characteristics of 22,256 persons with severe or profound mental disabilities residing in the state of New York. They found that cerebral palsy, convulsive disorders (epilepsy), cardiovascular (heart) diseases, respiratory diseases, eating disorders, and growth impairments affected many individuals in the population they studied. These conditions are briefly described below. Although not found with great frequency, spina bifida and hydrocephaly might also be present in the population of people with severe disabilities.

Cerebral Palsy Cerebral palsy is a neurological disorder resulting from the inability of the brain to control the voluntary muscles in a normal fashion, thus interfering with normal movement and posturing abilities. Depending on which region of the brain is damaged, different forms of this condition occur and affect different areas of the body.

The most common form of cerebral palsy is *spasticity*, which represents about 60% of all forms of cerebral palsy. The condition is characterized by muscle stiffness (or hypertonia) and originates in the pyramidal tract of the central nervous system (Bigge, 1991; Healy, 1990). Individuals who have spasticity have limited range of motion due to severe muscle contractures affecting their hands, elbows, hips, knees, and feet. They might also have misformed spines and hip dislocations.

About 20% of the population with cerebral palsy exhibit the form commonly known as *athetosis,* which is also referred to as dyskinesia, meaning unwanted or involuntary movement. This form of the disorder appears when neurological damage has occurred outside of the pyramidal tract (extrapyramidal). It is characterized by either slow, writhing movements or abrupt, jerky movements, which may occur in facial muscles, the wrists and fingers, the trunk of the body, or in one or more extremities.

Rigid cerebral palsy, or rigidity, also has its origin in the extrapyramidal region of the brain (Batshaw & Perret, 1986). This form of cerebral palsy is relatively rare and is often classified as a form of spasticity (Bleck, 1982a). The least common type of cerebral palsy is *ataxia,* which accounts for approximately 1% of the prevalence of the general disorder. Ataxia occurs primarily due to damage to the cerebellum and is characterized by a lack of balance and uncoordinated movement (Bigge, 1991; Bleck, 1982a).

A final diagnosis often applied to persons with cerebral palsy is *mixed.* As the term implies, more than one form of the disorder exists simultaneously when the "mixed" diagnosis is applied. Most often the mix includes spasticity and athetosis. Spasticity and ataxia may also occur together. As many as 30% of the persons diagnosed with any particular form of cerebral palsy also show evidence of another form.

Physical disabilities, including those due to cerebral palsy, are described clinically by the particular limbs that are affected. The different conditions are described in Figure 1–3.

Cerebral palsy, particularly in the spasticity form, is the most common type of physical disability to be found within the population of persons with severe disabilities.

From 50 to 60% of persons with cerebral palsy are also classified as mentally disabled (Batshaw & Perret, 1986; Hardman & Drew, 1977). The mental disability may be in the "mild" range (i.e., IQ of 50 or 55 to about 70 or 75) or within the moderate, severe, or profound range as described earlier. It is often difficult to specifically assess the degree of cognitive ability in persons with severe cerebral palsy because their motor disability often interferes with life experiences and their ability to communicate what they know.

- Monoplegia: only one limb is affected.
- Diplegia: the lower limbs are severely affected, the trunk and the upper limbs to a lesser extent.
- Hemiplegia: only the limbs on one side of the body are affected.
- Paraplegia: only the legs are affected.
- Quadriplegia: major involvement of all four limbs, as well as the neck and the trunk.

Figure 1–3
Clinical Terms for Effects of Physical Disabilities

Epilepsy Epilepsy is a disorder of the brain that results in recurrent seizures (Epilepsy Foundation of America, 1993). There are different types of seizures, but the most severe form, Generalized Tonic-Clonic seizures (formerly referred to as grand mal), occurs most often among persons with severe disabilities. Epilepsy is not a disease per se but a symptom of irregular activity within the brain. Seizures may have several known causes, but in many cases, the cause is unknown (Berg, 1982; Epilepsy Foundation of America, 1993).

When a Generalized Tonic-Clonic seizure occurs, the first visible sign is usually that the person appears to lose awareness of what is going on. He or she then ceases to engage in present activity, loses consciousness, and falls to the floor. First he or she becomes tonic (stiff), then clonic (jerking) movements occur.

When this happens the person becomes less rigid and shakes or jerks arms, legs, or both. At some point during the seizure, the individual may lose control of bowels or bladder, cry, or expel saliva from the mouth. After a few minutes of the seizure activity, the person usually becomes drowsy and disoriented or falls into a deep sleep that may last from several minutes to several hours (Bigge, 1991; Wolraich, 1990b).

Although the Tonic-Clonic seizure is the most common among persons with severe disabilities who have seizures, other types may also occur. These include Complex Partial Seizures (known previously as psychomotor or temporal lobe seizures) and Absence Seizures (previously called petit mal seizures). During Complex Partial Seizures, which originate in the temporal lobe of the brain, the person may carry out complex behaviors such as undressing or saying something over and over again, even though there is an altered state of consciousness. In Absence Seizures, which are very brief, lasting perhaps 1 to 10 seconds, the person experiences a loss of consciousness but otherwise remains fixed. Sometimes it is assumed that the individual is daydreaming (Berg, 1982; Bigge, 1991).

Prescribed anticonvulsant drugs might be used to control the occurrence of seizures. These primarily include Ativan, Depakene, Depakote, Mebaral, Klonopin, Mysoline, Tegretol, Phenobarbital, Dilantin, or Zarontin (Berg, 1982; Epilepsy Foundation of America, 1993; Wolraich, 1990b). The specific medicine depends on the nature of the disorder and the individual's reaction to it. Fox and Westling (1986) reported that nearly half the students with profound mental disabilities in one school district were receiving some type of anticonvulsant medication. Other studies have reported similar findings about the degree of medication used to control seizures in persons with severe to profound mental disabilities (Davis, Cullari, & Breuning, 1982; Tu, 1979).

Cardiovascular Disorders Many persons with severe disabilities have congenital heart disease. The causes are sometimes unknown, but they are often found to be the same factors that result in the primary disability, for example, chromosomal anomalies, viruses during the first trimester, genetic factors, chronic alcoholism, excessive radiation. A primary example of a heart disease that occurs often among persons with severe disabilities is *atrioventricular canal,* which occurs in about 40% of children with Down syndrome. This involves a lack of separation of the heart's four chambers due to holes in the heart's walls, and the incomplete formation of the valves between the chambers (Baum, 1982; Blackman, 1990a).

There are numerous other cardiac conditions that may affect persons with severe disabilities, including the occurrence of narrowed valves within the heart; a hole in a wall of the heart that allows blood to leak into another part of the heart; a lack of separation of the heart's chambers; arteries that are too narrow, causing the heart to pump harder; underdevelopment of part of the heart; the mixture of deoxygenated with oxygenated blood due to various defects; the abnormal development of major veins; and the attachment of arteries to the wrong part of the heart (Baum, 1982; Blackman, 1990a). These conditions result in shortness of breath, fatigue, poor growth and development, chest pain, blueness of the lips and nail beds (cyanosis), fainting, chest deformity, and rapid heart beat. Additionally, as a result of some forms of congenital heart defects, congestive heart failure may occur. This means the heart may not pump adequately, causing fluids to build up in the lungs, liver, and other organs (Baum, 1982).

Many children with heart defects die at birth or in the first year of life; others live fairly normal lives either with or without specific medical intervention (e.g., surgery or medicine). Most persons with heart defects must avoid overactivity, although otherwise normal involvement and participation in life is encouraged. The particular problem for persons with severe disabilities who have a congenital heart disease may be the degree of tiredness or fatigue they experience during the normal routine of the day. The opportunity for frequent rest periods should help alleviate this problem while still allowing involvement in many typical activities.

Respiratory Disorders Persons with severe disabilities often have respiratory disorders such as asthma, bronchitis, apnea, bronchopulmonary dysplasia, cystic fibrosis, respiratory distress syndrome, and chronic colds, flu, or pneumonia. Additionally, breathing difficulties may occur due to weakened muscles that result from cerebral palsy, muscular dystrophy, or spinal muscular atrophy (Blackman, 1990c; Bleck & Nagel, 1982).

Various respiratory disorders result in wheezing, breathing difficulties, and excess mucous. Persons with these conditions may need to undergo regular postural drainage, suctioning, and oxygen therapy and receive prescribed medication. Avoiding overactivity will also be necessary.

Some individuals who are severely disabled and who have chronic respiratory problems are considered "technology-dependent" or "technology assisted" (Bigge, 1991). These terms suggest that without some regular form of intervention using technical equipment, these persons would not be able to survive. The types of equipment used with persons with respiratory disorders include continuous or periodic ventilation to assist breathing (a ventilator using a battery-operated electric motor pushes air into the lungs); the provision of concentrated oxygen, using an oxygen tank or oxygen concentrator; or suctioning to remove excess mucous from the lungs, using manual suction or an electric suctioning machine. Some persons who have respiratory difficulties have a tracheostomy (an opening in the trachea), which allows breathing to occur more easily or accommodates the ventilator or suctioning device.

Eating Problems For most individuals, eating abilities progress in a normal fashion, beginning with reflexive sucking, progressing to normal chewing and swallowing, and maturing with the use of eating utensils. Persons with severe disabilities might develop eating problems that call for special attention if they are to consume enough nutrients to ensure adequate growth and have maximum cognitive development. The most critical time for this concern is the infant, toddler, and early childhood years.

There are a variety of problems that can result in inadequate eating or hinder the normal digestive process. Cerebral palsy may result in defective oral-motor functioning, causing a weak suck, poor lip closure, jaw thrusting, lack of tongue control, and difficulty in chewing and swallowing (Bigge, 1991; Curry, 1990). The increased muscle tone of individuals with spasticity may consume greater than normal calories and thus compound the problem. If, in addition, a child has a respiratory disorder or a cardiac disease, he or she may lack the energy to participate in the feeding process. This is clearly problematic because lack of adequate nutrition will result in even less stamina.

Some children exhibit voluntary or involuntary resistance to eating by having tantrums, gagging, or regurgitating. Gastroesophageal (GE) reflux (vomiting because of a weak muscle connecting the stomach and the esophagus) is correctable through surgery. In other cases these behaviors may occur as a response to an unpleasant eating experience, because of a strong preference or dislike for different foods, because of changes in the environment or the routine, or because of hunger (Curry, 1990).

Growth Impairments Children with severe disabilities often do not demonstrate normal rates of growth and in fact are often small for their age. There are several possible causes for this. One is that the child may not receive adequate nutrition. Because of eating difficulties and frequent illnesses that are often associated with developmental disabilities, a child may not receive the amount of food that is normally consumed. In other cases, such as in the occurrence of cerebral palsy, oral-motor development may be impaired. In still others, malabsorption of food and/or diarrhea may be a factor (Curry, 1990).

Some growth impairments are related to specific syndromes or to prenatal conditions that also result in mental disabilities. For example, Down syndrome and Cornelia de Lange syndrome are characterized by slow growth; generally individuals with these syndromes are below average in size. Additionally, rubella, cytomegalic inclusion disease, syphilis, and toxoplasmosis are all prenatal viral infections that can result in both mental disabilities and physical retardation (Horton & Rimoin, 1982).

Spina Bifida Spina bifida is a congenital disorder in which the spine does not develop normally during the first trimester of fetal development; it sometimes occurs in individuals with severe disabilities, but may also occur without adversely affecting cognitive development.

The most serious and most common form of spina bifida is *myelomeningocele.* When this condition occurs, the spinal cord (myelo) and its covering membrane (meninges) pouch out of the opening in the vertebrae. It is often accompanied by hydrocephalus and flaccid paralysis of the lower trunk. Besides lacking leg use, the person who has a myelomeningocele will lack bladder and bowel control, lack skin sensation in the lower body, and may have scoliosis (curvature of the spine).

Hydrocephaly Hydrocephaly accompanies the myelomeninges form of spina bifida 90 to 95% of the time it occurs, although it may also occur without the spinal disorder. Hydrocephaly occurs when the cerebrospinal fluid is not absorbed normally by the body and instead is trapped in the ventricles of the brain and causes the brain, and thus the head, to become enlarged. Brain cells and nerve fibers become compressed, sometimes leading to some degree of mental disability, often mild.

A shunt or tube may be surgically inserted into the ventricles, allowing the fluid to drain into the cavity of the abdomen, or, less often, into the heart (Wolraich, 1990a). Occasionally shunts cause infections that must be treated.

Hydrocephalus often results in motor, language, or perceptual disabilities and seizure disorders. Usually the condition is treated immediately upon its discovery during the first year of life, using the shunting procedure. Delayed treatment results in the condition becoming more serious, including a more serious degree of intellectual disability.

Other Physical Characteristics There are various other physical problems that persons with severe disabilities may have, involving bowel and bladder control, partial or complete loss of hearing or visual ability, congenital limb malformations or absences, juvenile rheumatoid arthritis, and susceptibility to infection. Like the other physical conditions discussed above, these present substantial challenges to persons with severe disabilities.

Learning Potential of Persons with Severe Disabilities

Given the learning characteristics, the personal-social difficulties, and the physical chal-

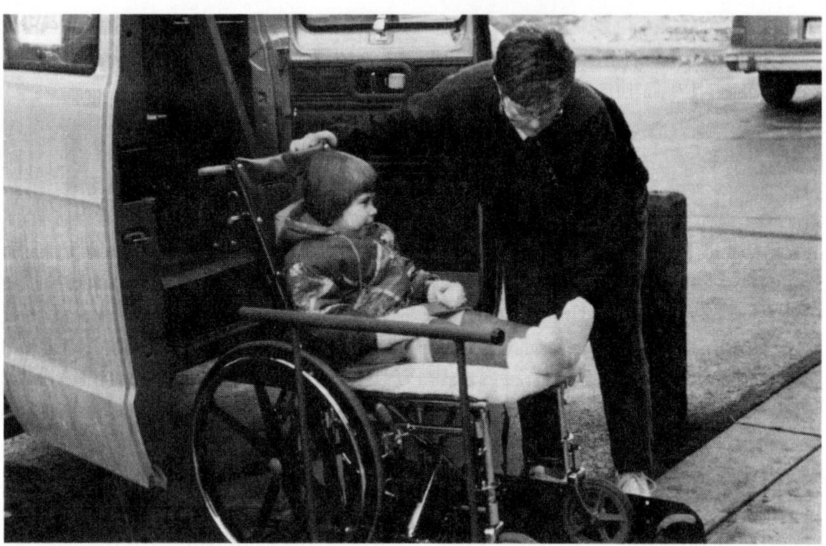

Students with severe disabilities can attend school with other children in the community.

lenges described in the previous sections, it would certainly be easy to conclude that there is little that persons with severe disabilities can learn, little that they can do. On the contrary, however, many studies and reports have demonstrated that this is not true. During the last several years, we have learned that given adequate opportunities and appropriate forms of instruction many persons with severe disabilities *can learn* and *can participate* in many life activities. When their involvement has been limited or when full participation has not been possible, partial, yet meaningful, participation has been the goal (Baumgart et al., 1982; Ferguson & Baumgart, 1991).

The potential areas of learning for persons with severe disabilities are far too numerous to present here. However, it is important that you acquire at least an indication of skill potential and how the skills have been learned. The areas of achievement discussed below are of great importance and are those in which recent research has demonstrated that people with severe disabilities can make substantial progress. We will briefly look at successful methods for teaching language skills, social skills, domestic and daily living skills, recreational and leisure skills, community skills, and skills for working in vocational settings. More details about providing instruction in these areas and others are presented throughout the text.

Language Skills

Persons with severe disabilities often exhibit few language skills, and therefore their communication can be very limited. It has been found, however, that different techniques and communication systems can result in the successful development and use of language (Caro & Snell, 1989; Mirenda, Iacono, & Williams, 1990). Some of these techniques include using environmental events to increase the probability that the person with the restricted language will exercise his or her verbal language skill. Other tactics include teaching the student to use signs or gestures or to communicate using pictures or symbols.

A very functional manner in which language has been taught to persons with severe disabilities requires that teachers, parents, and others identify naturally occurring opportunities such as arriving or departing from school, eating, or dressing and use these opportunities to prompt and reinforce the occurrence of language activity. Another natural strategy is skill clustering—teaching related skills in a natural sequence that will be functionally useful to the student, including a particular language skill. For example, the individual may be taught the steps necessary for entering a room, removing a coat, and then asking for a particular game to play (Caro & Snell, 1989; Halle, 1987).

The above language-training tactics attempt to develop necessary environmental conditions, primarily the responsiveness of other persons in the environment, in order to develop and increase natural speech. However, for some persons with severe disabilities, other methods of language or communication production are necessary because speech does not occur. Alternatives that have been successful include nonsymbolic or gestural communication, manual signing, and the use of static symbols or photographs. Usually the symbols will be attached to laptrays, communication boards, or even electronic communication devices that produce synthetic speech. Based on the individual's unique characteristics, the most suitable communication system will be developed (Mirenda, Iacono, & Williams, 1990).

Language training has been successful in increasing the frequency of language use, enlarging the number of language skills a person has, increasing the spontaneous and natural use of language in different environments, and providing alternative approaches to language production. After learning appropriate forms of language, some persons with severe disabilities have reduced their display of maladaptive, inappropriate, stereotyped, or self-injurious behaviors. These behaviors often serve as an attempt to communicate, but when other more acceptable forms of communication are introduced they are no longer necessary (Carr & Durand, 1985; Durand & Carr, 1987).

Whatever communication system is most appropriate, a major goal is to increase the responsiveness of key persons in the environment to attempts of these individuals to use language. Language is important because it allows us to exert some influence over our environment and the action of the people who are around us. Because this is true, we must work to increase our attention to the attempts by persons with severe disabilities to communicate with us and then reinforce those attempts. When this has been done, communication skills have generally improved.

Social Skills

The quality of a person's life may be defined by the nature of interaction with other people. Learning social skills allows us to live with others and to have different types and degrees of relationships with them. These relationships are important to most people and are no less important to persons with severe disabilities. However, because their abilities and circumstances often reduce their opportunities for normal social relations, it is most important that they participate in environments in which social behaviors and relations typically occur, and that they be taught the skills necessary to participate meaningfully in these environments. When this occurs, social skills improve.

The social behaviors of persons with severe disabilities have often been restricted by their segregation into environments that include only other persons with severe disabilities. In contrast, the development of social skills can improve if they are given the opportunity to interact with nondisabled persons. In a study that examined the effect of integrating persons with and without severe disabilities, Brinker (1985) found that there was more social behavior in the mixed groupings; that the students with severe disabilities made more positive social bids to the nondisabled students than to other students with severe disabilities; that those without disabilities made more positive social bids to the students with disabilities than did other students with disabilities; and that nondisabled students were more responsive to the social bids of the students with disabilities than were their peers with disabilities. All of this suggests that social behaviors by persons with severe disabilities are likely to increase in the presence of persons without disabilities.

To improve the skills necessary for people with severe disabilities to experience a full range of social relations, different forms of intervention might be necessary. Some that have been successful include direct instruction of social skills, teaching peers to initiate social interactions, and teaching social skills within the context of other functional behaviors. Research has shown that it is possible to use verbal directions, prompting, modeling, and role-playing to teach skills such as initiating interactions, acknowledging others' initiations, and elaborating on interactions and expanding them. As a result, students who have severe disabilities have been able to learn how to interact in a meaningful way with their nondisabled peers (Haring, 1991).

While learning specific social behaviors is important, it is more important to develop relations with nondisabled people that range from acquaintances to friendships. Recent reports suggest that people with severe disabilities can do so when given the opportunity (Kennedy, Horner, & Newton, 1989; Strully & Strully, 1985). In part, this is likely due to the ability of many people without disabilities to look past a person's mental and physical restrictions and toward the positive aspects of the person. It must be realized, however, that such occurrences are more likely to increase if we are able to teach persons with severe disabilities how to interact with others in a socially desirable fashion.

Domestic and Daily Living Skills

After 1967 the number of people with mental disabilities residing in large residential institutions began to decrease and, simultaneously, community-based residential programs began to expand. Today there are more options for where persons with severe disabilities may live, including private homes, group-living homes, and apartments in which they can live independently or semi-independently.

There has been a great deal of research reported that has demonstrated the ability of people with severe disabilities to acquire the skills necessary for self-care and daily living in their living environments (Browder & Snell, 1993; Snell & Farlow, 1993). These studies have shown that many people with moderate, severe, or profound mental disabilities can learn to use the toilet, bathe themselves, brush their teeth, shave, manage their menstrual care, dress themselves, eat appropriately, and perform most other self-care skills. They can also learn to do such things as wash their own clothes, use the telephone, clean their room, prepare meals, and perform other routine chores.

A portrayal of the typical domestic abilities of adult persons with mental disabilities was reported by Sullivan, Vitello, and Foster (1988). In their observational study, they described the activities of a group of six men with moderate mental disabilities over a 6-month period. The men resided in a group-living home and were observed as they engaged in their normal daily activities. Based on their extensive observations, Sullivan and her colleagues concluded that the men demonstrated quite skillful behaviors in virtually all of their daily routines, including personal care, domestic skills, and using appropriate manners and social behaviors.

Where a person lives and how he or she functions there is important. Natural homes are favored over institutional environments and provide the opportunities for persons with severe disabilities to function less dependently and more independently.

Recreational and Leisure Skills

Leisure and recreational activities are an important element of life for most people, and they are even more important for people with severe disabilities. Engaging in these activities is essential because it provides an opportunity to participate in an integrated world, demonstrate age-appropriate skills and social behavior, and make constructive use of free time. Thus an important goal for persons with severe disabilities—and a significant component of their instructional program—should be to develop appropriate leisure and recreational activities. Research has shown that many people with severe disabilities can make much progress in acquiring skills in this life domain (Dattilo, 1991).

Early studies found that persons with severe disabilities often engaged in no purposeful recreation and that their idle hours were spent in passive activities such as watching television. While to a certain degree this may be considered normal and acceptable, if it is the *only* way an individual spends free time, it may be less than desirable. Based on an apparent need for more suitable free-time skills, researchers developed a variety of instructional strategies and related interventions that have allowed persons with severe disabilities to develop more typical and enjoyable pursuits and to share many of the features of freedom that other persons have.

In a review of 17 studies, Nietupski, Hamre-Nietupski, and Ayres (1984) identified a number of recreational skills that researchers had been able to successfully teach different-aged persons who were moderately, severely, or profoundly mentally or multiply disabled. Some of the activities for children included riding a tricycle; using a trampoline; playing tic-tac-toe, checkers, and other table games; and playing with toys such as Legos, Brite-lite, Marble Rollway, and remote-control vehicles. Activities for adolescents and adults included calling and talking to people on the phone; doing physical fitness exercises; using a camera; playing Frisbee; playing darts; playing a pinball machine; playing video games; and buying soft drinks from a vending machine. Additional research may be expected to expand the skills and thus the opportunities for persons with severe disabilities to participate in different leisure-time activities.

Community Skills

One of the major effects of normalization, deinstitutionalization, and community living is that persons with severe disabilities have been able to make use of many of the facilities that exist throughout neighborhoods, towns, and cities. Many studies have shown that they can be taught the functional skills necessary for using such places as grocery stores, restaurants, department stores, laundromats, and community recreational facilities. Studies have also demonstrated that many adolescents and adults with severe disabilities can learn to cross the street safely, use public transportation, and withdraw money from automatic teller machines, among other skills that allow them to participate in communities (Snell & Browder, 1986; Westling & Floyd, 1990).

Aveno (1987) surveyed 436 community residences of persons with various severe disabilities to learn about the ways in which they participated in the community. Among the activities in which they engaged the most were using health-care services; walking, biking, or strolling in their wheelchairs; using restaurants; attending churches and synagogues; using grocery stores and supermarkets; using department stores; going to the barber shop or the beauty shop; visiting parks and zoos; and engaging in various recreational events including going to parties and dances, swimming, bowling, and attending movies, concerts, and plays. It is quite apparent that many persons with severe disabilities desire to take advantage of the many aspects of community life.

Teaching functional skills in community settings obviously requires a different instructional arrangement than has been used in the past by public school programs (Brown et al., 1983; Hamre-Nietupski, Nietupski, Bates, & Maurer, 1982). Teachers must take their students out of the schools and into community settings and conduct their instruction in the stores, restaurants, and other places in which the students will ultimately need to function. This will call for different public school staffing arrangements and instructional schedules and obviously will be a challenge for many educators and school administrators. However, the benefit will outweigh the additional effort because the students will be able to live much fuller, more normal lives in the community after learning how to operate in different settings.

Vocational Skills

One of the most typical aspects of adult life is being employed. Prior to the 1970s, the closest most people with severe disabilities came to employment was working in sheltered workshops. These workshops hired only people with disabilities and paid them far below the minimum wage (sometimes about one-tenth of it) to perform relatively simple tasks like folding letters and stuffing envelopes. While there are still such workshops today, there is clearly a different trend, one that encourages supported employment (or supported work) for people with severe disabilities in regular, integrated working environments (Rusch & Hughes, 1990; Wehman & Kregel, 1985).

The realization that people with severe disabilities could work in the regular world with different degrees of support occurred during the 1970s after several researchers, using the principles of applied behavior analysis, provided "illustrations of competence" by teaching people with moderate, severe, and profound mental disabilities to perform complex assembly tasks (Bellamy, Peterson, & Close, 1975; Gold, 1972). Following this, individual case studies began to appear in the literature, demonstrating that individuals with severe disabilities could learn to do jobs in community settings instead of in sheltered workshops (Rusch, Connis, & Sowers, 1978; Wehman, Hill, & Koehler, 1979). Today, supported employment models are used in most states in the United States (Shafer, Wehman, Kregel, & West, 1990).

A number of studies have been conducted that demonstrate the viability of supported employment in terms of the successful employment of people with disabilities and the financial benefit to both the person and the rehabilitation system. It has been shown that many persons with severe disabilities can perform various jobs, that they can get paid at least minimum wage for performing these jobs, and that they do not have to rely on sheltered workshop employment, which relies in turn on public funding (Rusch & Hughes, 1990). For example, a study by Wehman, Hill, Wood, and Parent

(1987) reported on the employment of 21 persons with severe mental disabilities (i.e., IQs under 40) over an 8-year period in various community settings. Although many demonstrated behavior difficulties that interfered with their work (e.g., worked slow, poor social skills), most also demonstrated positive characteristics (reliable attendance, good attitude) and remained employed for extended periods of time, earning at least minimum wage. The jobs were as entry-level service workers such as dishwashers and janitors. At the time of the study, as a group, these workers earned more than $230,000. One worker, whose IQ was 36, averaged more than $500 a month for more than 7 years (Wehman et al., 1987). Studies such as this demonstrate that having a severe disability need not preclude one from developing adequate vocational skills to function in the world of work.

Conclusion

People with severe disabilities are a heterogeneous group that have been placed in various traditional categories of disability. Regardless of the categorical placement, these individuals differ from one another, just as much as any two people without disabilities differ, perhaps even more. This variability makes it difficult to draw many general truths about people with severe disabilities. Nevertheless, there are certain characteristics and conditions that seem to explain the strengths and weaknesses of many individuals with severe disabilities. It is important to have knowledge of these in order to realize the types of services that need to be provided, although the specific needs of individuals can only be individually determined. When we know the learning difficulties experienced by people with severe disabilities, we can develop new ways for them to learn, and we can evaluate the effectiveness of these ways. By realizing some of the problems they face when interacting with others as well as when they are alone, we can look both to the individual with disabilities and to members of society and help both improve their behavior and accept each other. And by being aware of the many physical conditions that challenge those with severe disabilities, we can assist with their needs and find ways for them to have a fuller degree of participation and a better quality of life.

Prior to the last quarter of the 20th century, most people with severe disabilities were, in fact, denied the opportunity to participate in the world. They resided in institutions or were segregated in separate schools. But these conditions are rapidly changing. The last several years have seen tremendous advances in the knowledge we have about people with severe disabilities and how to educate them and assist them in learning to live. We are now better equipped to improve their functioning in many areas, such as using language, living in the community, and working on a job. All of this, and much else, assures that their lives will be better today and tomorrow than were the lives of persons with disabilities in past years.

Questions for Reflection

1. Several different concepts and definitions have been used for the term *severe disabilities*. What are some other ways to explain this condition?
2. Because people with severe disabilities are unique persons, is it appropriate to group them all together under one label? Why or why not?
3. Does the new definition of *mental retardation* by the American Association on Mental

Retardation improve the concept of this condition or make it more difficult to understand?

4. Given the learning characteristics shared by many people with severe disabilities, what would be one way to improve their learning potential?
5. How important is it for people to be able to generalize their skills? For which skills is generalizing most important? Are there any for which it is not important?
6. Many people with severe disabilities have significant physical problems or disabilities. Should we assume that people with very severe physical disabilities also have cognitive disabilities?
7. Unfortunately, some people with severe disabilities have relatively few friends. What could be done to improve this situation?
8. Research has shown that there is much potential for learning by individuals with severe disabilities. What additional areas of research might be important to expand upon this knowledge?

References

Abt Associates. (1974). *Assessment of selected resources for severely handicapped children and youth: Vol. 1. A state of the art paper.* Cambridge, MA: Abt Associates, Inc. (ERIC Document Reproduction Service No. ED 134 614.)

Agran, M., Fodor-Davis, J., Moore, S., & Deer, M. (1989). The application of a self-management program on instruction following skills. *Journal of the Association of Persons with Severe Handicaps, 14,* 147–154.

American Association on Mental Retardation. (1992). *Mental retardation: Definition, classification, and systems of supports* (9th ed.). Washington, DC: Author.

American Psychiatric Association. (1987). *Diagnostic and statistical manual of mental disorders* (3rd ed.). Washington, DC: American Psychiatric Association.

Aveno, A. (1987). A survey of activities engaged in and skills most needed by adults in community residences. *Journal of the Association for Persons with Severe Handicaps, 12,* 125–130.

Baker, D. (1979). Severely handicapped: Toward an inclusive definition. *AAESPH Review, 4*(1), 52–65.

Batshaw, M. L., & Perret, Y. M. (1986). *Children with handicaps: A medical primer* (2nd ed.). Baltimore, MD: Paul H. Brookes.

Baum, D. (1982). Heart disease in children. In E. E. Bleck & D. A. Nagel (Eds.), *Physically handicapped children: A medical atlas for teachers* (pp. 313–24). Orlando, FL: Grune & Stratton.

Baumgart, D., Brown, L., Pumpian, I., Nisbet, J., Ford, A., Sweet, M., Messina, R., & Schroeder, J. (1982). Principle of partial participation and individualized adaptations in educational programs for severely handicapped students. *Journal of the Association for the Severely Handicapped, 17*(2), 17–27.

Bellamy, G. T., Peterson, L., & Close, D. (1975). Habilitation of the severely and profoundly retarded: Illustration of competence. *Education and Training of the Mentally Retarded, 10,* 174–186.

Berg, B. O. (1982). Convulsive disorders. In E. E. Bleck & D. A. Nagel (Eds.), *Physically handicapped children: A medical atlas for teachers* (pp. 171–180). Orlando, FL: Grune & Stratton.

Bigge, J. L. (1991). *Teaching individuals with physical and multiple disabilities* (3rd ed.). New York: Macmillan.

Blackman, J. A. (1990a). Congenital heart disease. In J. A. Blackman (Ed.), *Medical aspects of developmental disabilities in children birth to three* (2nd ed.) (pp. 81–87). Rockville, MD: Aspen.

Blackman, J. A. (1990b). Congenital infections. In J. A. Blackman (Ed.), *Medical aspects of developmental disabilities in children birth to three* (2nd ed.) (pp. 89–95). Rockville, MD: Aspen.

Blackman, J. A. (Ed.) (1990c). Respiratory distress syndrome. In J. A. Blackman (Ed.), *Medical aspects of developmental disabilities in children birth to three* (2nd ed.) (pp. 243–245). Rockville, MD: Aspen.

Bleck, E. E. (1982a). Cerebral palsy. In E. E. Bleck & D. A. Nagel (Eds.), *Physically handicapped children: A medical atlas for teachers* (pp. 59–132). Orlando, FL: Grune & Stratton.

Bleck, E. E. (1982b). Rubella syndrome. In E. E. Bleck & D. A. Nagel (Eds.), *Physically handicapped children: A medical atlas for teachers* (pp. 431–432). Orlando, FL: Grune & Stratton.

Borthwick-Duffy, S. A. & Eyman, R. K. (1990). Who are the dually diagnosed? *American Journal on Mental Retardation, 94,* 586–595.

Brimer, R. W. (1990). *Students with severe disabilities: Current perspectives and practices.* Mountain View, CA: Mayfield.

Brinker, R. P. (1985). Interactions between severely mentally retarded students and other students in integrated and segregated public school settings. *American Journal of Mental Deficiency, 89,* 587–594.

Browder, D. M., & Snell, M. E. (1993). Daily living and community skills. In M. E. Snell (Ed.), *Instruction of students with severe disabilities* (4th ed.). New York: Merrill/Macmillan.

Brown, L., Nisbet, J., Ford, A., Sweet, M., Shiraga, B., York, J., & Loomis, R. (1983). The critical need for nonschool instruction in educational programs for severely handicapped students. *Journal of the Association of the Severely Handicapped, 8,* 71–77.

Caro, P., & Snell, M. E. (1989). Characteristics of teaching communication to people with moderate and severe disabilities. *Education and Training in Mental Retardation, 24,* 63–77.

Carr, E. G., & Durand, V. M. (1985). Reducing behavior problems through functional communication training. *Journal of Applied Behavior Analysis, 18,* 111–126.

Carter, C. H. (1975). *Handbook of mental retardation syndromes.* Springfield, IL: Charles C Thomas.

Crapps, J., Langone, J., & Swain, S. (1985). Quantity and quality of participation in community environments by mentally retarded adults. *Education and Training of the Mentally Retarded, 20,* 123–129.

Curry, P. A. S. (1990). Feeding problems. In J. A. Blackman (Ed.), *Medical aspects of developmental disabilities in children birth to three* (2nd ed.) (pp. 125–139). Rockville, MD: Aspen.

Dattilo, J. (1991). Recreation and leisure: A review of the literature and recommendations for future directions. In L. H. Meyer, C. A. Peck, & L. Brown (Eds.), *Critical issues in the lives of people with severe disabilities* (pp. 171–193). Baltimore: Paul H. Brookes.

Davis, R. R., & Rogers, E. S. (1985). Social skills with persons who are mentally retarded. *Mental Retardation, 23,* 186–196.

Davis, V., Cullari, S., & Breuning, S. (1982). Drug use in community foster homes. In S. Breuning & A. Poling (Eds.), *Drugs and mental retardation* (pp. 359–376). Springfield, IL: Charles C Thomas.

Demchak, M. A., & Halle, J. (1985). Motivational assessment: A potential means of enhancing treatment success of self-injurious individuals. *Education and Training of the Mentally Retarded, 20,* 25–38.

Downing, J., & Eichinger, J. (1990). Instructional strategies for learners with dual sensory impairments in integrated settings. *Journal of the Association for Persons with Severe Handicaps, 15,* 98–105.

Durand, V. M., & Carr, E. G. (1987). Social influences on "self-stimulatory" behavior: Analysis and treatment application. *Journal of Applied Behavior Analysis, 20,* 119–132.

Ellis, N. (Ed.). (1963). *Handbook of mental deficiency: Psychological theory and research.* New York: McGraw-Hill.

Ellis, N. (Ed.). (1979). *Handbook of mental deficiency: Psychological theory and research* (2nd ed). Hillsdale, NJ: Erlbaum.

Epilepsy Foundation of America. (1993). *Epilepsy: Medical aspects.* Landover, MD: Author.

Ferguson, D. L., & Baumgart, D. (1991). Partial participation revisited. *Journal of the Association for Persons with Severe Handicaps, 16,* 218–227.

Fox, L. (1989). Stimulus generalization of skills and persons with profound mental handicaps. *Education and Training in Mental Retardation, 24,* 219–229.

Fox, L., & Westling, D. L. (1986). The prevalence of students who are profoundly mentally handicapped receiving medication in a school district. *Education and Training of the Mentally Retarded, 21,* 205–210.

Fredericks, H. D., & Baldwin, V. (1987). Individuals with sensory impairments: Who are they? How are they educated? In L. Goetz, D. Guess, & K. Stremel-Campbell (Eds.), *Innovative program design for individuals with dual sensory impairments* (pp. 3–14). Baltimore: Paul H. Brookes.

Gaylord-Ross, R., & Peck, C. A. (1984). Integration efforts for students with severe mental retardation. In D. Bricker & J. Fuller (Eds.), *Severe mental retardation: From theory to practice* (pp. 185–207). Reston, VA: Division on Mental Retardation of the Council for Exceptional Children.

Gold, M. (1972). Stimulus factors in skill training of the retarded on a complex assembly task: Acquisition, transfer, and retention. *American Journal of Mental Deficiency, 76,* 517–526.

Grossman, H. J. (Ed.). (1973). *Manual on terminology and classification in mental retardation.* Washington, DC: American Association on Mental Deficiency.

Grossman, H. J. (Ed.). (1977). *Manual on terminology and classification in mental retardation.* Washington, DC: American Association on Mental Deficiency.

Grossman, H. J. (Ed.). (1983). *Classification in mental retardation.* Washington, DC: American Association on Mental Deficiency.

Halle, J. (1987). Teaching language in the natural environment: An analysis of spontaneity. *Journal of the Association for Persons with Severe Handicaps, 12,* 28–37.

Hamre-Nietupski, S., Nietupski, J., Bates, P., & Maurer, S. (1982). Implementing a community-based educational model for moderately/severely handicapped students: Common problems and suggested solutions. *Journal of the Association for the Severely Handicapped, 7,* 38–43.

Hardman, M., & Drew, C. (1977). The physically handicapped retarded individual: A review. *Mental Retardation, 15*(5), 43–48.

Haring, N. G. (Ed.). (1988). *Generalization for students with severe handicaps: Strategies and solutions.* Seattle, WA: University of Washington Press.

Haring, T. G. (1991). Social relationships. In L. H. Meyer, C. A. Peck, & L. Brown (Eds.), *Critical issues in the lives of people with severe disabilities* (pp. 195–217). Baltimore: Paul H. Brookes.

Healy, A. (1990). Cerebral palsy. In J. A. Blackman (Ed.), *Medical aspects of developmental disabilities in children birth to three* (2nd ed.) (pp. 59–66). Rockville, MD: Aspen.

Heber, R. (1959). A manual on terminology and classification in mental retardation. *Monograph Supplement of American Journal of Mental Deficiency* (No. 64).

Heber, R. (1961). Modifications in the manual on terminology and classification in mental retardation. *American Journal of Mental Deficiency, 65*(4), 499–500.

Horner, R. H., Sprague, J., & Wilcox, B. (1982). Constructing general case programs for community activities. In B. Wilcox & T. Bellamy (Eds.), *Design of high school programs for severely handicapped students* (pp. 61–98). Baltimore: Paul H. Brookes.

Horton, W. A., & Rimoin, D. L. (1982). Short stature and growth. In E. E. Bleck & D. A. Nagel (Eds.), *Physically handicapped children: A medical atlas for teachers* (pp. 451–468). Orlando, FL: Grune & Stratton.

Hughes, C., & Petersen, D. L. (1989). Utilizing a self-instructional training package to increase on-task behavior and work performance. *Education and Training in Mental Retardation, 24*, 114–120.

Hughes, C., & Rusch, F. R. (1989). Teaching supported employees with severe mental retardation to solve problems. *Journal of Applied Behavior Analysis, 22*, 365–372.

Jacobson, J. W. (1990). Do some mental disorders occur less frequently among persons with mental retardation? *American Journal on Mental Retardation, 94*, 596–602.

Jacobson, J. W., & Janicki, M. P. (1985). Functional and health status characteristics of persons with severe handicaps in New York State. *Journal of the Association for Persons with Severe Handicaps, 10*, 51–60.

Justen, J. E. (1976). Who are the severely handicapped? A problem in definition. *AAESPH Review, 1*(5), 1–11.

Kennedy, C. H., Horner, R. H., & Newton, J. S. (1989). Social contacts of adults with severe disabilities living in the community: A descriptive analysis of relationship patterns. *Journal of the Association for Persons with Severe Handicaps, 14*, 190–196.

Lennox, D. B., & Miltenberger, R. G. (1989). Conducting a functional assessment of problem behavior in applied settings. *Journal of the Association for Persons with Severe Handicaps, 14*, 304–311.

Mercer, C. D., & Snell, M. E. (1977). *Learning theory research in mental retardation: Implications for teaching.* Columbus, OH: Charles E. Merrill.

Meyer, L. H., Peck, C. A., & Brown, L. (Eds.) (1991). *Critical issues in the lives of people with severe disabilities.* Baltimore: Paul H. Brookes.

Mirenda, P., Iacono, T., & Williams, R. (1990). Communication options for persons with severe and profound disabilities: State of the art and future directions. *Journal of the Association for Persons with Severe Handicaps, 15*, 3–21.

Nietupski, J., Hamre-Nietupski, S., & Ayres, B. (1984). Review of task analytic leisure skill training efforts: Practitioner implications and future research needs. *Journal of the Association for Persons with Severe Handicaps, 9*, 88–97.

Paul, R. (1987). Communication. In D. J. Cohen & A. M. Donnellan (Eds.), *Handbook of autism and pervasive developmental disorders* (pp. 61–84). New York: John Wiley.

Reiss, S. (1990). Prevalence of dual diagnosis in community-based day programs in the Chicago metropolitan area. *American Journal on Mental Retardation, 94*, 578–585.

Rusch, F. R., Connis, R. T., & Sowers, J. (1978). The modification and maintenance of time spent attending to task using social reinforcement, token reinforcement, and response cost, in an applied restaurant setting. *Journal of Special Education Technology, 2*, 18–26.

Rusch, F. R., & Hughes, C. (1990). Historical overview of supported employment. In F. Rusch (Ed.), *Supported employment: Models, methods, and issues* (pp. 5–14). Sycamore, IL: Sycamore.

Rutter, M. (1985). The treatment of autistic children. *Journal of Child Psychology and Psychiatry, 26*, 193–214.

Sailor, W., & Haring, N. (1977). Some current directions in the education of the severely/multiply handicapped. *AAESPH Review, 2*(2), 67–86.

Salend, S. J., Ellis, L. L., & Reynolds, C. J. (1989). Using self-instruction to teach vocational skills to individuals who are severely retarded. *Education and Training in Mental Retardation, 24*, 248–254.

Schor, D. P. (1990). Autism. In J. A. Blackman (Ed.), *Medical aspects of developmental disabilities in children birth to three* (pp. 7–10). Rockville, MD: Aspen.

Shafer, M. S., Wehman, P., Kregel, J., & West, M. (1990). National supported employment initiative: A preliminary analysis. *American Journal on Mental Deficiency, 95*, 316–327.

Smithdas, R. (1981). Psychological aspects of deaf-blindness. In S. Walsh & R. Holzberg (Eds.), *Understanding and educating the deaf-blind/severely and profoundly handicapped* (pp. 38–42). Springfield, IL: Charles C Thomas.

Snell, M. E., & Farlow, L. J. (1993). Self-care skills. In M. E. Snell (Ed.), *Instruction of students with severe disabilities* (4th ed.) (pp. 380–441). New York: Merrill/Macmillan.

Snell, M. E., & Browder, D. M. (1986). Community-referenced instruction: Research and issues. *Journal of the Association for Persons with Severe Handicaps, 11,* 1–11.

Strully, J., & Strully, C. (1985). Friendship and our children. *Journal of the Association for Persons with Severe Handicaps, 10,* 224–227.

Sullivan, C. A. C., Vitello, S. J., & Foster, W. (1988). Adaptive behavior of adults with mental retardation: An intensive case study. *Education and Training in Mental Retardation, 23*(1), 76–81.

Tu, J. B. (1979). The survey of psychotropic medication in mental retardation facilities. *Journal of Clinical Psychiatry, 40,* 125–128.

U.S. Department of Education. (1990). *Twelfth annual report to Congress on the implementation of the Education of the Handicapped Act.*

Van Dijk, J. (1985). An educational curriculum for deaf-blind multi-handicapped persons. In D. Ellis (Ed.), *Sensory impairments in mentally handicapped people* (pp. 374–382). San Diego, CA: College-Hill Press.

Volkmar, F. R. (1987). Social development. In D. J. Cohen & A. M. Donnellan (Eds.), *Handbook of autism and pervasive developmental disorders* (pp. 41–60). New York: John Wiley.

Wehman, P., Hill, J. W., & Koehler, F. (1979). Placement of developmentally disabled individuals into competitive employment: Three case studies. *Education and Training of the Mentally Retarded, 14,* 269–276.

Wehman, P., Hill, J. W., Wood, W., & Parent, W. (1987). A report on competitive employment histories of persons labeled severely mentally handicapped. *Journal of the Association for Persons with Severe Handicaps, 12,* 11–17.

Wehman, P., & Kregel, J. (1985). A supported work approach to competitive employment of individuals with moderate and severe handicaps. *Journal of the Association for Persons with Severe Handicaps, 10,* 3–11.

Westling, D. L. (1986). *Introduction to mental retardation.* Englewood Cliffs, NJ: Prentice-Hall.

Westling, D. L., & Floyd, J. (1990). Generalization of community skills: How much training is necessary? *Journal of Special Education, 23,* 386–406.

Whitman, T. L. (1990). Self-regulation and mental retardation. *American Journal on Mental Retardation, 94,* 347–362.

Wolraich, M. (1990a). Hydrocephalus. In J. A. Blackman (Ed.), *Medical aspects of developmental disabilities in children birth to three* (2nd ed.) (pp. 175–179). Rockville, MD: Aspen.

Wolraich, M. (1990b). Seizure disorders. In J. A. Blackman (Ed.), *Medical aspects of developmental disabilities in children birth to three* (2nd ed.) (pp. 251–257). Rockville, MD: Aspen.

CHAPTER 2

Philosophy and Best Practices for Educating Persons with Severe Disabilities

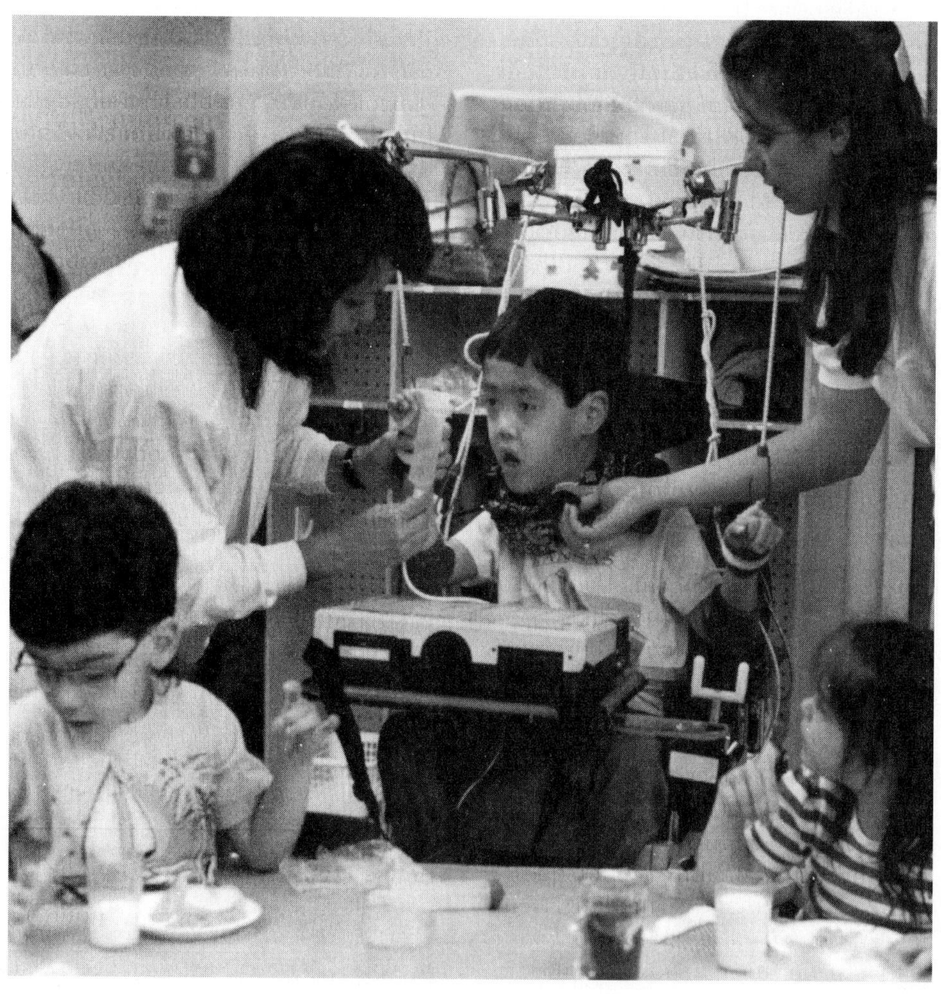

Chapter Overview

This chapter offers a philosophy and provides an overview of best practices for teaching students with severe disabilities. Also included are a definition of special education, characteristics of an appropriate special education program, and a rationale for why certain practices are appropriate. The chapter is intended to provide you with a snapshot of the types of services that should be offered and to serve as an advance organizer for subsequent chapters in the text.

No meaningful educational program can be developed for persons with severe disabilities unless it is directed by a philosophy and a corresponding set of guidelines for professional practice. Before a teacher begins to teach, there should be a clear understanding of the purpose of her or his activity. Once a philosophy is adopted, appropriate instructional practices will follow. Without a philosophy, however, the teacher's instructional activities will be unfocused and lack direction. Given the challenges faced by people with severe disabilities that were described in Chapter 1, the purpose of the present chapter is first to provide the philosophy that will permeate the instructional strategies and tactics presented throughout this text, and then to outline the currently accepted best practices for teaching students with severe disabilities, practices that reflect the philosophy.

> **A Philosophy for Providing Services to Students with Severe Disabilities**
>
> Students with severe disabilities should be provided with a quality of education that is no less than that offered to other students. The education should be individually designed to meet their needs but should not serve to isolate or segregate them from other people. It should begin as soon in life as possible after the recognition that there is a disability. As an integral part of the early intervention service, family involvement and support should occur. The education should continue through the school years and until the individual is adequately prepared to enter the adult world as a participating member, which should be the ultimate goal of an educational program. Special education and related services should maximize the learning, growth, and development of the individual while having the least possible degree of unnecessary intrusiveness. Simultaneously, special education should attempt to assist all nondisabled persons in understanding and developing a world that accommodates persons with severe disabilities.

Teachers and key professional personnel must recognize that each individual is of value and that each has the potential to learn. No student, with or without a severe disability, will learn if the persons responsible for promoting learning do not believe it is possible. It is therefore critical that teachers of these students have confidence in their ability to profit from instruction, regardless of the severity of their disability. The progress of a student with a severe disability will be directly related to the quality of education provided.

The Evolution of Philosophies and Practices for Teaching Students with Severe Disabilities

Since educational and related services began to be offered to persons with severe disabilities about two centuries ago, the philosophies that have guided professional practices have varied. Early in the 19th century, because practitioners thought that mental disabilities could be cured by exercising the central and peripheral nervous systems, their instructions consisted primarily of sensory and motor exercises. Later, toward the end of the century, professionals began to change their opinions. Deciding that cures were not possible, they felt that it would be better to protect and care for the needs of people with severe disabilities. The focus shifted from instruction to life management.

As the 20th century approached, Western society was swept by what has been referred to as the "genetic scare." There was great concern that persons with "inferior genes" would have a degrading effect on the quality of the human race. As a result of this type of thinking, people with mental disabilities and other disabilities were warehoused in distant large residential institutions so they would not pose a threat to the gene pool of society. Beginning with the turn of the century, then, the guiding philosophy was not to teach, and not even to care for, persons with severe disabilities, but to protect society from them. This most sorrowful and inhumane reasoning led to equally sorrowful and inhumane life conditions and living arrangements for most persons with mental disabilities and other severe disabilities.

Before the 1950s, there was little in the way of services for most persons with mental disabilities who remained in the community instead of being housed in institutions. Those that were available were provided by parents' organizations and private groups. It was not until the 1950s and 1960s that public schools began to provide instruction for persons with moderate and severe mental disabilities—and it was not until several years later that children and youth with the most severe disabilities, that is, with profound mental disabilities, began to receive public school services. This first occurred when Public Law 94-142 was passed in 1975. The reasons given by the public school personnel for these exclusionary practices were that schools were intended to teach academic skills and that persons not capable of learning at least the three Rs should not be served. This opinion—that some persons cannot benefit from education—was originally debated in the 1950s but has continued to be voiced since then (Bailey, 1981; Goldberg & Cruickshank, 1958).

When students with severe disabilities were finally accepted into public school systems, instructional practices were often guided by an ability-level philosophy. Students' developmental levels (i.e., mental ages, IQs) were determined, and they were taught skills that were considered to be within these levels. Instructional activities for students with moderate and severe mental disabilities, even those in their adolescent years, consisted of arts and crafts, preacademic and primary-level academic skills, language development, self-care skills, gross and fine motor skills, and prevocational skills. Regardless of the students' ages, most classrooms resembled kindergarten or nursery school classes.

When programs were developed for students with the most severe disabilities, instructional programming was intended to inch them forward on scales of normal human development. Teachers would attempt to increase the number of trials during which a student would make eye contact or put a block in a box, because this was the next step in the normal progression of human development.

Positive reinforcement (usually a small amount of food) was used to reward correct responses, and behavioral performances were recorded and charted on graph paper. Little thought was given to the usefulness of the behavior or how it would improve the student's life.

Current "best practices" for providing services to persons with severe disabilities did not spontaneously emerge but evolved over a period of time. During the late 1960s, the concept of *normalization* was introduced (Nirje, 1969; Wolfensberger, 1972). This policy called for agencies to provide persons with mental disabilities with living and learning experiences that were as normal as possible. Skills to be taught were those that would allow greater independence and life patterns that were parallel to those of people who did not have disabilities. Under the normalization principle, it was intended that the instructional procedures for teaching these skills were also to be as close to normal as possible.

At about the same time, the *deinstitutionalization* period began. This period was characterized by a decline in the number of persons living in large residential institutions and an increase in the number living with their families and in smaller community-based residences. Community facilities were intended to be "homelike" and included foster homes, group homes, intermediate-care facilities, and sheltered apartments. Much effort was made to move individuals out of large residential institutions into smaller facilities located in regular communities, where services that had traditionally been provided only in the institutions were to be provided.

As normalization and deinstitutionalization were occurring and public school programs were emerging, the focus gradually began to shift from simply providing services to improving the quality of instruction and related services. Many instructional programs lagged behind what was being proposed and implied by the normalization and deinstitutionalization movements. Students were *not* being educated for lives that were to be as normal as possible. They were *not* being educated for living with their families and in communities and being a part of those social systems. Often they were being taught activities that would not be of use to them, even though they may have been able to learn them and may have enjoyed doing them. In the worst cases, teachers were simply providing baby-sitting or custodial care and not teaching anything at all.

The question of the value and relevance of much special education was first raised in the 1960s. The most often cited paper was one written by Lloyd Dunn (1968), a prominent professor of special education at Peabody College. Dunn stated that too many minority children were being placed in self-contained special classes for students with mild mental disabilities and that this practice was discriminatory and did little good for the students. Dunn proposed that many of these students should not be considered mentally disabled, that general education should be able to serve them, and that so much special education was not justifiable. Following Dunn's paper, special education programs and related practices for students with mild mental disabilities started to change. But similar concerns about the practices of educating students with more severe disabilities did not begin to surface until a few years later, after the passage of P.L. 94-142.

Contemporary Best Practices for Students with Severe Disabilities

In 1976, Lou Brown of the University of Wisconsin and his colleagues published a paper that set the tone for most of what has evolved into current best practices for educating students with severe disabilities (Brown,

Nietupski, & Hamre-Nietupski, 1976). Brown et al. proposed the following:

- Students with severe disabilities should be educated in regular schools with students who do not have disabilities. "Placement in large multi purpose institutions, sustained maintenance at home, and/or sustained placement in self-contained classes within segregated schools is generally restrictive. The community must create other more educationally tenable developmental environments" (p. 3).
- The exclusive use of homogeneous ability grouping of students with severe disabilities should be avoided. Development and learning are more likely to occur if there is opportunity to interact with persons of different ability levels. "If severely handicapped students are to be expected to function effectively in heterogeneous community environments, as many preceding developmental experiences as possible should represent that heterogeneity" (p. 5).
- Teachers must directly teach the skills that students with severe disabilities are expected to learn and teach them in the settings in which they need to be performed. Referring to a "zero degree inference strategy," the authors wrote "Thus, teachers of severely handicapped students can rarely, if ever, infer that because a student performs a particular skill in an artificial setting, he or she can also perform that skill in other more natural settings" (p. 6).
- All educational efforts for persons with severe disabilities should be judged as they relate to the "criterion of ultimate functioning," that is, the ability to participate as fully as possible in integrated adult environments. Any activity that does not contribute to this type of personal development should not be pursued. We need to ask questions such as "Is this activity necessary to prepare students to ultimately function in complex heterogeneous community settings?" and "Could students function as adults if they did not acquire the skill?" (p. 9).
- Teaching procedures for students with severe disabilities should be natural. Instruction should be delivered to groups of students as opposed to an overreliance on one-to-one instruction. Massed-practice of behaviors in artificial circumstances (e.g., putting a block in a box for 10 consecutive trials) should be avoided in favor of distributed teaching of functional skills throughout the school day. Skills should be learned and practiced in different settings, with different people, and under different conditions so that the learner will be better able to use the skills in natural settings. Instructional materials and settings should be real. "However cumbersome, time consuming, inconvenient, or expensive it may be to do so, the pegs, felt squares, pictures of money, tokens, pictures, edible consequences, and many, if not all of the commercially available kits and irrelevant paper-and-pencil tasks should be faded out" (p. 14).

Since the publication of the paper by Brown and his colleagues, many subsequent authors have described or summarized best practices in papers and textbooks (e.g., Certo, Haring, & York, 1984; Ford et al., 1989; Fox et al., 1986; Horner, Meyer, & Fredericks, 1986; McDonnell, Wilcox, & Hardman, 1991; Meyer, 1987; Meyer, Eichinger, & Park-Lee, 1987; Rainforth, York, & Macdonald, 1992; Sailor et al., 1989; Salisbury & Vincent, 1990; Snell, 1988; Strain, 1990; Williams, Fox, Thousand, & Fox,

1990). These writings have outlined practices covering services for all ages of persons with severe disabilities, from infancy through adulthood. Together they describe state-of-the-art procedures for providing services to people with severe disabilities.

In the following sections of this chapter, an overview of many contemporary best practices is provided. This brief description is intended to orient you toward the content that will be provided throughout the remaining chapters of this text. We will begin with a definition of special education for students with severe disabilities and its features, and then look more closely at best practices in different areas.

The Meaning of Special Education

The following definition is proposed for special education for persons with severe disabilities. As can be seen, it is based on the previously presented philosophy.

Definition of Special Education

Special education for persons with severe disabilities consists of an instructional process by which persons with cognitive, social, and sometimes physical limitations are able to maximize their potential in such a way that they can enjoy a quality of life similar to that enjoyed by persons who do not have disabilities. As a result of this process, these persons would be able to experience life in their home and community very much like that experienced by others of the same chronological age.

Special education is *not* made special by the nature of the instructional materials used or by being provided in "special" settings in which there are only other students with severe disabilities. It is made special by the nature of the skills that are taught and the methods used to teach them. Special education should consist of supportive educational programs necessary to best ensure that a student with severe disabilities lives a normal life and learns normal behaviors to the degree he or she is most capable.

A high-quality special education program should be characterized by the following 11 features:

Characteristics of a Special Education Program

1. Students should be treated with dignity. The language and the attitudes of the teachers and others should reflect the value of the students as human beings. The professionals and paraprofessionals providing services should respect the humanity of the individual students whom they are teaching. They should also believe in the value of teaching them.
2. There should be a pervasive attitude that all students are capable of learning meaningful skills that will move them away from dependence and toward independence, away from isolation and toward involvement.
3. All students should be involved in the normal routines and schedules of the school along with the students who do not have disabilities. Interactions with students who do not have disabilities should occur for a substantial portion of the school day.
4. Meaningful learning activities should be planned and each student should be working toward individually prescribed objectives within those activities. Objectives should be taught that allow the student to function as well as possible in all current environments and to be prepared for operating in future environments. Instruction directed toward the achievement of specific objectives should be distributed throughout the day in a natural fashion, not presented in an artificial, massed array.
5. Instruction should occur in the most natural and least restrictive settings, including regular classes to the extent possible, different settings within the school, community settings, homes, and, in some situations, special education classrooms.

6. Materials used and instructional activities should be natural. They should be items and activities used in everyday life and not materials especially designed for special education, with the exception of technologically sophisticated devices designed to assist in areas such as communication or mobility.
7. Instructional procedures should be as precise as necessary, yet as natural as possible. The procedures should be those that best ensure that learning will occur but that show respect for the dignity of the individual and thus are not overly intrusive.
8. Student performance data on key, specific objectives should be collected on a regular basis in order to assess the student's progress.
9. Instruction should focus on skill acquisition, maintenance, and generalization. Targeted skills should not be "checked off" a checklist when "completed," but should become a part of the repertoire of functional skills possessed by the student.
10. Specific efforts to improve the knowledge and attitudes of other students and school employees toward people with severe disabilities should be made. Teachers should encourage students and other professionals, paraprofessionals, and nonprofessionals in the school to interact appropriately with students who have disabilities. Friendships between students with and without disabilities should be encouraged.
11. Parents should be acknowledged as the student's primary teachers and should be included in the educational program to the degree they wish. Most important, parents should be involved in the educational planning process.

Best Practices Within Educational Programs for Students with Severe Disabilities

In addition to the general characteristics listed above, other aspects of programs for students with disabilities are described in the following sections.

Collaborating with Other Professionals and Parents

The effectiveness of services for students with severe disabilities will be maximized if various professionals collaborate with each other and with parents and family members. In this way, services can be coordinated and goals and objectives can be developed that address students' needs holistically. Successful collaboration should reflect the practices described in Figure 2–1. Interactions among various professionals and parents are discussed in greater detail in chapter 3.

Assessment and Planning

In order that the most relevant instruction be provided to the student with severe disabilities, professionals and parents must cooperatively determine students' current skills, determine what skills are needed, prioritize those skills, and plan the specific objectives that should be achieved by the student to accomplish those skills. There are several types of assessment, but the most relevant forms involve the parents (and sometimes the student) indicating what the student can do and what skills he or she needs to function in important environments. Based on this information, different types of plans can be developed, including Individual Family Service Plans for infants and toddlers with disabilities and their families, Individual Educational Plans for school-age students, and Individual Transition Plans for students when they reach mid adolescence and are rapidly approaching adulthood. Alternative plans, such as Personal Futures Planning, can also be useful.

1. All persons participating in the collaborative process, including parents and professionals, are of equal importance.
2. All participants should be aware of the knowledge and expertise of other members of the collaborative team.
3. Representatives of various disciplines participate in the collaborative process. The needs of the student imply which professionals should participate.
4. Decisions are made through a consensus of the group.
5. Skills that are to be developed by various specialists (such as physical and occupational specialists) should be related to the functional skills needed by the student.
6. All disciplines should share knowledge and skills with all others so these can be applied to different needs and in different situations.
7. There are various degrees and types of participation appropriate for parents, and their right to choose how they want to be involved in their child's education must be respected. To the extent that they desire to participate, parents are given the necessary instruction for joining in the instructional process as it occurs in the home and community.
8. Parents should have frequent opportunities to visit the school and participate in activities with their child.
9. Communication between parents, teachers, and other members of the school system is extremely important. A system should exist for regular parent-school communication.
10. In addition to teaching their children, schools must recognize that they are a primary source of information for parents on other matters of support for their child. Parents should be provided with information about community services.

Figure 2–1
Best Practices for Collaboration with Professionals and Parents

Assessment and planning are thoroughly discussed in chapters 4 and 5. Some of the best practices associated with this process are listed in Figure 2–2.

Early Intervention and Preschool Programs

An early intervention program is an extremely important service that should be provided to infants and toddlers with disabilities. This should be followed by participation in a preschool program when the child is 3 years old. Since most children with severe disabilities are identifiable at birth or very early in life, it is possible to begin intervention early; to do so is critical to maximizing later development. Early intervention and preschool programs reduce the impact of the disability, promote the child's normalized development as much as possible, support the family in meeting the child's needs, and help coordinate all of the available sources of support for the child and the family. Complete discussion of early intervention and preschool programs is presented in chapter 18.

1. Planning should be a collaborative process with input from parents, professionals, and the student whenever possible. Friends of the student can also provide meaningful information. All of these persons can make important suggestions regarding what are appropriate objectives for students.
2. To aid in this planning process, consideration should be given to functioning in all life domains including areas of human activity that occur in *the school, the home, the community, recreational settings, and work environments*. Conducting *ecological inventories* in these settings is one way to determine what students need to function. Other methods include reviewing previous records, using adaptive behavior scales, and directly observing the student.
3. The student's current skill level in different settings and his or her needs should prescribe which specific skills should be listed as objectives for the student on the IEP. In addition to current environments, future environments should be considered when identifying specific objectives.
4. Planning for major moves or transitions should occur well in advance of the transition with attention being given to the needs of the person with disability and to the nature of the future setting or service. The transition out of the school system and into the adult world, including employment and often new residential arrangements, is often considered one of the most important. Planning for this transition should begin when the student is in early adolescence. All types of transition planning should be initiated at least a year prior to the change.
5. Special focus should be on planning for moving the learner to the least restrictive environment if he or she is not already there. This plan will include actions that are necessary for achieving as much inclusion as possible.

Figure 2–2
Best Practices in Assessment and Planning

Early intervention and preschool programs should have several characteristics, including those listed in Figure 2–3.

School Placement

Where students with severe disabilities go to school is important and can affect the skills they develop, their attitudes, and the attitudes of others toward them. It can influence the involvement of parents in the formal schooling process. For many years the argument has been made that students who have severe disabilities should receive their education in general school placements. Still, there are many locations in our country where this does not occur. It is hoped that policy changes in these school districts will come about in the near future so that students can be integrated with nondisabled peers in general schools and classrooms.

The guidelines in Figure 2–4 are suggested for placing students with severe disabilities in public school settings. Strategies and tactics for achieving inclusive programs are discussed in chapter 9.

1. Screening for children with disabilities, referral to programs, and initiation of services should all occur as soon as possible after atypical development has been identified.
2. Support of the family is an integral component of early intervention. The family's strengths and needs should be identified on the Individualized Family Service Plan (IFSP), and unique intervention plans should be developed accordingly.
3. In addition to family involvement, the extended family and other members of the family's social network should be considered a part of the support system for the child. Professional assistance should be provided to buttress the natural system of family support, not to supplant it.
4. The early intervention program should be developmentally based in that it encourages and fosters integrated development as opposed to "training" isolated skills. Children should be encouraged to make choices, be actively involved in the learning process, and learn how to effectively influence what happens in their environment.
5. Frequent assessment should occur and learning activities should be planned as a result of these assessments.
6. Because an important goal should be the introduction of the child into a normal kindergarten, the program should prepare the child for that environment and work with the family to plan a transition into the new program.
7. Program evaluation should occur on a regular basis with input from parents, teachers, and administrators regarding the satisfactory outcome of the program.

Figure 2–3
Best Practices for Providing Early Intervention and Preschool Programs

Curriculum and Instruction

Specific objectives must be developed for each student with severe disabilities, and these must be written into the student's individual educational plan. In order to have a framework in which to teach these objectives, the teacher must plan a series of daily activities, including activities in the regular classroom, and use a number of instructional methods to help students achieve their specific objectives within those activities. The objectives intended for the student with severe disabilities do not necessarily have to be the same for students without disabilities or for other students with mild or even severe disabilities.

The guidelines listed in Figure 2–5 suggest the preferred practices regarding what to teach and how to teach it. Most of the chapters in the text include these and other appropriate practices.

Community-Based Instruction

As was stated, training must occur in natural settings in order to develop skills that can later be applied in those settings. For several years, community-based instruction has been an integral part of special education programs for students with severe disabilities. This instruction takes students from classrooms and school

1. Students should be placed in regular schools for their education. The most preferred school will be the one that they would attend if they did not have a severe disability; that is, the home school appropriate for their chronological age.
2. The primary or "home room" classroom in the school should be a regular classroom. The student should be placed in a special classroom or other setting only if appropriate learning opportunities to achieve individual objectives are not possible in the regular classroom.
3. Placement in regular education schools and classrooms should be based on natural proportions of people with severe disabilities to people who do not have severe disabilities. Typically, no more than 1% of a school's population will have severe disabilities and there will be no more than one child with a severe disability in a regular classroom.
4. Students with severe disabilities will be better able to participate in classes that are activity-based and those that have more hands-on activities such as home economics, industrial arts, art, physical education, etc. As students become older, learning activities outside of the classroom, and often out of the school, will become more appropriate.
5. Whenever students are placed in separate special classrooms, they should have access to peers throughout the day, they should attend all special events with their peers, and they should have opportunities to learn in other settings besides the special class.
6. The special education teacher should work with the regular education teacher to develop activities that promote appropriate learning for students with severe disabilities and also foster social interactions between students with and without severe disabilities.
7. Students without disabilities may play different roles in interacting with the students with disabilities. They may participate with them in cooperative learning activities, they may provide them with physical assistance when such is required, and they may serve as tutors on certain learning tasks. Most importantly, they may become friends. It will be more appropriate for teachers to support relationships of interdependence rather than hierarchal roles.
8. The regular classroom teacher should be a part of the instructional team for the child with disabilities along with the special educator and the related services professional. This educator should participate in IEP planning, working with parents, and, of course, instructing students. It is important that all school personnel, especially classroom teachers, accept the philosophical position that students with severe disabilities do not "belong" to the special education teacher but are a part of the school population, even though they have need for special attention.

Figure 2–4
Best Practices for School Placement of Students with Severe Disabilities

grounds and into community settings where functional skills are needed to operate. The intention is to teach the students to be more independent. Even students with the most severe disabilities can learn to partially participate in community settings.

The practices listed in Figure 2–6 are recommended when providing community-based instruction. More in-depth discussion of this topic is presented in chapter 17.

Related Services

Related services are those that students receive in addition to their normal instructional services. Typical related services for students with severe disabilities include speech, communication, or language therapy; physical therapy; and occupational therapy. They may also require services from school psychologists or behavioral specialists, nurses, social workers,

1. The curriculum should be envisioned as a longitudinal sequence of skills that ranges from those appropriate for young children to those necessary for adulthood.
2. All objectives should focus on increasing the independence or participation of the individual, or making the individual less dependent and less isolated in the home, school, and community.
3. Students should not be excluded from instructional activities because they cannot learn a complete skill independently. Instead, objectives may be developed that allow students meaningful *partial participation.*
4. Objectives should be written so they describe specific observable behaviors and include criteria so that the student's skill level on a particular objective can be readily determined. Objectives should be written that target initial acquisition of skills and also skill maintenance and generalization.
5. Instructional programs for each student's specific objectives are written to describe setting, materials, cues, expected behavior, consequences for correct performance, correction procedure for incorrect performance, and the data collection and display system.
6. Settings, tasks, and materials used for instruction should be those found in natural environments, not artificially developed.
7. Important skills that contribute to functioning in all life domains, such as language, ambulation and mobility, motor skills, and social skills, are not to be considered as isolated instructional targets, but as targets for instruction within the broader framework of the domains.
8. Instruction in academic skills such as reading, writing, and arithmetic should be individually determined based on the student's need and desire to learn the skill. Depending on the student's age, learning ability, and accomplished skills, academic instruction may be given different degrees of emphasis.
9. Student performance data must be recorded and should be carefully observed. Instructional change decisions are to be based on students' performance as reflected in the data.

Figure 2–5
Best Practices in Curriculum and Instruction

rehabilitation engineers, and rehabilitation counselors.

Appropriate related services should be listed on each student's Individual Educational Plan (or, for preschool children, the Individual Family Service Plan) and should be an integral part of the educational process. They should be provided in a collaborative fashion, as described in Figure 2–7. Detailed information about the responsibilities of different professionals and their collaboration is described in chapter 3. Discussion of how related service professionals should be involved in students' learning and development is included in various relevant chapters.

Social Integration

Social integration is an extremely important component of educational programs for students with severe disabilities, because social skills are very difficult for them to learn, especially when they are segregated from good models of social behavior. They need every opportunity to develop social skills in socially integrated environments.

More than any other cluster of skills, social skills affect the degree to which persons with severe disabilities can participate in normal life routines and thus enjoy a good quality of life. The practices described in Figure 2–8 are sug-

1. The best and most natural way to teach community skills is in real community settings. Teaching skills only in simulated settings is usually not effective in that generalization to the actual community locations is poor.
2. There are community skills that are differentially important for different age groups. Young children, for example, may not need to shop for groceries, but they do need to learn to cross the street safely.
3. An ecological analysis of community sites should be conducted to determine the skills needed for the site. These skills may then be broken down and taught through the most appropriate instructional process.
4. Family members should be involved in selecting the community sites for which skills are needed and the specific objectives for those sites. Family members and friends may also participate in community learning activities whenever possible.
5. Probes of performance ability on community skills must be taken in community settings in order to determine if the student has actually learned the skill. Skills should not be considered learned until they have been adequately demonstrated in the environments for which they were trained.
6. The "community" in community-based training suggests that the skills be demonstrated in the community where the student lives. It will be most appropriate for skills to be taught and tested in the community settings that will be used in "real life."

Figure 2–6
Best Practices for Providing Community-Based Instruction

gested as optimal ways to improve social skills through social integration. Further discussion of strategies and tactics in this area is presented in chapters 9, 10, and 11.

Improving Challenging Behavior

Some individuals with severe disabilities, particularly those with the most severe disabilities (i.e., profoundly mentally disabled), demonstrate various forms of challenging, inappropriate behavior. These behaviors may include stereotyped acts, self-injurious behaviors, noncompliance with requests, and aggressive acts. Various theories have been put forth to explain these behaviors but only recently have researchers started to find positive, nonaversive behavioral supports that offer solutions for improvement in this area.

In Figure 2–9, several basic guidelines for improving inappropriate behavior are presented. Detailed discussion of methods for reducing inappropriate behaviors is provided in chapter 11.

The Bases of Best Practices

When we compare the best practices for teaching persons with severe disabilities today to those that existed 10, 20, or 30 years ago, we see great contrasts (Snell, 1988). In fact, many of the practices that existed in earlier periods (and in

1. Related services (as well as instruction) should be offered through a collaborative model that includes various professionals as well as students' parents.
2. Related services providers should be a part of the student's instructional team and contribute to the planning process and other key aspects of instruction besides the therapy service being provided.
3. Professionals should share knowledge about procedures with each other in order to increase the quality of services provided to students. There should be communication about various specific needs and interventions and how each person who works with the student can contribute holistically to the student's development as well as providing his or her unique contribution.
4. "Role release" will allow different professionals to provide some services that were traditionally only provided by certain therapists. This principle states that there are some functions of various professionals (for example, speech therapists) that can be taught to others (for example, teachers) so that appropriate services can be provided more often and in different relevant contexts.
5. All related services should be offered in the most natural, least restrictive environment possible. Providing related services in contrived environments such as small speech therapy rooms should generally be avoided except when therapists believe the restricted setting will better allow the student to accomplish new, difficult tasks that cannot be learned in more open environments.
6. If it is necessary to isolate the student for some aspect of a particular therapy, as indicated in the previous statement, the therapy should continue in the most natural setting as soon as possible.
7. Therapy goals should be integrated into the student's other objectives and vice versa. The more opportunity the student has to practice a particular skill, the better the chance for it to be learned, and learned sooner.
8. The therapist's expertise will be especially useful to teachers in explaining the student's limitations on certain tasks and how to circumvent or overcome them, and explaining the student's level of development and how to improve it. For example, an occupational therapist could explain the best way for the child to hold an eating utensil for self-feeding, while a language therapist could assist in identifying the vocabulary most necessary for immediate acquisition.

Figure 2–7
Best Practices for Providing Related Services

some places still exist today), are now judged to be wholly inappropriate by many professionals. What, then, makes the activities and procedures outlined above preferred over other approaches? Why are some practices praised while others are criticized? Are integrated placements truly better than segregated programs? Is early intervention really that important? Should our teaching always be directed toward the development of functional skills?

There are four bases that support the practices outlined in this chapter and elsewhere—social values, legal mandates, professional consensus, and empirical research.

Social Values

The values of any society, that is, the values that are held by a majority of its members, change with the passing of time. Most people have different attitudes toward different dimensions of the world and its people than those that were held by our ancestors. Our values are reflected in our attitudes toward the environment, health care, quality of life, public education, minorities, and other aspects of society. For some individuals, society's values have changed and are changing too fast; for others, change seems to occur too slowly. But

1. All current and future age-appropriate environments for social interaction should be identified and targeted for instruction. These environments will certainly include the school and the home, but may also include different community settings and vocational settings, depending on the age of the student.
2. Specific social skills that are to be taught should be identified for every student. These may include positive behaviors to be developed or increased, and/or negative social behaviors to be reduced or eliminated.
3. During all instructional activities and in all instructional environments, regardless of the instructional domains, social skills should be taught. This suggests a great deal of incidental teaching is appropriate.
4. Barriers and facilitators of social integration in natural environments should be identified. These may include particular individuals, physical structures, or some personal characteristics of the individual with severe disabilities.
5. The special education teacher should provide information to nondisabled individuals to assist them in interacting with students who have disabilities.
6. Teachers and other professionals who work with and interact with the students who have severe disabilities should be encouraged to set social behavior standards for them like those for other students without disabilities of the same ages. In other words, inappropriate social behavior should not be allowed because of their disability.
7. Prompts for appropriate social actions should be subtle but direct enough to improve the behavior. Prompts should be faded as soon as possible in order to allow natural environmental stimuli to influence the student's behavior.
8. Efforts to improve the *quality* as well as the quantity of social interactions between persons with and without disabilities should be continuous.

Figure 2–8
Best Practices for Developing Social Skills Through Social Integration

most of what changes in society's practices is shared by most members of that society, otherwise the changes would not occur.

One of the major changes that has evolved over the last 30 or 40 years is the value our society places on the rights of the individual. In the United States there has always been a basis for individual rights in our constitution; however, the interpretation of these rights was often limited. It must be remembered that only about 150 years ago, human beings were legally allowed to *own* other human beings in many parts of the world, including the United States. This was an acceptable social practice. Who had the right to own whom was simply determined by race.

For most of Western society, the world gradually improved, although slowly. In recent years, even after the end of slavery, we accepted without question or criticism the separation and derogation of persons for their race, their religion, their national origin, and their gender. Because of normal variations in human characteristics, people were denied human rights that were extended to others. In many instances, they were subjected to harassment, ridicule, and physical attack.

As history will note, however, beginning in the 1960s, significant positive changes in the course of society appeared. Civil rights legislation was passed, "separate but equal" schools for different races were ruled unconstitutional

Figure 2–9
Best Practices for Improving Challenging Behaviors

1. Although there often seems to be no readily apparent reason for stereotyped or self-injurious behavior, in many cases it is possible to identify the conditions under which the behavior occurs. Systematic observation can help to isolate influencing factors and conditions.
2. Although aversive stimuli (i.e., punishment) may result in rapid decrease in the behavior, its use is opposed because it subjects the individual with severe disabilities to abnormal and sometimes inhumane treatment. Additionally, the effects of punishment tend to be short-lived and do not generalize.
3. In contrast to punishment, efforts should be made to identify through a functional analysis the conditions under which the behavior occurs and either change those conditions or teach the individual a more appropriate way to respond to them.
4. Although the challenging behavior will be the behavior of greatest concern, attention must also be given to the effect of the intervention on collateral behaviors and on the occurrence of the behavior in different situations, with different people, and at different times.
5. Data must be taken in order to learn precisely about the influence of the intervention on the behavior of concern.

by the Supreme Court, and racial integration in society began to occur. Such changes as these, and many more, took place because the values of our society changed. People began to become more tolerant of others who varied from the norm, and the rights of the individual became more precious to society as a whole.

It is important to recognize all of this because we must understand that values related to the education and treatment of people with disabilities do not exist in a social vacuum. If we did not value the rights of minorities and other groups who have historically been disenfranchised by society, most likely the quality of education for persons with severe disabilities would not be where it is today. In fact, it is possible to draw parallels between the integration of minority students and the integration of students with severe disabilities (McDonnell & Hardman, 1989).

Although research has demonstrated the importance of many best practices, Peck (1991) discussed the need for linking values and science in social policy decisions affecting persons with severe disabilities. The traditional reliance on research data is now being supplemented by consideration for values, particularly by organizations such as The Association for Persons with Severe Handicaps (TASH). Peck suggested that "knowledge gained through scientific research should affect and be affected by knowledge from other sources, including personal and cultural values" (p. 2). To the extent that certain practices are in accord with the general values of society, we can expect that they will be considered as best practices for educating persons with severe disabilities.

Legal Mandates

One of the most apparent ways in which our society expresses its values is through the laws that are written by its representatives. Since the 1970s, a series of federal laws have been passed that support many of the best practices listed above. Several of these and their requirements are discussed below.

P.L. 94-142: The Education for All Handicapped Children Act Several years ago, in 1975, Public Law 94-142 was signed into law by President Gerald Ford. It is considered the most important piece of federal legislation ever passed related to the education of students with disabilities, perhaps especially students with severe disabilities (Gerry & McWhorter, 1991). The reason for this claim is that P.L. 94-142 gave *all* students with disabilities, including those with the most severe disabilities, the legal right to a free, appropriate public education (FAPE) in the nation's schools. Prior to this time, most public school systems in the United States did not provide services to individuals with severe disabilities, especially those with the most severe disabilities. P.L. 94-142 not only required that educational services be provided, but also required a host of "related services" (such as transportation, physical therapy, psychological services, etc.) pertinent to the student's development.

Another important requirement of P.L. 94-142 was that the education provided for students with disabilities be in the "least restrictive environment" (LRE). This requirement did not state that any particular setting was to be used, but it did place the responsibility on the public schools to show reason why a particular student had to be placed in a more restrictive setting as opposed to a less restrictive setting. Since this law was passed, it has often been demonstrated that students with severe disabilities can learn quite well in regular schools and often in regular classrooms (Sailor et al., 1989).

Other requirements of P.L. 94-142 are also reflected in the best practices listed above. These include the requirement that each student have an individual educational plan (IEP), that this plan state the annual goals and short-term objectives for the student, that an evaluation system be used at least once a year to monitor the student's progress, and that the student's parents be given the opportunity to participate in the educational planning process for their child. Also very important in the law was the guarantee of due process in decisions about placement and other educational matters. In other words, if the parents (or the student) disagreed with the action of the school system, a method of appeals that led to the federal court system could be used to resolve the conflict.

P.L. 99-457: The Education of the Handicapped Act Amendments of 1986 This law expanded upon what was required by P.L. 94-142 and other federal legislation. Its most important contribution was the creation of two new programs. The first was a *mandatory* requirement that children with disabilities between the ages of 3 and 5 be provided with free educational programs in the public schools. In other words, the requirements of P.L. 94-142 were extended to cover children beginning with their third birthday.

The second program established by P.L. 99-457 was a discretionary program to serve children between birth and 2: the Handicapped Infants and Toddlers Program. For states that opted to participate, funds were provided to create programs for children with disabilities and their families as soon as the children could be identified as having a disability. This federal program is extremely important for children with severe disabilities because appropriate early intervention can reduce the impact of the disability.

Under the Infants and Toddlers Program, several "best practices" were legislated. Perhaps most important was the family focus of the law. Similar to the IEP required under P.L. 94-142, P.L. 99-457 required that an Individual Family Service Plan (IFSP) be developed. This plan was to include eight components: (a) a statement of the child's present level of development; (b) a statement of the family's strengths and needs related to enhancing the child's development; (c) a statement of the major outcomes expected to be achieved for the child and the family; (d) the criteria, procedures, and timelines for determining progress; (e) the specific early intervention services necessary to meet the needs of the child and the family; (f) when the services will start and how long they will last; (g) the name of the case manager; and (h) procedures for transition from the early intervention program to the preschool program. Further, the assessment of the child, the development of the IFSP, and the implementation of the early intervention program was to be multidisciplinary. That is, it must include personnel from several professions, including special education, speech/language pathology, audiology, occupational therapy, physical therapy, psychology, counseling, and medicine. In order to not overwhelm families with professional input, one case manager must be designated to guide the family through the service system.

P.L. 101-476: Individuals with Disabilities Education Act The Individuals with Disabilities Education Act, or IDEA (P.L. 101-476), signed into law in October 1990, is the latest amended law in the series of federal laws governing the practices of public school education for children with disabilities. Like earlier laws, it also contributed to some of the best practices that have been identified. It is most important to note that IDEA changed the language of the previous "Education of the Handicapped" laws to "Individuals with Disabilities." The intention was to direct the focus first toward the individuality of persons with disabilities and then to note their unique challenge. This principle has guided our writing in this textbook as it does now most professional literature.

One important provision of the law is the allocation of funding to support special projects that address the needs of students with severe disabilities in integrated settings. These can be statewide projects intended to improve the quality of special education in integrated settings. The law also directs the U.S. Secretary of Education to place a priority on programs that improve the chances for the successful integration of students with severe disabilities into educational programs for nondisabled students (National Association of State Directors of Special Education, 1990).

Another significant contribution of IDEA is the inclusion of a definition of "transition services" and the requirement that a statement of the transition services be included in the student's IEP no later than age 16. These services must include "a coordinated set of activities . . . designed within an outcome-oriented process, which promotes movement from school to post-school activities, including post-secondary education, vocational training, integrated employment (including supported employment), continuing and adult education, adult services, independent living, or community participation." The law also notes the need to provide transition planning for other times of significant change in the life condition of the student with disabilities.

P.L. 101-336: Americans with Disabilities Act of 1990 (ADA) The final law that is considered here as a source of best practices is the Americans with Disabilities Act. The ADA is generally considered to be landmark legislation because it guarantees civil rights to all United States citizens with disabilities. These rights provide protection related to employment in the private sector, all public services, public accommodations, transportation, and telecommunications (Council for Exceptional Children, 1990).

According to the ADA, persons with disabilities cannot be discriminated against in hiring practices by companies that employ 15 people or more. In other words, if a person can do the job, the employer cannot refuse to hire him or her simply because of a disability. In addition, the employer is expected to make "reasonable accommodations" in the workplace if it will help the person with a disability to perform the job. In the area of public transportation, the ADA requires that all new vehicles be accessible to people with disabilities. Public accommodations must also be accessible; under ADA, it is illegal to exclude persons with disabilities from services used by the general public, such as hotels, restaurants, grocery stores, schools, and parks. If necessary, "reasonable" modifications must be put in place in order to better accommodate these persons. The law also covers all public buildings such as government facilities.

The relation of ADA to many of the best practices that are listed above is apparent: both are intended to foster the *inclusion* of persons with disabilities rather than excluding them. Both also have as a goal the maximization of individuals' human potential. The educational practices presented in this chapter will help persons with severe disabilities be able to better enjoy the rights assured them by the ADA.

There are many other laws that pertain to persons with disabilities. The ones that are discussed helped to establish some of the best practices discussed in this chapter, or, conversely, were written as a reaction to practices that came to be recognized as wrong by many professionals in the field.

Certainly it is good that laws have been developed to guide both professionals and the general citizenry in actions directed toward and on behalf of persons with severe disabilities. On the other hand, as Gerry and McWhorter (1991) pointed out, it is unfortunate that our society must establish a special set of laws to provide one segment of the population with rights that are provided to others under generic laws. As they stated:

> *In contrast to current practice, government policies toward persons with disabilities should be viewed in the context of an overall and* inclusive *American social policy. Rather than creating a separate set of policies for persons with disabilities, legislative and judicial strategies must be developed to ensure that the same basic goals of American social policy established for all of our nondisabled citizens are pursued with equal vigor for citizens with disabilities (Gerry & McWhorter, 1991, p. 496).*

Professional Consensus

Many of the best practices that we have listed in this chapter can be defended as such because they are supported by the opinions of a large number of professionals who have been involved for many years in developing programs, conducting research, writing policies, teaching, and providing other services to persons with severe disabilities. Two relatively recent studies using survey research methodology provide a general professional consensus about most of the practices we have recommended (Meyer, Eichinger, & Park-Lee, 1987; Williams, Fox, Thousand, & Fox, 1990).

The procedures for this research method generally begin with a listing of practices from the professional literature presumed to be the most promising. The authors then refine this list by exposing it to a limited number of persons with expertise in particular areas. Finally the list is sent to a large sample of professionals and parents who evaluate the significance or importance of each item.

Meyer et al. (1987) analyzed responses from 254 persons to a questionnaire listing what they considered to be 122 best practices related to the education and treatment of persons with severe disabilities. The individuals represented six areas, including: (a) behavior therapy experts; (b) experts in severe disabilities; (c) experts on deaf-blindness; (d) mental retardation researchers; (e) state directors of special education; and (f) parents of persons with severe disabilities who act as advocates on behalf of their children. Each item was scored by the respondents on a scale of 0 (not a consideration) to 20 (a very important consideration), with intermediate points at 5 (not an important consideration), 10 (undecided), and 15 (an important consideration).

In the second study, Williams et al. (1990) used a similar procedure, although it was limited to the state of Vermont. Their target responders included parents, special education administrators, special education teachers, general education teachers and principals, and related service providers. The special education teachers and administrators received a 64-item questionnaire; the other groups received abbreviated versions containing only selected items from the longer list. The responders were asked two types of questions: Does the item represent a "best practice"? and Is the item a current practice? Williams et al. received responses from 212 persons.

Both studies had important results. Most of the items considered by the researchers to be "best practices" (which were very similar to many of the items listed in this chapter) were rated by the respondents as being somewhere between important and very important (Meyer et al., 1987) or an appropriate "best practice" (Williams et al., 1990). However, there was some disagreement from different subgroups of the respondents as to the relative value of particular best practice indicators. For example, Meyer et al. found that items related to integration were rated higher by severe disabilities experts and parents than by the other groups, although the directors of special education gave a higher rating on the items in this factor than that given by the other groups. In the Vermont study, Williams et al. (1990) found that differential responses to questions about placing students with severe disabilities in regular classrooms or in special classrooms were closely related to whether or not the special education teachers and parents responding actually had experience with one setting or another. Those who had experience with regular classroom placements more often considered this placement as a best practice.

By examining these studies we can see that many practices suggested in this chapter and elsewhere as being most appropriate for the education of students with severe disabilities are supported by a strong degree of professional consensus. Of course, this consensus is not universal nor is it an implication that these practices enjoy widespread application. This matter is further discussed in the conclusion of this chapter.

Empirical Research The final basis for arguing that a particular practice is "best" is if research has been conducted to demonstrate its effectiveness. Several types of research may be conducted to test the effectiveness of a particular intervention or practice. The most traditional research designs used in education and the social sciences are group experimental designs (Campbell & Stanley, 1963). These designs typically include giving a pretest to determine subjects' skills, abilities, or characteristics before intervention begins; treating the experimental group of individuals in a specific way for a period of time; and then repeating the test (now called a posttest) to determine if the treatment had an effect. In order to control for threats to "internal validity" (that is, to make sure it was the treatment and not some other factor that resulted in the change in the subjects), a control group of equivalent subjects who do not receive the experimental treatment are also pretested and posttested on the same schedule. Even tighter experimental control (to protect against threats to "external" validity) can be maintained by randomly selecting subjects and randomly assigning them to the experimental or the control group. There are several variations in this design, but the one described is the most basic and should give you at least an idea of the nature of this research.

More commonly used in studies of persons with severe disabilities are single-subject or repeated measures research designs (Tawney & Gast, 1984). These studies use one or a few subjects to demonstrate the effect of a particular intervention. The most commonly used design for this type of research is the multiple baseline design, in which, typically, a few subjects, for example three, are simultaneously exposed to a situation in which the treatment or intervention to be evaluated does not exist, that is, the baseline condition. Within this condition, a direct measure is taken of the skill to be learned, usually on a daily basis. For example, the researcher may calculate the percentage of steps in a task completed by the learner, or the number of times a particular behavior (the target behavior) occurs. When all participants are demonstrating stable, typical behavior during baseline, one is selected for exposure to the treatment. The others continue under baseline conditions, and all the while, measures on the target behavior for each individual continue to occur. If the treatment has the effect that is expected, the behavior or skill of the subject who is exposed to it begins to change and the measurement system records this change. If only this subject's behavior changes, the change can be attributed to the experimental treatment. To further confirm the effect of the intervention, each of the remaining subjects is introduced to the treatment condition at different times but, prior to the times of their introduction, continue to be observed under baseline conditions. Each time a subject is exposed to the treatment, if the treatment has an effect and the behavior or the skill responds to the effect, there is evidence that the treatment or intervention is working. The systematic or varied replication of such research lends credence to the validity of the intervention. Over the years, a great number of these types of studies have been conducted and their results have allowed conclusions to be made about preferred interventions.

A third form of research that has become more common in recent years is qualitative or ethnographic research using methods of naturalistic observation (Bogdan & Biklen, 1982). The primary aim of this research is to gain an in-depth understanding of various processes and their interactions as they occur in natural situations. Unlike the other forms of research, ethnographic studies are more interested in determining the natural occurrence of phenomena (values, perceptions, actions) and how they affect individuals. This type of research usually does not look at the effect of a particular intervention; instead, the researcher is immersed in an environment, typically becoming a part of it, in order to discover the intricacies of the personal and social workings of the environment. Ethnographic research is often used to study the sociological aspects of disabilities.

During the last 10 to 15 years, research evidence has accumulated to support many of the practices discussed and listed in the figures in this chapter. Recent reviews of much of this research are available on many topics, including the effects of early intervention (Guralnick, 1990; Hanson & Hanline, 1989; Westlake & Kaiser, 1991); integrated school placements (Giangreco & Putnam, 1991; Lipsky & Gartner, 1989; Sailor, 1989; Sailor et al., 1989); curriculum and instructional practices (Ault, Wolery, Doyle, & Gast, 1989; Mirenda & Donnellan, 1987; Sailor, Gee, Goetz, & Graham, 1988;

Snell, 1988); the use of related services (Dunn, 1991); the development of communicative and social interactions (Caro & Snell, 1989; Haring, 1991; Mirenda, Iacono, & Williams, 1990); improving inappropriate behaviors (Doss & Reichle, 1989; Helmstetter & Durand, 1991; Horner et al., 1990; LaVigna, 1987; Lennox & Miltenberger, 1989; O'Brien & Repp, 1990); transitional planning and supported employment (McDonnell, Wilcox, & Hardman, 1991; Rusch, Chadsey-Rusch, & Johnson, 1991); community-based instruction (Snell & Browder, 1986; Westling & Floyd, 1990); and home-school partnerships (Singer & Irvin; 1991; Snell & Beckman-Brindley, 1984). What has been learned from these studies has provided much of the information that will be presented throughout the rest of this text.

Although there is apparently a substantial amount of research to support many of the practices that have been recommended, not all best practices are fully supported by research, nor would we expect them to be. The role of social science is probably better for the evaluation of social policy than for its invention (Peck, 1991). Thus some practices included on our list and elsewhere may not have evolved from research and, in fact, should not need to be subjected to research in order to provide a defense for them. (Does allowing women to vote make the country a better place? Should minority individuals be free to live and work where they want?) Obviously not all questions of social practice should be subjected to research. Instead, the more appropriate role of research is to improve practices that are socially valued.

Conclusion

We have advanced to a point where there is a relatively clear direction about what, when, where, and how we should be doing to provide the best, most humane services to persons who have severe disabilities. Because we are an evolving field, we can expect additional practices to be developed, given consideration, and perhaps added to the figures contained in this chapter.

Although the best practices have been identified, we must not conclude that they have been fully implemented. Over a million students with various disabilities in the United States are still served primarily in separate classes, separate schools, or residential facilities. Most of these students are classified as mentally retarded, multihandicapped, or deaf-blind (U.S. Department of Education, 1990). We also know that progress is lacking in other programmatic areas around the country. For example, only a few states have already implemented early intervention for children under 3; under P.L. 99-457, more are in the process of doing so (U.S. Department of Education, 1990). In the study by Williams et al. (1990) in Vermont, it was reported that while approximately 90% of the special educators surveyed agreed with most of the best practices on their list, each practice was implemented for all students only by 20 to 60% of the teachers. Were similar studies available from other locations, we might well find that even fewer best practices have been implemented.

Why do these conditions exist? There are no doubt several reasons. The long-time existence of separate special schools and the funding formulas used in many states may impede the integration of children with severe disabilities (U.S. Department of Education, 1990). Additional factors may include the lack of pre-service or in-service training for teachers (including both general and special educators) that would provide them with the skills to implement more appropriate practices; the lack of administrative support; inflexible scheduling of time and instructional activities;

poor or nonexistent interagency agreements; and the lack of sufficient funds (Brinker & Thorpe, 1985; Westling, 1989; Williams et al., 1990).

The responsibility of current and future professionals, administrators, parents, and citizens is to work to improve the status quo and move forward to the implementation of the most appropriate instructional and related practices. If this is achieved, the benefits will be realized not only by persons with severe disabilities, but by society as a whole. The remaining chapters of this text are devoted toward achieving that end.

Questions for Reflection

1. Of the "best practices" listed, which would you consider to be the most important? Why?
2. Are there any sets of "best practices" that you disagree with? Why?
3. Could you suggest other important practices that should be included when providing services to people with severe disabilities?
4. What are the reactions of some professional educators to the practices discussed in this chapter? How about nonprofessionals?
5. Of the various ways by which we conclude certain practices are preferred, which do you think is most important? Why?
6. From the point of view of a student with a severe disability, which of the practices described in this chapter would be considered most important?
7. Based on trends in society, what future "best practices" do you believe might emerge in the next few years?
8. What do you believe is the teacher's role in implementing best practices?

References

Ault, M. J., Wolery, M., Doyle, P. M., & Gast, D. L. (1989). Review of comparative studies in the instruction of students with moderate and severe handicaps. *Exceptional Children, 55,* 346–356.

Bailey, J. S. (1981). Wanted: A rational search for the limiting conditions of habilitation in the retarded. *Analysis and Intervention in Developmental Disabilities, 1,* 45–52.

Bogdan, R. C., & Biklen, S. K. (1982). *Qualitative research for education: An introduction to theory and methods.* Boston: Allyn & Bacon.

Brinker, R. P., & Thorpe, M. E. (1985). Some empirically derived hypotheses about the influence of state policy on degree of integration of severely handicapped students. *Remedial and Special Education, 6*(3), 18–26.

Brown, L., Nietupski, J., & Hamre-Nietupski, S. (1976). Criterion of ultimate functioning. In A. Thomas (Ed.), *Hey, don't forget about me!* Reston, VA: CEC Information Center.

Campbell, D. T., & Stanley, J. C. (1963). Experimental and quasi-experimental designs for research on teaching. In N. L. Gage (Ed.), *Handbook of research on teaching.* Chicago: Rand-McNally.

Caro, P., & Snell, M. (1989). Characteristics of teaching communication to people with moderate and severe disabilities. *Education and Training in Mental Retardation, 24,* 63–77.

Certo, N., Haring, N., & York, R. (Eds.) (1984). *Public school integration of severely handicapped students.* Baltimore: Paul H. Brookes.

Council for Exceptional Children. (1990). Americans with Disabilities Act of 1990: What should you know? *Exceptional Children, 57*(2) (Supplement).

Doss, S., & Reichle, J. (1989). Establishing communicative alternatives to the emission of socially motivated excess behavior: A review. *Journal of the Association for Persons with Severe Handicaps, 14,* 101–112.

Dunn, L. (1968). Special education for the mildly retarded—is much of it justifiable? *Exceptional Children, 35*(1), 5–24.

Dunn, W. (1991). Integrated related services. In L. H. Meyer, C. A. Peck, & L. Brown (Eds.), *Critical issues in the lives of people with severe disabilities* (pp. 353–377). Baltimore: Paul H. Brookes.

Ford, A., Schnorr, R., Meyer, L., Davern, L., Black, J., & Dempsey, P. (Eds.) (1989). *The Syracuse community-referenced curriculum guide for students with moderate and severe disabilities.* Baltimore: Paul H. Brookes.

Fox, W., Thousand, J., Fox, T., Williams, W., Lewis, P., Reid, R., & Creedon, S. (1986). *Proposed state guidelines for the education of students with moderate/severe handicaps.* Burlington, VT: Center for Developmental Disabilities, University of Vermont.

Gerry, M. H., & McWhorter, C. M. (1991). A comprehensive analysis of federal statutes and programs for persons with severe disabilities. In L. H. Meyer, C. A. Peck, & L. Brown (Eds.), *Critical issues in the lives of people with severe disabilities* (pp. 495–525). Baltimore, MD: Paul H. Brookes.

Giangreco, M. F., & Putnam, J. W. (1991). Supporting the education of students with severe disabilities in regular education environments. In L. H. Meyer, C. A. Peck, & L. Brown (Eds.), *Critical issues in the lives of people with severe disabilities* (pp. 245–270). Baltimore: Paul H. Brookes.

Goldberg, I., & Cruickshank, W. (1958). The trainable but not educable: Whose responsibility? *National Education Association Journal, 47,* 622–623.

Guralnick, M. J. (1990). Major accomplishments and future directions in early childhood mainstreaming. *Topics in Early Childhood Special Education, 10*(2), 1–17.

Hanson, M. J., & Hanline, M. F. (1989). Integration options for the very young child. In R. Gaylord-Ross (Ed.), *Integration strategies for students with handicaps.* Baltimore: Paul H. Brookes.

Haring, T. G. (1991). Social relationships. In L. H. Meyer, C. A. Peck, & L. Brown (Eds.), *Critical issues in the lives of people with severe disabilities* (pp. 195–217). Baltimore: Paul H. Brookes.

Helmstetter, E., & Durand, V. M. (1991). Nonaversive interventions for severe behavior problems. In L. H. Meyer, C. A. Peck, & L. Brown (Eds.), *Critical issues in the lives of people with severe disabilities* (pp. 559–600). Baltimore: Paul H. Brookes.

Horner, R. H., Dunlap, G., Koegel, R. L., Carr, E. G., Sailor, W., Anderson, J., Albin, R. W., & O'Neill, R. E. (1990). Toward a technology of "nonaversive" behavioral support. *Journal of the Association for Persons with Severe Handicaps, 15,* 125–132.

Horner, R. H., Meyer, L. H., & Fredericks, H. B. D. (Eds.) (1986). *Educating learners with severe handicaps: Exemplary service models.* Baltimore: Paul H. Brookes.

LaVigna, G. W. (1987). Non-aversive strategies for managing behavior problems. In D. J. Cohen & A. M. Donnellan (Eds.), *Handbook of autism and pervasive developmental disorders* (pp. 418–429). New York: John Wiley.

Lennox, D. B., & Miltenberger, R. G. (1989). Conducting a functional assessment of problem behavior in applied settings. *Journal of the Association for Persons with Severe Handicaps, 14,* 304–311.

Lipsky, D. K., & Gartner, A. (Eds.). (1989). *Beyond separate education: Quality education for all.* Baltimore: Paul H. Brookes.

McDonnell, A. P., & Hardman, M. L. (1989). The desegregation of America's special schools: Strategies for change. *Journal of the Association for Persons with Severe Handicaps, 14,* 68–74.

McDonnell, J., Wilcox, B., & Hardman, M. (1991). *Secondary programs for students with developmental disabilities.* Boston: Allyn & Bacon.

Meyer, L. (1987). *Program Quality Indicators: A checklist of most promising practices in educational programs for students with severe disabilities* (rev. ed.). Syracuse, NY: Syracuse University Division of Special Education and Rehabilitation.

Meyer, L., Eichinger, J., & Park-Lee, S. (1987). A validation of program quality indicators in educational services for students with severe disabilities. *Journal of the Association for Persons with Severe Handicaps, 12,* 251–263.

Mirenda, P. L., & Donnellan, A. M. (1987). Issues in curriculum development. In D. J. Cohen & A. M. Donnellan (Eds.), *Handbook of autism and pervasive developmental disorders* (pp. 211–226). New York: John Wiley.

Mirenda, P., Iacono, T., & Williams, R. (1990). Communication options for persons with severe and profound disabilities: State of the art and future directions. *Journal of the Association for Persons with Severe Handicaps, 15,* 3–21.

National Association of State Directors of Special Education, (1990). *Education of the Handicapped Amendments of 1990 (P.L. 101–476): Summary of major changes in Parts A through H of the Act.* Washington, DC: Author.

Nirje, B. (1969). The normalization principle and its human management implications. In R. B. Kugel & W. Wolfensberger (Eds.), *Changing patterns in residential services for the mentally retarded.* Washington, DC: President's Committee on Mental Retardation.

O'Brien, S., & Repp, A. (1990). Reinforcement-based reductive procedures: A review of 20 years of their use with persons with severe or profound retardation. *Journal of the Association for Persons with Severe Handicaps, 15,* 148–159.

Peck, C. A. (1991). Linking values and science in social policy decisions affecting citizens with severe disabilities. In L. H. Meyer, C. A. Peck, & L. Brown (Eds.), *Critical issues in the lives of people with severe disabilities* (pp. 1–15). Baltimore: Paul H. Brookes.

Rusch, F., Chadsey-Rusch, J., & Johnson, J. R. (1991). Supported employment: Emerging opportunities for employment integration. In L. H. Meyer, C. A. Peck, & L. Brown (Eds.), *Critical issues in the lives of people with severe disabilities* (pp. 1–15). Baltimore: Paul H. Brookes.

Rainforth, B., York, J., & Macdonald, C. (1992). *Collaborative teams for students with severe disabilities: Integrating therapy and educational services.* Baltimore: Paul H. Brookes.

Sailor, W. (1989). The educational, social, and vocational integration of students with the most severe disabilities. In D. K. Lipsky & A. Gartner (Eds.), *Beyond separate education: Quality education for all.* Baltimore: Paul H. Brookes.

Sailor, W., Anderson, J. L., Halvorsen, A. T., Doering, M. A., Filler, J., & Goetz, L. (1989). *The comprehensive local school: Regular education for all students with disabilities.* Baltimore: Paul H. Brookes.

Sailor, W., Gee, K., Goetz, L., & Graham, N. (1988). Progress in educating students with the most severe disabilities: Is there any? *Journal of the Association for Persons with Severe Handicaps, 13,* 87–99.

Salisbury, C. L., & Vincent, L. J. (1990). Criterion of the next environment and best practices: Mainstreaming and integration 10 years later. *Topics in Early Childhood Special Education, 10*(2), 78–89.

Singer, G. H. S., & Irvin, L. K. (1991). Supporting families of persons with severe disabilities: Emerging findings, practices and questions. In L. H. Meyer, C. A. Peck, & L. Brown (Eds.), *Critical issues in the lives of people with severe disabilities* (pp. 271–312). Baltimore: Paul H. Brookes.

Snell, M. (1988). Curriculum and methodology for individuals with severe disabilities. *Education and Training in Mental Retardation, 23,* 302–314.

Snell, M. E., & Beckman-Brindley, S. (1984). Family involvement in intervention with children having severe handicaps. *Journal of the Association for Persons with Severe Handicaps, 9,* 213–230.

Snell, M., & Browder, D. (1986). Community-referenced instruction: research and issues. *Journal of the Association for Persons with Severe Handicaps, 11,* 1–11.

Strain, P. S. (1990). LRE for preschool children with handicaps: What we know, what we should be doing. *Journal of Early Intervention, 14,* 291–296.

Tawney, J. W., & Gast, D. L. (1984). *Single subject design in special education.* New York: Merrill/Macmillan.

U.S. Department of Education. (1990). *Twelfth annual report to congress on the implementation of the Education of the Handicapped Act.* Washington, DC: Author.

Westlake, C. R., & Kaiser, A. P. (1991). Early childhood services for children with severe disabilities: Research, values, policy, and practice. In L. H. Meyer, C. A. Peck, & L. Brown (Eds.), *Critical issues in the lives of people with severe disabilities* (pp. 429–458). Baltimore: Paul H. Brookes.

Westling, D. L. (1989). Leadership for the education of students with mental handicaps. *Educational Leadership, 46*(6), 19–23.

Westling, D. L., & Floyd, J. (1990). Generalization of community skills: How much training is necessary? *Journal of Special Education, 23,* 386–406.

Williams, W., Fox, T. J., Thousand, J., & Fox, W. (1990). Level of acceptance and implementation of best practices in the education of students with severe handicaps in Vermont. *Education and Training in Mental Retardation, 25,* 120–131.

Wolfensberger, W. (1972). *The principle of normalization in human services.* Toronto, Canada: National Institute on Mental Retardation.

CHAPTER 3

Collaborative Teaming with Parents, Professionals, and Paraprofessionals

Chapter Overview

In order to work most effectively, professionals must collaborate with students' parents on transdisciplinary teams that include teachers, specialists in communication disorders, physical and occupational therapists, and sometimes others. This chapter discusses the organization and functioning of transdisciplinary teams and how teachers should collaborate with parents, other professionals, and paraprofessionals.

No teacher of students who have severe disabilities works in isolation. Every workday, teachers attend meetings, discuss problems, plan strategies, give and receive directions, offer advice, co-teach, and in various ways work with other key persons. Among the most important of these key persons will be the parents of the students with severe disabilities. Other professionals will also play critical roles. There can be many, but most professional interactions by teachers of students with severe disabilities are with general educators, physical therapists (PTs), occupational therapists (OTs), and communication disorder specialists (also called speech therapists or speech pathologists). Paraprofessionals (teacher aids or assistants) are also extremely important team players in most schools. Although all of these persons share a general goal—to improve the skills, abilities, and lives of the individuals about whom they are concerned—they vary in their perceptions, knowledge, experiences, and training, and they may have different philosophies about disabilities and different expectations about the students of interest. It will not always be easy for caregivers and service providers to maintain harmonious relations. Yet the greater the cooperation, the greater will be the success of the overall program and, therefore, the learning and well-being of the students. This chapter is devoted to improving the interactions of teachers and others who are significant in the lives of individuals with severe disabilities. It focuses on building collaborative teams comprised of three groups: parents, professionals, and paraprofessionals. We will consider the nature of collaborative teaming and the specific participants involved in teaming and their respective roles.

The Meaning of Collaboration

The complexity of characteristics of students with disabilities calls for the knowledge and skills of many different persons if maximum learning and development are to occur. In recent years, professionals have realized that collaboration among themselves and parents, that is *collaborative teaming* or *collaborative consultation,* should be considered a foundation for the planning and delivery of services (Rainforth, York, & Macdonald, 1992).

Collaboration is the process by which people with different areas of expertise work together to identify needs and problems and then find ways to meet the needs and solve the problems. All of the members of the collaborative team, including parents and professionals, are expected to contribute their expertise to the process in a cooperative manner. Each is considered to be of equal importance and is expected to work with the same end goal in mind.

In the formation of collaborative teams, there are several possible structures; all are not equal in terms of their potential success. Prior to the consideration of different team structures and their relative merits, five facts are worth noting. First, as stated previously, the complexity of the individual requires expertise in many areas. No one person possesses all the knowledge and skills necessary to provide the most beneficial program. Sometimes there is a need for certain areas of expertise to be included on a team; at other times different areas will be necessary.

Second, individuals in different areas of responsibility will vary in the amount of direct contact they have with a student. Some, such as special and general educators and paraprofessionals, have daily contact, others have contact only once or twice a week, and still others have even less frequent contact.

Third, the more the expertise of a particular professional can be applied to a student's life, the more that student benefits. There can be little doubt that a student who has ready access to the skills of a multitude of professionals fares better than one who does not. Again, however, the amount of direct interaction between students and different professionals varies.

Fourth, even though each professional has his or her unique function, each also performs some of the functions of some of the other professionals. This cannot be avoided in the real world. For example, a teacher teaches language; a communication specialist teaches social skills; a physical therapist or occupational therapist teaches recreational skills; and so on.

Finally, it is obvious that the better the communication is among key persons, the more likely it is that they will produce a cohesive program directed toward a beneficial end for the student. One can only imagine the less than satisfactory results that might occur if professionals carried out their duties in isolation. Realization of these facts should lead to the inexorable conclusion that a *team structure* must be developed and implemented if the goal is to maximize the learning of students with severe disabilities. Accepting this premise leads to questions regarding how the team should be structured and how it should function. Three common team models exist: the multidisciplinary model, the interdisciplinary model, and the transdisciplinary model.

The Multidisciplinary Team

The multidisciplinary model is the most traditional model of professionals working with individuals with disabilities. Each professional, primarily the teacher, the communication disorders specialist, the PT, and the OT, works separately and in isolation with each student, then, based on discipline-specific expertise, each one conducts an assessment, plans a program of intervention, implements the program, and evaluates the student's performance in the program (Campbell, 1987; Orelove & Sobsey, 1991).

The major advantage of this model is that it offers students the expert knowledge and skills of many professionals; beyond this, it has few advantages and several disadvantages. One major drawback is that it does not call for interaction or cooperation among professionals; it does not require that they go beyond what is considered their primary area of expertise. Another major problem is that services provided under the multidisciplinary model are delivered in isolation, using a "pull-out" model that takes the student out of relevant learning environments in order to provide brief episodes of therapeutic intervention. Sternat, Messina, Nietupski, Lyon, and Brown (1977) described a sequence similar to the following.

1. The student is taken from the classroom to the service area for the particular therapy.
2. The therapist uses formal and informal procedures to assess the student and determine therapeutic goals based on the student's current level of development.
3. The therapist designs a program to assist the student in progressing through a normal pattern of development.
4. Once or twice a week, the student is brought to the therapy area, where the therapist works with him or her for from thirty minutes to an hour.
5. The therapist returns the student to the classroom and, without much communication with the teacher, leaves him or her until the next therapy session. Neither the teacher nor the parents are aware of the student's needs within the particular therapy area.

The multidisciplinary team model originated in the medical service delivery system, which was the primary service available to individuals with severe disabilities prior to the passage and implementation of P.L. 94-142 with its mandate for a free and appropriate education in the least restrictive environment (Sears, 1981). As Sternat et al. (1977) pointed out, it is based on several assumptions: that the identification of therapeutic needs in an isolated therapy room provides a valid assessment of needs outside that environment; that the order of skills to be developed, based on the typical development for individuals without disabilities, is appropriate for individuals with disabilities; that brief periods of intervention will make a difference; and that skills that are acquired or improved in the therapy sessions will generalize and be used elsewhere when needed.

Today many professionals feel that the multidisciplinary model is inadequate because the isolated assessment, planning, and intervention procedures fall short of meeting the needs of students with severe disabilities. The approaches taken by different professionals are often in opposition to each other, and implementation beyond that provided by individual therapists is inadequate (Orelove & Sobsey, 1991).

The Interdisciplinary Team

The interdisciplinary model is a more sophisticated team approach, one that exceeds the multidisciplinary model in its ability to provide a more coordinated program. The primary characteristic of this model is the sharing of information by professionals at team meetings (Campbell, 1987; Orelove & Sobsey, 1991), which has the effect of improving organization and ensuring that all service needs are met.

Although the interdisciplinary model allows professionals of different disciplines to come together and make coordinated decisions about the educational and therapeutic needs of the student, it suffers many of the problems associated with the multidisciplinary model. Assessments and programs are carried out in isolation from each other; interventions are tied to the orientations of the individual disciplines; and all efforts are not necessarily going in the same direction.

Although communication between professionals is an improvement over the multidisciplinary model, the interdisciplinary model is still a clinical/medical, deficit-remediation model that works toward the improvement of select, isolated goals. Greater focus among the professionals working with the student is needed, and it is provided by the third model, the transdisciplinary team.

The Transdisciplinary Team

The transdisciplinary team model extends the potential effectiveness of the previous team models and is considered by many the preferred method of coordinating services and improving the functioning of students with severe disabilities (Bricker, 1976; Campbell, 1987; Dunn, 1988, 1991; Lyon & Lyon, 1980; Orelove & Sobsey, 1991; Rainforth & York, 1987; Rainforth, York, & Macdonald, 1992; Sears, 1981; Sternat et al., 1977). As its name implies, the transdisciplinary model provides coordinated services across disciplines rather than isolated services within disciplines. Table 3-1 compares the major features of the transdisciplinary model with the multidisciplinary and interdisciplinary models.

Under the transdisciplinary model, one professional, usually the teacher, referred to by Bricker (1976) as the "educational synthesizer," is responsible for coordinating and implementing most of the services, including those traditionally in the domains of other professionals. The teacher must be in regular contact with all the other professionals involved and, to the extent possible, incorporates the necessary therapies into students' daily learning routines.

Assessment and Planning

Implementing the transdisciplinary model in daily educational practice begins with team members participating in the assessment and planning process. Although therapists may conduct some forms of assessment in isolation, they also analyze the student's performance in natural settings. This process includes the following steps (Orelove & Sobsey, 1991; Rainforth & York, 1987):

1. One team member, usually the teacher, conducts an ecological inventory of the key environments in which the student needs to function currently or in the near future, then identifies the activities and skills the student needs to operate in these environments. The other team members, primarily the communication disorders specialist, the physical therapist, and the occupational therapist, review the inventory and suggest environmental modifications that might better allow the student to function.
2. The teacher and, when possible, team members representing the other professions then accompany the student to the appropriate settings and observe his or her attempts to complete the designated activities. During this observation, therapists note areas of individual performance that may warrant further assessment in a quieter, less distracting environment. Even professionals who could not participate in the direct observation might suggest tactics that could result in the most accurate performance by the student. They can also suggest key skills that should be observed by the teacher in the setting.
3. During the observation, the professional(s) attempt to determine the assistance and adaptations that will be necessary for the student to complete the activity as well as possible; they make a record of performance.
4. The results of the assessment in the natural environment are shared with all team members at a subsequent meeting. Campbell (1987) suggested that the following questions be addressed at this time:

Table 3–1
Comparison of Three Team Models

	Multidisciplinary	Interdisciplinary	Trandisciplinary
Assessment	Separate assessments by team members	Separate assessments by team members	Team members and family conduct a comprehensive developmental assessment together
Parent participation	Parents meet with individual team members	Parents meet with team or team representative	Parents are full, active, and participating members of the team
Service plan development	Team members develop separate plans for their discipline	Team members share their separate plans with one another	Team members and the parents develop a service plan based upon family priorities, needs, and resources
Service plan responsibility	Team members are responsible for implementing their section of the plan	Team members are responsible for sharing information with one another as well as for implementing their section of the plan	Team members are responsible and accountable for how the primary service provider implements the plan
Service plan implementation	Team members implement the part of the service plan related to their discipline	Team members implement their section of the plan and incorporate other sections where possible	A primary service provider is assigned to implement the plan with the family
Lines of communication	Informal lines	Periodic case-specific team meetings	Regular team meeting where continuous transfer of information, knowledge, and skills are shared among team members
Guiding philosophy	Team members recognize the importance of contributions from other disciplines	Team members are willing and able to develop, share, and be responsible for providing services that are a part of the total service plan	Team members make a commitment to teach, learn, and work together across discipline boundaries to implement unified service plan
Staff development	Independent and within their discipline	Independent within as well as outside of their discipline	An integral component of team meetings for learning across disciplines and team building

From *Educating Children with Multiple Disabilities: A Transdisciplinary Approach* (2nd ed.) (pp. 13 & 14) by F. P. Orelove & D. Sobsey, 1991, Baltimore: Paul H. Brookes Publishing Co., P.O. Box 10624, Baltimore, Maryland 21285-0624. Reprinted by permission.

- *What type of behavior will be selected for student performance in each of the targeted functional skill domains?*
- *What types of adaptive positioning equipment, adaptive materials, or other devices will be used to enable skill performance?*
- *What strategies will be used to teach certain skills?*
- *When and where will training be implemented and by whom?*
- *How will the effects of training be measured and reviewed? (Campbell, 1987, p. 109)*

Providing Integrated Therapy

Although some isolated forms of therapy may continue, a primary function of therapists operating within the transdisciplinary model is to provide direct therapeutic services to students in classrooms and natural settings. The *integrated therapy approach* is considered a significant complement to the transdisciplinary model (Rainforth et al., 1992). Throughout the day, there are natural opportunities for the student to exercise skills important for the development of physical functioning, communicative functioning, and so forth. At these times, therapists can provide direct therapy within the contexts in which the skills will be needed. This allows the student to benefit from therapy throughout the day and simultaneously to participate in various learning activities. All activities incorporate both functional goals and therapeutic goals.

Role Release by Professionals

Another important characteristic of the transdisciplinary model is *role release.* This aspect of the model allows different professionals to provide some of the services traditionally offered by other professionals. For role release to be successful, professionals must share information with each other about their activities and explain how certain procedures are carried out (Lyon & Lyon, 1980). Thus the teacher will perform some of the functions of the communication disorders specialist, the physical therapists, and the occupational therapists, and the therapists will perform some instructional functions of the teacher. It is this feature of the transdisciplinary model that makes the professionals participating more of a team than those working in other models. But in order for the model to be implemented, it is necessary for professionals, primarily therapists, to broaden their traditional roles. Three therapy models may be used appropriately within the transdisciplinary team model: direct service, monitoring, and consultation (Dunn, 1988, 1991).

Direct service from a therapist to a student is the most traditional form of intervention provided by a therapist and has usually been provided through pull-out practices. Although it is more desirable for therapy to be provided within natural learning environments, there are some circumstances when it is necessary for the therapist to work individually with a student in a nondistracting environment. In the area of physical or occupational therapy, for example, the therapist may need to operate directly on the student when specific knowledge of the neuromuscular system or the integrative functions of the sensory, perceptual, and motor systems is required (Dunn, 1988). Direct service is required when *ongoing* clinical judgment is required during exercises. Even when this is necessary, however, the therapeutic target should be relevant to the student's educational needs and transferred to natural learning environments for practice when possible.

There are many needs of students for which therapists can provide primarily a *monitoring* service as teachers, parents, and paraprofessionals provide the therapeutic intervention. When monitoring, the therapist is most involved in the initial assessment of the student and in determining the needs, planning the intervention program, and teaching the teacher and others how to implement the program in natural environments. Following this, the therapist maintains regular contact with the teacher (usually at least twice a month) to determine if any changes are needed in the intervention.

When monitoring, the therapist has demonstrated role release, a key component of the transdisciplinary model. However, therapists may undertake this level of intervention only under appropriate circumstances: if he or she feels the student's health and safety will be protected; if the teacher or another person implementing the procedure can be trained to demonstrate it without assistance; and if the person implementing the procedure can be trained to identify, without assistance, signs that call for it to be discontinued and the need to contact the therapist (Dunn, 1988).

A final form of service provided by the therapist in a transdisciplinary model is *consultation*, which may be provided for individual students (case consultation), for other professionals' needs (colleague consultation), or for the generic needs of a school system (system consultation). Obviously, in the transdisciplinary model, consultation is the most desirable form of involvement by a therapist when possible. When all therapists involved are serving primarily in consultative roles, there is opportunity for diverse expertise to be cooperatively applied to students' needs, which is both a cause and an effect of true team functioning.

Functioning as a Transdisciplinary Team

In order for the transdisciplinary team to function effectively, team members must undertake certain roles and responsibilities, which may be generic or discipline-specific (Rainforth et al., 1992). Generic roles include participating in decision-making activities about each student, contributing to problem-solving efforts, sharing knowledge and skills, supporting the contributions of others, and continuing to learn about successful methods for ensuring participation of students in family, school, and community life.

Discipline-specific roles, which are discussed in detail later in this chapter, are generally unique to the different members of the transdisciplinary team. In order for any group of professionals to function as a transdisciplinary team, it is important for each team member to be aware of the functions and expertise of other team members. Because historically educators and therapists have been trained in separate programs, isolated from each other and the respective skills that are being developed (Courtnage & Smith-Davis, 1987), the initial step in forming transdisciplinary teams might have to be for professionals to become familiar with the roles others play.

The next step is for the members to share their expertise with each other in an ongoing fashion through consultation and in-service training. Regular meetings are scheduled at which all members share information about specific students, and each member explains the functions he or she is carrying out. Decisions at these meetings will be reached by each individual and by the group as a whole regarding which operations can be shared and which must remain the prerogative of a particular professional.

It should not be expected that transdisciplinary teams will begin to function "by the book" at the outset. Bailey (1984) provided an important analysis of teams progressing through developmental sequences on three axes: dysfunctions related to team development, those related to team subsystems, and those related to whole-team functioning. Bailey suggested that a team that has only been together for a brief period is different from one that has been together for several months or years. As the team matures, its members can be expected to change their individual and group perspectives. For example, it may begin to function as a multidisciplinary team before ultimately maturing into an interdisciplinary and then a transdisciplinary model. Similarly, team subsystems may impede team functioning; one person may dominate the team instead of everyone working together. Finally, Bailey noted that whole-team functioning could be a problem in that the team might be too rigidly structured, have too little structure, be disorganized, or have poorly defined roles for its members. The longer any team works together, the better it will get and the better it will serve the students for whom it is responsible. Nevertheless, difficulties may be expected to continue to some extent. Professionals will have different knowledge, different philosophies, different language, and so forth. With time, learning, and acknowledgment of unique roles, many of these problems will be overcome.

It may be expected that parents might have difficulty understanding and accepting a transdisciplinary model, particularly the role-release aspect of the model. They may have the idea that the best way for their child to benefit is through daily direct service, not only from the teacher, but also from the communication disorders specialist, the PT, and the OT. When the functions of these other professionals are handled by the teacher, parents may feel that their child is not receiving maximum service. The teacher and other members of the team may have to explain the logic of team functioning and how it will benefit the child instead of being an impediment to progress (Orelove & Sobsey, 1991).

It must be acknowledged that some administrative requirements may not accommodate the transdisciplinary model. There are two major problems. The first is that in order for related services personnel in many administrative models to generate funds, they must be in contact with the students they are serving; that is, they must be applying direct service. As discussed previously, role release is a highly desirable form of indirect intervention by therapists in the transdisciplinary team model. However, these forms of involvement do not call for direct contact, and thus in some circumstances, funds to support the specialists will not be generated.

A second administrative problem is that time may not be allocated for teams to meet. Teachers are expected to be with their students except during planning sessions. Therapists must also be working with students, either individually or in small groups. Additionally, most therapists are itinerant, going from one school to another to provide services. Thus it is quite difficult for everyone to find time to meet unless administrative intervention has occurred that will allow meetings to be held on a regular basis (Dunn, 1991).

Benefits of Collaboration

Despite the problems, the advantages of the transdisciplinary model make it worth pursuing. The diversity of expertise that is brought together under this model makes it a very effective approach for working with students with severe disabilities. The expertise of each team member is applied more often to each student, fragmentation of services is decreased, the value of each instance of direct contact is increased, and there is greater continuity and consistency (Sears, 1981). The professional resources, combined with parent involvement, make it easier to solve difficult problems and recognize the unique needs of students. Rainforth et al. (1992) pointed out the following:

> *Each team member brings a unique perspective about an individual student's strengths and challenges. For example,* parents *have the greatest information about the student's daily life outside the school;* teachers *are most knowledgeable about requirements and opportunities in the classroom and about curricular and instructional adaptations;* physical and occupational therapists *bring to the team their knowledge of sensorimotor functioning; and* speech-language therapists *contribute strategies for alternative and augmentative communication, including use of language for social interaction (Rainforth et al., 1992, p. 21).*

Collaborative teaming, besides benefiting the student more than other service delivery models, also brings an important benefit to the professionals who participate. It promotes caring and commitment and aids in maintaining the psychological health of those working together. Professionals and parents can realize that being part of a team means that rewards and difficulties associated with their efforts are shared. Teamwork can help reduce stress and anxiety and promote "positive interdependence" (Johnson & Johnson, 1989).

Building Effective Teams

For most students with severe disabilities, a collaborative team requires parents, teachers, a physical and/or an occupational therapist, a communication disorders specialist, and a paraprofessional. However, the specific composition of a team may vary. Some authorities have suggested that these individuals should be considered a *core team* (Orelove & Sobsey, 1991; Rainforth et al., 1992), which may be expanded when necessary to include vision or hearing specialists, a nurse, a social worker, or others who may be required to contribute to the student's needs. Professionals whose expertise is required, but on a less frequent basis, may comprise a *support team,* which might include audiologists, psychologists, social workers, nurses, dietitians, and/or orientation and mobility specialists. The distinction between core team members and support team members is not so much their specific professions but how much participation is needed from them.

For the benefits of the team to be realized, there must be productive interaction among its members. Attitudes must be developed that invite cooperation; team members must be accessible to each other and must communicate openly with each other; isolating jargon must be reduced; and a commitment toward inclusion must be made by all members of the team (Bricker, 1976). When these commitments are made and when professionals work to achieve team functioning, it can be expected that students will benefit.

In the following sections, discussion of the team members is presented. We begin with parents, the most important participants on the team.

Collaborating with Parents

A most important professional responsibility of a teacher is cooperating with the parents or guardians of their students, whether or not the students have disabilities. All teachers should communicate with parents to inform them of the educational philosophy, goals, and objectives that affect their children and to listen to parents' concerns about the needs of their children so that, to the extent possible, these needs can be addressed during school hours. An important part of teacher-parent communication must include informing parents of their children's progress, usually through conferences and report cards. The frequency of these contacts should be increased if the student is experiencing uncommon difficulties in school, such as not getting along well with others or not keeping up with peers in one or more subjects.

Beyond these forms of interaction, there are many other opportunities for parents to be involved in school activities or in their child's education, but this is not required nor is it an integral part of the communication process. For example, many parents encourage and assist their child in the completion of homework. Some spend time as volunteers in the student's classroom working as tutors, are active in the parent-teacher organization, serve on a school (or school district) advisory council, or participate in a particular school activity, such as the annual fall festival. While all of these types of involvement are good and probably have a beneficial effect on parents, teachers, and students, they are not part of the basic type of interaction that parents and teachers must have.

When the student in question has a severe disability, all of the above parent-teacher-school relations remain true. Parents and teachers must communicate. Parents should inform the teacher about the student's unique needs, and teachers should inform the parents about the student's progress. The extent of parent involvement beyond that point is similar to that of other parents; some are involved more than others, some less.

Shea and Bauer (1991) suggested that there should be a "continuum of collaboration" between teachers and parents, ranging from written and telephone communication to participation by parents in classroom, school, and community activities. This point is very important. In the recent history of special education there has often been an emphasis placed on professionals telling parents what they must do (what they must learn, how they must be involved, how they should treat their children) in order for their children to progress. Although research has demonstrated that parents can be effective teachers for their children with disabilities (Baker, 1984), more recently professionals have come to realize that parents of children with disabilities are parents and their roles are not the same as teachers or other professionals (Lyon & Preis, 1984). This point is crucial and should serve as an important caveat for teachers and other professionals who work with students with severe disabilities.

With this understanding, however, it must also be understood that while parents of individuals with severe disabilities are far from a homogeneous group, they do share some common characteristics and experiences. By federal law, for example, they must approve of their child's Individual Educational Plan (IEP) and should be encouraged to participate in the

Frequent communication with parents is an essential element of collaboration.

planning process. If the child is under 3 years of age and is receiving services because of his or her disability, the parents will likely be asked to assist in the development of an Individual Family Service Plan.

There is a high statistical probability that parents of children with severe disabilities will experience more distress and personal and family difficulties than will other parents, particularly if there is not adequate formal or informal support to assist them with the unique challenges they face (Singer & Irvin, 1991). This is not necessarily true for all parents of individuals with severe disabilities, and it is not stated here with the intention of stereotyping these parents. In fact, in many cases the child with a severe disability improves the mental and emotional health of a family and results in much happiness (Turnbull, Guess, & Turnbull, 1988). However, this is most likely to be true if parents have adequate sources of support and have learned to cope with the difficulties that challenge them. Nevertheless, there are many stress-inducing situations, and teachers and other professionals should be aware of them.

Most professionals believe that working effectively with parents of individuals with severe disabilities is an important component of the overall program (Lyon & Preis, 1984). Educational and habilitation programs that coincide with family values, including their cultural values, have a better chance of meeting success than those that ignore them. The needs of families go beyond the provision of a public school education for the student with severe disabilities, and the extent to which these needs are met may influence the effectiveness of the program.

What Parents Often Need

The conditions that often result in parents experiencing personal difficulties, such as emotional distress, are generally related to the accessibility of different forms of support. Services such as health care for the child with severe disabilities, appropriate educational services, respite care (care of the individual with severe disabilities for short periods of time), financial assistance, in-home assistance (to help with problems related to caregiving or behavior problems), counseling and training in coping skills, and support from family, friends, or other parents of individuals with severe disabilities serve to reduce stress within families (Lyon & Preis, 1984; Singer & Irvin, 1991). The absence of these forms of support or the lack of coordination among them can result in dissatisfaction with "the system," greater stress, and consideration of placing the child in an out-of-home residence (Cole & Meyer, 1989).

In many cases, parents' ability to cope is improved if counseling and other more tangible forms of support are available. Singer, Irvin, Irvine, Hawkins, and Cooley (1989) described an "intensive support" program that offered the following services:

- Case management to help parents find and deal with various community agencies and to coordinate the services of those agencies.
- Respite care of up to 3 hours a week of free, in-home care for their child.
- Weekly 2-hour classes for parents on coping skills that created a "supportive environment" and "encouraged parents to assist one another, to show warmth and respect, and to use active listening skills" (p. 314).
- Community involvement activities for the parents' children provided by volunteers. (The children were taken to settings such as public swimming pools, malls, video arcades, and so forth. This was in addition to the in-home respite care.)

Singer et al. (1989) found that as a result of this level of intervention, the parents developed a lower level of distress as compared to a group of parents receiving less intensive support. The effect was still positive a year later when the researchers conducted a follow-up study.

While a program such as that described above would obviously be beneficial, less formal sources of support for parents and families, such as from friends, relatives, and neighbors, can also be very beneficial. Programs such as Project SHaRE (Source of Help Received and Exchanged) (Dunst, Trivette, Gordon, & Pletcher, 1989) was based on the notion that it is better for parents and families to help themselves and each other through an assistance-bartering system than to rely exclusively or even primarily on formal support systems. According to Dunst et al. (1989), personal social networks have several advantages. They serve as buffers against stress, enhance well-being, and lessen the likelihood of emotional and physical distress. When families have strong personal support systems, these sources of support may reduce time demands placed on the parents by the child; promote positive caregiver-child interactions; improve parent perceptions of child functioning; and indirectly influence positively several dimensions of a child's behavior. By encouraging parents to identify their own sources of support, both within the family and among their extra-family support network, the family unit is made stronger and better able to deal with difficult and stressful situations (Dunst, Trivette, & Deal, 1988; Dunst et al., 1989).

Unfortunately there are times when personal support is not available or when parents perceive this to be the case. When this occurs, parents are more susceptible to ill health and have a difficult time adapting to stress. Singer and Irvin (1991) state that parents and families of individuals with severe disabilities become isolated because (1) their caregiving has left them fatigued; (2) they have limited free time; (3) they encounter "misunderstandings" and "negative reactions" regarding their child; and (4) their child is often excluded from normal social settings and experiences.

What Teachers Should Know and Do

The relationship between a teacher and the parents of a child with severe disabilities is most important. Although services such as counseling and case management are usually provided by other professionals on the collaborative team (for example, counselors, psychologists, social workers), the teacher is most likely the professional with whom the parent has the greatest amount of direct contact. Additionally, the teacher is the primary link between the collaborative team (and the public school) and the parent. Teachers and other professionals who are perceived by parents as being most helpful are those with a pleasant disposition, those who are knowledgeable about their child's problems, those who treat parents as equals and involve them in making decisions, and those who are specific and practical when discussing how to address the child's needs (Singer & Irvin, 1991).

Communicating with Parents An open line of communication is the most important feature of teacher-parent relations. Parents can provide important information on a daily basis and likewise want to receive regular reports from the teacher. Parents and teachers who share information better understand how to interact with the student in matters ranging from communicative acts to medical problems.

Teachers and parents may communicate with each other, using any medium that is mutually satisfactory. Parents who drop their children off and pick them up at the end of the school day have frequent natural opportunities to talk with the teacher. Phone calls can also be used as long as there is agreement about when and where to call. Teachers should know whether or not calls to the parent's place of employment are acceptable and should let parents know if they (the teachers) are willing to accept calls at home and, if so, during what hours. (Of course, emergency phone calls about a student's well-being should be made whenever the need arises.) Recent communication devices such as electronic mail, telephone answering machines, and fax machines make communication easier and may be of use between some parents and teachers.

The oldest and probably most-used form of communication between teachers and parents is the daily log or journal, which is usually a spiral-bound notebook that goes between the home and the school with the student. In it, the teacher writes a brief report of the day's activities, focusing on any special positive highlights of the day (for example, "Emily selected a book in the library") or difficulties that occurred (for example, "Samuel had a seizure this morning; you may want to talk to his doctor about his blood levels"). When the book is returned via the student on the next school day, it may include a note from the parent indicating any current problems the student may be having and suggesting implications for the teacher ("Jamey did not sleep well last night, he may be tired today," or "Lucretia had a big breakfast at home, she probably won't eat anything at school this morning"). Teachers should send the notebook home each day, preferably with some positive message. Even if parents do not write a response, they will at least have the opportunity to do so and a useful line of communication will be kept open with relatively little effort.

Meeting with Parents Most schools encourage meetings between parents and teachers. Some of these are scheduled for all parents at the same time, such as during a school's open house; others are individually arranged. Teachers should plan their communicative activities with parents at these meetings accordingly.

Meetings with all parents at the same time allow the teacher to discuss general issues, such as his or her philosophy of education for students with severe disabilities; the types of activities that occur in the special class, the regular class, and other learning environments in the school and community; current or future projects to be undertaken; equipment and materials used; other professionals providing services to the students; and how the students' progress is monitored. The teacher can also discuss additional issues raised by individual parents that are likely to be of interest to all.

Meetings with individual parents may be arranged at the request of the teacher or the parent. The communication pathways discussed above, especially the student's personal communication notebook, is useful for arranging these meetings. When meetings are arranged and held, the guidelines outlined in Figure 3–1 should be followed.

When Parents Are Angry From time to time, all parents become angry with a school or a school district, or even with a particular teacher. When the child has a severe disability, this anger may arise from various sources. Although the teacher may or may not understand the cause of the anger and may or may not be able to rectify the situation, he or she must respond when approached by an angry parent and must do so in a professional manner. The suggestions presented in Figure 3–2 are intended to help a teacher reach a successful resolution with angry parents.

Offering Help to Parents Teachers or other professionals often become aware that parents

1. Whoever asks for the meeting, whether it is the teacher or the parent, should state why the meeting is requested. This may be very general ("I would like to update you on Richard's progress") or specific ("Please meet with me so we can discuss Rasheeda's moving into middle school next year").
2. If possible, it may be helpful to send questions or requests for information home in advance of the meeting so the parent may come prepared. For example, the teacher may ask the parent to bring relevant medical records or information about the student's favorite leisure activities.
3. When the time of the meeting is arranged, the teacher must make sure that enough time is allotted to fully discuss the issue and that both parties know when the meeting will begin and approximately how long it will last.
4. If appropriate, the teacher may want to arrange for other professionals to be present, such as the regular class teacher or the occupational therapist. If this is done, the parent should be notified before the meeting who will be there.
5. At the meeting, the teacher should listen carefully and take notes if necessary. At the conclusion, the teacher should feel confident that she or he understood what the parent was communicating. Rephrasing or summarizing the parent's comments may be helpful.
6. The teacher should make sure that any information given to parents is free from unnecessary jargon and easily understood by the parent. She or he should make an effort to determine if the parent understood all that was said and further explain any matter that was not fully comprehended.

Figure 3–1
Guidelines for Meetings with Parents

are facing unique difficulties associated with having a child with severe disabilities. When offering help in such situations, professionals should realize that certain forms of help-giving can have positive effects, while others can be negative. Dunst et al. (1988) suggested that offers of assistance be made with certain considerations. Most important, giving help should not undermine the family's use of its own resources to solve its problems, which can result in learned helplessness and reduced self-efficacy. Instead of solving the problem, the professional should encourage the parents to explore ways to solve it so that they see themselves as successful problem solvers. It is also very important that the help-giving professional never be patronizing or convey the notion that the parents seeking help are inferior or incapable of dealing with the problematic situation.

Dunst et al. (1988) also advised that the act of giving help should not foster a sense of indebtedness, which would interfere with the recognition of problems and might inhibit the person from seeking assistance in the future. Unsolicited help is likely to be harmful. Advice or help from someone who is not well known by the individual or from whom the individual does not want advice is not likely to be well received. Help will also not be well received if

1. If an angry parent calls on the telephone, the teacher should try to arrange a face-to-face meeting as soon as possible. Even if the parent wants to pursue the issue over the phone, personal contact will probably allow both to deal with the problem better by searching for both short-term and long-term solutions.
2. If a parent is extremely agitated at a personal meeting, the teacher should attempt to diffuse the present hostility. This may be done by assuring the parent of one's interest and concern about the problem, asking the parent to sit down, and offering the parent a soda or some coffee or tea. The intention is not to talk the parent out of being angry, but to help the parent attain a level of calmness so that the issue can be fully discussed.
3. The teacher must remain poised during the interaction. The teacher does not want to indicate that he or she is unconcerned, but that the problem will be addressed in a professional manner.
4. Most angry parents will want to be heard. Often the most important thing a teacher can do is let the parent fully air his or her grievance. After the teacher has listened carefully, he or she can discuss possible options to solve the dilemma.
5. When the source of the anger is something the teacher said or did, the teacher should explain to the parent why it was said or done. If it was a professionally acceptable action, the teacher should explain why it was undertaken. If the teacher made an error, then an apology is in order. In either event, the future course of the action's occurrence should be discussed and some agreement reached.
6. There will be some sources of anger that teachers will not be able to resolve. If the teacher cannot correct the problem, he or she may assist the parent by identifying the person who might do so and arranging a meeting with that person. When doing this, however, teachers must be sensitive of the parent's perception that they are "passing the buck" and should tell parents to contact them after the meeting to let them know if a satisfactory resolution was reached.

Figure 3–2
Suggestions for Assisting Angry Parents

it does not match the real need that an individual has or the need that the individual believes he or she has. Help-giving is likely to be most effective if it emphasizes building strengths within the family rather than remediating weaknesses.

With these thoughts about giving help in mind, there are several ways in which a teacher can serve as a source of support for parents. However, two points must be remembered. First, no one should assume that all parents of children with severe disabilities have personal problems related to their children. Some do and some do not, but creating situations that do not exist is detrimental to the students and their parents. Second, the teacher or other professional must realize that he or she can be helpful in some ways but not in all ways. For the most part, the objective when working with parents is to find ways to support them as they try to meet their own needs. Figure 3–3 presents a list of challenging occurrences (or stressful situations) and ways in which teachers can deal with them.

While it is helpful for families if some of the conditions that cause stress and personal difficulties can be reduced, it is also helpful if they can learn to accept the conditions that cannot be changed, realizing that all is not "their fault" and that all cannot be fixed. As Singer and Irvin (1991) stated, " . . . efforts to improve the situation have to be balanced with ways of

1. Parental difficulties are more likely to occur at times of transition or during major life events (divorce, moving into a new school). Teachers and other professionals should be most understanding of parents' needs at this time.
2. Smaller, more common events can also cause stress (i.g., the car breaking down, the checkbook running low, etc.). Teachers should be aware of these and should not contribute to them. They should avoid sending home "special requests" that may require extra effort in an already exhausting day.
3. To the extent that they are knowledgeable, teachers should inform parents of sources of support, particularly respite care services in the community and individuals or services that may help them in their home. Lack of respite care often is a factor related to parents seeking an out-of-home residence for their child. Other support services could provide health care, financial assistance, and counseling. The school social worker can assist in identifying these services.
4. There may be parent support organizations within communities and teachers should provide parents with information about them. Some organizations may include the local or state Association for Retarded Citizens, Association for Persons with Severe Handicaps, Autism Society of America, United Cerebral Palsy, or other parent/advocacy organizations. Teachers may also assist parents by helping them to form informal networks with parents of other students they teach.
5. Parents should also be encouraged by teachers to talk with other family members, friends, and relatives about their child and look to them as sources of informal support. These persons can help both emotionally and with the physical support of the individual with severe disabilities.
6. Teachers should place a high priority on targeting for improvement those aspects of the child's behavior that parents indicate are the most troublesome at home. For example, some parents would be helped if their child could learn to use the toilet appropriately or fix an after-school snack independently. When such targets are possible and appropriate, teachers should emphasize them.

Figure 3–3
Assisting Parents with Particular Needs

accepting it" (p. 283). Teachers and other professionals can provide important support by acknowledging this.

Collaborating with Other Professionals

The success of educational programs for students with severe disabilities may be directly related to the success with which various professionals work with each other as well as with parents.

Many professionals provide direct or indirect services to students with severe disabilities. Some of the professionals most commonly involved include special and general educators, physical and occupational therapists, communication (or speech/language) therapists, social workers, school psychologists, school nurses, vision specialists, audiologists, school administrators, and physicians. Descriptions of these roles have been provided by Orelove and Sobsey (1991) and Westling and Koorland (1988) and are summarized below.

Special Educators

As Bricker (1976) proposed, the special educator must be considered an educational synthesizer. In this role, a major function is to incorporate the skills and knowledge of other professionals collaborating on the transdisciplinary team and bring them to bear directly on the educational program for each student. The special educator is responsible for conducting a substantial portion of the student's assessment and participating in the planning process. On a daily basis, this professional is responsible for providing direct instruction to students with disabilities and communicating with other professionals and paraprofessionals who are doing so, giving them assistance and advice for conducting instructional activities. He or she also serves as the primary liaison between the school system and students' parents. Additionally, the special educator should serve as an advocate for students with severe disabilities.

The skills required by a special educator of students with severe disabilities are numerous (Fox & Williams, 1992; Whitten & Westling, 1985). Fox and Williams suggested that these teachers must have at the core of their activity a value system that acknowledges the dignity of individuals with severe disabilities and the appropriateness of providing an education that fosters a high-quality inclusive lifestyle.

General Educators

It would not be feasible to include students in regular classrooms and other general educational classes and environments without the cooperation and support of the professionals who operate in these settings. Although it cannot be assumed that these professionals have the depth of knowledge about the nature of severe disabilities that the special educator has (although some may), it can be expected that with support and some training, they can provide instruction to students with severe disabilities in integrated settings.

General educators have the primary responsibility for teaching subject matter to students who can acquire information primarily through verbal and written instruction and various learning experiences. In this process they plan lessons, prepare materials, organize instructional activities, and use instructional media and materials to teach the content of specific subject matter from the elementary level through high school. When students require alternative forms of instruction or have learning goals that fall outside of the norm, as do students with severe disabilities, the general educator often needs assistance in finding ways to instruct so that all students can benefit.

Some have proposed that the professions of general education and special education be merged so that all teachers will be trained to teach all students (Stainback & Stainback, 1985). Certainly there is much merit to this plan, but at this time few general educators can be assumed to have the knowledge and skills necessary to instruct students with severe disabilities in regular classrooms without substantial direct or indirect assistance from special educators. However, given adequate support, these educators should be expected to provide instruction to students with disabilities and therefore must be considered as an integral part of the educational team.

Physical and Occupational Therapists

The physical therapist is a health-care professional who has been trained to work with individuals who have physical disabilities. The PT possesses expertise in evaluating, planning, and intervening in posture and balance, preventing bodily misformations, and improving gross motor functioning, including ambulation. This professional provides exercises and positioning techniques to help align the spine, legs, and feet; fits students with positioning equipment and braces or prostheses; provides range of motion, relaxation, sensory stimulation, and postural drainage procedures; and develops methods that allow the student to function as independently as possible (Bigge, 1991; Orelove & Sobsey, 1991).

The PT can provide exercises that allow the student to increase the appropriate use of his or her body and its parts, and can prevent further limitations that may occur through misalignments, contractions, or primitive reflexes that persist. Equally important from the perspective of the teacher is the application of the knowledge of the PT to help the student participate in various common daily activities such as eating, dressing, and participating in recreational activities. By attending to concerns such as these, the PT helps the student function more in a normal life routine.

The occupational therapist possesses knowledge and skills similar to the physical therapist's but has an orientation toward providing purposeful activities or tasks that have meaning for the individual (Dunn, 1991). Practically speaking, OTs are more able to assist in using fine motor skills related to daily living activities (Orelove & Sobsey, 1991). For example, if a student with cerebral palsy is attempting to learn to eat independently using a spoon, an OT can provide specific suggestions regarding the type of utensil to use, how to place the plate or bowl for the best access, how to help the student learn to scoop the food, and how to improve oral-muscular control if necessary.

Most OTs and PTs have been trained in clinical models that call for in-depth evaluation of the physical development and needs of the individual followed by specific intervention to improve functioning or inhibit deterioration. Although traditionally these therapists have worked in isolated settings with individuals with disabilities, more recent practices consist of integrated therapy models. This approach is intended to bring the expertise of the therapist into areas of functional needs.

Communication Disorders Specialists

Most individuals with severe disabilities need special attention focused on communication skills—improving verbal language, developing and applying language skills to satisfy environmental needs, developing augmentative communication systems, or developing relatively basic forms of communication in order to express satisfaction or dissatisfaction, comfort or discomfort, or yes or no. Specialists in communication disorders (speech/language therapists, speech pathologists) can provide expertise in this area if they have received appropriate training.

The communication disorders specialist evaluates the student's language ability and needs and cooperates with other team members to suggest appropriate language-learning goals. Traditionally, the language specialist has provided direct therapy, but more recent approaches require the specialist to work through the teacher and others to help the student develop and improve functional language skills for use in natural environments (Caro & Snell, 1989; Mirenda, Iacono, & Williams, 1990).

Social Workers

A social worker's responsibility is to facilitate and coordinate the delivery of various social services to individuals and families who have needs beyond those that families normally have. When working for a school system or a social welfare agency, a social worker serves as a liaison between the family, the school, and different social services. He or she may provide counseling to parents and assist in locating sources of financial, medical, or nutritional support. Social workers are responsible for collecting case history information about a student and his or her family in order to provide services through special education or human services agencies.

Because social workers routinely visit homes to discuss needs and resources, they are often in a position to understand the unique situations of families and how these situations bear on the well-being of students with severe disabilities. If a teacher does not have a good communicative link with the student's parents, a social worker can help forge this relation by intervening with the family.

School Psychologists

The traditional role of the school psychologist has been to conduct assessments to determine the present level of functioning of students with disabilities. In order to be eligible for special education services in most school districts, students must score below predetermined criteria on standardized tests of intelligence and adaptive behavior. The school psychologist is the professional responsible for conducting these assessments, collecting other relevant types of information, and preparing a written report on the cognitive and behavioral functioning of the individual.

For students with multiple disabilities and the most severe disabilities, traditional forms of intellectual assessment may have little meaning insofar as planning an educational intervention. Likewise, because of a restricted range of ambulation and mobility, formal adaptive behavior assessment may have little meaning. Nevertheless, such assessments may be required to allow the individual to receive services.

Many school psychologists are trained in the area of applied behavior analysis and can analyze the relation between a student's behavior and environmental activities. With such analysis, plans may be developed to increase adaptive behavior and decrease less desirable forms of behavior. Serving in the role of behavior analyst, the school psychologist may directly observe the student in the classroom and may also ask the teacher(s) to provide information about the student's behavior. A strong cooperative relationship between teacher and psychologist can improve the quality of intervention used to facilitate a student's learning.

School Nurses

The school nurse is probably the professional most available to provide information and treatment related to a student's medical needs. Because many students with severe disabilities have sensitive physical conditions, the expertise of a nurse can be very valuable. He or she can provide direct treatment and also demonstrate to others how to respond to seizures, provide first aid when needed, give medication, and perform catheterization, suctioning, and tube feeding for students who need these services (Orelove & Sobsey, 1991).

Special and general educators should take advantage of the nurse's expertise by requesting in-service training and informal information related to medical needs. Teachers working with students with severe disabilities for the first time should arrange to receive an orientation from the nurse about general healthcare practices. When new students arrive, the teacher should seek medical information from the nurse about the unique characteristics or needs of each student.

Vision Specialists

Individuals trained in the area of visual disabilities may assist in the development and implementation of programs for students whose visual acuity or perception may be deficient. Because many children with severe disabilities also have single or dual sensory impairments (Fredericks & Baldwin, 1987), expertise in areas such as the use of residual vision, adaption of materials and activities, and mobility training can be very useful.

Audiologists

An audiologist is trained to assess hearing ability and loss, to determine the nature and extent of the loss if one exists, and to prescribe an appropriate hearing aid if one will be of use given the type of hearing loss. As stated above, many students who have severe disabilities also experience sensory impairments. If there is some indication that a student may not be hearing adequately, an audiologist is the professional who can assess the student's ability in this area.

On this matter, there are two important points. First, because many students who have severe cognitive disabilities may not be able to respond to common forms of audiological testing, an audiologist who works with these students must be able to use alternative methods of evaluation. Second, not all types of hearing loss can be remedied by the use of a hearing aid; even though it is determined that there is a hearing loss, the audiologist may not be able to prescribe an applicable device. Still, knowledge of a student's hearing ability will allow the teacher to modify environmental conditions when necessary.

School Administrators

All public school districts have well-developed administrative structures with various administrators serving in different roles (Westling & Koorland, 1988). School administrators, both from the central school district office (superintendents, assistant superintendents, and directors of special education, among others) and within the school (principal, assistant principal, and department heads) are responsible for developing policies, making decisions, and implementing programs. Without question, their commitment is vital to having successful, high-quality programs for students with and without disabilities. Individually and as a group, they make critical decisions on factors such as financing, service delivery arrangements, placement of students, IEP development procedures, community- and home-based instruction, in-service training needs, and so forth.

While their positions allow administrators to be very influential, like other professionals, they are held accountable for their actions. It is their responsibility to see that federal and state laws regarding educational services for students with disabilities are followed. They must also be responsive to parents, advocacy groups, and professional organizations. As the potential for quality services for students with severe disabilities continues to increase, so too does the demand for these services. Most successful administrators form strong alliances with these groups and individuals to develop high-quality programs.

Physicians

Finally, the role of medical doctors in the lives of persons with severe disabilities must be noted. Usually a physician is the first professional to provide parents with information about the disability of their child, including the initial diagnosis of the condition. From that point forward, parents have many interactions with physicians and these interactions often expand to include the student's teacher and other school personnel.

Specialists in pediatrics, neurology, ophthalmology, orthopedics, urology, dentistry, and other medical areas may all play a role in addressing the medical needs of individuals with severe disabilities. Communication between these professionals and the teacher, the school nurse, and/or the social worker is of great benefit to the student.

Others

The above list of professionals is extensive, but there are actually many others who play important roles although often their significance goes unrecognized. Some of these include the school guidance counselor, nutritionists and dietitians, respiratory therapists, pharmacists, rehabilitation engineers, bus drivers, music therapists, recreational therapists, and media specialists (Orelove & Sobsey, 1991; Westling & Koorland, 1988). The educational paraprofessional, a person who plays an extremely important daily and direct role in the lives of students with severe disabilities, warrants substantial attention, especially regarding his or her appropriate role in the educational program.

Collaborating with Paraprofessionals

Although not a trained professional, the paraprofessional makes a significant contribution on the transdisciplinary team and should be included in any discussion of collaborative interactions. Paraprofessionals work in special and regular classes with students with severe disabilities, performing many instructional functions similar to those carried out by the teacher. The primary differences between teachers and their aids or assistants are (1) teachers have been trained in colleges or universities, (2) teachers are considered to be the primary planners and decision makers in the classrooms, and (3) teachers, with other professionals on the transdisciplinary team, are responsible for developing instructional programs and are held accountable for students' learning and well-being.

Notwithstanding these important factors, the daily activities of teachers and paraprofessionals in learning environments are nearly indistinguishable. Both work directly with students to promote learning, both assist students with their needs, and both are concerned with the safety of the students. In order for the professional-paraprofessional relationship to be of greatest benefit to the student, there must be an understanding of the roles of the positions in relation to each other.

Delineating the Roles of Professionals and Paraprofessionals

The responsibility for maximizing the learning of students with severe disabilities rests with the members of the transdisciplinary team; the responsibility for implementing the appropriate learning activities on a daily basis rests primarily with the special educator and, to some extent, the other members of the team. In fulfilling these responsibilities, the professionals are the decision makers who determine, with the parents, the appropriate goals and objectives, the instructional strategies, and the therapeutic needs of students with disabilities. From this basis, the teacher designs the daily learning activities in the classroom and other environments, monitors students' progress through data collection and evaluation, and continues to collaborate with other team members as described previously.

Beyond these duties, many activities in programs for students with severe disabilities, whether they occur in the special or the regular classroom or in the home or the community, are performed by paraprofessionals

(Boomer, 1980, 1982; Frith & Lindsey, 1980; McKenzie & Houk, 1986). They work with individuals or with small groups, they implement instructional tactics, they collect performance data, they perform virtually all of the activities of the teacher, including those related to students' daily needs and hygiene.

Various tasks can be undertaken by paraprofessionals to assist in the integration of students with severe disabilities into regular classrooms and other environments. Frith and Lindsey (1980) suggested that a paraprofessional with adequate training and experience can provide assistance to the general educator when the student with severe disabilities is in an integrated setting. As the student participates or partially participates with other students, the paraprofessional can assist by arranging materials and equipment, helping with physical management, providing helpful cues or prompts, and recording performance data. He or she can also serve as a daily link between the general educator and the special educator as necessary. Figure 3–4 lists some typical functions of paraprofessionals employed in programs for students with severe disabilities.

Directing and Supervising Paraprofessionals

In order to have a paraprofessional fully participating in an educational program, the responsibilities of the teacher must be expanded. In addition to student-focused responsibilities, the professional must also assume responsibility for directing the activity of the paraprofessional placed in his or her charge, as well as supervising and evaluating this individual.

1. Supervise individuals and small groups in classrooms, lunchrooms, in community settings, etc., as directed by the teacher.
2. Position, lift, and carry students with physical disabilities as directed by the teacher, PT, and OT.
3. Implement self-care, feeding, dressing, and toileting programs as directed by the teacher.
4. Assist in the preparation of materials and arranging the classroom for learning activities.
5. Be responsible for keeping the classroom neat and orderly and clean material and equipment when necessary.
6. Assist the teacher in preparing materials, bulletin boards, adaptive equipment, classroom furniture, etc.
7. Collect student performance data as directed by the teacher.
8. Follow directions of the teacher and other team members when responding to inappropriate behavior.
9. Intervene in medical emergencies as directed and contact an appropriate individual for emergency medical services.
10. Communicate positively with students with and without disabilities, and with professional and paraprofessional personnel.
11. Assist students with mobility needs and transportation as directed by the teacher.
12. Provide instruction and assistance to individuals or groups as directed by the teacher.

Figure 3–4
Activities of Paraprofessionals in Programs for Students with Severe Disabilities

Often this task presents more of a challenge to new teachers than does directly teaching students with severe disabilities. Nevertheless, it is an important responsibility and must be undertaken with seriousness and deliberation.

Assignment of Duties

An individual working as a paraprofessional needs to perform a variety of tasks assigned by the teacher. It is important for the teacher to ascertain the paraprofessional's ability to perform certain tasks; if necessary skills are lacking, the teacher should demonstrate to the assistant how these tasks are to be done. In some cases, additional resources to help the paraprofessional learn the task requirements, such as in-service training, books, or videos, may be helpful (McKenzie & Houk, 1986).

As Figure 3–4 suggests, there are many appropriate tasks for the paraprofessional to perform. It is helpful and may offset future conflicts if these tasks or other specific responsibilities are written down and discussed with the paraprofessional at the beginning of employment with a teacher. In some school districts, paraprofessional requirements may already have been developed and these may be sufficient. However, it is important that paraprofessionals have a clear understanding of their duties regardless of who specifies those duties. Even if there are school-wide or school district policies, the teacher may wish to develop an individual assignment protocol for the paraprofessional unique to the needs of his or her program (McKenzie & Houk, 1986).

Supervision and Evaluation

A clearly written statement of the paraprofessional's job responsibility facilitates supervision and evaluation because there is little doubt by either the teacher or the teacher's assistant about what is expected. Given that there is mutual understanding of what the paraprofessional is to do, the job of supervising and evaluating can be very objective with job performance serving as the basis (Boomer, 1980).

To further facilitate supervision and evaluation, regular meetings between the teacher and the paraprofessional should be scheduled about once a week. This not only allows the teacher to evaluate the assistant's performance, but also allows the assistant to be involved in planning future activities for the students. Further, by scheduling regular meetings, discussions between the professional and paraprofessional are not limited to the times when the teacher is not satisfied with his or her assistant.

If the paraprofessional is not performing a task correctly, the teacher should be very explicit as to what must be done. Again the teacher may refer to the written job requirements. If this is not sufficient, the teacher may need to demonstrate how to perform the task. The teacher should make sure that the assistant has the opportunity to perform the task under close supervision and direction in order that he or she can do so independently in the future.

Regular feedback, both written and verbal, provides a paraprofessional with reinforcement for doing a job correctly or with information about what areas of job performance are in need of improvement. During weekly scheduled meetings, verbal evaluations may be sufficient; however, written evaluations should also be provided although they may come less often. Although schools or school districts may require teachers to provide annual written evaluations about paraprofessionals, more frequent notices about performance may be useful, particularly when new professional-paraprofessional relations are being established.

Personal Interactions

Because paraprofessionals are such an integral part of the teacher's daily activities, it is important for both, as well as for the students, that harmonious personal relations be maintained. Most often there are no problems in this domain, but there are potential sources of conflict. If the assistant has duties that are not clearly explained or that he or she does not know how to perform, if less pleasant duties are not shared equally by teacher and assistant, if the supervision by the teacher is critical in a nonconstructive fashion, or if the respective roles of the two are not clearly defined, personal conflicts may occur. The appropriate approach to supervision and evaluation as discussed above will help, but conflicts may still occur on some occasions.

Although avoiding these conflicts cannot always be assured, some efforts may be helpful. To begin, once again, the teacher must reinforce the fact that final decisions about operations in the classroom rest with him or her. This position needs to be taken early and often, but it must be presented diplomatically. The fact is that the paraprofessional is not employed or paid sufficiently to have this responsibility. So while input should be invited and welcomed, the paraprofessional must understand that ultimate decision-making is the teacher's responsibility.

Teachers should learn about and use the unique strengths of paraprofessionals, who have varied backgrounds and experiences that will allow them to provide unique types of assistance (Boomer, 1980). Discovering, using, and reinforcing individuals for their personal contributions will improve their self-esteem and make them more pleasant team players. It may also result in better service to the students because there may be some tasks at which the assistant may be more adept than the teacher.

As a final note on personal relations, teachers should always avoid arguing with a paraprofessional in the classroom or in other public locations. There may be times when the assistant and the teacher are clearly at odds as to what should be done or how a problem should be handled. For example, the teacher gives a direction to do something and the assistant ignores it or does something different. If the situation degenerates into an argument, students will be upset and nothing positive will occur. It is always more appropriate to delay discussion of the matter until a private meeting can be scheduled.

Conclusion

The professional responsibilities of a teacher of students with severe disabilities extend beyond the provision of direct services to those students. The teacher must collaborate with the parents of the students and other professionals by serving as a member of a transdisciplinary team and must work daily with a paraprofessional. The importance of the relationship between the special educator and these other individuals cannot be overstated. If the teacher does not work effectively with others, less than optimal services will be delivered to the students.

Understanding the unique circumstances of parents of students with severe disabilities will not only allow the teacher to better form the appropriate goals and objectives for students, but will also help her or him approach the educational process with an empathetic perspective. This is not to imply that the teacher should have an attitude of pity toward the parents or feel that they are superhuman because their child has a severe disability. In fact, the opposite is true. The better the interactions are between parents and teachers, the more likely it is that teachers will realize the unique characteristics of the parents and how the impact of their child affects each individually.

In the last several years, it has been acknowledged that many different professionals possess skills that can make substantial contributions to the development and learning of individuals with severe disabilities. Special and general educators, occupational and physical therapists, and specialists in communication disorders have the most frequent contact with students, but others also play important roles. It is not enough that the expertise of these persons be applied to the individual; it must be applied in a collaborative fashion, with the professionals each playing an important role on the transdisciplinary team. At times this role will call for the direct application of unique skills, at other times there will be role release (experts, through monitoring and consultation, encourage the application of their knowledge through the activities of another professional). This is the nature of the transdisciplinary model. It is a model that, to date, appears to offer the greatest benefit to students with severe disabilities.

Finally, the position of the paraprofessional must be acknowledged as one of great significance. Usually this individual has as much daily contact with students as does the teacher. Because the greatest degree of cooperation must exist between the teacher and the assistant, each should understand the proper role of the other and work within these parameters. The learning environments of the students will operate smoothly when this is the case and less so when it is not.

Questions for Reflection

1. What would be different for a teacher working on a transdisciplinary team as opposed to working independently or on a multidisciplinary team?
2. In what ways might professionals best learn from each other?
3. What might be some ways that professionals can gain a better understanding of parents' needs and concerns?
4. Why do professionals often expect more from parents of children with severe disabilities than from other parents?
5. What might be some creative ways for professionals and parents to meet and work together on a regular basis?
6. What type of characteristics would be most appropriate for a paraprofessional?
7. Should paraprofessionals who work with students with severe disabilities receive formal training? What should it include?
8. Should paraprofessionals be considered to have the same status on transdisciplinary teams as the specially trained professionals? Why or why not?

References

Bailey, D. B. (1984). A triaxial model of the interdisciplinary team and group process. *Exceptional Children, 51,* 17–25.

Baker, B. L. (1984). Intervention with families with young, severely handicapped children. In J. Blacher (Ed.), *Severely handicapped young children and their families: Research in review* (pp. 319–375). Orlando, FL: Academic Press.

Bigge, J. L. (1991). *Teaching individuals with physical and multiple disabilities* (3rd ed.). New York: Macmillan.

Boomer, L. W. (1980). Special education paraprofessionals: A guide for teachers. *Teaching Exceptional Children, 12,* 146–149.

Boomer, L. W. (1982). The paraprofessional: A valued resource for special children and their teachers. *Teaching Exceptional Children, 14,* 194–197.

Bricker, D. (1976). Educational synthesizer. In M. A. Thomas (Ed.), *Hey, don't forget about me!* (pp. 84–97). Reston, VA: Council for Exceptional Children.

Campbell, P. H. (1987). The integrated programming team: An approach for coordinating professionals of various disciplines in programs for students with severe and multiple handicaps. *Journal of the Association for Persons with Severe Handicaps, 12,* 107–116.

Caro, P., & Snell, M. (1989). Characteristics of teaching communication to people with moderate and severe disabilities. *Education and Training in Mental Retardation, 24,* 63–77.

Cole, D. A., & Meyer, L. H. (1989). Impact of needs and resources on family plans to seek out-of-home placement. *American Journal on Mental Retardation, 93,* 380–387.

Courtnage, L., & Smith-Davis, J. (1987). Interdisciplinary team training: A national survey of special education teacher training programs. *Exceptional Children, 53,* 451–458.

Dunn, W. (1988). Models of occupational therapy service provision in the school system. *American Journal of Occupational Therapy, 42,* 718–723.

Dunn, W. (1991). Integrated related services. In L. H. Meyer, C. A. Peck, & L. Brown (Eds.), *Critical issues in the lives of people with severe disabilities* (pp. 353–377). Baltimore: Paul H. Brookes.

Dunst, C., Trivette, C., & Deal, A. (1988). *Enabling and empowering families: Principles and guidelines for practice.* Cambridge, MA: Brookline Books.

Dunst, C. J., Trivette, C. M., Gordon, N. J., & Pletcher, L. L. (1989). Building and mobilizing informal family support networks. In G. H. S. Singer & L. K. Irvin (Eds.), *Support for caregiving families: Enabling positive adaptation to disability* (pp. 121–141). Baltimore: Paul H. Brookes.

Fox, L., & Williams, D. G. (1992). Preparing teachers of students with severe disabilities. *Teacher Education and Special Education, 15,* 97–107.

Fredericks, H. D. B., & Baldwin, V. L. (1987). Individuals with sensory impairments: Who are they? How are they educated? In L. Goetz, D. Guess, & K. Stremel-Campbell (Eds.), *Innovative program design for individuals with dual sensory impairments* (pp. 3–12). Baltimore: Paul H. Brookes.

Frith, G., & Lindsey, J. D. (1980). Paraprofessional roles in mainstreaming multihandicapped students. *Education Unlimited,* 2(2), 17–20.

Johnson, R., & Johnson, D. (1989). Cooperative learning and mainstreaming. In R. Gaylord-Ross (Ed.), *Integration strategies for students with handicaps* (pp. 233–248). Baltimore: Paul H. Brooks.

Lyon, S., & Lyon, G. (1980). Team functioning and staff development: A role release approach to providing integrated services for severely handicapped students. *Journal of the Association for the Severely Handicapped, 5,* 250–263.

Lyon, S., & Preis, A. (1984) Working with families of severely handicapped persons. In M. Seligman (Ed.), *The family with a handicapped child: Understanding and treatment* (pp. 203–232). New York: Grune & Stratton.

McKenzie, R. G., & Houk, C. S. (1986). The paraprofessional in special education. *Teaching Exceptional Children, 18,* 246–252.

Mirenda, P., Iacono, T., & Williams, R. (1990). Communication options for persons with severe and profound disabilities: State of the art and future directions. *Journal of the Association for Persons with Severe Handicaps, 15,* 3–21.

Orelove, F. P., & Sobsey, D. (1991). *Educating children with multiple disabilities: A transdisciplinary approach* (2nd ed.). Baltimore: Paul H. Brookes.

Rainforth, B., & York, J. (1987). Integrated related services in community instruction. *Journal of the Association for Persons with Severe Handicaps, 12,* 190–198.

Rainforth, B., York, J., & Macdonald, C. (1992). *Collaborative teams for students with severe disabilities: Integrating therapy and educational services.* Baltimore: Paul H. Brookes.

Sears, C. J. (1981). The transdisciplinary approach: A process for compliance with Public Law 94-142. *Journal of the Association for the Severely Handicapped, 6,* 22–29.

Shea, T. M., & Bauer, A. M. (1991). *Parents and teachers of children with exceptionalities* (2nd ed.). Boston: Allyn & Bacon.

Singer, G. H. S., & Irvin, L. K. (1991). Supporting families of persons with severe disabilities: Emerging findings, practices, and questions. In L. H. Meyer, C. A. Peck, & L. Brown (Eds.), *Critical issues in the lives of people with severe disabilities* (pp. 271–312). Baltimore: Paul H. Brookes.

Singer, G. H. S., Irvin, L. K., Irvine, B., Hawkins, N., & Cooley, E. (1989). Evaluation of community-based support services for families of persons with developmental disabilities. *Journal of the Association for Persons with Severe Handicaps, 14,* 312–323.

Stainback, S., & Stainback, W. (1985). The merger of special and regular education: Can it be done? *Exceptional Children, 51,* 517–521.

Sternat, J., Messina, R., Nietupski, J., Lyon, S., & Brown, L. (1977). Occupational and physical therapy services for severely handicapped students: Toward a natural public school service delivery model. In E. Sontag, J. Smith, & N. Certo (Eds.), *Educational programming for the severely and profoundly handicapped* (pp. 263–266). Reston, VA: Council for Exceptional Children, Division on Mental Retardation.

Turnbull, H. R., Guess, D., & Turnbull, A. (1988). *Vox populi* and Baby Doe. *Mental Retardation, 26,* 127–132.

Westling, D. L., & Koorland, M. A. (1988). *The special educator's handbook.* Boston: Allyn & Bacon.

Whitten, T., & Westling, D. L. (1985). Competencies for teachers of the severely and profoundly handicapped: A review. *Teacher Education and Special Education, 8,* 104–111.

PART II

Preparing to Teach: Planning and Assessment Procedures

CHAPTER 4	Planning Instructional Programs for Students with Severe Disabilities
CHAPTER 5	Conducting Assessments to Determine Instructional Needs

CHAPTER 4

Planning Instructional Programs for Students with Severe Disabilities

Chapter Overview

This chapter discusses the need for developing appropriate educational plans for students with severe disabilities. The requirements of the content for Individual Educational Plans, Transition Plans, and Family Service Plans are presented. The chapter concludes with a discussion of some of the inadequacies of the required plans and some alternative planning approaches that will allow more complete plans to be developed.

In order to provide an educational program appropriate for individuals with severe disabilities, the team of professionals described in chapter 3 must work in unison with the students' parents to develop effective educational plans. These plans must take into consideration the characteristics of the individual, including strengths and needs, the environments in which he or she currently functions and will function in the near future, and the types of skills necessary for functioning in these environments.

The teacher and other professionals must each conduct assessment activities in order to fully develop appropriate educational plans. The relationship between planning and assessment for students with severe disabilities is complex. Teachers often complain about the need to develop *individual educational plans* (IEPs, which are discussed later in this chapter) for students before they have had sufficient opportunity to conduct different types of assessment. How can one plan for instruction without being fully cognizant of the student's needs and abilities? On the other hand, it is difficult to conduct an appropriate assessment without first consulting with key individuals, including the student's parents, about information that may be necessary. So, in reality, planning and assessment are not separable events. Professionals plan what they are to assess (or find out about), conduct assessments (or inquire about the student's strengths and needs), and then plan for instruction. During the process of instruction they continue to assess the student's performance and plan for future instruction.

Although planning and assessment are intertwined, we will separate them for the sake of discussion. In this chapter we will discuss the process of planning and the types of plans that must be developed. In the next chapter we will discuss assessment procedures, or the types of information-gathering actions that must be taken to fully develop plans. At the completion of these two chapters, you should have a better understanding of the planning-assessment process.

Types of Plans

In the field of special education, the term *instructional plan* refers primarily to three types of plans: *individual educational plans* (IEPs), *individual transition plans* (ITPs), and *individual family service plans* (IFSPs). All of these plans are required by federal laws and regulations. In addition, there are alternative planning systems that are very suitable for the needs of persons with severe disabilities. These alternatives may be viewed as ways of strengthening required plans rather than supplanting them. As this chapter focuses on planning for individuals, it does not address planning that is required for daily instruction for a group of students, which is covered in chapter 9. Before addressing specific forms of planning, let's first consider the importance of planning for individuals with severe disabilities.

The Importance of Planning

During the years prior to the 1970s, teachers of students with disabilities were not required to plan individually for students as part of their instructional duties. Although accountability was considered an important component of special education (Jones, 1973), it was not until P.L. 94-142 was passed in 1975 that professionals were actually required to write formal instructional plans for students receiving special education services. Smith (1990) has noted that since IEPs were mandated, a general reluctance has developed among many professionals to write them and to use them as functional documents. Instead, many have moved toward processes that allow information about the student to be taken from formal assessment instruments, fed into a computer program, and generated into a document that satisfies the requirements of laws and regulations.

For some students, this process may be satisfactory, especially when the student's problems are primarily in learning academic skills. However, this type of planning is not appropriate for students with more severe disabilities, whose instructional needs are such that they are not readily determined through pencil-paper assessment. It may be hypothesized that the quality of the instruction provided is directly tied to the quality of the planning. The commitment by the persons involved in the planning process and the time this commitment calls for translate directly into how well the student will be taught and how well she or he will learn.

As in virtually all other activities that require planning, planning for the education of students with severe disabilities better ensures consumer satisfaction. Meals are better if they are planned, trips go more smoothly if they are preceded by planning, buildings are built correctly when detailed plans are developed, and so forth. If these activities were carried out without first thinking, reading, and writing about what was going to happen, the product would be less desirable and the consumer less satisfied. Planning helps meet the needs of the students, the parents, and the caregivers served by the educational system.

A written plan also helps keep professionals on a track of quality instruction. Assuming the plan is one of quality, the activities that occur based on it should be of a high caliber, and both the service provider and the consumer (students and parents) should know if what is being delivered is what was planned. In short, appropriate plans make the system and its employees accountable.

Plans also help professionals use time more efficiently. As was discussed in chapter 1, students with severe disabilities require more time than other persons for learning most skills. Therefore, it is critical that the teacher and other professional members of the transdisciplinary team work on skills that are essential to improving the quality of life or allow greater opportunities for participation in different activities. This does not mean that there is only time for teaching the exact and specific skills that appear on planning documents, but teachers as well as other professionals must be aware of the importance of maintaining an instructional focus.

Planning for students with severe disabilities must involve the entire transdisciplinary team. Parents, professionals, paraprofessionals, and the individual with disabilities must come together both mentally and physically to plan for the person's needs. Some forms of planning also encourage siblings, friends, extended family members, and advocates to join in the planning process to discuss what the individual should learn and what actions can be taken to improve his or her quality of life.

When considering the importance of planning, attention must also be given to what individualized planning should not be. A plan for teaching students with severe disabilities should not be seen as a restriction on what should be taught or what activities someone may participate in. If, for example, a trip from New York to California is planned with designated stops at points in between, the traveler would be certain to visit all those points. This doesn't mean, though, that all other areas of interest along the way would be ignored because this might limit learning and probably a lot of fun as well. It is the same when using an instructional plan: it should guide instructional actions but not limit them. This point should be kept in mind as various types of plans are considered.

Individual Educational Plans

Individual educational plans, or IEPs, are the sine qua non of educational programs for students with disabilities. When P.L. 94-142 became law in 1975, the following components were required to be included on an IEP.

- Current level of performance.
- Annual goals and short-term objectives.
- Special education and related services to be provided.
- The extent of participation in the regular classroom.
- Projected date for the initiation of services and the duration of the services.
- Annual evaluation procedures to be used to document the student's progress (Turnbull, Strickland, & Brantley, 1978, p. 35).

In addition, the 1990 Individuals with Disabilities Education Act (P.L. 101-476) required that the following elements be included on the plan:

> *Beginning no later than the age of 16, and as young as 14 when appropriate, a statement of the needed transition services be included annually in the IEP, including a statement of the interagency responsibilities or linkages before the student leaves the school. If an agency fails to provide the agreed upon service, the IEP team must reconvene to identify another source of the service. (Education of the Handicapped, 1991; National Association of State Directors of Special Education, 1990)*

After the initial IEP has been written, the school district must assume the responsibility for arranging a meeting at least once a year to review the IEP and its individual components. This meeting will usually take place on the anniversary date of the original IEP meeting.

Persons attending the IEP meeting must include the student's teacher(s), the parent(s), any individuals who have conducted an evaluation of the student (for example, a school psychologist), a representative of the school district administration, and, in the case of older students, representatives of other agencies participating in providing transition services. In addition to those required by law to attend, it is appropriate for the core members of the transdisciplinary team to be at this meeting. In many cases, it is also appropriate for the student to attend. This will be particularly important when the student grows older and acquires the right and responsibility to make decisions about his or her future. Additionally, parents may invite knowledgeable individuals who are not members of the school system to attend and provide advice or serve as advocates for the student. These persons may be lawyers or experts in special education procedures.

It is apparent that meeting to determine an individual's educational plan is an effort that requires the cooperation and input of many persons. The special education teacher's role in this process is very important. He or she is expected to provide input for all aspects of the IEP but, most importantly, the teacher should be able to offer relevant information about the student's current abilities, suggest appropriate goals and objectives, state an opinion about the need for related services, and discuss ways to integrate the student with severe disabilities into settings with students who do not have disabilities. These and the other components of the IEP are discussed below.

Current Performance Levels

This section of the IEP must specify the student's present level of ability, including strengths and needs. Various assessment activities undertaken by the teacher and other professionals (discussed in the next chapter) with input from the student's parents will help develop critical information about current performance level. Most often, the student's ability level in important life domains (domestic skills, community skills, leisure and recreational skills, and vocational skills), as well as in areas such as communication, social behaviors, and academic abilities, will be stated in this section of the IEP.

Many transdisciplinary team members will provide information about the student's current performance level. The parents may discuss the student's abilities and activities in the home, neighborhood, and community. The teacher will discuss the student's functioning in different areas during the school day. A communication disorders specialist, a physical therapist, and/or an occupational therapist may also provide input about the student's abilities if they have worked with the student over the course of the year or have evaluated the student prior to the IEP meeting. Other professionals who may be on the core team or the support team, such as a vision specialist or an audiologist, may also be present at the meeting to explain the student's abilities within their areas of expertise. A school psychologist may report the student's IQ or developmental level. (While this information may not be relevant for developing an educational program, it may be required in order to establish the student's eligibility and will therefore be reported at the meeting.)

Annual Goals and Short-Term Objectives

The student's annual goals and short-term objectives will be based on current performance level and his or her learning needs in immediate and future environments as perceived by parents and other team members. Each member of the team must consider available assessment data and give thought to factors such as the student's age and any pending changes in the living, schooling, or working environment. The goals and objectives to be developed must be functional and chronological-age appropriate, and they should be written to include learning in major life domains (community, domestic, recreational/leisure, and vocational) and key social, communicative, and academic skills.

The type, complexity, and difficulty level of specific goals and objectives must be individually determined and be geared toward the needs and abilities of each student. Students whose disabilities fall within the moderate range might have as an appropriate goal to learn independent shopping in a grocery store. In comparison, a student with a very severe disability, for example one who is profoundly mentally disabled, may have goals that will increase his or her degree of participation and quality of life. Lehr (1989) proposed that goals for students with the most severe disabilities should be selected from four continuums (see Figure 4–1). Such goals would move the student away from being dependent, not participating, being difficult to care for and unpleasant to be around and toward independence, full participation, and being easy to care for and pleasant.

The distinction between annual goals and short-term objectives is worth noting. Annual goals are usually rather broadly worded statements that describe a desired outcome in a certain learning area. For example, as stated above, a goal may be for a student to learn to shop in a grocery store independently. Another may be for a student to cooperate appropriately when being dressed by extending limbs, leaning forward, and so forth. Stated in this fashion, the goal is clear enough for another to know what the student is to learn. In contrast, writing that the student is going to "learn community skills" or "participate in daily activities" would be too vague; we would not have enough of an idea to know what we want to achieve within a year's time.

Dependence ◄-------► Independence
No participation ◄-------► Full participation
Difficult to care for ◄-------► Easy to care for
Unpleasant ◄-------► Pleasant

Figure 4–1
Curricular Goal Continuums for Students with Profound Mental Handicaps

From *Persons with Profound Disabilities: Issues and Practices* (p. 218) by F. Brown & D. H. Lehr (Eds.), 1989, Baltimore: Paul H. Brookes Publishing Co., P.O. Box 10624, Baltimore, Maryland 21285-0624. Reprinted by permission.

Another way to judge if the annual goal has adequate clarity is if it gives enough information for specific short-term objectives to be written. In contrast to the annual goals, short-term objectives, often referred to as behavioral objectives, must be very specific. Short-term objectives are the building blocks of annual goals; the objectives, when learned, indicate that the goal has been achieved.

A behavioral objective written in sufficient detail states *who* is going to do *what, under what conditions,* and *how often, for how long,* or *how quickly* it should happen. For example, an objective might be written for the goal of improving communicative/social skills at school. The objective may be as follows:

> Bill will greet at least one classmate by looking and smiling at the classmate or demonstrating some other appropriate social behavior within ten seconds after he enters a classroom or another setting in the school in which there are classmates.

In this example, Bill is *who,* looking and smiling at a classmate or demonstrating some other similar behavior is *what,* and when he comes into a classroom with other students is *the condition* under which the behavior should occur. Within ten seconds after coming into the room expresses *how quickly* the behavior should occur.

In addition, there must be a criterion or criteria for judging when the objective has been learned. How often or on how many days must Bill greet classmates before we decide that he has adequately learned this skill? How well does the skill have to be learned before we decide that we do not have to formally instruct Bill to greet others and collect data on his behavior? How many different classmates does he need to greet? In how many different school settings does he need to greet classmates?

Obviously there is no correct answer or absolute standard for determining these criteria or the performance standards for many other behavioral objectives. Instead we may consider how well others without disabilities can perform the action called for in the objective and make modifications in the criteria to the extent that it is necessary to do so. In other words, how often and in how many places do students without disabilities demonstrate this behavior? Based on this type of information, we may find that criteria for achievement may be like the following:

> Bill will greet a classmate at least 4 out of 5 days a week. Or: Bill will greet at least 3 of the 4 students he comes into contact with daily for 2 weeks.

A very important point about writing behavioral objectives is that they should focus more on function than on form. In many situations, how the behavior looks or is accomplished is not as important as whether it achieves the intention of the action. For example, it really would not matter whether Bill looked and smiled, waved his hand, or said "hi." What is most important is that some social greeting occurred and had an effect on the student's environment. In this example, we would expect that the student who was greeted would respond to Bill. If the behavior serves the function for which it is intended and does so by being topographically formed in a reasonable fashion (one that approaches normalcy as much as possible), the behavior called for in the behavioral objective will have been demonstrated.

In addition, behavioral objectives should be written in a way that expresses the need for generalization. Generalization is the demonstration of a learned behavior or skill across different appropriate settings, times, conditions, and/or people. Again in reference to the above example, it would not be sufficient to state that Bill should greet a classmate only when entering a single particular classroom. Although achieving such a behavior in such a limited environment may be an important accomplishment, it is not enough to increase Bill's social acceptability to a level that approaches that of other students his age. Therefore, behavioral objectives should be written that note a need for generalized behaviors and skills.

A common question is "how many goals and objectives should be written on an IEP?" The answer is that there is no specific number. In general, however, it is suggested that at least one goal should be written for each major life domain, including domestic, community, recreational/leisure, and vocational skills (if appropriate). Additional goals should be written for specific ability areas that include social skills, communication skills, and certain academic skills if the collaborative team feels that these are appropriate learning areas.

Special Education, Placement in the Regular Classroom, and Related Services

The IEP must state the special education services the student must receive, the related services that are required to meet the student's needs, and the extent of educational services the student with severe disabilities will receive in the regular classroom. Based on the goals and objectives that have been developed, federal law requires that the student be placed in the least restrictive environment that is appropriate to achieve those goals and objectives. Additionally, the law requires that necessary related services such as physical therapy, occupational therapy, and speech and language therapy be provided to the student.

In designing the most appropriate instructional arrangements for a particular student, the IEP planning team faces an important task. By law, there must be a "continuum" of placements available to support the individual needs of students. Which then is most appropriate? As discussed in chapter 2, many professionals generally accept as "best practice" the placement of students with severe disabilities into regular schools and classrooms, in contrast to placement in special classes or segregated, special schools.

It would be difficult to defend special school placement for any student based on educational needs. In some cases, professionals may find that parents feel that their child will be safer in special school environments and that other professionals support the parents in this choice; in such cases, placement in a special school will occur. However, there is no evidence that special schools are any safer than other schools. It is suggested, therefore, that students with severe disabilities be placed in regular schools for their education. Under ideal circumstances, this school will be the school they would attend if they did not have a disability, which will give them the opportunity to go to school with their brothers and sisters and neighborhood friends (Brown et al., 1989).

Assuming the regular home school is the school placement, the planning team must also address where services should occur within the school. Should the student be placed in a special education class? Should the student be in a regular classroom? How much time should students spend in different instructional settings? (Brown et al., 1989; Brown et al., 1991) Because it is desirable that students should be served in regular classes as much as possible, the questions raised are difficult to answer. Brown et al. (1991) offered some useful guidelines. These are summarized in Figure 4–2. In chapter 9, information is provided for creating inclusive environments in general education classrooms.

The provision of related services must also be addressed in this section of the IEP. As discussed in the previous chapter, there are various professionals besides the special educator who will be responsible for providing services to maximize each student's potential. The most common related services required by students with severe disabilities are speech therapy, physical therapy, and occupational therapy. The evaluation of the student by the professionals in these areas will indicate the type and amount of service that each should provide.

Of course, it will not suffice for each professional to provide his or her service in an isolated manner. On the contrary, an important consideration in the offering of related services is the degree to which they are integrated with each other and with the entire educational program, which is why the transdisciplinary model was proposed in chapter 3. Under this model, for example, it might be agreed by the team that a certain functional objective, such as selecting one's own clothing, is important for a student to achieve. Particular team members would then assist in designing instructional strategies that would allow the student to acquire such a skill given his or her sensory, motor, or cognitive abilities. As Campbell (1987) stated: "Methodologies from each discipline are integrated into one instructional program to minimize the impact of limitations in vision, hearing, movement, and cognition, on a student's performance of cognitive skills" (p. 109).

Projected Date for the Initiation of Services and the Duration of the Services

Services for students with severe disabilities will most often be initiated by the time the child is 3 years old, if not before, then will continue on an annual basis in the form called for by the IEP. One of the important features of the law's requirement for an annual review

1. *Chronological Age*. Placement in regular classrooms for individually determined amounts of time is generally more appropriate for children in elementary schools. As students get older, learning in nonschool settings becomes more important.
2. *Related Services*. There are many instances when therapeutic services can be delivered in the regular classroom. In other instances there may be time when the student and therapist work in private.
3. *Number of Environments in Which a Student Functions*. Students with severe disabilities must learn to function in a number of environments besides the regular class. If experience in these environments is not provided through the educational program, they may not occur.
4. *Personnel Qualities*. Many regular education classroom teachers are very competent and will operate classrooms in which the student with severe disabilities can learn important skills. Other teachers will have less competence. Time spent with competent persons should be maximized; time with incompetent persons, regardless of the setting, should be minimized.
5. *Effects on Social Relationships*. The regular classroom offers a rich environment for the development of social relationships. Students should not be removed from this environment without protecting the social relationships that exist.
6. *Parent/Guardian/Student Priorities*. Parents, guardians, or students who place a high priority on developing social relations with nondisabled peers should spend more time in regular classroom settings.
7. *Probability of Acquisition*. If there is a low probability that the student with severe disabilities will acquire certain knowledge and skills being taught because of their complexity, abstractness, or difficulty, then it is acceptable for the student to be in another setting for more appropriate activities.
8. *Functionality*. Many functional skills cannot be incorporated into the regular classroom program. Many important functional skills must be taught in home, community, and work environments.
9. *Preparation for Post-School Life*. As the student approaches graduation, skills that are important for adulthood must be given greatest priority. Many skills taught in regular high school classes will not be as useful for students with severe disabilities as those taught elsewhere.

Figure 4–2
Guidelines for Placing Students in Regular Classrooms
Adapted from "How Much Time Should Students with Severe Intellectual Disabilities Spend in Regular Education Classrooms and Elsewhere?" by L. Brown, P. Schwarz, A. Udvari-Solner, E. F. Kampschroer, F. Johnson, J. Jorgensen, & L. Gruenewald, 1991, *Journal of the Association for Persons with Severe Handicaps, 16*, pp. 39-47.

and rewriting of the IEP is that it provides an opportunity for the IEP team to reconsider the student's placement. As explained above, because placement considerations vary with age and educational needs, this factor should be considered on a regular basis.

The fact that the IEP must be reviewed and renewed at least once a year should not be interpreted to mean that changes cannot be made at other times. Whenever there is reason to believe that placement in a less restrictive environment is possible or that other objectives would be more appropriate, changes can be made. The specification of an annual review simply states that IEPs cannot be developed for more than a year at a time.

Annual Evaluation Procedures

The IEP must state how the student's performance will be evaluated on an annual basis.

Although students with mild disabilities often have their performance evaluated by means of standardized tests, such tests do not appropriately evaluate the performance of students with severe disabilities. Instead, the IEP should state that the student's performance will be evaluated based on the degree of completion of individual goals and objectives. The various data collection systems discussed in chapter 8 will be helpful in documenting the student's progress.

In addition to performance on specific objectives, related services professionals may evaluate the student on speech, language, and communication development; gross motor development; fine motor development; and so forth. Progress may be reported using developmental assessment instruments specific to these areas. A sample IEP is presented in Appendix A.

Individual Transition Plans

As stated earlier, when students with severe disabilities reach mid adolescence, the *Individuals with Disabilities Education Act* (P.L. 101-476) requires that the IEP contain a statement of the transition services to be provided. The transition initiative actually dates back several years before *IDEA,* when it was proposed that more emphasis be placed on assisting students with disabilities to make a successful transition from school to adult life because most such students were not employed upon leaving school (Will, 1984). Additional problems have been associated with the gradual entry into adulthood by persons with severe disabilities (Halpern, 1985; McDonnell & Hardman, 1985). For example, after public school services have reached a conclusion, there are often difficulties identifying and accessing community services, including those that would enhance participation in the community. When services are available, long waiting lists exist that cause delays in service delivery. It is unfortunate that when services are available, they may be ineffective in assisting the person to lead a life in the least restrictive environment. Instead, the person may have to wait for a service that places him or her in sheltered environments isolated from people without disabilities. As a result, the person with a severe disability does not have the opportunity to lead a typical life and the parents often experience undue financial and emotional stress.

To better prepare for postschool life, transition planning needs to begin when the student is no older than 16 years of age and perhaps as young as 14 years. The Individual Transition Plan (ITP), written as a part of the IEP when the student is in high school, must accomplish two major goals. It must identify the skills that the student must learn before leaving school to allow him or her to function most effectively as an adult, and it must simultaneously identify the postschool services that must be available to the individual with severe disabilities (McDonnell & Hardman, 1985). The latter should include a plan for meaningful employment, an appropriate place to live, and the opportunity to continue developing personal and social skills and a network of friends and acquaintances (Wehman, 1990).

Clearly the development and implementation of a successful ITP must involve all members of the transdisciplinary team and different agencies. The process is similar to developing an IEP except that there is need for participation by personnel and service agencies outside of the public school system. Besides the usual members of the team, therefore, the ITP team should include a vocational education teacher, a vocational rehabilitation counselor, a local representative of the appropriate state human services agency (such as the Department of Mental Health, Developmental Disabilities, or Mental Retardation) who will assume case management responsibilities, and representatives of private organizations such as the Association for Retarded Citizens (ARC) that may serve as vendors for supported employment or residential programs. It would also be appropriate for a representative of the disability community to assist by providing insight and keeping the group focused on developing outcome-oriented goals for the individual who will be experiencing the transition into adulthood (Everson & Moon, 1987).

Functioning as a team, this group must design an ITP, then individuals on the team must assume specific roles that will allow the plan to be implemented. Steps in this process have been outlined by several authors (McDonnell & Hardman, 1985; McDonnell, Wilcox, & Hardman, 1991; Wehman, 1990; Wehman, Wood, Everson, Marchant, & Walker, 1987). They are summarized in Figure 4–3.

Essential services that must be included on the ITP and ultimately provided during the adult years include employment, a living arrangement, leisure activities, supplemental income and medical support, transportation, and long-term support and care (McDonnell et al., 1991). It is especially important that various services and activities do not infringe upon the

1. Identify students needing an ITP.
2. Identify personnel who will serve on the ITP.
3. Identify adult service agencies that will be required to provide services and make certain that each is represented on the ITP.
4. Identify the skills needed to be learned by students prior to leaving school and how these skills will provide important benefits to the individual (such as socializing with friends, living and working in the least restrictive environment, and continuing to develop personal skills). Gather this information from parents, teachers, and therapists.
5. Schedule transition planning meetings at times when key persons can attend. These meetings should be a part of the IEP planning meeting.
6. At the meeting, discuss with the student his or her plans and desires for post-school life; ask parents about their views toward their adolescent child's future; ask agency representatives to discuss services they can provide and possible options; ask teachers and therapists to discuss specific skills that they will assist the student in developing to maximize participation as an adult.
7. Based on the above, write the formal ITP including (a) the services to be provided by specific agencies before and after the student leaves school; (b) the skills to be learned; (c) the individuals responsible for carrying out specific tasks; (d) the timeline for completing different steps in the task; (e) a system for monitoring achievement of the different tasks.
8. Subsequent to writing the initial ITP, plan follow-up meetings on an annual basis to report the achievement of tasks by different agency representatives of the ITP team. Make changes in assignments if tasks have not been satisfactorily completed.
9. Schedule an exit meeting and interview with parents and the student within six months of the time the student will leave the school system. At this meeting, reconfirm the roles to be played by adult service agencies and organizations in the community after the individual with severe disabilities leaves the school and enters adult life.

Figure 4–3
Steps in the Individualized Transition Planning Process

benefits of other services. For example, the committee should investigate and report to the parents if the level of income to be earned by their offspring will threaten supplemental security income (SSI) and associated medical benefits (McDonnell & Hardman, 1985). The committee should also provide parents with information about trusts and wills and the long-term care of their adult child after their death.

After the ITP has been developed, schools should implement as much of it as possible while the student is in school. Training should be provided on specific vocational skills in actual vocational settings. Leisure activities should be taught and practiced. Functional domestic and community skills should be taught in the most appropriate real settings, including those outside of the school. The exercising of transportation skills in the community will be very important. Contacts should be made with various agencies and necessary entry forms should be submitted to them at the earliest date. If possible, adult services from agencies such as vocational rehabilitation should begin while the student is still in school. Any problems associated with implementing any aspect of the ITP should be noted and corrected. The purpose is for the student and the agencies to be fully ready for success when it is time for the student to leave the school and enter the adult world.

The development of ITPs, now required by federal legislation, should do a great deal to facilitate successful adult lives for persons with severe disabilities. However, how these plans are developed and implemented may vary widely and some plans will assuredly not be as successful as others. In order to better ensure success in the transition process, Wehman (1990) suggested the following:

- Plan in the context of the local community. Understand the resources available and plan with them in mind.
- Strive for meaningful input from students and their parents. Let them know what their options are, what they could be, and how they can achieve what they want.
- Have clear agreements between agencies so that the resources of all are being shared fairly and directed toward specific outcomes.
- Place vocational rehabilitation counselors in the school settings to facilitate communication and cooperation.
- Develop good relationships with local businesses. They can provide input into what students need to learn, provide job sites, and support programs for individuals with disabilities.
- Use families, relatives, and friends of students with disabilities as sources of employment or for help in finding employment. Many follow-up studies have found that these persons play very important roles in helping secure employment. A sample Transition Plan is presented in Appendix B.

Individual Family Service Plans

Individual Family Service Plans (IFSPs) were first required under P.L. 99-457, Part H, as a significant element of the Handicapped Infants and Toddlers Program. As discussed in chapter 2, this law gives states discretionary authority to serve children with disabilities between birth and 2 years of age. If states implement this plan, they must develop an IFSP for the family of each child served. After the child reaches 3 years of age and is served in a preschool program, the legal requirement for an IFSP is dropped and it is replaced with an IEP.

The IFSP recognizes the importance of the family in providing services to infants and toddlers and specifies that it is the family (including the young child with the disability) that will be the service recipient as opposed to the child alone. It also recognizes that family representation is an essential element of the decision-making team (Krauss, 1990). When planning early intervention services for babies and young children with severe disabilities, it is particularly critical for family members to be considered part of the planning team as well as the potential recipients of services. The IFSP must include the eight components listed in Figure 4–4.

As can be seen by the components of the IFSP, there is much similarity between what must be included in this plan and what must be included in an IEP. Brown (1991) noted that there are four requirements for the IFSP that are not included on an IEP: (1) the provision for a service coordinator; (2) the need to consider family resources, priorities, concerns, strengths, and weaknesses as related to the child's development; (3) the inclusion of other nonearly intervention services; and (4) planning for transition into preschool programs. Notwithstanding these differences, it is important to consider how a system might move from serving the child with severe disabilities and his or her family via an IFSP when the child is younger than 3 years of age to focusing more directly on the child when the third birthday is reached. If it is assumed that the family focus is important for the development of the infant and toddler, how might services be best planned when this requirement ceases to exist, that is, when the child reaches 3 years?

This issue has been a concern for many professionals and has led some to ask whether or not the IFSP can legally serve as the IEP for the preschooler. In other words, instead of developing an IEP only when the child turns 3, continue planning under the guidelines for the IFSP. In fact, this is allowed if two conditions are met. First, the IFSP for the preschooler must contain all of the requirements normally included on the IEP. Second, all of the necessary individuals need to participate in the development (Schrag, 1990, as cited in Brown, 1991). The benefit of such an arrangement is that it will allow service providers to offer a "seamless" planning and delivery system that is focused on families and is in effect until the child reaches the typical age for beginning school.

It is a credit to those responsible for passing P.L. 99-457 that focus was directed toward the family unit instead of isolating the child for service. Children grow up in families, and parents almost always know more about their

1. A statement of the child's present level of development.
2. A statement of the family's resources, priorities, and concerns related to enhancing the child's development, and the criteria, procedures, and timelines for determining progress.
3. A statement of the major outcomes expected to be achieved for the child and the family.
4. The specific early intervention services necessary to meet the needs of the child and the family.
5. A statement of natural environments where the services will be provided.
6. When the services will start and how long they will last.
7. The name of the service coordinator.
8. The procedures for transition from the early intervention program to the preschool program.

Figure 4–4
Components of the Individual Family Service Plan
From *Early Intervention in Natural Environments: Methods and Procedures* by M. J. Noonan & L. McCormick, 1993, Pacific Grove, CA: Brooks/Cole.

child than do the various professionals who might serve the child. Yet, although there is clearly merit to the concept of an IFSP, there is also concern about how the requirement might be viewed and implemented by some (Beckman & Bristol, 1991; Krauss, 1990).

The IFSP requirement for assessment and possible intervention within the family is significant because it raises the question of how we determine a family's resources, priorities, and concerns. To what extent should professionals evaluate a family because one of its members has a disability? Further, what types of intervention are appropriate for a family and when and how should they be provided? Beckman and Bristol (1991) discussed the need for sensitivity in four areas when professionals develop IFSPs: cultural diversity, family assessment, intrusiveness, and establishing family outcomes.

Many infants with disabilities are born to families outside of the majority population, yet most of the professionals who respond to their needs under the requirements of P.L. 99-457 are of the majority culture. The challenge for professionals is that they must understand that practices that are different from theirs due to cultural diversity are not bad, only different. The service provider must acquire a sensitivity that will allow him or her to work effectively with a minority family without judging the family by his or her own cultural standards. This can best be done if the professional develops a self-awareness of his or her own cultural values and a realization of how they may influence judgments about the strengths and needs of a family.

When early interventionists collaborate with families to identify their priorities and concerns, regardless of the family's cultural values, they must avoid treating the family as if it has a disability. Some professionals have suggested that formal family assessments should be bypassed in favor of having informal discussions with family members to determine if there are specific needs that can be met to support the family in its efforts to support the child (Slentz & Bricker, 1992; Winton & Bailey, 1988, 1990). This approach is intended to reduce a perception that the family must be treated. As Krauss (1990) noted: "Families may chafe at the realization that because their child has Down syndrome or was born with a low birthweight, they, too, must be evaluated if their child is to receive services" (p. 390).

Finally, professionals need to be careful with regard to the types of family outcomes they specify on the IFSP. In some instances, there are more goals that are to be carried out by family members than by the professionals. It must be recognized that families vary a great deal in terms of extraordinary efforts parents can take because their child has a severe disability. More appropriate than stating several responsibilities that parents or families must achieve may be stating as goals on the IFSP what parents may expect from professionals (Beckman & Bristol, 1991). Most important will be the concentration on the *individuality* of the Individual Family Service Plan. A sample Family Service Plan is presented in Appendix C.

Alternative Approaches to Planning

Federal laws requiring IEPs, ITPs, and IFSPs should be recognized for what they are intended to accomplish. Instead of treating an individual based on a disability classification, these plans direct professionals to examine individual needs and develop intervention goals and objectives accordingly. As was noted earlier, however, some professionals have viewed these plans as laborious and bureaucratic. Instead of viewing them as opportunities for thinking carefully about what would be of benefit to specific students, they have sought ways to reduce the time they must invest in them (Smith, 1990).

Why is this so? There may be several reasons. One is simply that teachers would rather spend their time with students than with paper, and this is understandable. Most professional educators enjoy working with children or adolescents, and many have specifically entered this field because they dislike meetings and paperwork. Additionally, teachers may not see the need for plans. As discussed earlier, it seems difficult to make progress without knowing where you are heading, but many teachers may feel they know their students well enough and do not need to put on paper the goals and objectives for each individual student. Finally, it could be hypothesized that writing IEPs is not an activity that has been highly valued by many school systems. A federal law requiring such plans does not necessarily result in school districts liking them. What may be more true is that schools consider the task necessary to be in compliance with federal law. This will bear on the teachers' attitudes toward writing IEPs.

If planning is truly to be of value, there must be a greater commitment to it, not only by teachers but also by other professionals, parents, and administrators. To arrive at this commitment, it is necessary to ask some critical questions about the planning process and to consider ways in which it could be improved. Some important questions and proposed answers are presented below.

Who owns the plan? Does it belong to the school system or other service agency (or agencies)? The parents? The person with the severe disability?

It can be argued that the parents, the family, and the student with severe disabilities are the rightful owners of the individual plan that is developed. It is theirs because their lives are the ones it is intended to affect. The service agency should be viewed as assisting families to the degree necessary to write the plan, but the plan should be seen as belonging to the individual and the family.

Ownership is an important factor, and it should be understood by all who participate in the process. If families of individuals with severe disabilities and the individuals themselves accept that it is their plan, they will be more likely to address its development with deliberation. Further, if professionals understand that the plan is owned by the service consumer, they may give it more respect and appreciate their own role in assisting in its development.

What is an appropriate time frame for planning? One year? Three years? The school years? A lifetime?

Currently IEPs must be written for one year at a time. This is certainly better than week-to-week planning, but it should be realized that the one-year requirement is somewhat arbitrary. It is simply tied into the traditional school year calendar. It may be more beneficial to parents and their children to project for a longer period of time, to think further into the future. This is clearly the intention of the ITP, yet this longer-term planning does not begin until the student is into his or her adolescent years.

Many parents of children with severe disabilities approach life one day at a time because they feel that is about all they can emotionally cope with (Brotherson et al., 1988; Featherstone, 1980). Certainly each family must approach life in a way that it can best manage. However, many parents would like to know what the future holds and how they and their child with a severe disability can be best prepared for it. Although no one can say precisely what time frame should be used in planning, it is suggested that in many cases it should be beyond one year.

Who should be involved in the planning? Who knows the most about the child and has the "natural" responsibility for him or her?

The laws already state who is required to be a part of the planning team. But there may be other significant persons in the life of the child with disabilities who should also be included. Siblings, grandparents, neighbors, friends, ministers, and others who have a personal relationship with the individual and who care about what happens in his or her life could make an important contribution to developing individual plans.

What should affect the content of the plan? Existing programs and services, or those that are possible? Agency philosophy, or family, culture, and personal values?

Particular goals and objectives and, more broadly, the student's lifestyle can be affected by the circumstances surrounding the learning process. For example, many might agree that a particular student needs to learn age-appropriate recreational activities. In one situation, however, the student may be bound to learn activities in the context of a special school with only other students with disabilities. In another school district, the student may have the opportunity to learn the skills with nondisabled peers in community recreational facilities.

The plan that is developed, the one owned by the individual with severe disabilities and his or her family, should not be encumbered by current limitations in agencies' programs, practices, or philosophy. Certainly it may take time for service providers to make changes, but even so, this should not inhibit persons from making plans that suit their needs and desires for a quality life. This would be contrary to some of society's most cherished principles, particularly those that deal with the rights of persons to pursue happiness and lead productive lives. Instead, it is proposed that the plans developed should influence what is available to the individual with disabilities instead of vice-versa.

Given these views, it is important that alternative approaches to planning be considered. These are viewed as "alternatives" not because they are intended to replace current planning requirements, but because they can add significantly to the quality of planning. Three planning processes are discussed in the remainder of this chapter. Due to the limitations of space, if you are interested in implementing these alternative planning practices you will need to refer to the original publications of the material cited.

Personal Futures Planning

Personal futures planning (Mount & Zwernik, 1988) is a radical departure from traditional approaches. It was developed based on the work of O'Brien and Lyle (1987) and is intended to provide a positive approach for planning life activities for persons of various ages who have disabilities. Its primary goal is to help groups of people who are personally close to the person with disabilities plan ways in which that individual can "develop personal relationships, have positive roles in community life, increase their control of their own lives, and develop the skills and abilities to achieve these goals" (Mount & Zwernik, 1988, p. 1). The plan is intended to be dynamic, changing as changes occur in the individual's lifestyle. A critical aspect of personal futures planning is that it does not focus on a person's deficits (what he or she cannot do), but rather on the individual's gifts, talents, skills, and opportunities. The plan is also "person-centered" in that it continually focuses on the individual (referred to as the focus person) for whom the future plan is being developed. In this way, the plan is not limited by current services, but by what would be necessary to allow the individual to participate fully in society.

The personal futures planning system recognizes that there are three basic problems associated with traditional planning: It begins with an assessment that highlights the person's deficits; it establishes goals that are part of the existing service system; and it relies primarily on professional judgment and decision making. In contrast, the futures planning system offers an "interactive" style that involves people who are closest to the focus person and emphasizes the planning process more than the product. It has five important characteristics:

1. It describes capacities and opportunities in people and environments.
2. It seeks ideals.
3. It involves people who interact on a daily basis with the person with a severe disability.
4. It encourages experimentation with new courses of action.
5. It prompts people to act, to accept commitments to be involved in improving the quality of life for the person with the disability (Mount & Zwernik, 1988, p. 7).

The three steps that comprise the personal futures planning process are developing a personal profile of the focus individual; developing a plan for the person; and forming a network of support with the people in it making a commitment to support the individual in various ways to ensure the success of the plan. Each of these components is explained briefly below.

The Personal Profile In the first step of the process, the person with the disability and a few people who know and care about him or her come together for an interactive interview conducted by a facilitator. The facilitator is the person who will direct the group to address the key issues contained in the personal profile.

At this meeting, the group is directed to discuss key information about the individual and his or her capacities, upon which a plan can be built. First, basic information is gathered. This is not about results of formal assessments, but about the person's background, positive and negative experiences, major moves, critical events, the current situation, family issues, general health concerns, and relationships in the community. Second, information is gathered about the focus person's quality of life, including accomplishments, routines, and lifestyle patterns. Considered in this part of the personal profile are such areas as community participation and relationships with others, choices and rights, respect for the person by others, and skills the person has that allow others to view him or her in a positive manner.

In developing the final section of the personal profile, the third type of information is gathered, a list of what the individual enjoys and prefers and what is not enjoyable to him or her. The main questions to be addressed here are: What images does this person have for the future? What unrecognized dreams and hopes does this person have? What does this person want in life?

During the discussion, the facilitator uses colored pens to sketch the personal profile of the individual on large pieces of paper. Vivid symbols and words make the profile come alive. This description will then be used as a basis for the futures planning. Figure 4–5 provides an example of a portion of a personal profile showing an individual's background and history. Similar sketches are developed showing relationships, places visited, choices, preferences, and so forth.

The Personal Future Plan Following the meeting to develop the personal profile, another meeting is arranged to write the future plan for the individual. In addition to those who were present for sketching the personal profile, key people in the focus person's life should be in attendance. These should include family,

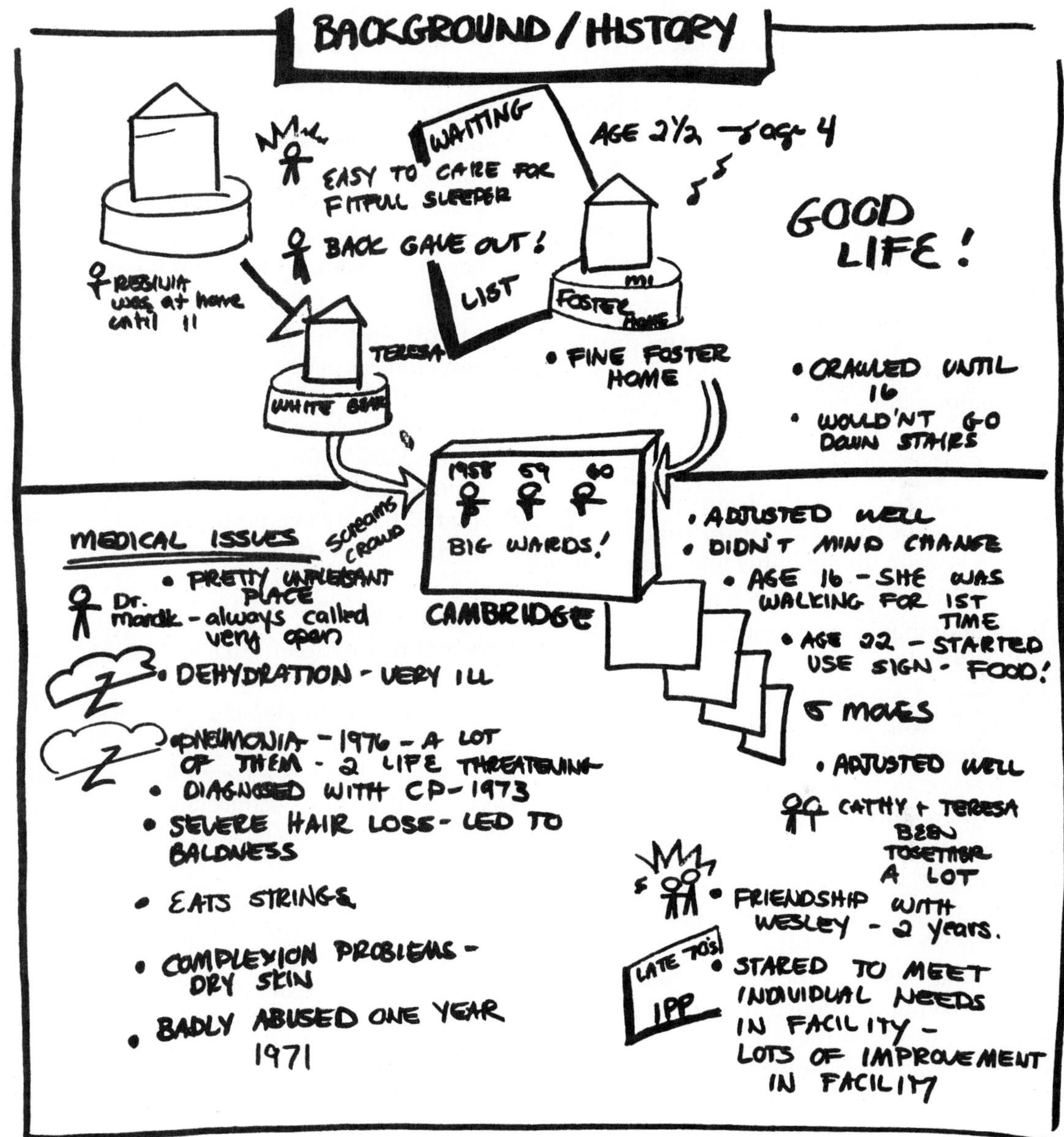

Figure 4–5
Individual Background and History Chart to Be Used in Futures Planning

From *It's Never Too Early, It's Never Too Late.* A Booklet About Personal Futures Planning (p. 10) by B. Mount and K. Zwernik, 1988, St. Paul, MN: Metropolitan Council. Used with permission.

friends, professionals, and others with whom the target person spends a great deal of time. Once again, the facilitator directs the meeting. If the person with the disability can communicate, he or she should be at the meeting as well. Mount and Zwernik also recommend that an advocate for the individual be present.

The process for developing the future plan consists of seven steps:

1. Reviewing the personal profile. The first step is for the group to look at the profile that has been developed and add other relevant information that has not been considered.
2. Reviewing trends in the environment. This consists of thinking about anything that may occur in the near future that might have a bearing on the individual (for example, graduation from high school).
3. Finding desirable images of the future. This is the key element of the plan; persons at the meeting present their ideas about the future. During this brainstorming session, participants are asked to imagine ways for the person to have more positive experiences than were identified in the personal profile. Ideas are clustered by the facilitator into major areas such as home, work, school, community activities, relationships, and so forth.
4. Identifying obstacles and opportunities. The clusters mentioned above are ranked by the group in terms of their importance, then obstacles and opportunities are identified beginning with the first area and continuing to each subsequent area. The group discusses ways to overcome obstacles, turning them into opportunities.
5. Identifying strategies. These strategies are the concrete "action steps" to be taken to implement the visions created in step 3. At this step, each member of the planning group must make a commitment to assist with particular efforts.
6. Getting started. Mount and Zwernik recommend that five specific strategies that can be implemented right away be identified. It is important to accomplish some parts of the plan immediately, even though they may be only small steps. Once these activities have been identified, a time for the next meeting should be agreed upon.
7. Identifying the need for system change. Sometimes existing systems (public schools, agencies) do not include structures or conditions that are supportive of the person's future plan. In this case, a commitment must be made to change the system or work around the existing obstacle. Regardless, it is important that system barriers be recognized.

Building a Network The final component of personal futures planning is building a network of support persons who will meet regularly to plan and implement strategies and tactics to improve the quality of life of the focus person. This group is referred to as a "circle of support." It includes family members, friends, neighbors, and others who are close to the person with disabilities.

Mount and Zwernik outlined several elements that they felt resulted in a strong support network. These included focusing on the individual and his or her dreams instead of directing the person toward something the support network wants; starting small and avoiding taking on too much at one time; and including at least one person in the support group who has good ties to the community and can serve as a bridge for the focus person to move outward toward more community involvement.

The circle of support is an essential element for making the future plan work for the individual with disabilities. As long as there is personal support, changes will occur, even though they may be gradual.

The McGill Action Planning System (MAPS)

The MAPS planning system (Forest & Lusthaus, 1987; Vandercook, York, & Forest, 1989) is another comprehensive planning process that clearly goes beyond what is required by law for individual plans. In many ways it is similar to the personal futures planning system. The primary difference is that the personal futures system may be more appropriate for adults, whereas the MAPS focuses specifically on developing IEPs for school-age individuals.

The MAPS targets full inclusion and participation in the regular classroom and other mainstream educational settings. Its primary purpose is to foster relationships for improving the quality of life of the individual with severe disabilities as well as his or her social skills and cognitive development. It calls for the involvement of a team that includes the individual with disabilities, family members, friends without disabilities, and general and special education personnel. During the planning sessions all gather in one setting to discuss the educational and life needs of the individual with severe disabilities. An important feature of the MAPS is the inclusion of the targeted individual's chronological-age peers on the planning team. Because of this, the MAPS process may not usually be undertaken unless there has been an opportunity for the student with disabilities to have had integrated experiences long enough to begin developing relationships.

As with the previously described system, a facilitator coordinates the planning session(s) by asking questions, encouraging open discussion, and writing down the key thoughts of those participating. According to Vandercook et al. (1989), this person must be "committed to building an integrated school community in which the individual is valued and provided the support necessary to be a member of the class with same age peers" (p. 207). The facilitator should be a good listener and one who can encourage interaction among those participating in the process. He or she is responsible for prodding group members to broaden their view of the community and also getting them to offer creative ideas that will allow the individual with disabilities to be a successful participant in integrated settings. Most important, the facilitator must be able to convince all of those involved in the MAPS process that their contribution is critical.

Although the process is flexible, seven questions serve to guide the discussion. These questions, presented one at a time by the facilitator, are as follows:

- What is the individual's history?
- What is your dream for the individual?
- What is your nightmare?
- Who is the individual?
- What are the individual's strengths, gifts, and abilities?
- What are the individual's needs?
- What would the individual's ideal day at school look like and what must be done to make it happen?

After each question is asked, those present are asked to respond and their responses are recorded by the facilitator. There are no rules as to what types of responses should occur. In fact, participants are encouraged to be creative, especially in discussing the individual's potential and future and ways to foster inclusion.

The MAPS procedures usually require about 3 hours and sometimes more than one session is needed. This can be contrasted with more typical IEP sessions that may be over in less than 30 minutes. However, as can be easily understood, the depth of the planning using MAPS is much greater. Table 4–1 demonstrates the priority needs of a student as identified by family, friends, and educators using MAPS. Table 4–2 displays a modified schedule for the student as she "moves toward an ideal school day."

Choosing Options and Accommodations for Children (COACH)

COACH is a system developed for assessment and planning that begins with the identification of "valued life outcomes" by family members and the student with disabilities, converts these desired outcomes into IEP goals and objectives, and then devises educational supports that will allow the student to achieve these objectives in inclusive educational environments (Giangreco, Cloninger, & Iverson, 1993). The COACH system is based on six assumptions:

1. Pursuing valued life outcomes is an important aspect of education.
2. The family is the cornerstone of relevant and longitudinal planning.
3. Collaborative teamwork is essential to quality education.
4. Coordinated planning is dependent on shared, discipline-free goals.

Table 4–1
Catherine's Priority Needs Identified by Family, Friends, and Educators

Family	Friends	Educators
For others to know she is not helpless	More friends	More friends
Music and time to listen to it	Support to get more places and learn things there	Support to get more places and learn things there
Affection	A lot of opportunity to walk and use her hands	A lot of opportunity to walk and use her hands
To be with people	As an adult, to live in a small home with friends in a community where she is accepted	Opportunity to let people know what she wants and a way to communicate that with more people
To change environments and surroundings often	Teachers to accept her	To increase the opportunity and skill to make more choices
Healthy foods	To learn to hang onto the book when a friend is reading with her	Affection
		People to know how to: deal with her seizures, help her stand up, and accept and deal with her drooling

From "The McGill Action Planning System (MAPS): A Strategy for Building the Vision" by T. Vandercook, J. York, & M. Forest, 1989, *Journal of the Association for Persons with Severe Handicaps, 14*(3), 205–215.

5. Using problem-solving methods improves the effectiveness of the educational plan.
6. Special education is a service, not a place.

COACH allows for the development of goals that are considered to be "cross-environmental" (communication, socialization, personal management, leisure/recreation, and applied academics), and those that are "environmental-specific" (for participating in activities in home, school, community, and vocational settings). The COACH system provides for planning three major components: IEP Goals, Breadth of Curriculum, and General Support (see Figure

Table 4–2
Tuesday Morning Schedule for Catherine: Moving Toward the Ideal School Day

Time	Catherine's Day (current)	3rd Grade Day (current)	Possibilities for Change (proposed)
9:00-9:30	Take off coat Use restroom Adaptive P.E.	Pledge of Allegiance Seat work directions Spelling	Breakfast (could eat with nondisabled peers if school arrival coincided)
9:30-10:00	Breakfast Work on lip closure, holding the spoon, choosing objects she wants	Reading Group I Others do seat work, write stories, read silently	Switch center (in 3rd grade reading) Transition to center, reaching, touching picture, activating tape player
10:00-10:45	Switch center Transition to center, reaching, touching picture, activating tape player using microswitch (leisure activity)	Physical education (10:00-10:20) Mousercize, Exercise Express, Use restroom Reading Group II (10:25-10:45)	Physical education (with 3rd grade) Skills related to maintaining ambulation and mobility (weight shifting, balance reactions, strength exercise) Cooperation with peer partner Rest time
10:45-11:10	Reading Group III (with 3rd grade) Makes transition to floor, responds to greeting from peer, reaches for peer's hand, holds onto book, looks at book, closes book, makes transition to standing	Reading Group III	Maintain current activity with 3rd grade
11:10-11:30	Library (with 3rd grade) Return book, choose book, look at it, check it out, return to class	Library	Maintain current activity with 3rd grade

From "The McGill Action Planning System (MAPS): A Strategy for Building the Vision" by T. Vandercook, J. York, & M. Forest, 1989, *Journal of the Association for Persons with Severe Handicaps, 14*(3), 205–215. Copyright 1989 by The Association for Persons with Severe Handicaps. Reprinted by permission.

4–6). The IEP Goals are identified by family members and the student with the disability, when appropriate, using the Family Prioritization Interview and are a limited number of the highest priority goals for the student. One member of the planning team works with the family to identify these priorities during an interview that lasts from one to one and a half hours.

The Breadth of Curriculum adds additional learning outcomes to the high priority outcomes identified by family members. These could include cross-environmental or environmental-specific goals, or they could include appropriate goals from the general education curriculum. Although goals from the Breadth of Curriculum sphere would be important, they would not be considered as important as IEP goals and would not have to be monitored as closely.

General Supports are planned to allow the student to participate as much as possible in the regular classroom setting. Within the COACH program, Giangreco et al. (1993) characterize the general supports in an important way. Whereas the IEP goals and the Breadth of Curriculum goals represent desired changes in the student's ability or behavior, the general supports section of the plan states the type of behavior or behavior change that those in the student's environments must demonstrate in order for the student to be successful. Five areas of support are included with the general support section:

1. Personal needs: feeding, dressing, giving medication, helping with personal hygiene needs, and so forth.
2. Physical needs: positioning and handling the student, helping the student move from place to place, managing special equipment such as braces or wheelchairs.
3. Sensory needs: accommodations that are necessary if the student has visual or hearing impairments, such as adjusting distance, location, lighting, and so forth.
4. Teaching others about the student, including other faculty, staff, and students.
5. Providing access and opportunities to a variety of integrated locations inside and outside of the school.

Using COACH to plan for a student's needs begins with the family interview, in which the parents are encouraged to think about "valued life outcomes" and provide a list of "family-centered priorities." These are then considered by the entire planning team and restated as IEP goals. The team also considers other needs and develops the Breadth of Curriculum and the general supports the student will need for access to a general education. After developing all of the components of the plan, the team identifies the most inclusive educational setting in which the student can be served, with the first preference being the regular classroom. The team also decides what types of related services will be necessary and how these should be delivered. Subteams may be used to develop short-term objectives, support plans, and lesson adaptations.

Like the other alternative planning approaches, COACH is family- and student-centered. The authors warn that the process should not be undertaken unless the team is "willing to accept and use the priorities of the family" (Giangreco et al., 1993, p. 24). They also suggest that during the interview the COACH system limits participants to family members and the individual with disabilities. The authors propose that the presence of too many people at the Family Prioritization Interview can interfere with the participation of the parents. The team member who conducts the interview reports the priorities to other team members.

COACH is a well-designed package for assessing students' needs and planning a comprehensive educational program. Professionals are guided through a process that begins with parent input and ends in a well-developed educational program to be carried out in inclu-

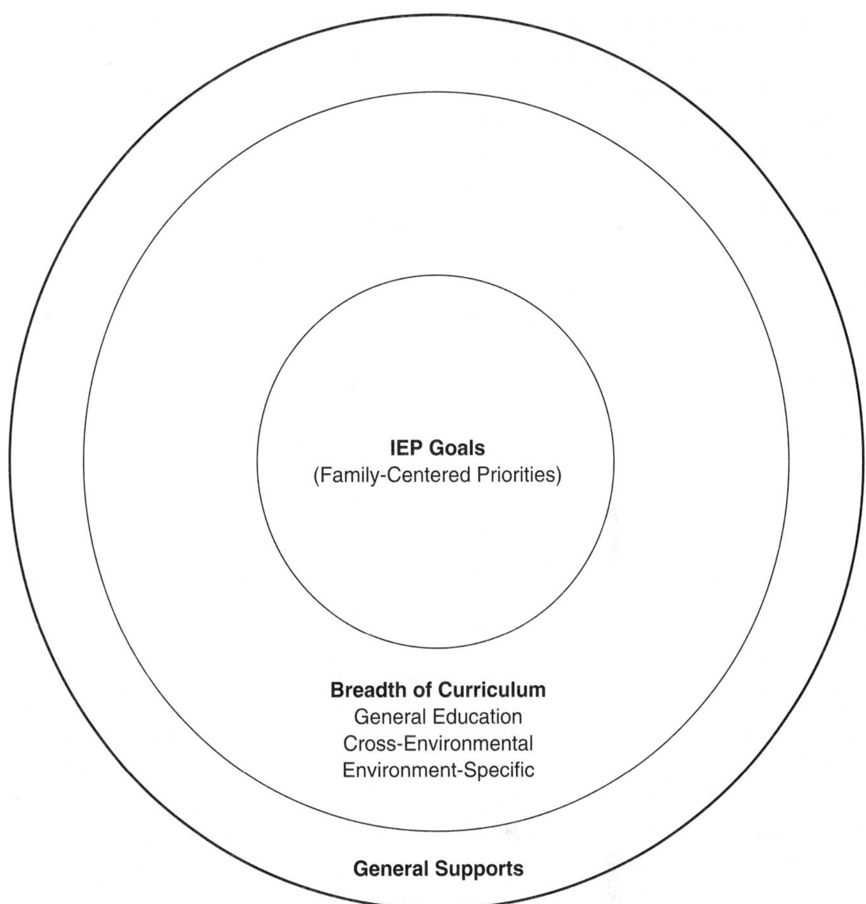

Figure 4–6
Educational Program Components of COACH
From *Choosing Options and Accommodations for Children: A Guide to Planning Inclusive Education* (p. 17) by M. F. Giangreco, C. J. Cloninger, & V. S. Iverson, 1993, Baltimore: Paul H. Brookes. Reprinted by permission of the author.

sive environments. It would be most helpful for developing Individual Educational Plans and Individual Transition Plans.

Conclusion

Individuals who experience severe disabilities will be the subject of considerable planning efforts. By law, during their lifetime as recipients of human services, these individuals will have Individual Family Service Plans, Individual Educational Plans, Individual Transition Plans, and perhaps other plans written on their behalf. If these are written with appropriate deliberation, they will serve a critical role in helping agencies identify and carry out services. Unfortunately, as Smith (1990) pointed out, too often this is not the case. Too often plans are developed solely to comply with the requirements of federal laws.

This condition is, of course, not satisfactory. In order to improve it, some alternative planning approaches have been developed. You are encouraged to explore these systems in more depth to understand fully what they offer and how they can be implemented. It is suggested that they can have an important role in increasing the meaningfulness of the plans required by law.

Questions for Reflection

1. Why do you believe (or not believe) that planning for individual students with severe disabilities is necessary?
2. Is it possible for teachers to do a good job teaching without developing individual plans?
3. What is the most important part of any educational plan?
4. What requirements with the IEP would you like to see changed? Would you add any? Remove any? Why?
5. Is it necessary that we have Individual Transition Plans? Couldn't IEPs be written appropriately for older students without having special planning for transition to adulthood?
6. Why is it important to have individual family plans for providing services to infants and toddlers with disabilities?
7. If you had a young child with a disability, what would be your reaction to having professionals inquire about your family's condition?
8. What type of alternative planning system would you like to see developed or what type would you like to develop?

References

Beckman, P. J., & Bristol, M. M. (1991). Issues in developing the IFSP: A framework for establishing family outcomes. *Topics in Early Childhood Special Education, 11*(3), 19–31.

Brotherson, M. J., Turnbull, A. P., Bronicki, G. J., Houghton, J., Roeder-Gordon, C., Summers, J. A., & Turnbull, H. R. (1988). Transition into adulthood: Parental planning for sons and daughters with disabilities. *Education and Training in Mental Retardation, 23,* 165–174.

Brown, C. W. (1991). IFSP implementation in the fourth year of P.L. 99-457: The year of the paradox. *Topics in Early Childhood Special Education, 11*(3), 1–18.

Brown, L., Long, E., Udvari-Solner, A., Davis, L., VanDeventer, P., Ahlgren, C., Johnson, F., Gruenewald, L., & Jorgensen, J. (1989). The home school: Why students with severe intellectual disabilities must attend the schools of their brothers, sisters, friends, and neighbors. *Journal of the Association for Persons with Severe Handicaps, 14,* 1–7.

Brown, L., Schwarz, P., Udvari-Solner, A., Kampschroer, E. F., Johnson, F., Jorgensen, J., & Gruenewald, L. (1991). How much time should students with severe intellectual disabilities spend in regular education classrooms and elsewhere? *Journal of the Association for Persons with Severe Handicaps, 16,* 39–47.

Campbell, P. H. (1987). The integrated programming team: An approach for coordinating professionals of various disciplines in programs for students with severe and multiple handicaps. *Journal of the Association for Persons with Severe Handicaps, 12,* 107–116.

Education of the Handicapped. (February 27, 1991). Special supplement: The new Individuals with Disabilities Education Act.

Everson, J. M., & Moon, M. S. (1987). Transition services for young adults with severe disabilities: Defining professional and parental roles and responsibilities. *Journal of the Association for Persons with Severe Handicaps, 12,* 87–95.

Featherstone, H. (1980). *A difference in the family.* New York: Basic Books.

Forest, M., & Lusthaus, E. (1987). The Kaleidoscope. Challenge to the cascade. In M. Forest (Ed.), *More education/integration* (pp. 1–16). Downsview, Ontario: G. Allen Roeher Institute.

Giangreco, M. F., Cloninger, C. J., & Iverson, V. S. (1993). *Choosing options and accommodations for children: A guide to planning inclusive education.* Baltimore: Paul H. Brookes.

Halpern, A. S. (1985). Transition: A look at the foundations. *Exceptional Children, 51,* 479–486.

Jones, R. L. (1973). Accountability in special education: Some problems. *Exceptional Children, 39,* 631–642.

Krauss, M. W. (1990). New precedent in family policy: Individualized family service plan. *Exceptional Children, 56,* 388–395.

Lehr, D. H. (1989). Educational programming for children with the most severe disabilities. In F. Brown & D. H. Lehr (Eds.), *Persons with profound disabilities: Issues and practices.* Baltimore: Paul H. Brookes.

McDonnell, J., & Hardman, M. (1985). Planning the transition of severely handicapped youth from school to adult services: A framework for high school programs. *Education and Training of the Mentally Retarded, 20,* 275–286.

McDonnell, J., Wilcox, B., & Hardman, M. L. (1991). *Secondary programs for students with developmental disabilities.* Boston: Allyn & Bacon.

Mount, B., & Zwernik, K. (1988). *It's never too early, it's never too late. A booklet about personal futures planning.* St. Paul, MN: Metropolitan Council.

National Association of State Directors of Special Education. (October, 1990). *Education of the Handicapped Amendments of 1990 (P.L. 101-476): Summary of major changes in parts A through H of the act.* Washington, DC: Author.

Noonan, M. J., & McCormick, L. (1993). *Early intervention in natural environments: Methods and procedures.* Pacific Grove, CA: Brooks/Cole.

O'Brien, J., & Lyle, C. (1987). *Framework for accomplishment.* Decatur, GA: Responsive Systems Associates.

Slentz, K. L., & Bricker, D. (1992). Family guided assessment for IFSP development: Jumping off the family assessment bandwagon. *Journal of Early Intervention, 16,* 11–19.

Smith, S. W. (1990). Individualized education programs in special education—From intent to acquiescence. *Exceptional Children, 57,* 6–14.

Turnbull, A. P., Strickland, B. B., & Brantley, J. C. (1978). *Developing and implementing individualized education programs.* Columbus, OH: Merrill.

Vandercook, T., York, J., & Forest, M. (1989). The McGill Action Planning System (MAPS): A strategy for building the vision. *Journal of the Association for Persons with Severe Handicaps, 14,* 205–215.

Wehman, P. (1990). School to work: Elements of successful programs. *Teaching Exceptional Children, 23,* 40–43.

Wehman, P., Wood, W., Everson, J., Marchant, J., & Walker, R. (1987). Transition services for adolescent age individuals with severe mental retardation. In R. N. Ianacone & R. A. Stodden (Eds.), *Transition issues and directions.* Reston, VA: Council for Exceptional Children/Division on Mental Retardation.

Will, M. (1984). *OSERS programming for the transition of youth with disabilities: Bridges from school to working life.* Washington, DC: Office of Special Education and Rehabilitative Services, U.S. Department of Education.

Winton, P. J., & Bailey, D. B. (1988). The family-focused interview: A collaborative mechanism for family assessment and goal-setting. *Journal of the Division for Early Childhood, 12,* 195–207.

Winton, P. J., & Bailey, D. B. (1990). Early intervention training related to family interviewing. *Topics in Early Childhood Special Education, 10,* 50–62.

CHAPTER 5

Conducting Assessments to Determine Instructional Needs

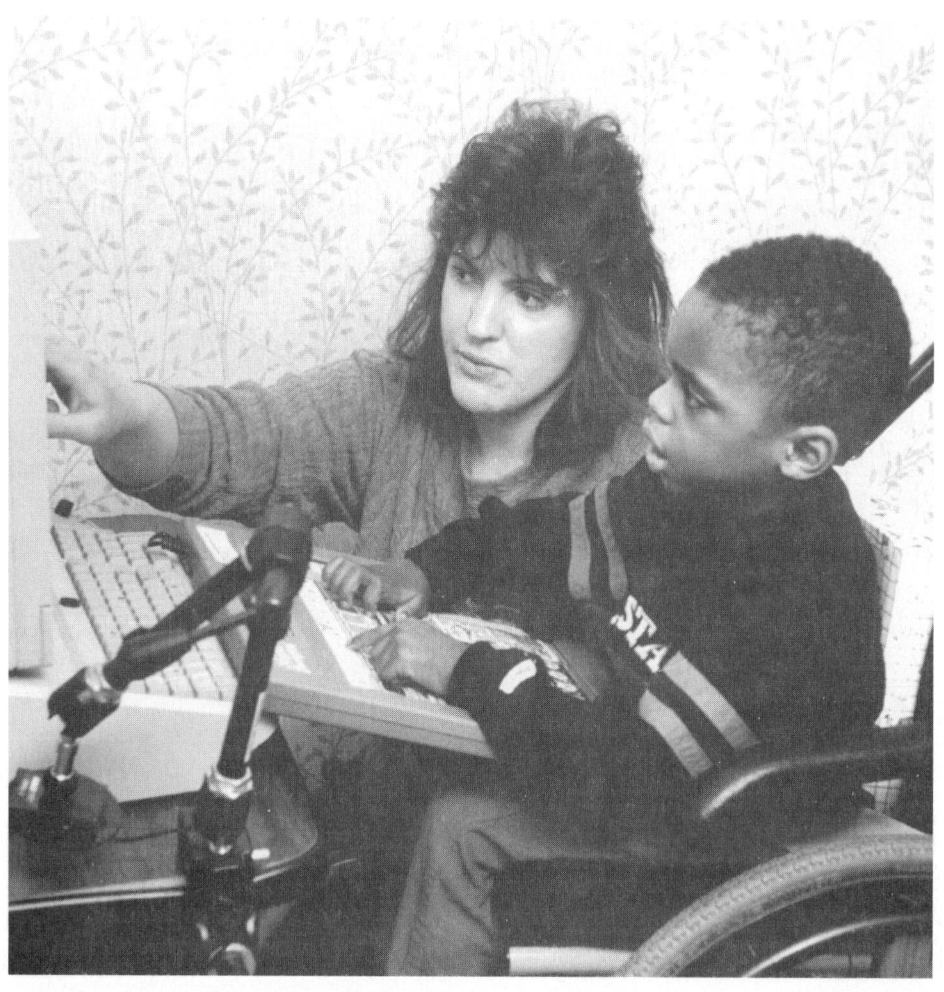

Chapter Overview

In this chapter, assessment of the student's needs through a variety of tactics is discussed. These include reviewing records, interviewing parents, using adaptive behavior scales and activities/skills checklists, conducting ecological inventories, conducting direct observations of the student during unstructured times and within structured activities, assessments conducted in the areas of language and physical functioning, and assessment of traditional academic skills when necessary.

Historically, in both special education and general education, student assessment (sometimes referred to as testing or evaluation) has had several purposes: to determine the student's ability for the purpose of assigning him or her to a particular category of disability, such as learning disabilities or mental disabilities; and then to calculate the progress the student has made over a period of time in order to assign grades or report in some other way how well he or she is doing. Additionally, sometimes students are assessed as part of educational experiments to see if a certain type of treatment or instruction is effective or to compare different types of treatment.

Perhaps the most important purpose of assessment, the one discussed in this chapter, is assessment that is intended to provide information to help plan for instruction. As was seen in the previous chapter, there are different types of plans that can or must be written. In this chapter, the discussion of assessment is intended to provide information that will help parents, teachers, and other team members make decisions about what the student needs to learn.

It should also be understood what assessment, as discussed here, is not intended to be. It is not intended to be deficit-oriented; it should not be conducted for the purpose of pointing out what the student cannot do. Further, the types of assessment discussed are not intended to result in a label or categorical designation. Most important, assessment is not being proposed to suggest a student's limitations in potential development. Instead, as stated above, the intention of assessment as presented here is to help with the planning process.

To that end we will present various types of information-gathering procedures that will prove helpful. The information gathered may include information about the student that comes from other people or reports, information about the student's needs in certain environments, and information about the student's skills and abilities as determined through direct observations and assessments. The specific processes that will be discussed include:

- Collecting information from existing records.
- Interviewing parents to determine educational goals.
- Using adaptive behavior scales and activities and skills lists to help decide students' needs.
- Ecological inventories of environments currently used or to be used by students to determine necessary skills.

- Direct observations of students in natural environments to determine existing skills and abilities.
- Direct observation of students' performance during targeted activities to determine specific capabilities and instructional needs on those activities.
- Assessment by team members to determine needs in communication and language and in physical functioning.
- Traditional academic assessments (with adaptations if necessary).

Although it is ultimately the responsibility of the planning team to decide which type or types of assessment should be used, it is suggested that generally the more information the team has, the better its decisions will be. It also should be noted that each member of the team will have an important role in the assessment process. However, a very significant role will be that of the teacher, who will collect much of the information directly and coordinate much of the rest of the process. Each of the methods of assessment presented above are discussed in the following sections. In chapter 8 the process of ongoing assessment to continuously evaluate the student's progress is discussed.

Reviewing Existing Records

An important activity that should be undertaken prior to determining instructional objectives is to review the student's existing records, especially his or her previous IEP (Browder, 1991). When a teacher will be working with a new group of students, this review should take place very early, during the preplanning days before students arrive (Westling & Koorland, 1988). It should be kept in mind, however, that not all the information in a student's cumulative folder will be useful. IQ scores, developmental screening test scores, and irrelevant goals and objectives may not provide the type of information that is helpful in forming new goals and objectives.

Useful information will include the objectives that the student has attempted to achieve in the past, information about whether or not they were achieved, and how well the student has maintained them and/or demonstrated their generalized use. Skills that have not been mastered may be viable candidates for continued instruction. Those that have been learned may need to be considered for maintenance (so they will not be forgotten by the student, perhaps as a part of a new objective) or generalization (so the skills may be used or applied across different people, times, places, and/or conditions). Chapter 7 discusses ways to promote skill maintenance and generalization.

In addition to previous objectives, the teacher should look for other pertinent data about the student, which would include information about his or her medical or physical condition, medicines taken, dietary restrictions, allergens, ongoing challenging behavior (particularly self-injurious behaviors or aggressive acts), evidence of likes and dislikes, physical and sensory abilities, and communication skills. This type of information might not only result in the development of instructional goals and objectives, it may also caution the teacher to be on the lookout for specific needs when the students arrive.

Interviewing Parents to Determine Educational Goals

As was seen in the previous chapter, contemporary approaches to planning for students with severe disabilities, such as *COACH, MAPS,* and *Personal Futures Planning,* call for the integral involvement of parents in determining skills that are appropriate for the student to learn. As a part of the team, parents can provide critical information about the student's current abilities and daily activities and about what the student needs to learn, particularly in the home and the community.

In order to learn about parent views, the teacher (and/or other professionals) will need to interview parents. This may be a part of one of the planning systems described in the previous chapter, or it may be a less formal activity. Regardless, when interviewing parents, teachers and other professionals should adhere to the guidelines offered in Figure 5–1 in order to complete their objective with the least amount of intrusion into the privacy of the family.

During the interview with the student's parents, the two major questions will be "what can your child do?" and "what do you want your child to learn?" These questions may be asked in different ways and using different formats. Two examples are presented in Figures 5–2 and 5–3. In the first, there is a sample of open-ended questions about what the student does at different times at home (Neel & Billingsley, 1989). In the second figure, the parent is given the opportunity to rate the importance of possible skills for the student to learn at school (Rainforth, York, & Macdonald, 1992).

The questions to ask the parents can be developed by the teacher and other professional members of the instructional team. There is a variety of commercially produced adaptive behavior scales and curriculum/activity guides that help direct the questioning. These products are described in the following two sections. Before selecting any one or more to use, the professional team should review them and determine their appropriateness for the student in question.

Adaptive Behavior Scales

Information about adaptive behavior skills, or skills that are especially useful for daily functioning, can be collected using one or more commercially produced adaptive behavior scales, which provide a broad overview of the student's skills and abilities in many areas of

Figure 5–1
Suggestions for Interviewing Parents

1. Make an appointment with the parents at a time that is convenient for them and at a location of their choice, usually the school or their home.
2. Try to determine the familial and cultural values that exist within the family and show respect for them.
3. Attempt to build a relation of trust, honesty, and openness with the family.
4. In order to facilitate the parents' opportunities to participate, if they wish, try to arrange child care for their child or children during the time of the meeting.
5. Avoid using professional jargon and displaying an air of arrogance. Show respect for the parents and be very open to their thoughts and opinions. Listen more than talk.
6. Arrive on time for scheduled meetings and only stay for a reasonable amount of time, usually no more than an hour.

What Does Your Child Do Most of the Time?

This section is designed to give us an idea about the number and types of activities your child participates in during the week. We are interested in where, when, and with whom your child interacts. We especially want to know the problems you and your child face on a day-to-day basis. Be sure to add any additional comments you feel will help us understand what goes on during a typical week. This information will be used to aid us in designing a functional program for your child.

What does your child usually do between school and dinner?

____

____

____

Which of these activities does your child do:

Independently ____

With members of the family __________________________________

____

With friends and/or neighbors ________________________________

____

What special problems, if any, occur during those times?

____

____

____

What does your child usually do between dinner and bedtime?

____

____

____

Which of those activities does your child do:

Independently ____

With members of the family __________________________________

____

With friends and/or neighbors ________________________________

____

Figure 5–2

Sample of Parent Interview Using Open-ended Questions

From *IMPACT: A Functional Curriculum Handbook for Students with Moderate to Severe Disabilities* (pp. 146–148) by R. S. Neel & F. F. Billingsley, 1989, Baltimore: Paul H. Brookes Publishing Co., P.O. Box 10624, Baltimore, Maryland 21285-0624. Reprinted by permission.

daily life. There are many such scales; some will be more useful than others. Usefulness will depend largely on the types of items contained on the scale and how well they apply to the student being evaluated. Typical items include daily living skills, some community skills, and functioning in specific ability areas such as demonstrating appropriate social behaviors, communicating, motor ability, and applying basic academic skills. Descriptions of specific adaptive behavior scales and their contents have recently been discussed by Browder

What special problems, if any occur during those times?

____
____
____

What does your child usually do on weekends?

____
____
____

Which of those activities does your child do:

Independently ____

With members of the family ____

____

With friends and/or neighbors ____

____

What special problems, if any, occur during those times?

____
____
____

Does your child play with other children? ____ Yes ____ No

If yes, with whom?

____
____
____

What activities does your family do for entertainment *at home*?

____
____
____
____

Figure 5–2, *continued*

(1991), Cone (1987), and Leland (1991). According to Cone (1987) the most commonly used scales are the *AAMD Adaptive Behavior Scales* (Nihira, Foster, Shellhaas, & Leland, 1974), the *Vineland Adaptive Behavior Scales* (Sparrow, Balla, & Cicchetti, 1984), *Scales of Independent Behavior* (Bruininks, Woodcock, Weatherman, & Hill, 1985), and the *Pyramid Scales* (Cone, 1984).

No formal training is required for the use of adaptive behavior scales, although it is very important that each scale be carefully reviewed before use. Each item may be directly rated (using the scale's designated rating system) by someone who is very familiar with the student, such as a parent or a caregiver. Alternatively, the scale may be filled out by the teacher while

What activities does your family do for entertainment *away from home*?

____

____

____

____

Which, if any, of these activities does your child enjoy?

____

____

____

____

When your child does participate in one of the activities that the family uses for recreation, does he or she participate in a special way, or with special rules, that are only understood by the members of the family? ____ Yes ____ No

If yes, please describe the special adaptations that you have made.

____

____

____

What, if any, are some of the problems you have with your child during vacation (when there is no school)?

____

____

____

What are some of the ideas you have that might make these times easier for your child and you?

____

____

____

Figure 5–2, *continued*

interviewing a person who is knowledgeable about the student's ability.

Although adaptive behavior scales do not always identify the most important skills to be taught, they do provide an important dimension of understanding about a student with severe disabilities. In essence, most adaptive behavior scales yield a profile of the "hills and valleys" that portray the student's overall strengths and weaknesses. If the instrument truly assesses "adaptive behavior" and this is behavior that allows the person to function within a typical environment, it would be important to know two things: areas that are lower than others that need special attention, especially if they interfere with the person's integration and participation in society, and areas that are strengths and that can help iden-

What Is Important for Your Child to Learn at School?

Parents want their child to go to a classroom where he or she will make progress. Children can make progress in different areas, and some areas may be more important than others. The list below contains different areas your child may progress in next year. Please circle the number to the right of the phrase to show how important it is for *your* child to progress in this area next year.

	NA	Not at all					extremely	RANK
1. Learn basic concepts such as colors, numbers, shapes, etc.	0	1	2	(3)	4	5	6	___
2. Learn prereading and reading skills such as letters.	0	1	2	3	(4)	5	6	___
3. Learn to use a pencil and scissors.	0	1	(2)	3	4	5	6	___
4. Learn to listen and follow directions.	0	1	2	3	4	(5)	6	___
5. Learn to share and play with other children.	0	1	2	3	4	5	(6)	1
6. Learn to be creative.	0	1	2	(3)	4	5	6	___
7. Learn more communication skills.	0	1	2	3	4	5	(6)	3
8. Learn confidence and independence.	0	1	2	3	4	(5)	6	___
9. Learn to work independently.	0	1	2	3	4	(5)	6	___
10. Learn to climb, run, and jump.	0	(1)	2	3	4	5	6	___
11. Learn self-care skills such as toileting, dressing, feeding.	0	1	2	3	4	5	(6)	2
12. Learn to follow classroom rules and routines.	0	1	2	3	(4)	5	6	___

Using the above list, place the numbers 1, 2, and 3 next to the three most important areas for your child to progress in next year.

Figure 5–3
Sample of Parent Interview Using a Rating Scale

From *Collaborative Teams for Students with Severe Disabilities: Integrating Therapy and Educational Services* by B. Rainforth, J. York, & C. Macdonald, 1992, Baltimore: Paul H. Brookes Publishing Co., P.O. Box 10624, Baltimore, Maryland 21285-0624. Reprinted by permission.

tify skills that fit within a range of social acceptability (Leland, 1991).

Cone (1987) suggested that five factors be considered when an adaptive behavior scale is used to make instructional programming decisions:

1. The scale should be relevant to different environments;
2. It should have a comprehensive listing of behaviors;
3. It should have items linked to instructional activities;

4. The items and their rating should be specific enough to help determine initial programming decisions; and
5. The instrument should be helpful in determining the scope, sequence, and content of instruction (Cone, 1987, p. 129).

Of greatest importance is whether or not the items reflect the typical abilities of the students in the program. A common criticism of adaptive behavior scales is that they do not have items suitable for assessing students with the most severe disabilities, that is, those with profound mental disabilities or severe multiple disabilities. For some of these students, the items are far beyond their behavioral repertoire and so they receive a completely "flat" profile. Information of this nature is not of much use.

After selecting an appropriate scale, the teacher must carefully read the directions and give particular attention to the scoring system that is used. Typically, a scale that reflects different performance levels is provided. For example, the Vineland has five levels of item rating: yes, usually (score 2), sometimes or partially (score 1), no, never (score 0), no opportunity (N), and don't know (DK). Each item on the scale is scored to reflect the most correct status of ability or knowledge about ability.

After the adaptive behavior assessment using the instrument has been completed, the test may be scored. Because many adaptive behavior scales are norm-referenced (the student's score may be compared to a standardization sample) and contain other technical properties such as validity and reliability, the scores for different sections, as well as the overall score, can be compared to the normative sample. This comparison allows the evaluator to develop the profile (draw the "hills and valleys") referred to above. This may provide some useful information, but the most applicable information will be that determined by analyzing individual items, which will help the teacher identify potential instructional objectives.

Curriculum/Activity Guides

In the last few years several curriculum/activity guides have been developed that can greatly assist teachers and planning teams in determining appropriate functional objectives for students with severe disabilities. Four such guides are *COACH* (Giangreco et al., 1993), which was described in the previous chapter for use as a planning instrument, *The Syracuse Community-Referenced Curriculum Guide* (Ford et al., 1989); *Community Living Skills: A Taxonomy* (Dever, 1988); and *The Activities Catalog: An Alternative Curriculum for Youth and Adults with Severe Disabilities* (Wilcox & Bellamy, 1987).

These guides are quite different from earlier ones, which presented lists of discrete behaviors sequenced according to the order of normal development in infants, toddlers, and children without disabilities. Instead, the most recent guides present an array of activities and skills that are functional and appropriate for the chronological age of the learner. The primary utility of these guides is to provide the teacher or service agency, working cooperatively with the student and his or her parents, with a broad array of activities in various domains. The guides can be used to help determine appropriate objectives for students through parent interviews. Key aspects of each of the guides are presented below.

COACH (Choosing Options and Accommodations for Children, Giangreco et al., 1993) was discussed in the previous chapter. However, it is listed here because as a part of its planning process it presents parents with a variety of possible learning needs that may be appropriate for their child with severe disabilities. COACH integrally relates the processes of assessment and planning by asking parents to evaluate their child's abilities on key skills and then rate the importance of learning the skill. To set the framework for this evaluation, the COACH system directs parents as well as professionals to consider important life values.

COACH helps parents and professionals identify learning needs, prioritize them, determine when they should be taught, where they should be taught, and what supports would be required for the student. It is a comprehensive planning system based on learning priorities determined by parents and professionals. Figure 5–4 displays one of the forms used in COACH to identify a student's abilities (in this example, language skills are listed) and whether or not the skill needs to be worked on by the instructional team. Refer back to chapter 4 for additional information about COACH as well as the original source.

Community Living Skills (Dever, 1988) is a list of functional community goals intended to allow the learner to live more independently. The skills are appropriate for a wide range of persons of different ability levels and would be useful both in public schools and in adult service systems.

The goals are presented within five major domains: personal maintenance and development, homemaking and community life, vocational, leisure, and travel. Each domain contains four major goals and several subgoals. Under each subgoal, several relevant skills are presented. One of the goals in each domain is dealing with "glitches," which is intended to teach the learner how to react when what is expected does not occur. The domains, goals, and subgoals were developed based on common weekday routines and special routines for weekend days and other "uncommon" days, (e.g., payday). The analysis of the routines led to the development of the goals and subgoals in the taxonomy, most of which are clearly beneficial for persons living independently in the community. Figure 5–5 is the Taxonomy of Community Living Skills, including all the major goals and subgoals within the different Domains.

The Activities Catalog, according to its authors (Wilcox and Bellamy, 1987), was developed to avoid the "readiness trap" by offering functional activities appropriate for learning by adolescents and young adults with severe disabilities. Instead of listing discrete skills to be identified as objectives, the catalog identifies whole activities as units of instruction. The critical feature of an activity is that it results in a natural effect or outcome. Table 5–1 provides illustrations of activity goals and distinguishes them from isolated skills.

One of the major features of the *Activities Catalog* is that it provides an assortment of choices for teachers, parents, and persons with disabilities to select for learning or participation. Wilcox and Bellamy point out that it is not important for the student to be able to learn all of the skills in an activity just to participate in an activity and enjoy it. It is also not expected that the individual will learn each of the activities, but that the catalog will serve as a convenient selection tool for reviewing various appropriate learning possibilities and selecting those that at the time seem to be the most suitable for learning.

The activities in the catalog are divided into three content domains: leisure, personal management, and work. These domains are further divided into different categories that reflect a common-sense grouping related to the benefits and functions of the activities.

The Syracuse Community-Referenced Curriculum Guide (Ford et al., 1989) is another guide that offers an array of functional activities appropriate for learning by persons with severe disabilities. The guide includes scope

COMMUNICATION*

PART 1.2

Check only one box:
ASSESS IN PART 1 (Potential Priorities this Year) ☒ ASSESS IN PART 2 (Breadth of Curriculum) ☐ SKIP FOR NOW ☐

		PART 1.3		PART 1.4		PART 2.2
#	ACTIVITIES	SCORE	NEEDS WORK	POTENTIAL PRIORITY	RANK	BREADTH OF CURR.
1	Indicates Continuation or Expresses More (e.g., makes sound or movement when desired interaction stops to indicate he or she would like eating, playing, and so forth to continue).	S	N (Y)			
2	Makes Choices when Presented with Options.	P	N (Y)			
3	Makes Requests (e.g., for objects, food, interactions, activities, assistance).	E	N (Y)			
4	Summons Others (e.g., has an acceptable way to call others to him or her).	E	N (Y)			
5	Expresses Rejection/Refusal (e.g., indicates when he or she wants something to stop or does not want something to begin).	S	(N) Y			
6	Greets Others.	P	N (Y)			
7	Follows Instructions (e.g., simple, one-step, or multi-step directions).	E	N (Y)			
8	Describes Events, Objects, Interactions, and so forth (e.g., uses vocabulary, nouns, verbs, adjectives).	E	N (Y)			
9	Responds to Questions (e.g., if asked a question he or she will attempt to answer).	E	(N) Y			
10	Asks Questions of Others.	E	(N) Y			
11	Sustains Communication with Others (e.g., takes turns, maintains attention, stays on topic, perseveres).	E	(N) Y			
			N Y			
			N Y			

Comments: Tommy has no consistent way to communicate that is easily understood by people other than his family.

Scoring Key: R = Resistant to the assistance of others; E = Early/emerging skills (1%-25%); P = Partial skill (25%-80%); S = Skillful (80%-100%). Use scores alone or in combination.

*Communication may be exhibited or received in any combination of ways (e.g., speaking, gestures, signing, keyboards).

Figure 5–4

COACH Assessment of Instructional Priorities in the Area of Communication

From *Choosing Options and Accommodations for Children: A Guide to Planning Inclusive Education* by M. F. Giangreco, C. J. Cloninger, & V. S. Iverson, 1993, Baltimore: Paul H. Brookes. Reprinted by permission of the author.

DOMAIN P: Personal Maintenance and Development

I. The learner will follow routine body maintenance procedures
   A. Maintain personal cleanliness
   B. Groom self
   C. Dress appropriately
   D. Follow appropriate sleep patterns
   E. Maintain nutrition
   F. Exercise regularly
   G. Maintain substance control

II. The learner will treat illnesses
   A. Use first aid and illness treatment procedures
   B. Obtain medical advice when necessary
   C. Follow required medication schedules

III. The learner will establish and maintain personal relationships
   A. Interact appropriately with family
   B. Make friends
   C. Interact appropriately with friends
   D. Cope with inappropriate conduct of family and friends
   E. Respond to sexual needs
   F. Obtain assistance in maintaining personal relationships

IV. The learner will handle personal glitches
   A. Cope with changes in daily schedule
   B. Cope with equipment breakdowns and material depletions

DOMAIN H: Homemaking and Community Life

I. The learner will obtain living quarters
   A. Find appropriate living quarters
   B. Rent/buy living quarters
   C. Set up living quarters

II. The learner will follow community routines
   A. Keep living quarters neat and clean
   B. Keep fabrics neat and clean
   C. Maintain interior of living quarters
   D. Maintain exterior of living quarters
   E. Respond to seasonal changes
   F. Follow home safety procedures
   G. Follow accident/emergency procedures
   H. Maintain foodstock
   I. Prepare and serve meals
   J. Budget money appropriately
   K. Pay bills

III. The learner will coexist in a neighborhood and community
   A. Interact appropriately with community members
   B. Cope with inappropriate conduct of others
   C. Observe requirements of the law
   D. Carry out civic duties

IV. The learner will handle glitches in the home
   A. Cope with equipment breakdowns
   B. Cope with depletions of household supplies
   C. Cope with unexpected depletions of funds
   D. Cope with disruptions in routine
   E. Cope with sudden changes in the weather

Figure 5–5
Taxonomy of Community Living Skills
From *Community Living Skills: A Taxonomy* (pp. 26–27) by R. B. Dever, 1988, Washington, DC: American Association on Mental Retardation. Copyright 1988 by the American Association on Mental Retardation. Reprinted by permission.

and sequence charts that cover the major community living areas: self management/home living; vocational; recreation/leisure; and general community functioning. There are also sections on functional academic skills, including reading and writing, money handling, and time management. Finally, there are three sections on "embedded" activities: social skills, communication skills, and motor skills. Figure 5–6 shows the scope and sequence for the

DOMAIN V: Vocational

I. The learner will obtain work
   A. Seek employment
   B. Accept employment
   C. Use employment service

II. The learner will perform the work routine
   A. Perform the job routine
   B. Follow work-related daily schedule
   C. Maintain work station
   D. Follow employer rules and regulations
   E. Use facilities appropriately
   F. Follow job safety procedures
   G. Follow accident and emergency procedures

III. The learner will coexist with others on the job
   A. Interact appropriately with others on the job
   B. Cope with inappropriate conduct of others on the job

IV. The learner will handle glitches on the job
   A. Cope with changes in work routine
   B. Cope with work problems
   C. Cope with supply depletions and equipment breakdowns

DOMAIN L: Leisure

I. The learner will develop leisure activities
   A. Find new leisure activities
   B. Acquire skills for leisure activities

II. The learner will follow leisure activity routines
   A. Perform leisure activities
   B. Maintain leisure equipment
   C. Follow leisure safety procedures
   D. Follow accident and emergency procedures

III. The learner will coexist with others during leisure
   A. Interact appropriately with others in a leisure setting
   B. Respond to the inappropriate conduct of others

IV. The learner will handle glitches during leisure
   A. Cope with changes in leisure routine
   B. Cope with equipment breakdowns and material depletions

DOMAIN T: Travel

I. The learner will travel routes in the community
   A. Form mental maps of frequented buildings
   B. Form mental maps of the community

II. The learner will use conveyances
   A. Follow usage procedures
   B. Make decisions preparatory to travel
   C. Follow travel safety procedures
   D. Follow accident and emergency procedures

III. The learner will coexist with others while traveling
   A. Interact appropriately with others while traveling
   B. Respond to the inappropriate conduct of others while traveling

IV. The learner will handle glitches during travel
   A. Cope with changes in travel schedule
   B. Cope with equipment breakdowns
   C. Cope with being lost

Figure 5–5, *continued*

major community living areas in the *Syracuse Curriculum.*

The primary philosophy guiding the Syracuse curriculum is that there are many typical school or general education activities applicable to the needs of students with moderate and severe disabilities, but there are others they must learn that often do not appear in the normal curriculum. These latter skills, therefore, are the ones presented in the guide.

Like the other guides, the Syracuse does not suggest that it includes all that a student needs to learn or that all of its contents should be taught to students with severe disabilities. The

Table 5–1

Illustrations of Skills and Activities from the Activities Catalog

Isolated Skills	Activity Goals
Given any price tag less than $15, Jason will count out bills and coins to equal that amount. John will match pictures, line drawings, rebuses to functional objects (e.g., clothing items, food items, classroom materials).	Tom will demonstrate the ability to shop at three different supermarkets: Safeway (2427 River Road), U Mart (416 Santa Clara Street), and Fred Meyer (3000 River Road) for up to 15 specific brand grocery items. Picture cards will be used as the grocery list. Performance includes travel to the store, selecting items, paying for the purchase using a next-dollar strategy, and transporting purchases back to school.
Heidi will learn to sign 25 functional words and word phrases (e.g., hamburger, milk, fries, I want, thank you) on request. Bianca will improve self-care skills in the areas of eating and meal preparation. Michael will independently cross uncontrolled intersections during low traffic periods.	Joe will use a communication notebook to order lunch at two fast-food restaurants (McDonald's and Arby's). Performance includes travel to the restaurant, entering, waiting in line as necessary, indicating desired lunch (sandwich, beverage, fries, dessert), paying using a next-dollar strategy, transporting food to table, eating, cleaning up, and returning to next activity.
Cindy will name, locate female body parts. Bob will demonstrate mature catching and throwing patterns using a variety of sizes weights of balls. Diane will demonstrate appropriate use of makeup. Jackie will independently wash her hair once a week.	Susan will use the YMCA twice weekly after school. Performance includes travel to the "Y," locating the correct locker room, finding a locker, changing clothes, using the weight room for at least 10 minutes, using the sauna, showering, dressing, and traveling home.
Bill will increase his understanding of areas of career interest relevant to his vocational potential. Matt will improve the social and communication skills needed for community vocational functioning.	Dan will participate as a member of a work crew responsible for after school cleanup. Performance includes arriving for work on time, greeting co-workers, putting on appropriate clothing, independently completing jobs designated by activity cards, changing out of work clothes, and returning home on designated bus.
Jeff will improve and maintain fine motor skills, bilateral coordination, spatial orientation, and equilibrium. Rob will increase his vocational skills and abilities. Allen will demonstrate an increased awareness of work values.	Shawn will participate in the Food Service Program at the Erb Student Union. Job cluster includes busing tables, washing dishes, washing pots, pans, and shelving clean dishes pans. Training will monitor social interactions, speed and quality prompts, and performance according to schedule.

From *The Activities Catalog: An Alternative Curriculum for Youth and Adults with Severe Disabilities* (p. 13) by B. Wilcox & T. G. Bellamy, 1987, Baltimore: Paul H. Brookes Publishing Co., P.O. Box 10624, Baltimore, Maryland 21285-0624. Reprinted by permission.

Community living areas		Age and grade levels					
			Elementary school				
		Kindergarten (age 5)	Primary (ages 6-8)	Intermediate (ages 9-11)	Middle school (ages 12-14)	High school (ages 15-18)	Transition (ages 19-21)
Self-management and home living	Eating and food preparation						
	Grooming and dressing						
	Hygiene and toileting						
	Safety and health						
	Assisting, taking care of others						
	Budgeting/planning/scheduling						
	Household maintenance						
	Outdoor maintenance						
Vocational	Classroom/school jobs and community work experiences						
	Neighborhood jobs						
	Community jobs						
Recreation/ leisure	School and extracurricular						
	Alone–home and in the neighborhood						
	Family/friends – home and in the neighborhood						
	Family/friends – community						
	Physical fitness						
General community functioning	Travel						
	Community safety						
	Grocery shopping						
	General shopping						
	Eating out						
	Using services						

Figure 5–6

Scope and Sequence of the Community Living Areas

From *The Syracuse Community-Referenced Curriculum Guide for Students with Moderate and Severe Disabilities* (p. 6) by A. Ford, R. Schnorr, L. Meyer, L. Davern, J. Black, & P. Dempsey (Eds.), 1989, Baltimore: Paul H. Brookes Publishing Co., P.O. Box 10624, Baltimore, Maryland 21285-0624. Reprinted by permission.

authors state that the guide "provides a framework for decision making that should be applied to individuals on a student-by-student basis. We would expect individualized decisions to vary considerably depending on a range of factors, including the student's age, present ability to participate in community living activities, personal and parental preferences and so forth" (Ford et al., 1989, p. 4).

Assessment of students' needs through parent interviews using commercially produced guides such as described in this section consists of similar procedures regardless of the guide. The decision-making process described below is based on the procedures presented in the guides reviewed in this section.

The first step of the process is for the parents or caregivers to become familiar with the pertinent contents of the curriculum guide. Gaining knowledge of the contents alone can be an important learning activity that will provoke thought on possible learning outcomes. Copies of the guide being used may be shared with the parents and caregivers, and the contents (or selected portions) may be shown to the student with disabilities if appropriate.

The next step should be for those who are familiar with the student to rate the student's skill level on the items in different sections or across different domains of the curriculum guide. The rating should be a system that reports the performance or ability of the student on the activity or skill. As an example, the Syracuse allows each skill to be rated using one of the following:

Needs assistance on most steps;

Needs assistance on some steps; or

Performs all steps independently.

It also allows the student's skill use to be rated in terms of whether or not he or she possesses the related social skills to perform the task and whether or not he or she demonstrates certain "critical features" in conjunction with the use of the skills (initiates as needed? makes choices? uses safety measures?). Finally, it allows a note to be made regarding the priority goal area.

The COACH uses a similar procedure. Each skill is rated on the following scale:

R—Resistant to assistance from others;

E—Early/emerging skill (1–25%);

P—Partial skill (25–80%);

S—Skillful (80–100%).

Once the skill level is determined, the COACH calls for a determination as to whether or not the skill should be taught and what level of priority it should be given.

Prioritization should be the next step regardless of the guide that is used. This is generally done by reviewing the ratings of the different items and establishing through parent and professional consensus the student's instructional priorities. The most important aspect of this phase of the process is that those skills that will be most immediately useful or enjoyable to the student are given top consideration. As Wilcox and Bellamy (1987) stated, the skills should be directed toward "building and maintaining a desirable lifestyle."

After interviewing parents or caregivers (or even previous teachers) and using adaptive behavior scales and activity and skills guides, the planning team has another source for determining potential objectives. An additional approach, analyzing the environments in which the student functions or may function in the future, is discussed below.

Conducting Ecological Inventories

One of the most important ways to determine potential instructional needs of students with disabilities is to analyze their current (and future) environments and lifestyle to observe the activities that occur and that might occur. This analysis of activities that are required within a particular setting is called an *ecological inventory* (Brown et al., 1979). Although it is preferable for the inventory to be conducted through direct observation in the setting, it may also be accomplished by interviewing someone who is very familiar with the setting or by asking someone to respond to a written survey about the setting.

To conduct an ecological inventory, the teacher, the parents, and the rest of the collaborative team must first identify which domains of learning are of interest. These might include the domestic environment, the community, the school, the workplace, and a leisure or recreational setting. Often, of course, all of these domains are appropriate. Next, the specific settings within the domains are identified, for example, the kitchen at home, the department store in the community, the school cafeteria, the grocery store where the person works, and/or the neighborhood recreational center. After specific environments have been identified, the subenvironments of greatest significance are identified and the important actions that are to occur in them: using the microwave to prepare a meal or the dishwasher to wash dishes, selecting clothes in the clothing department of the store, bagging groceries at the checkout counter, selecting food items in the cafeteria, and/or shooting pool in the recreation center. Once the key subenvironments and corresponding activities have been identified, the latter become the instructional targets. They will ultimately be written as *instructional objectives* and the components of the necessary activities will be listed in a *task analysis.* These items are discussed in chapter 6 as part of the topic of skill acquisition.

The ecological inventory is conducted to determine the types of activities an individual with severe disabilities might learn to perform in the settings. It is necessary to list all of the actions the individual must perform to successfully operate within the setting. Some of these may be identified by the team for immediate instruction; others may be considered appropriate for instruction at a later time.

When interviewing parents to determine students' instructional needs, the teacher can determine sites where ecological inventories would be necessary. The teacher should ask for information about learning needs necessary in the home and also needs for participating with the parents and family in places outside of the home. If this inquiry is being conducted by the teacher through a home visit, the teacher may take the opportunity to directly observe some of the student's living environments and learn about the student's abilities and difficulties in the home. The teacher can also ask the parents about the student's abilities in different community settings and later visit these settings to conduct more extensive ecological inventories through observation.

A variation of the ecological inventory to determine environmental needs is through an analysis of routines. This is similar to ecological inventories except that the focus is on typical activities that occur during a day rather than activities within particular environments. Dever (1988) suggested that if we identify the routine of a typical independent individual, we may be able to teach those skills to make another person more independent. Therefore he proposed that routines be developed such as the one presented in Figure 5–7.

This type of information may complement or broaden the data gathered through an ecological inventory. For example, if it is known that on a daily basis the individual can dress himself except for buttoning his shirt and zipping his trousers (two things his mother says she must always do), these tasks might become important learning objectives.

Figure 5–7
A Weekday Routine

From *Community Living Skills: A Taxonomy* (p. 29) by R. B. Dever, 1988, Washington, DC: American Association on Mental Retardation. Copyright 1988 by the American Association on Mental Retardation. Reprinted by permission.

1. Rise
2. Toilet
3. Groom self
4. Check weather conditions and select workday clothing
5. Dress
6. Make bed
7. Prepare breakfast
8. Eat breakfast
9. Prepare sack lunch
10. Clear table and wash dishes
11. Tidy kitchen
12. Brush teeth
13. Select outerwear for weather conditions
14. Check lights and appliances
15. Leave and secure house
16. Travel to work

•
•
•

(Perform work routine)

•
•
•

17. Travel home (see also payday routine)
18. Collect mail
19. Store outerwear
20. Exercise
21. Select evening clothing (for chore/leisure routine)
22. Bathe
23. Groom and dress
24. Store dirty clothing (and linen, if applicable)
25. Tidy bathroom
26. Set table
27. Prepare supper
28. Eat
29. Clear table and wash dishes
30. Tidy kitchen
31. Tidy living room
32. Perform chore/leisure routine
33. Toilet and dress for bed
34. Set alarm
35. Sleep

Another way to determine what the student needs to function in different environments is through a discrepancy analysis, which begins by looking at the behaviors and skills demonstrated in a particular setting by a person without disabilities who is about the same age as the person with the severe disability. The procedure then compares the skills of the person with the disability with those demonstrated by the person without disabilities. This may be done through direct observation or by questioning someone who knows the person. The discrepancy analysis can be used with very specific skills, such as buying a hamburger in a fast-food restaurant, or with entire routines, such as getting to the restaurant on a public bus, ordering the food, sitting down to eat, interacting socially, and so forth.

Analysis of the demands of the environment is essential for determining the specific learning goals and objectives most suitable for a student with severe disabilities. Although using published guides and adaptive behavior scales is useful to identify some potential learning targets, analyzing a student's actual needs in specific environments ensures that what is taught is functional and relevant to the student's progress toward independence.

Direct Observation of the Student in Natural Environments

All of the data-gathering procedures discussed to this point may be conducted through analyzing existing records, interviewing key persons, and observing and analyzing environmental demands. Although these are all extremely useful and necessary, only by spending time directly observing the student can the teacher develop a complete picture of the student's abilities and needs. Through such observations, additional possible learning objectives can be targeted, and the appropriateness of the potential objectives that have been learned through the procedures described above can be confirmed or questioned.

Direct observations of students in natural environments may occur during unstructured periods or when planned activities are occurring under the direction of a teacher, parent, or other person.

Observations of students in natural environments during unstructured activities are made by teachers at times when there is no attempt by the teacher or another person to get the student to demonstrate a particular skill or activity. Such observations of students should occur in both school and nonschool settings, including home and community locations. The more settings in which observations can be conducted, the more useful will be the information likely to be generated. Direct observations may be used to answer several important questions:

1. In what ways does the student participate in home, school, and community activities? Is participation complete or is partial participation encouraged?
2. With whom does the student spend leisure time and what types of activities does he or she enjoy? Do any particular toys, games, or activities seem to be especially interesting or reinforcing?
3. How does the student express himself or herself in different settings and with different people? Is the individual's language functional? Is communication adequate or is it difficult to understand the person's meaning or intention? Is an alternative form of communication used?
4. How are relationships with nondisabled peers manifested? Are there appropriate social behaviors? Are there friendships?
5. Does the student have limitations related to his or her physical or sensory abilities? Is he or she ambulatory or mobile? How much are arms and hands used? Are orthotic devices used?
6. Does the student exhibit any type of inappropriate behavior, such as self-injurious or aggressive acts? Do these occur in any particular circumstances? Do they appear to be related to communicative attempts or to express particular feelings?
7. How well does the student perform in the domains, environments, subenvironments, and activities that were identified through the ecological inventory process?

For the purpose of forming potential instructional objectives, the most appropriate time to conduct observations would be before the student begins to be served by the teacher, if this is possible. For example, if a student is moving into a new school program, such as from an elementary school to a middle school, it would be appropriate for the future teacher to go to the elementary school and observe the child in various applicable school environments. In addition, the teacher could arrange with the parents to observe the child in the home and in community settings visited by the family. Other possible observational settings could include previously identified settings such as a friend's house, a neighborhood playground, park, or recreational setting, the school bus, and so forth.

Although there are many formal data collection procedures used for direct observation, the most appropriate for this aspect of initial assessment is *anecdotal recording,* a relatively simple process in which the observer makes written notes about the targeted individual's behavior. During the observation, careful and continuous attention is given to the acts of the student and nearly all that occurs is written down on a pad of paper attached to a clipboard. Because the observer-recorder should not be a part of the ongoing action, an unobtrusive posture and position of observation should be taken whenever possible.

To add greater meaning to the information collected, an attempt should be made to record environmental events that precede or prompt certain behaviors (antecedent events) and those that follow or reinforce behaviors (consequences). A narrative recording that includes these elements has been referred to as an *A-B-C analysis* because it includes the antecedent, the behavior, and the consequence within a temporal framework.

Although the process is straightforward, it may become increasingly difficult during a lengthy observation for the teacher to remain focused on the student. For that reason, prompts, such as a list of questions concerning observational priorities, that can be attached to the clipboard will be useful.

Observation of the Student During Structured Activities

When specific skills or behaviors have been identified as potential targets for instruction through any of the previously outlined practices (analyzing the demands of the environment, assessing adaptive behavior, reviewing

Direct assessment of a student's performance offers important information about the student's current performance level.

published curriculum guides, reviewing prior records, observations during unstructured activities), it will be necessary to directly evaluate the student's ability to perform the task or activity. This aspect of the assessment process will be done during planned, structured activities. The purpose of this phase of assessment is to pinpoint specific instructional targets by seeing exactly what the student can do on particular tasks. Direct assessment is necessary because information obtained using the previously described procedures may not be specific enough or may be conflicting, or, because the person may not have had the opportunity to perform a skill, his or her true ability may not be known (Browder, 1991). In addition, what may have been true about a student's ability at another time or in other circumstances may not still be true. In other words, the student may no longer be able to do something or, conversely, may be able to perform a skill that someone did not think he or she could. For all of these reasons, direct assessment during structured activities is necessary.

Direct assessment procedures allow for the assessment of the student's skill level in specific situations and in specific circumstances. The situations and circumstances should be the areas of learning and performance where we expect certain skills to ultimately be demonstrated—in a classroom, in other school environments, in homes, or in community settings. If it is not possible to conduct on-site assessments, the best possible simulations should be used. Keep in mind, however, that to ultimately validate that a skill has been learned (i.e., after instruction) requires the examination site to be the actual setting in which the skill will be used.

The primary purpose of direct assessment is to observe the student's actual ability to perform certain tasks or activities. The level of competence or skill deficiency actually demonstrated will indicate whether or not the targeted behavior or skill should be considered for instruction. In order to conduct this assessment, the teacher needs to plan an activity that will provide the opportunity for the student to demonstrate the skills to be assessed. In most cases, this means the student will be enrolled in the teacher's class and the teacher will develop activities for the student in order to observe and record performance on specific tasks as the activities occur naturally during the school day. This does not mean that all of the opportunities for skill demonstration should occur in one area. Instead, the skill should be assessed where it will ultimately need to occur.

Direct assessment procedures must allow the student adequate opportunity to demonstrate whether or not the particular behavior, skill, or some parts of the skill can be performed; therefore, initial direct assessment of potential instructional targets must be more than a one-time evaluation. Typically the teacher will collect three to five days of performance data on the target behavior to validate the student's actual ability level. These data points are referred to as *baseline* data because they indicate the student's current performance level prior to instruction. They will be displayed on graph paper in order that the teacher may determine precisely which parts of the task the student can do and which need to be learned (see chapter 8).

The types of performance opportunities and the type of data to be collected depend on the type of behavior that is being observed. Given the heterogeneous characteristics of persons with severe disabilities, it is understandable that there will be a range of behaviors, skills, and activities that will need to be assessed and ultimately taught. This range of instructional needs will vary depending on severity and need. For students with the most severe disabilities, we may be looking for their ability to partially participate in an activity, to make a choice, or to reduce dependency (Lehr, 1989). Older or more capable students may be assessed to determine how well they can cook a meal or wash their clothes at a laundromat. Although the behaviors are different, the principles of direct assessment apply equally.

For the purpose of baseline data collection as well as continuous measurement during instruction (as discussed in chapter 8), we may consider each learning target as having one of four topographies or forms: *simple-discrete behaviors, continuous-ongoing behaviors, complex-chained skills* (comprised of multiple behaviors), or *routines* (also comprised of multiple behaviors but occurring when natural cues and reinforcers are in effect). Methods for collecting data on student performance on these types of behaviors include event recording, rate measures, partial interval and whole interval recording, momentary time sampling, latency recording, duration measures, and task analytic assessment. Since these data collection methods are explained in detail in chapter 8, they will not be discussed here. However, the four forms of behaviors that may be identified for baseline and ongoing assessment are explained below.

Simple-Discrete Behaviors

Behaviors within this group include simple movements that usually occur in and across different situations. Examples include smiling, eye contact, touching, holding, lifting, and so forth. These often appear in clusters with other behaviors, and the teacher may have several behaviors in one cluster that should be assessed. As is explained in chapter 8, event recording, rate measures, partial interval recording, momentary time sampling, and sometimes latency measures are used to measure these types of behaviors.

Continuous-Ongoing Behaviors

For some objectives or potential objectives, it is important not only to know that they occur, but also to know for how long they do so. For example, how long can a student work at a particular job or engage in a fitness activity? When such behavior is of concern, an appropriate measure, such as duration measures or whole interval recording, is used (see chapter 8).

Complex-Chained Skills

There are several possible instructional targets for evaluation that require the student to perform a chain of related behaviors in order to complete a task. Folding laundry, playing a pinball machine, setting a table, and vacuuming a room are a few examples of tasks that can be broken down into multiple individual behavior components. Breaking down a particular task in this way is referred to as a *task analysis.* When a student's ability to perform all of the steps in such a multicomponent task is evaluated, it is called a *task analytic assessment* (Browder, 1991). Assessment of students on such tasks requires that the teacher observe how well the student does on each component of the task and also what type of assistance the student needs in order to complete the task. Procedures for doing this are in chapter 8.

Functional Routines

Functional routines are similar to task analyses in that they list several behaviors in a chain that are to be evaluated as they occur in the chain. However, according to Neel and Billingsley (1989), routines differ in some important ways from traditional task analyses. First, routines are more complete acts in that they require all relevant behaviors necessary to "have access to a particular activity or event in the natural context" (Neel & Billingsley, 1989, p. 50). In other words, it is not sufficient during assessment only to determine whether or not the student can make a sandwich. Instead, it is necessary to observe the student when he or she is hungry and see if the student begins by going into the kitchen, finding the appropriate ingredients, arranging them for use, and then making the sandwich and eating it. As such a routine occurs, we may expect the student to use cognitive skills, communication skills, social skills, and motor skills.

Second, routines are initiated by a natural cue in the environment instead of by the teacher's direction to initiate the task (unless this is a natural cue). In addition, routines are finished when the student experiences the natural consequence that serves as a reinforcer for the entire event, which Neel and Billingsley refer to as a "critical effect." In the above example, this would be eating the sandwich and thus reducing the hunger that prompted the entire sequence. It is this idea of a critical effect that Neel and Billingsley suggest is the major difference between teaching through routines and the use of most task analyses.

Like traditional task analyses, routines may be relatively brief or they may be more elaborate. Although Neel and Billingsley recommend that the typical routine should have about 15 steps, the concept of the routine is broader than that of the task analysis. Because of the defining characteristics of a routine, we might envision routines that range from getting off the school bus and coming into the classroom to one that calls for a student to get on a bus, go to the grocery store, shop, and return home on the bus. While it is apparent that this would be quite extensive and we may need to break it into subroutines, it does possess the critical components of a routine.

Recording the student's performance on each step of routine can be the same as recording performance on steps in a task analysis. Again, these procedures can be found in chapter 8.

Recording and Charting Performance During Structured Assessment Activities

In order for the teacher to accurately monitor the student's progress, he or she should record the correct occurrences of the behavior, using the unit of measure most appropriate, and then transfer this information onto graph paper. Although the process of recording, graphing, and interpreting student performance should be started during initial assessment, it is also an important aspect of instruction (see chapter 6) and checking for maintenance and generalization (see chapter 7). The discussion of this topic is presented separately in chapter 8.

Assessing Related Skills

The process of assessing students to determine instructional needs, as has been demonstrated thus far, is an extensive and complicated process, but if a student is to be taught the skills that are most important to daily and future quality living, it is important that the process be undertaken and continued.

As was discussed in chapter 3, collaborative, transdisciplinary teaming is essential to offering the best possible educational service to students with severe disabilities. During the assessment process, key members of the team should be involved to determine students' abilities in related areas, particularly *communication* and *motor development*. In the first area, the communication disorders specialist (speech/language therapist) will have the lead role; in the second area, a physical therapist or an occupational therapist (or both) will analyze development and suggest to the team important needs that should be addressed.

Related skills, such as communication and motor skills, are referred to as such because they may be related to most functional targets that will be taught. Ford et al. (1989) call them "embedded skills." Although they are not taught in isolation from other skills, it is still necessary to have a clear understanding of a student's abilities and needs in these areas so that communication and motor skills can be given the appropriate attention when teaching any and all functional skills. In this way, the student can learn to function less dependently or more independently in his or her environment by working on the specific functional activity and the related skill that is a part of it.

Communication Skills

Determining current and needed functional communication skills will measure the ability of the individual with severe disabilities to influence the behavior of other people. The assessment of communication skills must be a team effort led by the specialist in this area, and must include information provided by parents, teachers, and other professionals and paraprofessionals. Each will contribute to the understanding of the student's abilities and needs.

Assessment of communication requires information about three areas (Neel & Billingsley 1989; Noonan & Siegel-Causey, 1990):

1. Communicative functions: What does or will the student need to express to participate more fully in current and future environments? In what way does the student currently attempt to control the environment? What would be important for him or her to learn to do so?
2. Communicative form: How does the student communicate now? Is this system adequate? Is it understood by others in the student's environment?
3. Communicative context and situations: What does the student communicate about and with whom does he or she communicate? What aspects of the environment stimulate communication?

In order to answer these questions, several different types of evaluation are required, including commercially available assessments, communication/language samples, oral motor assessment, and behavioral assessment (Noonan & Siegel-Causey, 1990). The speech/language therapist conducts the first two forms of assessment, a physical or occupational therapist may conduct the oral-motor assessment, and the teacher is in the best position to conduct a behavioral assessment by using the anecdotal recording or A-B-C analysis system described previously. For very specific language behaviors, the teacher may also use event recording or take frequency measures.

Motor Skills

A significant number of students with severe disabilities have physical disabilities, or perhaps multiple disabilities, that present extraordinary challenges to their participation in many life activities. Their motor skills may be both delayed and disorganized. The most typical students with disabilities of this nature will have cerebral palsy in addition to a moderate, severe, or profound mental disability (Rainforth, Giangreco, & Dennis, 1989). It is very important, therefore, that their motor skills be assessed and that the assessment lead to functional improvements in participatory skills. In the assessment of motor skills and physical abilities, the teacher's primary responsibility is to determine the functions that the student must acquire that require motoric involvement. That is, in various areas of functioning, what type of physical movement or participation must the student develop in order to achieve more independence or less dependence? (Browder, 1991)

The evaluation conducted by the therapist should provide the teacher and others with this type of information. The physical and/or occupational therapist, like the teacher, is concerned about functional performance and therefore observes the student during normal activities. Additionally, in-depth evaluations are conducted in the areas of self-help and general motor development. The outcome of the assessment by the PT or OT will be to identify motor skill deficits, suggest environmental modifications to improve participation, and perhaps restructure the job or task so that the intended function can be achieved.

Although therapists, like teachers, are very concerned with functioning, they are also concerned with the underlying physical dysfunctioning associated with functional performances. Because of this, the therapist conducts evaluations of reflexes and reflex patterns, the conditions of muscle tone, range of motion, motor patterns, limb length discrepancy, limb girth (circumference), muscle strength, sensation, gait, posture, and sensory integration (Carpignano & Bigge, 1991). As a result of these assessments, information is provided that will help the student maintain health and increase participation in current and future integrated environments (Rainforth et al., 1989).

Assessing Traditional Academic Skills

The academic skills that teachers of most students with severe disabilities are interested in assessing include reading, writing, and arithmetic (primarily money handling and time management) (Ford et al., 1989). Although acquisition and application of skills in these areas may not be possible or may not be the most important area of instruction for some students with severe disabilities, for others it would be inappropriate not to teach certain academic skills. Some students with severe disabilities are capable of learning some useful academic skills (Rynders & Horrobin, 1990), and such skills may enrich the quality of their lives and increase their ability to participate more fully in normal environments. Teachers should not make assumptions about the student's ability in this area, but should undertake a careful analysis to determine the extent that academic skills should be taught.

The first step in the assessment of academic skills for students with severe disabilities is to develop an estimation of the type of academic curricular focus appropriate for the student. This is based on five primary considerations about the student:

1. What is the age of the student and how much time does he or she have remaining in school?

The younger the student, the more likely it is that he or she will benefit from instruction in academic skills. The skills that are taught are relatively simple during the first few years of school and the student may be at an age when cognitive abilities and academic objectives coincide maximally. As students get older and the number of years left in school decrease, there must be more concern about how well particular skills will serve him or her in the adult world. The functionality of the skills that are taught becomes critical at some time between the beginning of the middle school years and the high school years. Continuing to focus on basic academic skills may not be functional at this time.

2. What amount of success has the student had thus far in learning academic skills?

If a good attempt has been made to teach the student academic skills but he or she has made little progress, this will be an indication that instruction should take another form or be terminated. In this area, as in other curricular areas, the value of what is being taught must be questioned and the success or lack of success must be judged. All students with severe disabilities can benefit from instruction, but we must decide what are the most appropriate objectives. Through the experience the teacher has with the student and the experience that other teachers have had, the decision must be made whether to continue or move to other areas of instruction.

3. What type of academic skills are needed for functioning in relevant environments and also for leisure and recreational activities?

Given the student's current and near future life situation, different types of academic instruction will be useful. For example, a student who is learning to participate in community activities (e.g., shopping for groceries or clothes) will need certain skills, whereas other skills may be needed for leisure activities (e.g., reading magazines, looking at books, reading the television or movie listings). If there is difficulty teaching academic skills for one type of activity, it still may be appropriate to teach for another.

4. What is the relative value or significance of academic skills when compared to other skills? Are there other skills that will reduce dependence or increase independence?

If a student cannot brush his teeth, pull up his pants, or use appropriate social responses and also lacks basic academic skills, which is more important to teach? The answer to this is simply based on which type of skill will allow the person to be more independent and be viewed more as a valued member of society. Academic skills may be important, but if the individual does not have an adequate repertoire of more basic skills, he or she is more likely to be shunned by others. On the other hand, many persons with severe disabilities have many functional, generalizable self-care and other daily living skills. For them, it may be most appropriate to teach academic skills.

5. What are the wishes of the student and the student's parents regarding instruction in academic skills?

This is the final question, but certainly not the least important. Students may express an interest in learning academic skills in some form and this should not be ignored. Parents may say that it is their responsibility to teach "functional" skills and that it is their wish that the school system teach their child academic skills to the extent possible. In cases of this type, consideration should certainly be given to their wishes, especially if the student does indeed demonstrate that many skills have been taught in the home by the parents.

After careful consideration of the above questions, the teacher, along with the parents and other members of the planning team, will likely choose one of four forms or types of academic curriculum for the student (Browder & Snell, 1993; Ford et al., 1989). These are:

1. the general education curriculum;
2. the general education curriculum adapted to focus on the most essential skills;
3. a sequenced functional skills curriculum;
4. an embedded functional skills curriculum.

These approaches and instructional methods in different areas of academic instruction are discussed in chapter 16. How assessments should be conducted within each area is explained below.

The general education curriculum is most likely to be appropriate for students with severe disabilities who are young and/or who have shown a history of success with academic skills. These students may be classified as having a moderate mental disability that may be accompanied by severe and/or multiple physical or sensory disabilities. Some students classified as being autistic may also benefit from the general education curriculum.

Assessment of students on general curriculum may be done using commercially produced tests that are appropriate for students with mild disabilities or for nondisabled students, such as the Peabody Individual Achievement Test-Revised (Markwardt, 1989), school district checklists of academic skills, or curriculum-based assessment using grade-level curriculum material (Deno, 1985).

For students with multiple sensory and/or physical disabilities, evaluation of academic skills may require adaptations to the normal procedures so that speaking and writing are not required. In cooperation with specialists in communication disorders, physical disabilities, and sensory disabilities, the teacher may modify these tests to allow the student to respond to multiple choice items by pointing to the correct response in an array of options; by using eye glances to indicate his or her response; by matching objects and symbols; or by signaling yes and no (perhaps with eye blinks or other facial expressions). Using such adaptations of standard procedures will require several test sessions to complete the assessment. There will also be concern about the test maintaining its validity when nonstandard procedures are used in its administration. For more details, see Carpignano and Bigge (1991).

Some students with severe disabilities will work on academic skills by pursuing objectives in the general education curriculum with adaptations to focus on the most essential skills. According to Ford et al. (1989), such modifications in the curriculum would allow the teacher to focus on parts of the curriculum that are more essential and applicable to everyday life. It would be expected that the student could achieve about a 2nd-grade reading level, which would allow for both functional reading and pleasure reading. The student would also have functional mathematics computational skills and be able to learn to use time skills to read schedules, use a calendar, and tell time from a clock face or a digital clock or watch. Students who do not appear to be making adequate progress in the general curriculum may be appropriate candidates for the adapted curriculum.

A *sequenced functional skills curriculum* calls for an instructional emphasis that helps the student acquire academic skills that will have a direct bearing on life's daily needs. As Ford et al. (1989) ask: "If a student . . . could learn to handle money, manage time, and read and write some of the words that are encountered in everyday life, would that not be a more desirable outcome than his or her having acquired a few rudimentary math and reading skills that were never developed to a point of becoming useful?" (pp. 90-91) A decision is made to pursue this curriculum when too much time would have to be spent on academic skills that would not lead to a degree of usefulness. Students who developed skills at this level could read functional words and phrases such as those found in recipes and menus, could write short notes and lists, could use numberlines and calculators to shop for items, and could understand time from clocks and watches. Instruction of these skills occurs in the classroom during normal periods of reading, writing, and math. The skills learned are then practiced in applied settings outside of the classroom.

Ford et al. (1989) have provided a series of inventories for use in determining key skills appropriate for students to learn at this curricular level. Similar information could be gathered from ecological inventories with a particular focus on the academic skills that appear in them.

The fourth level of academic instruction is an *embedded functional skills curriculum.* For these skills, no time is spent in the classroom on direct instruction. Instead, instruction occurs when the skills are needed naturally during other activities—it is embedded within the instruction in other areas. Students may interpret the meaning of words, pictures, or line drawings as they occur in various contexts; they may enjoy looking at pictures and drawings; they can pay for objects by matching coins to a money card or using a predetermined amount of money; and they may use picture symbols to follow schedules (Ford et al., 1989). Determining the academic skills to teach students at this curricular level is the same as stated above.

Conclusion

The assessment of persons with severe disabilities as described in this chapter provides a starting point for deciding what skills should be taught. The process does not end here, but is ongoing. Not only must the teacher continuously monitor the student's learning on specific objectives, she or he must also stay abreast of the environmental needs of the student.

As students get older, change schools, change interests, visit different places in their community, acquire new responsibilities, get new jobs, and so on, their learning needs change. The teacher must communicate with the student (when possible), with parents or caregivers, and with other team members to determine what the student should be learning at a given time.

The student's needs, having been determined through different forms of assessment, will ultimately be discussed and prioritized through the planning processes discussed in the previous chapter.

Questions for Reflection

1. What do you believe is the most important way for determining what students with severe disabilities need to learn?
2. In what ways might reviewing existing records be detrimental to assessment and planning procedures?
3. What do you believe would be the most useful type of information that parents could provide?
4. Do you believe that the norm-referenced status of a student based on an adaptive behavior scale is useful information? Why or why not?
5. With several fellow students or colleagues, review the curriculum/activity guides referenced in this chapter and discuss their strengths and weaknesses.
6. What are various ways to determine locations where ecological inventories should be conducted for students with severe disabilities of different ages (e.g., elementary school age, high school age, etc.)?
7. Direct observations of students during structured activities take up a great deal of time. In what ways might a teacher conduct such observations in the most efficient manner?
8. How could the expertise of different professionals be used during unstructured observations and observations during structured activities?

References

Browder, D. M. (1991). *Assessment of individuals with severe disabilities: An applied behavior approach to life skills assessment* (2nd ed.). Baltimore: Paul H. Brookes.

Browder, D. M., & Snell, M. E. (1993). Functional academics. In M. E. Snell (Ed.), *Instruction of students with severe disabilities* (3rd ed.) (pp. 442–479). New York: Macmillan.

Brown, L., Branston-McLean, M. B., Baumgart, D., Vincent, L., Falvey, M., & Schroeder, J. (1979). Using the characteristics of current and subsequent least restrictive environments as factors in the development of curricular content for severely handicapped students. *AAESPH Review, 4,* 407–424.

Bruininks, R. H., Woodcock, R. W., Weatherman, R. F., & Hill, B. K. (1985). *The scales of independent behavior.* Allen, TX: DLM Teaching Resources.

Carpignano, J., & Bigge, J. (1991). Assessment. In J. Bigge (Ed.), *Teaching individuals with physical and multiple disabilities* (pp. 280–326). New York: Merrill/Macmillan.

Cone, J. D. (1984). *The pyramid scales.* Austin, TX: PRO-ED.

Cone, J. D. (1987). Intervention planning using adaptive behavior instruments. *Journal of Special Education, 21*(1), 127–148.

Deno, S. (1985). Curriculum-based measurement: The emerging alternative. *Exceptional Children, 52,* 219–232.

Dever, R. B. (1988). *Community living skills: A taxonomy.* Washington, DC: American Association on Mental Retardation.

Ford, A., Schnorr, R., Meyer, L., Davern, L., Black, J., & Dempsey, P. (Eds.) (1989). *The Syracuse community-referenced curriculum guide for students with moderate and severe disabilities.* Baltimore: Paul H. Brookes.

Giangreco, M. F., Cloninger, C. J., & Iverson, V. S. (1993). *Choosing options and accommodations for children: A guide to planning inclusive education.* Baltimore: Paul H. Brookes.

Lehr, D. H. (1989). Educational programming for young children with the most severe disabilities. In F. Brown & D. H. Lehr (Eds.), *Persons with profound disabilities: Issues and practices* (pp. 213–237). Baltimore: Paul H. Brookes.

Leland, H. (1991). Adaptive behavior scales. In J. L. Matson & J. A. Mulick (Eds.), *Handbook of mental retardation* (2nd ed.) (pp. 211–221). New York: Pergamon Press.

Markwardt, F. C. (1989). *Peabody individual achievement test—revised.* Circle Pines, MN: American Guidance Service.

Neel, R. S., & Billingsley, F. F. (1989). *IMPACT: A functional curriculum handbook for students with moderate to severe disabilities.* Baltimore: Paul H. Brookes.

Nihira, K., Foster, R., Shellhaas, M., & Leland, H. (1974). *AAMD adaptive behavior scale.* Washington, DC: American Association on Mental Deficiency.

Noonan, M. J., & Siegel-Causey, E. (1990). Special needs of students with severe handicaps. In L. McCormick & R. Schiefelbusch (Eds.), *Early language intervention: An introduction* (pp. 383–425). New York: Merrill/Macmillan.

Rainforth, B., Giangreco, M., & Dennis, R. (1989). Motor skills. In A. Ford, R. Schnorr, L. Meyer, L. Davern, J. Black, & P. Dempsey (Eds.), *The Syracuse community-referenced curriculum guide for students with moderate and severe disabilities* (pp. 211–230). Baltimore: Paul H. Brookes.

Rainforth, B., York, J., & Macdonald, C. (1992). *Collaborative teams for students with severe disabilities: Integrating therapy and educational services.* Baltimore: Paul H. Brookes.

Rynders, J. E., & Horrobin, J. M. (1990). Always trainable? Never educable? Updating educational expectations concerning children with Down syndrome. *American Journal on Mental Retardation, 95,* 77–83.

Sparrow, S. S., Balla, D. A., & Cicchetti, D. V. (1984). *Vineland adaptive behavior scales.* Circle Pines, MN: American Guidance Service.

Westling, D. L., & Koorland, M. A. (1988). *The special educator's handbook.* Boston: Allyn & Bacon.

Wilcox, B., & Bellamy, T. G. (1987). *The activities catalog: An alternative curriculum for youth and adults with severe disabilities.* Baltimore: Paul H. Brookes.

PART III

General Instructional Procedures

CHAPTER 6 Teaching Students to Acquire New Skills
CHAPTER 7 Teaching Skills for Maintenance and Generalization
CHAPTER 8 Monitoring and Evaluating Student Progress
CHAPTER 9 Creating Inclusive Educational Environments

CHAPTER 6

Teaching Students to Acquire New Skills

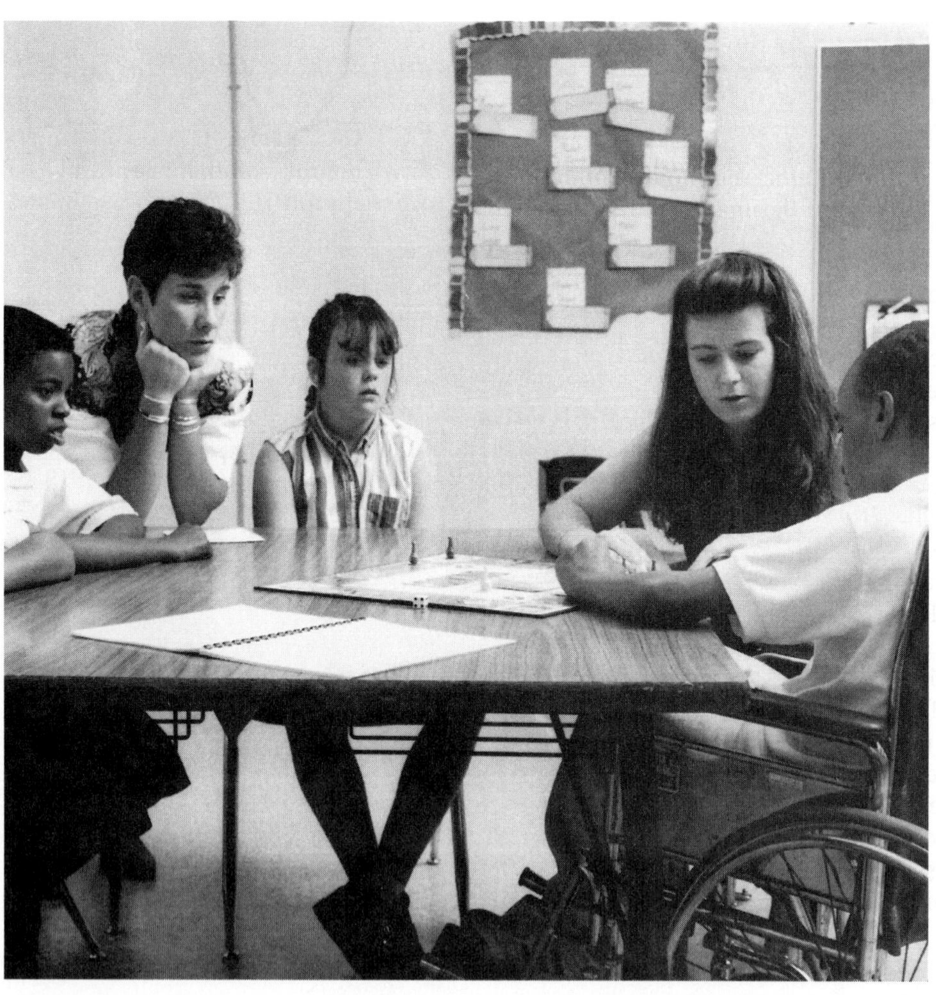

Chapter Overview

Instructional procedures for teaching students with severe disabilities to learn new skills are discussed in this chapter. The chapter begins with a brief overview of appropriate general instructional strategies, then continues with specific procedures to be used for skill acquisition methods, including prompting methods, stimulus modifications, using natural cues, and reinforcement and error correction procedures.

Effective instruction of students with severe disabilities requires using strategies and tactics that will result in students learning new behaviors or skills. The teacher of students with severe disabilities, whether that person is a special educator or a general educator, must use both sound general teaching strategies and effective specific instructional tactics if students with severe disabilities are to have successful learning experiences. The planning and assessment procedures explained in previous chapters should lead parents, teachers, and other members of the collaborative team to arrive at a minimum set of objectives for the student. These will be the primary targets for instruction. Additionally, of course, instruction on nontargeted objectives may occur (Giangreco, Cloninger, & Iverson, 1993).

This chapter begins with a brief overview of developing instructional or behavioral objectives, followed by a discussion of appropriate general teaching practices. Next, a paradigm for understanding the process for learning is presented to provide a context for the major section of the chapter, where specific tactics are presented for teaching students with severe disabilities how to learn new skills. The chapter concludes with a format for writing instructional plans for specific objectives. In the two chapters that follow, ways to achieve skill maintenance and generalization are explained (chapter 7) and procedures for continuously monitoring learning of students with severe disabilities are discussed (chapter 8).

Types of Objectives to Teach

The objectives that will be written and taught are usually those that students were unable to demonstrate adequately during the baseline period in structured activities or that appeared to be important based on other types of assessment information. Most importantly, all team members must agree on the objectives that are to be prioritized for instruction. The format for writing behavioral objectives was presented in chapter 4 when writing IEPs was discussed. In addition, you will recall from chapter 5 that four types or categories of behaviors are appropriate for assessment and instruction: *simple-discrete behaviors, continuous-ongoing behaviors, complex-chained skills,* and *functional routines.* Depending on the student's needs and abilities, objectives may be written to teach one or more of these types. If necessary, you should review the structure of these behavioral objective forms as discussed in chapter 5. The following are some examples:

- Jesus will shake his head up and down to indicate when he wants an offered item or activity 90% of the time that something is offered. He will do this throughout the school day in different locations with different people for 5 continuous days (Simple-discrete behavior)
- Sara will take an item in her hand when it is offered to her 80% of the time for 3 consecutive days. (Simple-discrete behavior)
- Joan will hold her head erect for 5 minutes when engaged in cooperative learning activities with her fellow 4th graders. This will occur in her regular classroom throughout the semester. (Continuous-ongoing behavior)
- Huan will remain actively involved in physical education exercises for 20 minutes after the exercises begin every day during PE class. (Continuous-ongoing behavior)
- Mac will play the pinball machine at the recreation center, completing all of the necessary steps until the game has been completed 2 days a week after school. (Complex-chained skill)
- Rhonda will fold all of the laundry after it has been taken out of the dryer both in her training apartment and at home when requested by her father or mother. (Complex-chained skill)
- Alexis will complete all necessary bathroom activities after appropriately using the toilet, including pulling up pants, flushing the toilet, and washing and drying hands. He will do this in any location where he must use the bathroom. (Functional routine)
- When Jeff is hungry after school, he will prepare an appropriate snack, eat it, and clean up after he has finished. (Functional routine)

As you read each of the above objectives, notice that each states who the learner is and what he or she is expected to be able to do, under what conditions, and how often. All objectives should include these dimensions. In some cases it is also important to add a time dimension stating how long the behavior should occur or how quickly.

Of course, these characteristics do not tell what is an appropriate objective and what is not. That decision must occur as part of the assessment and planning processes. As part of this process, when parents and professionals are considering the importance of objectives, they should try to answer the following questions:

- Is the skill functional in that it will allow the student to have more independence, less dependence, greater participation, or a better quality of life?
- Is the skill appropriate for the chronological age of the individual?
- Is the skill something that the student will use in his or her present living condition or in the near future?
- Is the skill something that will help the student be better accepted by others?
- Will the skill allow the individual to live and participate in more life environments?
- Is the skill considered important by the individual with severe disabilities and by those close to the person?

Answers to such questions as these will help parents and the rest of the team decide which objectives are most important. Other considerations about writing behavioral objectives are discussed below.

Function over Form

For many objectives, if not for all, more concern should be placed on the student's learning well enough to achieve a critical effect instead of demonstrating a behavior in a way that is typical for people without disabilities. In other words, function is more important than form. This is especially important in complex-chained objectives or functional routines in which there are multiple steps necessary for achieving the objective. Brown, Evans, Weed, & Owen (1987) made a distinction between "fixed" and "substitutable" routines and the specific behaviors that comprise them. Although some skills, such as "brushing teeth," require certain very specific behaviors to occur (although not necessarily in a particular order), other skills may have different forms and yet achieve the same *function*. For example, "spending leisure time with a friend" may have the form of listening to CDs together, walking in the park, playing cards, or hanging out at the recreational center. Each will achieve the same function, but each will take a different form. An important implication is that it is possible in some cases to achieve the *critical effect* of a function without engaging in specific behaviors.

Extending the Objective

Although behavioral objectives represent the most critical learning targets for students, they should not be limited or taught in an isolated fashion. Instead, "extension" activities can be added, particularly to task-analyzed behaviors or skills (Brown et al., 1987). Extension activities such as *initiating* the activity, *preparing* for the activity, *monitoring the quality* of one's performance, *monitoring the tempo* of performance, *problem solving* if necessary, and *terminating the activity* when appropriate may be applied to extend different core skills. Additionally, during many activities it is possible for the student to work on "enrichment" skills that may not be directly related to the task. These could include skills in communication, social interaction, and expression of choice (Brown et al., 1987).

Partial Participation

In some cases it is appropriate for objectives to reflect a desire for a student to learn to partially participate in some activities (Baumgart et al., 1982; Ferguson & Baumgart, 1991). Simply because a student cannot learn to cook a meal, wash his or her face, or engage independently in activities in a community recreational center does not mean that he or she cannot participate in some part of the activity or participate using a form different from the form others use. By employing even simple discrete behaviors such as reaching, touching, holding, or looking, the student may participate in a wide variety of activities. Suppose, for example, that a group of 3rd-grade students is making a cake as part of a lesson on foods. Each student may have a particular assignment he or she must perform. If a child has a severe disability it may be difficult for him or her to perform the activities that the other children are doing, but it may be possible to participate by holding a utensil or a bowl, pouring an ingredient, or pressing the switch on an electric mixer. The student may be able to make such actions alone or with the assistance of the teacher, the teacher's assistant, or another student. Regardless, this form of participation by the student can represent an important aspect of the educational experience and at the same time contribute to the group activity in a meaningful way.

Four strategies can assist teachers in making partial participation meaningful for students, especially for students with the most severe disabilities (Ferguson & Baumgart, 1991). First, the student should be engaged in an active manner rather than in a passive way. Even though a student may have a restricted repertoire of skills, objectives may be developed for those skills to be used in different ways. Second, the teacher must make sure that the type of participation, albeit partial, is responsive to a multiple- perspective view of the student's needs. The perspectives should be family- and community-based and related to the daily life of the student. Teachers should monitor the student's learning from the view of others by asking key people about how the student is performing in their view and whether or not his or her quality of life is being positively affected. Third, teachers should avoid "piecemeal" partial participation (i.e., the student is partially participating only some of the time) by devising daily schedules that continuously involve the student. Finally, the teacher or another person should always be as involved as necessary to ensure that participation occurs. In some cases, as discussed later in this chapter, it will be appropriate for the teacher to fade assistance, but this should not be done if it jeopardizes the student's opportunity to be involved.

Good General Teaching Practices

There are teaching strategies that should be used regardless of whether or not students have disabilities, regardless of the instructional objectives, and regardless of particular characteristics or ages of students. The following are summarized from those suggested by the U.S. Department of Education (1986) and Wolery, Ault, and Doyle (1992).

- *Manage instructional time efficiently.* The more time a student spends participating in instructional activities, the more he or she is likely to learn. Teachers, therapists, and aides must coordinate their time in order to maximize students' learning time. Daily activities should be planned in advance so that every minute is used in the most productive way.
- *Manage student behavior effectively.* Teachers should develop simple rules and reinforce students for appropriate behavior. Students should learn that they must participate in learning activities and not behave in ways that are socially unacceptable.
- *Carefully present instructional stimuli and procedures.* Teachers must give clear directions and other forms of input, review previously learned skills, keep instruction occurring at a steady pace, and make smooth transitions from one activity to another.
- *Provide frequent feedback to the student.* Performance will improve if the student knows if he or she is performing a task correctly; the teacher needs to provide reinforcement for correct responses and correct those responses that are incorrect.
- *Monitor students' performance.* Teachers must have a system that allows them to track the performance of students on the objectives they should be working toward achieving. When a student is not making satisfactory progress, a change is needed in the objective or in the instructional method being used.
- *Have appropriately high expectations for students.* What teachers believe about students' learning ability can have a bearing on how much or how little students can learn. It is sometimes assumed that when a student has a severe disability many skills cannot be learned. Although some limitations exist, a positive attitude toward students' learning ability may increase what is actually learned.

These approaches to daily instruction will increase the productivity of the teacher's teaching and the students' learning. However, specific forms of instruction have been found to be useful for students with severe disabilities. Before examining them, however, a general paradigm for learning should be considered in order to provide a context for the specific tactics that will be discussed.

How Behaviors and Skills Are Learned

Over the years many theories and concepts have been developed to explain learning: what it is, how it occurs, how it is impaired, and conditions that are associated with it (Ellis, 1963, 1979; Mercer & Snell, 1977). All of these theories cannot be discussed at this time. However, when we consider learning specific skills by persons with severe disabilities, it may be most useful to do so within the paradigm of *operant learning* (Wolery et al., 1992).

Operant learning considers behavior to occur primarily as a function of the external environment. Particular behaviors, whether they are motoric or verbal, simple or complex, occur because of a history of reinforcement. That is, the behavior has occurred and has been followed by a positive consequence, resulting in an increase in the probability that the behavior will occur again in the future (Alberto & Troutman, 1990; Sailor & Guess, 1983). This condition is depicted by the following formula:

> Behavior + Consequence (positive) = High probability of future occurrence

An example might be greeting people by saying hello, because just about every time we say hello to someone, it is positively reinforced by that person saying hello to us. If there were not such a response, there would be a lower probability that we would say hello in the future. Virtually any behavior that exists in an individual's behavioral repertoire has been reinforced on several occasions. (The exception to this is physiologically based behavior such as a seizure.)

But it is also obvious that not only do previously reinforced behaviors occur with regular frequency, but they usually occur under certain conditions and not others. These conditions are in existence prior to or at the time of the behavior and are therefore called *behavioral antecedents.* Since they tend to trigger or prompt certain behaviors and not others, they are also referred to as *discriminative stimuli.* The addition of this component to the behavioral formula changes it to the following:

> Antecedent (discriminative stimuli) + Behavior + Consequence = High probability of future occurrence when antecedent is present

This suggests that a particular behavior is more likely to occur when the corresponding antecedent (discriminative stimuli) is present and when there is a positive consequence that follows the behavior. Extending the example used above illustrates this condition.

The greetings we usually extend are to particular people we know or occur in certain situations when greetings are appropriate. For example, if we are walking down the street and we see someone we know, we will probably say hello. Or if we walk into a clothing store and see a salesperson, again it is likely that we will say hello. Under both circumstances the behavior is appropriate and most often will be reinforced with a response from the other person. In contrast, if we are walking down a busy avenue we are not likely to greet everyone we see. Essentially we *discriminate* the conditions under which certain behaviors should occur and those that indicate that behaviors should not occur. We learn to make these discriminations based on experiences that teach us the relationship between antecedents, behaviors, and consequences.

But what is the origin of a new behavior or new skill? If we stop to think about all that we know and know how to do—daily living skills, socially interacting with others, communicating, performing academic exercises, and so on—we realize that, despite the presence of a broad skill repertoire, at some earlier time in life these did not exist.

Normally individuals learn their many skills in several ways. One way is through the *differential reinforcement* of existing behaviors only when they occur under certain environmental circumstances. At the outset, these behaviors may not have any intention or purpose, but when they occur in certain contexts and are reinforced in those contexts, they become "learned" behaviors, that is, they become controlled or influenced by certain stimuli. Take, for example, the infant who randomly says "dada." This behavior occurs initially without any particular intention. However, the parents will generally reinforce the behavior only when it is appropriate, for example, when daddy is present, or is expected, or is wanted, and so forth. On the other hand, when it is not appropriate for the situation, the parent(s) will say "No, that's not daddy." Sooner or later the child will learn to say "dada" under the appropriate circumstances. When a behavior is appropriately influenced by environmental conditions, both antecedents and reinforcers, *stimulus control* has been established and the behavior has been learned.

Another way in which initial learning generally occurs is through the observation and imitation of others. The ability to follow a model is very important for learning verbal skills, social skills, and many other things. The learner attends to what another is doing, imitates it under a similar circumstance, is reinforced, and ultimately demonstrates the behavior or skill after the model is no longer there. Since reinforcement has occurred in the presence of certain stimuli, these stimuli take over as the environmental elements that influence the subsequent occurrence of the behavior. Learning through imitation is critical to early learning but also continues throughout life. Future teachers, for example, learn many of their teaching behaviors by observing and imitating the teaching of veteran teachers.

People can also develop new skills by being verbally directed to perform the skills. Appropriate directions tell what to do, when to do it, and/or how to do it. Sometimes the verbal directions may also tell why. If a skill has not been learned (for example, how to solve an algebra problem), the verbal direction must tell the student first to "solve the problem," then explain how the problem-solving behavior is to occur, that is, how the student should respond given the elements of the problem. The ability to acquire skills from others through the use of language is, of course, what makes humankind such a remarkable and accomplished species. When we broaden this form of input to include written language as well as spoken language, we have indeed an extremely broad mechanism for people to learn new skills and behaviors. Of course, after acquisition of these skills, the same antecedent-behavior-consequence paradigm maintains the subsequent occurrence and continuation of the behaviors.

Finally, some new skills may be learned through direct physical contact and guidance. Young children learning to use a knife to cut up their own food may need to have someone guide their hand, directing them through a slicing motion. As the child becomes a little more skillful, verbal directions may be sufficient, for example, "Turn the knife over and slice back and forth. Press down hard." A person learning to skate is another case in which direct physical contact may be necessary during the initial stage of skill acquisition, and this guidance may occur until the person learns to skate appropriately. Again, however, once the skill has been learned, it will occur when other stimuli are present—uncut food, a skating rink, and so forth.

As people grow older, they usually develop an adequate ability to learn new skills through verbal input (either oral or written) and/or modeling and rely less and less on physical contact to guide them through a specific movement. However, there are some circumstances when some form of physical contact may help in the initial learning process, especially when the behavior being learned is physical. For example, a coach might tell or show a new football player how to block, but might also need to physically position the player to get the best performance. In most situations, however, most persons can learn most skills by watching them occur and/or receiving verbal directions.

Instructional Tactics for Teaching New Skills to Students with Severe Disabilities

The operant paradigm provides a functional model in which to develop instructional practices for teaching new skills to individuals with severe disabilities. Various antecedents will provide cues or prompts for behaviors to be learned, and positive reinforcement will consequate the behaviors. As the behavior develops, the instructional plan will be to move away from obtrusive and artificial stimuli as much as possible and toward maintenance of the behavior by natural stimuli. Numerous instructional strategies and tactics can be used to take an individual from a level of not being able to perform a specific act or skill to being able to do so with some degree of independence. The facility with which the student learns will depend on both the learning ability of the student and the teaching ability of the teacher. Clearly, as discussed in chapter 1, students who have severe disabilities will not be able to learn as efficiently as students who do not have disabilities or those who have relatively mild disabilities. Nevertheless, all students are capable of learning and at least part of their success depends on how well they are taught. Instructional tactics that lead toward success are discussed in the following sections.

Instructional Prompts

Several prompting tactics are useful for teaching students new behaviors. Prompts may be defined as "any teacher behaviors that cause students to know how to do a behavior correctly. In a more precise sense, response prompts are teacher behaviors presented to increase the probability of correct responding" (Wolery et al., 1992, p. 37). In reference to the operant paradigm, the difficulty in learning experienced by a student with a severe disability may be considered a low probability of attending to a particular stimulus (or a group of stimuli), responding in a normally acceptable manner, and being reinforced in the normal fashion. Response prompting is intended to assist the student in making the correct response in the presence of a particular discriminative stimulus so that reinforcement can occur. There are several forms of prompts that may be used. Again, however, it should be kept in mind that these prompts are intended to assist the student in initially acquiring a behavior; they should give way to less intrusive or more natural stimuli as learning improves over time.

Gestural Prompts Some behaviors may be prompted with hand motions, pointing, head nodding, or other nonverbal prompts that are intended to provide a supplemental cue to a student so that he or she will perform a behavior that is appropriate for a particular situation and normally prompted by a natural cue in that situation. A student learning to bus tables in a restaurant who does not notice a table that needs to be cleared could be prompted by a job coach using a slight nod of the head. Normally the cluttered table would serve as a natural stimulus, but in this case the additional prompt may be required to get the student to act. Similarly, a student who has removed his coat but does not know where it should be placed could be easily prompted by a gesture to hang the coat on a hook.

Gestures are events that commonly occur among people without disabilities. For this reason, using a gesture as a prompt is a tactic that a teacher can do easily and in a natural fashion. If gestures are used as behavioral prompts, however, the teacher must be aware of their limitations. A gesture may not work; it may not exert sufficient stimulus control over the student to initiate the desired behavior. This would suggest that a more direct form of prompting should be used. Another problem, one that is exactly opposite, is that the gesture may exert too much control. When this occurs, the student may become overly reliant on the artificial cue and respond appropriately only after seeing the teacher give the gestural prompt instead of responding to the natural cue. Of course, because this type of prompt dependency may occur for other types of prompts as well, teachers must attempt to eliminate all artificial prompts through systematic instructional procedures.

Verbal Prompts The use of a specific verbal statement that tells a student what to do and how to do it (as opposed to simply telling a student to do something) is a verbal prompt. If, for example, a student is learning to play checkers, the person teaching him or her might say, "When my piece is right next to yours like that, you need to jump it. Go ahead and jump my piece now." It is important to note that verbal prompts are specific to the performance of particular behaviors. A verbal statement that is more general, like "let's play checkers," would be considered a suggestion or direction, but not a verbal prompt.

Wolery et al. (1992) point out that there are five types of verbal prompts: those that tell how to do a behavior; those that tell how to do part of a behavior; those that give a rule to follow; those that give a hint; and those that provide options. When a verbal prompt is given, it must be clear, as natural as possible, and effective (i.e., the student must be able to respond correctly to the prompt). It is understandable that some students with severe disabilities may not have acquired a level of receptive language sufficient to allow them to respond to a verbal prompt. In such cases, the teacher must use other forms of prompts along with the verbal prompt until the student can respond to the verbal prompt.

Pictorial (Two-Dimensional) Prompts In some situations, students may be prompted to perform a particular behavior through the use of pictures or other two-dimensional stimuli (e.g., words, symbols, signs, and so forth). Depending on the situation in which these visual prompts may be required, they may be formatted or arranged in different ways. One example would be to provide a picture or drawing of a clock with the clock hands arranged to indicate a particular time. Attached to the clock picture would be a picture showing individuals engaging in a certain activity appropriate for the time shown on the clock, for example, relaxing at break time. The picture prompt could be located at or near the work site so the student could use it as a reminder that when the wall clock looked like the clock in the picture, it would be time to take a break. Another example is the use of picture recipe books for a person learning to cook.

These books would display photographs or line drawings in a sequence showing how to prepare a particular food item.

Pictorial prompts have advantages and disadvantages. They have the potential for being used without the intervention of another person. In some cases they can be used in a very unobtrusive fashion and can be made available to the student in ways that only he or she needs to be aware of. However, the student must initially learn to attend to the two-dimensional prompt when it is appropriate to do so and remember to attend when necessary; otherwise picture prompts will not serve adequately as stimuli. Finally, of course, the student must be able to "interpret" the prompt. In other words, the visual images that are presented must not be of a level of complexity that is too difficult for the student to respond to appropriately.

Model Prompts As discussed earlier, imitation is a natural form of learning, and some behaviors that need to be learned may be prompted by an instructor's modeling or demonstration of the behavior. A teacher attempting to teach a 5-year-old how to put on a coat might do so by demonstrating how to do it as the child watches. Of course, because the prerequisite to modeling is attending, the teacher would have to be certain that the child is looking or "paying attention." In addition to visual models, verbal models may also be used and are particularly useful in teaching speech and language skills.

Model prompts alone may not be effective for some students with severe disabilities who do not readily imitate the actions of others. In such cases, model behavior may be combined with other forms of prompts to cue the occurrence of a behavior.

Partial and Full Physical Prompts If a student does not respond with the appropriate physical movement called for by a natural stimulus (e.g., the student is thirsty, there is a glass of

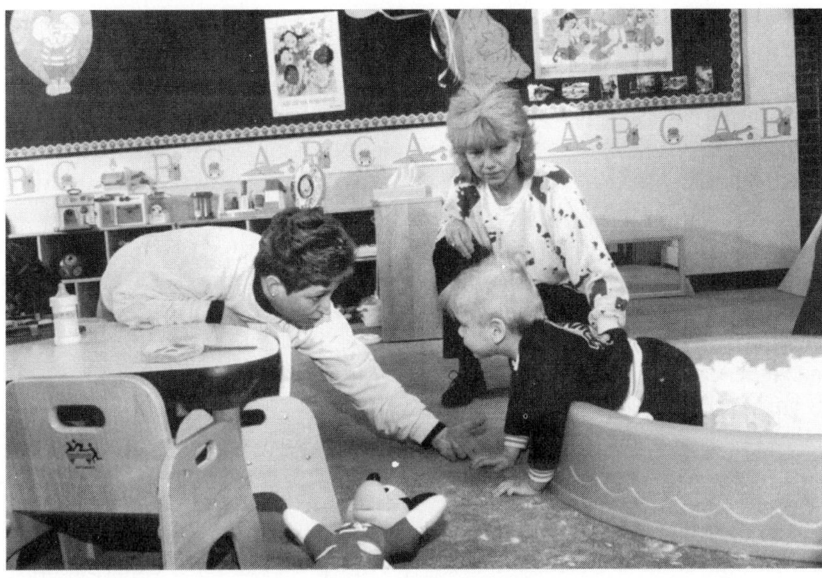

Physical prompts assist the student with severe disabilities to perform and practice new skills.

water on the table, the student does not lift the glass and take a drink of water) or does not respond when other prompting techniques are used, physical prompts may be used to teach that student how to respond. These prompts may be partial or full.

In the above example, a full physical response would require that the instructor place her or his hand over the student's hand and guide the student's hand to grasp the glass, pick it up, take a sip of water, and then return the glass to the table. Essentially, the use of the full prompt is the most intrusive and controlling prompt because the person providing the prompt is performing the behavior, not the student himself or herself. Generally, full physical prompts should be used only when it does not seem that the student will respond to less direct methods of prompting.

Like full physical prompts, partial physical prompts require the teacher to touch the student, but the touch may be a nudge, a tap, guidance partially through the movement, or contact on a part of the arm (the wrist, the forearm); it is less manipulative and less intrusive than guiding the hand. Sometimes full prompting is used until the student begins to show some volitional movement; then it is faded to partial physical prompts.

Full and partial physical prompts should always be paired with less intrusive prompt forms, particularly verbal or gestural prompts. When the physical prompts are gradually eliminated or faded, it may be necessary to continue to cue the behavior with the less intrusive prompts. The pairing technique may facilitate this because as the physical influence is diminished, the verbal or gestural prompt may gain stimulus control.

Mixed Prompts The various forms of prompts (e.g., verbal and physical, verbal and model) may be mixed or combined to better ensure the occurrence of a behavior. Combinations of prompts seem more natural and are often more effective. When using such combinations, however, teachers should remain cognizant of what types of prompts are being used so that they can fade components of the multiple prompts systematically.

Applying Prompts During Skill Acquisition Training

To the extent that it is possible, the ultimate goal of an instructor using any of the types of prompts described above is to eliminate the artificial, "teacher-made" prompts so that the student will respond to the natural environmental conditions (stimuli) by demonstrating the behavior or skill when it is typically required (Ford & Mirenda, 1984). Sometimes complete elimination of artificial prompts is possible; sometimes only partial elimination can be achieved. Nevertheless, prompt reduction is the goal, and there are several methods that can be used.

During the last several years researchers have developed and studied different ways students with severe disabilities can learn to acquire new skills through prompt reduction methods. These methods are designed to initially prompt behaviors but then to eliminate the prompts. Reviews and additional information about the tactics are available from several sources (Ault, Wolery, Doyle, & Gast, 1989; Billingsley & Romer, 1983; Demchak, 1990; Doyle, Wolery, Ault, & Gast, 1988; Schoen, 1986; Wolery, Ault, & Doyle, 1992; and Wolery & Gast, 1984). As will be seen in the explanations provided below, these tactics combine prompts in different arrangements in order to get behaviors and skills to occur independently.

Before considering these techniques, two important concepts must be understood: *target stimuli* and *controlling stimuli* (Wolery et al.,

1992). A target stimulus is the discriminative stimulus that is expected to ultimately control the occurrence of a behavior or group of behaviors after training has been completed. It may be a verbal direction or cue from an individual (e.g., "Put all your toys away"; "Set the table"), or it may be a natural environmental situation that normally cues the occurrence of behavior (e.g., walking across a street at an intersection when the signal says "walk"; smiling or waving at someone when he or she smiles or waves at you).

In many instructional practices with students with severe disabilities, teachers have identified verbal directions as the target stimulus. In other words, it has been their primary intention to teach the student to respond in a certain way when told what to do. While this is appropriate for some behavioral objectives, for many others it is better if the target stimulus is a natural aspect of the environment, one that would normally be a discriminative stimulus in the natural environment. Learning to respond appropriately to such a stimulus makes it possible for the student to ultimately function as normally and independently as possible in the natural environment, which often means doing what is appropriate without being told to do so. Therefore, whenever possible, teachers should identify the natural aspects of the environment that prompt behavior as the target stimuli to which they wish to have the student respond.

In contrast to the target stimulus, a controlling stimulus is one that will control a student's responsiveness to the target stimulus given the student's current skill or ability level. In other words, at the start of training the student may not have learned to respond to the target stimulus, so a controlling stimulus, one that the student *can* respond to, is used either simultaneously with the target stimulus or shortly after it in order to get the behavior to occur. For example, a student with a severe disability may not have learned to brush her hair when she looks in a mirror and sees that it is mussed (the natural target stimulus). However, when the teacher points to the hair and tells the student she needs to brush it while she is looking in the mirror, and she does so, then the verbal direction serves as a controlling stimulus. Ultimately, however, we want the reflection in the mirror (the target stimulus) to be sufficient to get the student to brush her hair.

Further examples of target stimuli and controlling stimuli are presented in the tactics described below. In each case, the goal is to ultimately eliminate the controlling stimulus so the target stimulus will have the desired effect.

Constant Time Delay The application of constant time delay calls for the presentation of a *task direction* (the target stimulus, a verbal or nonverbal environmental stimulus indicating what behavior is to occur), followed by a *delay period* of a few seconds, followed by an effective *controlling stimulus* that will have enough impact to result in the completion of the behavior by the learner. The controlling stimulus may be a verbal model, a gesture, a physical prompt, or any other appropriate prompt, but most important, it must have enough control over the student's behavior so that the behavior that was called for by the target stimulus (task direction) will occur when the controlling prompt is given (Snell & Gast, 1981). Usually, constant time delay is used to teach single, discrete behaviors such as saying the name of an object or pointing to an object.

If the target behavior does not occur within the allocated delay period following the target stimulus, the prompt, or controlling stimulus, is delivered by the teacher. After the prompt is given and the behavior occurs, the student is reinforced. When the behavior does occur during the delay period (i.e., the student performs the task during the delay period), the prompt is withheld and the student is reinforced immediately. This procedure allows the student to learn that the initial task direction is calling for a particular behavior to occur. Ultimately the student learns the relation between the initial direction (target stimulus), the behavior, and the reinforcement.

In order to facilitate the process, during initial trials (perhaps the first 5 or 10 times the target stimulus or task direction is given), there is a "no delay" period (zero-seconds delay) and the controlling stimulus is applied immediately following the direction. This is done so that a correct response may be virtually guaranteed during early learning. After these initial trials, the delay period (typically 4 or 5 seconds) is inserted between the direction and the prompt. When the task direction begins to appropriately control the behavior, there is no need for the subsequent prompt and it (the prompt) can be eliminated. Then the student will respond appropriately to the initial task direction or stimulus, which, of course, is the objective.

The initial task direction should be a direction or cue that would naturally be given to get the student to do what is desired. It may be verbal ("It's time to go, get your coat") or visual (the clock shows that it's 5 o'clock). The controlling stimulus prompt may be any of those that have been previously described. However, it must be controlling enough to assure that the behavior occurs. If a verbal prompt or a model is sufficient, such a prompt may be used, but if, for the particular behavior or skill being taught, the student will only respond to a more direct prompt, such as physical guidance, then this form of prompting must be used.

An example of using a constant time delay procedure is a teacher who wishes a student to ask for a particular item using verbal language. Initially the teacher presents the item (perhaps a toy or something to eat) by holding it out to the student and saying "Would you like to have the toy?" The target response for the student is "Toy, please." For the first 5 or 10 trials, after presenting the item and asking the question, the teacher immediately provides a verbal prompt or a model ("Say 'toy'" or simply, "toy"), waits for the student's response, and reinforces the student when it occurs. Once the student is responding correctly and consistently under the zero-second delay period, the teacher moves to a four-second delay, inserting the interval between the first question (task direction) and the prompt. This gives the student time to respond appropriately before the prompt and be reinforced by receiving the toy.

In order for time delay to be effective, the student must be able to wait for the prompt if he or she does not know the correct response. In the above example, the student would need to have imitative ability. This is not always necessary; it simply depends on the type of response that is desired. Generally verbal responses require that the student be able to imitate the model. An alternative would be to teach the student to point to (or touch) the desired item following a direction to "Show me what you want." Since the desired response in this case is physical, the teacher could use full or partial physical guidance or a physical model instead of a verbal model. In all other ways the procedure remains the same, that is, after correct responding occurs through the use of no time delay, the fixed time interval is inserted between the direction and the prompt. Again, when the behavior occurs during the interval, there is no need to provide the prompt and the student is reinforced. The prompt is used when the behavior does not occur or occurs incorrectly.

Progressive Time Delay Progressive time delay is very similar to constant time delay, but it may be more effective for students with severe disabilities (Wolery et al., 1992). The only difference between constant and progressive time delay is that the progressive procedure gradually increases the delay period between the initial task direction and the prompt. Instead of going immediately from a zero-second time delay to a 4- or 5-second delay period, as in constant time delay, the progressive procedure requires that the instructor follow the zero-second trials by introducing several 1-second trials, followed by several 2-second trials, then 3-second trials, 4-second trials, and so forth. Because the delay period is gradually increased, it is more likely that the student will not be "lost" between the initial task direction and the controlling prompt.

Except for the variation of the time interval between the task direction and the prompt, the progressive time delay procedure is just like the constant time delay procedure—the most important ingredient is that the controlling stimulus must be effective enough to influence the student to perform the behavior if he or she does not do so within the allowed number of seconds following the initial direction. When increasing the number of seconds of delay, care should be taken to make the increases gradually. Although there is no hard rule governing the amount of time by which to increase the delay period, usually 1- or 2-second increments are appropriate. Increases in the delay intervals may occur after each session of instruction, after a certain number of trials, or after a certain number of trials in which correct responses occur.

The number of increased intervals is also somewhat arbitrary ("Should I increase up to 4 seconds?" "Up to 6 seconds?" "To 8 seconds?"). Again, there is no rule to determine this. The teacher must judge the task to be learned and the student who is learning the task to decide on the maximum amount of delay time that would be acceptable in an environment in which the behavior normally occurs. If, for example, the situation called for a student to look at the price on a grocery item and enter that amount into a hand-held calculator, the teacher would have to ask "How much time is sufficient from when the student sees the price and when it is punched into the calculator?" If the teacher decides that the response should occur within 5 seconds, then the final amount of wait time would be 5 seconds. In the trials leading up to that time the teacher would allow for perhaps 10 trials of zero time delay, 10 for 1-second delay, 10 for 2-second delay, and so on. If the target behavior did not occur before the wait time was over, the teacher would prompt the student to respond, using a prompt such as "When you see the price, you need to punch it in on the calculator. Do it now."

System of Least Prompts Both constant time delay and progressive time delay are based on the premise that the behavior will occur following a particular target stimulus or task direction; if it does not occur within the allowed period of time, then it will be prompted, using a single prompt that is virtually guaranteed, that is, a controlling stimulus. The system of least prompts (or least-to-most prompting) also uses a brief waiting period following the initial stimulus, but then provides the student with a hierarchy of prompts that move progressively from having a minimal influence to having a maximum, controlling influence (a controlling stimulus). The intention is to provide a prompt on each trial with only the minimum intensity necessary to get the behavior to occur. This skill acquisition training system is one of the most commonly used for teaching individuals with severe disabilities and, in contrast to time delay, has been used more often to teach chained tasks (task- analyzed skills) than discrete behaviors (Doyle et al., 1988). As the teacher moves from one step to the next in a task analysis or functional routine, she or he presents the target stimulus, and if no response occurs, the next stimulus, and then the next, until finally a controlling stimulus is used if necessary. Having completed that step, the teacher moves on to the next step in the chain and repeats the hierarchical process. This continues until instructions have been provided for all steps (whole task instruction). The following example demonstrates how the system of least prompts is applied to teach a complex, chained task.

Suppose a teacher wants to teach a student to use a drip coffee maker to make coffee. The teacher begins by conducting a task analysis of the coffee-making process such as the following:

1. Remove the container of coffee from the cupboard.
2. Remove the coffee filters from the cupboard.
3. Plug in the coffee maker.
4. Remove the filter tray from the coffee maker.
5. Place a coffee filter in the filter tray.
6. Place 3 scoops of coffee from the container into the filter in the filter tray.
7. Return the filter tray to the coffee maker.
8. Fill the water container with 8 cups of water.
9. Pour the water into the opening in the coffee maker.
10. Turn on the switch.
11. Return the material to the cupboard.

Following this, the teacher determines a least-to-most hierarchy of prompts. In this case, the teacher uses the following:

1. No prompt (completion of prior step is to serve as the cue to do the next step).
2. Verbal direction (will tell the student what to do).
3. Partial physical prompt (will nudge the student's hand in the direction of the action that should occur).
4. Full physical assistance (will fully guide the student through the behavior that is to occur).

The teacher begins instruction at a time that is appropriate for making coffee and in a location where coffee-making should occur, let's say in the home ec room. The teacher might say something like "Why don't you make some coffee for us?" and then wait for the student to start making the coffee. (This would be a natural cue to start the process.) From this point the teacher observes, prompts, and reinforces as appropriate and necessary.

If the student does not begin to remove the coffee container from the cupboard within an allotted period of time (for example, 4 seconds), the teacher gives the verbal prompt appropriate for the step in the task analysis, such as "Get the coffee." If the student does not respond, the teacher repeats the verbal direction and simultaneously provides a partial physical prompt by moving the student's hand toward the coffee. Finally, if necessary, the teacher repeats the verbal direction and fully guides the student through the step in the task analysis. For each step in the task analysis, the teacher proceeds in the same fashion, progressing through the prompt hierarchy only to the extent necessary for the student to complete the step. Once the student has successfully completed a step, regardless of the prompt required to do so, the teacher provides reinforcement.

An important consideration is what specific prompts should be in the hierarchy and how many there should be. The prompts to be used are determined by the teacher. They should be natural for the situation, with each prompt being a little more intrusive than the preceding one. The final prompt must be as direct and intrusive as necessary to get the behavior to occur. Often this is full physical assistance but it does not have to be if the teacher knows from experience that the student will respond consistently to another prompt form such as a model or a clear verbal direction. The types of prompts that may be used in the hierarchy will be those described earlier, including:

- Gestural prompts (e.g., pointing)
- Verbal prompts (e.g., "put your toys away")
- Pictorial prompts (e.g., written or drawn directions)
- Model prompts (e.g., demonstrating how to tie a shoe)
- Partial physical prompts
- Full physical prompts

Different types of prompts might be included in the hierarchy or the same type of prompt. Table 6–1 displays possible combinations of prompt types. Usually no more than three or four prompts will be used in the sequence in addition to the target stimulus.

At each level of prompt, the target stimulus must be repeated to allow the student to learn the association between the stimulus and the prompt. In situations such as the coffee-making example, the completion of the previous step in the task should serve as the stimulus for the next step to occur and thus it would always be present. Beyond this stimulus, however, the teacher could include the verbal prompt alone and then at each of the subsequent prompt levels (partial and full physical assistance). Ultimately, however, the teacher would want the student to complete each step without the verbal or the physical prompts.

When using the system of least prompts (or other behavior acquisition methods) to teach chains of behaviors, it is preferred to teach the whole task at each teaching opportunity. In past experiments, researchers have taught single steps in the task analysis (using backward or forward chaining) and as each was learned, additional steps were added. However, whole-task teaching has generally been shown to be more effective and is a more natural teaching

Table 6–1
Combinations of Prompt Types at Levels in the System of Least Prompts Hierarchy

Level	Different Type Each Level	Multiple Types Each Level	Single Type Each Level
1	Target stimulus	Target stimulus	Target stimulus
2	Target stimulus + Verbal prompt	Target stimulus + Verbal prompt + Gestural prompt	Target stimulus + Physical prompt at shoulder
3	Target stimulus + Model prompt	Target stimulus + Verbal prompt + Model prompt	Target stimulus + Physical prompt at wrist
4	Target stimulus + Physical prompt	Target stimulus + Verbal prompt + Model prompt + Physical prompt	Target stimulus + Physical prompt hand on hand

From *Teaching Students with Moderate to Severe Disabilities: Use of Response Prompting Strategies* (p. 101) by W. Wolery, M. J. Ault, & P. M. Doyle, 1992, New York: Longman Publishers USA. Used with permission.

approach (Kayser, Billingsley, & Neel, 1986; Zane, Walls, & Thvedt, 1981). Of course, learning occurs more rapidly if there are more opportunities for learning. In the above example, the student might be given the opportunity to make coffee twice a day instead of just once.

Most-to-Least Prompts The most-to-least prompting system, which is essentially the opposite of the system of least prompts, is another tactic that may be used to establish new behaviors. Also known as the "decreasing assistance" procedure, this tactic calls for the teacher to begin teaching a new behavior by simultaneously providing both a target stimulus and a controlling prompt on the first set of trials. (This is the same as the time delay procedure when there is a zero-second delay.) When the student has experienced the behavior after being exposed to the stimulus and the controlling level of prompting, subsequent prompts with lesser degrees of control or intrusiveness are used. As the influence of the controlling prompt is gradually lessened over subsequent trials, the target stimulus increases its controlling effect. The advantage of this instructional model is that it can eliminate most errors that tend to occur in the early learning trials. For this reason this instructional method is often used with individuals with very severe disabilities with the first prompt level being full physical assistance.

Use of the most-to-least model requires that the teacher establish a hierarchy of prompts, just as in the least-to-most procedure. However, instead of starting with the least intrusive prompt and going to the prompt ultimately required to cause the behavior to occur within a single trial, the teacher establishes a criterion for correct performance at each level of prompting (e.g., 80% correct for a certain number of trials). When that criterion is achieved, the teacher (at the following instructional session) moves to the next prompt on the hierarchy, one that is less intrusive than the previous one. This process continues until the student can complete the behavior given only the target stimulus and no additional prompt.

One potential disadvantage to the most-to-least model is that there is the possibility that the student may be learning faster than the prompting hierarchy requires and thus the teacher may be using a more intrusive prompt than is necessary. In order to resolve this problem, Wolery et al. (1992) suggested that periodic probes be provided to see if the student can perform the required task at less intrusive prompt levels or given only the initial direction or target stimulus. Probes are opportunities for the student to perform the skill given only the target stimulus and no other input from the instructor. A student who demonstrates the behavior or skill adequately under the probe condition, that is, to the level of satisfaction specified in the instructional or behavioral objective, would not need further instruction to acquire the skill.

To better understand how the most-to-least intrusive procedure is implemented, consider an example of a student learning to feed himself with a spoon. Using the most-to-least method, the teacher first conducts a task analysis of self-feeding with a spoon and then decides on the prompts to be included in the hierarchy. These may be prompts such as the following:

1. Full physical assistance (will fully guide the student through the behavior that is to occur).
2. Partial physical prompt (will nudge the student's hand in the direction of the action that should occur).
3. Verbal direction (will tell the student what to do).

Note that these prompts are like those listed in the previous example, but their order is reversed; instead of going from least to most, they go from most to least. The teacher decides on the criterion for moving from one prompt (more intrusive) to another (less intrusive). She may decide, for example, that she will require a minimum of 2 days of correct performance with a minimum of 4 opportunities (or trials) per day for each step in the task analysis.

When the teacher has made the relevant decisions and is ready to begin training, she approaches the student, provides the necessary material for eating with a spoon, and in some way tells the student that he should begin eating. Then, for each step in the task analysis, the teacher simultaneously gives an appropriate, predetermined verbal direction ("pick up your spoon") and physically guides the student through the task, using full physical assistance, the first level of assistance in the prompting sequence as listed above. The teacher provides this level of assistance on each step of the task analysis until criterion has been achieved on the step, using the present prompting system. If criterion for a task analysis step is achieved after 8 trials (let's assume it was 80% correct responding with the prompt), the student can move forward to the next lesser intrusive level of assistance (partial physical guidance) on the next learning opportunity. (Each step in the task analysis must be treated independently of other steps when deciding to move forward to lesser levels of assistance.) The process continues until each step of the task analysis is occurring when only the target stimulus is being used—in this example, a verbal direction.

It should be noted that the criterion for success is somewhat arbitrary. In this example the teacher or the collaborative team decided that 80% correct performance on 8 attempts over 2 days was necessary before moving to a lesser level of assistance. However, it might have been decided that 70% or 100% would be necessary. Depending on the target behavior, the usual criterion of successful performance is set between 80% and 100%.

Antecedent Prompt and Test Procedures In all of the preceding tactics, the order of instructional events has consisted of providing a prompt after the task direction or target stimulus (constant time delay, progressive time delay, system of least prompts) or during the presentation of the task direction (most-to-least procedure). Antecedent prompt and test procedures allow for the delivery of the prompt preceding a test or probe to determine if the student can perform the task as the prompt indicated (Wolery et al., 1992). Usually this consists of telling, showing, or physically guiding the student to do something before he or she is tested to see if the task has been learned. There are three prompt and test procedures: antecedent prompt and test, antecedent prompt and fade, and graduated guidance.

The *antecedent prompt and test* procedure calls for the simultaneous presentation of a controlling prompt (one that assures that the student will correctly perform the task) and the stimulus being taught. Several trials or opportunities are presented for the student to perform the target task under this condition, and then the prompt is totally removed and only the stimulus is presented. Under this test (or probe) condition, the student is observed to see if the control of the behavior is shifted to the stimulus, that is, if the behavior occurs in the presence of the stimulus instead of the stimulus and the prompt. An example of this procedure follows.

Rodney is requested to separate plastic containers from glass containers so that they may be recycled. In order to teach Rodney how to do this, his job coach says "Rodney, put the glass containers over here (indicating one bin) and the plastic ones over here (indicating the second bin)." Then the job coach begins separating the items while Rodney watches. As he works, the job coach says, "plastic here, glass here." After the job coach separates many items, he stops (removes the prompt) and tells Rodney to do it (provides the stimulus). As Rodney performs the task, the job coach reinforces correct separation.

In this example, the prompt was totally dropped, but in some cases it is possible to gradually fade the prompt until the student is being tested on the activity without the presence of the prompt. This is the *antecedent prompt and fade* procedure. Initially, the controlling prompt is presented along with the stimulus but then it is gradually withdrawn or reduced in intensity while the stimulus remains present. Ultimately the prompt is entirely removed and the stimulus is sufficient to cause the behavior to occur. Unlike the most-to-least procedure, the fading of the controlling prompt is not previously specified but occurs based on the teacher's judgment about whether or not the student is capable of responding with a less intrusive prompt.

An example of the antecedent prompt and fade procedure could be seen in a student learning to feed herself with a spoon and requiring assistance to complete all the steps of lifting the spoon, scooping the food, putting the spoon in her mouth, and so forth. The teacher provides a full physical guidance prompt of holding the student's hand and fully guiding it through the required movement. Obviously this would be a very intrusive, fully controlling prompt. If after only a few successful trials of doing this, the teacher were to terminate all prompting, the student would most likely not be able to complete the movement, or at least not all of it. Instead, the teacher decides to fade the prompt by gradually providing less assistance when it is perceived that the child is making more independent movements. The teacher might fade assistance in several ways. She may provide assistance on some attempts but not all; she may provide assistance through the initial portion of the movement but allow the student to complete more and more of the latter portion; or she may provide physical support at the hand for several trials, then at the wrist, at the forearm, at the elbow, and so forth. The important feature of the system is that the prompt is faded gradually until the student acquires enough prompted experience to successfully complete the movement independently.

Graduated Guidance Graduated guidance is very similar to the antecedent prompt and fade procedure except that the teacher is making moment-to-moment decisions about the amount of support the student needs to complete any particular part of the movement (Wolery et al., 1992). For example, if the teacher were teaching a student how to reach for an object, she might place her hand over his and gradually move it toward an object, but in the process feel the student beginning to reach and thus "back off" her physical guidance. She would keep her hand near the student's (that is, "shadow" the student's movement) but physically guide the student only when needed. Graduated guidance is often used with students with very severe disabilities to teach correct movements for particular skills.

Modifying Stimulus Materials

Often when we talk about target stimuli and controlling stimuli, we are referring to the teacher's verbal or physical actions that will better ensure the learning of particular behaviors or skills. For some learning situations, however, it is possible to modify stimulus materials in order to increase the probability of correct responding. This may occur when students are learning to discriminate between materials or when they are learning to manipulate materials in a particular way. Two techniques may be used: *stimulus shaping* and *stimulus fading* (Ault et al., 1989; Schoen, 1986).

Stimulus Shaping and Fading Stimulus shaping consists of the gradual changing of the shape (or topography) of a particular stimulus from one the student responds to correctly to one that the student cannot respond to correctly at the start of training but needs to learn to respond to. Stimulus fading involves changing a particular element of a stimulus gradually (one that the student is responsive to) so that the normally controlling element of a stimulus (one that the student is not initially responsive to) will ultimately influence the student's behavior. Some examples will clarify these procedures.

In many daily activities, individuals are required to make discriminations, for example, selecting a bowl to hold ice cream is preferred over selecting a plate because the latter will not hold the ice cream as well. Selecting a heavy coat to wear when a light sweater would do may result in being hot and uncomfortable or carrying the coat around instead of wearing it. The ability to discriminate which item is most appropriate for a particular need or situation is sometimes difficult for persons with severe disabilities because they do not know what particular aspect of the item warrants their attention. It may be helpful to take steps to better ensure that correct discriminations occur.

A practical way to improve discrimination ability is to use stimuli or cues that the student can easily recognize to identify the different items or materials that are to be selected. As the student learns to make the discrimination based on the more familiar cues, they can be faded or shaped so that the student's attention gradually shifts to the relevant dimensions and cues of the stimulus.

Stimulus shaping can be used in situations where it is possible to gradually change the features of a particular stimulus. For example, suppose it is desired that a student learn to select spoons instead of forks to be used for eating dessert. In order to do this, normally the student would have to attend to the *shape* of the two items and then make the choice. In this situation, the shape is considered the *relevant dimension* of the stimuli because it possesses the information about what the correct item is. But if the student does not attend well to shape, errors will occur. Assume, however, that the student has a better ability to discriminate between large and small than between the shapes of objects. One way to get the student to learn the shape discrimination more easily would be to initially allow discrimination based on the size dimension instead of the shape dimension. To do this, one would make all of the spoons large (say, for example, using large tablespoons) and the forks small (e.g., salad forks). This would make the discrimination easier because instead of attending to shape, the student could attend to size. Once the student learns to select the correct item (the spoon for dessert), the relevance of the size dimension can be decreased, with the aim of shifting the student's attention to the shape dimension. This can be done in three stages—by first replacing the salad forks with dinner forks, then replacing the tablespoons with long-handled teaspoons, and finally replacing the long-handled spoons with regular spoons appropriate for eating dessert. Throughout the process, the verbal direction to "get the spoons" is used. At each stage, the student is given enough opportunities to perform until an adequate criterion of success is achieved.

Stimulus shaping is difficult in many cases because it requires the gradual changing of some dimension of the stimulus. Therefore it is often easier to use stimulus fading. Consider again the previous situation. If the student cannot attend well to shape, but is able to attend to the dimension of color, the teacher might simply mark the forks with red and the spoons with blue, and then, over several trials, *fade* the colors gradually so that the student's attention is shifted from the color dimension to the shape dimension. The effect would be the same, but stimulus fading may be an easier process for this learning task as well as for others.

Modifying Material Difficulty Materials can be modified to make some manipulation tasks easier in early stages of learning, then slowly changed to make the tasks more difficult in later stages. In the final stage, the material will be of a nature that is normally required for a task. Learning to dress oneself serves as a good example. When a child with a severe disability is first learning to button a shirt, the small buttons on the shirt may be extremely difficult to manipulate. When the teacher is just beginning to teach the task, a higher probability of success may be possible if larger buttons and correspondingly larger buttonholes are provided during early learning trials. As the child begins to achieve criterion in early phases, learning to successfully use the material that is easier to handle, the material can gradually be changed, going through several stages, until finally the child can successfully button the buttons that he or she will use in daily life.

Although the sequential modification of materials can be a helpful tactic for acquiring many skills that require materials to be used, there is an important caveat for teachers and others. If the materials in use appear to be inappropriate for the age of the individual in a particular situation and call negative attention to the individual's disability, it will not be appropriate to use them. For example, it would not be appropriate for an adolescent to wear a coat in public that had oversized buttons on it simply because he or she could better manipulate those buttons. Instead, for such occasions, assistance with normal-size buttons would be preferred—or another material that is easy to manipulate and also age appropriate, such as Velcro, might be used.

Use of Natural Cues

In all objectives, it is very important to remember one thing. The ultimate accomplishment for the student when learning new behaviors or skills is to respond appropriately to the natural cues available in the environment (Dever, 1988; Ford & Mirenda, 1984). For example, individuals usually put on their socks and shoes in the morning after putting on their other clothes and before going to breakfast. Most people do not put on shoes and socks only when given a verbal direction, a gesture, a model, or a physical prompt to do so. Because of their relative general learning disabilities, persons with severe disabilities often require systematic instruction, using the tactics described in this chapter, when initially learning some skills, but this does not mean that these artificial prompting techniques should be continued without end. If we consider the environment to be full of natural stimuli that call for certain behaviors to occur, we would hope that these stimuli would assume their normal function for individuals with severe disabilities. But how is this to occur?

The most important consideration is that skills must be taught in the presence of natural stimuli. Usually this means teaching in those environments where the stimuli exist and considering the natural stimuli to be the ultimate cue, or target stimulus, in our sequence. Even though prompting may occur in several ways, whenever possible all prompts should ultimately be eliminated so that the student responds to naturally existing stimuli. Consider the following example.

Suppose there is an objective for a student to learn to order a hamburger at a fast-food restaurant. An instructional plan is designed to use the system of least prompts as described previously by (a) asking if she would like to order a hamburger, (b) suggesting to the student that she order a hamburger, and (c) directly telling the student to order a hamburger. The problem with this sequence is that normally there would not be someone around to complete even step (a) of the least-to-most system. Therefore, there should be one step that precedes (a). That is, the student must be in the location, smelling the food, seeing the large menu on the wall (reading ability is not important here), and have the counter attendant ask: "Can I help you?" These are all natural cues that the student must learn to attend and respond to if the behavior (ordering a hamburger) is going to occur in the natural setting.

Unless such conditions can be arranged for learning all functional objectives, the student may learn to respond only when there is an initial artificial prompt. When certain conditions inhibit training in the natural environment, it is important that relevant conditions be incorporated into the training situation. Nietupski, Hamre-Nietupski, Clancy, and Veerhusen (1986) offered several suggestions for creating simulated learning conditions to enhance training that cannot occur in the natural environment. These suggestions include taking inventories of community settings to determine the range of stimuli, using various simulations, changing simulations that do not improve performance in the natural environment, using simulations to provide for intensive practice that cannot be provided in natural environments, and providing training in simulations close in time to when the skill will be practiced in the natural environment.

Although it is clearly desirable for students with severe disabilities to respond to natural cues, there are some students who will not be able to do so, or at least not be able to do so in all circumstances. For these students, it is more important that they participate in some meaningful manner—even if uncommon prompting and support must be continued indefinitely—than not to participate at all (Ferguson & Baumgart, 1991). Still, when possible, teachers should work to develop appropriate skills and behaviors that occur when natural stimuli are present.

Reinforcing Correct Responses

Only if behaviors are reinforced will they tend to recur. This is referred to as the "law of effect," and it is true for all individuals whether they have a disability or not. Therefore, when individuals with severe disabilities exhibit appropriate behaviors, regardless of the stimulus that prompts the behaviors, the behaviors must be reinforced. If they are not, ultimately they will cease to occur. In the initial stages of learning, when a skill is first being acquired, reinforcement should occur immediately after each appropriate or desired behavior, or at least after most behaviors. Once the behavior has been established, a "thinner schedule" of reinforcement can be used, that is, not every instance of the behavior will have to be reinforced. (For a complete discussion on schedules of reinforcement, the reader is referred to Alberto and Troutman, 1990.)

Selecting Reinforcers In the general population, different people like different things and effective reinforcers are not the same for everyone. This can also be said about reinforcers that consequate the occurrence of specific behaviors of persons with severe disabilities; therefore, it is necessary to discover what will serve as an effective reinforcer for each student and then use that reinforcer during instruction for skill acquisition.

Wolery et al. (1992) suggested four tactics for selecting effective reinforcers. The first is to use reinforcers that are effective for other students. The second is to identify possible reinforcers by asking parents, family members, and others who know the student what they believe to be most desirable or favored by the student. This could be done during assessment and planning. Third, the student may be observed over a period of time to determine what objects he or she seeks, holds, or manipulates for a period of time or what activities are preferred. Finally, reinforcers may be identified by presenting different stimuli to the student on several occasions (distributed across several days) and note which the student prefers (Mason, McGee, Farmer-Dougan, & Risley, 1989; Pace, Ivancic, Edwards, Iwata, & Page, 1985).

Even after particular reinforcers are identified, however, it must be remembered that reinforcers tend to lose their effectiveness. The teacher should always be looking for new stimuli that may serve as effective reinforcers. Various items and activities may be effective, such as items with visual or auditory appeal, verbal statements, and physical expressions.

The most desirable types of reinforcers to use will be those that are most natural for the behavior and those that occur in the natural environment. For example, the reinforcer that typically keeps one involved in performing personal grooming behaviors is the reaction of others, such as "you look nice today." The difficulty with relying solely on natural reinforcers is that they may not occur often enough to maintain the behavior, particularly when the behavior is first being learned and/or the student may not fully comprehend the meaning of some social or verbal reinforcers. The teacher or another person may need to supplement the natural schedule of reinforcement by using other items and activities that are selected based on the individual likes of the student.

Using Food and Drink as Reinforcers During the relatively brief history of teaching persons with severe disabilities, particularly those with the most severe disabilities, food and drink items have often been used as reinforcers. Even though they have typically been effective when used this way, for several reasons this is not a good idea. First, individuals have a natural right to food and drink when they are hungry and thirsty; to deliver them contingently seems to diminish this right. Second, dietary concerns may admonish against the use of food as reinforcement. This may include possible allergic reactions to certain foods. Third, the student may learn to respond only in the presence of food and become overly responsive when food is available. For example, the student may hold out his or her hand continuously in the presence of food. Fourth, the responsiveness of the student may decrease after snacks, lunch, and other natural eating opportunities. Although the potency of food as a reinforcer for many individuals cannot be denied, for these reasons the teacher should search for and use other reinforcers.

Delivery of Reinforcement The way in which reinforcers are delivered following a behavior is as important as the reinforcer itself. Reinforcement must come immediately after the correct behavior (regardless of the prompt level required) so that the student learns the association between the stimulus, the behavior, and the reinforcer. If reinforcement is delayed, this association may not occur. It is also important to tell the student, in a natural way, why he or she is being reinforced. For example, "you look really nice, your hair looks good" may provide reinforcement and also tell why the student is being reinforced. Also, when reinforcing students, teachers and others should be sincere in their expressions. All learners, even those with severe disabilities, recognize insincerity. Finally, and of great importance, the delivery of supplementary reinforcement in natural, nonschool environments should be paired with the natural reinforcement and be presented in an unobtrusive fashion, one that does not call attention to itself. As the natural reinforcer begins to acquire more influence, the supplemental reinforcement should be reduced and eliminated (Ford & Mirenda, 1984).

Correcting Errors

As one may expect, there will be errors when new behaviors or skills are first being acquired. The instructional tactics described in this chapter were designed to reduce the occurrence of these errors and sometimes even eliminate them altogether. For example, the most-to-least prompting system has a very low error-producing rate because it requires an initial controlling prompt that will exert much control over the student's behavior when it is first being learned. This tends to reduce student errors. This is also the case with time delay when the controlling prompt occurs at the zero-second delay interval.

Types of Errors Even though instructional tactics are intended to result in few student errors, errors (or no responses) will occur and they will occur in different forms, including the following:

- The behavior does not occur when the target stimulus is presented alone, either after prompts have been eliminated or before the prompt can be delivered (unprompted, no response error).
- An incorrect behavior occurs when the target stimulus is presented alone, after prompts have been eliminated or before the prompt can be delivered (unprompted error).
- The behavior does not occur when the target stimulus and the prompt are presented together (prompted, no response error).
- An incorrect behavior occurs when the target stimulus and the prompt are presented together (prompted error).

As can be seen, there are both prompted and unprompted errors as well as errors of no response. In contrast, of course, there are prompted and unprompted correct responses. A prompted correct response occurs when the student performs the correct behavior when a prompt is used, whatever its form. An unprompted correct response occurs only when the target stimulus is provided.

Error Correction Procedures When incorrect responses occur, the teacher has several possible *correction procedures* she or he may use depending on the nature of the error and the instructional tactic being used. Generally the purpose of any correction procedure is to cause the behavior to occur correctly when a student either does not respond or gives an incorrect response, whether prompted or unprompted.

If a *time delay* procedure is being used (either constant or progressive), it is important that the prompt that is delivered at the end of the delay interval be a controlling prompt that the teacher is certain the student will respond to. If errors occur when using time delay, they are most likely to do so during the delay interval, between when the target stimulus occurs and when the teacher intends to use the prompt. This is considered an unprompted error. When this occurs the teacher should use a verbal direction, a gesture, and/or a physical prompt to interrupt the incorrect behavior and then provide the target stimulus again.

If a pattern of responding incorrectly before the prompt is given develops, the teacher may need to introduce "wait training" (Wolery et al., 1992), which is done by switching to progressive time delay procedure and gradually moving from a zero-second delay to 1-second delay, 2-second, and so forth. In order to improve the chance of the student's learning to wait, Wolery et al. suggested that special tasks that are too difficult for the student to perform without a controlling prompt be used so that the student must wait for the prompt before responding.

When an error occurs after the controlling prompt is delivered using a time delay procedure, whether the error is an incorrect behavior or no response at all, it is an indication that the "controlling prompt" is not adequately "controlling" to get the behavior to occur. In this case, a more effective prompt is necessary.

When an error occurs using the system of least prompts, regardless of the level or type of prompt being provided (including no prompt at the first delivery of the target stimulus), the appropriate correction procedure is to repeat the target stimulus and go immediately to the next, more intrusive prompt on the hierarchy. If the error is an incorrect behavior, the teacher should interrupt the movement and provide the next prompt. If the error is no response within the allotted time interval, the teacher should repeat or re-present the target stimulus and the next more intrusive prompt. The final prompt used in the sequence must be a controlling prompt; if its use does not result in a correct response, a stronger, more directing prompt is required.

Errors are also possible with the most-to-least prompting procedure; they include both prompted and unprompted errors and no responses. Since the first level of assistance provided is assumed to be a controlling prompt, errors at this time indicate that the prompt is inadequate and needs to be changed to exert more influence. If errors occur at subsequent, less intrusive levels of prompting, the teacher should either revert to the most intrusive prompt to correct the error or to a prompt more intrusive than the one at which the error occurred but less intrusive than the controlling prompt.

Regardless of the prompting system that is being used, when an error occurs on a particular trial, the teacher should implement an error correction procedure. Whatever form of reinforcement is being used should be withheld and the correction of the error should be carried out in a matter-of-fact manner without any anger or hostility shown toward the student. Before going on to the next trial, the teacher might pause briefly (10 to 20 seconds) before repeating the target stimulus.

Writing an Instructional Program

Every behavioral objective for every student with severe disabilities requires that an instructional program be written. This program is a comprehensive description of the plan of instruction for a particular objective. It begins with the behavioral objective (and task analysis or functional routine if appropriate) and the material and setting used to teach the skill. It then states all of the elements of the instructional process that have been discussed in this chapter as they will be used in the instruction of the objective. This includes a statement of the skill acquisition training procedure to be used with the levels of prompting if they are part of the procedure, the reinforcement procedure, and the error correction procedure. (Plans for maintenance and generalization of the behavior as well as for data collection and recording should also be included. See chapters 7 and 8 for discussion of these topics. Figure 6–1 provides an example of an instructional plan for a student who is learning how to clean a bathroom in a motel.

As can be seen in Figure 6–1, the teacher has developed a complete description of the instructional plan that will be followed to teach the student to clean a bathroom.

A complete plan of instruction for each student with a severe disability should include at least six written instructional programs such as the one presented in Figure 6–1. This is not intended to imply that this is all that the student will learn, but it is a precise way of detailing how the student will acquire certain behaviors or skills that have been prioritized by the collaborative team. The plan for each objective is to be developed regardless of the exact nature of the objectives to be taught, whether the objective is to teach simple discrete behaviors or complex skills with task analysis or functional routines.

Conclusion

For each skill or behavior to be learned by a student, the teacher has a variety of skill acquisition training techniques that might be used. The teacher should select procedures that seem to be most effective for getting the job done. Although it is not possible to say which specific procedure will be effective for which

Student: James

Behavioral object: James will clean the bathroom in a motel where he is working by completing all of the steps of the task analysis. He will begin within 10 seconds after entering the bathroom and will complete the entire task within 10 minutes.

Setting and materials: Any bathroom within a motel where James is learning to work.

Task analysis/functional routine:

1. Gather all towels, bath mats, and wash cloths and place them in the laundry cart in the hallway.
2. Gather old soap and trash basket and empty into the container in the hallway.
3. Turn on the cold water and wet the inner portion of the bathtub.
4. Sprinkle cleanser in the bathtub.
5. Use sponge to wipe the bathtub thoroughly.
6. Rinse tub and dry.
7. Sprinkle cleanser in toilet bowl and on the outside of the toilet.
8. Wipe inside and outside of the toilet.
9. Use second damp cloth to wipe cleanser off toilet.
10. Sprinkle cleanser on sink.
11. Wipe sink clean.
12. Rinse sink.

Figure 6–1
Instructional Plan for Cleaning a Bathroom

13. Clean mirror with glass cleaner and cloth.
14. Damp-mop bathroom.
15. Put clean towels, bath mats, and wash cloths in bathroom.

Instructional procedure:

(Including prompting sequence)

Use the system of least prompts for each step in the task analysis beginning when James enters the bathroom. Wait 5 seconds between prompts.

1. No prompt.
2. Gesture by pointing to the materials of the activity to occur. (Point to the tub and the cleanser and the cloth.)
3. Verbally suggest the step in task analysis that is to be completed, using an indirect statement ("What are you supposed to do with the sink now?")
4. Tell James what step in the task analysis he is to do. ("Throw away the old soap and the trash.")

Reinforcement: During the first 3 days of training, reinforce James after each step in the task analysis is completed correctly by saying "looks good" or something similar. On the next 3 days, reinforce only after every other step. Continue reducing comments until a point is reached where James is congratulated for a good job after he has finished the entire task. If amount of time required for task completion is greater than called for in objective, reinforce more often for faster performance.

Figure 6–1, *continued*

student or skill to be learned, Wolery et al. (1992) provided the following suggestions:

- Teachers should study the research literature to determine the effectiveness of different techniques. Ault et al. (1989) and Demchak (1990) provide recent reviews.
- Teachers should select tactics that have the least potential for harming the student and are the least likely to call attention to the student when being used in public settings.
- The tactics used should be those that require the least amount of intrusiveness or restrictiveness and that seem to be the most natural for the situation.
- Consideration should be given to the student and to what has been effective with the student in the past. Students respond differently to prompting systems; the more the teacher knows about students, the better he or she may be able to select effective instructional systems.
- Teachers should select the simplest system that will be effective. It is best to avoid developing elaborate instructional systems that will be difficult to implement if simpler systems will work just as well.
- Finally, teachers should be concerned about using only systems that are socially valid. This means that the method of instruction should be acceptable to the student, the parents, members of the community, other professionals, and the instructional team.

During the process of instruction the teacher must consequate behaviors appropriately by using correction procedures when errors occur and by reinforcing appropriate behaviors. However, as this is done, the teacher should remember that the importance of the task is likely to be more effective in motivating the student than the reinforcement and error correction procedure. Thus, again it is suggested that objectives be written to develop important skills that will decrease dependence, increase independence, and improve the student's quality of life.

Questions for Reflection

1. How important is it for all team members to agree upon the objectives for a student? What if they do not?
2. Why must objectives be stated in rather specific terms? When developing objectives, why is "function" often more important than "form"?
3. Develop some sample objectives that allow for partial participation. Explain in what ways these would be meaningful for the student.
4. Are there any additional good general teaching practices that can be added to those discussed in this chapter?
5. How would you describe the purpose and structure of the prompting techniques presented in this chapter?
6. Why is it desirable that students learn to respond to natural cues and consequences? What should the teacher do if this does not occur?
7. Do you believe there are circumstances in which it would be appropriate to use food or drink as reinforcement for students with severe disabilities?

References

Alberto, P. A., & Troutman, A. C. (1990). *Applied behavior analysis for teachers* (3rd ed.). New York: Merrill/Macmillan.

Ault, M. J., Wolery, M., Doyle, P. M., & Gast, D. L. (1989). Review of comparative studies in the instruction of students with moderate and severe handicaps. *Exceptional Children, 55,* 346–356.

Baumgart, D., Brown, L., Pumpian, I., Nisbet, J., Ford, A., Sweet, M., Messina, R., & Schroeder, J. (1982). Principle of partial participation and individualized adaptations in educational programs for severely handicapped students. *Journal of the Association for the Severely Handicapped, 7*(2), 17–27.

Billingsley, F. F., & Romer, L. T. (1983). Response prompting and the transfer of stimulus control: Methods, research, and a conceptual framework. *Journal of the Association for the Severely Handicapped, 8,* 3–12.

Brown, F., Evans, I. M., Weed, K. A., & Owen, V. (1987). Delineating functional competencies: A component model. *Journal of the Association for Persons with Severe Handicaps, 12,* 117–124.

Demchak, M. (1990). Response prompting and fading methods: A review. *American Journal on Mental Retardation, 94,* 603–615.

Dever, R. B. (1988). *Community living skills.* Washington, DC: American Association on Mental Retardation.

Doyle, P. M., Wolery, M., Ault, M. J., & Gast, D. L. (1988). System of least prompts: A literature review of procedural parameters. *Journal of the Association for Persons with Severe Handicaps, 13,* 28–40.

Ellis, N. R. (Ed.). (1963). *Handbook of mental deficiency: Psychological theory and research.* New York: Adaption-Hill.

Ellis, N. R. (Ed.). (1979). *Handbook of mental deficiency: Psychological theory and research* (2nd ed.). Hillsdale, NJ: Erlbaum.

Ferguson, D. L., & Baumgart, D. (1991). Partial participation revisited. *Journal of the Association for Persons with Severe Handicaps, 16,* 218–227.

Ford, A., & Mirenda, P. (1984). Community instruction: A natural cues and corrections decision model. *Journal of the Association for Persons with Severe Handicaps, 9,* 79–87.

Giangreco, M. F., Cloninger, C. J., & Iverson, V. S. (1993). *Choosing options and accommodations for children: A guide to planning inclusive education.* Baltimore: Paul H. Brookes.

Kayser, J. E., Billingsley, F. F., & Neel, R. S. (1986). A comparison of in-context and traditional instructional approaches: Total task, single trial versus backward chaining, multiple trials. *Journal of the Association for Persons with Severe Handicaps, 11,* 28–38.

Mason, S. A., McGee, G. G., Farmer-Dougan, V., & Risley, T. R. (1989). A practical strategy for on-going reinforcement assessment. *Journal of Applied Behavior Analysis, 22,* 171–179.

Mercer, C. D., & Snell, M. E. (1977). *Learning theory research in mental retardation: Implications for teaching.* New York: Merrill Macmillan.

Nietupski, J., Hamre-Nietupski, S., Clancy, P., & Veerhusen, K. (1986). Guidelines for making simulations an effective adjunct to in vivo community instruction. *Journal of the Association for Persons with Severe Handicaps, 11,* 12–18.

Pace, G. M., Ivancic, M. T., Edwards, G. L., Iwata, B. A., & Page, T. J. (1985). Assessment of stimulus preference and reinforcer value with profoundly retarded individuals. *Journal of Applied Behavior Analysis, 18,* 249–255.

Sailor, W., & Guess, D. (1983). *Severely handicapped students: An instructional design.* Boston: Houghton Mifflin.

Schoen, S. A. (1986). Assistance procedures to facilitate the transfer of stimulus control: Review and analysis. *Education and Training of the Mentally Retarded, 21,* 62–74.

Snell, M. E., & Gast, D. L. (1981). Applying time delay procedure to the instruction of the severely handicapped. *Journal of the Association for the Severely Handicapped, 6*(3), 3–14.

U.S. Department of Education. (1986). *What works: Research about teaching and learning.* Washington, DC: Author.

Wolery, M., Ault, M. J., & Doyle, P. M. (1992). *Teaching students with moderate to severe disabilities: Use of response prompting strategies.* New York: Longman.

Wolery, M., & Gast, D. L. (1984). Effective and efficient procedures for the transfer of stimulus control. *Topics in Early Childhood Special Education, 4,* 52–77.

Zane, T., Walls, R. T., & Thvedt, J. E. (1981). Prompting and fading guidance procedures: Their effect on chaining and whole task teaching strategies. *Education and Training of the Mentally Retarded, 16,* 125–135.

CHAPTER 7

Teaching Skills for Maintenance and Generalization

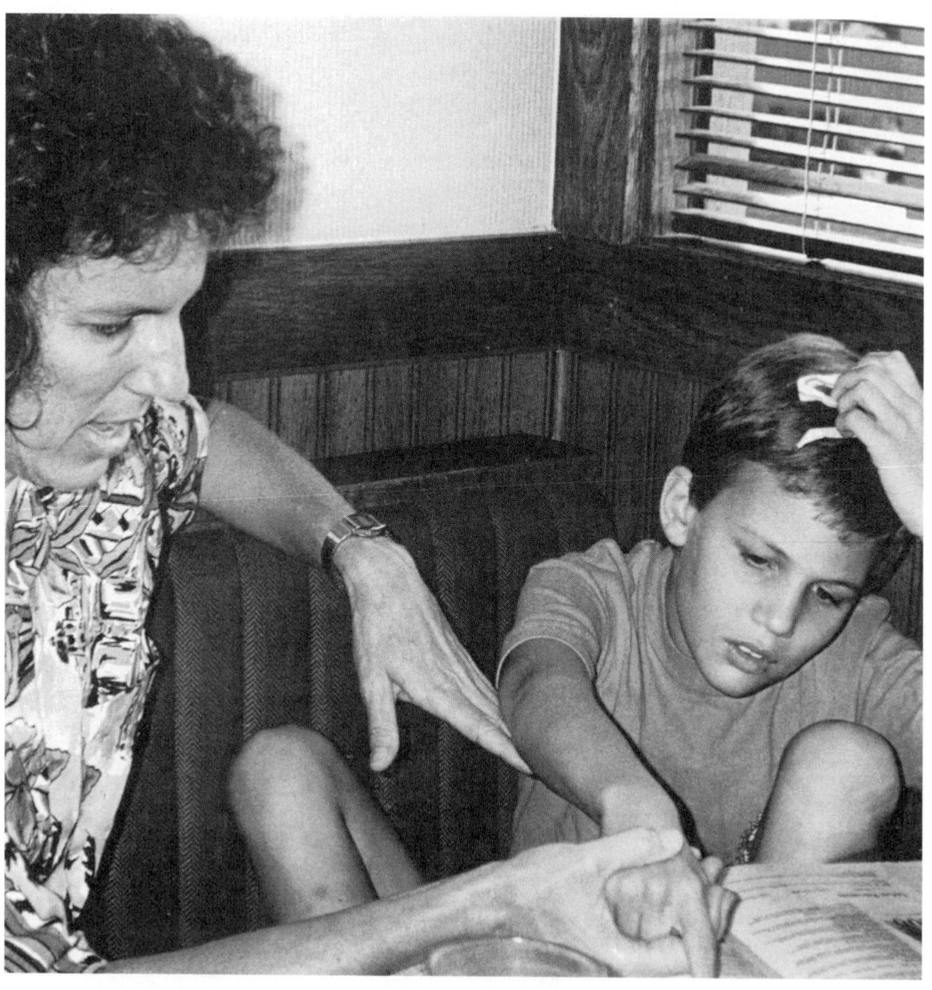

Chapter Overview

In addition to initially learning new behaviors or skills, students must also learn how to apply the skills in new situations or locations and must retain the skills over a period of time so they can use them. This chapter describes procedures that will help achieve skill generalization and maintenance. Greater focus is placed on generalization because there has been much recent research in this area.

In chapter 6, methods for skill acquisition were discussed. These methods are designed to allow students to initially acquire behaviors or skills that they did not previously possess. Key to learning these skills is the systematic use of cues, prompts, positive reinforcement, and correction procedures. It was implied that the employment of these procedures would result in students with severe disabilities acquiring new functional behaviors or skills. It is essential to realize, however, that acquiring a new skill or learning how to perform a particular task in one situation or under one limited set of conditions is only half the battle. In addition, the student must learn to use the skill as often as it is needed and in all situations when it is appropriate and necessary to do so. Conversely, the student must also learn not to exhibit skills or behaviors in situations or environments when they are not necessary or would be considered inappropriate. When individuals can apply skills in different environments or situations or under different circumstances from those in which they were initially learned, it is referred to as skill *generalization*. When students can use skills at times beyond the point that they were originally learned, it is referred to as behavioral *maintenance*. Another way to think of maintenance is as generalization of the behavior across time.

Traditionally, one of the most often recognized learning weaknesses of individuals with severe disabilities is their poor ability to apply learned behaviors to new environmental conditions, that is, to use the behaviors with different people, in different places, with different materials, and at different times (Fox, 1989; Haring, 1987; Haring, 1988; Horner, Dunlap, & Koegel, 1988; Stokes & Baer, 1977). A student might acquire certain shopping behaviors, but fail to use the behaviors when taken to a grocery store, or learn to correctly use a communicative act at school, but not at home or in the community. A similar problem occurs when the student has successfully learned a skill in one school year, but during the next year seems to have forgotten what was learned. Such outcomes, of course, result in the learned skills having little practical utility. Unfortunately, this learning weakness is often compounded by the fact that teachers do not always plan for or use instructional tactics that result in generalization or maintenance (Billingsley, 1984). Instead, teachers often work on a skill until it has been mastered under one condition or in one situation (usually the classroom) and then, considering it as learned, check it off the IEP or the curriculum checklist. The following year a new teacher has to reteach the behavior and the cycle starts over.

The problem in this type of situation is that the behavior has not been learned to a level of functional utility because the student did not learn how to use the new behavior beyond the site or time of initial acquisition. The behavior was not maintained and did not generalize.

Fortunately, in recent years, researchers and practitioners have begun to identify methods of instruction that will help solve these problems of limited skill utility, particularly in the area of generalization (Donnellan & Mirenda, 1983; Fox, 1989; Haring, 1987; Haring, 1988; Haring et al., 1985; Horner, Dunlap, & Koegel, 1988; Horner, McDonnell, & Bellamy, 1986; Horner, Sprague, & Wilcox, 1982; Westling & Floyd, 1990; White et al., 1988). They have suggested that with these methods, students with severe disabilities can enjoy life more because they can use functional skills when and where they are needed.

In the following pages of this chapter, strategies and tactics for achieving generalization and maintenance will be discussed. Most of the attention will be placed on generalization because much research has been conducted in this area. It should be realized that because maintaining a behavior over a period of time may be considered a form of generalization, information relevant to promoting skill generalization is also applicable to maintaining behaviors.

Defining Generalization

In broad terms, *generalization* is "appropriate responding in untrained situations" (Haring, 1988). A student who has learned a generalized skill is able to demonstrate the skill in a variety of situations and conditions when it is appropriate to do so. These "situations and conditions" could include *different persons, different objects or materials, different settings and stimuli, different reinforcers,* and *different times of the day* (Haring, 1988). Albin and Horner (1988) point out that it is equally important for a particular behavior not to occur when it is not appropriate.

Strategies That Have Been Used to Achieve Skill Generalization

Perhaps the most important paper to initially address strategies undertaken to promote generalization was published by Trevor Stokes and Donald Baer in 1977. In this paper, Stokes and Baer examined many applied behavior analysis research articles in which there was an attempt to measure the occurrence of generalization. In each of these studies, they identified the method that was used to teach the participants and noted the amount of success that was achieved, that is, how successful the approach was in resulting in generalization. They identified nine strategies, including those described below.

Train and Hope

The "train and hope" approach teaches someone to acquire a skill and then hopes that it will generalize. In other words, there is no specific programming to promote generalization. Using "train and hope," the teacher focuses on teaching a behavior to the level of acquisition and then expects that it will generalize to those environments and conditions in which it will be needed. While this outcome does occur in some instances, this is the approach least likely to be successful. Unfortunately, it is an approach that seems to be used quite often.

Sequential Modification

Sequential modification is an approach that teaches the individual to generalize if he or she fails to do so following initial acquisition training. After a train and hope approach has been used and a follow-up test for generalization in another setting, time, or other condition is presented to the learner, *if generalization does not occur,* training is conducted in the novel setting, at the new time, or under another desirable new condition.

Sequential modification is limited to generalization of the behavior occurring only in the new condition in which subsequent training is provided. For example, if the teacher taught a student to use one video game and then tested the student to see if she could play another, it would be a (limited) test for generalization. If the student was not successful on the new game and the teacher then taught the student the new game, the teacher would have used sequential modification.

Introduce to Natural Maintaining Contingencies

This approach teaches an individual a skill during the acquisition period that will later be reinforced by natural contingencies in the environment in which the behavior will occur, instead of through the artificial reinforcers that were used during acquisition training. Since initial training often occurs in an environment other than the one in which the behavior or skill is needed, generalization to the criterion environment may be improved if the reinforcers in that environment can be applied to the behavior as it is being learned initially.

Train Sufficient Exemplars

Because the lack of generalization is associated with training in limited settings or under limited conditions, improved generalization should occur if training occurs under several sufficient conditions with various stimuli. White et al. (1988) offered an example of teaching an individual to put on a sweater. Instead of teaching only a long-sleeved crew-neck sweater, this would suggest that sleeveless sweaters, v-neck sweaters, cardigan sweaters, and other types should also be taught.

Train Loosely

In order to avoid having the person learn to respond under strict stimulus conditions, variations in stimuli, responses, and reinforcers are allowed. This may be considered an "informal technique" with "relatively little control over the stimuli presented" (Stokes & Baer, 1977, p. 357).

Use Indiscriminable Contingencies

A behavior is much more likely to continue to occur if the learner is reinforced on an intermittent schedule of reinforcement. If the individual does not know when reinforcement will occur, or in what settings, or under what stimulus conditions, he or she is likely to demonstrate the behavior with greater frequency and also in different settings and conditions. The behavior is less likely to be susceptible to extinction.

Program Common Stimuli

Generalization to a new setting will be more likely to occur if the training setting contains stimuli that are also contained in the generalization setting. "Programming common stimuli" refers to having in the training environment those stimuli that will appear in the environment(s) in which it is desirable for the learned behavior to occur. In order to use this approach, a teacher would attempt to strictly recreate many of the conditions in the initial teaching environment that would appear in the generalization environment(s). This is often difficult to accomplish.

Mediate Generalization

This requires teaching a cobehavior with the target behavior during initial training so that the cobehavior can facilitate (mediate) the new behavior during generalization training. For example, the learner may learn *to say* the particular behavior that is to occur so that he or she may remind himself or herself what to do in the new setting. Liberty (1987) reported that some studies have shown that such "self-management" or "self-control" strategies may be helpful in achieving generalization.

Train to Generalize

This approach differentially reinforces the student for behaviors that occur outside of the initial setting or condition and stops reinforcement when the behavior occurs only under the original condition. In this way the student learns that it is the generalized behavior that is to occur.

Since the Stokes and Baer (1977) publication, additional methods for better ensuring the occurrence of generalization have been identified (Chandler, Lubeck, & Fowler, 1992; White et al., 1988). These include:

Teach Functional Target Behaviors

This strategy suggests that generalization will be more likely if the instructional targets (behaviors or skills) are relevant and functional. If they are, they are more likely to occur and be reinforced in the natural environment. On the other hand, if something is being taught that has little practical utility for the learner, it will cease to occur when the individual is no longer in the training environment. Developing functional objectives for students with severe disabilities enhances the chances that they will be used in various settings and other various conditions.

Specify a Fluency Criterion

The degree of successful generalization may be dependent on how fluently or proficiently someone performs a task at the time of initial learning. Thus some researchers have studied the relationship between teaching the student to acquire a particular skill performance fluency criterion and later generalization. Skills that the student learns to perform faster and with greater ease during initial teaching may generalize better.

Train in the Natural Setting

This strategy calls for training in at least one natural setting in which the skill will be used. The current emphasis on nonschool, community-based training (Brown et al., 1983; Falvey, 1989) is based on the premise that training that occurs in natural environments is likely to generalize to other natural environments.

Use General Case Programming

General case programming applies the practice of using several exemplars of a very specific nature. It calls for the teacher to identify the "universe" of desired generalization conditions, identify the variations of the relevant stimuli and responses in the universe, and then teach the student to respond appropriately under all appropriate stimulus conditions. Although it is a complex procedure, it has met with a great deal of success in achieving generalization (Westling & Floyd, 1990; White et al., 1988). The merits of this approach and others are discussed below.

Effectiveness of Generalization Strategies

Although several approaches have been identified to promote skill generalization, not all have been equally effective. Several writers have examined the extensive research literature on generalization and have made distinctions between more effective and less effective strategies. Chandler et al. (1992) analyzed 51 studies in which strategies were used to teach social skills to preschool children with special needs. Their concern was which strategies were associated with greater degrees of generalization and which with less. The children who were subjects in the reviewed studies all had social behavior problems and included those with a disability or developmental delay, those at risk for developmental or social delay, those who were aggressive or passive, and those who were developing normally but had social behavior problems. White et al. (1988) examined 172 studies that assessed the effects of different strategies on the generalization of behaviors. Most of the studies included persons with severe disabilities, but studies of individuals without disabilities were also included. Fox (1989) was interested in determining the extent to which individuals with the most severe disabilities (profound mental disabilities) could generalize learned behaviors. She examined 25 studies that included individuals with this degree of disability and identified factors that appeared to be related to successful generalization. Finally, Westling and Floyd (1990) analyzed 27 studies of teaching functional community skills to persons with severe disabilities to determine what training strategies would be necessary for achieving generalization in community settings. They reported the relative degrees of success achieved within the studies and what contributed to the outcomes. The conclusions that may be drawn from these reviews are discussed in the following sections.

Train and Hope

As stated previously, the "train and hope" approach is the least likely to result in generalization. White et al. (1988) concluded that individuals with severe disabilities would generalize only about 25% of the skills taught with this approach. In examining generalization of community skills, Westling and Floyd (1990) determined that about 30% of the time learners with severe disabilities were able to generalize acquired skills without specific efforts being made to help them do so. In 6 of the 25 studies on the generalization of skills by individuals with the most severe disabilities reviewed by Fox (1989), or about 25%, she found that some degree of generalization occurred when only the train and hope model was used.

It is not clear why some individuals with severe disabilities are able to generalize their skills without specific preparation to do so and others are not. Westling and Floyd (1990) speculated that the successful persons may have had some relevant experiences prior to the experimental studies in which they participated that ultimately helped them generalize. Fox (1989) and, earlier, Stokes and Baer (1977) suggested that instructional models that appear to be only of the train and hope variety may actually, perhaps inadvertently, include programming efforts to improve the potential for generalization that are not reported.

Regardless, the fact is clear that if teachers simply teach a skill, using one of the skill acquisition methods described in the previous chapter without employing a strategy for generalization, their hope will not be realized for the majority of students. Thus the effectiveness of different types of interventions intended to result in generalization must be considered. In the sections that follow, training strategies to improve generalization are grouped according to whether they are *consequences* or *antecedents* used during initial instruction. We will consider first the use of consequences as a method for improving skill generalization.

Arranging Consequences During Initial Training to Improve Generalization

In the above list of generalization strategies there are three that pertain to behavioral consequences: introduce natural maintaining contingencies, use indiscriminable contingencies, and train to generalize. Unfortunately, relatively few studies have examined the effectiveness of these strategies with learners who have severe disabilities while controlling for the influence of other factors. Those that have been reported, however, have reported only moderate success.

White et al. (1988) found that when students with severe disabilities were taught skills that were functional and thus more likely to be reinforced in the natural environment, they were more likely to generalize them than when the skills were nonfunctional and thus not likely to be frequently used or reinforced. The analysis of research conducted by Chandler et al. (1992) led to the same conclusion. In fact, Chandler et al. found that one of the most successful factors for achieving generalization was the use of functional target behaviors.

White et al. (1988) cautioned, however, that the student must have enough opportunity in the natural environment to practice the skill; that he or she must be proficient enough with the skill for it to result in the natural reinforcer; and that reinforcement must be available for successful performance. Without these conditions, the application of natural contingencies may not be effective.

Another effective consequational strategy for promoting generalization is the use of indiscriminable contingencies. Chandler et al. found in the studies they reviewed that this was an important distinction between studies in which generalization occurred more often and those in which it occurred less often. White et al. noted that this strategy calls for continuous (1:1) schedules of reinforcement to be gradually replaced by intermittent, unpredictable, more natural occurrences of reinforcement. (Intermittent reinforcement is discussed later in this chapter.)

The train to generalize method for attempting to improve generalization skills has not been used a great deal except in combination with other approaches to improve generalization. Thus its individual effectiveness is difficult to determine. However, in their review, White et al. (1988) found that only 10% of the individuals with whom this procedure was used generalized well as a result. Similarly, Chandler et al. (1992) found that the approach was used more often in unsuccessful studies of generalization than in successful ones.

Arranging Antecedents During Initial Training to Improve Generalization

In comparison to studying the effects of consequences during acquisition learning, researchers have been much more interested in studying how well individuals generalize as an effect of what occurs *prior to* the demonstration of the behavior or skill when it is being learned, that is, the effect of behavioral antecedents. As the term is used here, behavioral antecedents include the setting where the training occurs, the use of sufficient exemplars, training loosely (i.e., providing various cues or prompts), programming common stimuli, and using the general case method.

A relatively recent trend in the field of special education for students with severe disabilities is providing training in the natural environment, particularly in nonschool, community environments (Brown et al., 1983; Falvey, 1989). The assumption is that students who are taught in the natural environment will be able to learn functional skills and generalize them to other natural environments. However, if the teacher provides training only in one natural environment, without undertaking additional activities to promote skill generalization, it may not occur. In summarizing the research they reviewed on this subject, White et al. (1988) stated:

> *An analysis of the overall impact of those studies indicates that merely shifting the location of instruction without incorporating other strategies to facilitate generalization will not be effective for many students. In studies with severe subjects, training in the natural setting is only as effective as train and hope. (White et al., 1988, p. 21)*

In their analysis of studies on the generalization of community skills, Westling and Floyd (1990) came to a similar conclusion. They found that training in simulated conditions could be effective in achieving generalization but that the degree of generalization improved if this training was paired with community site-based training. They also found that training in multiple community settings was generally more effective than training in single community settings.

The use of sufficient exemplars may also be considered an aspect of training important for improving generalization. Teaching skills using this method requires providing enough exemplars (or examples) until the concept or induction is formed. Using sufficient exemplars is defined by White et al. (1988) as the sequential introduction of new target stimuli within an environment. These authors found only three studies using this procedure with individuals who had severe disabilities. In these studies, about half of the subjects with severe disabilities generalized well as a result of using this approach. Chandler et al. (1992) found that the use of sufficient exemplars as a strategy to improve generalization of social behaviors was approximately equal in more successful and less successful studies.

One problem with simply employing multiple exemplars is that the exemplars may not be adequately representative of the stimuli that will exist in various generalization circumstances. In order for the stimuli to be effective, therefore, there must be some criteria for their selection. Without such, simply using multiple stimuli in the training has not been found to result in effective generalization. The general case method (discussed below) was developed to provide the criteria for the selection of the exemplars.

Training loosely allows for unplanned variation in both the stimuli used to prompt the skill or behavior during initial training and the form of the behavior as exhibited by the learner. It has had only modest success in promoting generalization by individuals with disabilities and those without (Chandler et al., 1992; White et al., 1988). Programming common stimuli, which means to ensure that stimuli that will exist in the generalization settings also exist in the initial training setting, has resulted in somewhat more success than training loosely when teaching individuals with severe disabilities (White et al., 1988). Part of the effectiveness of this approach is dependent on how similar the "common stimuli" are in the training condition in comparison to the generalization condition. If there is much similarity, generalization will probably be more successful than if there is little (Westling & Floyd, 1990).

Based on the analyses of the available research, the general case method is considered the most successful antecedent training strategy for promoting generalization (Fox, 1989; Westling & Floyd, 1990; White et al., 1988). This approach uses multiple exemplars that are representative of the universe of conditions or settings in which the learner is to successfully demonstrate the learned skill (Albin, McDonnell, & Wilcox, 1987; Horner, McDonnell, & Bellamy, 1986; Horner, Sprague, & Wilcox, 1982). In the various reviews of studies, this approach was consistently reported to result in high levels of generalized performance. It has been employed with much success in developing generalized skills in areas such as purchasing food in fast-food restaurants (McDonnell & Ferguson, 1988), in the operation of vending machines (Sprague & Horner, 1984), in purchasing groceries (McDonnell, Horner, & Williams, 1984), in selecting grocery items (Horner, Albin, & Ralph, 1986), and in street crossing (Horner, Jones, & Williams, 1985). Because the general case method has been more successful than others, it is described in more detail later in this chapter.

Mediation During Generalization Training

An approach that has not been studied a great deal but that has met with some amount of success is the use of mediated events to help generalization occur. Liberty (1987) noted that generalization strategies such as those presented above are based on the control of environmental stimuli, either antecedents or consequences, by someone other than the learner. In contrast, she proposed that "self-control" by the learner through the use of mediational techniques (for example, reminding oneself what is being done and what is to be done later) may be an effective method to improve skill generalization.

Liberty (1987) examined the effect of self-control on 34 skills by various individuals, some with severe disabilities and some without. She found that the use of this strategy improved the generalization ability for 90% of the persons without severe disabilities and for 50% of those with severe disabilities. The analysis by Chandler et al. (1992) of the social behavior of young children also found that the use of mediators was an effective strategy in that it was used more often in studies that resulted in successful generalization than in those that were not as successful.

Summary of the Effectiveness of Generalization Strategies

Six of eight strategies examined by White et al. (1988), when used in isolation, produced statistically better results than the success generally achieved using the "train and hope" approach (e.g., 25%). These included using natural contingencies, indiscriminable contingencies, programming common stimuli, using sufficient exemplars, training loosely, and using the general case method. Training in the natural environment did not produce better results than the "train and hope" approach, nor did using mediation techniques to achieve generalization. However, in the latter case, White et al. looked at relatively few subjects (six) in few studies (two) and this low number probably precluded finding statistically significant differences. In contrast, Liberty (1987) found the use of mediational techniques to be effective for about half of the persons with severe disabilities with whom they were tried.

Although the above conclusions can be drawn about strategies when they are used in isolation (i.e., no other strategy is used to help promote generalization), most of the studies reviewed by White et al. used combinations of strategies intended to promote generalization. While this makes the effect of individual strategies difficult to determine, it provides useful information for the practitioner because most teachers would use more than one strategy at a time to promote generalization. Interestingly, counter to what one might intuitively conclude, White et al. found that some strategies decreased in their effectiveness when used in combination with other strategies. It should be realized, however, that to conclude that the use of multiple strategies reduces the probability of generalization is risky. Various reasons may be proposed as to why this result occurred, including the relative role of a particular generalization strategy in specific studies. Notable is the fact that the effectiveness of training in the natural environment increased when it was combined with other methods intended to increase generalization.

Chandler et al. (1992) found that in studies that resulted in most successful generalization, the most common strategies used were addressing functional target behaviors, using indiscriminable contingencies, and specifying a fluency criterion. In contrast, each of these strategies was used in relatively few of the studies that resulted in the least amount of generalization success. Chandler et al. also analyzed most and least successful combinations of generalization strategies. They found that the most successful combinations of two promotion strategies included the following: addressing functional target behaviors and using indiscriminable contingencies; using indiscriminable contingencies and teaching mediation strategies; and addressing functional target behaviors and teaching mediation strategies. The studies analyzed by Chandler et al. that used three or four generalization promotion strategies most often included some combination of addressing functional target behaviors, specifying a fluency criterion, using indiscriminable contingencies, and using mediational strategies.

As can be seen, the practitioner has many generalization strategies that can be useful when teaching skills to students with severe disabilities. In the planning process, it is important to realize the significance of generalization and plan for it prior to the beginning of instruction. Without such planning, the instruction may help the student acquire a particular skill, but the usefulness of the skill may be limited to the situation in which it has been learned.

Applying Generalization Strategies

Implementing various methods to assist in the achievement of generalization by persons with severe disabilities should be considered an important aspect of instruction by teachers. Fortunately, as seen from the previous descriptions, the practicing teacher has several strategies that can be used to help the student progress beyond the level of skill acquisition.

Stokes and Osnes (1988) suggested three principles that they considered to be important for achieving generalization. The first was to take advantage of natural communities of reinforcement, meaning that within an individual's environment there exist natural reinforcers (generally social reinforcers) that may be successfully applied to promote generalization of particular skills. Second, it was proposed that instructors should train diversely (or train loosely). Stokes and Osnes acknowledged that more tightly controlled training activities may influence behaviors more quickly during the acquisition phase of learning, but suggested that more variation in stimuli may ultimately result in better generalization. They suggested that only the least amount of control necessary for successful acquisition be applied. Finally, as a principle for instruction, Stokes and Osnes suggested that functional mediators be used during initial instruction that could be applied to the generalization settings or conditions. They stated that these could be either physical stimuli, such as objects, or stimuli "carried by" the learner, such as verbal instructions one could use as a self-control or self-reminder technique.

Tactics of Generalization Programming

Going beyond general principles, Stokes and Osnes (1988) suggested multiple tactics for improving generalization based on research literature such as that presented above. These tactics include the following.

Teach Relevant Behavior As has been stated throughout this text, the primary focus of instruction for students with severe disabilities should be teaching behaviors that can be applied to improve their lives. But teaching relevant or functional behaviors also means that these behaviors will be more likely to generalize, because such behaviors are more likely to result in reinforcement than are behaviors that are irrelevant or nonfunctional.

Modify Environments Supporting Maladaptive Behaviors Functional and appropriate behaviors are less likely to occur if inappropriate behaviors are occurring. Thus it is important that reinforcement is available for appropriate behavior but not for maladaptive behavior. More information for decreasing inappropriate behavior in a positive fashion is presented in chapter 11.

Recruit Communities of Natural Reinforcers As the earlier principle stated, natural reinforcers should be used to promote generalization. However, because the occurrence of these reinforcers in the natural environment may be less than sufficient, the learner with severe disabilities may be taught to seek reinforcement for positive generalized behavior by prompting members of his or her environment to provide it by asking such questions as "How am I doing?"

Use Sufficient Stimulus Exemplars In order to improve generalization, Stokes and Osnes suggested that one of the most important things that can be done is to vary the instructional materials and settings. It will also be helpful to use various persons during the training process.

Use Sufficient Response Exemplars In order to allow for more functional success, Stokes and Osnes suggest that variations in the nature of the behavior being learned be reinforced so that it may be more applicable to all of the different generalization situations. This is referred to as response generalization.

Use Indiscriminable Contingencies It is easy for particular behaviors or skills being learned by individuals with severe disabilities to be linked to particular reinforcers and schedules of reinforcement. In order to enhance generalization, therefore, contingencies of reinforcement should become progressively less discriminable. Stokes and Osnes suggested that the sooner this happens in the instructional process, the better it will be for the student.

Use Common Physical and Social Stimuli When the learner moves beyond the initial learning environment and into the generalization environment, his or her success in the new environment will be related to the stimuli in the new environment that were present in the previous environment. Such stimuli may be physical, such as signs, furniture, or equipment, or social, such as friends, peers, siblings, and so forth.

Stokes and Osnes (1988) felt that application of the above principles and tactics from the onset of the instruction for particular skills or behaviors was critical. They summarized:

> *Generalization programming needs to be built in to any serious behavior management program from the beginning of any behavior change procedure. If the focus of attention and effort turns to issues of generalization only after a successful but well-discriminated behavior change, it may be too late. It may be more complicated to work on such programming from the outset, but it is probably more efficient in the long run. (Stokes & Osnes, 1988, p. 15)*

Applying Decision Rules About Generalization Strategies

Although blanket application of the principles and tactics suggested by Stokes and Osnes would seemingly increase the likelihood of generalization, Liberty and her colleagues offered an alternative. They have suggested that "decision rules" would allow practitioners to determine the most appropriate strategies to use to help students with severe disabilities learn to generalize skills (Liberty, 1988; Liberty, Haring, White, & Billingsley, 1988). These decision rules rest on four assumptions:

1. Generalization must be a target of instruction, and criteria for measuring generalization and the conditions under which generalization is expected should be specified in the IEP.
2. Direct assessment of student performance in the target generalization situations is required to make decisions about generalization.
3. Some learners with severe disabilities may generalize some skills before, during, or after instruction without the need for special strategies, and
4. If a learner does not generalize a skill once it has been acquired, special strategies are needed (Liberty et al., 1988, pp. 316–317).

The decisions about which strategies might be used to improve generalization are based on the answers to a series of questions that are asked about the student's performance. These questions, the procedures used to acquire the answers, and the next step or decision to make based on the answers are presented in Table 7–1.

As the entries in Table 7–1 indicate, the first question to be answered is whether or not the skill has generalized in all desired situations when assessed in initial probes. This implies that these situations have been identified through the planning process and that probes have been taken in these situations to see if the skill is present. It would obviously not be necessary to plan a generalization instructional strategy if the individual already could demonstrate the behavior or skill under all desirable conditions, situations, or settings. Assuming that the answer to this item will most often be "no" (the student cannot demonstrate the behavior in a generalized fashion), the next question is whether the student has acquired the skill. In other words, in a single instructional setting, has the student been able to demonstrate the skill to a level of satisfaction? If not, the instructor is to continue instruction leading toward skill mastery using acquisition training procedures such as described in the previous chapter.

If the student is able to demonstrate the skill under a single training condition, the next question is to what extent generalization is desired. This is an important consideration. There will sometimes be situations when generalization to only a few settings or conditions

Table 7–1
Decision Rules for Generalization

	Question	Procedures	Answer	Next Step/Decision
A.	Has skill generalized at the desired level in all target situations?	Probe for generalization in all desired situations, then compare performance with criteria (IEP objective).	yes	1 SUCCESSFUL INSTRUCTION * Step ahead to a more difficult level of skill * Choose a new skill to teach. EXIT sequence
			no	CONTINUE with question B.
B.	Has skill been acquired?	Compare performance in instructional situation with criteria for acquisition or performance levels specified in IEP objective. Answer yes if student has met performance levels in training situation but not in generalization.	yes	CONTINUE with question C.
			no	2 SKILL MASTERY PROBLEM * Continue instruction. EXIT sequence
C.	Is generalization desired to only a few situations?	Analyze function of skill in current and future environments available to student.	yes	CONTINUE with question D.
			no	CONTINUE with question E.
D.	Is it possible to train directly in those situations?	Are all situations frequently accessible for training so that training time is likely to be adequate to meet aim date in IEP objective?	yes	3 LIMITED GENERALIZATION SITUATIONS * Train in desired situation * Train sequentially in all situations (sequential modification). EXIT sequence
			no	CONTINUE with question E.
E.	Does student perform inappropriate or other behaviors instead of the target skill *and* is the student reinforced? OR Does the student fail to respond *and* is reinforced (accesses reinforcers)?	Observe student behavior during probes and note events which follow appropriate, inappropriate, target, and non-target skills. Determine if those events are those which should follow the target skill, or have been shown to reinforce other skills.	yes	to either question, CONTINUE with question F.
			no	to both questions, CONTINUE with question G.

	Question	Procedure	Answer	Result
F.	Reinforcers contingent on others?	Observe how student is reinforced. If other people deliver the reinforcement, answer YES. If student accesses reinforcer directly, answer NO.	yes	4 COMPETING REINFORCER PROBLEM * Alter generalization contingencies * Amplify instructed behavior. EXIT sequence
			no	5 COMPETING BEHAVIOR PROBLEM * Increase proficiency * Amplify instructed behavior * Alter generalization contingencies. EXIT sequence
G.	Did the student generalize once at or close to criterion performance levels and then not as well on other opportunities? (Consider performance in current and past probes.)	Compare student performance for each response opportunity with performance level specified in objective. If near criterion performance occurred on the first response opportunity, and performance was poor or non-existent after that, answer yes.	yes	6 REINFORCING FUNCTION PROBLEM * Program natural reinforcers * Eliminate training reinforcers * Use natural schedules * Use natural consequences * Teach self-reinforcement * Teach to solicit reinforcement * Reinforce generalized behavior * Alter generalization contingencies EXIT sequence
			no	CONTINUE with question H.
H.	Did the student respond partially correctly during at least one response opportunity?	Analyze anecdotal data and observational notes from probes.	yes	7 DISCRIMINATION FUNCTION PROBLEM Vary stimuli: * Use all stimuli * Use frequent stimuli * Use multiple exemplars * Use general case exemplars EXIT sequence
			no	CONTINUE with question I.
I.	Did the student fail to perform any part of the target skill?	Analyze student performance during probe situation.	yes	8 GENERALIZATION TRAINING FORMAT * Increase proficiency * Program natural reinforcers * Use natural schedules * Use appropriate natural stimuli * Eliminate training stimuli EXIT sequence
			no	*STOP.* You have made an error in the sequence. Begin again at Question A.

From "A Technology for the Future: Decision Rules for Generalization" by K. A. Liberty, N. G. Haring, O. R. White, & F. Billingsley, 1988, *Education and Training in Mental Retardation, 23,* pp. 315–326. Copyright 1988 by the Division on Mental Retardation and Developmental Disabilities, The Council for Exceptional Children. Reprinted by permission.

is desirable. For example, since a person usually shops in a limited number of grocery stores or convenience stores and uses the same brand of sanitary napkins, how much generalization is actually necessary? When only a few specific locations or conditions are necessary to ensure functional performance and extensive generalization will not improve the quality of life, it will most likely be sufficient to teach the individual to operate only in those select settings or under the desired specific conditions. When this is the training need, a sequential modification approach to teaching generalized skills will be adequate and appropriate.

If a sequential modification approach will not be sufficient, Liberty et al. suggest that the next issue to be considered is the existence of competing reinforcers. In other words, the individual's behavior may be affected by reinforcement for inappropriate behavior or simply be reinforced for not performing the desired target objective. If this is the case, the contingencies of reinforcement must be changed so that the student is not reinforced when demonstrating nontargeted behavior and is reinforced when the behavior occurs.

Reinforcement may also be a problem if the student does not appear to be motivated to perform the behavior or task in the generalized settings even though he or she has done so in the past or has come close to doing so. When the situation is "she can do it if she wants to; she just doesn't want to," then reinforcement strategies to improve generalization should be considered. As Table 7–1 indicates, these strategies could include providing natural reinforcers while eliminating reinforcers used for initial instruction, teaching the person to use a mediational strategy to provide self-reinforcement, teaching the person to ask for reinforcement ("Do you think I did a good job on this?"), and reinforcing generalized behavior.

If the problem in achieving generalization is not related to reinforcement but to adequately attending and responding to correct stimuli ("Did the student respond partially correctly during at least one response opportunity?"), Liberty et al. refer to this as a "discrimination function problem" and offer accommodating solutions. These include varying the stimuli, using multiple exemplars, or using the general case method. Finally, the option of the student's not generalizing at all is presented; if this is the outcome, a "generalization training format" is suggested that calls for increasing proficiency, using natural reinforcers and natural schedules of reinforcement, and using natural stimuli while fading training stimuli.

Using the General Case Method

The general case method or general case programming is undoubtedly the most successful method that has been used to promote generalization by persons with severe disabilities. Because of the detail of its procedures and the extensiveness of the successful research associated with it, it warrants a more detailed report.

The general case method was developed by Horner and his colleagues and has been explained in several publications (Albin & Horner, 1988; Albin, McDonnell, & Wilcox, 1987; Horner, McDonnell, & Bellamy, 1986; Horner, Sprague, & Wilcox, 1982). The strategy requires that the practitioner undertake a relatively complicated process to ensure that skills that are acquired can be demonstrated in any environment or under any condition in which they are called for. The six steps of the general case method are described below. For more detail, the reader is referred to one of the references listed above.

Step 1: Define the Instructional Universe The first step of the general case method is to define the instructional universe. This means the teacher must determine all of the locations,

In general case instruction, teaching occurs in situations that provide the range of conditions that are present in generalization settings.

persons, conditions, and/or other situations in which the student is expected to demonstrate the learned behavior and also what type of variation in the behavior may be necessary. Certainly this could be an extensive task, but it directs the teacher to answer the question: "Under what circumstances is the behavior or skill expected to occur and what different forms could the behavior take?" For example, the parents and the teacher may decide that it is desirable for the student with severe disabilities to shop in all of the convenience stores within a three-block radius of his or her home and be able to buy any combination of snacks up to two dollars. These stores and the various items within them would then be considered the *instructional universe* of convenience stores in which the student would be expected to generalize. Other examples of instructional universes could include cleaning all of the tables in a restaurant that are ready to be cleaned, but not cleaning those that people are using; selecting clothing that would be appropriate for the weather; and selecting and using a board game from all of those in the apartment.

Step 2: Define the Range of Relevant Stimulus and Response Variation In this step, the teacher must consider all of the relevant aspects of all of the settings or conditions in the instructional universe in which generalization is to occur and also the variations in behaviors that may need to occur. There must be an identification of aspects of the environment that are likely to influence the successful performance of the learner, how these will vary, and the ways in which the learner will respond to the different stimuli. In reference to the convenience stores, for example, the teacher may note where the entrance doors are located (center or side), where the checkout counter is located (middle of the store or side), whether or not the store serves food, and so on. There may be several important stimuli that exist within the store and the teacher must know what they are and how the student must respond to them. Table 7–2 provides an illustration of an activity analysis for fast-food restaurants (Albin et al., 1987). As can be seen, there are five considerations: first, the generic responses are identified; second, all of the discriminative stimuli that could prompt the target responses are listed; third, the possible variations of stimulus classes are listed; fourth, ways in which the learner might respond are

Table 7–2
Illustration of Activity Analysis for Using a Fast-Food Restaurant

Generic Response Components	Discriminative Stimuli	Range of Stimulus Characteristics	Response Variation	Anticipated Problems/Errors/ Exceptions
1. ENTER	Door	Door type (single, double, automatic)	Push or pull door Walk through automatic door	Door location varies
	People entering or exiting	People present (entering before, entering after)	Follow others in/out Wait Push or pull and hold open for others	Student may hold door for too many people
2. APPROACH COUNTER	Counter	On the right On the left Straight ahead after entering	Walk to counter at register	Separate order and pick-up counters
	Register	Tan register on counter		Visibility of register varies Shape of register varies
	People waiting in line	One too many people waiting in line	Walk to end of line and move up with the line	
	Entry lane	Railings for entrance lane	Walk though lane	
3. ORDER	Verbal request for order	Can I help you? What will it be? Yes. Can I take your order? Have you been helped? What would you like? Will that be to stay or go?	Show communication notebook for a drink or lunch Verbally order Request condiments if desired Answer "stay" or "go"	Other employees behind counter not taking orders
	Clerk at counter	Clerk at register eye contact with customer		Number of people in restaurant varies with time of day
	Item choices	Drinks only		

outlined; finally, there is a list of anticipated problems, errors, and exceptions.

Step 3: Select Examples for Teaching and Probe Testing Having identified relevant stimuli and response variations, the teacher must select one set of examples from the instructional universe for use in teaching and one set for probe testing. Both sets must reflect the range of conditions that exist within the universe and all behaviors that may be required. Again considering the convenience store, the teacher

Table 7–2, *continued*

Generic Response Components	Discriminative Stimuli	Range of Stimulus Characteristics	Response Variation	Anticipated Problems/Errors/Exceptions
		Preselected choices in prosthetic Hamburger, french fries, cola, etc.		Menu changes with time of day
4. PAY	Displayed cost	Amounts .15-$4.99 Color of numerals on register Red or green LED Readout location Near top of register No readout	Count out X + 1 dollars and hand to counter person Money from wallet and/or pocket	
	Verbal cue	.XX Cents		Other prices being stated in close proximity
5. OBTAIN ORDER	Order payment made	Clerk may say "Thank you" Give receipt or number Put money in register Give direction to move to next window	Step aside and wait for order to come up Move to pick-up window and wait for order	Other orders will come up before student's order
6. EAT	Requested items in hand	Tray (no tray, single item)	Picks up order Locates condiments, gets what needed	Food or drinks may be dropped or spilled
	Empty table	Table (2 chairs, 3 chairs, 4 chairs) Table (empty)	Locates table, sits down, and eats	No empty tables
7. EXIT	All finished eating	Food and beverage gone	Bus table if required	Other customers may or may not bus table
	Time up	Time management prosthetic (watch or clock)	Exit building	

From "Designing Intervention to Meet Activity Goals" by R. W. Albin, J. J. McDonnell, & B. Wilcox (pp. 63–88), in B. Wilcox & G. T. Bellamy (Eds.), *The Comprehensive Guide to the Activities Catalog,* 1987, Baltimore: Paul H. Brookes Publishing Co., P.O. Box 10624, Baltimore, Maryland 21285-0624. Reprinted by permission.

would have to select some that have the door on the side and others that have the door in the center; some that have the checkout counter in the center of the store and some that have it on one side of the store; some that serve food and some that do not, and so on. It is not necessary that the teacher select all of the stores for instruction, but the ones that are selected must adequately represent the variations of important stimuli and responses. The list is then divided equally, with some stores being used for teaching and others for testing. Each list must reflect an adequate array of stimulus conditions and requisite behaviors.

In teaching the generalization of some skills, it is important to have two types of teaching examples: positive examples and negative examples (Albin & Horner, 1988). Positive examples are used to teach the learner the conditions appropriate for when the behavior should occur; negative examples are presented so the learner will know when not to enact the behavior. The table- clearing situation suggests the type of occasion when negative as well as positive teaching examples are necessary. Typically, when it is possible for the student to "overgeneralize," there should be adequate examples of the negative conditions or stimuli in order to teach the student not to do so. Albin and Horner (1988) point out that the greater the differences are between the positive and negative stimuli, the easier it will be for the learner to make the discrimination. However, the smaller the differences, the more precise in discrimination ability will the learner ultimately become. Therefore, they suggest that in initially teaching discrimination-generalization tasks, the teacher start with positive and negative samples that are very different, then reduce their differences over progressive instructional opportunities.

Additional guidelines for selecting instructional examples are (Albin et al., 1987):

1. Select the smallest number of teaching examples that will sample the full range of stimulus and response variation in the instructional universe.
2. Select teaching examples that provide equal amounts of new information to the learner.
3. Provide adequate negative teaching examples (that teach the learner what not to do).
4. Select examples that vary irrelevant stimuli (characteristics that do not provide information about whether or not the behavior should occur).
5. Select examples that include significant exceptions.
6. Select examples that are logistically feasible.

Step 4: Sequence the Teaching Examples Having selected appropriate examples for instruction, the teacher must sequence these in an appropriate order for instruction. Albin et al. (1987) offered five guidelines for sequencing instruction.

1. Teach multiple components of an activity within a training session (do not teach isolated components).
2. Present variations within individual sessions. Teach as many of the examples as possible with training sessions.
3. Juxtapose the most similar positive and negative examples to improve discrimination ability.
4. Use cumulative programming. If all teaching examples cannot be taught in one session, work on a few at a time, adding new examples to already learned examples in each new session.
5. Teach the general case before teaching exceptions.

Step 5: Teach the Sequence That Was Developed The instructional activities required would employ the methods of skill acquisition described in the previous chapter. The important aspect required by the general case method is the use of appropriate stimuli to ensure proper generalization.

Step 6: Test the Nontrained Probe Examples In order to determine if generalization has occurred, the teacher must examine the student's performance under each of the relevant conditions initially identified.

The general case method of teaching is rather complex because it forces the teacher, the parents, and other members of the collaborative team to consider various settings or conditions in which the behavior or skill needs to occur. Then it asks that all of the relevant variations be identified, taught, and tested. Although the process is complicated, it provides the most empirically validated method for achieving generalization. Teachers may wish to consider various methods for achieving generalization, but the general case method is likely to be the most effective. Certainly it provides a framework for thought about the factors that affect generalization and at least for this reason merits attention.

Maintenance

Maintenance is discussed in the following sections. Unfortunately, there does not exist much research on the long-term retention of skills by persons with severe disabilities (separate from that which appears in the generalization literature), so there is no opportunity to validate the effectiveness of different approaches.

Defining Maintenance

Maintenance refers to a behavior or skill continuing to occur for as long as it is needed without having to be taught again, for example, learning to ride a bicycle, then being able to use that skill whenever it is required or desired. A student with a severe disability who maintains a behavior or skill for a long period of time (e.g., more than a year) will have the advantage of being able to apply the skill when it is needed. Several strategies may improve the chance of this occurring.

Strategies for Teaching Skill Maintenance

In order for students with severe disabilities to maintain learned skills over a long period of time, they must learn the skills to a functional degree of usefulness and use the skills in many situations over a long period of time. Therefore, the strategies that can be used to teach skill generalization will also help achieve skill maintenance. The error often made is that a skill is learned, and even generalized to some degree, but then is not practiced sufficiently beyond the initial learning period. Or a skill is learned, but not well enough for it to be practical or used after the teaching sessions have ended. In order to avoid these problems, several strategies are suggested. They should be used in addition to strategies that will facilitate skill generalization (Alberto & Troutman, 1990).

Skill Overlearning

Students should learn the skill to an adequate level of performance and then continue practicing the skill beyond that point, a practice referred to as "overlearning." It suggests that an appropriate criterion statement for an objective should be the correct performance of the behavior or skill many times after the first time it is performed. Alberto and Troutman (1990) suggested that overlearning opportunities be at least 50% of the opportunities that were necessary for the student to initially learn the objective.

Learning Through Distributed Practice

Another way to help make sure the skill is maintained is to practice it during distributed learning sessions. This means instead of working with a student to see some skill practiced ten times in a row in a very short period of time (i.e., massed practice), practice is spread out across the day. When the student is given many opportunities to practice a skill at different times instead of all at once, the skill is likely to be maintained for a longer period of time after it has been initially learned.

Intermittent Reinforcement

As discussed in the chapter on skill acquisition, providing the student with reinforcement after the completion of a particular behavior increases the chance of that same behavior recurring in the future when similar stimuli are present. During acquisition training, it is important to reinforce the behavior nearly every time it occurs so the student can learn the connection between the stimulus conditions, the behavior, and the reinforcer. However, in order for a behavior to strengthen (to be more resistant to extinction), the teacher should use positive reinforcement on an intermittent basis after the behavior has been pretty well established.

There are four main intermittent schedules of reinforcement: fixed ratio and variable ratio (FR and VR) schedules and fixed interval and variable interval (FI and VI) schedules. Ratio schedules reinforce the behavior based on a count of the behavior. For example, the teacher may determine that for every five dishes washed correctly, the student will receive a reinforcer. This would be a ratio schedule of reinforcement; more precisely, it would be a *fixed* ratio five (FR: 5) schedule because the reinforcement would be delivered following every fifth dish washed. If the reinforcement delivery schedule was calculated so that the reinforcer was delivered *on an average* of every five dishes washed but not precisely on each fifth dish, this would be a *variable* ratio five (VR: 5) schedule of reinforcement.

Interval schedules of reinforcement are based on time instead of number of behaviors occurring. Consider again the student learning to wash dishes. If the teacher decided to reinforce the student after a 2-minute period of dishwashing without regard to the number of dishes washed, this would be an interval schedule of reinforcement. The reinforcer would be delivered after the first dish was finished, following a 2-minute period; this would be referred to as a fixed interval 2-minute (FI: 2 min.) schedule. Variable interval schedules are like variable ratio schedules except that the reinforcement delivery is based on an average amount of time passage instead of an average number of behaviors occurring. For example, the student washing dishes would be reinforced on a schedule that has an average of 2 minutes passing between reinforcement delivery.

All intermittent schedules have the effect of making behavioral occurrences more frequent simply because the learner must exhibit more behavior before it is reinforced. They will also make the behavior less vulnerable to extinction. Variable schedules are more effective than fixed schedules because the learner does not know when the reinforcement is coming and thus tends to work more to get it. Use of intermittent schedules of reinforcement can be of great practicality in building strong behavioral and skill repertoires. As the behavior develops more and more, the schedules can be "leaned out" so that more and more behavior (or time) must occur before the reinforcement. This again will produce stronger behaviors that will be more likely to maintain over longer periods of time.

Building on Learned Skills

Another strategy that may help prevent the loss of learned skills is to incorporate the newly acquired skills into different, new skills. Likewise, skills can be linked together through different activities. For example, a student may have learned to participate in home economic activities by holding utensils or being responsible for mixing various ingredients. These activities may help achieve the student's need to hold items with her hand and improve fine motor skills. These same motor skills can be practiced during different classroom activities, art activities, physical education, or during some leisure-time activities. The more opportunities for practice the student is given, the greater the likelihood will be that the behavior will be maintained.

Another way to consider the application of this guideline is by inserting newly learned skills into existing tasks or routines. For example, a student may know how to go into a movie and enjoy watching it, but may not know how to use public transportation. Learning to ride a bus or subway may be targeted for instruction, and, once it has been satisfactorily learned, should be included in the routine of going to a movie.

Using a Maintenance Schedule

Students with severe disabilities may learn skills that are functional, but may be used infrequently or on an irregular basis. Going to a dentist's office, using a sanitary napkin, and responding to a fire alarm are examples of skills that may be considered important by parents and other team members. However, skills such as these are easy to forget if they are not practiced often enough.

Obviously some of these skills will be naturally practiced on a regular basis and it is very likely that they will be maintained. Others, however, should be placed on a "maintenance list" and practiced on a regular timetable, say once a month, after they have been learned initially. If this provision is not made, the skill is likely to be forgotten, which would indicate the need for reteaching it and then practicing it more often.

Using the Skill at Home and Elsewhere

If a skill has been identified as an important target for instruction there is probably a need for it outside of the classroom or other initial learning environments, and it might be expected that the skill would be practiced in settings and at times when it is needed. If this is the case, the additional practice is likely to help the skill be maintained. Skills that are not useful or helpful to an individual with severe disabilities are likely to neither generalize nor be maintained. This point is made so that during the initial identification of skills for instruction efforts are made by all involved to agree that practice outside of the primary learning environment is encouraged and coordinated with learning new skills.

Skills can be maintained through regular practice after initial training. Varying the location or other conditions of the practice setting will also help ensure that generalized use of the skill is being maintained. A major error that is often made is that a skill is learned to an acceptable level of criterion as specified within the instructional objective, but then is not adequately practiced and is forgotten. This is certainly a common problem, but one that teachers should avoid if possible.

Writing Instructional Programs to Include Generalization Training and Promote Maintenance

In the previous chapter, an outline was provided for writing instructional plans for individual objectives (see Figure 6–1). The suggested plan was to include the objective, setting and material, a task analysis or elements of a routine, an instructional procedure, and reinforcement and error correction procedures. It is also proposed that the plan include a description of how generalization will be taught and how the behavior or skill might be maintained over a period of time.

The first step toward teaching skills that will generalize and be maintained is to *plan* adequately. Generally, it is not sufficient to plan to teach a particular skill to an individual with severe disabilities; the plan should also include provisions for generalizing the skill. Whether the skill is an individual behavior that will allow the student to participate more, a complex chained skill, or routine, such as going shopping in department stores, adequate planning will include a strategy for generalization. This will require that the parents, the teachers, and the rest of the collaborative team raise questions about where the skill needs to occur, with what people, under what conditions, at what times, with what variations and exceptions, and what behavioral changes may be expected. Addressing questions such as these will result in objectives that include generalized outcomes (Billingsley, 1988; Billingsley, Burgess, Lynch, & Matlock, 1991).

The objective presented as an example in Figure 6–1 in the previous chapter can be redesigned to include generalization and maintenance in its format. The intention was for the student to be able to clean a bathroom by completing each of the steps in a task analysis. But could it be concluded that if a student successfully cleaned one bathroom that this objective would have been achieved? Based on the criteria presented in the original objective, the answer would be "yes." However, two facts should be apparent. The first is that satisfactorily cleaning one bathroom does not indicate that the student can clean all of the bathrooms in several motels or even in one motel. Second, unless the student can learn to clean all of the motel bathrooms requiring cleaning, it cannot be expected that he or she will be successful at a job that requires this skill. Therefore, the objective should be rewritten to reflect the appropriate degree of generalization required, for example:

> *James will clean all of the bathrooms in the motel where he is working . . .*

Or,

> *James will clean all of the bathrooms in the six motels on the interstate highway. . . .*

In this way, generalization becomes an expected part of the objective. Once the need for generalization has been established and written into the objective, a generalization plan can be incorporated into the instructional plan. To do this the various strategies discussed in this chapter could be reviewed to see what might be helpful in achieving generalization, for example, the general case method. The plan for achieving generalization would then require following the six steps called for by that strategy.

In addition to generalization, the question of skill maintenance must be considered when the planning is being done. Once again, to use the previous example as an example, the plan might include a statement that the student will be able to successfully clean the bathrooms over a one-year period of time:

> *James will be able to continue cleaning bathrooms successfully for one year without additional instruction after initial learning and successful generalization.*

If the student were to be working cleaning hotel rooms for that period of time (one year), there would be no special difficulty in monitoring the maintenance of the skill. However, for other objectives, continued practice after the initial learning had been achieved would need to be specified. This would state the number of times per week, month, or semester, for example, that it would be necessary for the student to practice the behavior and in what locations or under what circumstances. As this practice was done, the teacher would record the student's performance. Appropriate procedures for continuously monitoring students' performance is discussed in the following chapter.

Conclusion

People without cognitive disabilities acquire certain skills in their lives either through direct instruction or incidental learning. In the process, they also learn new and different circumstances in which it is appropriate to apply the skills and, conversely, circumstances in which the skills do not apply. The learning and generalization continue throughout their lives and important skills are maintained for a long time.

People with cognitive disabilities have learning abilities that are not as efficient. It takes longer periods of time for them to learn and then they often do not know the circumstances in which to use the skills they have learned, or they forget how to use the skills before they have been practiced enough. For many years teachers and parents have been frustrated by the fact that students did not remember or did not apply previously learned skills to new or different situations.

Part of the problem of such shortcomings is due to the learner, but part is also due to the instructional process. The "train and hope" strategy is not effective for achieving generalization or helping to maintain the newly learned skill for most students. Parents and professionals must actively plan and implement strategies that will ensure that generalization and maintenance occur to a desired degree.

Some of the current best practices are likely to result in more generalization and maintenance. The fact that there is much greater focus on functional skills is very important and will do much more to ensure that what is taught is going to be reinforced in the natural environment. In addition, teaching in nonschool natural environments is going to be helpful. Although teaching in only one such environment does not necessarily result in generalization, multiple sites of the appropriate variety are likely to do so. Using natural reinforcers and natural schedules of reinforcement also help generalization and maintenance occur more often. But foremost in importance is the idea that generalization and maintenance are important and desirable outcomes, no less important than initial skill acquisition. Given this assumption, during initial training there must be a plan that will achieve these components of the instructional objective. The strategies and tactics presented in this chapter are intended to help achieve this outcome.

Questions for Reflection

1. Why is generalization so difficult to achieve when only the "train and hope" approach is used? How might student characteristics be related to this result?
2. What type of reinforcement procedures might best result in generalization and maintenance? Why?
3. What are the most important decisions that must be made using the "decision rules"?
4. Why has research found the general case method to be so successful? What would be the most difficult aspect of this method for a teacher to implement?
5. How would the relevance or functionality of a behavior help achieve maintenance and generalization?
6. Why would it help students to maintain certain skills by incorporating them into other skills?

7. How can successful generalization of a skill also help achieve successful maintenance?
8. Describe a plan that would allow a teacher to simultaneously work on generalization and maintenance.

References

Alberto, P. A., & Troutman, A. C. (1990). *Applied behavior analysis for teachers* (3rd ed.). New York: Merrill/Macmillan.

Albin, R. W., & Horner, R. H. (1988). Generalization with precision. In R. H. Horner, G. Dunlap, & R. L. Koegel (Eds.), *Generalization and maintenance: Life style changes in applied settings* (pp. 99–120). Baltimore: Paul H. Brookes.

Albin, R. W., McDonnell, J. J., & Wilcox, B. (1987). Designing intervention to meet activity goals. In B. Wilcox & G. T. Bellamy (Eds.), *The comprehensive guide to the* Activities Catalog (pp. 63–88). Baltimore: Paul H. Brookes.

Billingsley, F. F. (1984). Where are the generalized outcomes? (An examination of instructional objectives). *Journal of the Association for Persons with Severe Handicaps, 9,* 186–192.

Billingsley, F. F. (1988). Writing objectives for generalization. In N. G. Haring (Ed.), *Generalization for students with severe handicaps: Strategies and solutions* (pp. 123–128). Seattle: University of Washington Press.

Billingsley, F. F., Burgess, D., Lynch, V. W., & Matlock, B. L. (1991). Toward generalized outcomes: Considerations for writing instructional objectives. *Education and Training in Mental Retardation, 26,* 351–360.

Brown, L., Nisbet, J., Ford, A., Sweet, M., Shiraga, B., & York, J. (1983). The critical need for non-school instruction in programs for severely handicapped students. *Journal of the Association for the Severely Handicapped, 8,* 71–77.

Chandler, L. K., Lubeck, R. C., & Fowler, S. A. (1992). Generalization and maintenance of preschool children's social skills: A critical review and analysis. *Journal of Applied Behavior Analysis, 25,* 415–428.

Donnellan, A. M., & Mirenda, P. L. (1983). A model for analyzing instructional components to facilitate generalization for severely handicapped students. *Journal of Special Education, 17,* 317–331.

Falvey, M. A. (1989). *Community-based curriculum: Instructional strategies for students with severe handicaps* (2nd ed.). Baltimore: Paul H. Brookes.

Fox, L. (1989). Stimulus generalization of skills and persons with profound mental handicaps. *Education and Training in Mental Retardation, 24,* 219–229.

Haring, N. G. (Principal investigator). (1987). *Investigating the problem of skill generalization: Literature review III.* Seattle: University of Washington, Washington Research Organization.

Haring, N. G. (Ed.). (1988). *Generalization for students with severe handicaps: Strategies and solutions.* Seattle: University of Washington Press.

Haring, N. G., Liberty, K., Billingsley, F., White, O., Lynch, V., Kayser, J., & McCarty, F. (1985). *Investigating the problem of skill generalization* (3rd ed.). Seattle: University of Washington, Washington Research Organization.

Horner, R. H., Albin, R. W., & Ralph, G. (1986). Generalization with precision: The role of negative teaching examples in the instruction of generalized grocery item selection. *Journal of the Association for Persons with Severe Handicaps, 11,* 300–308.

Horner, R. H., Dunlap, G., & Koegel, R. L. (Eds.). (1988). *Generalization and maintenance: Life style changes in applied settings.* Baltimore: Paul H. Brookes.

Horner, R. H., Jones, D. N., & Williams, J. A. (1985). A functional approach to teaching generalized street crossing. *Journal of the Association for Persons with Severe Handicaps, 10,* 71–978.

Horner, R. H., McDonnell, J. J., & Bellamy, G. T. (1986). Teaching generalized skills: General case instruction in simulation and community settings. In R. H. Horner, L. H. Meyer, & H. D. Fredericks (Eds.), *Education of learners with severe handicaps: Exemplary service strategies* (pp. 289–314). Baltimore: Paul H. Brookes.

Horner, R. H., Sprague, J., & Wilcox, B. (1982). Constructing general case programs for community activities. In B. Wilcox & G. T. Bellamy (Eds.). *Design of high school programs for severely handicapped students* (pp. 61–98). Baltimore: Paul H. Brookes.

Liberty, K. (1987). Behaver-control of stimulus events to facilitate generalization. In N. G. Haring (Principal investigator), *Investigating the problem of skill generalization: Literature review III* (pp. 1-16). Seattle: University of Washington, Washington Research Organization.

Liberty, K. (1988). Characteristics and foundations of decision rules. In N. G. Haring (Ed.), *Generalization for students with severe handicaps: Strategies and solutions.* Seattle: University of Washington Press.

Liberty, K. A., Haring, N. G., White, O. R., & Billingsley, F. (1988). A technology for the future: Decision rules for generalization. *Education and Training in Mental Retardation, 23,* 315–326.

McDonnell, J., & Ferguson, B. (1988). A comparison of general case in vivo and general case simulation plus in vivo training. *Journal of the Association for Persons with Severe Handicaps, 13,* 116–124.

McDonnell, J. J., Horner, R. H., & Williams, J. A. (1984). Comparison of three strategies for teaching generalized grocery purchasing to high school students with severe handicaps. *Journal of the Association for Persons with Severe Handicaps, 9,* 123–133.

Sprague, J. R., & Horner, R. H. (1984). The effects of single instance, multiple instance, and general case training on generalized vending machine use by moderately and severely handicapped students. *Journal of Applied Behavior Analysis, 17,* 273–278.

Stokes, T. F., & Baer, D. M. (1977). An implicit technology of generalization. *Journal of Applied Behavior Analysis, 10,* 349–367.

Stokes, T. F., & Osnes, P. G. (1988). The developing applied technology of generalization and maintenance. In R. H. Horner, G. Dunlap, & R. L. Koegel (Eds.), *Generalization and maintenance: Life style changes in applied settings* (pp. 5–19). Baltimore: Paul H. Brookes.

Westling, D. L., & Floyd, J. (1990). Generalization of community skills: How much training is necessary? *Journal of Special Education, 23,* 386–406.

White, O. R., Liberty, K. A., Haring, N. G., Billingsley, F. F., Boer, M., Burrage, A., Connors, R., Farman, R., Fedorchak, G., Leber, B. D., Liberty-Laylin, S., Miller, S., Opalski, C., Phifer, C., & Sessoms, I. (1988). Review and analysis of strategies for generalization. In N. G. Haring (Ed.), *Generalization for students with severe handicaps: Strategies and solutions.* Seattle: University of Washington Press.

CHAPTER 8

Monitoring and Evaluating Student Progress

Chapter Overview

Methods for assessing students' progress as they are engaged in learning are discussed in this chapter. Most of the focus is on direct measurement of behavior, using quantifiable units of measure. Alternative continuous assessment practices using indirect measures and portfolio assessment are also discussed.

Developing instructional plans based on students' needs and implementing teaching tactics that will result in new skills being learned, maintained, and generalized requires a great deal of effort by teachers and other members of the team. However, only if some form of ongoing, continuous evaluation or assessment is implemented will the teacher, the parents, and other professionals know if important goals and specific instructional objectives are being met. Continuous assessment is a system that in some way measures each student's progress on a regular and frequent basis. It provides data that allows the teacher and others to know if adequate progress is being made, if certain teaching strategies are working, if there is a need to change to other approaches that may be more successful, or if there is a need to develop new instructional objectives. During all phases of the instructional process, including baseline (after an instructional target has been identified but before instruction), initial skill acquisition, and generalization and maintenance, the student's progress should be monitored and written records developed. Review of these records will then allow important decisions to be made.

There are different ways to approach the task of continuous assessment; all require the teacher to regularly observe and record the student's performance. The data must be written so that the teacher can observe over a period of time whether or not progress is sufficient and will not have to rely on memory to make important judgments. The task of data collection is often neglected, but available research suggests that teachers who collect student performance data make better decisions about instruction (Farlow & Snell, 1989; Fuchs & Fuchs, 1986). This means that students learn more because less time is spent on ineffective teaching practices.

There are three approaches presented in this chapter that may be employed to regularly monitor the learning of students with severe disabilities. These are:

- Direct measures of student performance
- Indirect measures of student performance
- Portfolio assessment of student performance.

Of these, the first has both the longest history and the greatest complexity, and therefore it will be discussed first and in relatively more detail. Teachers should become knowledgeable about all three approaches and then select the one (or perhaps a combination) that will best meet their needs as well as the needs of their students.

Direct Measures of Student Performance

The most traditional form of continuous assessment or data collection is a quantitative method that assesses progress through direct measurement of student behavioral performance. This method, based on the principles of precision teaching and usually attributed to the early work of Ogden Lindsley (1971), counts the occurrence of certain behaviors, or parts of behaviors, or takes other quantifiable measures of human behavior. The behaviors targeted for measurement are usually those that are specified on the IEP to be learned or improved in some way. In addition, behaviors that are considered to be challenging or targeted for decreasing (see chapter 11) may also be measured using direct measurement techniques.

Using direct measurement, the teacher or another observer makes a record of the student's performance during instruction, during "probe" periods (attempts by the student to perform the task without instruction), or at other times when the behavior may be expected to occur, then transfers the written data to a graph or chart. By adding data points on a daily (or frequent) basis and using straight lines to connect the points, the teacher (as well as others, such as the student or the parents) can easily observe the student's progress on a particular behavior or skill over a period of time. This type of continuous measurement system has been used for many years in the fields of applied behavior analysis and special education (Alberto & Troutman, 1990; Browder, 1991; Brown & Snell, 1993; Sailor & Guess, 1983; White & Haring, 1980).

Types of Behaviors and Units of Measure

As discussed in chapter 5, direct measurement of student performance begins as part of the initial assessment process. It requires that the teacher first identify the topographical types of behaviors that will be measured and then use an appropriate unit of measure. The behaviors were described as being *simple-discrete, continuous-ongoing, complex-chained skills,* or *functional routines.* Respectively, these could be objectives such as touching to indicate choice, jogging for a period of time, assembling a model car, or shopping for clothes in a department store. The units of measure that could be used include event recording, rate, partial interval recording, momentary-time sampling, and latency for simple-discrete behaviors; duration measures and whole interval recording for continuous on-going behaviors; and task analytic recording for both complex-chained and functional routine types of objectives.

Defining the Behavior

Before measurement of student performance through direct assessment begins, it is very important that the behaviors to be observed and measured be precisely defined. Once the measurement process begins, the teacher must take the same type of measure from day to day. If one day the teacher interprets the behavior to have occurred because it was demonstrated in a particular way, but on another day the form of the behavior is different yet still counted as occurring, the measurement system will not be consistent. This type of inaccuracy could result in the behavior being counted at some times but not at other times, defeating the purpose of direct measurement. Thus a primary rule is to adequately define (or pinpoint) the behavior so there is no mistake about when it occurs and when it does not. This is true for all types of behaviors to be measured, including one-component behaviors (simple-discrete and ongoing) and multiple-component behaviors (complex-chained and functional routines). With multiple-component behaviors, each component or part of the chain must be specified well enough so that accurate and consistent measurement can occur.

In order to know if a behavior has been well enough defined, the teacher may provide the definition to another person (another professional or paraprofessional) and ask him or her to record the occurrence of the behavior simultaneously with the teacher for a brief period of time. If the two people arrive at the same result, then the measurement system is said to be *reliable.* Reliability is always higher when the behavior being measured is well defined.

Observation of the Behavior

When the behavior has been identified and adequately defined, the teacher (or another trained individual) observes the student at predetermined times and circumstances in order to note the occurrence of the behavior or skill. The time and circumstance depend on the instructional objective and the daily schedule. For some behaviors, the teacher may need to observe for an extended period of time, perhaps an hour or maybe even an entire day. For example, a student may be working on a social skill such as offering a toy to another child or asking for a favorite item instead of grabbing it. In this type of situation, it would be important for the teacher to observe for at least enough time so that the behavior has an adequate opportunity to occur. In addition, some functional routines may require a couple of hours or longer to complete (e.g., planning a dinner menu and shopping in a grocery store). In circumstances such as these, much time would have to be spent in direct observation. Other behaviors or skills, however, may require less time. Putting on one's coat, reading sight words, or sweeping a kitchen, for example, can be completed in a relatively brief period and thus require relatively little observation time.

The most desired frequency of observing student's behaviors is on a daily basis, but this is not likely to happen, especially for behaviors that take longer to observe. With these, once or twice a week may be all that it is possible.

Recording the Data

Behavioral data may be recorded in several ways. In each, the basic process requires that the teacher make a written note or place a mark on a data collection sheet, then transfer the mark to a corresponding graph or chart. The type of data collected depends on the unit of measure being used. Procedures for different types of data collection are explained in the following sections.

Event Recording Discrete behaviors are those with clear beginning and ending points, such as various social, communicative, or motor behaviors. They can be recorded as they occur throughout a typical day or within a certain period of time during the day. The teacher can make hash marks on a piece of paper to note the occurrence or may use other simple tactics such as counting on a golf counter strapped to the wrist, changing paper clips from one pocket to another, or using any other simple technique that will allow an accurate count to be kept.

The teacher (or another capable person, such as the paraprofessional) may need to count several behaviors of one student or several behaviors of several students. This process can be facilitated by using a data collection form such as shown in Figure 8–1. As can be seen in the figure, the teacher wishes to monitor several behaviors for each student. It may be assumed that each of these represents one of the objectives that is included in the student's IEP or that has been considered by the teacher, parent, or other member of the team to require some type of intervention for improvement. The teacher is recording the number of times the events occur within a specified amount of time in order to have an accurate record of each student's progress on each behavior.

Rate Measures Any behavior that may be counted during event recording may also be measured in terms of rate. *Rate* is defined as the number of behaviors that have occurred divided by the number of minutes of observation or simply behaviors per minute. The use of rate as a measure results in a consistent unit of measure (behaviors per minute) being calculated, recorded, and analyzed. It is like speed measured using the unit *miles per hour:* the speed is not affected by either the actual number of miles driven or the number of hours. Using rate, the amount of time spent recording the behavior may vary, but the unit of measure is consistent from day to day.

To measure a behavior using rate, the teacher begins by noting the starting time, counts the target behavior and records the number of occurrences, and writes the ending time of the observation period, noting the total number of minutes of observation. Finally, the teacher divides the number of behaviors that occurred by the number of minutes. The result is the rate of the behavior or behaviors per minute. It should be noted that unless the behavior is occurring at a high rate (more than one behavior per minute), the result of the calculation will be a number less than one.

Figure 8–2 displays the collection of rate data for the same behaviors displayed in Figure 8–1 for event recording. Note the different amounts of time that were used during the counting period and how the count was divided by time to result in the rate data.

Partial Interval Recording Interval recording notes whether or not a behavior occurred within a specific interval of time. The time of

Date 6/5/94

Student / Behavior(s)		Number of Events	Length of Observation	Total
Jill	Raises hand for help	~~IIII~~ III	1 hr.	8
	Responds to classmate's greeting	III	1 hr.	3
Ricardo	Looks toward someone calling his name	IIII	30 min.	4
	Points toward desired object	~~IIII~~ IIII	30 min.	9
Andrea	Throws objects	II	30 min.	2
	Comes to seat when requested	III	30 min.	3
Nino	Passes an item when requested	I	20 min.	1
	Touches classmate	~~IIII~~	20 min.	5
	Pinches classmate	III	20 min.	3

Figure 8–1
Data Collection Form for Event Recording

the intervals may vary according to the frequency of the behavior and the flexibility of the observer for recording the data. Intervals may be 1 minute, 5 minutes, 10 minutes, and so on, even up to a half hour or an hour. Typically, strings of contiguous intervals are arranged so the observer may note the occurrence of the behavior over a period of time. For example, there may be twelve 5-minute intervals linked together during a 1-hour period. The teacher will need to judge the occurrence of the behavior and determine the interval length as well as the number of intervals in a way that will show the occurrence of the behavior in its truest form. There are two forms of interval recording, partial interval and whole interval. Partial interval is discussed here because it is more appropriate for recording discrete (as opposed to ongoing) behaviors. Whole interval recording will be discussed later.

Partial interval recording means that the observer records the behavior as occurring if it occurs at least once at any time during the present observation interval. As shown in Figure 8–3, unlike the previous recording forms for event recording and rate measures, each discrete behavior being observed is given a series of small cells representing time intervals. (Again, these intervals can be of any appropriate length and are shown to be various lengths in Figure 8–3.) At the end of the interval period, if the behavior has occurred at least once at some time during the interval observation period, the teacher makes a check mark in the cell. Afterwards, the observation begins again and continues to the end of the next interval and again a mark is made if the behavior occurs. It is important to note that only one mark is made per cell regardless of the actual number of behaviors that occurred. Herein lies both the advantage and the disadvantage of

Date 4/3/94

Student /	Behaviors	Number of Events	Beginning/ Ending Time	Total Minutes	Number/Minute = Rate
Jill	Raises hand for help	~~IIII~~ III (8)	9:30–10:15	45	$^{8}/_{45}$ = .18
	Responds to greeting	III (3)	9:30–11:30	120	$^{3}/_{120}$ = .02
Ricardo	Looks toward someone calling his name	IIII (4)	8:00–9:30	90	$^{4}/_{90}$ = .04
	Points toward desired object	IIII ~~IIII~~ (9)	9:00–10:00	60	$^{9}/_{60}$ = .15
Andrea	Throws objects	II (2)	8:30–11:30	180	$^{2}/_{180}$ = .01
	Comes to seat when requested	III (3)	10:00–11:00	60	$^{3}/_{60}$ = .05
Nino	Passes an item when requested	I (1)	2:00–2:20	20	$^{1}/_{20}$ = .05
	Touches classmate	~~IIII~~ (5)	2:00–2:20	20	$^{5}/_{20}$ = .25
	Pinches classmate	IIII (4)	2:00–2:20	20	$^{4}/_{20}$ = .20

Figure 8–2
Data Collection Form for Rate Data

partial interval recording. The teacher only needs to know if the behavior occurred once and therefore does not need to record each individual occurrence of the behavior as with event recording or rate recording, but because of this recording rule, the teacher sees only an *estimate* of behavior occurrence. Thus, if Jill raises her hand once, twice, or more during the 5-minute interval (see Figure 8–3), the data in the particular cell would show only one mark.

Momentary Time Sampling Another recording system that provides only an estimate of the actual occurrence of a particular behavior is momentary time sampling. This technique uses an interval cell system just as does partial interval recording as shown in Figure 8–3, but the rule for making a mark in the cell is different. Instead of making the mark if the behavior occurs at least once at any time in the interval, when using momentary time sampling, the mark is made only if the behavior is occurring precisely at the time the interval ends. If it occurs at any other time during the interval but is not occurring at the time the interval ends, no mark is made. In order for momentary time sampling to be useful, the behavior must be occurring often enough so that on at least some occasions it occurs at the time the observer is allowed to record.

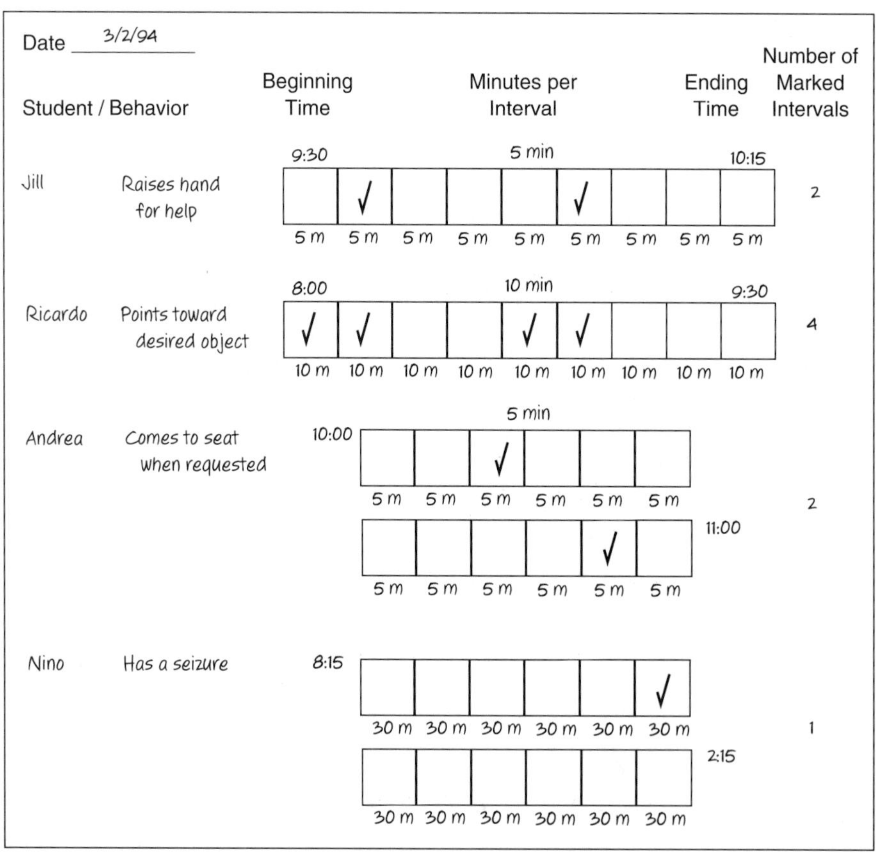

Date 3/2/94

Student / Behavior		Beginning Time	Minutes per Interval	Ending Time	Number of Marked Intervals
Jill	Raises hand for help	9:30	5 min	10:15	2
			5 m, 5 m ✓, 5 m, 5 m, 5 m, 5 m ✓, 5 m, 5 m, 5 m		
Ricardo	Points toward desired object	8:00	10 min	9:30	4
			10 m ✓, 10 m ✓, 10 m, 10 m, 10 m ✓, 10 m ✓, 10 m, 10 m, 10 m		
Andrea	Comes to seat when requested	10:00	5 min	11:00	2
			5 m, 5 m, 5 m ✓, 5 m, 5 m, 5 m		
			5 m, 5 m, 5 m, 5 m, 5 m ✓, 5 m		
Nino	Has a seizure	8:15		2:15	1
			30 m, 30 m, 30 m, 30 m, 30 m, 30 m ✓		
			30 m, 30 m, 30 m, 30 m, 30 m, 30 m		

Figure 8–3
Partial Interval Data Recording Form

Measuring Latency Measures of latency are not often used, but in some cases this could be a useful unit of measure. Latency is the period of time between when a stimulus occurs or is presented and when the behavior it is intended to prompt occurs. If an individual is particularly slow at responding to a cue and it is considered important to decrease the time interval between the cue and the response, one might wish to measure the latency of the response.

Measuring latency requires that a count of seconds be made between the cue and the response. This can be done by simply counting or by using a stopwatch or a watch with a second hand. At each opportunity, after the cue occurs the teacher measures and records the response time. An example of this measure being used might be when a student is learning to respond to natural inquiries in the community during a shopping trip. The store clerk or counter attendant could ask "May I help you?" and the student would be expected to respond in a reasonable amount of time. In such a situation the teacher would count the number of seconds that elapse between the natural cue ("Can I help you?") and the response. Figure 8–4 shows a data collection form that could be used to record latency.

Duration Measures Unlike the previous measures, duration is a measure that is useful for measuring how long a continuous-ongoing behavior lasts. Like event recording and rate measures, duration is a direct measure of the actual behavior, not an estimate like interval recording or momentary time sampling.

There may be several instructional objectives that target increasing the amount of time a student can be engaged in an activity, such as working on a particular job, playing at a recreational activity, exercising during a physical activity, and so on. When these types of objectives occur, measures of duration are appropriate because they indicate to the teacher if progress is being made; positive behaviors should show an increase in duration whereas negative behaviors should show a decrease. Figure 8–5 displays an example of a data sheet used for recording the duration of a behavior.

The most precise way to observe and record duration of a behavior is to use a stopwatch or, if this is not possible, a watch with a second hand. As discussed previously, as with all behaviors, it is important that the behavior being measured with duration be accurately defined with a clear beginning and end so that the observer knows when the record should begin and when it should end.

Whole Interval Recording Whole interval recording is like partial interval recording except for one important difference. In order for the observer to place a mark in the cell, the behavior must occur *continuously* throughout the interval instead of occurring at least once during the cell interval. This is why whole interval recording is a better measure of continuous-ongoing behaviors. Only if the behavior continues to occur for the entire time of the interval is the mark made. When it is not possible to use duration recording, it may be possible to use whole interval recording to provide an estimate of the continuity of a behavior.

Using a measure of duration, the teacher would know exactly how long a behavior occurred. Using whole interval recording, however, the observer can only record the behavior (make a mark in the interval) if the behavior occurred throughout the entire interval. The disadvantage of whole interval recording is that if the behavior occurs for up to 99% of the time represented by the interval, it is not recorded. Obviously this can result in a false picture of accomplishment. For example, a student learning to shovel snow (a relatively continuous behavior) may be observed using a whole interval recording system with intervals set at 2 minutes. Each time 2 minutes pass during which the student has continu-

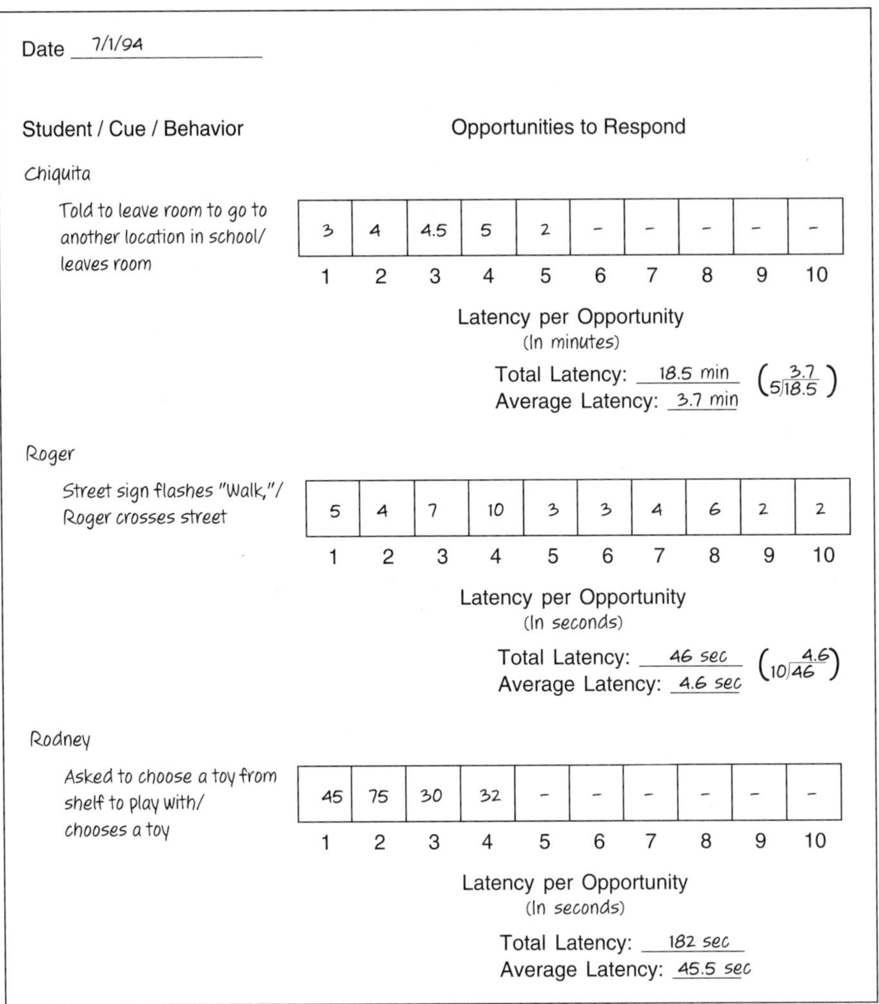

Date 7/1/94

Student / Cue / Behavior — Opportunities to Respond

Chiquita

Told to leave room to go to another location in school/ leaves room

1	2	3	4	5	6	7	8	9	10
3	4	4.5	5	2	-	-	-	-	-

Latency per Opportunity
(In minutes)

Total Latency: 18.5 min (5)18.5 = 3.7)
Average Latency: 3.7 min

Roger

Street sign flashes "Walk,"/ Roger crosses street

1	2	3	4	5	6	7	8	9	10
5	4	7	10	3	3	4	6	2	2

Latency per Opportunity
(In seconds)

Total Latency: 46 sec (10)46 = 4.6)
Average Latency: 4.6 sec

Rodney

Asked to choose a toy from shelf to play with/ chooses a toy

1	2	3	4	5	6	7	8	9	10
45	75	30	32	-	-	-	-	-	-

Latency per Opportunity
(In seconds)

Total Latency: 182 sec
Average Latency: 45.5 sec

Figure 8–4
Latency Data Recording Form

ously shoveled the snow, a mark would be made in an interval cell. During the next 2-minute period, if the student paused, the cell would not be marked because the behavior was not continuous. The process would continue through all of the intervals for which recording was planned.

Even though the need for a continuous display of the behavior may be considered a major disadvantage of the whole interval recording system, the advantage of it is that it does not require continuous measurement using a stopwatch or second hand as is required for duration recording. For this reason, whole interval recording may be a useful data recording system in some situations. The same form as used for partial interval recording would be used for whole interval record-

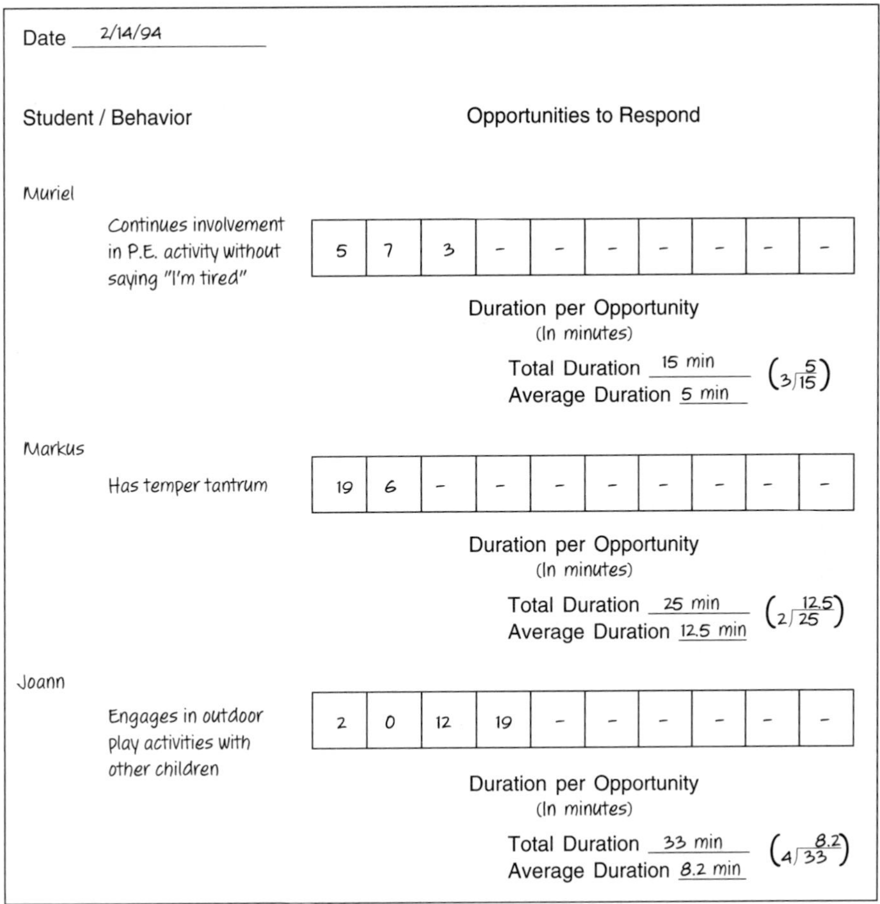

Date 2/14/94

Student / Behavior — Opportunities to Respond

Muriel

Continues involvement in P.E. activity without saying "I'm tired"

5	7	3	-	-	-	-	-	-	-

Duration per Opportunity (In minutes)

Total Duration 15 min ($3\overline{)15}$ = 5)
Average Duration 5 min

Markus

Has temper tantrum

19	6	-	-	-	-	-	-	-	-

Duration per Opportunity (In minutes)

Total Duration 25 min ($2\overline{)25}$ = 12.5)
Average Duration 12.5 min

Joann

Engages in outdoor play activities with other children

2	0	12	19	-	-	-	-	-	-

Duration per Opportunity (In minutes)

Total Duration 33 min ($4\overline{)33}$ = 8.2)
Average Duration 8.2 min

Figure 8–5
Duration Data Recording Form

ing (see Figure 8–3), but the difference would be the rule stipulated above for marking the cell.

Task Analytic (Multiple Component) Recording Each of the previously discussed units of measure were developed for recording individual behaviors, either simple-discrete behaviors or continuous-ongoing behaviors. However, many of the skills that are taught to individuals with severe disabilities have multiple components. As explained in chapter 5, they are either complex-chained skills or functional routines. Thus it is necessary to have a measurement system that will allow the teacher to record students' performance on objectives that have several components or behaviors chained together. The measurement process begins by constructing a task analysis or list of the individual behaviors that constitute the entire action. Such a list is presented in Figure 8–6 for putting on pants, an objective that may need to be taught to a student with severe disabilities.

1. Get pants from closet, drawer, or wherever they are located.
2. Place pants within reach of a place where you can sit (near a chair, the bed, a stool, etc.).
3. Sit down on the chair, bed, or stool.
4. Pick up the pants from the nearby location.
5. Adjust the pants so they are being held in front of you with two hands holding the pants at the waist with one hand on each side of the pants.
6. Bend over as much as possible and lower the pants down to almost floor level.
7. Push one foot through the appropriate pants leg.
8. Push the second leg through the other pants leg.
9. Pull the pants up as high as possible while sitting.
10. While still holding on to the pants, stand up.
11. While standing, pull the pants up all the way around the waist.
12. Button the pants.
13. Pull up the pants zipper.
14. If appropriate, find a belt for the pants.
15. Adjust the belt so that it can be inserted into the first loop on the pants.
16. Pass the belt through each loop on the pants.
17. Buckle the belt.

Figure 8–6
Task Analysis of Putting On Pants

During the continuous assessment process, the student's performance on each component of the instructional target is recorded. Typically, recording of the student's performance occurs at least once a day. (In the case of learning to put on pants, the most normal time to teach this is probably during physical education.) The data collection form that is used is based on the task analysis and includes all of the steps of the behavior and spaces for recording the student's performance. Figure 8–7 shows the data collection form used for recording how well the student puts on pants. (Note that the steps have been abbreviated.) All other multicomponent instructional objectives will use a similar form.

As can be seen in Figure 8–7, all of the steps are listed with spaces for recording performance on each step during each day. There is also a section on the bottom of the form to indicate the type of prompt or other assistance that was required for each step.

During the baseline period, as discussed in chapter 5, the teacher is interested simply in whether or not the student can perform any of the steps independently and records this performance on the data collection form. During instruction, however, the teacher wants to know not only which steps the individual can demonstrate independently, but also what level or type of assistance is necessary to get the student to complete each step when he or

Objective: Josh will put on his pants independently by completing all of the steps listed in the task analysis independently for at least three days in a row.

Steps	Days or Sessions									
	M	T	W	Th	F	M	T	W	Th	F
1. Get pants.	PP	VC								
2. Place pants within reach.	PP	PP								
3. Sit down.	VC	G								
4. Pick up the pants.	FP	PP								
5. Adjust the pants.	FP	FP								
6. Lower the pants to floor level.	PP	FP								
7. Push one foot through.	FP	X								
8. Push the second foot through.	FP	FP								
9. Pull the pants up while sitting.	PP	VC								
10. Stand up.	G	VC								
11. Pull pants up around the waist.	PP	PP								
12. Button the pants.	FP	PP								
13. Pull up the zipper.	FP	FP								
14. If appropriate, find a belt.	VC	VC								
15. Adjust the belt.	PP	FP								
16. Pass the belt through each loop.	FP	FP								
17. Buckle the belt.	FP	FP								

Prompts or Assistance:

NA: No assistance. Student completes step following completion of previous step with no assistance from teacher.
G: Gesture. Student completes step following a gesture from the teacher indicating what the student should do.
VC: Verbal cue. Student completes the step after the teacher provides a cue as to what to do, e.g., "pull them up!"
PP: Partial physical assistance. Student completes the step after teacher provides partial physical assistance.
FP: Full physical. Student completes the step only after teacher completely physically guides the student through it.
X: The student did not perform the step correctly with any level of assistance.

Direction: Use least-to-most assistance with delay of 4 to 5 seconds before moving to greater level of assistance.

Figure 8–7
Data Recording Form for Multicomponent Behaviors (Putting On Pants)

she cannot do so independently. This is usually done by constructing a least-to-most prompting sequence, as discussed in chapter 6, and listing the sequence on the recording form (see Figure 8–7).

To begin the instructional sequence, the teacher waits until the environmental circumstances provide a natural cue for putting on pants or, if necessary, gives a general verbal direction for the student to put on the pants. If the student does not begin the first step (getting the pants and bringing them to the location where they are to be put on), the teacher provides a gesture, such as pointing to the pants. If the student does not respond in four to five seconds, the teacher moves to the second level of assistance, which calls for a specific verbal cue. Again the teacher waits for the student to respond. If there is still no response or an incorrect response is initiated, the teacher proceeds to an even greater level of assistance, which in this case would be providing partial physical assistance. Finally, if the student is not responsive to this level of assistance, the plan calls for the teacher to provide total physical guidance.

Each multicomponent objective follows the same type of format. Of course, as discussed in chapter 6, the instructional assistance plan varies depending on the objective and the student. Regardless of plan, on each day or during each instructional session, the teacher records after each step the level or type of input that was necessary for the student to successfully complete the behavior. As indicated in Figure 8–7, levels of assistance are coded and the codes can be used to show how the student performed on each day or during each session. If the student was unable to perform a step regardless of the level of assistance, an *X* could be used to indicate that the step was not completed.

Data Collection During Baseline

Baseline is the time when the teacher observes the student's ability to demonstrate certain behaviors or perform skills that have been identified as being instructional objectives but before providing instruction for the student to learn the objective. As discussed in chapter 5, the instructional objectives may have been identified by the teacher, parents, and other members of the collaborative teams using various techniques. Baseline observations are then conducted for each objective to confirm that the student cannot actually perform the targeted behavior or skill. In single subject research, it is the relative improvement in the individual's behavioral performance beyond the baseline level during the intervention phase that is used to confirm the effectiveness of the intervention (independent variable) on the target behavior (dependent variable). In the instruction of students with severe disabilities, however, baseline may be considered more a demonstration of the student's need for instruction in a particular area than a way to demonstrate that the instruction affected the behavior.

Collecting baseline data requires that the teacher place the student in situations in which the behavior has the opportunity to occur and record the occurrence of the behavior, using one of the methods described previously. A low or zero measure of the behavior over several days suggests that instruction should be given. During experimental research, a minimum period of baseline is usually considered to be 3 to 5 days or until the baseline is stable (shows little variability). This is also a good rule of thumb for collecting baseline data for instruction unless the baseline data is very low or nonexistent. In this case common sense would suggest that instruction should be initiated sooner in order to avoid wasting time.

Data Collection During Instruction

Data collection and instruction should usually occur simultaneously. For discrete and ongoing behaviors, the time of observation to record the data is when instruction can be provided for the targeted behavior. For example, suppose the objective is for a student to use words to ask for certain objects. Each time the student needs something, the teacher uses event recording to note if the student makes an appropriate verbal request. The teacher keeps nearby a data collection form such as the one shown in Figure 8–1 on which to record the data. Because part of the objective is to increase such verbal statements, the instructional plan that has been developed may call for time delay or least-to-most prompting or other tactics for skill acquisition (see chapter 6) to be used when there is a natural opportunity for the student to demonstrate the behavior. When the behavior is demonstrated correctly, reinforcement is provided. After such a sequence of events the teacher records the student's performance on the data collection sheet.

When there is opportunity for the behavior to occur at any time, as in the case described above, the teacher should implement the instructional plan whenever possible. Sometimes, however, the recording that is done is limited to a representative portion of the day, for example, from 9 to 10 o'clock in the morning. This allows the teacher to collect representative data for analysis but does not require him or her to record data during every occurrence of the behavior.

What is important is that enough time be allotted for data collection so that the record can reflect the results of the intervention. In a large way, this will depend on how often the behavior can and does occur. Behaviors or skills that have the opportunity to occur at high frequencies require less time for observation and recording because only short time periods are required to see occurrence; essentially, a "snapshot" of the student's performance may be taken. On the other hand, low-frequency behaviors require longer observation periods because they cannot always be detected in short periods of time. For example, a student who is learning to control angry outbursts may demonstrate such outbursts only once or twice a day. Monitoring would have to take place throughout the entire day to record the occurrence of the behavior.

Multicomponent behaviors, complex-chains, or functional routines that are broken down into their component parts are taught at specific times with the entire skill being taught in its natural sequence. In this process, data collection can be recorded during the instructional process as described above and as displayed in Figure 8–7. However, data should also be collected during noninstructional probe sessions.

Probes are opportunities for the student to demonstrate the behavior or skill in natural circumstances without teacher assistance, instruction, or reinforcement. A probe may be thought of as a test to see how well the student has learned the skill. During probe sessions, the teacher observes the student in the context in which the behavior would normally occur and records his or her performance on each component of the skill. The type of form that is displayed in Figure 8–7 could be used, but the teacher would only record whether or not each step of the behavior was demonstrated correctly. Since it is a probe, there is no opportunity for the teacher to provide different types of instructional input. Essentially, probes are conducted in the same way that baseline data is collected, without any form of instruction.

Data Collection During Generalization

One special form of probe that must be conducted tests how well generalization has occurred. As discussed in chapter 7, skill generalization is often an important goal for individuals with severe disabilities. In order to find out how well the student can perform learned tasks in different situations, probes should be conducted in targeted generalization conditions or settings.

The data collection procedures discussed in the previous sections may be applied to assessing students' efforts to generalize their skills. However, there are some considerations that the teacher should keep in mind (Browder, 1991; White, 1988). First, as discussed in chapter 7, it is necessary to determine what adequately constitutes appropriate generalization sites or conditions for the purpose of assessment, and this should be done when objectives are being written. Natural times and natural places must be used. In addition, the number of times the generalized skill is assessed, the people present when the condition is assessed, and the stimuli in the environment should all be normal for the condition. The teacher should keep in mind that the purpose of a generalization probe is to determine if the student can demonstrate the behavior in the "real world" (White, 1988).

As with other probes, generalization probes are conducted without the use of any of the instructional cues or prompts such as those used in the training phase. However, stimuli that are natural to the environment are allowed because they will be present when the learner is expected to demonstrate the behavior after training. If artificial prompts or supports are provided by a teacher or another during observations in generalized settings, it should be noted on the data collection form, because it would not be accurate to conclude that the student could independently perform the skill.

One concern about the collection of data during generalization probes is the presence of the person who conducted the initial instruction of the skill, usually the teacher (Westling & Floyd, 1990; White, 1988). The problem is that this person may serve as a prompt and/or reinforcer for the individual learning the task. Even though this occurs unintentionally, it nevertheless inhibits the teacher from knowing if the student possesses the skill and can perform it independently. For this reason, it is often useful to have someone whom the student does not know be present to observe the student and report on how well the behavior or skill was demonstrated in the natural environment. White (1988) suggested that if someone else does this observation, the teacher should clearly inform that person what to look for, define examples of the behavior, and explain how to collect data on the behavior.

Graphing the Data

The data that are recorded using the units of measures on the forms represented in Figures 8–1 through 8–5 and 8–7, as already explained, provide the teacher with significant information about the progress of students on their individual objectives as well as the effectiveness of instruction. However, in order to be able to interpret progress (or the lack of it) the teacher must look at student data occurring over many learning opportunities. One way to do this would be to examine all of the daily data collection forms over many days. A more efficient way would be to transfer the raw data onto graphs or charts and observe students' progress, using these graphic displays. In this way the teacher may discern important trends on particular skills.

Graph paper with four or five squares to the inch may be used to construct simple graphs to display each student's performance on particular behaviors or skills that have been observed and recorded on the data collection forms. Figure 8–8 displays such a chart with the vertical axis and the horizontal axis drawn in at right angles to each other and with spaces to add other pertinent information (name, target skill, etc.).

The horizontal lines on the graph represent the unit of measure that is being used for the targeted behavior or skill. The appropriate label to place beside the vertical axis will thus depend on what is being observed and measured. Based on the types of measures that have been discussed, the following units of measure may be appropriate:

- The number of certain events that occur during the day.
- The rate of certain events (number/minutes).
- The number of intervals in which the behavior appeared at least once (partial intervals).

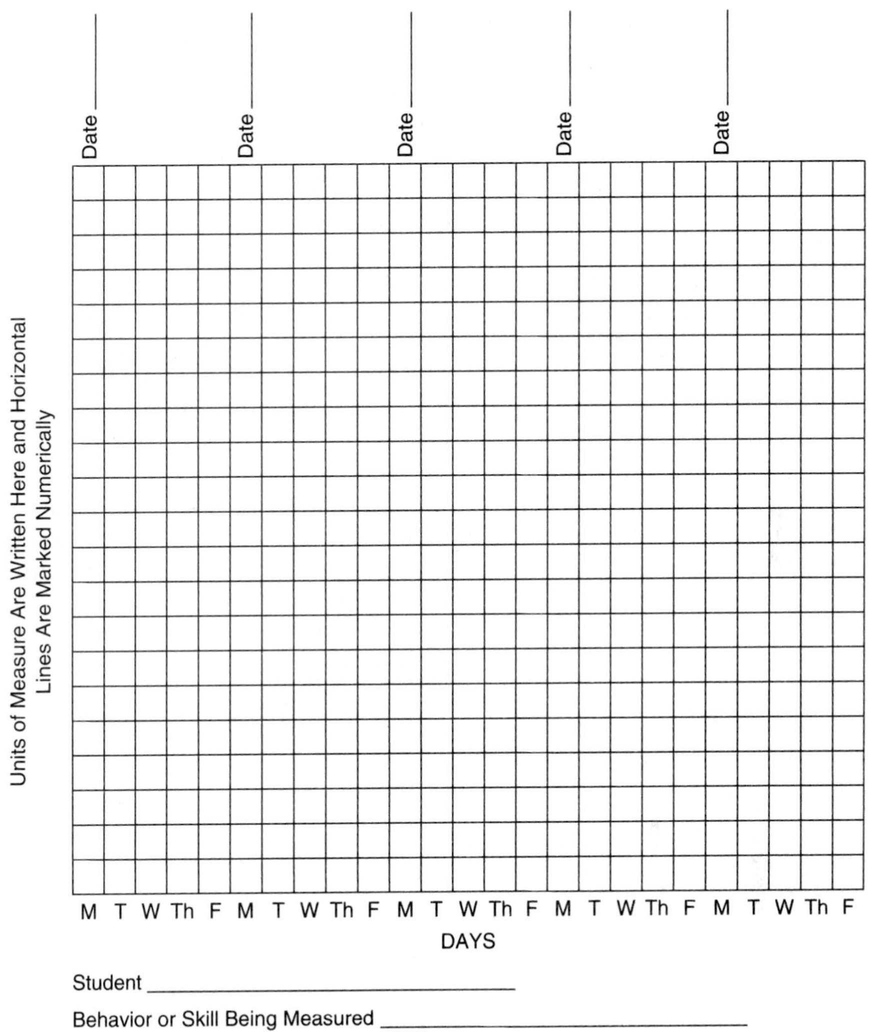

Figure 8–8
Graph Paper Used to Chart Student Performance on Individual Objectives

- The number of momentary observations at which the behavior was observed (time sampling).
- The total or average latency that occurred between a certain cue and the initiation of the behavior (in minutes or seconds).
- The total or average duration of the behavior (in minutes or seconds).
- The number of intervals in which the behavior occurred continuously (whole intervals).
- The number (or percentage) of steps in the task analysis or routine successfully completed.

After the appropriate unit of measure is written on the side of the chart, each horizontal line will be given a numerical value so that the entire possible range of performance levels can be recorded on the graph. For example, a behavior that is likely to occur no more than ten times during a day would require the horizontal lines to be numbered from 1 to at least 10. Similarly, a task analysis or routine with 15 steps would require the numbering of lines 1 to 15.

Under the bottom horizontal line on the graph, the word *days* is written and each of the ascending vertical lines represents a particular day and should be labeled beneath accordingly, that is, *M, T, W, Th, F.* If it is possible to collect data on the weekend, *S* and *Su* should also be included. At the conclusion of the instructional day, the teacher or the paraprofessional transcribes the data collected on the data form to a corresponding graph by using a pencil to place a dot at the intersection of the current day line (vertical line) and the unit of measure line (horizontal line). As each dot is placed, a straight line is drawn between it and the previous dot. If the previous dot was on the preceding day, obviously, this will be only a short line. However, if several days have passed since data were collected, the days that were missed will have nothing marked on them and the line will go from the present data point to the last previous data point. Figure 8–9 displays six graphs, on each of which a different unit of measure has been used. Graphs constructed by the teacher would be similar.

Interpreting the Graphs

During the baseline period, data points representing the student's performance prior to instruction are placed on the first few vertical lines. These data are analyzed in order to make decisions regarding instruction. Uniformly low performance indicates that instruction is warranted. Data points that are high or ascending suggest that the student already has learned much of the skill and instruction is necessary only to achieve mastery and then maintenance and generalization.

After the completion of collecting, recording, and graphing baseline data points, subsequent data points are added following the beginning of the instructional phase. When there is a change from baseline condition to the instructional phase condition, a straight vertical line should be drawn between day lines. This "phase change" line indicates that there has been an important change and, by observing the following data points, the teacher will know if the change (in this case going from baseline conditions to instructional conditions) has resulted in improved performance by the student. Any changes in important aspects of the environment that might affect the student's performance should also be indicated with phase change lines. Typical important phase changes include changes in reinforcement, the location or time of instruction, the materials, and so forth. The critical purpose of this technique is that the person observing the graph will see what happens to the student's performance during different phases of instruction and/or observation.

When the graphic display of the data is examined, various patterns may emerge and the teacher must know how to interpret them in order to make instructional decisions. A pattern that usually occurs at the beginning of instruction shows a very low level of performance (see Figure 8–9 a and b), meaning that few steps in the task analysis or routine are being recorded, few events are occurring, there is a low rate of behavior, and so forth. The teacher should realize that this is typical and should continue instruction for several days to see if performance starts to improve. If this occurs, the teacher is on the right track with regard to instructional practices.

When the data points on the graph are ascending but have not reached their highest

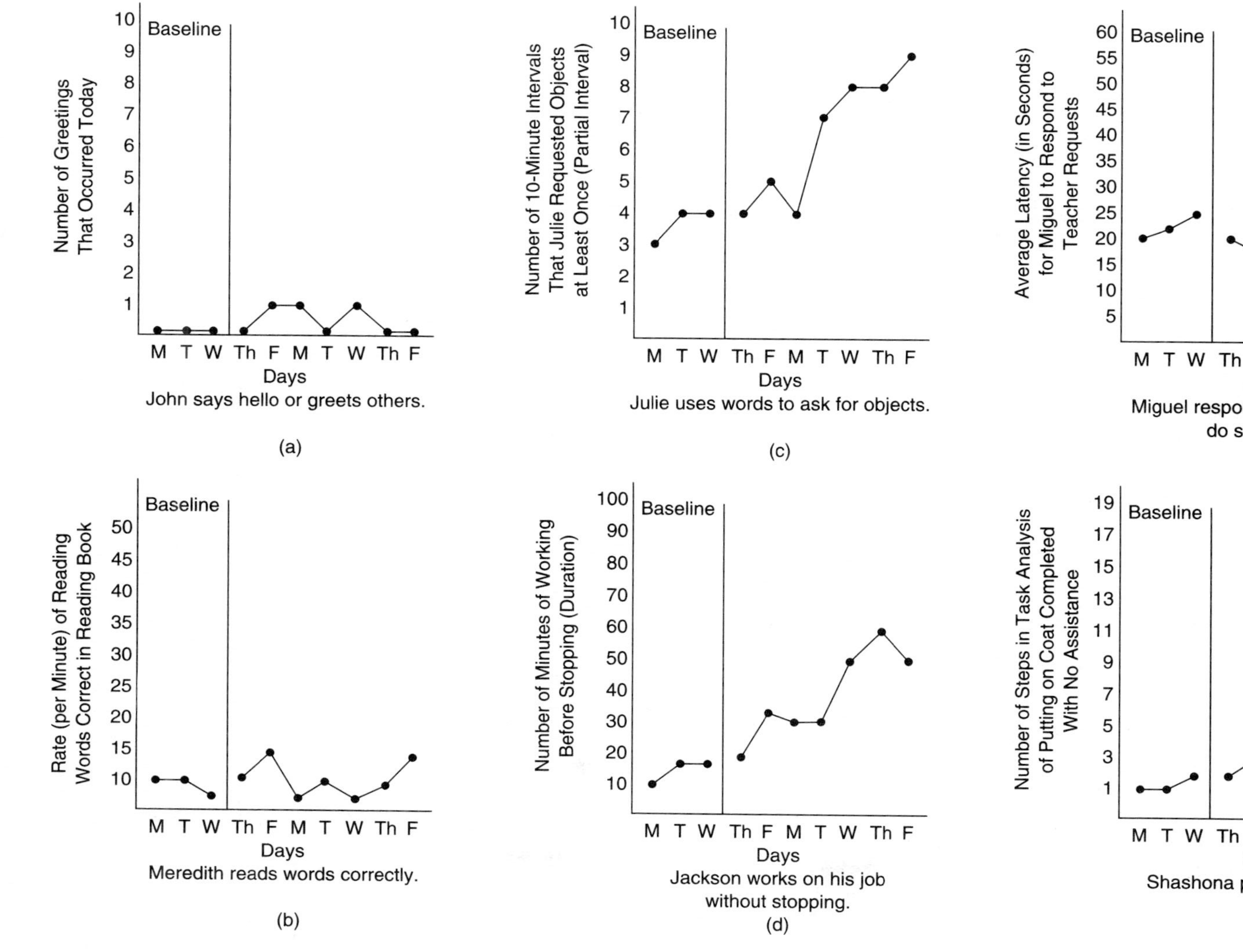

Figure 8–9
Charts of Student Performance on Individual Objectives

possible level, learning is occurring (see Figure 8–9 c and d). What is happening is that over several days, the student has steadily demonstrated more correct steps, longer durations, higher rates of performance, and so forth. When this occurs, it indicates that the teacher should continue under current conditions until criterion performance is achieved. Ultimately the student may show a uniformly high level of performance across all days of direct assessment. When this is the case, the teacher should conclude that the target skill has been learned and does not require further instruction. It is being demonstrated adequately, at least under the conditions in which it is currently being taught and assessed. For example, the teacher may see that a student smiles quite often throughout the day and therefore conclude that this does not need to continue as an instructional objective. The teacher would then work on skill maintenance and generalization, as discussed in chapter 7.

The data pattern that indicates that something is very wrong with the teacher's instructional practice or something else is one in which the student is showing a gradual decrease in performance (see Figure 8–9 e and f). In other words, from day to day there is a drop in data points. This may suggest several conditions. The cues or prompts are not working effectively, the reinforcement is not effective, or perhaps something else in the student's life, something not a part of instruction, is affecting learning. The teacher must take note of this pattern and attempt to find methods to improve student performance. Of course, if the goal is for a decrease in the measure to occur, as it would be in Figure 8–9 e, then this pattern would be desirable.

Direct measurement of students' behaviors and skills offers a complex yet thorough method for documenting progress on instructional objectives or the need for changes in the instructional process. Using the procedures presented in this chapter will allow teachers and others to note whether students are learning and, if they are not, whether new forms of intervention can be more effective. Direct measure of behavior has a long history in special education and is used successfully by many special educators (Farlow & Snell, 1989). However, there are other types of information that can be useful in making decisions about instructing students with severe disabilities (Grigg, Snell, & Loyd, 1989), and the alternative practices of ongoing assessment methods should be considered.

Indirect Measures of Student Performance

Meyer and Janney (1989) developed procedures that they referred to as being "user-friendly" to document student progress. They are not direct measurement procedures like those described in the previous sections of this chapter, but instead are types of records of a less formal nature that the teacher may keep in order to monitor the progress of students with severe disabilities. However, like direct measures, these records must be kept and reviewed regularly. The authors of these methods pointed out that many teachers do not keep direct measurement data on their students (Burney & Shores, 1979; Haring, Liberty, & White, 1980) and that more convenient methods are necessary. They described the measurement tools discussed below.

Schedule of Student Activities

Since various instructional efforts and interventions are often intended to broaden the activities and inclusive opportunities available to students with severe disabilities, a weekly schedule of students' activities can be used to monitor progress. Meyer and Janney (1989) explained that "a diary of student activities completed by program staff before, during, and after the intervention can be used to document broad changes in the nature of the student's school day and staff perceptions of the behavior change" (p. 265). An example of the type of student schedule proposed is presented in Figure 8–10. Using this schedule would allow one to see the types of activities the student is engaged in, grouping arrangements, staff assignments, the amount of time the student is integrated, and the level of success achieved.

In analyzing student progress based on the weekly schedule presented in Figure 8–10, the teacher would look to see if the student had been involved in more integrated learning opportunities, fewer 1:1 teaching arrangements, and more varied instructional groupings, with a higher number of activities being rated as more successful.

Daily Log

Another relatively simple approach to monitoring student progress proposed by Meyer and Janney is the daily log. Entries into this log could reflect several kinds of data; some of these may be listed as prompts on preprinted log forms to remind the record keeper to address them. They might include the following or some that are similar:

- Overall, what kind of day did the student have? Circle one of the following: A very good day; okay; not sure; not okay; a very bad day.
- How well did the student do on tasks in school today? Circle one of the following: A very good day; okay; not sure; not okay; a very bad day.
- How well did the student do on tasks in the community today? Circle one of the following: A very good day; okay; not sure; not okay; a very bad day.
- Comment briefly on the day's events and the student's behavior. Note any incidents that occurred that seemed important to you (positive and negative).
- Describe tasks or activities that the student enjoyed or worked well on.
- Describe tasks or activities that the student *did not* enjoy or work well on.

In order that the log be as true an indicator of student performance as possible, Meyer and Janney recommended that log entries be made two days a week and that these days be randomly preselected to avoid bias in deciding to make an entry. This would require entries to be made without regard to the type of day that the student had. To ensure a degree of reliability, the authors also recommended that separate entries be made by two different people on some days (e.g., the teacher and the paraprofessional or two teachers). Of course, whoever makes an entry must be very familiar with the student's performance on that day.

Incident Record

The third form of measurement recommended by Meyer and Janney is the incident record, a document that is designed to record serious problems such as self-injury or other challenging behaviors. The incident record would include information relevant for conducting a functional analysis of the problematic behavior (see chapter 11 for an explanation of this procedure) and the following objective information:

- A description of the behavior, how intense it was, how long it lasted, and so forth.
- The activity taking place when the behavior occurred.

STUDENT SCHEDULE

STUDENT ____________________ STAFF: ____________________ ____________________ ____________________

name/role name/role name/role

SCHOOL ____________________ ____________________ ____________________ ____________________

name/role name/role name/role

DATE ____________________

Time	Monday	Tuesday	Wednesday	Thursday	Friday	1:1 Independent Small group Large group	Staff	+ = Usually Successful – = Usually Unsuccessful V = Varies	✓ If Integrated

Figure 8–10
Student Schedule Used to Show Changes in Student Participation

From "User Friendly Measures of Meaningful Outcomes: Evaluating Behavior Interventions" by L. H. Meyer & R. Janney, 1989, *Journal of the Association for Persons with Severe Handicaps, 14*(4), p. 267.

- Where the behavior occurred.
- Professional staff and other students present when the behavior occurred.
- What was happening immediately before the behavior occurred.
- What happened immediately following the behavior that may have been a consequence of the behavior (e.g., How did people react? Were task demands reduced? Could anything else have served as a reinforcer for the behavior?)

The recorder could also add subjective information to the record, such as:

- Why do you think the incident occurred?
- How do you think the behavior could have been prevented or handled differently?

A form that could be used to record incidents is presented in Figure 8–11. It is important to remember that the incident record was designed only to record the occurrence of serious challenging behaviors.

The indirect measurement procedures described above allow teachers to keep relevant records, although not in the quantified forms used in direct measurement. For some teachers they may be preferable as an alternative approach to measuring students' progress; for others they may supplement the direct measures described in this chapter. Another measurement alternative is described below.

Portfolio Assessment of Student Performance

Assessment portfolios are collections of evidence reflecting the development and learning of individual students over a period of time. "It is a means of assessment that provides a complex and comprehensive view of student performance in context" (Grace & Shores, 1992, p. 5). Like the types of measures discussed previously in this chapter, portfolio assessment is intended to provide information that will be useful for making decisions about student performance in a variety of curricular areas (Meisels & Steele, 1991; Paulson, Paulson, & Meyer, 1991).

Several different types of information may be stored in a student's portfolio. Examples of information appropriate for student portfolios include the following (Meisels & Steele, 1991):

- Samples of student's written work.
- Logs of activities completed by student.
- Photos of student's completed art or work products or actual samples.
- Written records about the student's thoughts and ideas that he or she has commented on.
- Anecdotal records about the student's performance on different activities.
- Video recordings of the student engaged in certain activities.

Essentially, any evidence of student performance that reflects his or her ability and that can be captured on paper or on audio or video recordings can be included in assessment portfolios as well as data collected using the procedures described in the previous sections on direct and indirect measurement practices.

Meisels and Steele (1991) suggested that no less than once or twice a month teachers should gather evidence to be included in the portfolio. They recommended that the students be given the opportunity to assist in the selection of information to be included, with the teacher prompting the students to select items that were especially pleasing or difficult for them. Most important, the included items should reflect the student's progress on individually developed goals or objectives (Grace & Shores, 1992).

Although portfolio assessment has not been used broadly in educating students with severe

INCIDENT RECORD

COMPLETED BY________________

STUDENT________________ ACTIVITY TAKING PLACE ________________

WHERE ________________ DATE/DAY OF WEEK ________________ TIME ______

STAFF PRESENT WHEN INCIDENT OCCURRED ________________

STUDENTS PRESENT WHEN INCIDENT OCCURRED ________________

1. Describe what happened just before behavior occurred: (Was the student prompted? Was a staff person attending to the student? Was the student alone? Etc.)

2. Describe what the student did and what happened through the incident: (How intense was the behavior? How long did it last? Etc.)

3. Describe what happened to the student immediately after the incident: (include any "consequences" deliberately applied and also those that occurred without planning. Did people gather around? Did task demands stop? Did people get excited or stay calm? Etc.)

4. Why do you think the incident occurred?

Figure 8–11
Incident Record Used to Monitor Challenging Behaviors
From "User Friendly Measures of Meaningful Outcomes: Evaluating Behavior Interventions" by L. H. Meyer & R. Janney, 1989, *Journal of the Association for Persons with Severe Handicaps, 14*(4), p. 268. Copyright 1989 by The Association for Persons with Severe Handicaps. Reprinted by permission.

disabilities, it has much potential as a means of documenting student progress. In one study of two young children with disabilities, Hanline and Fox (1994) documented the progress of the children over a period of one year, collecting information for inclusion in the portfolios at the beginning, middle, and end of the year. They examined and evaluated photos of block construction, photos of free-form art products, results of systematic observations of sociodramatic play during both outdoor and indoor play periods, and systematic observations of social and cognitive play behavior during fluid play periods (i.e., with water and sand). Based on their observations, they noted the developmental progress of the children, which was determined by changes in the quality of block construction and art products; an improvement in motor skills, spatial awareness, and symbolic abilities; an increase in social interactions; and an increase in dramatic play. Hanline and Fox (1994) reported that the type of information they included in the portfolio assessment proved to be especially useful for communicating with parents about the students' progress.

Conclusion

Some type of measure is taken on just about all the important things in life, and many things that are not so important. Electricity, water, and gas used in a home are measured so we know how much to pay. Some of us monitor our weight so we know whether or not we should modify our diet and exercise routines. In general education, students' performance is measured so grades can be awarded.

Measuring the progress of students with severe disabilities is also very important. It is not conducted so that we can compare one student's progress with that of others, but so that we can compare the student to himself or herself over a period of time. This allows us to answer questions about the effectiveness of our interventions and whether we should keep using the same form of instruction or try something different. If we want students with severe disabilities to learn and to experience many of the pleasures of life that others enjoy, instruction must have a clear impact on their skills and abilities. The measurement procedures we use should reflect this impact or direct us to improve instruction so that a greater effect will occur.

Questions for Reflection

1. Why should the assessment of students with severe disabilities be more frequent than the assessment of students without disabilities?
2. What are some advantages and disadvantages of quantifying human behavior for the purpose of assessment?
3. In assessment, what is meant by the concept of reliability and how can it be achieved during direct measurement of student behavior?
4. Why would a measure of the rate of behavior usually be preferred to event recording?
5. Why can partial and whole interval recording and momentary time sampling be considered only "estimates" of true behavioral occurrences?
6. Is baseline data always important? Why or why not?
7. Would you prefer to use direct or indirect methods of recording student performance? Why?
8. What are some ingredients that could be included in an assessment portfolio for adolescents with severe disabilities?

References

Alberto, P. A., & Troutman, A. C. (1990). *Applied behavior analysis for teachers* (3rd ed.). New York: Merrill/Macmillan.

Browder, D. M. (1991). *Assessment of individuals with severe disabilities: An applied behavior approach to lifeskills assessment* (2nd ed.). Baltimore: Paul H. Brookes.

Brown, F., & Snell, M. E. (1993). Measurement, analysis, and evaluation. In M. E. Snell (Ed.), *Instruction of students with severe disabilities* (4th ed.). New York: Merrill/Macmillan.

Burney, J. P., & Shores, R. E. (1979). A study of relationships between instructional planning and pupil behavior. *Journal of Special Education Technology, 2*(3), 16–25.

Farlow, L. J., & Snell, M. E. (1989). Teacher use of student instructional data to make decisions: Practices in programs for students with moderate to profound disabilities. *Journal of the Association for Persons with Severe Handicaps, 14*, 13–22.

Fuchs, L. S., & Fuchs, D. (1986). Effects of systematic informative evaluation: A meta-analysis. *Exceptional Children, 53,* 199–208.

Grace, C., & Shores, E. F. (1992). *The portfolio and its use: Developmentally appropriate assessment of young children.* Little Rock, AR: Southern Association on Children Under Six.

Grigg, N. C., Snell, M. E., & Loyd, B. (1989). Visual analysis of student evaluation data: A qualitative analysis of teacher decision making. *Journal of the Association for Persons with Severe Handicaps, 14,* 23–32.

Haring, N. G., Liberty, K., & White, O. (1980). Rules for data-based strategy decisions in instructional programs: Current research and instructional implications. In W. Sailor, B. Wilcox, & L. Brown (Eds.), *Methods of instruction for severely handicapped children* (pp. 159–192). Baltimore: Paul H. Brookes.

Hanline, M. F., & Fox, L. (1994). The use of assessment portfolios with young children with disabilities. *Assessment in Rehabilitation in Exceptionalities, 1*(1), 40–57.

Meisels, S. J., & Steele, D. M. (1991). *The early childhood portfolio collection process.* Ann Arbor, MI: Center for Human Growth and Development, University of Michigan.

Meyer, L. H., & Janney, R. (1989). User friendly measures of meaningful outcomes: Evaluating behavior interventions. *Journal of the Association for Persons with Severe Handicaps, 14,* 263–270.

Paulson, F. L., Paulson, P. R., & Meyer, C.A. (1991). What makes a portfolio a portfolio? *Educational Leadership, 48,* 60–63.

Sailor, W., & Guess, D. (1983). *Severely handicapped students: An instructional design.* Boston: Houghton Mifflin.

Westling, D. L., & Floyd, J. (1990). Generalization of community skills: How much training is necessary? *Journal of Special Education, 23,* 386–406.

White, O. (1988). Probing skill use. In N. G. Haring (Ed.), *Generalization for students with severe handicaps: Strategies and solutions.* Seattle: University of Washington Press.

White, O. R., & Haring, N. G. (1980). *Exceptional teaching.* Columbus, OH: Merrill.

CHAPTER 9

Creating Inclusive Educational Environments

Chapter Overview

In this chapter, strategies for organizing and supporting the instruction of students with severe disabilities within inclusive programs are presented. The chapter begins by providing information on practices that are related to successful school inclusion and the facilitation of acceptance of the student with severe disabilities. The second section of the chapter describes procedures that may be used for organizing and managing instruction. The final section of the chapter addresses scheduling issues and the role of the special educator in the school.

An important task for teachers is to organize instruction in a manner so that the needs of every student are met. The Individual Education Plan provides direction to the teacher on the goals of instruction and the support services that can be provided, but the teacher must determine how, where, and when instruction will occur. In this chapter, guidelines for organizing instruction in inclusive school settings will be provided. The chapter begins with an explanation of the importance of inclusive schooling and then provides strategies for developing optimal inclusive environments. The next section of the chapter moves from the "big picture" of inclusive schooling to the specifics of when and where to provide instruction on individual goals. The chapter ends with a description of the changing role of the special educator in programs that are moving toward inclusive education.

The Importance of School Inclusion

A variety of terms have been used over the last decade to describe the education of students with disabilities with their nondisabled peers. When students with severe disabilities were primarily educated in separate special schools, *integration* was the term used to describe the successful placement of students with disabilities into regular schools. In situations where students with disabilities attended the regular school but were primarily instructed in separate special classes, the term *mainstreaming* was used to describe the placement of students with disabilities in regular education classes. In both integration and mainstreaming, students with disabilities were viewed as the newcomer to the school or class who had to be accommodated.

Since the mid-1980s professionals and parents have worked to achieve education programs that include all students without the presumption that some students do not belong or must be labeled to receive support services. *Inclusion* describes much more than the acceptance of students with disabilities into the mainstream. Inclusive education programs do not focus on the accommodation of students with disabilities into a general education setting, but are focused on the restructuring of schools to accept and provide for the needs of all students. *Inclusive education* is used to describe the development of schools where every student belongs and is supported (Stainback & Stainback, 1990). In inclusive education, mainstreaming and integration are viewed as intermediary steps to the ultimate goal of teaching all students together. In inclusive programs, specialized instruction and support are provided to any student who is in need of support.

Currently, educational programs for students with severe disabilities may be provided in segregated special schools, in self-contained classrooms located at a regular school with minimal contact with nondisabled students, in self-contained classrooms with informal and formal opportunities for interaction with nondisabled students, or in inclusive schools. There is great variability between and within states. In this text, practices will be presented for educating students within inclusive programs because they represent best practice for students with severe disabilities and also apply to more restrictive settings. Teachers who educate students in self-contained classrooms or special schools may find that their role as the primary educator of students with severe disabilities is more explicitly defined, but they may also feel isolated from the support of colleagues in general education.

It is important for the teacher to understand why inclusion is best practice. The teacher who is trained in practices needed to support students with severe disabilities in the inclusive school will have to be able to articulate the benefits of inclusive schooling to school and community members who may be unaware of its importance. The rationale for integrating students with disabilities with nondisabled students is based on legal, moral, and educational reasons (Bricker, 1978).

Legal Rationale

The Education for All Handicapped Children Act (P.L. 94-142) of 1975, now known as the Individuals with Disabilities Education Act (P.L. 101-46), was the culminating legislation of a struggle to legally mandate the education of all students with disabilities. Included in the mandate was the provision that students with disabilities should be educated with their nondisabled peers. This provision requires that:

> *To the maximum extent appropriate, handicapped children, including children in public or private institutions or other care facilities, are educated with children who are not handicapped, and that special classes, separate schooling, or other removal of handicapped children from regular educational environment occurs only when the nature or severity of the handicap is such that education in regular classes with the use of supplementary aids and services cannot be achieved satisfactorily.* (20 U.S.C. 1415 [5][B])

The passage of P.L. 94-142 marks a time in history when there was a philosophical shift in the way society regarded people with disabilities. Prior to this time students with disabilities were educated in segregated settings if at all. The prevailing theme in educational and social services was that individuals with disabilities needed to be sheltered and protected from others in society. When the efforts of parents, professionals, and legal advocates pushed issues regarding the inclusion of people with disabilities into public view, the shift in philosophy about the need to include and integrate persons with disabilities followed, closely paralleling the civil rights movement, in which society was forced to confront issues surrounding the inclusion of minorities (McDonnell & Hardman, 1989).

The right to be educated with students who are not disabled is supported by litigation and has been affirmed by several court decisions (*Greer by Greer v. Rome City School District, Holland v. Sacramento City School District,* and *Oberti v. Board of Education of Clementon School District*). The decision made in 1993 by the United States Court of Appeals for the Third Circuit in the case of *Rafael Oberti v. Board of Education of Clementon New Jersey* used guidelines established by both *Holland v. Sacramento City School District* and *Greer by Greer v. Rome City School District* to uphold the right of students with disabilities to be included in general education classes with students who are not disabled. In the Oberti case, the court found that the school district violated the rights of Rafael Oberti, an 8-year-old with Down syndrome, when it refused to allow him to attend regular classes in his neighborhood school. The district had argued that Rafael's behavioral problems and immaturity made placement in a regular class inappropriate and recommended placement in a segregated, self-contained special class for students classified as "multihandicapped." The Obertis contended that Rafael would not have presented such severe behavior problems had he been provided with adequate supplementary aids and services in the regular class as stipulated in the Individuals with Disabilities Education Act.

In the Oberti decision, the Court of Appeals established that the school district must give serious consideration to including the student with disabilities in the regular class with supplementary aids and services and modifications in the curriculum. In addition, the Oberti decision directs the court to carefully consider the unique benefits that the student with disabilities may obtain from an integrated setting that are not available in a segregated setting. The promise of greater academic progress in a segregated setting may not warrant the exclusion of a student from the regular classroom.

Philosophical Rationale

The legal mandates for inclusion are based on the philosophical or moral value held by our society that the segregation of persons because of a physical attribute is not appropriate. We have made a philosophical commitment to equality of rights for all humans. The inclusion of students with disabilities into their neighborhood schools is an application of the right to equality. Inclusion is also based on the concept of normalization (Nirje, 1969) for persons with disabilities. Normalization has been described as making available the patterns and conditions of everyday life to people with disabilities. The concept of normalization serves as a criteria for service providers when decisions are made about designing interventions for people with disabilities. The placement of students with disabilities into the school they would attend if they were not disabled is the application of the concept of normalization.

Educational Rationale

In addition to the philosophical and legal reasons for the inclusion of students with disabilities, there are important educational ones. Many special educators view an integrated setting as interdependent with a quality program for students with disabilities (Snell, 1988). The regular school environment offers such students a rich setting in which to learn skills in natural contexts. Because students with severe disabilities have slow rates of learning and difficulty retaining and generalizing what is learned, they must be taught personally relevant skills that are useful in a variety of present and future environments. The need for functional skill attainment illuminates the importance of providing instruction in integrated environments, for it is in those types of environments that students with severe disabilities must learn to function (Snell, 1988).

The Benefits of Inclusion

Instructional Benefits

In addition to the logical arguments for the appropriateness of educating students with severe disabilities in an inclusive environment, there is ample empirical evidence that confirms the practice as beneficial (Halvorsen & Sailor, 1990). Brinker and Thorpe (1984) investigated the educational impact of integration on the achievement of learners with severe disabilities and found that rate of interaction with nondisabled students was a significant predictor of the number of IEP objectives achieved by a student with severe disabilities. Integrated settings have also been linked to increased social and communication skills (Gaylord-Ross & Peck, 1985; Strain & Kerr, 1981). Social and communication skills are learned within interactions with other individuals. Students who attend schools where all of their peers have communication and social skill deficits do not have as many opportunities for interaction as students who are educated with peers who are not disabled. Frequent interaction opportunities are essential to communication and social skill development. Episodic interactions with nondisabled peers do not offer enough practice for mastery (Snell & Eichner, 1989).

A study conducted by Hunt, Goetz, and Anderson (1986) found that the IEPs written for students in integrated settings were technically superior to ones written for students in segregated settings. This may be because teachers in segregated settings are less likely to view their students by chronological age and that placement in a segregated program may influence teachers to work to remediate skill deficiencies rather than develop community-referenced skills.

Friendship Formation

Most important, the general education environment offers an opportunity for students with severe disabilities to build friendships with nondisabled peers. Strully & Strully (1989) have described friendships as being critical to inclusion in the community. Little attention has been paid to how friendships are formed and ways to facilitate friendship building, although few persons would argue about the importance of friendship to a quality life (Stainback & Stainback, 1987). There are numerous accounts by parents and professionals that describe the advantages of inclusion for the student with severe disabilities in the development of friendships (Forest & Lusthaus, 1989; Peck, Donaldson, & Pezzoli, 1990; Strully & Strully, 1985). Clearly, opportunities for friendship formation with nondisabled students are restricted when students with severe disabilities are segregated from their nondisabled peers.

When discussing the value of inclusion, it is important to distinguish between the physical integration and the social integration of students with disabilities. Physical integration occurs when students with disabilities attend regular public schools. Physical integration is necessary for inclusion in the school community, although inclusion does not always follow physical integration. If students with disabilities are placed in a temporary classroom far from other classrooms or are in a wing of the school for special education, opportunities for sustained and intimate contact with students who are not disabled are minimal. If students with disabilities are given no opportunity to interact with nondisabled peers or if no effort is made to facilitate those interactions, social integration is unlikely to occur. It is critical that schools not only physically integrate, but also plan ways to promote the inclusion of the student with disabilities into the school community.

Impact on Nondisabled Peers

When inclusion occurs, students with disabilities are not the only ones to benefit. The most important benefit to nondisabled students and to society in general is that the inclusion of students with disabilities in the school positively influences the attitudes of nondisabled students toward people with disabilities (Gaylord-Ross & Peck, 1985; Voeltz, 1980, 1982). The current school population will be the next generation of adults (e.g., bus drivers, grocery-store clerks, apartment managers, doctors, lawyers, architects, and parents of children with disabilities) who will interact with people with disabilities in the community. Their exposure to individuals with disabilities and subsequent positive attitudes should result in a generation of citizens who understand and accept peers with disabilities (Brown et al., 1983).

In addition to promoting positive attitudes toward people with disabilities, nondisabled students who have had direct and sustained contact with students with severe disabilities have experienced other benefits. Peck et al. (1990) interviewed 21 adolescents who had contact with students with moderate and severe disabilities in their school programs. Using qualitative analysis of the interviews, the researchers found that the high school students perceived the following six benefits from their social relationships with peers who had severe disabilities (Peck et al., 1990, p. 244):

1. Self-concept: growth in their understanding and appreciation of their own personal characteristics.
2. Social cognition: growth in their understanding of the feelings and beliefs underlying the behavior of other people.
3. Reduced fear of human differences: reduced anxiety and fear of people who look or behave in an unusual fashion and/or increased confidence in their ability to respond appropriately and effectively in interpersonal interactions with such people.
4. Tolerance of other people: increased acceptance of the feelings, behavior, and personal limitations of other nondisabled people, including family and friends.
5. Development of personal principles: relationships with students with disabilities contributes to reflection and/or action toward the further formation, clarification, or commitment to personal moral or ethical principles.
6. Experiencing relaxed and accepting friendships.

Although there is a wealth of evidence that inclusive educational programs are desirable, change from segregated special programs to a more progressive model of instruction has not occurred as rapidly as desired by many advocates, parents, and professionals. It is important to remember that school systems are large bureaucracies that do not respond immediately to innovation and reform. The development of an inclusive school is not simply the adoption of a new curricular approach; it involves major school restructuring that goes far beyond meeting the needs of students with disabilities. Salisbury (1991) describes the inclusive elementary school as " . . . a value that is manifested in the way we plan, promote, and conceptualize the education and development of young children" (p. 147).

Despite the slow and uneven pace in which some school districts are moving to inclusive models of education, there is little question among professionals and researchers that progress toward the widespread adoption of inclusive schooling will continue to occur. Schools across the country are concerned with the ability of public schools to meet the needs of a diverse at-risk school population. The inclusive schooling movement should be viewed as a school restructuring innovation that can meet the needs of all students, not just students with disabilities. In the following section of this chapter, the inclusive education model is described, and practices that should be implemented for successful inclusion are presented.

The Inclusive Education Model

The term *full inclusion* has been used to describe educational programs where a student's primary placement is in general education. This means that all students report to a regular homeroom or have a primary placement in a grade-level classroom. The schedule of classes for the remainder of the day depends on the student's Individual Education Program and is developed by the IEP team. The principle of natural proportion, the distribution of individuals with disabilities in a school that reflects the natural diversity in the community, is adhered to in the enrollment of students with severe disabilities in individual schools and in involvement with the regular class (York, Vandercook, MacDonald, & Wolff, 1989).

Full inclusion programs that have been described in the literature are located in Syracuse, New York (Biklen, Corrigan, & Quick, 1989; Knoblock & Harootunian, 1989); Vermont (Thousand et al., 1986); and the Northwest Territories and New Brunswick, Canada (Forest & Lusthaus, 1989). Full inclusion programs are based on the philosophy that every student is a genuine member of the school community and that the school community has a responsibility to meet all of the students' needs (Williams, Villa, Thousand, & Fox, 1989). General educators work in partnership with special educators in providing for the individual needs of students with disabilities.

Some advocates of inclusive schooling wish to eliminate the use of the term *full inclusion* because it suggests that inclusion is an entity that is measurable and that can occur partially or fully. They propose that if inclusive programs are truly supportive of every student's individual needs, a range of supports will be provided that may involve full-time regular classroom placement or may involve instruction in the community or other settings. In this chapter, inclusive schooling will be defined as providing the supports necessary to promote the learning of every student in the neighborhood or home-zone school without the use of separate special education classrooms.

The partnership of general and special educators is essential to the success of the inclusion model (Stainback & Stainback, 1990). The development of an individual education program for a child in an inclusion program requires the collaboration of a variety of people as a team (Vandercook & York, 1990). This team is not composed of only the classroom teacher and the student's parents, but also may include the student, important family members, a support teacher with training in instructional adaptations and meeting the needs of students with disabilities, an administrator or a designee, support personnel from related services, and classmates of the student.

The mission of the team is to identify, evaluate, and implement the supports and adaptations needed by the student with disabilities for meaningful inclusion in the school community. Stainback & Stainback (1989) suggest that a person be designated as a support facilitator to enhance the success of inclusion programs. The support facilitator would most likely be a trained special educator whose role is to promote natural networks of support for the student with disabilities (particularly friendships), locate needed instructional resources (curricula, assessments, equipment, consultants), and provide direct help as a team teacher.

The primary placement of students with severe disabilities in regular classes is an idea that has been received with controversy (Brown et al., 1989b). People who have resisted this model are concerned that the placement of students with severe disabilities is too radical a model and that general educators will receive it with resistance, that students with severe disabilities will not be provided with the appropriate supports and services they need in a regular class, that special education is better configured in ratio and technology to meet the needs of these students, and that the curricula provided to students in general education is often inappropriate for students with disabilities (Brown et al., 1989b). Proponents of full inclusion argue that it is better for a student to belong in a regular class and leave for some periods than to be an outsider who comes in, that adjustments can and should be made in classroom ratio and the resources needed to support the student with disabilities, and that regular class placement does not preclude instruction in more relevant environments and activities when necessary (Brown et al., 1989b).

Facilitating School Acceptance

A primary challenge to implementing an inclusive educational program is ensuring school acceptance of students with disabilities. Strategies must be used to promote an environment of acceptance and inclusion. The school district and individual schools must prepare for and work together to achieve this goal. It is also necessary to use strategies to facilitate peer interactions. Nondisabled students who have been denied exposure to people with disabilities may not know how to interact with their peers with disabilities or may enter into interactions with fears and biases that hinder the development of personal relationships.

In successful inclusion programs, inclusion is viewed as a schoolwide effort, not just another specialized program of exceptional student education. Strategies that have been used to foster school inclusion are listed in Figure 9–1 and are discussed below. It is important to note that every school community is unique and that strategies that will work in some settings may not be applicable to others.

Classroom Placement

In order for inclusion programs to be successful, the school must accept students with disabilities as members of the school community. Students with disabilities should be placed in a grade-level classroom or homeroom with nondisabled peers. When students are placed in a separate classroom, a message is transmitted to the school community that students with severe disabilities don't really belong in the regular classroom although they may be invited to join their nondisabled peers with special arrangements. A classroom that is used to instruct students with severe disabilities separately from a grade-level class should not be identified as a special class; rather it should be a room that is used as a resource for students who have a variety of needs, for example, students in a Chapter One program or those who need individualized tutoring. If the classroom served a variety of students, students with severe disabilities would not ever be excluded from what was provided to the general school population.

Awareness Training

In successful inclusive schools, the entire school population is aware of the need to support students with disabilities. Information about students with disabilities can be presented to nondisabled students through awareness training (Sailor et al., 1989). Some awareness activities that have been used are the "Kids on the Block" puppet show, movies about persons

Place students with disabilities in general education homerooms and classrooms

Specialized instruction should occur in environments that are also used by nondisabled peers

Provide for initial and ongoing ability awareness activities

Provide information to everyone in the school community about the importance of inclusion

Model positive and respectful interactions with students with disabilities

Use curriculum infusion to increase student and teacher knowledge about supporting students with disabilities

Develop collaborative teams to support school inclusion and individual student support

Involve the parents of all students in supporting inclusion

Develop peer tutoring, special friends, and peer networks to support the inclusion of students with disabilities

Facilitate the interactions and friendship development of students with disabilities and their non-disabled peers

Figure 9–1
School Inclusion Strategies

with disabilities, reading books about disabilities, disability simulation exercises, and workshops in classrooms. When presenting awareness-training activities, it is important to conduct them in ways that promote positive images of persons with disabilities. The purpose of the awareness training is not to generate sympathy or charitable feelings toward the student with disabilities, but to encourage an understanding of their capabilities and needs (accessibility, adaptations, assistance). Teachers should carefully review films, movies, books, and awareness kits to make sure that the language used is appropriate and that a desirable image of persons with disabilities is portrayed.

Awareness training should become part of the school's effort to provide a multicultural antibias curriculum—an approach to instruction that directly addresses issues of stereotyping, bias, and discrimination. In such a curriculum students are taught to understand and value diverse cultures and differences and to recognize and combat racism, sexism, and handicapism. Students do not learn these concepts in an isolated fashion with a thematic or unit focus on a particular cultural group or difference; rather, they are provided with information on diversity in an integrated curriculum. Teachers who embrace a multicultural antibias approach seek to provide realistic images of people from diverse backgrounds in relevant, everyday situations. This approach provides an awareness of disability by including wall displays and books that picture persons with disabilities engaging in everyday activities, instructional materials such as books and toys (dolls, play props) that include persons with disabilities, and instructional activities that assist students in understanding the concepts of disability, accessibility, and handicapism.

Awareness training is an important component of developing an inclusive school, but it should not represent the only effort (Fritz, 1990). Awareness activities should be ongoing and conducted in conjunction with the other strategies listed in Figure 9–1. Awareness should not be encouraged for students only; it will also be necessary for the special educator or designated professional involved in the inclusion effort to educate general educators and the parents of students in the school about inclusion and students with severe disabilities. For many general educators, inclusion is a new idea that may be initially met with apprehension.

Professionals with knowledge of inclusion can provide in-service training to colleagues, lead faculty discussions on the issues related to inclusion, disseminate relevant literature about inclusion from special education resources and journals and magazines that are familiar to general educators (e.g., *Young Children, Elementary School Journal, Phi Delta Kappan),* and provide presentations to the parent-teacher organization. In building an awareness of the importance of inclusion, educators have found that showing videos depicting successful inclusion efforts (e.g., *Regular Lives, Educating Peter, Choices)* or providing presentations from teachers and families of successful inclusion stories can be beneficial.

Teacher Modeling

In addition to formal presentations on the importance and implementation of inclusion, the special educator should provide modeling of appropriate interactions with students who are disabled. The attitude of the special educator, the person who is presumed to be the expert, influences the way others will view those students. If the special educator appears to be protective of the students or apologetic for their presence, others in the school will react accordingly. The teacher should emphasize the positive attributes of students with disabilities, model social interactions with them, and use appropriate and normalizing language when talking about them. For example, if the special educator refers to them as the "handicapped students" or speaks to them using the tone of voice and phrasing used with young children, the perceptions of others in the school will be that students with disabilities should be treated in a protective or condescending manner.

Curriculum Infusion

Curriculum infusion is a strategy that is aimed at promoting understanding and acceptance of students with disabilities (Hamre-Nietupski et al., 1989). It is accomplished by expanding the general education curriculum to include reference to disability-related issues. Curriculum infusion is a project that both special educators and general educators do collaboratively. Hamre-Nietupski et al. (1989) suggest a 4-step implementation procedure: (1) establish a core team to work on the infusion project; (2) select general education units for infusion; (3) develop and implement infusion activities; and (4) evaluate infusion activities. An example of infusion activities are provided in Figure 9–2.

Collaborative Teaming

The education of students and staff about the importance of inclusion is only the foundation for success. Awareness and curriculum infusion activities must be accompanied by some

Unit: Genetic/Environmental Influences on Development

A. Class discussion
   1. Genetic and environmental causes of disabilities
   2. Identification of similarities between disabled/nondisabled individuals
   3. Past (segregated) versus present (integrated) educational model
B. Teams debate segregated vs integrated education
   1. Four-person teams are formed.
   2. Teams visit integrated/segregated programs.
   3. Teams gather written information on integration/segregation.
   4. Guest speakers, one pro-integration, one pro-segregation, debate before the class.
   5. Teams debate before the class using previously gathered information.
C. Each student writes a position paper on integration/segregation.
D. All students visit students with severe disabilities to get to know them better.

Figure 9–2
Seventh Grade Fusion Activities
From "Enhancing Integration of Students with Severe Disabilities Through Curricular Infusion: A General/Special Education Partnership" by S. Hamre-Nietupski, B. Ayres, J. Nietupski, M. Savage, B. Mitchell, & H. Bramman, 1989, *Education and Training in Mental Retardation, 24,* pp. 78–88. Copyright 1989 by the Division on Mental Retardation and Developmental Disabilities, The Council for Exceptional Children. Reprinted by permission.

type of formal mechanism to provide ongoing support and problem solving as students with disabilities are integrated into the school. One method for providing such support is the use of collaborative teams (Fox & Williams, 1991; Stainback & Stainback, 1990; Thousand & Villa, 1990). In collaborative teaming, team members work together as equal partners to achieve a common goal. The team assists with school inclusion by developing solutions to problems and challenges and developing strategies to support the school goal of inclusion.

The school planning team is a collaborative team whose goal is to improve the educational program for all students (Fox & Williams, 1991). Members of the community, instructional personnel, administrators, and families should be involved in the team, whose tasks may include developing a shared vision and mission statement for inclusive schooling, assessing school practices and identifying areas for improvement, and developing action plans that provide for the changes needed to promote the inclusion and appropriate instruction of all students in the school.

Individual Student Planning Teams In addition to the school planning team, inclusive schools should also form individual student planning teams, collaborative teams that are formed to support the education and inclusion of each student with severe disabilities (Fox & Williams, 1991). The special educator will find that he or she is a member of several individual planning teams; the general educator would be a member only of the planning team concerned about the student who is placed in his or her class.

The individual student planning team is composed of persons who have frequent contact with the student with severe disabilities and who are directly involved in the education of the student, typically the student, parents, general educator, special educator, paraprofessional, and related service providers (e.g., speech therapist). The tasks of the individual student planning team are to assess and develop the supports needed by the student with severe disabilities by determining the skills that should be taught to the student, designing accommodations to meet the student's individual needs, monitoring the student's progress, and designing supports to assist the student with transitions.

Fox and Williams (1991) recommend that the individual student planning team meet each week for an hour, using a structured agenda with time limits for each topic discussion to facilitate an efficient teaming process. Because it is likely that the special educator or inclusion facilitator will initiate the collaborative teaming process, it is important for the special educator to keep in mind that the team members must share equal roles in the planning process. This activity should not be perceived as being led by special education. The goal is for all team members to actively participate in the support of students with intensive needs.

Community and Family Involvement

A school inclusion program will not work well without community support and involvement. The parents of all of the students in the school must be aware of the goals of inclusive schooling and may also assist in the implementation of the integration program. In some schools parents have conducted disability awareness activities, shared their views of inclusion to students, and assisted as volunteers with inclusion activities. There may be initial resistance or anxiety in the community when inclusion is first being discussed, so it is important to give community members an opportunity to express their fears and for professionals to provide reassurance. In time, most families will see the positive aspects of the program.

Peer Programs

Because the physical placement of students with disabilities in regular schools and classrooms may not be enough to promote social interaction between nondisabled students and their peers with disabilities, there must also be an effort to promote such interaction. Peer tutoring and Special Friends are two commonly identified programs that have been successfully used by many schools to implement inclusion programs. Peer tutors are students who volunteer to assist other students in achieving their instructional goals; special friends are volunteers who socially interact with students who are disabled in fun and leisure activities.

Facilitating Interactions

Social interactions between students with severe disabilities and their nondisabled peers may not spontaneously occur. Typically, the student with severe disabilities has limited social and communication skills, and the student without disabilities has limited experiences in interacting with peers with disabilities. Because of this, social interaction is a primary goal of inclusive schooling. Brown et al. (1989a) have identified 11 types of nonmutually exclusive relationships that should be part of the life of a student with disabilities. Those relationships are: peer tutor, eating companion, art/music/p.e./industrial arts/home economics companion, general class companion, during-school companion, after-school companion, friend, extracurricular companion, after-school project companion, travel companion, and neighbor. They recommend that individual educational programs be designed to develop, maintain, and enhance a healthy range of these social relationships.

Several strategies have appeared in the literature for facilitating peer interaction in inclusion settings. These strategies are listed in Figure 9–3 and discussed below. It is important to note that the research that supports the use of these strategies was usually conducted in situations that are not considered full inclusion. Most of what is known about social integration comes from research in situations where students with severe disabilities were present in unnatural proportions or who had only limited interaction time (e.g., during a planned play group) with nondisabled students. It is possible that in inclusive education programs, fostering social interactions may become less difficult as students with disabilities are fully accepted and have the opportunities for sustained and longitudinal relationships with their peers.

Environmental Arrangement

Teacher Mediation

Peer-Mediated Interactions

Peer Tutoring

Special Friends

Peer Support Networks

Figure 9–3
Strategies for Facilitating Peer Interaction

Environmental Arrangement A first step to promoting interactions between the two groups of students is to examine the environment for interaction opportunities and to create opportunities through environmental arrangement. There are times in the school day when students have opportunities to be social (e.g., recess, lunchroom, gym, music class, media center) that should be used to facilitate interactions. The teacher may also want to create activities that promote joint participation; for example, a teacher may assist students in developing a collaborative enterprise (such as selling popsicles or school supplies) that offers opportunities for peer interaction and a shared goal. Teachers can make use of adapted materials, toys, and games such as computers with electromechanical switches, video games, remote control or electromechanical switch toys, or race car sets that can be operated by the student with disabilities and are attractive to nondisabled students. Providing the student with disabilities with an interesting toy or activity (e.g., bubbles and giant bubble wand, kite, classroom pet) when on the playground is an effective way to encourage other students to approach the student with disabilities.

Teacher Mediation When students approach peers with disabilities the teacher can use facilitation procedures to assist with the interaction. These procedures include modeling social interactions, prompting peers to initiate and interact with the student with disabilities, prompting the students with disabilities to initiate and maintain interactions with their peers, and providing reinforcement to both sets of students for appropriate social interaction. These procedures may be used when opportunities for interactions occur, or the teacher may want to use peer tutoring or special friends programs to schedule interaction time.

Peer-Mediated Interventions Many researchers have been successful at facilitating social interaction by providing nondisabled students with prompts and reinforcement to interact with their peers with disabilities (Hendrickson, Strain, Tremblay, & Shores, 1982; Kohler & Fowler, 1985; Lancioni, 1982). This is typically done by providing a brief training program to the peer in social interaction prompting techniques. Unfortunately, researchers have had a difficult time achieving maintenance of the behavior by the nondisabled peer (Lancioni, 1982; Sasso & Rude, 1987). Another challenge of peer-mediated interventions is teaching the student with disabilities to respond and initiate back to the nondisabled peer so that true social reciprocity in the interaction results (Odom & Strain, 1986). Procedures that have been used in peer mediation that may be successful include teaching peers to reciprocate to the initiations of students with disabilities (Odom & Strain, 1986), training peer mentors in methods to adapt play activities for the students with disabilities (Knapczyx, 1989), and providing training to peers in ways to use prompts to encourage untrained peers to interact with the target student (Sasso, Hughes, Swanson, & Novak, 1987).

Peer Tutoring Peer tutoring programs involve the recruitment of nondisabled students to work with students with severe disabilities. Most peer tutoring programs (Donder &

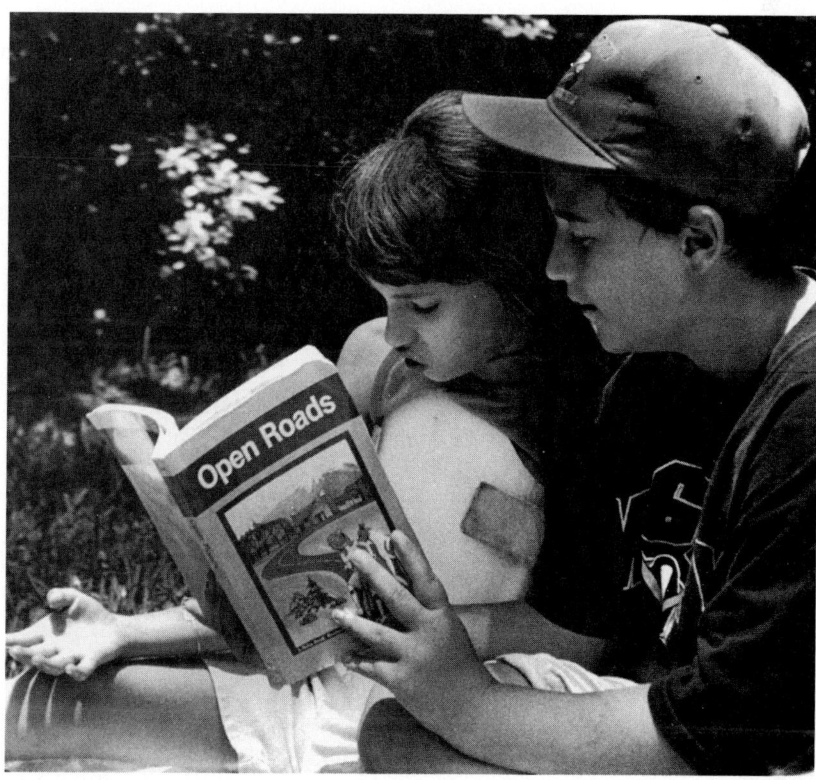

Students with severe disabilities may receive instruction from peer tutors.

Nietupski, 1981; Kohl & Stettner-Eaton, 1985; Kohl, Moses, & Stettner-Eaton, 1983; Lancioni, 1982) have focused on training nondisabled students as instructors of the students with disabilities.

Peer tutors have been used to teach a variety of skills including playing games, performing classroom jobs, preparing a snack, cooking, using cafeteria skills, and operating a tape player or record player. It is important for peer tutors to be trained by the teacher on how to work with the student with disabilities and to be provided with information on how to appropriately prompt and reinforce their tutees. Training for peer tutors usually includes information presented prior to the tutoring, modeling and instruction by the teacher with the student and peer tutor, and feedback to the tutor on his or her performance (Sailor et al., 1989).

Some researchers have expressed concern that peer tutor relationships are hierarchical in nature and may inhibit true friendship formation (Meyer & Putnam, 1987; Voeltz, 1980, 1982). Others (Sailor et al., 1989) contend that peer tutor and special friends programs are very similar and that friendships have evolved from relationships that began as tutorial. Haring, Breen, Pitts-Conway, Lee, and Gaylord-Ross (1987) used a pretest-posttest experimental design to examine the effects of peer tutoring and special friend participation on the attitudes and social exchanges of the nondisabled peer toward persons with disabilities. They found that there were no significant differences in attitude or interaction styles for the two groups except that the nondisabled students who served as special friends were more likely to initiate a social interaction toward an unfamiliar peer with autism.

Special Friends Voeltz (1984) described a peer interaction program, Special Friends, where students with disabilities and nondisabled students were encouraged to develop "positive, mutually rewarding relationships . . . that will generalize to nonschool environments and maintain over time" (p. 176) and to develop the social competence of the child with disabilities.

The first activity of the Special Friends program was a short slide/tape presentation that was about the Special Friends program and the students with disabilities. The slide show was presented to all of the classes in the school and students were told that they could volunteer for the Special Friends program in about a week. The volunteers then attended eight 15- to 30-minute weekly group sessions. Examples of the session titles were "What is a disability?" "How do we communicate?" and "How can we play together?" Each Special Friend volunteer spent free-time periods and recess with a selected peer with disabilities. The interactions of the Special Friend were structured by the special educator to promote social peer exchange.

A study conducted by Cole, Meyer, Vandercook, and McQuarter (1986) lends support to the idea that the teacher should be nonintrusive in facilitating peer relationships. The researchers compared two approaches to peer interaction. One group of nondisabled peers received social instruction; the other received friendly comments as they interacted with a student with severe disabilities. The nondisabled peers in the social instruction group were prompted to engage in cooperative play; in the friendly comments group peers were rewarded for attendance, encouraged to practice the game, or received friendly comments about miscellaneous unrelated topics. Initially, the social instruction group showed higher levels of social interaction as measured by a revised version of the Social Interaction Observation System (Voeltz, Kishi, & Brennan, 1981), but by the middle of the study these differences disappeared, and by the end of the study the friendly comment group was more interactive. The authors postulate that high rates of teacher intervention may lead to habituation of the cooperative play behavior of peers.

Both peer tutor and special friend programs have proved to be successful strategies for promoting peer interaction. Teachers should note that these programs were developed in the era of integration programs (i.e., where students with severe disabilities were clustered in self-contained special classrooms) and may not be applicable to the inclusive school. However, the teacher may wish to use some of the components of peer tutoring and special friends programs to ensure that students with disabilities receive the support of peers in the regular classroom. General guidelines for implementing these programs are presented in Figure 9–4.

Peer Support Networks

In some programs, educators collaborate with peers in designing ways to support the student with disabilities in the regular school (Ford & Davern, 1989; Forest & Lusthaus, 1989; Stainback & Stainback, 1990; Vandercook & York, 1990). This procedure, building peer networks, has been a key component of inclusion programs. The peer network is a group of students who are actively involved in encouraging, supporting, and helping the student with

1. Obtain permission from school administrator.
2. Give program presentation to faculty members.
3. Provide faculty and parents with written materials describing the program.
4. Develop participation criteria with teachers who wish to be involved.
5. Make presentations in individual classrooms to recruit students.
6. Send permission forms and parent letter home with students wishing to participate.
7. Develop schedules with students and classroom teachers. You may wish to assign students to support students with severe disabilities in general education classes, individualized instruction, community-based instruction, lunchtime, or playground activities.
8. Meet individually with peer tutor/special friend to discuss role in the classroom, expectations desired, etc. Develop a contract with student if appropriate.
9. Allow student several warm-up visits to observe and meet students with disabilities.
10. Meet with peer tutor/special friend to discuss students and activities he or she would like to assist with.
11. Train peer tutor in procedures he or she should use, review student's likes and dislikes, communication system, when to ask for assistance, how to assist physically; model interactions with the student with disabilities for the special friend/peer tutor.
12. Provide ongoing feedback to the special friend/peer tutor and his or her classroom teacher.
13. Promote the activities of the program in the school.

Figure 9–4
Guidelines for Implementing Special Friends/Peer Tutor Programs

disabilities become a member of the school community.

The peer support network is classroom-based and is comprised of volunteers who have a genuine interest in supporting the student with disabilities. Forest & Lusthaus (1989) describe the "circle of friends" process that they have used to establish peer networks. A facilitator visits the classroom before a student is integrated and talks to the other students about the arrival of the student with disabilities and the apprehensions that some adults have about the experience. He or she elicits from the students that some of the fears may be that the student won't be treated well or have friends. The facilitator then draws four concentric circles on the chalkboard with a stick figure in the center, gives each student a worksheet with the circles, and asks the students to fill in the circles with the people who are in their lives, using the first circle for people closest to them, the second circle for friends, and so forth. The facilitator completes the circle on the chalkboard, shares it with the group, and asks the students to share their circles. Then she draws the circles and describes a fictional person who has only a mother in the first circle and then service workers (doctor, teacher, therapist) in the last. The facilitator asks the students how that person must feel, then uses that example to discuss the student who is arriving and how that student will need a network of people to welcome him or her to the classroom. She explains that she hopes that friendships will evolve from the network, but says that for the moment the network should concentrate on ways to welcome the new student.

The peer support network can be used to brainstorm ways to include students with disabilities in the general education curriculum and extracurricular activities. Because peers are more knowledgeable about what is current fashion or is "in," they can be a good resource for assisting the student with disabilities to fit in socially with peers. In some programs, the peer support network works formally with other team members in the development of instructional goals and activities.

Meaningful Instructional Arrangements

The acceptance of students with disabilities is a critical component of a successful inclusive education program. In addition to being accepted in school, the student with disabilities must be learning efficiently. Techniques for teaching students with severe disabilities were presented in chapter 6. In this chapter, the methods for organizing and arranging instruction are discussed.

When students with severe disabilities were first taught in the public schools, teachers often used a developmental perspective to determine instructional goals. These goals were based on the development of young children and were usually not relevant to life in the community. The instructional procedures used were based on principles of operant conditioning and often involved artificial cues (teacher verbal instruction) and consequences (e.g., material or food reinforcers). The use of materials designed for preschoolers (stacking rings, shape sorters, etc.) and rigidly designed systematic instruction procedures were not uncommon in the 1970s. Typically, skills that were targeted for instruction were taught using a one-to-one instructional format that involved many instructional trials on the skill presented in a massed fashion within a contrived context.

It did not take many years for researchers and teachers of students with severe disabilities to realize that a developmental approach to skill selection would not lead to the acquisition of important life skills by learners with severe disabilities. As a result, the use of ecological inventories became prevalent as a method to identify skills that are relevant to the current and future activities of the student. The use of ecological inventories to determine functional curriculum content for the student is only one piece of the puzzle, however. Teachers were also challenged with determining a method for conducting instruction so that it was effective, functional, and meaningful for the student with severe disabilities. In the following sections, methods are presented for arranging instruction so that it is effective and functional.

Basic Principles of Instructional Arrangements

There are several principles of instruction for educating students with severe disabilities that are applicable to students of all ages in all instructional situations. These principles should be considered as the foundation of appropriate practice and should be evident regardless of the targeted goals, curriculum, or educational placement.

One of the most important of these principles is to provide students with severe disabilities with instruction in meaningful contexts; instruction should be conducted within relevant daily activities rather than in isolated or contrived training situations. Another critical principle is to provide instruction on skills that are functional for the student; skills should be taught that will be useful to the student in both current and future environments.

In the late 1970s, Guess et al. (1978) introduced one of the first formal descriptions of a systematic method of providing functional skill instruction in meaningful contexts called the Individualized Curriculum Sequencing Model (ICS). The ICS provided a model for instructing skills within functional activity routines. The theoretical orientation of the ICS model has been described as a holistic model (Holvoet, Mulligan, Schussler, Lacey, & Guess, 1984) that is based on the assumption that "learning is best achieved through the teaching of skill clusters that are meaningful for the learner" (Helmstetter & Guess, 1987, p. 255). The key components of the ICS model are presented below. These components are regarded by most professionals as universal guidelines and are reflected in most contemporary curricula that are focused on students with severe disabilities.

Functional Skill Instruction Because students with severe disabilities are able to learn a restricted number of skills and need intensive support to learn them, teachers must carefully select the skills that are taught. Functional skill instruction has been used to describe the instruction of skills that are related to independent living in the community. Many teachers select functional skills by examining the routines of nondisabled adults and selecting skills and activities from those repertoires without reflecting on the value of the selected skills to the individual student with severe disabilities. For example, teaching a student to operate a sewing machine has little value for the student who is unlikely to use a sewing machine at home or in the future.

Independence in daily living skills must not be used as the only test of functional skill instruction. Teachers, working in collaboration with the student's individual planning team, must examine the student's individual situation. Instruction should result in the acquisition of skills but also must assist students in the achievement of valued life outcomes (Giangreco, Cloninger, & Iverson, 1993; Meyer, 1991) such as living in the community, having a network of social relationships, choice and self- determination, having an active lifestyle, and being healthy (Giangreco et al., 1993).

When valued life outcomes are used as a defining guideline of functional instruction, skills such as taking turns with peers (needed for building a social network) and learning a community job skill (needed for an active lifestyle) may be important instructional targets, and skills such as sorting silverware or stuffing envelopes may not relate to the achievement of a valued life outcome and, although they appear to be functional, may not be relevant to an individual student.

Distributed Practice In distributed practice, trials of skill instruction occur throughout the day rather than one after another. Massed trials (the repeated practice of one response) were commonly used when skills were taught in an isolated fashion. For example, a teacher using massed trials might have a student practice using a pincer grasp 10 times in a row. When skills are taught within meaningful routines and in combination with related skills, massed trials become logistically difficult for most skills.

Scheduling instruction by developmental domains contributed to the use of massed practice and the instruction of skills without linking them to related skills. It was not uncommon 10 years ago to see a class schedule that consisted of 9:00 Fine motor skills, 9:30 Communication time, 10:00 Gross motor skills, and so forth. When instruction was scheduled by domains, the teacher might teach a goal, such as making a request, only during that time of day. In the distributed trial format a student might be taught to signal a request (with an augmentative communication system or using a natural gesture) during morning arrival, small group instruction, free choice leisure time, lunch, and any other time of the day when requesting is appropriate.

A review of the literature by Mulligan, Guess, Holvoet, and Brown (1980) offers convincing evidence that distributed trial training is preferred to massed trial training. Research also substantiates that distributed trial instruction results in a decrease in nonresponding to tasks (Dunlap & Koegel, 1980) and higher response rates (Mulligan, Lacy, & Guess, 1982).

Skill Clustering Current educational approaches recognize that teaching skills in isolation does little to promote the use of those skills in meaningful contexts. Skills should be taught with the skills from other domains that are related. For example, peer interaction skills should be taught at the same time that a student is learning to purchase lunch in the cafeteria. Guess & Helmstetter (1986) describe the instructional format as "horizontal" rather than the "vertical" format that had been traditionally used. For example, in the traditional model a student was taught communication skills separately from motor skills, although communication is typically used in combination with motor or some other skill domain. In a skill cluster model, a communication skill is taught in combination with the related motor skill; for example, a student raises his head, looks at his communication partner, and says "hi."

Multiple Exemplars Instruction is distributed within activities throughout the day, with multiple examples of materials, in multiple locations, using different responses, and with multiple instructors. The use of varied stimuli in skill acquisition increases the likelihood that the skill will be generalized by the learner (Stokes & Baer, 1977). In the traditional instructional model, instruction occurred using the same stimuli until mastery was achieved. Efforts were not made to ensure generalization, and, typically, generalization was not achieved (Stokes & Baer, 1977). This issue and other strategies that may be used to promote generalization are presented in chapter 7.

Natural Cues and Consequences In an effort to make instruction more meaningful for the student, the training of nonfunctional skills and activities has been abandoned and skills are taught in ways that result in meaningful skill acquisition. For example, you can teach a student to throw away a piece of paper that you have just crumpled and given to him on the verbal cue of "throw it away" followed by a piece of cereal as a reinforcer, or you can teach him to throw a paper towel away after he has dried his hands with it. Instructing skills in a functional manner (natural cues and consequences) results in the acquisition of skills that can be used in meaningful activities in response to naturally occurring stimuli.

Choice-Making Providing learners with choices is identified as an important component of teaching students with severe disabilities, but there is no room for providing opportunities for choice-making when instruction is highly controlled. Professionals in the field have expressed their concern about the conspicuous lack of choice-making opportunities for students with disabilities (Guess & Siegel-Causey, 1985; Shevin & Klein, 1984). Central to the argument of why choice-making is an essential component of instruction is that it is the way that valued members of our society should be treated. In addition to acknowledging the learner's humanness, choice-making enhances instruction and may increase student motivation. The opportunity for choice-making is also an opportunity for communicative expression; every time the student is offered a choice, there is an opportunity to use whatever form of expressive communication he or she has. Students who choose the activities they engage in, the people they work with, and the materials they use are likely to be more motivated and engaged in instruction.

Meaningful Environments When students with severe disabilities were first educated in the public schools, their instruction took place in the special education classroom. This is somewhat compatible with the concept of normalization, that is, students learn in school, therefore students with disabilities should learn in school. But the need to teach students with severe disabilities functional life skills necessitates instruction in settings other than the classroom. If a student needs to learn to prepare a simple snack, purchase items at a grocery store, play a game with a friend, or ask for assistance from a store clerk, it isn't likely that he or she can learn those skills in the special education classroom. Students need to learn skills in the real-life setting where they will be required to use the skill.

Providing Individualized Instruction

The ICS model provides a format for organizing and instructing curriculum content called the activity/skills matrix (Guess & Helmstetter, 1986). The matrix, shown in Figure 9–5, is a format for examining a student's individual goals and the activities of the day in order to determine when skills will be taught.

To develop an activity/skills matrix, the teacher and the individual student planning team first list the activities of the instructional day in the order that they occur. In an inclusion classroom, the activities that are scheduled for the regular class are listed on the matrix with the addition of any individualized events planned for the target student. In a special education classroom where there is mainstreaming into the regular class, typical peers coming into the special education class, and community-based instruction, all of those events will be listed on the matrix. Although the class schedule may change or may not be finalized at the outset of the school year, filling out the matrix prior to instruction is essential. It should be viewed as a worksheet to assist the teacher with planning instruction rather

student ____________________
teacher ____________________

Activity (location)	Time Instructor	skills to be taught

Figure 9–5
Activities/Skills Matrix

than as a rigorous schedule that cannot be changed. The matrix can be revised and readdressed by the teacher or the individual student planning team as the student schedule changes or as goals are changed.

If the teacher is determining the activities that will occur (rather than following the regular class routines) it is important to naturalize the order of activities (e.g., clean-up after snack time) and to make sure that the locations of activities are natural to the activities (e.g., dressing skills in the locker room). The location of the activity should be listed under each activity.

The next step is listing the student's instructional goals across the top of the matrix, then filling in the individual cells of the matrix. Some teachers simply determine if the skill can be functionally taught during the activity and

student Amy
teacher Lisa

Activity (location)	Time Instructor	skills to be taught: greet	raise head	extend elbow	use photo book for request	stand in standing frame	take turns	mechanical switch
arrival	8:30 peer	X	X					
homeroom	8:45 Mike	X	X	X	X			
computer	9:00 Chris	X	X		X		X	X
special (art, music)	9:30 Lisa	X	X	X			X	
snack leisure	10:15 10:45 Lisa	X	X	X	X	X	X	X
library	11:15 Beth	X	X	X	X			X
lunch	12:00 peer	X	X		X		X	
community	1:00 Lisa/peer	X	X	X				
project	2:00 S.T/Lisa/peer		X	X	X		X	X
clean-up	2:30 Lisa/peer	X	X		X			
departure								

Figure 9–6
Activities/Skills Matrix for Amy

put an *X* in the cell. Another procedure is to write in materials or events that will be used to teach the skill. The teacher may want to also list choices that can be made in each cell. A completed activities/skills matrix is shown in Figure 9–6.

Skill clusters, sequences of two or more related target skills, are built from the activities/skills matrix. In Figure 9–6, the teacher has indicated that she can instruct Amy on the simple-discrete behaviors of greeting, extending her elbow, and the continuous ongoing behavior of holding her head up during arrival time. A skill cluster that would include these skills would be:

Teacher Cue: Teacher greets Amy by saying "Hi, Amy."

Student Response: Amy responds by *vocalizing a greeting* and *raising her head.*

Teacher Cue: Teacher prompts Amy to hang up her backpack by pointing to hook and placing backpack in hand.

Student Response: Amy responds by *extending elbow* holding backpack.

This skill cluster could be repeated in music class, where Amy is prompted by a peer to say hello and must extend her elbow to receive the instrument mallet.

There will be skills that are not clustered but are task analyzed or that naturally involve massed practice. The skill of brushing one's teeth or preparing a simple snack involves many chained steps that should be task-analyzed. The task of stapling together the school assembly program is one that naturally involves massed practice.

The activities/skill matrix addresses the organization of instruction for skills and activities that are listed as educational goals on a student's IEP. These goals are targeted for the achievement of valued life outcomes and should be specifically addressed, using systematic instructional techniques. Students with severe disabilities will be exposed to much more instructional content than what is listed on the IEP. In the regular classroom, the student with severe disabilities may participate in a social studies lesson on Martin Luther King or a science class on the influence of gravity on matter. The content in those activities may not appear on the IEP or the matrix, although the student may be learning some of the content with his or her peers. In those situations, the student with severe disabilities may also be working on the acquisition of skills such as working cooperatively with peers, attending to a group presentation, or following 2-step directions. The purpose of the activities/skills matrix is to provide the teacher and the individual student planning team with a mechanism to examine the activities of the day and the IEP and to determine when those targeted goals will be instructed.

Instructional Arrangements in the Regular Classroom

Instructional arrangements in the regular classroom must be approached flexibly. The support of the individual student planning team is essential in determining the ideal arrangement for the student, his or her peers, and the teacher. Inclusion does not mean the instruction of the student with disabilities in a one-to-one situation on content that is different from what is taught to nondisabled students. The activities of the regular classroom should be analyzed by the teacher or the individual student planning team; then accommodations can be made to support the student with severe disabilities. A plan that assists the individual student planning team in analyzing the compatibility of the class activity with the needs and skills of the student with disabilities that is used by teams in Vermont (Fox & Williams, 1991) is provided in Figure 9–7.

In inclusive education programs, the role of the special educator is expanded to include more consultation and collaboration activity. The expansion of the special educator's role, or rather the transformation of the role of the special educator to a support facilitator, means that the role of directly instructing the student with severe disabilities becomes the responsibility of other instructional team members. The individual student planning team must examine all of the instructional situations to determine who will be responsible for instruction within specified activities. When doing this, they must not assume that the paraprofessional will shoulder most of the responsibility for instruction. Instead, they must determine ways to accommodate the needs of the student with severe disabilities within instructional activities

ACTIVITY COMPATIBILITY PLAN

Student________________ Class __________________ Teacher__________________

Description of Class Activities (e.g., lecture, drill)	Does the Activity have Instructional Value
1.	1. Yes No
2.	2. Yes No
3.	3. Yes No
4.	4. Yes No
5.	5. Yes No
6.	6. Yes No

OUTCOMES FOR GROUP

	STUDENT CAN BENEFIT

OUTCOMES FOR STUDENT

	OTHER STUDENTS USE/PRACTICE DURING CLASS

ARRANGEMENT

	CURRENTLY USED IN THE GROUP	STUDENT CAN WORK IN	CHANGES NEEDED
Large Group			
Small Group - Teacher Directed			
Small Group - Student Directed			
Cooperative Group			
Independent			
1:1 in a Small Group Context			
Other			

Comments

Figure 9–7

Activity Compatibility Plan

From *Implementing Best Practices for All Students in Their Local School* by T. J. Fox & W. Williams, 1991, Burlington, VT: Vermont Statewide Systems Support Project, Center for Developmental Disabilities, The University Affiliated Program of Vermont.

TEACHING METHODS	CURRENTLY USED IN THE GROUP	STUDENT CAN BENEFIT FROM	CHANGES NEEDED
Verbal Directions			
Lecture			
Questioning			
Discussion			
Teacher Demonstration / Model			
Coaching			
Drill and Practice			
Computer Aided			
Shaping			
Fading			
Time Delay			
Other			
Comments			

MATERIALS	CURRENTLY USED IN THE GROUP	STUDENT CAN BENEFIT FROM	CHANGES NEEDED
Real Items			
Photographs			
Miniature Objects			
Line Drawings			
Work Books / Work Sheets			
Textbooks			
Audio / Visual			
Concrete Experience			
Paper and Pencil			
Test Forms			
Other			
Comments			

Figure 9–7, *continued*

so that he or she is being taught by the general educator along with nondisabled peers.

It is also important for the individual student planning team to examine the academic content of the regular classroom and to determine the nature of the instructional goals of the student with disabilities within the academic scope and sequence. The fol-

STUDENT RESPONSE	CURRENTLY USED IN THE GROUP	STUDENT CAN USE	CHANGES NEEDED
Look At			
Touch			
Pick Up			
Point At			
Mark Choice			
Draw Line to Connect			
Underline			
Color			
Write Short Answers			
Write Long Exercises			
Write Numerals, Math Problems			
Label Items			
Reply "Yes/No" or "Don't Know"			
Simple Words or Phrases			
Say Short Answers			
Read Aloud			
Express Thoughts and Feelings			
Make Formal Presentations			
Other			

Comments

Figure 9–7, *continued*

lowing categories have been offered as the types of instructional goals that may appear on an IEP (Davern & Ford, 1989, p. 252):

Regular: The student with disabilities is learning the same goals from the general curriculum with modifications made on a lesson-by-lesson basis if needed.

Regular-adapted: The student participates in the regular curriculum with goals adapted for the student's level. Often the goals selected for the student with disabilities may be in the same subject but will be at a level far below the student's peers'.

Embedded: The student participates in the activities of the regular curriculum, working on embedded social, motor, and communication goals, but is not expected to master the goals of the general curriculum.

Functional: Goals and objectives are set that are not part of the regular curriculum but are skills the student needs to function in current and subsequent environments.

The intent of inclusive education is not to bring the traditional special education perspective of instructing students with severe disabilities into the regular classroom, but regular classes offer advantages to the student with severe disabilities, such as opportunities to learn to interact with peers, to learn the common components of the routines in a regular classroom, and to learn about subject areas (e.g., social studies, science) that may not be part of the curriculum in a self-contained special education classroom (York, Vandercook, Caughey, & Heise-Neff, 1989).

Peer Interaction During Instruction

The primary advantages of inclusive educational programs are the opportunities for intensive and sustained interactions with nondisabled peers. These interactions should not be viewed as occurring exclusively during noninstructional times; peer interactions can and should be promoted during instruction as well. The collaborative team should examine classroom practices to determine if different instructional arrangements can result in the meaningful participation and inclusion of students with severe disabilities. Two strategies that might be used as alternatives to traditional instructional practices are partial participation and cooperative learning groups.

Partial Participation An important strategy for facilitating social interaction is the use of partial participation (Baumgart et al., 1982; Ferguson & Baumgart, 1991) in designing instructional activities. The principle of partial participation means that students are not excluded from activities because of their inability to complete them independently. The application of this principle in fostering interactions between students guides the teacher to look for ways to adapt activities or their components to allow the student with severe disabilities to participate. A student who cannot understand the rules of a game does not have to be excluded from playing if he or she can do part of the game with or without assistance. In applying the principle of partial participation to interactions, the teacher looks for activities that students without disabilities engage in and enjoy with their peers and then develops adaptations or strategies so that the student with disabilities can also participate. For example, the seventh-grade students usually play an informally organized soccer game at lunch and recess. Chris, a seventh-grader with disabilities, loves to watch but is unable to keep up with his peers. His teacher asks the students if they can find some way that Chris can be included. His peers suggest that Chris throw in the foul balls. In another class, Amy watches her peers using a computer to write a report for social studies. Amy does not comprehend the content of a report on the rain forest but, with assistance, can use a mouse to operate a computer. The teacher adapts the lesson criteria for her, and Amy (with the assistance of a peer) uses the computer to put together a picture report on the same topic.

Cooperative Learning Cooperative learning (Johnson & Johnson, 1989) is a technique that has proved successful in promoting interaction between students with and without disabilities in instructional activities. Cooperative learning is different from academic lessons that are structured competitively (students work against each other to achieve a goal and are graded on a curve that compels them to work harder and perform better than their peers) or lessons that are structured individualistically (students' goal achievements are independent of one another and students work at their own speed to achieve a preset criteria). In cooperative learning, students' goal achievements are positively correlated, and students only achieve their goal if all students in the learning group also reach their goals (Johnson & Johnson, 1989).

Elements of Cooperative Learning There are five critical elements that are essential to cooperative learning (Johnson & Johnson, 1989). The first is that students clearly perceive their positive interdependence. Positive interdependence is achieved by goal interdependence, the structuring of the task so that the members of the group realize that they can attain their goals only if other members of the group also attain their goals. In addition to goal interdependence, teachers may also use reward interdependence (group members receive the same reward for completing a joint task), resource interdependence (group members must combine their individual resources to complete the task), or role interdependence (members are assigned interconnected roles that the group needs to complete the task).

The second element is that students work in small groups that are structured in a way to facilitate interaction and discussion (Johnson & Johnson, 1989). The third element is individual accountability. By assessing each group member and reporting to the group and individual, all members know that they must contribute to the process and also know which group members will need support to complete the assignment. The fourth element is the use of interpersonal and small-group skills. Collaborative social skills are taught to students so that they will be able to function effectively in cooperative learning groups.

The last element is the use of group processing to focus on the behaviors needed to enable the cooperative group to function. In group processing, members describe to each other member actions that are helpful and unhelpful and receive feedback on participation from their peers.

Designing a Cooperative Lesson The first step in designing a cooperative lesson is to decide on the lesson objectives. Two types of objectives should be specified—an academic objective and a collaborative skills objective. Once the objectives are determined, the teacher determines the most effective group size (usually two to six students) and assigns students to groups, making sure that the groups are heterogenous. The classroom may need to be rearranged to accommodate a cooperative group structure. The cooperative group needs to sit close together in a seating arrangement that allows members to share materials and engage in face-to-face discussion. The lesson materials are distributed in ways that promote the notion that this is a group effort—by giving each member part of the materials that are needed to complete the activity or lesson or by giving only one copy of the materials to the group so that they will have to work together. The teacher should assign roles to group members to promote interdependence. Roles that are typically assigned are: checker (who makes sure everyone can correctly explain how the group arrived at the answer), summarizer (who will report the group's conclusions), facilitator (who makes sure that group processes are followed and that everyone participates), a recorder (who writes down the conclusions), an evaluator (who collects evaluation data on the participation of group members), and an accuracy coach (who corrects mistakes made in members' explanations or summaries).

Presenting the Cooperative Lesson The teacher first presents a cooperative lesson by explaining the academic task and how the students will work collaboratively in their groups to produce a product or report. He or she explains the criteria for success and specifies the behaviors that are appropriate for the cooperative lesson (e.g., taking turns, talking quietly).

When the cooperative groups begin working, the teacher moves from group to group, observing students' work and assisting with problems. When monitoring groups that include students with severe disabilities, the teacher may have to intervene and model ways to prompt the participation of the student with disabilities or to adapt the task. He or she may also have to intervene in groups where students are having problems in collaboration and suggest ways for the group to work together. When the lesson is complete, each student should be able to describe what he or she learned. The teacher assesses the quality and quantity of the work and provides feedback to the students, and, finally, the learning group performs a self-assessment on the group's ability to work collaboratively and productively.

There is a wealth of research on the effectiveness of cooperative learning (Johnson, Johnson, & Maruyama, 1983; Slavin, 1984) and some data on the application of cooperative learning to successfully instruct students with mild disabilities in the mainstream (Madden & Slavin, 1983). A few studies have examined the application of cooperative learning to individuals with severe disabilities. Eichinger (1990) found that when students with severe disabilities participated in cooperative goal-structured activities they were more socially interactive with their peers than in individualistic goal-structured activities. Cooperative activities were cooking and art activities in which students were each given a part of the materials needed to reach the goal.

Putnam, Rynders, Johnson, and Johnson (1989) used the Social Interaction Observation System (SIOS) developed by Voeltz, Kishi, and Brennan (1981) to examine the social interaction behaviors of children with moderate/severe mental handicaps and their nondisabled peers working on a science lesson. One group of children was instructed in collaborative skills; the other was not. Students who had been instructed in collaborative skills were trained to use cooperative skills and were given feedback on their use. Nondisabled students in this group showed a significant superiority in orienting to the student with disabilities, in commenting to the students with disabilities, and in cooperative participation. There were no overall differences in the frequency of social behavior directed toward the nondisabled students by the students with disabilities in the two groups.

Implementing Inclusive Instruction

Inclusive instruction involves bringing together the many components of appropriate practice and support that have been discussed in this and earlier chapters. The collaborative team should realize that inclusive instruction is a complex endeavor that is composed of many variables. An example of one child's inclusive instructional program is provided in this section to assist you in understanding how the elements of inclusive education fit together.

Paul is a 10-year-old student with severe disabilities who is being educated in the elementary school he would attend if he were not disabled. He attends a regular fifth-grade class and is the only student labeled severely disabled in the class, although the classroom of 28 students also includes five students who are labeled mildly disabled.

He is supported by a support facilitator who is certified as a teacher of students with severe disabilities and who provides instructional support for five students with moderate and severe disabilities in Paul's school of 520 students. The support facilitator provides some instruction to Paul, coordinates the activities of Paul's individual student planning team, and provides consultation to Paul's classroom.

Paul's individual student planning team is composed of the support facilitator, his fifth-grade teacher, his mother, the speech therapist, and the paraprofessional in his class. The team developed the following IEP goals for Paul:

1. Paul will indicate a choice by visually scanning objects offered by peers or a teacher and directly selecting his preference.
2. Paul will spontaneously sign an approximation of "finished" to indicate a desire to change activities.
3. Paul will point to a picture from an array of four options to indicate a request for an object or activity.
4. Paul will increase his social interaction with nondisabled peers during free play situations from 33% to 50% of observed intervals.
5. Paul will take out materials independently upon natural verbal cues in the classroom and on the playground.
6. Paul will increase the number of turns to 50% above baseline level within a 10-minute play sequence with a nondisabled peer.
7. Paul will prepare a simple snack (place cookie on plate, place chips in bowl, put juice in cup) independently.
8. Paul will independently move through cafeteria food line with peers at breakfast and lunch.
9. Paul will throw a ball to a peer in a play sequence.
10. Paul will make a purchase in the community by handing the cashier a predetermined amount of money and waiting to receive his change.
11. Paul will use a stamp of his name to identify his work, check out library materials and work, and sign in on the computer log book.
12. Paul will independently select a computer program from a choice of three and place the disk in the drive.

Once the instructional goals were determined, Paul's team examined the activities of his classroom to pinpoint when instruction could occur. In the design of Paul's instructional day, the team made recommendations for the use of cooperative learning, large-group instruction, peer instruction, community-based instruction, and activity-based instruction. Examples of how those approaches are applied to Paul's IEP goals are listed below:

Cooperative Learning Paul is placed in a group of 5 fourth graders. They've been given a science assignment to plan a day's menu and to calculate the number of calories and the grams of fat, protein, and carbohydrates that their menu includes. The students will work in cooperative groups to decide on the menu, cut out magazine pictures that illustrate the item selections, and display the menu and nutritional information on a poster. The group will then complete a worksheet on nutrition and diet.

In the group, Paul will work on the following IEP goals: visually indicating a choice when a peer holds up two pictures; spontaneously signing "finished" after he glues a picture to the poster board; going to the shelf and getting magazines to bring to the group; and stamping his name on the group worksheet.

Large-Group Lesson with Individualized Goals A group of 28 students are learning about the solar eclipse. Paul is assisting a student who is making an eclipse viewer. The goals Paul works on in this activity are pointing to an array of pictures to show the peer what he wants to do next (tape, glue, cut); taking turns with the peer; taking out materials independently; and signing "finished."

Peer Instruction During the free-play part of physical education class, a peer throws a ball with Paul. Paul works on his IEP goals of increasing social interaction; increasing turns taken; throwing a ball; and signing "finished." The peer has been coached on how to redirect Paul to the activity and how to prompt him to sign "finished." When they return to class, the peer reports to the teacher how many turns Paul took before he wanted to quit playing.

Community-Based Instruction Paul and three classmates go to the community shopping center across the street from school. Paul's classmates have been given a social studies assignment to interview people in management roles about their expectations of employees. This assignment is part of a 9-week unit on careers and job skills. Paul accompanies his peers and, with the supervision of a paraprofessional, receives instruction and practice on his goals of visually indicating a choice and making a purchase.

Activity-Based Instruction Every day during math, Paul is assigned to work in the computer area. Five other students are allowed to work in the computer area each day; they are allowed to use a program for math drills or can work on developing a program. Paul keeps the computer log book; after he stamps his name on the log, the other students sign in. Paul is prompted by a peer to select the computer program he wishes to work on and is assisted with turning on his terminal. When Paul stops working on the computer, a peer prompts him to sign "finished" and then assists him with taking the disk out and selecting another program.

Organizing Individualized Support

The success of inclusive schooling hinges on the provision of adequate supports to the students with disabilities so that they may be active and successful learners. Educators often fall into the trap of thinking about support as an additional person who will take on the responsibility for an activity or a student. If the realization of support is an additional person who shadows the student with disabilities, that person can end up being a barrier to the student's social inclusion in the classroom.

It is helpful to view supports from the perspective of what the student needs rather than assigning personnel to students. Needs may include teaching support, prosthetic support, and interpretive support (Ferguson, Meyer, Jeanchild, Juniper, & Zingo, 1992). Teaching support, the instruction of skills and concepts, may be provided by peers, general educators, related service personnel, paraprofessionals, or special educators. Prosthetic support, such as adaptive equipment, correct positioning, physical assistance, and adaptations of activities and materials, may be needed by students with severe disabilities so that they can learn effectively. Such supports will always be needed by the student and are most effective when everyone in the school is familiar with them (Ferguson et al., 1992). Interpretive supports are supports to the general educator or peers who do not have intimate knowledge of the student with disabilities and who may need assistance in designing or adapting activities to facilitate the student's learning and social inclusion. Interpretive supports are usually provided by the special educator or related service personnel.

The Role of the Special Educator

In the special education classroom, the role of the special educator is fairly easily determined; he or she is the primary person to provide instruction, train and supervise paraprofessionals, collaborate with families, and, typically, is the team coordinator of the transdisciplinary team. In inclusive education programs, the special educator's role is changed; he or she becomes a support person for the student with disabilities and other educators. The titles of support facilitator, consulting teacher, method and resource teacher, or inclusion facilitator have been used in inclusive education programs rather than the title of special educator.

The role of the special educator in an inclusive education program is collaboratively determined by the individual student planning team. However, it is likely that as special educators move into inclusive education programs that have been newly designed, they will be the lead professionals, coordinating the efforts to support the student with severe disabilities, including such activities as scheduling and information sharing with related service personnel, ongoing contact with the student's family, managing student paperwork, training and supervising paraprofessionals, facilitating information exchange between team members and other school personnel, securing and maintaining adaptive equipment, and adapting instructional materials (Giangreco et al., 1993).

Inclusive education programs should be viewed within a dynamic framework. The role of the special educator will change as other team members become comfortable with the model and take on new responsibilities. It is highly unlikely that a school can transform from segregated special education classrooms to an inclusive school overnight; the process of restructuring the school will be a gradual one. The flexibility of special education personnel will be required as schools attempt to move to inclusionary practices.

Scheduling Support Personnel

As students are integrated into general education classes, there will be times in the day that the teacher is not with them. It is important that appropriate techniques be used in such situations and that others who interact with them know those strategies. Before a student with severe disabilities is left under the supervision of another adult (general educator, paraprofessional) or typical peer, the teacher should review the goals of the student, instructional strategies to be used, and any specialized positioning or handling techniques that are necessary. The teacher may want to develop a manual for the adult that includes an activities/skills matrix focusing on the period of time that the student is with them, photos of the student in the correct position or being assisted with movement, and guidelines for emergencies.

Often the teacher finds that some of the day is spent in activities that are not traditionally regarded as instructional, but are related to the student's physical and health needs. Students who are not toileting independently need to be assisted with toileting or changed. Students who are not eating independently need to be assisted at mealtimes. Some students may need specialized health-care procedures such as suctioning, postural drainage, and catheterization. Other students have to be assisted in changing physical positions and be placed in adaptive equipment. It is critical that these activities, which can consume so much of the day, become instructional routines. The teacher should include them in the activities/skills matrix and use them for instructing targeted skills. For example, Naomi is a student who is learning to extend her arms and make choices. She also must stand in a standing frame for 20 minutes a day. Her teacher has integrated her therapy routine of standing in the standing frame into a leisure activity. When Amy is placed in the standing frame, which is next to a table, she works on extending her arms and making choices by using a mechanical switch to activate several toys while she interacts with a peer for the 20 minutes.

Many students with severe disabilities receive related services such as occupational therapy, speech therapy, and physical therapy. The traditional model of service delivery has been for the therapist to pull the student out of the regular classroom to work on therapy goals in isolation of other skills. A more desirable arrangement is to integrate therapy into the situations where the student is working on meaningful, functional skills (Sternat, Messina, Nietupski, Lyon, & Brown, 1977). Dunn (1991) defines functional integration as the most desirable integrated therapy arrangement. When functional integration occurs, "professionals apply therapeutic strategies to an individual's life environments" (Dunn, 1991, p. 354). An ideal arrangement would be to have the therapist work in the classroom or in community training sites alongside the educator. In this arrangement the therapist can train the educator in strategies and techniques that can then be applied in other activities and throughout the school day. Block scheduling, where the therapist works in one classroom or school for an extensive amount of time (e.g., 2 hours), enables the therapist to work on therapy goals as they are embedded in routine activities (Rainforth, York, & Macdonald, 1992). When block scheduling is used, the therapist reduces the frequency of student/therapist contacts but increases the number of environments and activities in which facilitation can occur.

When the therapist is with the teacher, it is important to maximize the time for the best therapeutic benefits. This does not mean that the therapist should spend that time in direct therapy with a student. On the contrary, a more appropriate use of the time may be for the therapist to consult with the teacher, address new concerns, examine data on treatment plans, demonstrate techniques, conduct evaluations, and develop therapeutic programs. These tasks involve providing direct therapy but, more important, they include training the educator and others to use specialized techniques.

Two case studies are provided to illustrate the different roles that the special educator may assume as a teacher of students with severe disabilities in two very different inclusion programs.

Case Study One: Sarah

Sarah was hired as the teacher of a class for students with severe disabilities in a regular elementary school. This was the first integrated class for her school district and was implemented in response to the advocacy efforts of parents and professionals. In order to accommodate the students, a portable classroom was placed on the school grounds.

On the first day of the preschool planning week, Sarah requested 20 minutes to discuss her program at the faculty meeting. During this session she explained who she is, why students with severe disabilities were being placed on the campus, gave information about the need to create an environment of inclusion on the campus, and requested that teachers who might be interested in working with her or having their students participate in a special friends/peer tutor project meet with her later that afternoon in the lounge. That afternoon, two teachers came to the lounge and talked with Sarah about the inclusion of her students. They discussed the need to enlist more teacher involvement and the development of awareness activities. One of the teachers offered to work with the PTO in the development of some schoolwide awareness efforts. Both teachers expressed interest in a peer tutor/special friend program.

Sarah wrote up a description of the peer tutor/special friend program and put a copy in each of the teacher's mailboxes on the second day of planning week. She invited the teachers to meet with her for a coffee break in her room to discuss the program on the last day of planning week. Five teachers attended the meeting. Sarah explained the program and offered to come to the teachers' classrooms to do an awareness workshop and to recruit volunteers. The teachers helped her develop permission forms and provided her with the times when their students would be able to come to her class for peer tutoring/special friends activities. At this time Sarah would have liked to request that her students attend some of the activities in the regular classes, but sensed that this might be moving too quickly for some of the teachers.

School began and Sarah was able to do workshops in the five classrooms and to begin her peer tutoring/special friends programs. She made a short presentation in the faculty meeting, asking if some of the classrooms would volunteer to be a "buddy classroom" to her students—to find ways to include one of her students in special activities and field trips, and to find times in the day (reading, project time, sharing) when her student could be integrated. Sarah was pleased to have enough teachers volunteer that each of her students would have a "buddy classroom."

The PTO came through with a committee that wanted to develop the awareness training program. They consulted Sarah about their plans and she guided their selection of films and literature. She also gave them a short lesson in using language that is sensitive to persons with disabilities.

By the middle of the school year the peer tutor/special friends program was going well and there had been several awareness training activities. Sarah had worked hard to make sure that the classroom teachers' efforts were appreciated, writing articles for the school newsletter and sending thank-you notes to helpful parents and faculty. But Sarah was concerned that her students were still not perceived as full members of the school community and were seen as a special project.

She asked three of the teachers with whom she had worked closely to meet with her to talk about these concerns. They recognized that the students with severe disabilities were still seen as outsiders and discussed with Sarah some remedies to the problem. They met again and developed a plan that they intended to present to the principal for discussion and implementation. Included in the plan was the assignment of every student with severe disabilities to a regular classroom at the beginning of the next school year, the movement of Sarah's classroom into the main building, the movement of a special area class into the portable classroom, and the formation of an inclusion committee as one of the formal school committees for the next school year.

Case Study Two: Ray

Ray is a first-year special educator in a school that is implementing a full inclusion program. Ray received some training in integration in his university coursework and interned in a classroom for students with moderate and severe disabilities on a regular school campus. He is very skilled in working with students with severe disabilities and came highly recommended, but he had no direct experience in full inclusion.

Ray was assigned responsibility for coordinating the education program for six students with moderate and severe disabilities of different ages in a regular elementary school. Each student was assigned to a regular classroom teacher who teamed with Ray, the related services professionals, and the parents in the development of each student's Individual Education Program.

On the first day of preschool planning, Ray was given the school folders of the students he would be assisting. He reviewed the folders and scheduled home visits with each student's family. That afternoon all of the teachers who would be including students with disabilities and the special educators who were hired as support facilitators met to discuss the logistics of the program. At that meeting it was decided that a letter explaining the full inclusion program should be sent to all of the parents and that the usual formal awareness activities would not be conducted in school assemblies but rather in individual classrooms in more subtle ways.

During the remainder of the planning week Ray divided his time between becoming acquainted with the students he would be supporting and assisting their teachers in developing schedules and adapted lessons for inclusion. All but one of the teachers had been assigned a paraprofessional to assist in the increased demands of including students with disabilities. The teacher who did not receive paraprofessional support is fairly experienced in mainstreaming students with disabilities and would be including a student who is independent in his mobility and self-care skills.

On the first day of school, Ray positioned himself at the bus arrival area to make sure all of his students found their way to their homerooms. By prior arrangement, the fifth-grade students were available to help all new students find their way around school. Ray hooked each of his students up with a fifth grader and requested that he or she be assisted to the proper homeroom. When the first bell rang, Ray moved to classroom 6. He had promised to show the teacher how to position a student in an adapted chair. After he demonstrated the transfer and positioning, he stayed in the classroom and assisted the student in the social studies lesson that was being taught. In second period, he went to classroom 18 to pick up Manny, a student who was learning to dress independently. Because it took Manny a longer time to change into his PE clothes, Ray took him to the gym locker room about 15 minutes before the rest of the class came down. By the time the other boys arrived, Manny was ready to put on his T-shirt, which he did independently. The rest of Ray's morning was spent in the classrooms of the other three students, conducting assessments of their performance in the regular class, to be used in working with the individual student planning teams in designing instructional programs. The speech therapist asked Ray to come with her to the cafeteria so that she could teach him some of the techniques she uses to promote expressive communication and socialization with two of the students.

In the afternoon, Ray spent time in three classrooms, observing lessons and writing down ideas for adaptations. When the students went home for the day, he wrote a note to each of the grade-level teachers, suggesting activity adaptations and offering assistance. He developed a schedule of his activities for the rest of the week and provided it to all of the teachers he works with. He also made some notes about things he wanted to work on in the next few weeks: developing peer support networks for each student, working with the teacher in developing a data collection system to monitor instructional goals, and collaborating with the speech therapist on developing expressive communication systems that can be used at home and at school for two of the students.

Conclusion

The nature of instruction for students with severe disabilities has changed dramatically in the last 25 years. The teacher of students with severe disabilities must be aware of much more than just what he or she wants to plan for the special education classroom. Instruction must be designed to take place in a variety of relevant environments for each individual student—in activities that are meaningful for the student and that have a direct relationship to the student's present and future lifestyle. The curriculum has shifted from a developmental, isolated model to a functional, inclusive one. Teacher roles have also shifted. The special educator working with students with severe disabilities today must be able to plan, develop, and implement instruction in many different settings while working with a variety of people.

The instruction of students with severe disabilities in regular schools and regular class environments is an achievable and beneficial arrangement. Probably the greatest inhibitor to successful inclusion is the prevailing attitude of adults that students with disabilities do not belong and need specialized settings for instruction. Attitudinal barriers can be overcome. The special educator's best defense in response to resistive attitudes is to show that students with disabilities can belong and to find creative ways to develop inclusive school communities.

Questions for Reflection

1. What evidence do you see in the media that the acceptance of persons with disabilities is gaining widespread attention?
2. How do teacher education programs inhibit or promote the ability of teachers to provide inclusive education programs?
3. Do you feel that inclusive education programs are more appropriate for students of a specific age range? What ages? Why?
4. What personal characteristics might enhance a special educator's success as a support facilitator?
5. Do you feel that there are some skills that cannot be taught in a regular classroom? What are they? Could they be taught with nondisabled peers?
6. What do you think are the most significant challenges in implementing an inclusive program for special educators? General educators? School administrators?

References

Baumgart, D., Brown, L., Pumpian, I., Nisbet, J., Ford, A., Sweet, M., Messina, R., & Schroeder, J. (1982). Principle of partial participation and individualized adaptions in education programs for severely handicapped students. *Journal of the Association for Persons with Severe Handicaps, 7*(2), 17–27.

Biklen, D., Corrigan, C., & Quick, D. (1989). Beyond obligation: Students' relations with each other in integrated classes. In D. Lipsky & A. Gartner (Eds.), *Beyond separate education: Quality education for all* (pp. 207–221). Baltimore: Paul H. Brookes.

Bricker, D. (1978). A rationale for the integration of handicapped and nonhandicapped preschool children. In M. Guralnick (Ed.), *Early intervention and the integration of handicapped and nonhandicapped children* (pp. 3–26). Baltimore: University Park Press.

Brinker, R. P., & Thorpe, M. E. (1984). Integration of severely handicapped students and the proportion of IEP objectives achieved. *Exceptional Children, 51,* 168–175.

Brown, L., Long, E., Udvari-Solner, A., Davis, L., VanDeventer, P., Ahlgren, C., Johnson, F., Gruenewald, L., & Jorgensen, J. (1989a). The home school: Why students with severe intellectual disabilities must attend the schools of their brothers, sisters, friends, and neighbors. *Journal of the Association for Persons with Severe Handicaps, 14,* 1–7.

Brown, L., Long, E., Udvari-Solner, A., Schwarz, P., VanDeventer, P., Ahlgren, C., Johnson, F., Gruenewald, L., & Jorgensen, J. (1989b). Should students with severe intellectual disabilities be based in regular or in special education classrooms in home schools? *Journal of the Association for Persons with Severe Handicaps, 14,* 8–12.

Brown, L., Nisbet, J., Ford, A., Sweet, M., Shiraga, B., York, J., & Loomis, R. (1983). The critical need for nonschool instruction in educational programs for severely handicapped students. *Journal of the Association for the Severely Handicapped, 8,* 71–77.

Cole, D. A., Meyer, L. M., Vandercook, T., & McQuarter, R. J. (1986). Interactions between peers with and without severe handicaps: The dynamics of teacher intervention. *American Journal of Mental Deficiency, 92,* 160–169.

Davern, L., & Ford, A. (1989). Scheduling. In A. Ford, R. Schnorr, L. Meyer, L. Davern, J. Black, & P. Dempsey (Eds.), *The Syracuse community-referenced curriculum guide for students with moderate and severe disabilities* (pp. 247–255). Baltimore: Paul H. Brookes.

Donder, D., & Nietupski, J. (1981). Nonhandicapped adolescents teaching playground skills to their mentally retarded peers: Toward a less restrictive middle school environment. *Education and Training of the Mentally Retarded, 16,* 270–276.

Dunlap, G., & Koegel, R. L. (1980). Motivating autistic children through stimulus variation. *Journal of Applied Behavior Analysis, 13,* 619–627.

Dunn, W. (1991). Integrated related services. In L. H. Meyer, C. A. Peck, & L. Brown (Eds.), *Critical issues in the lives of people with severe disabilities* (pp. 353–378). Baltimore: Paul H. Brookes.

Eichinger, J. (1990). Goal structure effects on social interaction: Nondisabled and disabled elementary students. *Exceptional Children, 56,* 408–416.

Ferguson, D. L., & Baumgart, D. (1991). Partial participation revisited. *Journal of the Association for Persons with Severe Handicaps, 16,* 218–227.

Ferguson, D. L., Meyer, G., Jeanchild, L., Juniper, L., & Zingo, J. (1992). Figuring out what to do with the grownups: How teachers make inclusion "work" for students with disabilities. *Journal of the Association for Persons with Severe Handicaps, 17,* 218–226.

Ford, A., & Davern, L. (1989). Moving forward with school integration. In R. Gaylord-Ross (Ed.), *Integration strategies for students with handicaps* (pp. 11–31). Baltimore: Paul H. Brookes.

Forest, M., & Lusthaus, E. (1989). Promoting educational equality for all students. In S. Stainback, W. Stainback, & M. Forest (Eds.), *Educating all students in the mainstream of regular education* (pp. 43–57). Baltimore: Paul H. Brookes.

Fox, T. J., & Williams, W. (1991). *Implementing best practice for all students in their local school.* Burlington, VT: Vermont Statewide Systems Support Project, Center for Developmental Disabilities, The University Affiliated Program of Vermont.

Fritz, M. F. (1990). A comparison of social interactions using a friendship awareness activity. *Education and Training in Mental Retardation, 25,* 352–359.

Gaylord-Ross, R., & Peck, C. A. (1985). Integration efforts for students with severe mental retardation. In D. Bricker & J. Filler (Eds.), *Severe mental retardation: From theory to practice* (pp. 185–207). Reston, VA: Council for Exceptional Children, Division on Mental Retardation.

Giangreco, M. F., Cloninger, C. J., & Iverson, V. S. (1993). *Choosing options and accommodations for children: A guide to planning inclusive education.* Baltimore: Paul H. Brookes.

Greer by Greer v. Rome City School District, 950 F.2d 688 (11th Cir. 1991).

Guess, D., Horner, D., Utley, B., Holvoet, J., Maxon, D., Tucker, D., & Warren, S. (1978). A functional curriculum sequencing model for teaching the severely handicapped. *AAESPH Review, 3,* 202–215.

Guess, D., & Siegel-Causey, E. (1985). Behavioral control and education of severely handicapped students: Who's doing what to whom? and why? In D. Bricker & J. Filler (Eds.), *Severe mental retardation: From theory to practice* (pp. 230–244). Reston, VA: The Council for Exceptional Children.

Guess, D., & Helmstetter, E. (1986). Skill cluster instruction and the individualized curriculum sequencing model.

In R. H. Horner, L. H. Meyer, & H. D. Fredericks (Eds.), *Educating learners with severe handicaps: Exemplary service strategies* (pp. 221–248). Baltimore: Paul H. Brookes.

Helmstetter, E., & Guess, D. (1987). Application of the individualized curriculum sequencing model to learners with severe sensory impairments. In L. Goetz, D. Guess, & K. Stremel-Campbell (Eds.), *Innovative program design for individuals with dual sensory impairments* (pp. 255–282). Baltimore: Paul H. Brookes.

Halvorsen, A., & Sailor, W. (1990). Integration of students with severe and profound disabilities: A review of the research. In R. Gaylord-Ross (Ed.), *Issues and research in special education* (Vol. 1, pp. 110–172). New York: Teachers College Press.

Hamre-Nietupski, S., Ayres, B., Nietupski, J., Savage, M., Mitchell, B., Bramman, H. (1989). Enhancing integration of students with severe disabilities through curricular infusion: A general/special education partnership. *Education and Training in Mental Retardation, 24,* 78–88.

Haring, T. G., Breen, C., Pitts-Conway, V., Lee, M. & Gaylord-Ross, R. (1987). Adolescent peer tutoring and special friend experiences. *Journal of the Association for Persons with Severe Handicaps, 12,* 280–286.

Hendrickson, J. M., Strain, P., Tremblay, A., & Shores, R. E. (1982). Functional effects of peer social initiations on the interactions of behaviorally handicapped children. *Behavior Modification, 6,* 323–353.

Holland v. Sacramento City School District, 786 F. Supp. 874 (E.D. Cal. 1992).

Holvoet, J., Mulligan, M., Schussler, N., Lacy, L., & Guess, D. (1984). *The Kansas individualized curriculum sequencing model: Sequencing learning experiences for severely handicapped children and youth.* Portland, OR: A.S.I.E.P. Education Co.

Hunt, P., Goetz, L., & Anderson, J. (1986). The quality of IEP objectives associated with placement on integrated versus segregated school sites. *Journal of the Association for Persons with Severe Handicaps, 11,* 125–130.

Johnson, R., & Johnson, D. (1989). Cooperative learning and mainstreaming. In R. Gaylord-Ross (Ed.), *Integration strategies for students with handicaps* (pp. 233–248). Baltimore: Paul H. Brookes.

Johnson, D. W., Johnson, R. T., & Maruyama, G. (1983). Interdependence and interpersonal attraction among heterogenous and homogenous individuals: A theoretical formulation and a meta-analysis of the research. *Review of Educational Research, 53,* 5–54.

Knapczyx, D. R. (1989). Peer-mediated training of cooperative play between special and regular class students in integrated play settings. *Education and Training in Mental Retardation, 24,* 255–264.

Knoblock, P., & Harootunian, B. (1989). A classroom where differences are valued. In S. Stainback, W. Stainback, & M. Forest (Eds.), *Educating all students in the mainstream of regular education* (pp. 199–209). Baltimore: Paul H. Brookes.

Kohl, F. L., Moses, L. G., & Stettner-Eaton, B. A. (1983). The results of teaching fifth and sixth graders to be instructional trainers with students who are severely handicapped. *Journal of the Association for Persons with Severe Handicaps, 8,* 32–40.

Kohl, F. L., & Stettner-Eaton, B. A. (1985). Fourth graders as trainers of cafeteria skills to severely handicapped students. *Education and Training of the Mentally Retarded, 20,* 60–68.

Kohler, F. W., & Fowler, S. A. (1985). Training prosocial behaviors to young children: An analysis of reciprocity with untrained peers. *Journal of Applied Behavior Analysis, 22,* 77–83.

Lancioni, G. E. (1982). Normal children as tutors to teach social responses to withdrawn mentally retarded school mates: Training, maintenance, and generalization. *Journal of Applied Behavior Analysis, 15,* 17–40.

Madden, N. A., & Slavin, R. E. (1983). Mainstreaming students with mild handicaps: Academic and social outcomes. *Review of Educational Research, 53,* 519–569.

McDonnell, A. P., & Hardman, M. L. (1989). The desegregation of America's special schools: Strategies for change. *Journal of the Association for Persons with Severe Handicaps, 14,* 68–74.

Meyer, L. H. (1991). Guest editorial—Why meaningful outcomes? *Journal of Special Education, 25,* 287–290.

Meyer, L., & Putnam, J. (1987). Social integration. In V. B. VanHasselt, P. Strain, & M. Hersen (Eds.), *Handbook of developmental and physical disabilities* (pp. 107–133). New York: Pergamon.

Mulligan, M., Guess, D., Holvoet, J., & Brown, F. (1980). The individualized curriculum sequencing model (I): Implications from research on massed, distributed, or spaced trial learning. *Journal of the Association for the Severely Handicapped, 5,* 325–336.

Mulligan, M., Lacy, L., & Guess, D. (1982). The effects of massed, distributed, and spaced trial sequencing on severely handicapped students' performance. *Journal of the Association for the Severely Handicapped, 7,* 48–61.

Nirje, B. (1969). The normalization principle and its human management implications. In R. Kugel & W. Wolfensberger (Eds.), *Changing patterns in residential services for the mentally retarded* (pp. 179–195). Washington, DC: President's Committee on Mental Retardation.

Oberti, 789 F. Supp. at 1327.

Odom, S. L., & Strain, P. S. (1986). A comparison of peer-initiation and teacher-antecedent interventions for promoting reciprocal social interaction of autistic preschoolers. *Journal of Applied Behavior Analysis, 19,* 59–71.

Peck, C. A., Donaldson, J., & Pezzoli, M. (1990). Some benefits nonhandicapped adolescents perceive for themselves from their social relationships with peers who have severe handicaps. *Journal of the Association for Persons with Severe Handicaps, 15,* 241–249.

Public Law 94-142, *Education for All Handicapped Children Act of 1975,* 20 U.S.C. 1412-1415 (5)(B), 1975.

Public Law 101-46, *Individuals with Disabilities Education Act of 1989.*

Putnam, J. W., Rynders, J. E., Johnson, R. T., & Johnson, D. W. (1989). Collaborative skill instruction for promoting positive interactions between mentally handicapped and nonhandicapped children. *Exceptional Children, 55,* 550–557.

Rainforth, B., York, J., & Macdonald, C. (1992). *Collaborative teams for students with severe disabilities.* Baltimore: Paul H. Brookes.

Sailor, W., Anderson, J. L., Halvorsen, A. T., Doering, K., Filler, J., & Goetz, L. (1989). *The comprehensive local school.* Baltimore: Paul H. Brookes.

Salisbury, C. L. (1991). Mainstreaming during the early childhood years. *Exceptional Children, 58,* 146–154.

Sasso, G. M., Hughes, G. G., Swanson, H. L., & Novak, C. G. (1987). A comparison of peer initiation interventions in promoting multiple peer initiators. *Education and Training in Mental Retardation, 22,* 150–155.

Sasso, G. M., & Rude, H. A. (1987). Unprogrammed effects of training "high status" peers to interact with severely handicapped children. *Journal of Applied Behavior Analysis, 20,* 35–44.

Shevin, M., & Klein, N. K. (1984). The importance of choice-making for students with severe disabilities. *Journal of the Association for Persons with Severe Handicaps, 9,* 159–166.

Slavin, R. E. (1984). Review of cooperative learning research. *Review of Educational Research, 47,* 633–650.

Snell, M. E. (1988). Curriculum and methodology for individuals with severe disabilities. *Education and Training in Mental Retardation, 23,* 302–314.

Snell, M. E., & Eichner, S. J. (1989). Integration for students with profound disabilities. In F. Brown & D. H. Lehr (Eds.), *Persons with profound disabilities: Issues and practices* (pp. 109–138). Baltimore: Paul H. Brookes.

Stainback, S., & Stainback, W. (1990). Inclusive schooling. In W. Stainback & S. Stainback (Eds.), *Support networks for inclusive schooling* (pp. 3–23). Baltimore: Paul H. Brookes.

Stainback, W., & Stainback, S. (1987). Facilitating friendships. *Education and Training in Mental Retardation, 22,* 18–25.

Stainback, W., & Stainback, S. (1989). Practical organizational strategies. In S. Stainback, W. Stainback, & M. Forest (Eds.), *Educating all students in the mainstream of regular education* (pp. 71–87). Baltimore: Paul H. Brookes.

Sternat, J., Messina, R., Nietupski, J., Lyon, S., & Brown, L. (1977). Occupational and physical therapy services for severely handicapped students: Toward a naturalized public school service delivery model. In E. Sontag (Ed.), *Educational programming for the severely and profoundly handicapped* (pp. 263–278). Reston, VA: Council for Exceptional Children.

Stokes, T. F., & Baer, D. M. (1977). An implicit technology of generalization. *Journal of Applied Behavior Analysis, 10,* 349–367.

Strain, P. S., & Kerr, M. M. (1981). *Mainstreaming of children in schools: Research and programming issues.* New York: Academic Press.

Strully, J., & Strully, C. (1985). Friendship and our children. *Journal of The Association for Persons with Severe Handicaps, 10,* 224–227.

Strully, J. L., & Strully, C. F. (1989). Friendships as an educational goal. In S. Stainback, W. Stainback, & M. Forest (Eds.), *Educating all students in the mainstream of regular education* (pp. 59–68). Baltimore: Paul H. Brookes.

Thousand, J. S., Fox, T. J., Reid, R., Godek, J., Williams, W., & Fox, W. L. (1986). *The homecoming model: Educating students who present intensive educational challenges within regular education environments.* Burlington, VT: University of Vermont, Center for Developmental Disabilities.

Thousand, J. S., & Villa, R. A. (1990). Sharing expertise and responsibilities through teaching teams. In W. Stainback & S. Stainback (Eds.), *Support networks for inclusive schooling* (pp. 95–122). Baltimore: Paul H. Brookes.

Twelfth Annual Report to Congress on the Implementation of the Education of the Handicapped Act (1990). Washington, DC: U.S. Office of Special Education and Rehabilitation Services.

Vandercook, T., & York, J. (1990). A team approach to program development and support. In W. Stainback & S. Stainback (Eds.), *Support networks for inclusive schooling* (pp. 95–122). Baltimore: Paul H. Brookes.

Voeltz, L. M. (1980). Children's attitudes toward nonhandicapped peers. *American Journal of Mental Deficiency, 84,* 455–564.

Voeltz, L. M. (1982). Effects of structured interactions with severely handicapped peers on children's attitudes. *American Journal of Mental Deficiency, 86,* 380–390.

Voeltz, L. M. (1984). Program and curriculum innovations to prepare children for integration. In N. Certo, N. Haring, & R. York (Eds.), *Public school integration of severely handicapped students: Rational issues and progressive alternatives* (pp. 155–183). Baltimore: Paul H. Brookes.

Voeltz, L. M., Kishi, G., & Brennan, J. (1981). *The social interaction observation system (SIOS).* Honolulu: University of Hawaii.

Williams, W., Villa, R., Thousand, J., & Fox, W. L. (1989). Is regular class placement really the issue? A response to Brown, Long Udvari-Solner, Schwarz, VanDeventer, Ahlgren, Johnson, Gruenewald, & Jorgensen. *Journal of the Association for Persons with Severe Handicaps, 14,* 333–334.

York, J., Vandercook, T., Caughey, E., & Heise-Neff, C. (1989). Regular class integration: Beyond socialization. In J. York, T. Vandercook, C. MacDonald, & S. Wolff (Eds.), *Strategies for full inclusion* (pp. 117–120). Minneapolis, MN: University of Minnesota, Institute on Community Integration.

York, J., Vandercook, T., MacDonald, C., & Wolff, S. (1989). *Strategies for full inclusion.* Minneapolis: University of Minnesota, Institute on Community Integration.

PART IV

Specific Instructional and Management Procedures

CHAPTER 10 Teaching Communication Skills

CHAPTER 11 Providing Behavioral Supports to Improve Challenging Behaviors

CHAPTER 12 Managing Sensory and Motor Disabilities

CHAPTER 13 Providing Support for Health and Medical Needs

CHAPTER 14 Meeting the Needs of Young Children

CHAPTER 15 Teaching Self-Care and Daily Living Skills

CHAPTER 16 Teaching Leisure and Recreational Skills

CHAPTER 17 Teaching Appropriate Academic Skills

CHAPTER 10

Teaching Communication Skills

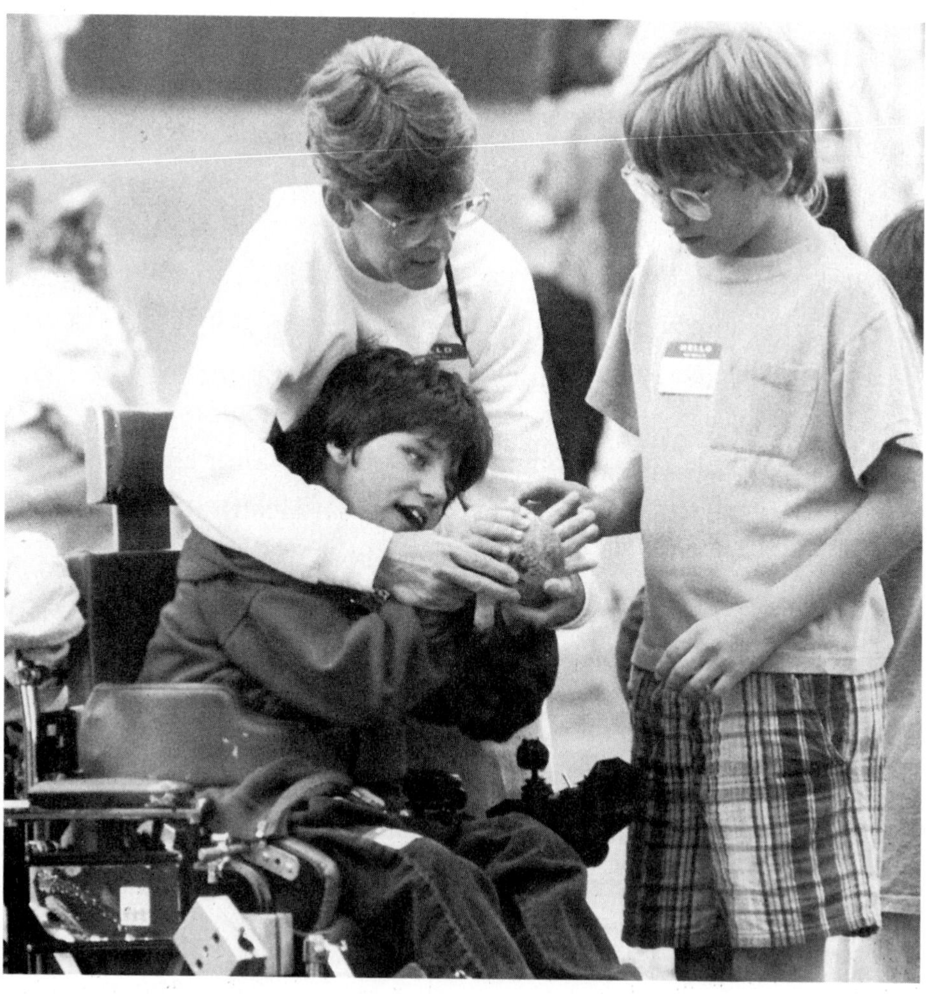

Chapter Overview

In this chapter, communication skill development is discussed and methods for assessing a student's communication abilities are presented. You are provided with information on how to match a communication system to a student's abilities and techniques for the instruction of communication skills.

The skill of communication is one of the most important and most difficult to teach students with severe disabilities. The difficulty stems in part from practitioners' lack of knowledge about designing communication interventions and the myriad problems associated with the student's disability. Successful communication is a result of the integration and performance of cognitive, social, and motor skills. Students with severe disabilities are likely to display difficulties in some or all of these areas.

The knowledge and technology related to communication skill instruction has grown significantly in the last decade. Important milestones that have been achieved include a shift in assessment practices from identifying appropriate candidates for communication instruction to a belief that communication instruction is appropriate for all students, a shift from a focus on the development of isolated speech and language skills to the development of functional communication, and an understanding of the importance of multimodal communication (Mirenda & Iacono, 1990).

Because learners with severe disabilities have severe cognitive impairments and usually additional physical handicaps, the instruction of communication skills is a very complicated and dynamic process. The speech therapist, the teacher, and other collaborative team members will spend a significant amount of time analyzing a student's communicative behavior and trying different types of interventions and communication systems to assist the student in achieving success. The areas of knowledge that are essential to appropriate instruction in communication are communication skill development and assessment, augmentative communication systems, instructional strategies, and generalization procedures.

Communication Skill Development

In the past, developmental milestones were used as a guide in examining the development of communication skills by individuals with severe disabilities. Emphasis was placed on the development of expressive and receptive communication skills with a focus on the acquisition of language. Students with disabilities were assessed using communication inventories or language assessments based on normal developmental milestones and then taught the skills indicated as deficits by the assessment. This resulted in the instruction of language skills that were often meaningless for the student with disabilities. For example, a student might have been taught to imitate speech sounds without being taught to use those sounds as a request or a comment. In addition, the focus on teaching language skills excluded instruction for the learner who was at a prelinguistic or nonsymbolic level of language development.

Early Communication Development

In the late 1970s researchers in communication development began to focus on the normal development of prelinguistic skills (i.e., communication skills that develop before speech) with infants and toddlers (Alvares, Falor, & Smiley, 1991). More recently, researchers interested in children with disabilities have applied the research on prelinguistic communication development of infants and toddlers to students with severe disabilities (Siegel-Causey & Guess, 1989; Wetherby & Prizant, 1989). An important result of the study of prelinguistic communication has been a focus on the pragmatics of communication. *Pragmatics* can be defined as the use of communication indices within the social context. What has been learned from the research on the development of prelinguistic communication skills is that these skills develop within the context of a social relationship, predictably the relationship between the primary caregiver and the child. The application of a pragmatic orientation requires the evaluation of communication skills by examining the social context in which the exchange occurs, and it often results in targeting both the learner and the communication partner for intervention (Alvares et al., 1991).

The interest in pragmatics has been very important to understanding the communication skill development of learners with severe disabilities. In the past, when language researchers and practitioners were concerned with the structure of language rather than the social aspects of communication, students with severe disabilities who were not talking were often not included in intervention. In addition, there was very little guidance in the literature for ways to assist the skill development of students who were at a nonsymbolic or prelinguistic stage of development.

Intentionality

Researchers have been particularly interested in the development of intentionality in the prelinguistic communication exchanges of children and their caregivers. *Intentionality* may be defined as "the deliberate pursuit of a goal" (Wetherby & Prizant, 1989, p. 77). A child who exhibits intentionality is one who knows that if a message is sent to the listener, the listener will receive and act on it. A common approach to identifying intentionality is to use behavioral criteria (Bates, 1979; Harding & Golinkoff, 1979). Behavioral evidence that may signal intentionality includes alternating eye gaze between the goal and the listener, persistent signaling or changing the signal until the goal is met, awaiting a response from the listener, and indicating satisfaction when the goal is met (Wetherby & Prizant, 1989).

Bates (1979) proposed a three-stage model for describing the development of communication and intentionality. The first stage of the model, the perlocutionary stage occurs from birth until there is evidence of intentionality in the child's communicative utterances or gestures. In this stage the child has an effect on the listener without intending to. An example of communication at the perlocutionary stage is the interpretation by the caregiver that an infant's crying means that the infant wants to be held. The second stage of the model, the illocutionary stage, occurs when the child uses gestures and sounds to intentionally affect the listener. An example of a communication expression at the illocutionary stage is a toddler's pointing to a carton of juice to indicate to his caregiver that he wants a drink or repeating a vocalization (i.e., not words) until his caregiver provides his favorite toy. The third stage of the model, the locutionary stage, occurs when language emerges and the child communicates with words.

The Bates (1979) framework offers useful distinctions between communicative stages, but does not fully explain the development of intentionality. A child with disabilities may evidence intentionality when reaching for a toy that is on a shelf to signal a request to a caregiver but may also cry or shift his eye gaze during a play activity without intentionality. It would be difficult to determine if this child is in the perlocutionary or illocutionary stage. Wetherby and Prizant (1989) discuss the emergence of intentionality as occurring along a developmental continuum rather than only being present or absent. In their model, they describe intentionality as developing from children having no awareness of the goal to an ability to send a message and then repair or change the form of the signal if their needs are not met. For example, when a child in the early perlocutionary stage cries, a caregiver might respond by interpreting the cry to mean that the child wants to be picked up. A child in the illocutionary stage who has an awareness that the listener will respond to a message and has the capacity to plan a message, may pull the caregiver to the refrigerator to request a bottle, and, if the goal is not met, may begin patting the refrigerator or vocalizing. Thus, the child has persisted in signaling and has changed the signal form for achieving the desired goal.

Communicative Means and Functions

The development of the child's ability to signal by examining intentionality is one important aspect of communication development to be considered. In addition, the interventionist should consider the child's ability to use different means of communication (forms of the communication signal, such as crying, vocalizing, gesturing, or talking) to express himself or herself. Wetherby and Prizant (1989) explain that sophistication in the means to express intentionality develops in a horizontal direction during the prelinguistic stage. In this stage, typically developing children progress from nonverbal to verbal means of communication within the three major categories of communication functions that are described in Figure 10–1.

In learners with severe disabilities, means used for communicative functions can range from nonverbal, idiosyncratic behavior (eye-poking, slapping) to a variety of conventional means (pointing, words) that are more easily understood by the communication partner. These communicative means are used to express the communicative functions of behavioral regulation (to request objects or actions, to protest), social interaction (to attract and maintain someone's attention for affiliative purposes), and joint attention (to direct someone's attention to an object or entity) (Wetherby & Prizant, 1989).

Teachers can use information on the development of intentional communication and the description of communication functions to understand the communication behavior of students with severe disabilities who are in the prelinguistic or nonsymbolic stage of communication development. This framework will assist the teacher in analyzing the range of means (the form of communication) and functions (the reason for communicating) and the level of intentionality the student exhibits. For example, when Andy, a 10-year-old student with severe disabilities, wants a drink he brings his cup to his mother and looks at her and at the refrigerator. If she does not get a

I. ***BEHAVIORAL REGULATION***:
acts used to regulate the behavior of another person for purposes of obtaining and restricting an environmental goal

- to request an object or action
- to protest an object or action

II. ***SOCIAL INTERACTION***:
acts used to attract or maintain another's attention to oneself for affiliative purposes

- to request a social routine
- to greet or call another person
- to show off
- to request another's permission
- to acknowledge another's action or utterance

III. ***JOINT ATTENTION***:
acts used to direct another's attention to an object, action, or utterance for purposes of sharing the focus on an entity or event

- to label or comment on an object or event
- to clarify a previous utterance
- to request information about an object or event

Figure 10–1
Communicative Functions Emerging in the First Two Years
From "Communicative Profiles of Handicapped Preschool Children: Implications for Early Identification" by A. M. Wetherby, D. G. Yonclass, & A. A. Bryan, 1989, *Journal of Speech and Hearing Disorders, 54*(2), pp. 148-158. Copyright by the American Speech-Language-Hearing Association. Adapted by permission.

drink immediately, he cries but does not engage in any additional behavior such as pulling her to the refrigerator or pointing to the refrigerator. Andy also pushes away objects that he does not want and shakes his head back and forth. If the object is not removed immediately, he bangs his forehead on the table or on his knee. In examining Andy's behavior from the Wetherby and Prizant (1989) framework, the teacher can conclude that Andy uses bringing his cup to his mother as a request function and uses shaking his head and banging his forehead as a protest. Both of these functions fall into the category of behavior regulation. In examining the level of intentionality, the teacher can conclude that Andy shows an ability to use alternative plans to achieve his goal by changing his signal (crying, headbanging) after an unsuccessful attempt to achieve that goal.

Assessment Issues

Before communication intervention begins, the educator must determine the student's current repertoire of communication behavior. It is essential to know what current communicative functions are exhibited by the learner, what means are used to express these functions, under what conditions different communicative means and functions are exhibited, and what level of intentionality is present in communicative attempts. In addition, the educator will want to assess the student's capabilities in motoric skills, sensory functioning, cognitive functioning, and receptive language comprehension.

Communication Skill Assessment

A traditional approach to assessment involves the administration of standardized language or communication inventories that are based on normal development and focused on expressive and receptive language skills. However, these instruments are rarely helpful in examining the communication skills of students with severe disabilities (Schuler, Peck, Willard, & Theimer, 1989), who may be at a prelinguistic level in communication development or who may not have the physical capacity to speak. The process for assessing the communication skills of students with severe disabilities involves an array of informal and nonstandardized procedures.

Several inventories have been developed for evaluating the communication behavior of students with severe disabilities, including the Communication Programming Inventory (Sternberg & McNerney, 1988), the Communication Intention Inventory (Coggins & Carpenter, 1981), and the Communication Interview (Schuler et al., 1989). In addition to these measures, Neel and Billingsley (1989), Wetherby and Prizant (1989), Siegel-Causey and Downing (1987), and Donnellan, Mirenda, Mesaros, and Fassbender (1984) offer formats for determining a student's communication abilities.

The procedures for determining the current communication abilities of a student may involve the direct assessment of skills in a traditional skill checklist format such as the *Communication Programming Inventory* (Sternberg & McNerney, 1988), the use of an interview procedure like that shown in Figure 10–2 (Schuler et al., 1989), or by collecting a communication sample (Wetherby & Prizant, 1989). The communication interview developed by Schuler et al. provides questions that can be asked of a person familiar with the student with disabilities to determine the student's communicative means and functions. The functions (reasons) of communication that are examined are requests for objects, actions, and interaction; protests; and comments. Across the top of the interview is a listing of different communicative means that range from the idiosyncratic and problematic, such as tantruming or aggression, to the conventional, such as using complex speech. The assessor probes the person familiar with the student or fills out the interview by determining what means are used for each communicative function.

Wetherby and Prizant (1984) offer guidelines for an informal procedure that may also assist in determining a student's communicative means and functions. They describe a procedure that uses "communicative temptations" to elicit communicative behavior. An example of a communicative temptation is to eat a desired food item in front of a child without offering the child some, which may elicit request behavior. Another example is to show the child a toy that requires activation, activate the toy without letting the child see how it was done, and then hand the child the toy when it has stopped. This may elicit a request for help or a comment from the child. A communication sample can be collected by videotaping the reactions of the child to a series of communicative temptations. The videotape can be

CUE QUESTIONS	Crying	Aggression	Tantrums, Self-Injury	Passive Gaze	Proximity	Pulling Other's Hands	Touching Moving Other's Face	Grabs, Reaches	Enactment	Removes self, Walks away	Vocalization, Noise	Active Gaze	Gives Object	Gestures, Pointing	Facial Expression	Shakes "no"/Nods "yes"	Intonation	Inappropriate Echolalia	Appropriate Echolalia	One-Word Speech	One-Word Signs	Complex Speech	Complex Signs
1. Requests for affection/interaction: WHAT IF S WANTS																							
adult to sit near?																							
peer to sit near?																							
non-hand. peer to sit near?																							
adult to look at him?																							
adult to tickle him?																							
to cuddle/embrace?																							
to sit on adult's lap?																							
other:																							
2. Requests for adult action: WHAT IF S WANTS																							
help with dressing?																							
to be read a book?																							
to play ball/a game?																							
to go outside/to store?																							
other:																							
3. Requests for Object, Food, or Things: WHAT IF S WANTS																							
an object out of reach?																							
a door/container opened?																							
a favorite food?																							
music/radio/tv?																							
keys/toy/book?																							
other:																							
4. Protest: WHAT IF																							
common routine is dropped?																							
favorite toy/food taken away?																							
taken for ride w/out desire?																							
adult terminates interaction?																							
required to do something doesn't want to?																							
other:																							
5. Declaration/Comment: WHAT IF S WANTS																							
to show you something?																							
you to look at something?																							
other																							

Figure 10–2
Communication Interview

From "Assessment of Communicative Means and Functions Through Interview: Assessing the Communicative Capabilities of Individuals with Limited Language," by A. L. Schuler, C. A. Peck, C. Willard, & K. Theimer, 1989, *Seminars in Speech and Language, 10,* pp. 51–62. Reprinted with permission from Thieme Medical Publishers Inc.

analyzed later to determine the communicative means, functions, and levels of intentionality that the child displays. Other temptations that may be used are presented in Figure 10–3.

It is important for the teacher to realize that students with severe disabilities may express communicative functions using means that are viewed as aberrant or problematic behavior. A student who has not developed a conventional signal for protest may engage in aggression or self-injury to communicate a signal for "no" or "stop." Methods for discerning the communicative functions of problem behavior and the procedures for intervention are discussed at length in chapter 11. In fact, the most current work in intervening with problem behavior suggests that an understanding of pragmatics is important in behavior intervention (Carr, McConnachie, Levin, & Kemp, 1993; Donnellan et al., 1984).

Assessing the communication abilities of the student is essential to the development of intervention strategies. In addition to understanding the learner's capacities, the interventionist should also seek to understand what communication demands and supports are provided by the student's environments.

Ecological Assessment

Ecological inventories (as described in chapter 5) can be used to collect information about the unique communicative demands and opportunities of the environments the student will encounter. This information will assist the interventionist in understanding the communicative needs of the student, what modes of communication may be needed (e.g., sign language vs. communication book), and how the learner currently functions in those situations. In addition to information on the activities and skills needed in various subenvironments, information should also be collected on the communicative demands and opportunities of various environments and the communicative functions, vocabulary, and modes that will be needed by the learner to communicate effectively in those environments (Sigafoos & York, 1991). For example, an ecological inventory of

1. Eat a desired food in front of the child without offering any to the child.
2. Activate a wind-up toy, let it deactivate, and hand it to the child.
3. Give the child a book and encourage him or her to look at the book and turn the pages, then repeat this with a second book.
4. Open a jar of bubbles, blow bubbles, then close the jar tightly and give the closed jar to the child.
5. Initiate a familiar and unfamiliar social game with the child until the child expresses pleasure, then stop the game and wait.
6. Hold a food item or toy that the child dislikes out near the child to offer it.
7. Place a desired food item in a clear container that the child cannot open while the child is watching, then put the container in front of the child and wait.

Figure 10–3
Communicative Temptations

From "The Expression of Communicative Intent: Assessment Guidelines" by A. M. Wetherby & B. M. Prizant, 1989, *Seminars in Speech and Language, 10,* pp. 77–90. Reprinted with permission from Thieme Medical Publishers Inc.

a fast-food restaurant might indicate that the learner must be able to respond to "May I help you?" by placing an order. If the learner uses sign language for most of his communication expression, he may need to be taught an alternate mode (such as picture cards) to effectively meet the communication demand in this setting.

Selecting a Communication Mode

When information has been collected on the student's communicative repertoire and opportunities for communication interaction, the collaborative team should determine whether the student's current communication system is understandable to others, socially acceptable, and not a part of an existing behavior repertoire that is inappropriate (Reichle, 1991). If the behavior is understood by others and socially appropriate, the collaborative team may choose to focus on the expansion of means or vocabulary and the level of intentionality the learner displays in his or her present mode of communication. If the behavior is not understandable or socially acceptable, the focus of the intervention may be to replace the current mode of communication with a more conventional and acceptable form (Reichle, 1991).

For many students with severe disabilities, speech is not the most effective mode of communication (Romski & Sevcik, 1988). Determining that a student should use an augmentative or alternative communication system or that the focus on the intervention should be increasing language skills is a decision that must be made by the collaborative team, including the family. The speech therapist, physical therapist, audiologist, and occupational therapist may be able to contribute essential information on the student's language, sensory, and motoric abilities that will guide decision making. A poor prognosis for the effectiveness of natural speech is evident if the student has physical difficulty in the production of speech sounds as evidenced by the evaluation of oral reflexes, eating patterns, vocal patterns, and neuromuscular status of the oral mechanism, if the student has not developed speech by 5 years of age, if the student is unable to imitate words verbally, and if the student has a hearing impairment (Musselwhite & St.Louis, 1988). Some students may be using limited speech to express some functions. The interventionist should consider the efficiency of speech for the student's communication repertoire. Perhaps an additional mode of communication expression is necessary to allow the student to expand the range of functions and level of intentionality that he or she can express.

The decision to teach the use of an alternative or augmentative mode of communication should not be viewed as giving up on the student's eventual use of language. Researchers have found that the use of augmentative communication does not inhibit speech production (Romski & Sevcik, 1992). The goal for the collaborative team is to develop a communication intervention plan that will allow the student with severe disabilities to express himself or herself and affect others. Unlocking the student's access to the social world, using whatever strategy necessary, is of primary importance.

Augmentative and Alternative Communication

For students who will not be using natural speech or who need an additional mode of communication to communicate effectively, the interventionist needs to select an appropriate augmentative or alternative system of communication. Augmentative systems involve the use of aids that supplement existing vocal communication skills; alternative systems are methods of communication that are used by a person without vocal ability (Mustonen, Locke, Reichle, Solbrack, & Lindgren, 1991). The many types of symbols, methods, techniques, and systems that can be used for augmentative and alternative communication can be classified as either gestural or graphic modes of communication (Mustonen et al., 1991).

The selection of an augmentative or alternative system will depend in part on the student's motor, cognitive, and sensory abilities. A student who does not appear to understand symbolic representation of objects is an unlikely candidate for a complex symbol system. A student with vision impairments will need a communication system with enhanced visual symbols, tactile cues, or auditory feedback. A student with limited fine motor skills would not be an appropriate candidate for sign language instruction. Knowledge of the student's capabilities in motor skills, visual skills, and cognitive skills will assist the collaborative team in selecting an appropriate system. A communication system should be developed with symbols placed in the student's reach or visual field. A communication system must be designed specifically for the student with knowledge of the whole individual and a commitment to continuous modification until success is met.

In addition to matching a communication system to a student's capacities, the collaborative team must be concerned with family preferences because family support of the proposed system is essential to the student's success. The team should pay close attention to any family concerns that are voiced when communication systems are proposed. If there are concerns, the team should work with the family to determine where the problem sources are and to find solutions that meet the agreement of the entire team.

Gestural Communication

Gestural communication ranges from the use of natural gestures to indicate communicative functions to formal sign language systems. There are a variety of natural gestures that children and adults use to communicate. Pointing is a natural gesture that directs attention to an object or event for the purpose of requesting or commenting. Another natural gesture frequently used is holding an object out to the communication partner for the purpose of showing. Handing a person an object, such as an empty cup or a favorite book, is a natural gesture that is used by young children to signal a request (e.g., a drink or a story). Pulling a communication partner toward an activity or an object is another natural gesture that may serve as a request or a comment. A well-recognized natural gesture that is used in adulthood is head nodding to signal a yes or no response. These natural gestures work effectively to communicate one's needs and may be potential targets for acquisition by students with severe disabilities. If a student with severe disabilities grabs objects he or she wishes to have, it may be possible to shape the grabbing into a point to indicate requests. For example, the interventionist could reinforce the student for reaching for objects by providing the object contingently on the reach. Then the interventionist could model or physically assist the student in pointing to desired objects that are out of reach and reinforce the behavior by providing the object. The same type of process could be used if a student moves his face away when shown an undesired toy or food item, shaping the head turning into a head shaking to indicate no.

For some learners, gestural communication may take the sophisticated form of sign language. Sign language and sign systems have been developed to offer nonverbal communicators a symbol set for communication.

American Sign Language (Ameslan), a sign language system used by persons who are deaf, involves signals for letters (fingerspelling) and words or phrases. Ameslan has its own semantic and syntactic rules, many of which differ from English. Signing Exact English (Gustason, Pfetzing, & Zawolkow, 1972) draws its basic signs from Ameslan but uses English word order and includes signs to represent syntax (arrangement of words to convey meaning) and morphology (the structure of words). Amer-Ind is a gestural set that is derived from the gestures used by American Indians (Skelly, 1979). Amer-Ind signs are more understandable to others with guessability (ability for the naive to interpret the sign) ranging from 50% (Vanderheiden & Lloyd, 1986) to 80% (Skelly, 1979).

The ease with which signs are learned is dependent on several features of the sign language or system. The easiest signs to learn are those that take two hands to produce with physical contact between the hands, are symmetrical, are produced within the communicator's visual field, and resemble their referents (Dennis, Reichle, Williams, & Vogelsberg, 1982; Doherty, 1985). Although sign language has the advantage of not needing any equipment to communicate and offering an unlimited vocabulary potential, it also has several disadvantages in its potential use by learners with severe disabilities. It depends on understanding by the listener. The majority of people in the community are not trained in manual sign language and would have difficulty interpreting communication by sign language. In addition, the production of sign language requires a level of manual dexterity that many individuals with severe disabilities do not have. Signs are also dynamic displays of language rather than graphic symbols, which are static. Because they are dynamic, the learner with severe cognitive impairments may be unable to maintain a mental representation of the communication utterance when attempting to form the sign symbol. Although sign language is frequently taught as an augmentative system, few studies have shown that learners with severe disabilities acquire generalized sign language systems that involve more than one- or two-word utterances or generalization (Iacono & Parsons, 1986).

Aided Systems

The use of an aided system of communication will be an effective communication alternative for many students with severe disabilities. Aided systems include a range of alternatives from the use of objects and picture to communicate to complex electronic communication devices. When selecting an aided communication system, the interventionist must consider if the student is capable of using a representational communication system, the type of symbols that will be used, the format in which the symbols will be displayed, and the method the learner will use to select the symbol for communication expression.

Symbol Selection Symbols used in aided communication systems vary in symbol guessability, ease of acquisition, and how well the symbol use is generalized and maintained in nontraining settings. Real objects or tangible symbols have been successfully used by individuals with severe disabilities and vision impairments for communication (Rowland & Schweigert, 1989; Stillman & Battle, 1984). Tangible symbols are permanent, manipulable, tactually discriminable, require simple motor responses for use, and have an obvious relationship to the object they represent (Rowland & Schweigert, 1989). An example of the use of a tangible symbol may be the presentation of a block to indicate a desire to play with blocks or the presentation of a cup to indicate a desire for a drink. Because the use of real objects limits the expandability and portability of a communication system, miniature objects or parts of objects can be used with a student who is capable of representational thought. For example, a student may use a piece of a milk carton to indicate a request for milk or a tiny spoon to indicate a request for cereal. Students can also be taught to associate unrelated symbols to activities or objects to use for communication by attaching the tangible symbol. For example, the teacher could glue a sandpaper shape to a game box and provide the student with a similar sandpaper shape to use as a request for the game.

Representations of objects, activities, places, and expressions by photographs, product logos, and line drawings have also been used for expressive communication. There are several types of line-drawn symbol systems that have been developed for augmentative and alternative communicators. Picsyms (Carlson, 1984) are black line-drawn symbols that represent 1,800 words. Rebus symbols, line drawings that represent words or parts of words, have been used to teach reading skills to young children and children with mental disabilities (Woodcock, 1968; Woodcock, Clark, & Davies, 1969). Rebus symbols are easier to learn, remember, and decode than spelled words (Clark, Davies, & Woodcock, 1974).

Blissymbols are another type of pictographic system that was developed for use as an international communication system (Silverman, 1980). There are approximately 100 symbols, which represent general concepts or ideas. When symbols are combined with other elements, the meaning of the symbol is changed. For example, when the symbols for person, mouth, and musical note are combined, the representation would mean the concept "singer" (Silverman, 1980). Symbols used in the Bliss system are pictographic (the referent is shown in an outline drawing), ideographic (idea is represented with shapes associated with the referent), and arbitrary (Mustonen et al., 1991). Because Blissymbols are not easily intelligible to untrained communication partners, they are displayed with the written language equivalent.

The learnability of graphic symbol sets has been investigated by researchers (Hurlbut, Iwata, & Green, 1982; Mirenda & Locke, 1989; Sevcik & Romski, 1986). Empirical evidence indicates that a hierarchy of difficulty from easiest to most difficult to learn appears to be: real objects, color photographs, black-and-white photographs, miniature objects, black-and-white line drawings, rebuses, and Blissymbols.

Symbol Display and Organization There are several ways for communication symbols to be displayed, organized, and carried by the communicator (see Figure 10–4). Communication wallets can be designed by placing the symbols on cards that are inserted into the vinyl credit card sleeves of a wallet (Mustonen et al., 1991). Symbols on laminated cards can be put on a ring that can be attached to the learner's belt loop or carried.

Communication books allow for a greater number of symbols to be stored, but are less portable than wallets. A communication book can easily be made from a photo album or three-ring binder. Symbols are displayed and arranged in a format that facilitates quick access by the learner. For example, a communication book may be arranged by symbols the learner uses at home, school, and work or by symbols representing people, objects, foods, and activities. A more portable version of a communication book can be made by reducing the size of the book so that it can be carried by the learner in a pack attached to the waist.

Communication boards, flat surfaces on which the symbols are placed, are frequently used by individuals who spend most of their

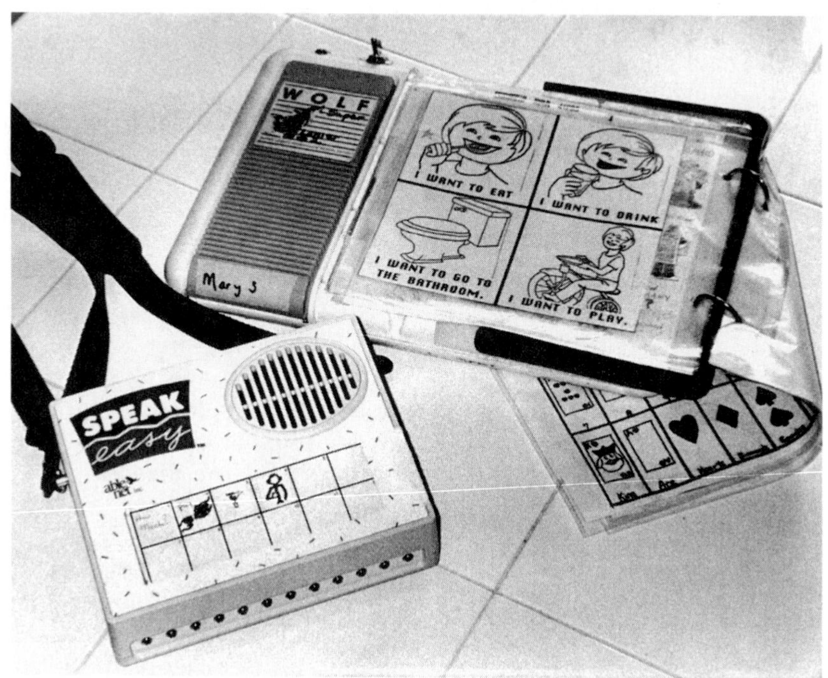

Figure 10–4
Organizing and Displaying Symbols
SpeakEasy™ voice output communication aid is available from AbleNet, Inc. Wolf available from Wayne County, Michigan Resa Adam Lab.

time in a wheelchair. The communication board can be placed directly on the lap tray. Communication boards that are specific to an area or activity may also be used. For example, a communication board may be designed for use just at the lunch table with symbols of items the student typically requests; another student may have a communication board specific to a vocational task. With the use of these mini-boards in activities that involve specified vocabulary, more symbols are made available to the learner.

Communicating with Symbols When developing a communication system, the teacher should examine the system and determine whether the student will be able to gain the attention of a listener effectively. If the student does not have a reliable mechanism to call for the listener's attention, the teacher should consider adding a component to the communication system. Examples of methods that a learner might use include vocalizing, pressing a buzzer, and pressing an icon that will activate a message (e.g., "I want to tell you something"). Once the listener's attention has been gained, the learner can select a communication symbol.

Learners who use a graphic system to communicate must have a means to indicate their selection of a symbol to their communication partners. Touching or pointing to the symbol is called direct selection; it can be done by using the hand or finger but can also be accomplished through directed eye gaze, by using another body part (toe, elbow, etc.), or by using a pointer attached to the body (mouthstick, head pointer). If the learner is physically capable of direct selection, it is the preferred method of indicating the symbol (Mustonen et al., 1991).

Scanning is a technique that can be used by learners whose physical impairments prevent direct selection. In scanning, the learner indicates a selection by signaling to the listener that the desired symbol has been reached. One version of scanning, auditory scanning, is the use of "twenty questions" (Shane & Cohen, 1981). In "twenty questions" the learner uses a signal to respond to questions that the listener asks to determine what the learner is trying to communicate. In manual scanning, the listener touches the symbols sequentially until the learner signals to stop, thereby indicating the symbol selection. For learners with many symbols, group/item scanning or page/item scanning may also be used. In group/item and page/item scanning, the learner uses scanning first to indicate the set of symbols (arranged by topic, environment, etc.) and then the item selection. For example, Jacob uses page/item scanning with a communication book. His communication partner opens the book to a menu page. On that page is a symbol for toys, positions, food, activities, and people. The communication partner points to each symbol and asks "Do you want ____?" Jacob blinks when the desired symbol is touched. The communication partner then turns to the page in the communication book that has symbols for the selected topic. The communication partner begins scanning those symbols until Jacob indicates his selection by blinking.

Encoding is a type of scanning that may be useful for students who are able to memorize and perform complex representational and sequencing skills (Miller & Allaire, 1987). In encoding, the learner memorizes a coded vocabulary and then communicates a message by using the code. For example, the learner uses eye gaze to point to a code system of numbers, colors, or letters displayed around the edge of the board. The student may eye point to the color red, which means he wishes to use the red group of words and messages and then eye points to a number, which means he wishes to use the word in the red group with the designation *5*.

Scanning may also be used with electronic communication devices. Because such devices continue to become more affordable, students with the cognitive capacity to use the encoding system described before are increasingly more likely to use them. Electronic scanning is accomplished through the use of a switch that controls the scanning. For many devices the switch activates a light that moves through the symbol array until the switch is hit again. There are a variety of patterns that can be used for scanning. In linear scanning, the cursor moves across the row of symbols one symbol at a time in a left-to-right movement. In circular scanning, the cursor moves in a circular fashion around the display. In row/column scanning, the cursor moves down a column until it is stopped and then moves across the row of symbols that was selected. Directed scanning can also be used with switches or a joystick controlling the cursor. In directed scanning, the learner uses the joystick to move the cursor directly to the symbol being selected.

There are a variety of switches that can be used to control the cursor of an electronic device for scanning. Electromechanical switches allow the learner to control the movement of the cursor by interrupting the electrical current that operates the machine. They work the same way a light switch works, allowing a person to turn the light on or off. Push switches are activated by physical pressure and can be designed for activation by almost any body part. Common push switches are push buttons, push plates, paddles, joysticks, and squeeze bulbs. Position switches are activated by a change of position in space and usually are made of a globule of mercury in a tube that opens and closes the switch when the learner moves the body part to which it is attached. Pneumatic switches (sip and puff, suck and blow) are activated by blowing or sucking on the end of a tube. Sound-controlled switches are activated by sound energy that is converted to electrical energy by a microphone and can be designed so that only a particular sound at a particular intensity will activate them (Silverman, 1980). Light-controlled switches work by directing a beam of light to a photoelectric cell or by interrupting a beam of light (Silverman, 1980).

In the last 10 years, the cost of electronic devices has dropped and practical applications have increased, including watches that store data, electronic date books, and even wallet-size computers. There has also been a boom in the development of electronic aids for communication. The advantages of electronic devices include the capacity to produce speech, visual displays, and written output; the capacity to produce a message beyond the student's capability (e.g., the symbol for *play* results in the phrase "can I play with you?"); the capability to store messages; and the ease in which scanning can be used with the system (Mustonen et al., 1991).

Selecting an Alternative or Augmentative Communication Mode

There has been much discussion in the literature about candidacy for augmentative communication and decision rules for selecting communication modes. Decision rules often involve a dichotomous system that separates speech potential from alternative modes and then suggests the type of alternative system that may be most appropriate (Reichle & Keogh, 1986). Decision rule strategies typically consider the student's physiological capacity for speech, success with vocal training, and cognitive level of functioning (Chapman & Miller, 1980; Shane & Baskir, 1980). Alpert (1980) and Reichle (1991) discuss the risks of decision rules by pointing out that some learners may have the physiological capacity for speech but may not have the potential for functional communication through a speech mode and yet are not introduced to nonspeech modes until vocal communication training has failed.

Reichle (1991) feels that there are no cognitive prerequisites to communication and that there is no evidence to suggest that instruction in an alternative system will inhibit speech. Reichle (1991) offers the flow chart in Figure 10–5 to describe the questions that must be asked in establishing and monitoring the augmentative or alternative system that is selected.

The first step in developing an augmentative or alternative communication system is to conduct an ecological analysis in an effort to determine the environments, activities, and situations that demand communicative behavior from the learner (Reichle, 1991). The ecological inventory will also assist in examining the behavior of the learner's communication partners and may pinpoint changes they can make to facilitate the communicative efforts of the learner.

An examination of the learner in different environments will yield information on how he or she currently meets communication obligations and opportunities. The communication situations the learner is exposed to and his or her communicative effectiveness in those situations will guide the interventionist in determining the communicative intents that should be taught.

The intents that are selected for instruction come from the communicative functions of behavior regulation, social interaction, and joint attention (see Figure 10–1), which emerge in the first two years of typical development (Wetherby, Cain, Yonclass, & Walker, 1988). The ecological inventory may reveal that students have idiosyncratic or unconventional means for some of these functions. For exam-

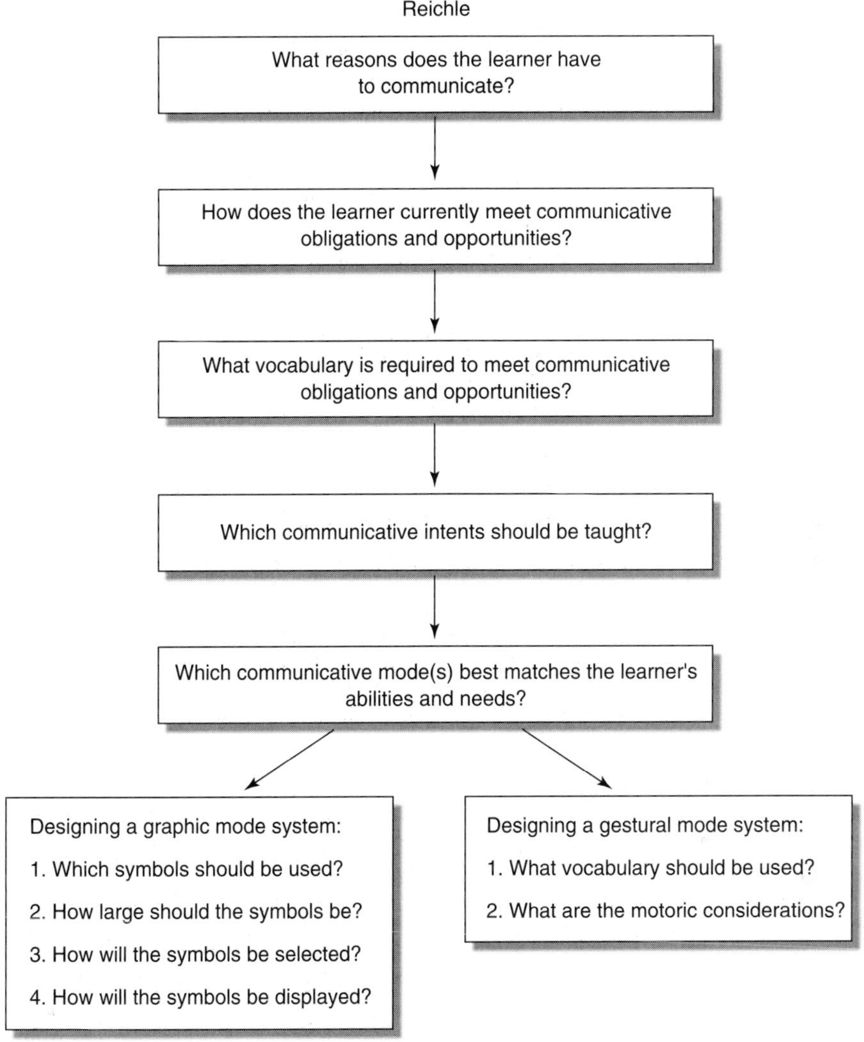

Figure 10–5
Decisions Involved in Designing Augmentative or Alternative Communication Systems
From "Defining the Decisions Involved in Designing and Implementing Augmentative and Alternative Communication Systems" by J. Reichle, in *Implementing Augmentative and Alternative Communication* (p. 40) by J. Reichle, J. York, & J. Sigafoos, 1991, Baltimore: Paul H. Brookes Publishing Co., P.O. Box 10624, Baltimore, MD 21285-0624. Reprinted by permission.

ple, a student may hit his face to request a drink or throw materials to communicate a protest. When students have idiosyncratic means, the goal is to teach a socially acceptable, interpretable means for the communication function. The ecological inventory may also reveal that the student is not exhibiting behavior that can be interpreted as communication. In such a case, the behavioral regulation functions would be the first area to focus on when establishing communication behavior.

When selecting the mode of communication it is likely and often desirable for mixed modes to be taught (Reichle, 1991). The selection of mode depends on the demands of the environments and the intent that is being taught. For example, if a learner wants to be able to request a certain type of sandwich at a fast-food restaurant, the most efficient mode of communication may be to hand the cashier a picture card describing the sandwich (e.g., Big Mac, please) but the same learner may be taught to use a natural gesture to express rejection or no. The use of two different modes for the same vocabulary is discouraged (Reichle, 1991). If two modes are taught for one word, the learner may become confused about which mode to use and should work on expanding rather than duplicating vocabulary.

The work of selecting and designing a communication system is never complete. The approach that is selected should build on the student's current skills and needs and expand to meet more needs over time (Mirenda & Iacono, 1990). Communication interventions from this perspective are "always ongoing and dynamic" (Mirenda & Iacono, 1990, p. 12).

Facilitated Communication

There have been reports of the success of a controversial method of aided communication called facilitated communication (Biklen, 1990), which involves the use of a letter board or keyboard (computer, typewriter, communicator). In this method the learner is provided with physical support under the forearm or hand to isolate the index finger and make a selection of a letter. One report describes the successful application of this method with 21 students labeled autistic (Biklen & Schubert, 1991). The researchers report that with facilitated communication, students with autism were able to communicate by spelling words and sentences and that many of them revealed unexpected literacy and numeracy skills through their typing. Biklen (1990) has hypothesized that facilitated communication allows individuals with autism to overcome neuromotor difficulties they have in communication as well as lack of confidence when communicating.

The term *facilitated communication* was introduced by educator Rosemary Crossley (Crossley & McDonald, 1980), who initially used the method to assist individuals with cerebral palsy and later discovered its application for individuals with autism (Biklen, 1990). Biklen and Schubert (1991) describe the basic elements of the method as: (1) physical support under the hand or forearm, (2) initial training and introduction through a series of activities and choices, (3) assisting the learner to maintain focus by ignoring excess behavior and reminding the student to look at the keyboard or resume typing, (4) providing support for typing but not testing the student for competence, (5) providing initial set-work (fill in the blank, questions, etc.) to help the student develop fluency with the method, and (6) fading the physical support over time.

Professionals have expressed concern about the limited empirical information available—information that is needed to understand the process and theoretical basis of the method (Calculator, 1992; McLean, 1992). Research that offers objective procedures, complete subject descriptions, generalization data, and reliable measures is needed to document the success of the method, although initial efforts (Biklen, 1990; Biklen & Schubert, 1991) indicate that this method holds great promise as a communication intervention.

Instructional Strategies

In recent years there has been a focus on the instruction of communication skills in natural contexts, which developed in response to operant training interventions that employed one-to- one, massed-trial instructional formats and failed to result in generalized and spontaneous language use (Goetz & Sailor, 1988). The use of natural contexts for communication instruction necessitates that the natural environment promotes communication, that communication partners in the environment can facilitate communication expression, and that specific procedures are developed and used to prompt and consequate communication use.

It is essential that opportunities for communication expression are provided in the student's daily environments. Typical children develop language without planned and systematic intervention, but students with severe disabilities do not. It is only through an intensive and systematic effort that communication interventions are successful for many students with severe disabilities. Unfortunately, teachers often lose sight of the importance of repeated practice in natural contexts. They work with a student and an augmentative communication system in the classroom and then neglect to take it out to the playground or they teach communication gestures at school without providing the student's family with a vocabulary list of gestures so that they can be used at home. It is critical that repeated practice on communication targets is provided and that communication systems are used in every environment.

An intervention plan designed to promote the communication skills of a student with disabilities is not focused solely on the development of skills by the student; it should also be aimed at creating an environment that encourages and supports the student's communication efforts.

Interaction Style

Communication partners (teachers, caregivers, peers) of the student with severe disabilities need to interact with the student in a manner that facilitates communication use. Halle (1984) discussed ways in which caregivers are not facilitative by preempting language use. Environmental preempting is arranging the physical environment so that toys, materials, and activities are freely provided to students in a way that eliminates the need to make requests. Nonverbal preempting occurs when caregivers give materials, toys, and activities freely without expecting communication from the student. Verbal preempting occurs when caregivers use specified prompts and cues for communication that eliminate the opportunity or need for a student to initiate communication.

Methods to inhibit preempting in the classroom or at home are

1. Use time delay. Wait silently with an expectant look for the child to initiate a request or indicate a need (Halle, 1984). For example, the teacher begins passing out cookies to the student's peers and uses time delay to elicit a request from the target student by holding the cookie and looking expectantly at him or her.
2. Use sabotage. The caregiver withholds an essential tool or material that makes completing the activity impossible and creates an opportunity for communication expression. For example, the teacher gives a child a bowl of ice cream but does not provide a spoon or gives a student a toy but withholds the electromechanical switch (Halle, 1984).

3. Out of reach. Place desirable toys and materials within the student's sight but out of reach to elicit a request (Halle, 1984).
4. Inadequate portions. Provide only small portions of materials or food so that the student will have to request more (Ostrosky & Kaiser, 1991).
5. Choice-making. Choices of materials, food, activities present the child with an opportunity to use communication skills for requesting (Ostrosky & Kaiser, 1991).
6. Assistance. Provide toys (e.g., battery-operated game, windup toy) that will need assistance to activate and result in the need for requesting help (Ostrosky & Kaiser, 1991).

The strategies described above provide opportunities for students to practice and strengthen communication skills or behaviors that they have learned. They do not replace instructional techniques that will be described later in this chapter.

There are many students with severe disabilities who do not socially initiate and seem to lack the basic skills necessary for a social exchange. Before these students can learn to communicate effectively, they need to develop the basic pattern of back-and-forth turntaking with a partner (MacDonald & Gillette, 1986). Turntaking interactions are difficult to establish when adults do not see the need for becoming social partners with students who are disabled. Strategies that adults may use to build social interactions are playing in routines, taking turns, using wait time, imitating the student's actions and sounds, progressively matching the student by acting like the student and adding one step, playing in the student's world, being animated and interested, and responding acceptingly to any social behavior (MacDonald & Gillette, 1986). The goal for adults is to become sensitive communication partners who facilitate and expand on the communication attempts of the student.

Once the student is communicative, adults must engage in an interactional style that encourages the building of language and conversation. Often adults dominate the communication interactions by talking at a student without expecting a response or by focusing on questions and commands (MacDonald & Gillette, 1986). It is critical that the adult allow the student to be both initiator and responder in communicative exchanges. Some strategies that can be used at this stage are commenting on what the student is experiencing, keeping on a student's topic, keeping the student on your topic, showing the student that you expect him or her to communicate, and using open-ended comments (MacDonald & Gillette, 1986).

Interacting with Learners Who Are Nonsymbolic

Siegel-Causey and Guess (1989) developed an intervention approach for learners who are nonsymbolic communicators and function with limited intentionality. Their approach stresses the reciprocal nature of communication exchanges and is intended to enhance the learners' understanding and expand their use of nonsymbolic communication. These strategies were developed after examination of the wealth of research literature on the communication development of infants, which reveals the types of behaviors caregivers use to facilitate the early nonsymbolic communication behaviors of infants.

Siegel-Causey and Guess (1989) recommend that the strategies listed in Table 10–1 be used in natural contexts and functional, relevant activities to facilitate nonsymbolic communication.

The five strategies of developing nurturance, increasing opportunities, utilizing movement, sequencing experiences, and enhancing sensitivity can be used by the interventionist to create an environment that

Table 10–1
Intervention Guidelines and Strategies Illustrated in Dialogues

Guidelines	Strategies
Developing Nurturance	Provide support, comfort, affection Create positive setting for interactions Expand on child-initiated behavior Focus on individual's interest
Enhancing Sensitivity	Recognize nonsymbolic behaviors Respond contingently Recognize individual's readiness for interaction Respond to individual's level of communication
Increasing Opportunities	Utilize time-delay Provide choices Create need for requests Provide opportunities to interact
Sequencing Experiences	Establish routines Utilize patterns in games Provide turn-taking opportunities Encourage participation
Utilizing Movement	Respond to movements as communicative behaviors Use movements matched to the level of the learner's actions Select movements that accommodate the learner's immediate ability to respond and interact within particular contexts/moments Use movements as communicative behaviors

From *Enhancing Nonsymbolic Communication Interactions Among Learners with Severe Disabilities* (p. 56) by E. Siegel-Causey & D. Guess, 1989, Baltimore: Paul H. Brookes Publishing Co., P.O. Box 10624, Baltimore, Maryland 21285-0624. Reprinted by permission.

expects communication and promotes reciprocal exchanges between the student and others.

Developing nurturance is used to create in the student a sense of trust that others in the environment will be responsive, warm, and caring. Adults develop nurturance by responding to students warmly, focusing on students' interests, and expanding on students' initiations (Siegel-Causey & Guess, 1989).

Increasing opportunities is accomplished by providing learners with many opportunities for interaction with others. Strategies that may be used to increase opportunities are to provide choices, create needs for requests, and use time delay (Siegel-Causey & Guess, 1989).

Utilizing movement is intended to convey to students with severe disabilities that their movements may be used for communication.

Adults can use the movements of students by matching student movement with language, modeling the use of movement (gestures, pointing) for communication, and responding to student movement that is communicative.

Sequencing experiences refers to the use of routines, games, and turntaking exchanges that provide learners with the opportunity to participate in reciprocal dialogues. Routines provide the learner with a context in which they learn turntaking skills and how to initiate, maintain, and terminate interactions.

Enhancing sensitivity is used by the interventionist to become aware of the learner's nonsymbolic behavior and early communicative efforts. Interventionists enhance sensitivity by becoming aware of and responding contingently to a learner's behavior and individual level of communication.

Designing Instructional Strategies

Providing a supportive environment is important to facilitate communication development, but it is not enough. Specific instructional goals must be selected and instructional strategies must be used to strengthen and expand the individual's communication ability. This is not to suggest that language interventions should adopt a didactic approach to instruction. Communication interventions must be conducted in contexts and activities that are meaningful for the student and employ both natural cues and consequences (Bricker, 1993).

Because of the importance of the natural context to communication development, instruction must take place in a variety of environments throughout the day. This approach has direct implications for the manner in which the speech-language therapist delivers services. One approach to the delivery of therapy that uses natural contexts for communication instruction is integrated therapy, which is the use of therapeutic intervention methods in real-life situations across the student's day (Rainforth, York, & Macdonald, 1992). In this model (as discussed in chapter 3) the therapist provides some direct therapy but is primarily involved in consultation. The therapist works with the student in daily activities (rather than taking the student to another environment for instruction), so that the classroom teacher is able to observe techniques that are used and to work collaboratively with the therapist. The therapist demonstrates intervention methods and assists the teacher in the evaluation of instructional needs and student performance.

Many of the instructional strategies that are described in chapter 6 may also be applied to the instruction of communication skills. Response prompting procedures (most-to-least prompt system, least-to-most prompt system, graduated guidance, and chaining) and stimulus prompting procedures (stimulus shaping and stimulus prompting) can be used to teach the acquisition of communication skills.

In Table 10–2, examples of the use of response and stimulus prompting procedures in the instruction of a request function are provided. A more detailed discussion of the features and applications of these training procedures is presented in chapter 6.

Naturalistic Teaching Procedures

A set of naturalistic teaching procedures, referred to as milieu teaching procedures, were developed specifically to promote communication and language skill development. These procedures, which include the use of time delay (Halle, Marshall, & Spradlin, 1979), mand-model (Warren, McQuarter, & Rogers-Warren, 1984), and incidental teaching (Hart & Risley, 1975), share the common features of (1) being based on the child's interest, (2) embedding brief episodes of instruction within natu-

Table 10–2
Stimulus and Response Prompting Procedures

Method		Application
most-to-least prompting procedure to teach a "want" symbol	Step 1:	The teacher places desired object in front of student. The teacher provides full physical assistance to the student to touch the "want" symbol. The teacher provides the desired object to the student.
	Step 2:	The teacher places desired object in front of student. The teacher provides a physical prompt by touching the student's hand and the symbol to cue the student to touch the "want" symbol. If the student touches the symbol, the teacher provides the object. If the student does not touch the symbol, the teacher applies step one and provides the object.
	Step 3:	The teacher places desired object in front of student. The student touches the "want" symbol to receive object. If student does not touch symbol, the teacher applies step two.
least-to-most to teach a natural gesture for request	Step 1:	The teacher presents desired object and waits for the student to use gesture. If student produces gesture, the teacher provides object. If student fails to produce gesture, the teacher applies step two.
	Step 2:	The teacher presents desired object and gives student physical prompt to produce gesture by pushing hand toward object. If student produces gesture, the teacher provides object. If student fails to produce gesture, the teacher applies step three.
	Step 3:	The teacher presents desired object and gives student full assistance to produce gesture. The teacher provides object after assisting the student to produce gesture.
graduated guidance to teach a student to touch a symbol for "drink" to receive a drink	Step 1:	The teacher presents the drink. The teacher uses hand over hand assistance to guide the student to touch the drink symbol, using as much assistance as necessary. The teacher provides the drink.
	Step 2:	The teacher presents the drink and reduces the assistance to touching the student's wrist but returns to hand over hand assistance if needed by the student.

rally occurring contexts, (3) being focused on explicit skill goals, and (4) providing natural consequences (Kaiser, Yoder, & Keetz, 1992).

Milieu procedures have been shown to be effective in the instruction of sign language, one-word responses, multiword phrases, and spontaneous speech (Kaiser, Yoder, & Keetz, 1992). There is also theoretical and correlational evidence that modified milieu procedures may be effective with prelinguistic communi-

Table 10–2, *continued*

Method		Application
	Step 3:	Over successive trials the teacher reduces assistance by shifting from support to the wrist to support to the forearm, elbow, shoulder, and finally to no support at all. Support is increased and faded according to the subtle movements of the student. The teacher provides the drink after the symbol has been touched.
backward chaining to teach a student to touch a symbol of a toy	Step 1:	The teacher presents a highly desired toy to the student and, as the student reaches for the toy, provides the symbol so that the student touches the symbol immediately prior to touching the toy.
	Step 2:	The teacher places the symbol on the table in front of the toy and prompts the student (using least to most or most to least) to touch the symbol prior to receiving toy.
	Step 3:	The teacher places the symbol on the student's lap tray and prompts the student to touch the symbol prior to receiving toy.
	Step 4:	The teacher presents the toy and waits for response of student to touch symbol prior to receiving toy.
interrupted behavior chain to teach the use of a communicating book symbol for *eat*	Step 1:	Teacher selects snack routine as chain sequence for interruption because it occurs twice a day, causes moderate levels of distress when interrupted, and results in student trying to complete the sequence.
	Step 2:	The teacher interrupts the snack routine by holding the snack item on the table until the student points to the symbol for *eat*. If the student touches the symbol within 5 seconds, the teacher provides the snack. If the student does not touch the symbol, the teacher models touching the symbol and then provides physical guidance to the student. If the student touches the symbol, the teacher provides the snack item. If the student fails to touch the symbol, the snack item is removed and the procedure is tried again in 5 minutes.

cators (Yoder & Warren, 1993). In Table 10–3 milieu teaching procedures to teach a request function by natural gesture and a communication board are described; descriptions of the steps for each milieu procedure follow.

Time Delay To use time delay, the interventionist must identify the response desired by the student. For example, the teacher wants to teach a student to make a request for more by saying the word *more*. The teacher should

Table 10–3
Using Milieu Procedures to Teach Communication Skills

Procedure	Natural Gesture	Communication Board
Time Delay	The teacher holds up a cup of juice that the student wants and looks expectantly at the student. When the student makes eye contact with the teacher, the teacher waits for 5 seconds (time delay). If the student does not gesture for the drink, the teacher models the action.	The teacher holds up a toy that the student wants and looks expectantly at the student. When the student makes eye contact with the teacher, the teacher waits 5 seconds (time delay). If the student does not touch the appropriate icon, the teacher models or mands the action.
Mand-Model	The teacher is playing with a favorite toy of the student. The student moves to the teacher and looks from the toy to the teacher. The teacher says "What do you want?" The child looks from the toy to the teacher. The teacher says "Show me want" (mand). The student reaches for the toy. The teacher provides the toy and says "You showed me want, here is the toy."	The teacher and three students are making a cake. The teacher gives two students a turn to hold the mixer. The teacher turns to the third student and says "What do you want?" The student looks expectantly at the teacher. The teacher provides a mand "touch 'my turn now.'" The student touches the correct icon. The teacher provides the mixer and says "you told me, 'my turn now'. Now it is Ricky's turn."
Incidental Teaching	Several students are eating a snack. The student pulls the teacher to the table. The teacher says "Want what?" The student points to the box of cookies. The teacher provides a cookie and says "Ricky wants a cookie too."	It is a free choice play time. The student touches the icon on his board representing "play". The teacher says "play what?" The student touches the play icon and then the car icon. The teacher moves to the shelf to get the car and says "O.K., Chris wants to play with the car."

identify occasions when the student is likely to need to use the target utterance, such as activity time or snack time. The teacher first establishes joint attention with the student and then introduces a time delay. During snack time, the teacher shows the student the cookie container (establishing joint attention) and waits for a response (time delay). If the student produces the desired behavior, the teacher consequates the response with praise, verbal expansion, and the requested item. If the student fails to produce the behavior, the teacher can provide a correction by modeling the desired response (e.g., "say more") or manding (instructing) the behavior (e.g., "tell me what you want"). Providing the model may be more appropriate if the student is not sure of the desired response; the mand may be more useful for students who know the answer.

Mand-Model Procedure The mand-model procedure was developed to assist students who know language responses to generalize their use to new contexts (Warren, McQuarter, & Rogers-Warren, 1984). In this procedure, the teacher identifies the response that is desired and then arranges materials in a way to promote child interest. When a student expresses interest in the material, the teacher mands (verbally instructs) the student to respond. For example, if the teacher wants the student to use object labels with *want* to make requests, she may say "Tell me what you want." If the student fails to respond with the desired utterance, the teacher would then model the desired response (e.g., "want ball"). If the child provides the appropriate response, the teacher provides praise, an expansion on the response (e.g., "Tony wants the big ball"), and the desired material.

Incidental Teaching In incidental teaching, the interventionist arranges the environment to create the need for students to request materials by placing them out of reach or in visible containers. When the student is verbally or nonverbally requesting a material, the interventionist establishes joint attention with the student and then prompts more elaborate language by using the mand-model procedure or time delay. For example, a student approaches a shelf, looks at the interventionist, and points to a radio. The interventionist follows the student response by using the mand "show me what you want." The student continues to point; the interventionist models the desired response. The interventionist makes a manual sign for music and says to the student "show me, music." The student signs *music* and the interventionist provides the radio, saying, "Here it is. You want to listen to music."

Interrupted Chains

Interrupted chaining is a teaching strategy that involves inserting a communication instructional trial into a routine activity (i.e., chain of behaviors) that the student is completing (Alwell, Hunt, Goetz, & Sailor, 1989). The interrupted chain strategy was shown to be more effective than placing the instructional trial just before the student began a familiar chain of behaviors (Goetz, Gee, & Sailor, 1985). In addition, students who learned communication skills using the interrupted chain strategy were able to generalize the skills learned to other activities, including those where no interruption occured.

To use the interrupted chain strategy, the teacher must first identify the instructional goal. The interrupted chain strategy has been successful at teaching students to use a natural gesture, signs, "want" card, and communication book. The teacher then develops a list of behavior sequences that: (1) the student engages in at least twice a day, (2) have at least three steps, and (3) are initiated by the student (Alwell et al., 1989). The teacher interrupts the student at various points in those behavior sequences to determine the amount of distress the interruption precipitates from the student and the student's attempts to complete the behavior chain. The behavior sequences that are appropriate to use for training cause a moderate level of stress (i.e., the student is motivated to complete the chain) and result in consistent attempts by the student to complete the activity.

When the training sequences have been identified, instruction occurs during the routines when they naturally take place. To interrupt the behavior chain, the teacher can delay presenting a needed item (e.g., spoon to stir cake mix), place a needed item out of reach (e.g., tape player on a high shelf), or block the behavior (e.g., hold the door closed). After the interruption, the teacher waits 5 seconds for a response (e.g, sign *want,* point to needed item, sign *open).* If there is no response, the teacher models the response, physically guides the student through it, and does not let the student finish the routine. The teacher waits for the student to attempt the routine again and interrupts again. If the student responds correctly, the teacher provides reinforcement, gives the student the needed item or removes the block, and allows the student to complete the routine. If the student does not respond correctly, the teacher removes the needed item or removes the student from the situation and does not allow the student to complete the routine.

Conversational Skill Training

Conversational skill training, which was developed to teach students with severe disabilities to initiate and maintain a conversation with peers (Hunt, Alwell, & Goetz, 1991; Hunt, Alwell, Goetz, & Sailor, 1990), makes use of a communication book that includes pictures of objects, places, and people associated with activities that the student enjoys and may wish to talk about (e.g., going to the bowling alley). The conversation book should be small enough to be portable and the pictures should be grouped by environments. Topics in the conversation book should be changed weekly.

Peer partners are instructed briefly about their role in the conversation skill training. They should be told to (1) make comments on the pictures in the book, (2) cue the student to take a turn by asking a question, and (3) wait for the student with severe disabilities to respond. The peer partner should be given an opportunity to role-play the use of the conversation book with the teacher before training begins. The sequence of the turntaking within the conversation skill training is shown in Figure 10–6.

Training the student with severe disabilities involves a most-to-least prompting sequence that is tailored to the individual student. The teacher may initially verbally prompt the student to initiate (e.g., "Tell Mara about bowling"), then fade the direct verbal prompts to verbal reminders (e.g., "Is there something you want to tell Mara about?"). Some students may

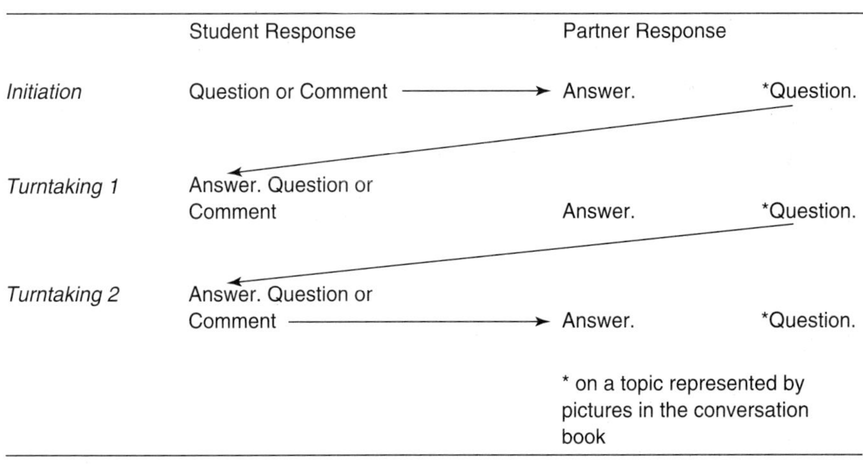

Figure 10–6
Conversation Turntaking Structure
From "Generalized Effects of Conversation Skill Training" by P. Hunt, M. Alwell, L. Goetz, & W. Sailor, 1990, *Journal of the Association for Persons with Severe Handicaps, 15*(4), pp. 250-260. Copyright 1990 by The Association for Persons with Severe Handicaps. Reprinted by permission.

initially require a direct verbal prompt plus a gestural prompt (e.g., pointing), which may be faded to the verbal prompt, then to the verbal reminder. If the student does not respond correctly, increasing assistance should be provided until the student is successful.

Van Dijk Method

There is growing interest among interventionists in the use of the Van Dijk method to promote communication development by students with severe disabilities (Lang & Uptmor, 1991; Sternberg & McNerney, 1988). The Van Dijk approach was developed in Holland by Jan van Dijk as a communication intervention for students who are deaf and blind. Although there is little empirical research on the efficacy of the procedures, and Van Dijk does not apply the method to students with severe multiple disabilities (Writer, 1987), educators in this country have begun to apply the principles to students with severe disabilities (Guess & Thompson, 1991; Sternberg & McNerney, 1988; Writer, 1987).

In the Van Dijk method the student is moved from an egocentric level of not relating to people or objects to the ability to use communication intentions with others (Lang & Uptmor, 1991). The method involves six major levels of communication development: nurturance, resonance, coactive movement, nonrepresentational references, deferred imitation, and natural gestures (Writer, 1987). In the first level, nurturance, the caregiver focuses on the development of a warm social bond between himself and the child. In the second level, resonance, the caregiver and the student move together with body-to-body contact. When students are in the resonance level, the caregiver responds to their movements as if they are communicative rather than attempting to teach specific communication behaviors (Stillman & Battle, 1984). The student moves from a resonance level to coactive movement, where the caregiver and the student move together although they are physically separated. In the coactive stage, complexity is gradually introduced to the movement sequences. The student progresses from the resonance stage of body-to-body contact movements to anticipating the order of a movement sequence and using movement sequences with objects. Anticipation shelves are introduced in the coactive movement stage as a communication device (Sternberg & McNerney, 1988; Stillman & Battle, 1984). Anticipation shelves are a series of boxes that are arranged horizontally on a shelf. Each box represents a different activity and contains an object that represents that activity (e.g., a bar of soap to represent handwashing). Before the activity begins, the student and the caregiver go to the shelf, pick up the object, and complete the activity. When the activity is completed, the student replaces the object in the box and picks up the object that signals the next activity. The purpose of the anticipation shelves is to evoke anticipatory responses from the student and for the student to understand the representation of activities by objects (Stillman & Battle, 1984).

The fourth stage in the Van Dijk method is nonrepresentational reference, in which the student develops an understanding of his body parts and, later, the body parts of a doll. In the following stage, imitation, the student is prompted to imitate the familiar movement actions of the caregiver. Imitative movements usually begin with gross motor movement and progress until the student can imitate limb and hand movement (Writer, 1987). The activities in the imitation stage are conducted within the natural daily routine. The sixth stage is the use of natural gestures as communication signals within routines. Natural gestures evolve from a student's experience with the motor qualities of things and first represent what the student does with an object (Sternberg & McNerney, 1988). After the student begins to use a variety of gestures in daily routines, the gestures are gradually shaped into manual signs (Writer, 1987).

Generalization Issues

The generalization of communication skills learned by students with severe disabilities is of great concern. The focus on teaching communication skills in natural contexts and the increased emphasis on milieu teaching strategies represent an effort to instruct communication behavior in a way that will result in generalization. Communication instruction is often successful in the instructional setting, but spontaneous use of the instructed communication behavior in other environments is rarely evident (Calculator, 1988; Halle, 1987; Kaczmarek, 1990).

The spontaneous use of communication skills by the learner with severe disabilities is an important outcome. The ability to spontaneously communicate allows the learner to initiate communication about topics that are personally relevant and important and select the time, place, and conversation partner for social interaction (Kaczmarek, 1990). Halle (1987) defines spontaneous language as language for which an observer cannot identify the controlling conditions.

Halle (1987) addresses the issue of spontaneous communication by defining spontaneity as utterances that occur in the presence of conditions that are not easily discerned. He offers a continuum of controlling stimuli that clarifies the idea of spontaneity (Figure 10–7). Communication is considered more spontaneous when it occurs under conditions that are less easily discerned. This continuum may also be a helpful guide in thinking about instruction of communication skills and the fading of prompts.

On the continuum in Figure 10–7, physical guidance represents the most restricted level of controlling stimuli. Physical guidance is often used in the early stages of communication training in the use of aided communication systems and natural gestures. The next point on the continuum is modeling. Modeling is frequently used in vocal training or is used as a less intrusive prompt following physical guidance. Questions or mands are less restricted stimuli that set the occasion for a response from the learner. The last three points on the continuum, presence of objects, presence of listener, and contextual and interoceptive stimuli, describe the diminishing discernability of controlling stimuli to stimuli that are within

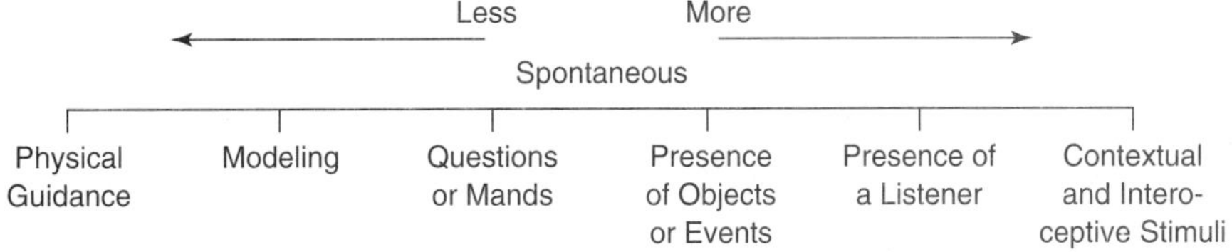

Figure 10–7
Continuum of Controlling or Discriminative Stimuli in the Presence of Which Responses Appear More or Less Spontaneous

From "Teaching Language in the Natural Environment: An Analysis of Spontaneity" by J. W. Halle, 1987, *Journal of the Associaiton for Persons with Severe Handicaps*, 12(1), pp. 28-37. Copyright 1987 by The Association for Persons with Severe Handicaps. Reprinted by permission.

the setting or learner and represent spontaneous communication use.

Kaczmarek (1990) addresses the learner's need to select a listener, establish proximity, and obtain attention in order to deliver a message in a matrix model for teaching spontaneous communication. The ability to perform those skills, described as listener preparatory behavior, gives the learner "more communicative" power to display spontaneous language than the learner who does not (Kaczmarek, 1990, p. 161). These behaviors do not occur in a set sequence, but may vary dependent on the environment in which communication is occurring, the response of the listener, and the nature of the message that is being communicated. There are also contextual variables that influence spontaneous communication. Kaczmarek (1990) suggests the use of a matrix model to understand all the possible contextual and listener preparatory variables that could affect the spontaneous use of a communicative function. An example of the matrix is presented in Figure 10–8.

The matrix can be used for intervention by first assessing the student's abilities within each condition and then developing an instructional sequence based on the student's entry repertoire. The interventionist can periodically probe in the cells that have not been targeted for intervention to test for generalization. These probes would indicate the conditions that should be targeted for additional training.

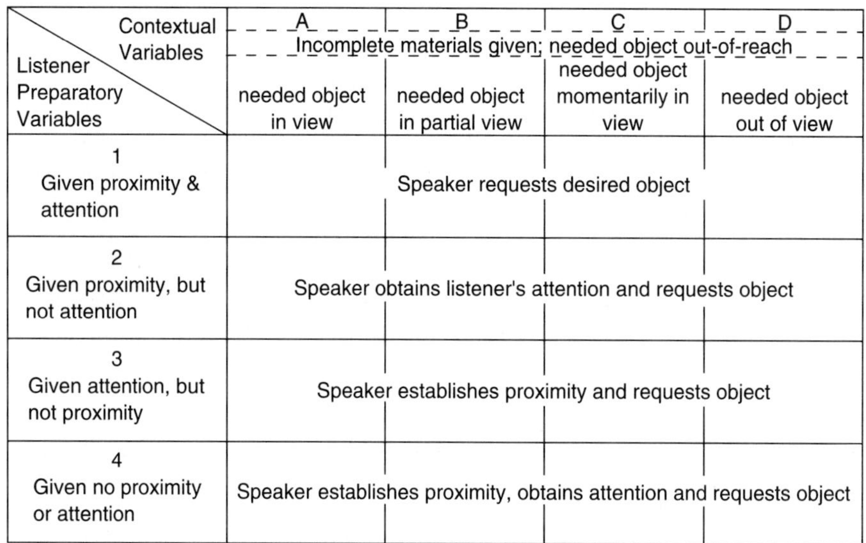

Contextual Variables / Listener Preparatory Variables	A	B	C	D
	Incomplete materials given; needed object out-of-reach			
	needed object in view	needed object in partial view	needed object momentarily in view	needed object out of view
1 Given proximity & attention	Speaker requests desired object			
2 Given proximity, but not attention	Speaker obtains listener's attention and requests object			
3 Given attention, but not proximity	Speaker establishes proximity and requests object			
4 Given no proximity or attention	Speaker establishes proximity, obtains attention and requests object			

Figure 10–8

Example of a Matrix Model Defining a Possible Instructional Universe for Requesting Needed Objects When Materials Needed to Complete a Task Are Not All Accessible

From "Teaching Spontaneous Language to Individuals with Severe Handicaps: A Matrix Model" by L. A. Kaczmarek, 1990, *Journal of the Association for Persons with Severe Handicaps, 15*(3), pp. 160–169. Copyright 1990 by The Association for Persons with Severe Handicaps. Reprinted by permission.

Conclusion

In this chapter strategies for assessing communication abilities, selecting communication modes, and instructing communication skills in natural contexts were presented. The foundation for all of these activities must be the belief that all behaviors communicate and that every individual has a right to become a more competent communicator. If these beliefs are in place, the interventionist will continue to seek new ways to understand and teach communication skills.

Questions for Reflection

1. What are some of the environmental variables that the collaborative team may wish to consider in the design of communication intervention plans?
2. What are the positive features of teaching students with severe disabilities multiple modes of communication?
3. What behaviors might be observed in a student who is moving from the perlocutionary stage to the illocutionary stage of development? What strategies would facilitate these behaviors?
4. What might be appropriate instructional goals for a student who is nonsymbolic?
5. What similarities do you see between the discussion in this text of general best practices for instruction and the use of naturalistic teaching procedures for communication development? How do these similarities fit into society's changing view of persons with disabilities?
6. What role does inclusion play in facilitating communication skill development?

References

Alpert, C. L. (1980). Procedures for determining the optimal nonspeech mode with autistic children. In R. L. Schiefelbusch (Ed.), *Nonspeech language and communication: Analysis and intervention* (pp. 389–420). Baltimore: University Park Press.

Alvares, R., Falor, I., & Smiley, L. (1991). Research on nonlinguistic communication functioning of individuals with severe or profound handicaps. In L. Sternberg (Ed.), *Functional communication: Analyzing the nonlinguistic skills of individuals with severe or profound handicaps* (pp. 18–37). New York: Springer-Verlag.

Alwell, M., Hunt, P., Goetz, L., & Sailor, W. (1989). Teaching generalized communicative behaviors within interrupted behavior chain contexts. *Journal of the Association for Persons with Severe Handicaps, 14,* 91–100.

Bates, E. (1979). *The emergence of symbols: Cognition and communication in infancy.* New York: Academic Press.

Biklen, D. (1990). Communication unbound: Autism and praxis. *Harvard Educational Review, 60,* 291–314.

Biklen, D., & Schubert, A. (1991). New words: The communication of students with autism. *Remedial and Special Education, 12,* 46–57.

Bricker, D. (1993). Then, now, and the path between: A brief history of language intervention. In A. P. Kaiser & D. B. Gray (Eds.), *Enhancing children's communication: Research foundations for interventions* (pp. 3–31). Baltimore: Paul H. Brookes.

Calculator, S. N. (1992). Perhaps the emperor has clothes after all: A response to Biklen. *American Journal of Speech-Language Pathology, 2,* 18–20.

Calculator, S. N. (1988). Promoting the acquisition and generalization of conversational skills by individuals with severe disabilities. *Augmentative and Alternative Communication, 4,* 94–103.

Carlson, F. (1984). *Picsyms categorical dictionary.* Lawrence, KS: Baggeboda Press.

Carr, E. G., McConnachie, G., Levin, L., & Kemp, D. C. (1993). Communication-based treatment of severe behavior problems. In R. Van Houten & S. Axelrod (Eds.), *Effective behavioral treatment: Issues and implementation* (pp. 231–267). New York: Plenum.

Chapman, R., & Miller, J. (1980). Analyzing language and communication in the child. In R. L. Schiefelbusch (Ed.), *Nonspeech language and communication: Analysis and intervention* (pp. 159–196). Baltimore: University Park Press.

Clark, C. R., Davies, C. D., & Woodcock, R. W. (1974). *Standard rebus glossary.* Circle Pines, MN: American Guidance Service.

Coggins, T., & Carpenter, R. (1981). The communication intention inventory: A system for observing and coding children's early intentional communication. *Journal of Applied Psycholinguistics, 2,* 235–251.

Crossley, R., & McDonald, A. (1980). *Annie's coming out.* New York: Penguin Books.

Dennis, R., Reichle, J., Williams, W., & Vogelsberg, T. (1982). Motoric factors influencing the selection of vocabulary for sign production programs. *Journal of the Association for the Severely Handicapped, 7,* 20–33.

Doherty, J. E. (1985). The effects of sign characteristics on sign acquisition and retention: An integrative review of the literature. *Augmentative and Alternative Communication, 1,* 108–121.

Donnellan, A., Mirenda, P., Mesaros, R., & Fassbender, L. (1984). Analyzing the communicative functions of aberrant behavior. *Journal of the Association for Persons with Severe Handicaps, 9,* 202–212.

Goetz, L., Gee, K., & Sailor, W. (1985). Using a behavior chain interruption strategy to teach communication skills to students with severe disabilities. *Journal of the Association for Persons with Severe Handicaps, 10,* 21–30.

Goetz, L., & Sailor, W. (1988). New directions: Communication development in persons with severe disabilities. *Topics in Language Disorders, 8,* 41–54.

Guess, D., & Thompson, B. (1991). Preparation of personnel to educate students with severe and multiple disabilities: A time for change? In L. H. Meyer, C. A. Peck, & L. Brown (Eds.), *Critical issues in the lives of people with severe disabilities* (pp. 391–398). Baltimore: Paul H. Brookes.

Gustason, G., Pfetzing, D., & Zawolkow, E. (1972). *Signing exact English.* Rossmoor, CA: Modern Signs Press.

Halle, J. W. (1984). Arranging the natural environment to occasion language: Giving severely language-delayed children reasons to communicate. *Seminars in Speech and Language, 5,* 185–196.

Halle, J. W. (1987). Teaching language in the natural environment: An analysis of spontaneity. *Journal of the Association for Persons with Severe Handicaps, 12,* 28–37.

Halle, J. W., Marshall, A. M., & Spradlin, J. E. (1979). Time delay: A technique to increase language use and facilitate generalization in retarded children. *Journal of Applied Behavior Analysis, 12,* 431–439.

Harding, C., & Golinkoff, R. (1979). The origins of intentional vocalizations in prelinguistic infants. *Child Development, 50,* 33–40.

Hart, B., & Risley, T. R. (1975). Incidental teaching of language in the preschool. *Journal of Applied Behavior Analysis, 8,* 411–420.

Hunt, P., Alwell, M., & Goetz, L. (1991). Interacting with peers through conversation turntaking with a communication book adaptation. *Augmentative and Alternative Communication, 7,* 117–126.

Hunt, P., Alwell, M., Goetz, L., & Sailor, W. (1990). Generalized effects of conversation skill training. *Journal of the Association for Persons with Severe Handicaps, 15,* 250-260.

Hurlbut, B. I., Iwata, B. A., & Green, J. D. (1982). Nonvocal language acquisition in adolescents with severe physical disabilities: Blissymbol versus iconic stimulus formats. *Journal of Applied Behavior Analysis, 15,* 241–258.

Kaczmarek, L. A. (1990). Teaching spontaneous language to individuals with severe handicaps: A matrix model. *Journal of the Association for Persons with Severe Handicaps, 15,* 160–169.

Kaiser, A. P., Yoder, P. J., & Keetz, A. (1992). Evaluating milieu teaching. In S. F. Warren & J. Reichle (Eds.), *Causes and effects in communication and language intervention* (pp. 9–47). Baltimore: Paul H. Brookes.

Lang, L., & Uptmor, E. (1991). Intervention models to develop prelinguistic communication. In L. Sternberg (Ed.), *Functional communication: Analyzing the nonlinguistic skills of individuals with severe or profound handicaps* (pp. 38–56). New York: Springer-Verlag.

MacDonald, J. D., & Gillette, Y. (1986). Communicating with persons with severe handicaps: Roles of parents and professionals. *Journal of the Association for Persons with Severe Handicaps, 11,* 255–265.

McLean, J. (1992). Facilitated communication: Some thoughts on Biklen's and Calculator's interaction. *American Journal of Speech-Language Pathology, 2,* 25–27.

Miller, J., & Allaire, J. (1987). Augmentative communication. In M. Snell, *Systematic instruction of persons with severe handicaps* (3rd ed.) (pp. 273–297). Columbus, OH: Merrill.

Mirenda, P., & Iacono, T. (1990). Communication options for persons with severe and profound disabilities: State of the art and future directions. *Journal of the Association for Persons with Severe Handicaps, 15,* 3–21.

Mirenda, P., & Locke, P. (1989). A comparison of symbol transparency in nonspeaking persons with intellectual disabilities. *Journal of Speech and Hearing Disorders, 54,* 131–140.

Musselwhite, C., & St.Louis, K. (1988). *Communication programming for persons with severe handicaps: Vocal and augmentative strategies.* Boston: College-Hill.

Mustonen, T., Locke, P., Reichle, J., Solbrack, M., & Lindgren, A. (1991). An overview of augmentative and alternative communication systems. In J. Reichle, J. York, & J. Sigafoos, *Implementing augmentative and alternative communication: Strategies for learners with severe disabilities* (pp. 1–37). Baltimore: Paul H. Brookes.

Neel, R. S., & Billingsley, F. F. (1989). *IMPACT: A functional curriculum for students with moderate to severe disabilities.* Baltimore: Paul H. Brookes.

Ostrosky, M. M., & Kaiser, A. P. (1991). Preschool classroom environments that promote communication. *Teaching Exceptional Children, 23,* 6–11.

Rainforth, B., York, J., & Macdonald, C. (1992). *Collaborative teams for students with severe disabilities.* Baltimore: Paul H. Brookes.

Reichle, J., & Keogh, W. J. (1986). Communication instruction for learners with severe handicaps: Some unresolved issues. In R. H. Horner, L. H. Meyer, & H. D. Fredericks (Eds.), *Education of learners with severe handicaps: Exemplary service strategies* (pp. 189–219). Baltimore: Paul H. Brookes.

Reichle, J. (1991). Defining the decisions involved in designing and implementing augmentative and alternative communication systems. In J. Reichle, J. York, & J. Sigafoos, *Implementing augmentative and alternative communication: Strategies for learners with severe disabilities* (pp. 39–60). Baltimore: Paul H. Brookes.

Romski, M., & Sevcik, R. (1988). Augmentative and alternative communication systems: Considerations for individuals with severe intellectual disabilities. *Augmentative and Alternative Communication, 4,* 83–93.

Romski, M. A., & Sevcik, R. A. (1992). Developing augmented language in children with severe mental retardation. In S. F. Warren & J. Reichle (Eds.), *Causes and effects in communication and language intervention* (pp. 113–130). Baltimore: Paul H. Brookes.

Rowland, C., & Schweigert, P. (1989). Tangible symbols: Symbolic communication for individuals with multisensory impairments. *Augmentative and Alternative Communication, 5,* 226–234.

Schuler, A. L., Peck, C. A., Willard, C., & Theimer, K. (1989). Assessment of communicative means and functions through interview: Assessing the communicative capabilities of individuals with limited language. *Seminars in Speech and Language, 10,* 51–62.

Sevcik, R., & Romski, M. (1986). Representational matching skills of persons with severe retardation. *Augmentative and Alternative Communication, 2,* 160–164.

Shane, H., & Baskir, A. (1980). Election criteria for the adoption of an augmentative communication system: Preliminary considerations. *Journal of Speech and Hearing Disorders, 45,* 408–414.

Shane, H., & Cohen, C. (1981). A discussion of communicative strategies and patterns by nonspeaking persons. *Language, Speech, and Hearing Services in Schools, 12,* 205–210.

Siegel-Causey, E., & Downing, J. (1987). Nonsymbolic communication development: Theoretical concepts and educational strategies. In L. Goetz, D. Guess, & K. Stremel-Campbell (Eds.), *Innovative program design for individuals with dual sensory impairments* (pp. 15–48). Baltimore: Paul H. Brookes.

Siegel-Causey, E., & Guess, D. (1989). *Enhancing nonsymbolic communication interactions among students with severe disabilities.* Baltimore: Paul H. Brookes.

Sigafoos, J., & York, J. (1991). Using ecological inventories to promote functional communication. In J. Reichle, J. York, & J. Sigafoos, *Implementing augmentative and alternative communication: Strategies for learners with severe disabilities* (pp. 61–70). Baltimore: Paul H. Brookes.

Silverman, F. H. (1980). *Communication for the speechless.* Englewood Cliffs, NJ: Prentice-Hall.

Skelly, M. (1979). *Amer-Ind gestural code based on universal American Indian hand talk.* New York: Elsevier.

Sternberg, L., & McNerney, C. (1988). Prelanguage communication instruction. In L. Sternberg (Ed.), *Educating students with severe or profound handicaps* (2nd ed.) (pp. 311–341). Austin, TX: ProEd.

Stillman, R. D., & Battle, C. W. (1984). Developing prelanguage communication in the severely handicapped. An interpretation of the Van Dijk method. *Seminars in Speech and Language, 4,* 159–170.

Vanderheiden, G. C., & Lloyd, L. L. (1986). Communication systems and their components. In S. W. Blackstone (Ed.), *Augmentative communication: An introduction* (pp. 49–161). Rockville, MD: American Speech-Language-Hearing Association.

Warren, S. F., McQuarter, R. J., & Rogers-Warren, A. K. (1984). The effects of mands and models on the speech of unresponsive socially isolated children. *Journal of Speech and Hearing Disorders, 47,* 42–52.

Wetherby, A. M., & Prizant, B. M. (1989). The expression of communicative intent: Assessment guidelines. *Seminars in Speech and Language, 10,* 77–90.

Wetherby, A. M., Cain, D., Yonclass, D., & Walker, V. (1988). Analysis of intentional communication of normal children from the prelinguistic to the multi-word stage. *Journal of Speech and Hearing Research, 31,* 240–252.

Woodcock, R. W. (1968). Rebuses as a medium in beginning reading instruction. *IMRID Papers and Reports, 5*(4).

Woodcock, R. W., Clark, C. R., & Davies, C. O. (1969). *The Peabody rebus reading program teacher's guide.* Circle Pines, MN: American Guidance Service.

Writer, J. (1987). A movement-based approach to the education of students who are sensory impaired/multihandicapped. In L. Goetz, D. Guess, & K. Stremel-Campbell (Eds.), *Innovative program design for individuals with dual sensory impairments* (pp. 191–223). Baltimore: Paul H. Brookes.

Yoder, P. J., & Warren, S. F. (1993). Can developmentally delayed children's language development be enhanced through prelinguistic intervention? In A. P. Kaiser & D. B. Gray (Eds.), *Enhancing children's communication: Research foundations for intervention* (pp. 35–61). Baltimore: Paul H. Brookes.

CHAPTER 11

Providing Behavioral Supports to Improve Challenging Behavior

Chapter Overview

In this chapter, strategies for intervening with challenging behavior are presented. The chapter begins by describing the types of problem behavior that are often targets of intervention programs. Following the description of problem behavior, you are provided with the orientation that problem behavior occurs for a reason and that the teacher must first understand the behavior before an intervention plan can be designed. Strategies for determining why the behavior may be occurring are provided, followed by the steps needed to design a behavior-support plan.

One of the most difficult challenges that teachers encounter is instructing learners who exhibit problem behaviors. Students with severe disabilities often are members of this group. The types of behavior problems that have been observed in persons with severe disabilities include stereotypic, self-injurious, aggressive, and socially inappropriate behavior. The prevalence of problem behavior is particularly high among individuals who live in institutional settings (Borthwick, Meyers, & Eyman, 1981).

Current approaches to behavior intervention differ dramatically from earlier views. In the past, behavior interventions were focused solely on eliminating behavior with little consideration given to the context in which the behavior occurred and the need to replace problem behavior with new appropriate skills. In recent years, behavior interventionists have focused on the analysis of the function of these behaviors by examining the context in which they occur and linking interventions directly to the analysis. There is also an increased emphasis on considering aspects of an individual's lifestyle and developing an intervention plan that includes changes in social and ecological conditions that will support meaningful outcomes for the individual.

It is important at this point to discuss the beliefs that serve as a foundation of the approach to problem behavior that is presented in this chapter. There are two concepts that the interventionist should remember when designing behavior interventions. First, many of these behaviors have a communicative message, and it is essential that the interventionist try to understand and respond to that underlying message. Second, interventions that are designed to simply eliminate a behavior or replace it with another skill while ignoring the entire context in which a problem behavior occurs will not demonstrate long-term effectiveness. The approach that is presented in this chapter is based on a lifestyle perspective (Evans & Meyer, 1990; Horner et al., 1990; Meyer & Evans, 1989) in which the interventionist examines all aspects of an individual's lifestyle and seeks not only to change behaviors but also to enhance the lifestyle so that meaningful outcomes will result and be maintained.

In this chapter, strategies for analyzing problem behavior and developing intervention programs within a functional approach are presented. The chapter begins with a discussion of the types of problem behavior that may be associated with persons with severe disabilities. Although the topography of the behavior (what the student actually does) does not appear to have a systematic relationship with why persons with severe disabilities engage in problem behavior, it is relevant to define and describe these categories of behavior (Meyer & Evans, 1989). In the second section the rationale for using a functional approach to intervening with problem behavior is discussed with research presented to support the method. The third section presents the methods of functional assessment and hypotheses development, the fourth section presents intervention strategies and how they may be used within the behavior support process, and the final section describes how an intervention plan is developed and applied.

Defining Problem Behavior

Problem behavior can take many forms. An act that may not be considered a problem behavior in one setting, for example, screaming and stamping one's feet at a football game, can be very problematic in a setting such as the classroom. Researchers have used classifications to define and describe problem behavior, and these definitions are useful for the purpose of facilitating discourse about such behavior. In this section the major categories of problem behavior are described and the common hypotheses about why the behavior occurs are presented. These are provided as an explanation of how researchers have traditionally viewed problem behavior. It is important to emphasize that defining a problem behavior by topography (e.g., self-injurious behavior or stereotypic behavior) will not lead directly to a method for reducing the behavior. The definitions and examples of categories of problem behavior are presented here so that you will be knowledgeable about the terminology that is commonly used to discuss problem behavior.

Stereotypic Behaviors

Stereotypic behaviors are repetitive cycles of behavior that consist of idiosyncratic rhythmic movements of the body or body parts. Many people engage in stereotypic behaviors such as cracking their knuckles, twirling their hair, or swinging their feet. These behaviors become problematic when they occur in such excess that the individual is unable to participate in other activities when engaged in the behavior or when the behaviors result in negative reactions from others. Examples of problematic stereotypic behavior include head-weaving, finger-flapping, mouthing hands, and rocking.

There are several theories about why persons with severe disabilities engage in stereotypic behavior in amounts or intensity that is problematic. One theory is that the behavior serves a self-stimulatory function, which means that the behavior provides the individual with sensory input that is reinforcing. Some research supports this hypothesis in that when the sensory consequences of the behavior were decreased, the behavior also decreased (Rincover & Devany, 1982). A related theory is that the behavior serves a self-regulatory function, meaning that the behavior might serve to increase stimulation or decrease arousal (Meyer & Evans, 1989).

Self-Injurious Behaviors

Self-injurious behaviors are responses that inflict harm on the individual engaging in the behavior. Examples of such injurious behaviors that have been treated by researchers are head-banging, face-slapping, eye-gouging, and hand-biting. Four general explanations for why individuals engage in self-injurious behavior have been described by Gast and Wolery (1987). One explanation is the psychoanalytic position, which postulates that individuals engage in self-injury to reduce their guilt or to distinguish themselves from their inner world. The neurophysiological explanation suggests that the self-injury has reinforcing stimulatory features and that the initiation of pain provides an opiate through the production of endorphins in the central nervous system (Cataldo & Harris, 1982). The organic explanation is related to the relationship of self-injurious behavior to specific syndromes. Both Cornelia de Lange and Lesch Nyhan syndromes appear to be related to self-injury. Another organic explanation of self-injury is the presence of otitis media (Demchak & Halle, 1985). The fourth explanation is that the behavior is learned through environmental contingencies. For example, an individual may have learned through reinforcement that self-injury results in a decrease of instructional demands (Carr, 1977).

Self-injury can be one of the most horrifying categories of problem behavior in persons with disabilities. As a result, interventionists may resort to behavior reduction interventions that are also extreme in nature. Self-injury has been treated with the use of contingent shock, water misting, restraint, and lemon juice in the mouth (Guess, Helmstetter, Turnbull, & Knowlton, 1987). The occurrence of self-injurious behavior is higher (by 10 to 17%) among individuals who are institutionalized (Baumeister & Rollings, 1976; Schroeder, Schroeder, Smith, & Dalldorf, 1978). It also appears to be related to the severity of retardation, indications of neurological impairments, and the rate of stereotypic behavior (Maisto, Baumeister, & Maisto, 1977).

Aggression

Aggressive and disruptive behavior can be defined as behavior that results in injury or damage to others and/or their property. It often occurs as part of a general tantrum and includes a combination of behaviors (e.g., screaming, crying, destroying property, and attacking others). In addition, some authors include passive-aggressive behavior, such as noncompliance, running away when called, and so forth, as aggressive acts when they are attempts to counter-control (Meyer & Evans, 1989).

There are a variety of explanations for why individuals with disabilities engage in aggressive and disruptive behavior. In some individuals, this pattern of behavior is evidenced in reaction to demand situations or complex tasks (Carr & Durand, 1985; Carr, Newsom, & Binkoff, 1980; Weeks & Gaylord-Ross, 1981). There is also evidence that aggression can be influenced by environmental conditions. Aggression may increase as materials decrease or environmental conditions become uncomfortable.

Inappropriate Social Behavior

Inappropriate social behavior describes a category of behavior that is regarded as antisocial (Meyer & Evans, 1989). Examples include public masturbation, inappropriate affectionate behavior, laughing hysterically, shouting or swearing, hoarding possessions or food, and inappropriate or irrelevant conversations. These behaviors appear to result from failure to learn more appropriate social skills (Meyer & Evans, 1989).

The current approach to intervening with problem behavior moves beyond a simple identification of the behavior and the selection of a method of intervention. Labeling a behavior (e.g., stereotypic, self-injurious) does little to assist the interventionist in selecting a treatment. For example, one student may engage in aggression because he has an ear infection; another may engage in aggression to express her frustration with a task. A functional approach, in which the relationship of variables to the behavior is individually examined, is most likely to lead to effective intervention (Carr, Robinson, & Palumbo, 1990).

A Functional Approach to Changing Behavior

It has only been since the late 1980s that interventionists and researchers have stressed the importance of approaching problem behavior from a functional assessment perspective. Before then, behavior modification was used for intervention but the interventions were usually not developed by analyzing the cause of the behavior (Carr et al., 1990). Functional assessment was not neglected because the technology did not exist. To the contrary, there are early papers that describe functional assessment (Skinner, 1953, 1959) and examples of the successful application of the technique (Ullmann & Krasner, 1965). The concept of functional assessment is quite simple: Before interventions are designed to reduce the occurrence of problem behavior, hypotheses are developed and tested to determine why the behavior occurs. Thus, an intervention can be designed that fits the circumstances surrounding the problem behavior. Despite knowledge of functional assessment, researchers appeared to abandon the technique in favor of interventions that offered a quick suppression of the problem behavior (Deitz, 1978; Hayes, Rincover, & Solnick, 1980; Lennox, Miltenberger, Spengler, & Erfanian, 1988; Lundervold & Bourland, 1988). The desire to eliminate problem behavior quickly may have taken precedence over making an effort to understand the source of the behavior (Carr et al., 1990).

Eliminative Approach

Meyer and Evans (1989) used the term *eliminative approach* to describe the use of behavior modification to reduce behaviors without the benefit of a functional assessment. In this approach the interventionist is interested only in eliminating the problem behavior and designs interventions that are focused on behavior reduction. Although this approach appears to be a logical response to problem behavior, there are several difficulties inherent in its use. First, it fails to recognize that problem behavior serves a function for the individual (Donnellan, Mirenda, Mesaros, & Fassbender, 1984), and when the means for that function is eliminated, the individual may find an alternative way to express the function, which is often expressed as another problem behavior. For example, Bill is a student with severe disabilities who bangs his head frequently. If a functional assessment had been done, the interventionist would have discovered that this behavior occurs when Bill is not engaged in an activity and appears to be an expression of boredom. Because a functional assessment was not done, the interventionist tried a variety of methods to reduce the behavior while increasing the intrusiveness of the methods each time. Finally, the interventionist implemented a behavior reduction program where Bill was misted with water (from a spray bottle) each time he engaged in head-banging. Bill stopped head-banging in an effort to avoid the water mist procedure, but within several days he began screaming and biting his hand when he was bored.

A second problem with the eliminative approach is that the problem behavior is often reduced in one setting or with one interventionist but persists in other situations. For example, Susan would bite her hand when an activity became frustrating or when she wished to escape a situation. The teacher implemented a program where Susan was assisted in raising her hands in the air and then to the side for three repetitions following every incident of hand-biting, followed with redirection to the task. Susan stopped biting her hand at school, but continued to exhibit the behavior with increased frequency in the home and in community settings.

An additional problem is that once the behavior-change program is phased out the target behavior returns, often with greater intensity. Richard engaged in episodes of extreme aggression when he was not feeling well or was not provided with activities or objects when he requested them. He had hurt several adults and peers by hitting, kicking, and biting them. After an array of treatment approaches, including positive reinforcement and water mist, had been tried, he was treated by being placed in restraints following every episode of aggression. The restraints were permanently fastened to a chair and then placed on his arms, legs, waist, and forehead when he was seated in the chair. His episodes of aggression decreased until efforts were made to decrease the use of the restraints. Within two months the aggressive episodes were occurring with the same frequency as before and, in addition, included acts of property destruction.

Finally, interventionists who use the eliminative approach may withhold positive programming or instructing new skills until the problem behavior is controlled (Evans & Meyer, 1985). Often when behavior interventionists or teachers encounter individuals who exhibit high levels of problem behavior, they work on controlling the behavior before shifting their focus to teaching new skills. The eliminative approach is singularly focused on the reduction of problem behavior without considering the need to teach new skills to the individuals and provide them with the support they need to engage in new patterns of behavior (Evans & Meyer, 1985).

A common feature of behavior intervention programs designed by professionals who are focused solely on behavior reduction is the use of aversive consequences. There is a wealth of literature that documents the use of a great variety of consequences (e.g., electric shock, water mist, slapping, restraint, pinching) that are considered to be aversive (Guess et al., 1987). The use of such consequences in behavior intervention programs has been a controversial issue and the subject of great concern for professionals and professional groups.

In this chapter, only positive approaches to intervening with problem behavior are presented. In a functional approach to behavior intervention, the interventionist focuses on the instruction of new skills and changes that can be made in environments to support appropriate behavior.

Functional Approach

A functional approach to behavior intervention is based upon an effort to understand problem behavior before trying to change it (Carr et al., 1990). Donnellan et al. (1984) used pragmatics to explain the relationship of problem behavior to communication. Pragmatics is the study of language within the social context (Schuler & Goetz, 1981). Within the pragmatics perspective, all behavior is viewed as having a functional message value. For example, if a child approaches his mother with his hand outstretched when his mother is eating a cookie, one would view this behavior as a request for a cookie. The meaning is inferred by viewing the behavior in the social context. If the same child held his hand outstretched while playing in the sandbox with a friend, one might infer that the child is commenting or directing the play interaction. Although the behavior is the same, we infer different meanings by understanding the context in which the behavior occurs.

Behavior interventions that are based on a pragmatics perspective are designed to expand the repertoire of the individual with severe disabilities rather than limiting it (Donnellan et al., 1984). These interventions are based on determining the message conveyed by the behavior and replacing the behavior with an alternative communication behavior or an alternative response that results in the desired consequences. For example, in a study conducted by Carr and Durand (1985), an assessment procedure was used to discover why several students engaged in hitting, tantrums, self-injurious behavior, and other inappropriate behavior. They found that some of the students exhibited this behavior when the tasks given to them were difficult; others exhibited the behavior to solicit attention from the interventionist. The experimenters taught the overwhelmed students to request assistance verbally, and they taught those whose problem behavior was associated with attention to request the attention they needed by asking "Am I doing good work?" The problem behaviors dropped to nearly zero after the students learned to use a functionally equivalent communication behavior to serve the same function as the problem behavior.

Pragmatically oriented interventions may also involve a change in antecedent conditions to decrease the problem behavior. When a functional assessment is conducted to determine the message of the behavior, the interventionist might discover a relationship between the context and the behavior that could be manipulated to result in the desired changes in the behavior.

For example, in a study conducted by Touchette, MacDonald, and Langer (1985), the experimenters assessed the relationship of a student's program to her aggressive behavior. The functional assessment revealed that she was most aggressive between 1:00 and 4:00 p.m., Monday through Thursday. The events that occurred at this time were group prevocational and community living classes. To intervene in the behavior, the experimenters revised her schedule and replaced the afternoon activities with activities not associated with aggression (i.e., activities from the morning schedule). Elements of the student's original schedule were slowly reintroduced into her activities. As she became more tolerant of the conditions of the afternoon activities, the expectations of the student were gradually increased. This intervention resulted in a dramatic decrease in the aggressive behavior.

The functional approach to behavior intervention considers all aspects of an individual's lifestyle that may lead to problem behavior. In the eliminative approach, the focus of the intervention was mainly on the consequences that maintained a behavior rather than consideration of the antecedents that might contribute to the behavior. For example, imagine a classroom where activity choices are limited and students are directed in all of their activities. Suppose there is a student with severe disabilities in that classroom who is unable to expressively communicate in ways that others can understand. When he is directed to an activity that he does not want to do, he becomes aggressive with the teacher to let her know that he does not want to engage in the activity. In this situation, the lack of choices in the classroom has set the stage for the problem behavior to occur. In a functional approach, enriching the classroom with activity choices becomes part of the behavior intervention plan.

A functional approach to the treatment of problem behavior contrasts to nonfunctional treatment in the way treatments are selected, when treatment is implemented, the purpose of the treatment, and how long the treatment is carried out (Carr et al., 1990). These contrasts are described in Table 11–1.

In a functional approach, interventions are selected after an understanding of the behavior is reached through functional assessment. Intervention strategies that are selected are not

Table 11–1
Distinctive Features of Functional Versus Nonfunctional Approaches to Treatment

Functional Treatment	Nonfunctional Treatment
1. Treatment selection is explicitly based on functional analysis. The focus is on understanding.	1. Treatment selection is implicitly based on behavior topography and/or general diagnostic category. The focus is on technology.
2. Treatment is proactive. It takes place when the individual is not engaging in behavior problems.	2. Aversive treatment is reactive. It takes place when the individual is engaging in behavior problems.
3. The purpose of treatment is to make desirable responses more probable. The focus is on education and behavior enhancement. Behavior problem reduction is an important side effect.	3. The purpose of treatment is to make undesirable responses less probable. The focus is on crisis management and behavior control. Behavior problem reduction is the main effect.
4. Treatment is carried out indefinitely (long-term focus) because the main concern is with maintenance of increases in desirable behavior.	4. Treatment is carried out for relatively brief periods of time (short-term focus) because the main concern is with crisis management of undesirable behavior.

From "The Wrong Issue: Aversive versus Nonaversive Treatment. The Right Issue: Functional versus Nonfunctional Treatment," by E. G. Carr, S. Robinson, & L. W. Palumbo, in A. C. Repp & N. N. Singh (Eds.) (1990), *Perspectives on the Use of Nonaversive and Aversive Interventions for Persons with Developmental Disabilities* (p. 372). Copyright © 1990 by Sycamore Publishing Co. Reprinted by permission of Brooks/Cole Publishing Company, Pacific Grove, CA 93950.

reactive to the problem behavior when it occurs, but are focused on the prevention of problem behavior through the manipulation of antecedent events, intervention contexts, and the instruction of new skills. Functional intervention strategies are always based on increasing desirable skills and responses rather than focusing solely on the elimination of problem behavior. Finally, because the functional approach to changing problem behavior is concerned with the acquisition of new skills and behavior patterns, intervention programs are designed to be long-term.

Conducting a Functional Assessment

Because the functional approach to behavior intervention is based on understanding the behavior, the assessment of problem behavior is an essential first step. This assessment is conducted not only to document the behaviors the individual engages in, but also to develop hypotheses about why the behavior occurs. Before conducting such an assessment, the collaborative team should gain an understanding of the individual's lifestyle.

Lifestyle Understanding

The first step to understanding an individual's behavior is to examine all of the conditions and patterns of his or her life. A collaborative team that wishes to understand the nature of a student's challenging behavior must look into aspects of the student's life that might contribute to the challenging behavior or assist in developing a behavior-support plan.

When the behavior-support plan is developed, changes in the individual's lifestyle are important outcomes. Those outcomes cannot be identified without first understanding the student's lifestyle patterns. For example, if the collaborative team is concerned about a student's self-injurious behavior, one of the outcomes they may target is improved health and safety. In addition, they may want the student to be able to experience a broader array of social activities in the community as he or she becomes less in need of constant supervision.

Lifestyle issues that are particularly relevant to the challenging behavior of individuals with severe disabilities include leisure activities; opportunities for choice-making; friendships and social relationships; community activities; health status; and the nature of the classroom, residential, and work environments. Some individuals with severe disabilities have very few leisure activities, little control over their environment, and very few affectionate relationships. When such conditions exist, the team must examine the relationship of those variables to the challenging behavior of the individual. If you had a lifestyle that included few friends and limited activities, would your mood or behavior patterns be affected?

One method for examining a student's lifestyle is to use the personal futures planning process that is described in chapter 4. It is likely that in an instructional situation the collaborative team is already familiar with the lifestyle issues of the student. If that knowledge is already accessible, the team should ensure that those issues are discussed as part of the functional assessment process.

Methods that have been developed to conduct a functional assessment of problematic behavior can be classified as (1) indirect methods, which include behavioral interviews, checklists, and rating scales; (2) direct methods, which rely on observation of the behavior in natural contexts; and (3) experimental analysis, which involves the manipulation of controlling variables to determine the functional relationship of an array of variables to the problem behavior (Lennox & Miltenberger, 1989).

Indirect Assessment

Several tools have been developed to gather information on problem behavior and the context in which it occurs. Behavioral interviews, which are frequently the first step in conducting a functional assessment, provide a series of questions that are designed to identify and describe the problem behaviors, identify and describe the ecological and consequence events that surround the occurrence of the behavior, and develop initial hypotheses about the functions of the problem behavior (Iwata, Wong, Reardon, Dorsey, & Lau, 1982; Meyer & Evans, 1989; Miltenberger & Veltum, 1988; O'Neill, Horner, Albin, Storey, & Sprague, 1990). Questions that are often asked in behavioral interviews include:

- What are the problem behaviors?
- Which of the problem behaviors are the most serious?
- What is most likely to occur before the problem behavior?
- What is most likely to occur after the problem behavior?
- Why do you think the individual engages in the behavior?
- What medications is the individual taking?
- Describe the eating, sleeping, and activity routines of the individual.
- When is the problem behavior least likely to occur?
- What activities or objects are most preferred by the individual?
- What methods does the individual use to communicate a protest, request an activity or object, and request social attention?

- What intervention strategies have been used in the past to attempt to change the problem behavior?

Another method for collecting information about problem behavior is the use of behavior rating scales and checklists. The Motivation Assessment Scale (Durand & Crimmins, 1988) is designed to provide information to analyze the variables related to self-injurious behavior. The Motivation Assessment Scale lists 16 questions about the nature of the behavior that will lead to indicating possible motivational sources. Once the questions have been answered, the scoring system indicates if the function of the behavior is to escape, to obtain sensory input, to obtain a tangible reinforcer, or to obtain social attention.

Although the Motivation Assessment Scale can be a reliable instrument that is easily implemented, it is limited in the functions of the behavior it can identify. When it is used to develop initial hypotheses about the functions of behavior, additional observations, interviews, and systematic manipulations may be needed for a comprehensive assessment.

Indirect methods for assessing problem behavior can yield important information in the functional assessment process, but it is important to note that interviews and checklists rely on informants' impressions of the behavior and may be influenced by their personal perspectives (Iwata, Vollmer, & Zarcone, 1990; Lennox & Miltenberger, 1989). It is possible that the interview alone will provide enough information to develop an intervention plan, although it is more likely that direct observation will need to follow the interview. Direct observation of the behavior in naturally occurring contexts can offer important additional information about the nature of the antecedents, behavior, and maintaining consequences.

Direct Observation Assessment

Direct observation assessment involves the observation of behavior and the contexts in which it occurs. "ABC analysis" is used to record the events that occur before and after the behavior in an effort to understand the variables that are functionally related to the behavior (White, 1971). In an ABC analysis, the observer records the antecedents that are present, the behaviors that follow antecedent events, and the consequences that follow the target behavior. An example of an ABC analysis is provided in Figure 11–1.

When conducting an ABC analysis, the observer should first identify the target behavior that is the focus of the functional analysis. Although there may be many behaviors that are of interest, it is important for accuracy to narrow the scope of the observation. In the antecedent column, the observer lists aspects of the setting as well as actions and requests of others that may have a relationship to the target behavior. This is followed by a precise description (in the second column) of the observed student's behavior following the antecedent events. The consequences that follow the behavior are noted in the consequence column, where all events that follow the behavior should be described, including actions by others, changes in the setting, and actions by the observed student.

The ABC analysis is a fairly easy method to use, although the accuracy of the assessment is highly dependent on the accuracy of the observer and the objectivity of the events that are recorded. Because of the potential subjectivity of the measure, the interventionist may want to follow the descriptive information provided in an ABC analysis with more controlled observation techniques, such as the "Scatter Plot" method or the communicative function observation tool described below.

Name: Jon
Observer: Rick
Date: May 3, 1993
Target Behavior: aggressive tantrums that include hitting, kicking, and screaming
Observation Setting: classroom, activity-time
Time Begins: 9:00 A.M.
Time Ends: 9:25 A.M.

Antecedent	Behavior	Consequence
Teacher directs Jon to go to the shelf and select an activity.	Jon rolls wheelchair to shelf.	Teacher waits for Jon to make toy selection.
Jon reaches for toy Kim is holding. Kim pulls toy to self.	Jon screams and hits Kim.	Teacher reaches for identical toy and gives it to Jon.
Jon takes toy to table.	Jon plays with toy alone.	Teacher watches and moves to another group.
	Jon plays with toy for several minutes.	
Kim brings identical toy to table.	Jon reaches for her toy.	Kim pulls toy to herself.
	Jon screams, hits, and kicks Kim.	Teacher runs over and pulls Kim away.
	Jon becomes calm and plays with Kim's toy.	
Teacher says to put toys back.	Jon puts toy under table and head down.	Teacher directs Jon to take the toy to the shelf.
	Jon sits up.	
Teacher tries to physically assist Jon with picking up toy.	Jon screams and hits teacher.	Teacher holds Jon's hands down for 20 seconds.

Figure 11–1
ABC Analysis of Jon's Aggressive Tantrums

The Scatter Plot method provides information on the frequency of the behavior within time intervals over the course of a day (Touchette et al., 1985). In this method, a grid is designed that segments time into units on the vertical axis and days across the horizontal axis. Each blank cell represents a frequency of zero occurrences of the problem behavior. If the behavior occurs within the time interval, the cell is marked with a slash to indicate a low frequency or is shaded to indicate a high frequency. The differentiation of high or low fre-

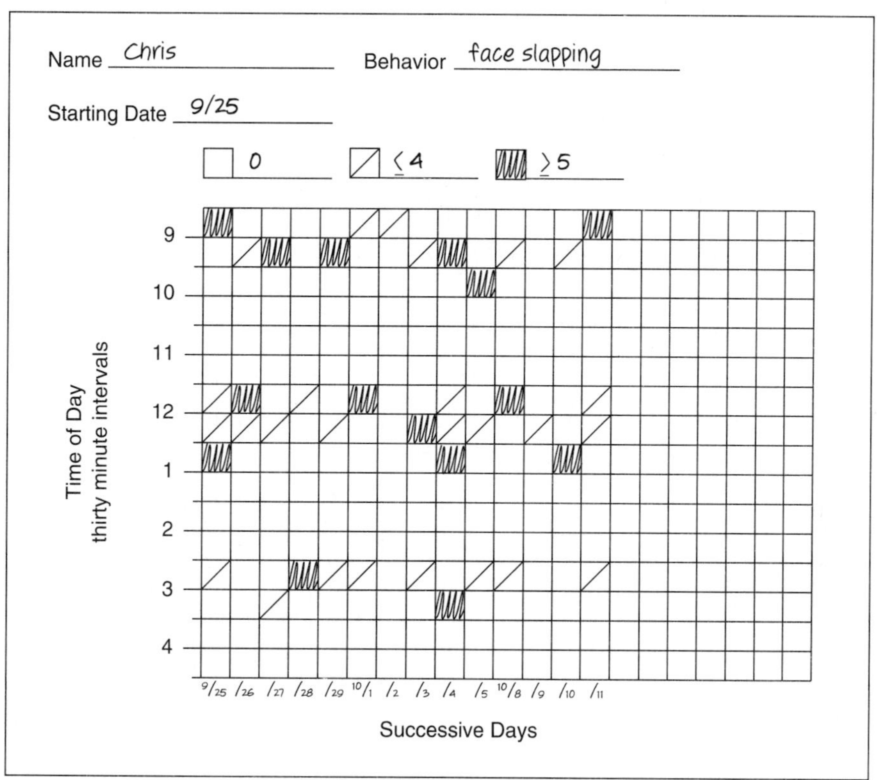

Figure 11–2
Completed Scatter Plot Grid for a Student Who Engages in Face-Slapping

quency is determined before the observation occurs and is based on the nature of the problem behavior that is being observed. An example of a completed scatter plot grid is provided in Figure 11–2.

When the grid has been filled with observations, a visual array of the density of the problem behavior and the times of day that problem behavior occurs is evident. When this information is supplemented with an analysis of the events that occur during those time periods, hypotheses about the relationship of controlling variables to the behavior can be developed.

Another tool that can be used for observing and analyzing problem behavior is the communication functions observation tool (Donnellan et al., 1984). This tool, shown in Figure 11–3, is designed to record the observer's impressions about the communicative functions of behavior when it occurs. The observer notes behaviors that occur (they are listed across the top of the form) and then identifies the possible function(s) that the behavior may serve (the functions are listed on the vertical axis). Possible functions are determined by asking the question "In the present context, what does the student seem to be communicating and how does he or she do it?" (Donnellan et al., 1984, p. 47). A mark is then made at the intersect of the behavior and the function. After the observation period, the data

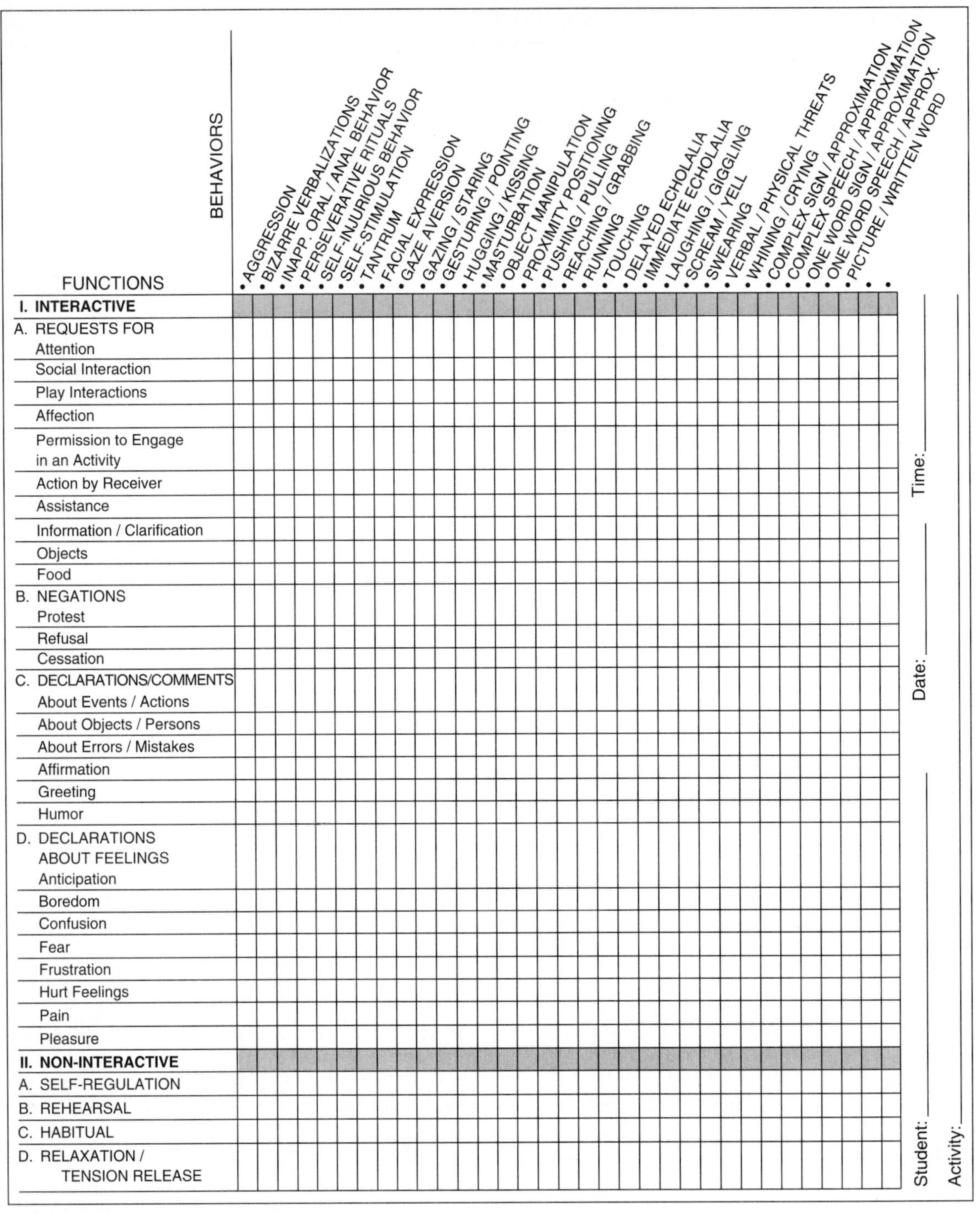

BEHAVIORS

- AGGRESSION
- BIZARRE VERBALIZATIONS
- INAPP. ORAL / ANAL BEHAVIOR
- PERSEVERATIVE RITUALS
- SELF-INJURIOUS BEHAVIOR
- SELF-STIMULATION
- TANTRUM
- FACIAL EXPRESSION
- GAZE AVERSION
- GAZING / STARING
- GESTURING / POINTING
- HUGGING / KISSING
- MASTURBATION
- OBJECT MANIPULATION
- PROXIMITY POSITIONING
- PUSHING / PULLING
- REACHING / GRABBING
- RUNNING
- TOUCHING
- DELAYED ECHOLALIA
- IMMEDIATE ECHOLALIA
- LAUGHING / GIGGLING
- SCREAM / YELL
- SWEARING
- VERBAL / PHYSICAL THREATS
- WHINING / CRYING
- COMPLEX SIGN / APPROXIMATION
- COMPLEX SPEECH / APPROXIMATION
- ONE WORD SIGN / APPROXIMATION
- ONE WORD SPEECH / APPROX.
- PICTURE / WRITTEN WORD
- •
- •

FUNCTIONS

I. INTERACTIVE

A. REQUESTS FOR
- Attention
- Social Interaction
- Play Interactions
- Affection
- Permission to Engage in an Activity
- Action by Receiver
- Assistance
- Information / Clarification
- Objects
- Food

B. NEGATIONS
- Protest
- Refusal
- Cessation

C. DECLARATIONS/COMMENTS
- About Events / Actions
- About Objects / Persons
- About Errors / Mistakes
- Affirmation
- Greeting
- Humor

D. DECLARATIONS ABOUT FEELINGS
- Anticipation
- Boredom
- Confusion
- Fear
- Frustration
- Hurt Feelings
- Pain
- Pleasure

II. NON-INTERACTIVE

A. SELF-REGULATION

B. REHEARSAL

C. HABITUAL

D. RELAXATION / TENSION RELEASE

Student: ____________ Date: ____________ Time: ____________

Activity: ____________

Figure 11–3

An Observation Tool for Analyzing the Communicative Functions of Behavior

From "Analyzing the Communicative Functions of Aberrant Behavior" by A. M. Donnellan, P. L. Mirenda, R. A. Mesaros, & L. L. Fassbender, 1984, *Journal of the Association for Persons with Severe Handicaps, 9,* pp. 201–212. Copyright 1984 by The Association for Persons with Severe Handicaps. Reprinted by permission.

that have been recorded assist the observer in generating hypotheses about the communicative functions of the target behavior.

The Functional Analysis Observation Form (FAOF) shown in Figure 11–4 is an observation tool that was developed to provide information on the antecedents, behavior, consequences, time, setting, and possible functions of the behavior (O'Neill et al., 1990). It combines the important features of the ABC analysis, scatter plot, and the communicative functions observation tool in one form.

To use the FAOF, the observer first records the name of the person being observed and the dates of the observation. The second step is to fill in the times of the observation intervals. Predictable activities (e.g., morning arrival, snack, physical education) may be recorded with the time. If activities are different over the days (e.g., 9:00 on Monday is community-based instruction and on Friday it is physical education), activities may be listed under the setting events/discriminative stimuli column.

The third step is to record the behaviors that will be observed in the behaviors column. The observation form may be used as an event-recording tool to document the occurrence of an episode of a behavior (e.g., crying tantrum) or the frequency of a behavior (e.g., hitting others). When the behavior occurs, the observer records the first instance, placing the number 1 under the behavior that occurred, the setting event or stimuli it occurred in response to, the observer's impression of the function of the behavior, and the consequences that followed the behavior.

Observations should continue through the day with behaviors numerically recorded. When a new day of observations begins, the observer makes a hash mark after the last number assigned to the last behavior recorded that day and then continues the observations and numerical tracking. In this manner, there is a method for tracking what behavior occurred on specified days. Observations should continue until there is a clear pattern to the data suggesting the likely antecedents, functions, and maintaining consequences of the behavior.

All of the direct observation methods that are described in this section allow the observer to make hypotheses about the relationship of variables to problem behavior. These types of observations have been described as "descriptive" rather than "functional" to emphasize that they do not yield the type of data needed to confirm a functional relationship between variables and behavior (Iwata et al., 1990). Experimental analyses, in which a functional relationship is directly tested and verified, may need to follow the descriptive information that is generated through observational assessment techniques, although there will be many occasions where the interview and observations clearly indicate the direction of the intervention. In those cases, an intervention plan may be developed and then evaluated for effectiveness. The effectiveness of the intervention will confirm if the hypotheses were correct.

Hypotheses Development

Hypotheses are informed guesses about why the student engages in the behavior. They are generated through an analysis of the information generated from the functional assessment process and should be developed about the antecedents that predict the behavior and the consequences that maintain the behavior. For example, "the cooking activity is difficult for Josh so he throws materials on the floor to escape the task." Hypotheses may also relate to more distal antecedents (setting events) such as environmental variables, mood of the student, physical status, or incidents that occurred prior to the immediate context of the behavior. For example, "When Susan has not slept well the night before,

Functional Analysis Observation Form

Person: Jean
Dates: 2-20 to 2-21

	Behaviors							Settings Events / Discriminative Stimuli																									Perceived Functions: Get / Obtain					Perceived Functions: Escape / Avoid						Actual Conseq.					
Time	Screaming		Pinch / Scratch		Rip / Destroy			Demand / Request	Difficult Task	Transition (task-task)	Transition (settings)	Interruption	Alone (no attention)		Teacher		Aide														Don't Know / Unclear	Attention	Desired Item / Activity	Self-Stimulation			Demand / Request	Activity ( )	Person			Other / Don't Know	Ignore		Time-out			COMMENTS: (If nothing happened in period, write initials.)
8:30 – 9:00 H.R.	6		6		6			6									6																				6								6			
9:00 – 10:00 Self-care	1 2 7		1 2					1 2					7		7		1 2															7					1 2						1 7		2			
10:00 – 11:00 P.E.																																																T.R.
11:00 – 11:30 Office	3				3			3									3																				3								3			
11:45 Lunch	8		4		8								4 8				4															4 8											4		8			
12:45 Meal prep	5		5 9		9			5 9							5 9																						5 9						5 9					
1:45 Street cross																																																T.R.

~~1~~ 2 ~~3~~ ~~4~~ ~~5~~/~~6~~ ~~7~~ ~~8~~ ~~9~~ 10 11 12 13 14 15 16 17 18 19 20 21 22 23 24 25 26 27 28 29 30 31 32 33 34 35 36 37 38 39 40 41 42 43 44 45 46 47 48 49 50

2-20 2-21

Figure 11–4

Functional Analysis Observation Form

From *Functional Analysis of Problem Behavior: A Practical Assessment Guide* by R. E. O'Neill, R. H. Horner, R. W. Albin, K. Storey, and J. R. Sprague.

she is more likely to hit peers when she becomes frustrated with an assignment."

It is important to develop hypotheses statements that are specific and lead directly to an intervention. Vague statements, such as "Susan hits peers when she is angry," will not provide enough information for an intervention plan.

Hypotheses Testing

An experimental analysis of the relationship of specified variables to the problem behavior may be conducted to verify assumptions or hypotheses that have been made about the functions of the problem behavior. When these hypotheses are verified or rejected, a meaningful behavior intervention plan can be developed.

Confirmation of the relationship of variables to behavior can be done by manipulating antecedent and consequent conditions to decipher the meaning of problem behavior. For example, if the hypothesis about tantrum behavior is that the individual is using it to express a desire to escape a particular work activity, conditions can be manipulated in a way to confirm that hypothesis. The interventionist could provide several activities, allow the individual a choice, and then see if the tantrum behavior continues, or the interventionist could systematically present the hypothesized problem task to see if the problem behavior only occurs when that task is presented. A functional analysis to confirm the relationship of identified variables to problem behavior requires at minimum two conditions, one in which the variable of interest is present and one where it is absent (Iwata et al., 1990). These conditions are then alternated to demonstrate the relationship between conditions and the behavior.

For many individuals, problem behavior may be generalized to serve more than one function. For example, an individual may use the problem behavior of hand-biting to signal boredom, frustration, and excitement. In such instances, the interventionist will need to manipulate many conditions to sort out all the variables that are related to the behavior.

In a study conducted by Dunlap, Kern-Dunlap, Clarke, and Robbins (1991), functional assessment was used to determine the relationship between curriculum features and the severely disruptive behavior of an adolescent female with multiple disabilities. Over a period of five weeks, the investigators used a variety of indirect measures and direct observation to develop hypotheses about the student's behavior. The four hypotheses that were developed were that the student was better behaved when engaged in large-motor rather than fine-motor activities, that she did better when activities were brief rather than lengthy, that she did better within functional activities with concrete and preferred outcomes, and that she did better when she had choices about the activities she was asked to complete.

The four hypotheses were tested within rapidly changing reversal designs over 4 days with one hypothesis tested each day in a 15-minute session. Figure 11–5 shows the results of the functional analysis for the four hypotheses. Once these hypotheses were confirmed, curricular revisions were made in response to the information gained from the functional analysis. The guidelines for changes in the curriculum included providing short activity sessions when the student was engaged in fine-motor and concentrated academic activity, interspersing fine-motor activities with gross-motor activities, arranging work activities so that the content was meaningful to the student and resulted in concrete outcomes, and providing a menu of choices to the student. These changes resulted in decreases in the student's disruptive behavior and an increase in her on-task responding.

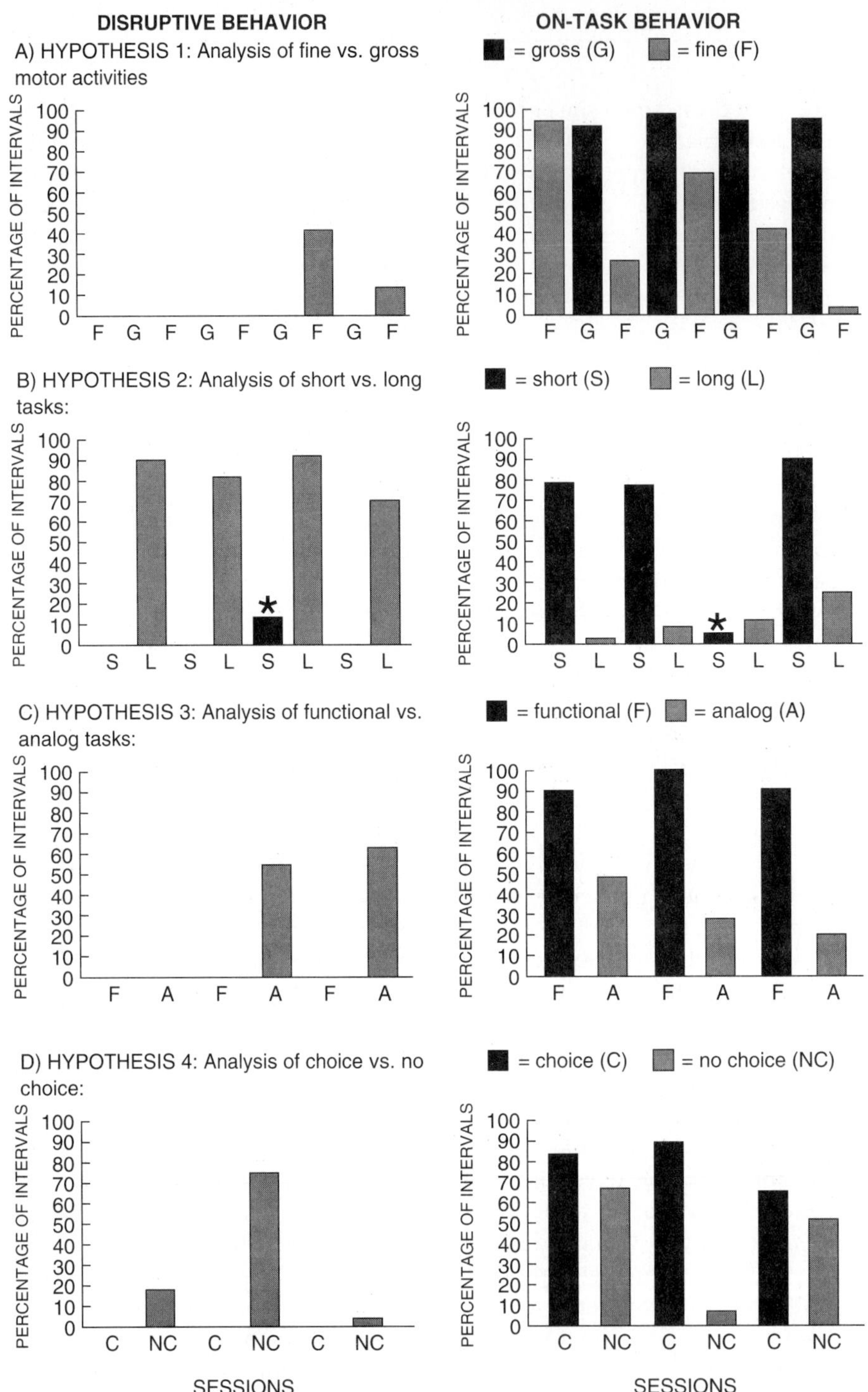

Figure 11–5

Results of the Hypothesis-Testing Phase of the Functional Assessment Process. Levels of disruptive behavior (left) and on-task responding (right) are shown for each of the four hypotheses.

From "Functional Assessment, Curricular Revisions, and Severe Behavior Problems" by G. Dunlap, L. Kern-Dunlap, S. Clarke, & F. R. Robbins, 1991, *Journal of Applied Behavior Analysis, 24,* pp. 387-397. Copyright 1991 by the Journal of Applied Behavior Analysis. Reprinted by permission.

Intervention Strategies

Once hypotheses are developed, an intervention plan is designed that is comprehensive and multicomponent. The intervention plan should be broad enough to address issues of lifestyle, ecological variables, immediate antecedents and consequences, and the instruction of new skills.

In the following sections, strategies that may be used to address issues of ecological and setting events, antecedents, consequences, and the instruction of functionally equivalent communication skills are provided. These strategies are not intended to be used as the comprehensive list of appropriate interventions; they are provided as examples of what may be included in a multiple component plan. Strategies must be selected based on the information yielded by the functional assessment and must match the hypotheses statements that are developed about the student's behavior.

Ecological and Setting Event Strategies

Ecological and setting events may have a significant impact on an individual's behavior and should not be viewed as beyond the scope of a behavior intervention plan. For example, if an individual who lives in a group home with several other persons with disabilities has a difficult time coping with the noise and bustle of congregate living as evidenced by tantrums, a move to a more comfortable living environment should be considered by the team. Such a major change may be warranted if the behavior is significantly impacting the individual's ability to function in community environments.

Other ecological variables that may be considered and manipulated are the activity schedule of the individual, the frequency and nature of social relationships, and health issues. For example, if the hypotheses developed indicate that a student's limited activity schedule contributes to boredom that is expressed by stripping for attention, an appropriate intervention would include enriching the student's activities and social contacts.

When health issues are a concern, medical remedies should be pursued, although there are conditions that cannot be eliminated by medical intervention and that may persist, such as menstrual discomfort or headaches. If a student is more likely to exhibit problem behavior because of menstrual discomfort, the intervention plan may include a component that is aimed at making her more comfortable during those times (e.g., heating pad, back rub) or decreasing demands in empathy for the student's discomfort.

Antecedent Strategies

If the functional assessment pinpoints specific antecedents as predictors of problem behavior, manipulation of the antecedents is warranted. For example, if a student always tantrums during transitions from activity to activity, a manipulation of the antecedent should be a part of the plan. A strategy may be to provide the student with a warning that the transition is coming, using a system that the student can comprehend, such as a timer with a bell or a picture schedule. Some teachers feel that this approach is "giving in" to the student, but it is important to realize that the intervention plan will include components to decrease the occurrence of the problem behaviors while the student is simultaneously taught new skills. Providing a warning to a student may be a strategy to decrease the occurrence of the problem behavior until he or she learns new communication or self-management skills and can be gradually taught to handle unexpected changes in activities.

Other strategies that may be used to decrease the occurrence of problem behavior are changing the demands of a task to make it less difficult or using prompting techniques to make a task easier; eliminating stimuli that trigger the behavior (e.g., loud music) or providing adaptations that allow the student to avoid triggering stimuli (e.g., transition to a different classroom before the halls fill with students); and embedding trials of difficult tasks within tasks that are easy for the student (Winterling, Dunlap, & O'Neill, 1987).

A very important antecedent strategy is to teach the student an alternate form of communication that matches the function of the behavior. For example, if a student is throwing materials across the room to signal that he wants a break, an effective strategy would be to teach him to signal for a break and then reinforce him for using an appropriate form of communication.

Consequence Strategies

In the functional approach to behavior intervention, more attention has been focused on the antecedents and ecological variables that are related to the behavior. This focus does not mean that consequences are no longer an important aspect of the functional assessment or that consequence strategies will not be used in the intervention plan. Listed below are consequence strategies that may be used as a component of the behavioral intervention plan. What has changed with the functional perspective is that these strategies alone do not constitute a comprehensive behavior intervention plan.

Reinforcement Teachers often use praise or activity reinforcers without individually assessing their reinforcement value to particular students. Reinforcers should be identified for each student, using a systematic assessment process. A simple method for identifying reinforcers is to expose the student to different objects or activities and observing if he or she interacts with the item, displays positive affect, and tries to retrieve the item when it is removed. It is also important to remember that reinforcers change and that satiation is possible.

When the functional assessment indicates that reinforcement is available and maintaining the problem behavior, a strategy that should be used is to eliminate the reinforcement for the problem behavior and provide reinforcement for an adaptive alternative or appropriate behavior.

Differential Reinforcement of Other behavior (DRO) is providing reinforcement for not engaging in the target behavior for a specified interval of time. This procedure has been used to intervene with aggression, self-injury, tantrums, self-biting, and a variety of other problem behaviors (Carr, Robinson, Taylor, & Carlson, 1990). To use DRO, the interventionist must first define the target behavior to be changed and take baseline data on the frequency with which the behavior occurs. The next step is to define the time interval that will be used for the DRO procedure. Donnellan, LaVigna, Negri-Shoultz, and Fassbender (1988) recommend that the interval selected should be one-half the interresponse time under baseline conditions. Interresponse time is calculated by observing the behavior and counting the number of times the behavior occurs within a time interval and then calculating the average length of time between responses. For example, if a student engaged in an average of six tantrums in a 1-hour period, the interresponse time would be one tantrum every 10 minutes. When selecting an interval for reinforcement, the interventionist would divide the interresponse time of 10 minutes in half to determine a reinforcement interval of 5 minutes.

After a time interval is selected, the interventionist should select the reinforcement to be used with the procedure and develop a plan to fade the reinforcement. The reinforcer that is selected should be one that is only available through meeting the criterion of the DRO schedule (Donnellan et al., 1988). Fading the reinforcement can be accomplished by changing the interval schedule. For example, the interventionist may start by using a fixed interval schedule with the DRO procedure and then move to an increasing interval schedule once positive changes in the behavior are established.

The interventionist must also determine the actions that will be taken if the target behavior occurs during the DRO procedure—ignoring the behavior, providing feedback to the student, or using a crisis-intervention procedure if the behavior is very dangerous (Donnellan et al., 1988).

Differential Reinforcement of Incompatible behavior (DRI) and *Differential Reinforcement of Alternative behavior (DRA)* refer to the reinforcement of behaviors that are topographically different from the target behavior. In DRI, the student is reinforced for engaging in a behavior that is physically incompatible with the behavior targeted for reduction. By increasing the targeted incompatible behavior, the target behavior is guaranteed to decrease in frequency (Foxx, 1982).

In using the DRI procedure it is important to address several variables (Donnellan et al., 1988). First, an alternative behavior should be identified rather than reinforcing the student for not displaying a behavior. The goal is not passivity, but rather a reduction in the target behavior and an increase in the incompatible or alternative behavior. Second, the more dissimilar the chosen incompatible behavior is to the target behavior, the better the method will work. Third, the identified incompatible behavior and the target behavior must cover the universe of possible behavior. For example, if the student is reinforced for interacting appropriately with others in order to decrease the incompatible behavior of interacting inappropriately by shouting at adults and peers, the universe of possible behavior has been covered. The student can only interact appropriately or inappropriately. But if the teacher had identified raising one's hand to ask a question as the incompatible behavior for shouting, there would be times when the student could be not doing either of those behaviors. Although reinforcement for raising his hand would result in an increase in that behavior, there would be many opportunities when hand-raising would not occur and the shouting could happen (e.g., on the playground). An appropriate alternative behavior, when increased, will directly result in the decrease of the target behavior.

To implement the DRI procedure, the interventionist must first define the target behavior to be reduced. The second step is to identify an alternative behavior that is topographically different and physically incompatible from the target behavior. The alternative behavior and the target behavior should cover the universe of possible behaviors. The third step is to identify the reinforcer to be used for the alternative response and to select a schedule of reinforcement.

Differential Reinforcement of Low rates of behavior (DRL) is a reinforcement procedure used to reduce behaviors that occur at a high frequency rate. In DRL the student is reinforced if the response rate is below an established criterion (Donnellan et al., 1988).

One variation of DRL is to reinforce the response if a specified interval of time has occurred since the last response and then gradually increase the interval. Another variation is to reinforce the behavior if the frequency is below baseline rate during a specified interval of time. When using the DRL procedure it is helpful to provide a tangible feedback system to the student so that he or she is aware of the contingency in place. One method of tangible feedback may be to have a container with marbles in it that correspond in number to the frequency of the behaviors that are allowed within the interval. Every time the behavior occurs, a marble is moved from one container to another. At the end of the interval, if marbles remain in the container the student is reinforced. If no marbles are left, the student does not receive reinforcement for that interval.

In implementing the DRL procedure, the teacher must first collect baseline data and establish the rate of the problem behavior. The second step is to select a monitoring system that will provide feedback to the learner about the contingency that is in place. The third step is to determine the initial interval size and reinforcement criteria. Donnellan et al. (1988) recommend that the initial criterion for reinforcement be the baseline rate. For example, if the student throws materials on the floor an average of 15 times a day, the teacher may begin the procedure by using 60-minute intervals within the 5-hour school day and reinforcing the student if the behavior occurs no more than three times per interval. Once a steady rate has been established, the criterion for reinforcement is lowered.

Response interruption procedures are used to prevent a behavior from occurring (Meyer & Evans, 1989). This can be done through the use of prosthetic devices, manual blocking, or cuing the learner. Prosthetic devices have been used to prevent the individual from being successful at exhibiting a behavior. For example, helmets have been used to prevent individuals who head-bang from hitting surfaces, and mittens have been used to prevent an individual from being successful at chewing his fingers. The use of prosthetic devices for this purpose is difficult because they often restrict the movement or sensory awareness of the individual and can be reacted to as if they are aversive. If prosthetic devices are used, every effort should be made to ensure that they do not restrict participation in functional activities, that they are normalized in appearance (e.g., a helmet that is covered by a baseball cap), and that they are not used as a contingent restraint or punishment procedure (Meyer & Evans, 1989).

In manual blocking, a procedure that involves physically blocking the individual from engaging in the target behavior, the interventionist interrupts the behavior by holding the individual's hands down briefly (e.g., when hitting) or preventing contact by blocking the physical action (e.g., hand to head) of the individual. Manual blocking is more effective if a staff person is assigned to shadow the individual when the behavior is likely to occur and to move in and block the behavior when it occurs. This shadow person does not socially interact with the individual but applies the procedure whenever necessary and reacts to the behavior in a completely neutral manner (Meyer & Evans, 1989).

A cuing procedure may be used if the individual shows some signs that indicate that the problem behavior is likely to occur. In this procedure, a verbal and/or physical cue is used to interrupt the behavior chain that leads to the problem behavior. For example, Mary began her tantrums by wringing her hands and reciting the schedule of events that were to occur that day. To prevent the tantrums, her teacher would say to her softly, "It's OK, Mary. Put your hands down. Everything will be fine."

Verbal reprimand is a punishment procedure in which an individual is provided with a firm reprimand following the target behavior. Verbal reprimands can be effective with even very serious behavior when the individual engaging in the behavior is motivated to please others (Meyer & Evans, 1989). A verbal reprimand is not yelling or berating the individual; it is a firm brief statement that is calmly delivered and describes the behavior that is not appropriate (e.g., "No, stop biting").

Time-out is a punishment procedure that is used for behavior that is motivated by social attention. In time-out the student is removed from the situation where reinforcement is available for a short amount of time. The student may be moved to a chair in the corner of the classroom or to an area that is away from the other students and activity. Time-out should be relatively brief, 3 to 5 minutes, with no activity or interaction with the student occurring during the period. When the time-out period is ended, the staff person should ask if the student is ready to return to the activity and, upon receiving a neutral or an affirmative answer, move the student back (Meyer & Evans, 1989). If the student is not calm or has persisted in the behavior, the time-out period should begin again. Time-out should reduce the behavior within several days if the procedure is the correct intervention selection. If no changes in the behavior are apparent after several days, a different procedure should be selected.

Brief contingent restraint is a punishment procedure that is used after a behavior occurs; it involves holding the individual's hands down briefly after he or she has engaged in an inappropriate behavior (Meyer & Evans, 1989). This type of procedure has been used for stereotypic hand movements or hitting behavior. It is important that the individual's hands are held down briefly (e.g., less than 30 seconds) and that the procedure does not provoke an escalation of the behavior (Meyer & Evans, 1989). When the interventionist releases the individual's hands, an opportunity for a positive alternative behavior should be provided.

It is important to note that all of the methods described in this section are only tools that can be used within an overall plan to change problem behavior. It is highly unlikely that any of these techniques used in isolation of a functional assessment or a comprehensive approach to behavior change will result in meaningful outcomes.

Teaching Functionally Equivalent Communication Skills

A critical component of the intervention plan is the instruction of new communication skills that are functionally equivalent to the problem behavior. To teach the new skill, the teacher must first identify skills that are equivalent to the problem behavior. For example, a student may scream and throw materials to indicate that he wants a break or he may ask for a break by holding up a card with *break* written on it. The selection of the functional equivalent is dependent on the functional assessment process. If that has been thoroughly conducted, the selection of the behavior to be taught is relatively straightforward.

The goal in the selection of a functionally equivalent communication skill is to give the student a more socially acceptable and easily understood mechanism for getting his or her needs met. When selecting skills to teach, the teacher should select responses that will be easy for the student to perform, easy for others to interpret, and usable in a variety of environments. In addition, the teacher must be sure that the new behavior will be efficient in achieving the desired response. For example, if a student pushes peers and adults to request a social interaction, the teacher may try to teach him or her to say "play with me." If the student has difficulty with speech and takes a long time to deliver the phrase, others will not consequate his behavior quickly, and he is likely to continue pushing, which will result in some kind of social response. In this situation, the teacher may want to teach the student a simple gesture, such as patting himself on the chest, and teach others how to respond to the gesture. This gesture may be paired with teaching the verbal request ("play with me"), but initial reinforcement (i.e., social contact) will be delivered on any approximation of the gesture.

When a functionally equivalent skill has been selected, the teacher must determine a method of instruction that will result in acquisition and generalization of the skill. It is essential that many opportunities for instruction or skill use be presented and that reinforcement be highly salient and immediate. For example, if a student cries and bangs her head to reject toys and activities, the teacher may decide to teach her to signal protest by using a push-away gesture. But if the only opportunities that are available to use the skill are during free play and center time, it is likely that the acquisition of the skill will be slow and that the problem behavior will persist. The teacher should try to increase the opportunities to use the protest gesture by offering items that she anticipates the student will reject. Increasing opportunities will give the student more trials of instruction and a higher density of reinforcement for appropriate skill use.

Developing Intervention Plans

When a functional assessment of problem behavior has occurred and hypotheses are defined, a behavior intervention plan may be developed. The plan should include components that will provide immediate interventions and solutions for problem behaviors as well as strategies to bring about long-term change in behavior and the acquisition of new skills (Meyer & Evans, 1989).

In one of the few "how to" manuals published on a functional approach to behavior intervention, Meyer and Evans (1989) describe four components of a behavior intervention plan (see Figure 11–6).

The first component, *short-term prevention procedures,* is a set of strategies that are used to prevent the behavior from occurring. These strategies, which are determined from the

1. Short-Term Prevention Procedures — Strategies that are used to reduce the frequency of occurrence of negative behaviors. Examples of strategies include schedule changes, modifications to the environment, and close supervision.
2. Immediate Consequences — Procedures that will be used if the behavior occurs. Examples of procedures may be ignoring, verbal reprimand, and crisis management procedures.
3. Adaptive Alternatives — Instruction in adaptive behaviors that are precise alternatives to the problem behavior. Examples of adaptive alternatives include specific communication utterances and social skills that match the function of the problem behavior.
4. Long-Term Prevention — Long-term goals that will support a decrease in the problem behavior and support the individual in new patterns of interaction with others. An example of long-term prevention procedures for a student who uses physical aggression to initiate social interactions are the long-term goals of establishing multiple friendships and enriched social activity schedule.

Figure 11–6

Four Components of a Behavior Intervention Plan

From *Nonaversive Intervention for Behavior Problems: A Manual for Home and Community* (pp. 63–84) by L. H. Meyer & I. M. Evans, 1989, Baltimore: Paul H. Brookes Publishing Co., P. O. Box 10624, Baltimore, Maryland 21285-0624. Reprinted by permission.

functional assessment of the behavior, reduce the frequency of the problem behavior until the student can learn replacement skills (Meyer & Evans, 1989). Short-term prevention strategies may include reinforcement strategies, response interruption techniques, or altering ecological and setting events. The second component of the behavior intervention plan is the description of procedures to be used when the behavior occurs. This component, *immediate consequences,* outlines what will occur if the student exhibits the target behavior. One option is to ignore the behavior if it occurs, which is effective if the function of the behavior is to gain attention and if the behavior is one that can be ignored. If the behavior is too disruptive or harmful to be ignored, a crisis management procedure such as behavior interruption or personal restraint may be used to prevent or interrupt the behavior.

The third component is the teaching of adaptive behaviors that are alternatives to the problem behavior. These *adaptive alternatives* may include teaching the student to request a break instead of throwing objects to express his frustration with a task or teaching him a more socially appropriate way to gain social attention than by hitting peers. Adaptive alternatives may involve the instruction of social, communication, and leisure skills. The selection of the adaptive alternatives is determined by the functional assessment of the problem behavior. If the problem behavior is related to task demands and lack of more conventional forms of communication, two adaptive alternatives may be to teach the student to become tolerant of work activities of increasing difficulty and to use a system of communication that others will recognize. This component is essential to the behavior intervention plan. Without the instruction of adaptive alternatives, the intervention plan will be focused only on reducing the problem behavior without replacing the behavior with new skills.

The fourth component of the intervention plan expands the focus on developing adaptive alternatives to the problem behavior to teaching the basic skills needed by the individual with disabilities to prevent the occurrence of problem behavior. If the individual has difficulty with task demands and communicating when he wants a break, a more general training program in self-regulation, work skills, and social interaction is needed. These *long-term prevention strategies* may include lifestyle changes in the areas of community integration, employment, or living that are needed to support the individual in the development of new behavior and the reduction of problem behavior.

In many situations, one individual (such as the teacher or the behavior specialist) is charged with responsibility for designing a behavior intervention plan. This approach is not desirable for these reasons: (1) functional assessment should involve a variety of individuals to gain a variety of perspectives, and (2) the persons who are involved in day-to-day interactions should be invested in the behavior intervention plan in order to be motivated to carry it out. When a team approach is used to develop an intervention plan, the likelihood of the plan's success is increased.

One of the first tasks of the team is to examine the individual's lifestyle. One method for accomplishing this may be to gather together people who know the individual well (e.g., parents, friends, therapists, teacher) and discuss the patterns of the individual's life. The processes suggested for personal futures planning (Mount & Zwernik, 1988) or lifestyle planning (O'Brien & Lyle, 1987) may be helpful in facilitating this discussion. Meyer and Evans (1989) suggest that the team discuss the individual's history, including an identification of the problem behavior, and then generate a "wish list" of the ideal program options and life experiences for the individual and a "now list" that includes goals from the "wish list" that can be implemented immediately.

Once the team has addressed the lifestyle issues of the individual who engages in problem behavior, the behavior intervention plan can be developed. The creation of the intervention plan is a dynamic process that should include the diverse perspectives of the collaborative team. As the plan is developed, the team should ensure that it:

1. Includes recommendations for lifestyle outcomes;
2. Focuses on the acquisition of skills rather than on behavior reduction;
3. Is matched to the functional assessment and hypotheses;
4. Includes procedures that are respectful and dignified.

The behavior plan should include all of the components previously discussed, as well as an identified process for evaluating its effectiveness. The process for evaluation should include data on the occurrences of the problem behavior and measures of skill acquisition and lifestyle changes.

Conclusion

In this chapter, the rationale and procedures for intervening in problem behavior have been presented. What is more difficult to convey, but as important, is the attitude of the interventionist as behavior intervention programs are designed. If the interventionist is going to be successful at meaningful behavior change, using positive intervention strategies, he or she must be ready to be persistent and creative. The methods for determining the functions of problem behavior and the design of intervention plans are only a process. This approach will not provide a cookbook of solutions to problem behavior. The interventionist must use his or her knowledge about the individual and ability to take the individual's perspective to develop an effective intervention plan. It may take many hours of analysis, brainstorming, and problem-solving to ultimately develop a behavior plan that is effective and respectful of the individual with disabilities.

Questions for Reflection

1. Why would understanding the history of interventions that have been tried with a student be important to the functional assessment process?
2. How important will knowledge of the student's expressive and communication abilities be in the functional assessment?
3. Think of a behavior of yours that you have successfully or unsuccessfully tried to change. Did you change ecological or setting events? Did you manipulate antecedents or consequences? Did you learn a new skill? If you were successful in changing your behavior, what outcome was the hallmark of your success?
4. If a student engages in behavior that may be dangerous to others, such as hitting or biting, should he or she be restricted from contact with other students until the behavior changes? Why or why not?
5. Some schools have schoolwide discipline plans, such as going to the office or suspensions after a specified number of rule infractions. Should these consequences also apply to students with severe disabilities? Why or why not?
6. A parent might use corporal punishment at home with a child with severe disabilities and request that the teacher use the same

procedures. How would you react to that request?

References

Baumeister, A. A., & Rollings, J. P. (1976). Self-injurious behavior. In N. R. Ellis (Ed.), *International review of research in mental retardation* (vol. 6, pp. 59–96). New York: Academic Press.

Borthwick, S. A., Meyers, C. E., & Eyman, R. K. (1981). Comparative adaptive and maladaptive behavior of mentally retarded clients of five residential settings in Western states. In R. H. Bruininks, C. E. Meyers, B. B. Sigford, & K. C. Lakin (Eds.), *Deinstitutionalization and community adjustment of mentally retarded people* (pp. 351–359). Washington, DC: American Association on Mental Deficiency.

Carr, E. G. (1977). The motivation of self-injurious behavior: A review of some hypotheses. *Psychological Bulletin, 84,* 800–816.

Carr, E. G., & Durand, V. M. (1985). Reducing behavior problems through functional communication training. *Journal of Applied Behavior Analysis, 18,* 111–126.

Carr, E. G., Newsom, C. D., & Binkoff, J. A. (1980). Escape as a factor in the aggressive behavior of two retarded children. *Journal of Applied Behavior Analysis, 13,* 101–117.

Carr, E. G., Robinson, S., & Palumbo, L. W. (1990). The wrong issue: Aversive versus nonaversive treatment. The right issue: Functional versus nonfunctional treatment. In A. C. Repp & N. N. Singh (Eds.), *Perspectives on the use of nonaversive and aversive interventions for persons with developmental disabilities* (pp. 361–379). Sycamore, IL: Sycamore Publishing Co.

Carr, E. G., Robinson, S., Taylor, J. C., & Carlson, J. I. (1990). *Positive approaches to the treatment of severe behavior problems in persons with developmental disabilities: A review and analysis of reinforcement and stimulus-based procedures.* Seattle, WA: The Association for Persons with Severe Handicaps.

Cataldo, M. F., & Harris, J. (1982). The biological basis for self-injury in the mentally retarded. *Analysis and Intervention in Developmental Disabilities, 2,* 21–39.

Deitz, S. M. (1978). Current status of applied behavior analysis: Science versus technology. *American Psychologist, 33,* 805–814.

Demchak, M. A., & Halle, J. W. (1985). Motivational assessment: A potential means of enhancing treatment success of self-injurious individuals. *Education and Training of the Mentally Retarded, 20,* 25–38.

Donnellan, A. M., LaVigna, G. W., Negri-Shoultz, N., & Fassbender, L. L. (1988). *Progress without punishment: Effective approaches for learners with behavior problems.* New York: Teachers College Press.

Donnellan, A. M., Mirenda, P. L., Mesaros, R. A., & Fassbender, L. L. (1984). Analyzing the communicative functions of aberrant behavior. *The Journal of the Association for Persons with Severe Handicaps, 9,* 201–212.

Dunlap, G., Kern-Dunlap, L., Clarke, S., & Robbins, F. R. (1991). Functional assessment, curricular revisions, and severe behavior problems. *Journal of Applied Behavior Analysis, 24,* 387–397.

Durand, V. M., & Crimmins, D. B. (1988). Identifying the variables maintaining self-injurious behavior. *Journal of Autism and Developmental Disorders, 18,* 99–117.

Evans, I. M., & Meyer, L. H. (1985). *An educative approach to behavior problems: A practical decision model for interventions with severely handicapped learners.* Baltimore: Paul H. Brookes.

Evans, I. M., & Meyer, L. H. (1990). Toward a science in support of meaningful outcomes: A response to Horner et al. *Journal of the Association for Persons with Severe Handicaps, 15,* 133–135.

Foxx, R. M. (1982). *Decreasing behaviors of severely retarded and autistic persons.* Champaign, IL: Research Press.

Gast, D. L., & Wolery, M. (1987). Severe maladaptive behaviors. In M. Snell (Ed.), *Systematic instruction of persons with severe handicaps* (3rd ed., pp. 300–332). Columbus, OH: Merrill.

Guess, D., Helmstetter, E., Turnbull, H. R., & Knowlton, S. (1987). *Use of aversive procedures with persons who are disabled: An historical review and critical analysis.* Seattle, WA: The Association for Persons with Severe Handicaps.

Hayes, S. C., Rincover, A., & Solnick, J. V. (1980). The technical drift of applied behavior analysis. *Journal of Applied Behavior Analysis, 13,* 275–285.

Horner, R. H., Dunlap, G., Koegel, R. L., Carr, E. G., Sailor, W., Anderson, J., Albin, R. W., & O'Neill, R. E. (1990). Toward a technology of "nonaversive" behavioral support. *Journal of the Association for Persons with Severe Handicaps, 15,* 125–132.

Iwata, B. A., Vollmer, T. R., & Zarcone, J. R. (1990). The experimental (functional) analysis of behavior disorders: Methodology, applications, and limitations. In A. C. Repp & N. N. Singh (Eds.), *Perspectives on the use of nonaversive and aversive interventions for persons with developmental disabilities* (pp. 301–330). Sycamore, IL: Sycamore Publishing Co.

Iwata, B. A., Wong, S. E., Reardon, M. M., Dorsey, M. F., & Lau, M. M. (1982). Assessment and training of clinical interviewing skills: Analogue analysis and field replication. *Journal of Applied Behavior Analysis, 15,* 191–204.

Lennox, D. B., & Miltenberger, R. G. (1989). Conducting a functional assessment of problem behavior in applied settings. *Journal of the Association for Persons with Severe Handicaps, 14,* 304–311.

Lennox, D. B., Miltenberger, R. G., Spengler, P., & Erfanian, N. (1988). Decelerative treatment practices with persons who have mental retardation: A review of five years of the literature. *American Journal on Mental Retardation, 92,* 492–501.

Lundervold, D., & Bourland, G. (1988). Quantitative analysis of treatment of aggression, self-injury, and property destruction. *Behavior Modification, 12,* 590–617.

Maisto, C. R., Baumeister, A. B., & Maisto, A. A. (1977). An analysis of variables related to self-injurious behavior among institutionalized retarded persons. *Journal of Mental Deficiency Research, 12,* 232–239.

Meyer, L. H., & Evans, I. M. (1989). *Nonaversive intervention for behavior problems: A manual for home and community.* Baltimore: Paul H. Brookes.

Miltenberger, R. G., & Veltum, L. (1988). Evaluation of an instruction and modeling procedure for training behavioral assessment interviewing. *Journal of Behavior Therapy and Experimental Psychiatry, 19,* 31–41.

Mount, B., & Zwernik, K. (1988). *It's never too early, it's never too late. A booklet about personal futures planning.* St. Paul, MN: Metropolitan Council.

O'Brien, J., & Lyle, C. (1987). *Framework for accomplishment.* Decatur, GA: Responsive System Associates.

O'Neill, R. E., Horner, R. H., Albin, R. W., Storey, K., & Sprague, J. R. (1990). *Functional analysis of problem behavior: A practical assessment guide.* Sycamore, IL: Sycamore Publishing Co.

Rincover, A., & Devany, J. (1982). The application of sensory extinction procedures to self-injury. *Analysis and Intervention in Developmental Disabilities, 2,* 67–81.

Schroeder, S. R., Schroeder, C. S., Smith, B., & Dalldorf, J. (1978). Prevalence of self-injurious behaviors in a large state facility for the retarded: A three-year follow-up. *Journal of Autism and Childhood Schizophrenia, 8,* 261–270.

Schuler, A. L., & Goetz, L. (1981). The assessment of severe language disabilities: Communicative and cognitive considerations. *Analysis and Intervention in Developmental Disabilities, 1,* 333–346.

Skinner, B. F. (1953). *Science and human behavior.* New York: Free Press.

Skinner, B. F. (1959). Current trends in experimental psychology. In B. F. Skinner, *Cumulative record* (pp. 23–241). New York: Appleton-Century-Crofts.

Touchette, P. E., MacDonald, R. F., & Langer, S. N. (1985). A scatter plot for identifying stimulus control of problem behavior. *Journal of Applied Behavior Analysis, 18,* 343–351.

Ullmann, L. P., & Krasner, L. (Eds.). (1965). *Case studies in behavior modification.* New York: Holt, Rinehart, & Winston.

Weeks, M., & Gaylord-Ross, R. (1981). Task difficulty and aberrant behavior in severely handicapped students. *Journal of Applied Behavior Analysis, 14,* 449–463.

White, O. R. (1971). *A glossary of behavioral terminology.* Champaign, IL: Research Press.

Winterling, V., Dunlap, G., & O'Neill, R. (1987). The influence of task variation on the aberrant behavior of autistic students. *Education and Treatment of Children, 10,* 105–119.

CHAPTER 12

Managing Sensory and Motor Disabilities

Chapter Overview

In this chapter, techniques are provided that may be used to support students who have motor and sensory disabilities. The chapter begins with a description of motor and sensory development and describes the need for intervention when there are disabilities in these areas. Basic positioning and handling techniques for students with motor disabilities are described and intervention approaches that may be recommended are explained. A general overview of the impact of hearing and vision impairments on students with severe disabilities is presented and methods for supporting students with sensory impairments are described.

Teachers who work in the field of severe disabilities are encountering an increase among students who may be labeled multiply disabled because they have physical and/or sensory impairments in addition to mental disabilities. This increase may be due to several factors: the increasing number of children who are low birth weight and survive, the use of medical intervention procedures in the neonatal period that affect sensorimotor development, the increase in enrollment of students with multiple disabilities in public schools, and the ability to diagnose sensory impairments with students who in the past were thought to be untestable. Students with multiple disabilities may experience cerebral palsy, skeletal deformities, sensory disorders, seizure disorders, respiratory difficulties, and other medical problems (Orelove & Sobsey, 1991). The needs of such students require that special educators team with professionals from a variety of fields (e.g., physical therapy, occupational therapy, respiratory therapy, nursing) and implement systematic instruction and physical management that is sensitive to the unique needs of the student.

Collaborative teaming is an essential component of instruction of students with multiple impairments whose unique needs require the expertise of professionals who are trained in a variety of disciplines. The term *collaborative teaming* reflects the combination of an integrated therapy approach and transdisciplinary teaming (Rainforth, York, & MacDonald, 1992). The transdisciplinary team model is one where team members work across discipline boundaries to train each other in the skills and techniques needed to best meet the needs of the student. The integrated therapy approach adds to the transdisciplinary model by emphasizing that instruction and therapy should take place in natural contexts.

The goal of the collaborative team is to design and implement instructional programs for students with severe disabilities. The team is structured in such a way that decisions are made through consensus with equal participation of all team members, including the family. The team members infuse their discipline-specific knowledge into the design of instructional programs that will provide for the instruction of embedded sensorimotor and communication skills within instructional interventions. Family members on the collaborative team provide their intimate knowledge of their child's development, personality, skills, and needs in different environments. An educational program that is designed through collaborative teaming offers the student with disabilities the advantages of the knowledge and skills of professionals from diverse disciplines who work together with the family to provide an appropriate program. Educational programs that are provided by collaborative teams are more likely to have less duplication of services, provide more consistent attention to student needs, and are more likely to result in the integration of discipline-specific knowledge and skills into instructional programs (Albano, Cox, York, & York, 1981).

In this chapter, basic information on the management of sensorimotor and physical disabilities is presented. The chapter begins with a description of the development of the sensorimotor systems and the impact of disability on movement ability. Techniques for facilitating the posture and movement of students are described, and suggestions are given for the provision of systematic instruction that addresses the movement needs of the student. The chapter also describes the effect of sensory impairments on the student with severe disabilities, addressing the needs of the student with sensory impairments and offering techniques for instruction.

The Sensory Systems

People move by integrating the motor and sensory areas of the central nervous and muscular systems (Cusick, 1991). The sensory system integrates information from environmental stimuli, creating complex maps of the person and the environment (Dunn, 1991). The motor system uses these maps to execute movements in response to environmental demands (Dunn, 1991). It is important to understand the interdependence of the motor and sensory systems when designing interventions for students with multiple disabilities. Individuals with multiple disabilities may show evidence of atypical development or involvement in any of those systems. When instructional personnel understand the functioning of the motor and sensory systems, they can adapt activities that build on intact systems and minimize the effects of involved systems (Dunn, 1991).

Sensations from the environment provide the individual with information to facilitate the development of skills. The *somatosensory* system responds to touch input through receptors on the skin (Dunn, 1991). Variations of touch by changes in pressure, temperature, duration, and so forth provide information to the individual about himself or herself and the environment. The *proprioceptive* system responds to the positioning of the body in space and the movement of muscles. Proprioceptive input provides the nervous system with the input needed to create maps of the body as it moves in space. The *vestibular* system's receptor is housed in the inner ear and serves to orient the head in space. When the vestibular receptors are activated through shifts in balance or equilibrium, the vestibular system generates muscle actions to maintain the person in an upright position.

The *gustatory* (taste) and *olfactory* (smell) systems use chemical receptors to discriminate sensory input. The *auditory* system uses receptors housed in the ear to process sound, which is used by an individual to map the environment and to communicate with people in the environment. The *visual* system uses receptors housed in the eyeball to decode and transmit images from the environment. It assists the individual in motor movement and depends on the proprioceptive and vestibular system as an interface between the visual and motor systems.

Students with severe disabilities often experience and integrate sensory input in atypical ways. Damage to the central nervous system, specific genetic abnormalities, and the lack of experiences of students with severe disabilities may result in responses to sensorimotor input

ing position, is activated by turning the head to one side, which causes the arm and leg of the side of the body toward which the head is turned to extend. The arm and leg on the side of the body toward which the back of the head is turned are flexed. The ATNR reflex can interfere with feeding, use of the hands in a midline position, and symmetry of the body. For example, a student who has an active ATNR reflex may have difficulty when a switch toy is presented to the side for activation. If the student turns his head to look toward the object, his arm and leg extend, making it difficult to activate the switch. A better way to present the switch toy would be in a midline or when the student is in a side-lying position.

The Symmetrical Tonic Neck Reflex is activated by bending the neck forward and back. When the neck is bent backward (extended), the arms straighten and the legs bend; when the neck is bent forward (flexed), the arms bend and the legs straighten. The STNR can interfere in crawling, using the arms when sitting, and maintaining a functional sitting position.

The Tonic Labyrinthine Reflex (TLR) is triggered by the position of the head in relation to gravity. When the individual is supine (placed on his or her back), an attempt to lift the head results in leg extension. When the individual is in a prone position (placed on his or her stomach), an attempt to lift the head results in leg flexion. The presence of a TLR keeps the individual from shifting positions when supine or prone. Supine positioning with the head, shoulders, and hips flexed will help decrease or minimize the effects of the TLR.

Posture and Movement

The movements that people perform are composed of a complex array of components. Individuals with physical disabilities who have atypical muscle tone, primitive reflexes, difficulties with postural balance and stability, and deformities may not be able to perform some of the motor components of tasks or may use abnormal posture or movement patterns in performing those tasks. Continued practice of abnormal movement patterns can lead to secondary problems of changes in muscle length and subsequent orthopedic problems (Campbell, 1987b, 1989). Thus, early intervention in motor problems is particularly critical.

Early motor development during the infancy period is focused on establishing movement against gravity. For example, an infant learns to lift his or her head against gravity. These movements are accomplished through muscle contraction. To move the head from side to side requires the activation of the neck muscles and the co-contraction of muscles to maintain postural stability against gravity (Campbell, 1987b). If the infant has atypical muscle tone, the movement that results is often atypical. For example, one way individuals with low tone compensate for the lack of muscle strength in the head and neck is by elevating the shoulders so that less effort is needed to maintain the head erect.

The use of atypical postures is the beginning of a cycle (see Figure 12–1) that results in impaired posture and movement and, for some individuals, permanent deformities. If compensatory motor patterns are allowed to become habitual, they can result in secondary problems of muscle shortening or elongation. These changes in muscle length can result in orthopedic changes or deformities that may be correctable only through surgery (Campbell, 1987b).

The goal of the intervention team is to develop a consistent intervention program of positioning, handling, and facilitating movement in an effort to elicit more normal muscle tone and facilitate normal posture and move-

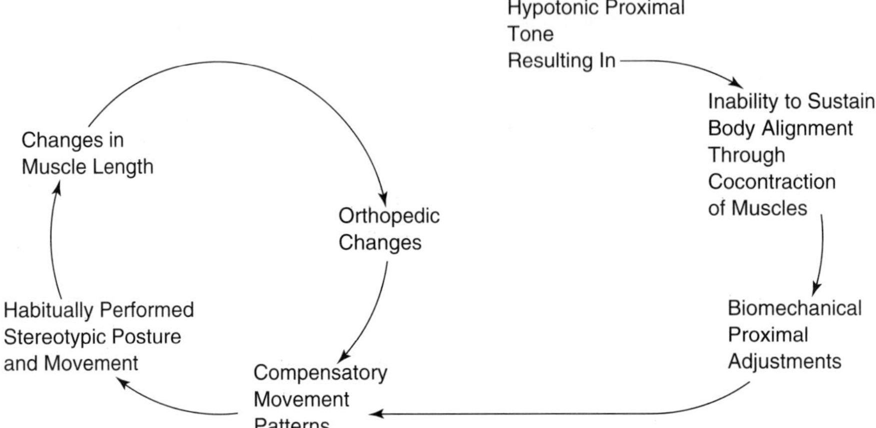

Figure 12–1
Cycle of Development of Abnormal Movement
From "Integrated Programming and Movement Disabilities" (p. 268) by P. H. Campbell & S. Forsyth, in *Instruction of Students with Severe Disabilities*, Fourth Edition, by Martha Snell. Copyright © 1993 by Macmillan College Publishing Company. Reprinted with permission.

ment patterns (Rainforth & York, 1991). A common approach that has been used to enhance functioning in posture and movement is based on a remedial perspective (Campbell, 1989). In this approach the individual is assessed by examining current levels of functioning in gross motor milestones and then determining goals and objectives. In cases where individuals have disorders that will not respond to remedial interventions because of the severity of the disorder, the quality of previous intervention efforts, or the age of the individual, a compensatory approach may be more effective (Campbell, 1989). In a compensatory approach, the intervention team designs programming that includes strategies that will compensate for existing impairments and prevent secondary disorders. The areas of concern for team members will be methods for positioning the individual to prevent secondary disorders (muscle overlengthening or shortening, orthopedic deformities) and to enhance independent functioning and methods for handling the individual that will facilitate functional movement and normalized patterns. In the next sections, procedures for using appropriate body mechanics while repositioning the individual with physical disabilities, ways to position the individual, and methods for facilitating appropriate posture and movement will be presented.

Positioning and Handling

Students with multiple disabilities require an educational program that is designed with the expertise of a team of professionals, which should include a physical therapist and/or an occupational therapist. These therapists will recommend treatment methods that include preparation to attain tone normalization and muscle lengthening for body alignment, control of environmental and sensory influences, facilitation of movement through space, and the maintenance of body alignment and muscle length (Campbell, 1987b). Proper procedures for teachers to use are discussed in the following sections, beginning with the use of body mechanics when handling the student with disabilities. It is important to note that all of the procedures described in this chapter should be performed only after instruction or training has been provided by the therapist. Teachers place themselves and their students at risk of injury if appropriate guidance has not been received. Subsequent sections include facilitating posture and movement and the use of therapeutic physical management techniques and positioning.

Body Mechanics

It is critically important to your safety and the safety of the student with disabilities that good body mechanics be used when lifting and transferring the student. An unsafe lift or transfer can cause permanent damage to the lifter's back and can jeopardize the safety of the student. The most important rule to remember when lifting is to keep your trunk in an erect posture, bending your legs rather than your back. The second rule is to keep the load that is lifted as close to your body as possible and within the safe work zone, which is between your hips and mid-chest.

Before lifting or transferring an individual, you should plan the transfer, arrange the environment so that the transfer can occur easily, and decide if assistance is needed to conduct the lift (Rainforth & York, 1991). Assistance may be needed if the student is heavy, is unable to assist in the lift or transfer, or has movement patterns that may make handling difficult.

If the student is positioned on the floor, you should squat or kneel beside the child as closely as possible. Tell the student that you are going to lift him and request his assistance if he is capable. It is extremely important to tell the student what you are going to do before you do it so that he can anticipate the movement, prepare himself, and partially participate in the transfer. Bring the child onto your lap or close to your trunk, distribute his weight over your hips, and then conduct the lift. When two adults are needed to conduct the lift, one adult can lift the child's arms and upper body while the other holds the student's hips and legs. Principles for using good body mechanics when lifting are presented in Figure 12–2.

One person can lift and carry a student who is small. A young student who is spastic (predominantly high tone) and primarily extended should be assisted to sit up and assume a symmetrical position before being lifted. A student with a strong extensor pattern should be rolled to the side slightly to make bending his or her head and hips easier before lifting. One way to hold the student with an extensor pattern is in a sitting position with his or her hips and knees bent and arms over the adult's shoulders, as shown in Figure 12–3.

The young student who is athetoid (writhing movement within the muscles) should be lifted by first flexing her hips and legs next to her trunk and gathering her arms across her chest or around her legs. The athetoid child who has uncontrolled and continuous unwanted movements should be provided with steady and firm handling that provides as much stability as possible (Finnie, 1974). Support the student with one or both arms under her knees. If you have one arm under the student's knees, your free arm can be used to secure her arms, as in Figure 12–4. An alternative is to secure the student's hands around her flexed lower extremities with your hands over hers as shown in Figure 12–5.

The low-tone child should be provided with steady handling at the shoulders and arms so it is easier for him to control his head and should be carried in a way that provides adequate stability and support at the hips to

1. If the student is able to assist you with the transfer, move at his pace so that he can work with you.
2. If you are unsure of your ability to lift alone, ask someone to help you.
3. When lifting a student, always know his abilities first. Explain what you plan to do before lifting or transferring and encourage the student to assist wherever possible.
4. Assess the environment and make sure your pathway is clear. Arrange equipment and situations so the least amount of work is required.
5. Stay close to the student you are lifting. If necessary, squat or kneel on the floor next to him to gather him up.
6. Maintain a wide, stable base of support by planting your feet flat on the floor and spreading them apart.
7. Line yourself up with the student so that you can maintain a straight back throughout the lift.
8. Never twist your trunk while lifting. Instead, pivot on your feet, keep your back straight, and move your feet, legs, and trunk as a unit.
9. Use your leg muscles when lifting and lowering. Actively tighten your abdominal muscles to establish good pelvic stability and continue to breathe regularly.
10. When two people lift together, make sure the lift is smooth and well-timed to prevent sudden, jerky movements. Plan the lift together and coordinate your movements by counting aloud, "one, two, three."
11. Make sure the student you are transferring feels as secure as possible.

Figure 12–2
Principles of Correct Body Mechanics
From *Teaching Nontherapists to Do Positioning and Handling in Educational Settings* by N. Cicirello, J. Hyltm, P. Reed, & S. Hall, 1989, Portland, OR: Child Development and Rehabilitation Center Publications, Oregon Health Sciences University. Adapted by permission of CDRC Publications.

encourage him to extend his head and back. Holding the child so he faces the direction in which he is moving will increase his motivation to hold his head erect, as shown in Figure 12–6.

Facilitating Posture and Movement

Although there are many times that a student must be lifted or carried by an adult, it is essential that students with physical disabilities be helped and encouraged to participate in the movement as actively as possible. The teacher usually supports and handles the student from key points of control; the head, shoulders, trunk, and pelvis are the areas of the body where abnormal postures and movement patterns are most easily interrupted and more normal postures and movement patterns can be facilitated (Finnie, 1974; Rainforth & York, 1991).

The touch that the teacher uses when handling the student depends on the student's muscle tone, reaction to tactile stimulation, and the nature of the motor movement. The therapist on the collaborative team should provide team members with guidance on the touch to use with each individual student. In general, a firm, deep touch should be used with students who have high tone or who are hypertonic; a light, active touch should be used with students who are hypotonic or low tone to awaken the muscles and initiate postural adjustments. Quick light touches cue muscles to

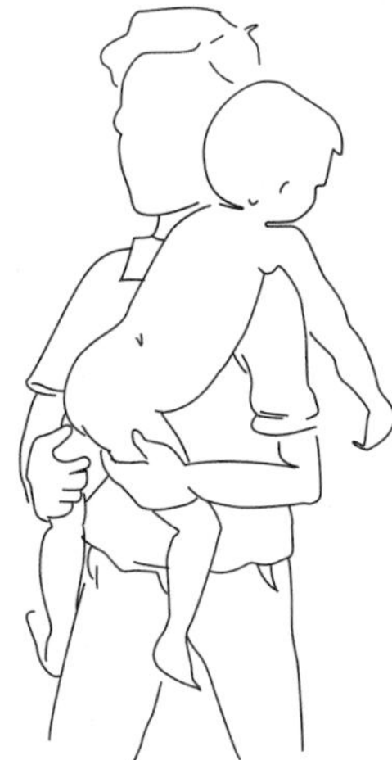

Figure 12–3
Carrying a Child with Spasticity
From *Handling the Young Cerebral Palsied Child at Home* (2nd ed.) by Nancie R. Finnie. Copyright © 1974 by Nancie R. Finnie, F.C.S.P.; additions for U.S. Edition, copyright © 1975 by E. P. Dutton & Co., Inc. Used by permission of Dutton Signet, a division of Penguin Books USA Inc.

move; firm sustained touches cue muscles to hold a position.

When facilitating a movement, the teacher should first consider where the student's center of gravity is prior to the movement, where the student is bearing weight before the movement, what reactions are desired from the student when a weight shift occurs, which muscles have been properly elongated, what the next movement will be, and the final destination point of the movement. For example, to assist a student to move from a bench to sitting on the floor, the student would first be facilitated to place his hands on the side of the bench and pivot onto his hands so he turns onto his stomach, and then facilitated to lower himself to his knees. Once on his knees, he is helped to place one hand on the floor and lower his trunk, then place the other hand on the floor so that he assumes a four-point position on the floor. The student is then facilitated to rotate his pelvis and lower himself into a side-sit position.

Therapists should teach team members the techniques they need to assist students in changing position and maintaining appropriate postures. Techniques that may be used include: (1) rolling a student who exhibits a strong extensor pattern to the side to inhibit the extension, (2) flexing and rotating the student to inhibit extension, (3) stimulating the muscle tone of a low-tone child to elicit participation in movement, and (4) using key points of control to facilitate movement. Therapists should also train team members in techniques to prevent secondary disabilities. Those techniques include positioning the student appropriately and providing therapeutic activities intended to maintain muscle length.

Positioning

The student with physical disabilities must be placed in varied positions to: (1) promote active participation in activities; (2) prevent the development or progression of deformities and

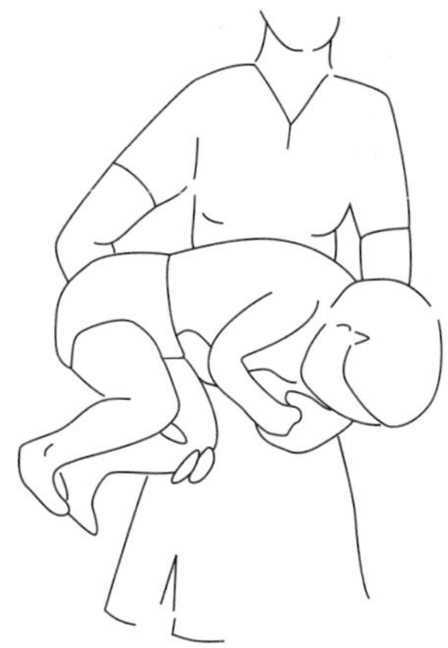

Figure 12–4
Lifting the Child Who Is Athetoid
From *Handling the Young Cerebral Palsied Child at Home* (2nd ed.) by Nancie R. Finnie. Copyright © 1974 by Nancie R. Finnie, F.C.S.P.; additions for U.S. Edition, copyright © 1975 by E. P. Dutton & Co., Inc. Used by permission of Dutton Signet, a division of Penguin Books USA Inc.

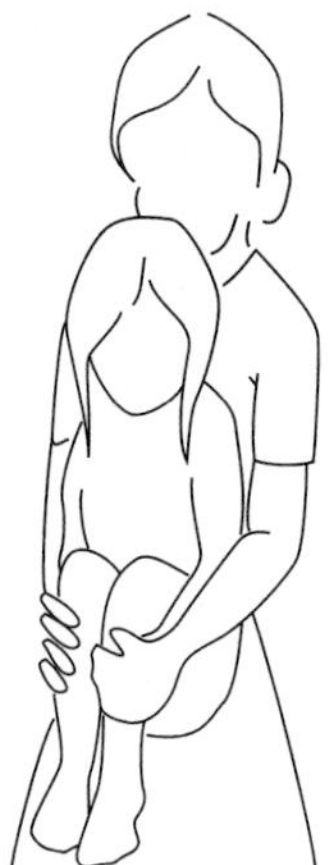

Figure 12–5
An Alternative Way of Lifting the Child Who Is Athetoid
From *Handling the Young Cerebral Palsied Child at Home* (2nd ed.) by Nancie R. Finnie. Copyright © 1974 by Nancie R. Finnie, F.C.S.P.; additions for U.S. Edition, copyright © 1975 by E. P. Dutton & Co., Inc. Used by permission of Dutton Signet, a division of Penguin Books USA Inc.

skin breakdowns; (3) provide weight-bearing experiences; (4) facilitate circulatory, respiratory, and digestive functions; and (5) allow mobility. Often individuals who are nonambulatory are positioned in a sitting position for most of the day, which enhances the individual's ability to participate in activities, but may also affect muscle length and spinal musculature that can lead to deformities (Campbell, 1989). Alternate positions must be provided to place the muscle groups that are at risk for muscle overlengthening or shortening into the opposite length (Campbell, 1989). For example, a student who is low tone and spends a large amount of time in an upright position may develop shortened lateral flexors or lower back muscles because he or she leans to the side or falls forward over the pelvis. This student should also spend time in a supported weight-bearing position (standing or side-lying) that will promote muscle stretching and lengthening.

The positioning of a student can be described as dynamic or static (Rainforth & York, 1991). Dynamic positioning refers to the use of techniques to modify tone, stabilize and align body parts, and facilitate the active movement of the student. Static positioning is performed with adaptive equipment and has the advantage of freeing the team member from having to provide one-to-one assistance.

The collaborative team should decide on the positions that are most appropriate for the student with disabilities. Positions that are selected should be functional, comfortable, and therapeutic. It is essential that the adaptive equipment that is selected for use as positioning aids be well fitted to the student. The positions that are selected for use in the classroom and community must also be age-appropriate and functional for the activity. For example, standing and sitting are the most age-appropriate and functional positions for most classroom activities, although a prone position on the floor or supine lying might be used while reading or

Figure 12–6
Carrying the Child with Low Tone
From *Handling the Young Cerebral Palsied Child at Home* (2nd ed.) by Nancie R. Finnie. Copyright © 1974 by Nancie R. Finnie, F.C.S.P.; additions for U.S. Edition, copyright © 1975 by E. P. Dutton & Co., Inc. Used by permission of Dutton Signet, a division of Penguin Books USA Inc.

during recreational time if nondisabled students assume those positions as well. Rainforth and York (1991) suggest that the team use the following considerations in selecting a position and positioning equipment:

1. What positions do nondisabled peers use when they engage in that activity?
2. Which of these positions allow easy view of and access to activity materials and equipment?
3. Do the positions allow for proximity to peers?
4. Do the positions promote efficient movement as needed to perform the task?
5. What positions provide alternatives to overused postures or equipment?
6. If positioning equipment is required, is it unobtrusive, cosmetically acceptable, and not physically isolating?
7. Is the positioning equipment safe and easy to handle?
8. Is the equipment individually selected and modified to match individual learner needs?
9. Is the equipment available in and/or easily transported to natural environments?

When positions that use adaptive equipment are selected for students, it is helpful to take a Polaroid photograph of the student appropriately positioned. This photograph can be used for reference when he or she is being positioned and the therapist is not available to monitor correct placement. In addition to having access to such a photograph, the teacher should know why the position is being used, what activities are appropriate for the position, how long the student can remain in the position, if there are special precautions associated with the position, and what physical conditions of the student (e.g., placement, pressure points) should be monitored (Cicirello et al., 1989). Common positions and their advantages and disadvantages are described in Table 12–1.

Students with physical disabilities often spend most of the school day in a seated position (Hulme, Poor, Schulein, & Pezzino, 1983; Kohn, Enders, Preston, & Motloch, 1983). Because adapted wheelchairs do not always meet the physical needs of these students (Rainforth & York, 1991), educators should have a thorough understanding of the principles of seating so problems can be minimized.

The optimal position for the pelvis in a seated position is with the hips flexed to 90 degrees and the pelvis symmetrical and tilted slightly forward. The pelvis can be supported in this position by using a lap belt across the hip joint. The weight of the student should be evenly distributed across both buttocks and thighs. A firm seat (rather than a sling) will support the symmetrical positioning of the hip and pelvis. Each thigh should be fully supported, with the seat extending to one inch back from the calf (Rainforth & York, 1991). Students with leg-length differences or a deviation of both legs to one side require lengthening the chair seat to fully support both thighs. The trunk should be held in a symmetrical, midline position. Some students may need to use chest support in addition to the lap belt to hold the trunk upright.

Feet should be positioned flat with the toes forward on a footrest. The footrest should be low enough so the thighs are resting flat on the seat but not so low that the feet hang or so high that the thighs are lifted from the seat. Heel straps, when prescribed, help secure the foot to the footrest. When trays are placed on adapted chairs, they should be high enough that the student can rest his elbows and forearms on the tray (Rainforth & York, 1991) without raising his shoulders. A tray offers the student with poor head and trunk control a surface to lean on and provides greater stability. The tray can also provide a place to support a

Table 12–1
Positions for Students with Physical Disabilities

Position	Advantages	Disadvantages
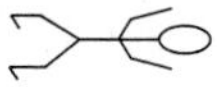 Prone	Normal resting position; requires no motor control; promotes trunk and hip extension	Possibility of suffocation; stimulates asymmetry if head turned to side; may stimulate flexor tone; functional activities limited
 Supine	Normal resting position; requires little motor control; no danger of suffocation; symmetry can be maintained	May stimulate extensor tone; prolonged position inhibits respiration; possibility of aspiration; ceiling view; functional activities limited
 Prone on elbows	Encourages head, arm, and trunk control; allows improved view	May stimulate flexor tone; may stimulate excessive extension; tiring position; limits hand use
 Side-lying	Normal resting position; usually does not stimulate abnormal tone; improves alignment, brings hands together at midline	May require bulky equipment; sideward view; few functional activities; pressure on bony prominences (hips)
 Side-sitting	Easy to assume from lying, hands and knees, kneeling; promotes trunk rotation, range of motion in hips, trunk if sides alternated	May reinforce asymmetry; may require one or both hands for support; difficult with tight hips or trunk
 Indian or ring sitting	Wide base of support; symmetrical position; easier to free hands	Difficult transition to/from other positions; may reinforce flexed posture
 Long sitting	May provide wide base of support; may prevent hamstring contractures	Impossible with tight hamstrings; may stimulate trunk flexion, flexor spasticity
 Heel or W-sitting	Easy transition to/from other positions; stable base of support; frees hands	Reinforces hip, knee, and ankle deformity; reduces reciprocal movement, weight-shifting, and trunk rotation
 Chair sitting—standard chair	Normal position and equipment; easy transition to/from other positions; minor adaptations can be added to improve position	May not provide adequate position for feet, trunk, hips; may be overused

Adapted from "Handling and Positioning" by B. Rainforth and J. York, 1991, in *Educating Children with Multiple Disabilities: A Transdisciplinary Approach*, Second Edition (pp. 89-90), by F. P. Orelove & D. Sobsey, Baltimore: Paul H. Brookes Publishing Co., P.O. Box 10624, Baltimore, Maryland 21285-0624.

communication device or serve as a work surface.

A challenge when positioning a student with multiple handicaps upright is maintaining the head in an upright position. The ideal head position is erect with the chin in a tucked position. Some students may benefit from headrests that serve to guide head placement (Fraser, Hensinger, Phelps, & Jacques, 1987); others may need head support equipment that is more elaborate and support the head completely.

Instructional Programming

In addition to physical management and positioning, individuals with multiple disabilities should be provided with intervention and therapy to assist in maintaining and developing motoric skills. In a collaborative team, the person who is with the student during instruction (the teacher or the paraprofessional) is primarily responsible for carrying out intervention plans. Through the collaborative teaming process, therapists work with other team members to select the approaches that are appropriate for individual students and provide training in the use of intervention techniques. In addition, the family members and educator on the team show the therapist techniques that may be effective and evaluate with the therapist the functional utility of proposed interventions. Some of the common approaches to motor intervention are neurodevelopmental treatment, sensory integration, and behavioral programming.

Sensory Integration

Sensory integration therapy is a neurobiological model of intervention that was designed to be used with individuals with learning disabilities (Arendt, MacLean, & Baumeister, 1988; Dunn, 1991). Sensory integrative approaches have also been extended to applications with individuals with multiple disabilities, although there is little research documenting benefits for that population (Arendt et al., 1988; Horn, 1991).

Sensory integration, which involves sensory stimulation to the individual to improve the way the brain processes and organizes sensations (Ayres, 1979), is based on the theory that sensory stimulation is necessary to improve the sensory processing capabilities of the brain that are needed for subsequent learning tasks.

Interventions that use a sensory integrative approach may involve adapting a learning activity to provide sensory integrative experiences within the activity or may involve activities that are specifically designed to match the sensory input needs of an individual student. The techniques used may involve rubbing the student with textured items to provide tactile stimulation; moving the child on a therapy ball, in a net, or on a scooter board to provide vestibular stimulation; or positioning the student in a way to accommodate sensory input within a learning activity.

Neurodevelopmental Treatment

Neurodevelopmental Treatment (NDT) involves identifying the posture and movement problems of individuals with neurological dysfunction and designing interventions that will decrease the effects of abnormal muscle tone and increase the normal muscle action for functional movement (Bobath, 1980). Intervention strategies that use an NDT approach consist of inhibiting abnormal patterns of posture and movement, normalizing muscle tone, and facilitating equilibrium reactions (Bobath, 1980).

The NDT approach involves direct intervention to affect muscle tone and guide patterns of posture and movement. The interventionist is first concerned with establishing body alignment and normalized muscle tone. He or she moves the child through movement patterns that facilitate desired muscle actions and inhibit atypical movement patterns. These patterns are embedded in functional routines and skills. Many therapists report that an NDT approach results in qualitative changes in the student's movement, although little empirical evidence exists to support these claims (Horn, 1991; Stern & Gorga, 1988).

Behavioral Programming Intervention

The behavioral programming approach to motor intervention involves the use of behavioral principles to train motor behavior. The motor skills are taught using prompting, shaping, and contingent reinforcement (Horn, 1991).

In the behavioral programming approach, which is common to educators and psychologists but less familiar to therapists, behavioral principles are used to establish changes in motor behavior. There is substantive research that supports the use of this approach with students who have multiple disabilities (Ball, McCrady, & Hart, 1975; Filler & Kasari, 1981; Grove & Dalke, 1976; Horn & Warren, 1987; Lee, Mahler, & Westling, 1985; Leiper, Miller, Lang, & Herman, 1981; Richman & Kazlowski, 1977; Skrotzky, Gallenstein, & Osternig, 1978). Through collaborative teaming, therapists and educators can design motor intervention programs that combine knowledge from different disciplines to design maximally effective programs.

Integrated Programming

Regardless of the intervention approach recommended by a therapist, it is critical that intervention techniques be integrated into instructional and activity routines (Campbell, 1987a) and that the strategies that are used are developed by the collaborative team including the family. Team members must combine their expertise to develop a functional instructional program that will enhance the student's participation and independent functioning in natural settings. Any adaptations, positions, or therapy techniques that are selected must be carefully considered in regard to how they can be used in natural environments (including the home and community) by a variety of interventionists. Techniques that require isolated treatment or specialized equipment may not provide enough benefit to outweigh the isolation that will be imposed upon the student with severe disabilities. If the techniques, positions, and adaptations that are selected can be used by a variety of interventionists in a variety of natural environments, positive outcomes are far more likely to occur.

Sensory Impairments

The prevalence of vision and hearing impairments among persons with severe disabilities is not well determined (Fredericks & Baldwin, 1987; Sobsey & Wolf-Schein, 1991). The accuracy of a prevalence figure is affected by the differences in definitions used by prevalence surveys and differences in sampling procedures (Sobsey & Wolf-Schein, 1991). Despite the difficulty in achieving an accurate estimate of prevalence, it is clear that vision and hearing impairments occur more frequently in individuals with multiple disabilities than in other persons (Sobsey & Wolf-Schein, 1991). The conditions that result in severe and multiple disabilities are frequently related to visual and hearing impairments. Teachers of students with severe disabilities should expect to encounter students with sensory impairments and must be able to work with team members in the assessment of sensory impairments as well as in determining adaptations that can be made to enhance students' learning potential. In the following sections of this chapter, hearing and visual impairments are described and strategies for assisting the learner with sensory impairments are discussed.

Hearing Impairments

Hearing impairments are described by the type of loss and the degree of impairment. There are four types of hearing loss:

1. Conductive: an impairment that results from an obstruction in the pathway from the ear canal to the inner ear. Conductive losses are caused by otitis media (middle ear infection), ear wax, or structural abnormality.
2. Sensorineural: an impairment that is caused by damage to the inner ear or to the auditory (vestibulocochlear) nerve. Sensorineural losses are caused by infections, genetic conditions, or ototoxic (harmful to hearing) drugs.
3. Mixed: impairments that are both conductive and sensorineural.
4. Central Auditory Disorders: impairments that are caused by damage to the central nervous system in a way that prohibits the individual from responding meaningfully to sound.

Degree of hearing loss is defined as mild, moderate, moderately severe, severe, and profound. Decibel ranges are used to describe hearing sensitivity. Most people with normal hearing can hear tones of 10 to 20 decibels in a quiet room (Niswander, 1987); persons who have a hearing threshold that is no poorer than 25 decibels are considered to have normal hearing.

Individuals with mild loss have a hearing sensitivity that falls in the 25- to 40-decibel range. A moderate hearing loss involves a sensitivity threshold in the 40- to 55-decibel range; individuals with a moderate loss may have to strain to hear conversational speech, which is usually in the 40- to 45-decibel range. A moderately severe loss is comprised of a sensitivity threshold of 55 to 70 decibels; individuals with a hearing loss in this range are unable to hear normal conversational speech, but may be able to hear if the speaker is close by and shouting. A severe hearing loss involves a hearing threshold of in the 70- to 90-decibel range; individuals with a severe hearing loss are unable to discriminate speech sound and are able to hear only very intense sounds such as a car horn (Niswander, 1987). A profound hearing loss involves a hearing threshold of greater than 90 decibels; individuals with this level of a loss would not be expected to develop functional hearing for speech and should be provided with nonspeech communication alternatives.

A teacher may suspect hearing loss by observing behavioral signs such as language delays, poor articulation, poor response to verbal instruction, requests to repeat what was said, distractibility, inattention, failure to localize to sounds, failure to imitate vocalizations, avoidance of task with auditory demands, and hyperactivity (McCubbin, 1986; Sobsey & Wolf-Schein, 1991). When a hearing loss is suspected, the teacher can use noisemakers and observations of response in an informal testing situation to probe if a hearing loss may be present.

An accurate assessment of hearing loss is typically performed by an audiologist, who may use one of a variety of audiological assessments to determine the extent of the hearing impairment and an intervention plan. The Visual Reinforcer Auditory (VRA) Procedures assess response to sound by pairing a visual stimulus with an auditory signal. A typical VRA uses a mechanical toy that is housed in a Plexiglas box. An auditory signal is activated and at the same time the box is lit and the mechanical toy is turned on. The child is reinforced for looking at the box by the illumination and the toy. After a few paired trials, the sound is presented and the child is observed to see if he anticipates the appearance of the illuminated toy. If the child turns toward the box, it is assumed that he hears the sound. This procedure may not be effective for children with visual impairments, children who do not localize to sound, and children who are unable to turn their head from side to side (Sobsey & Wolf-Schein, 1991).

The Tangible-Reinforcer Operant-Conditioning Audiometry (TROCA) method uses an operant discrimination paradigm for determining hearing ability (Niswander, 1987). TROCA is conducted by using equipment that dispenses a reinforcer when a button is pushed. The individual is reinforced for pressing a lighted bar or button when it is paired with an auditory signal. Once the response is conditioned, the illumination is faded and the auditory stimulus cues the response. This procedure may not be effective with students who have motor delays or cognitive disabilities that inhibit the button-press response or acquisition of stimulus-response relationships (Niswander, 1987).

Auditory Brainstem Response (ABR) examines the brain-wave response to auditory stimuli. To assess auditory functioning through brain-wave response, three electrodes are attached to the head. These electrodes detect electric activity and display them on a screen for analysis. The testing requires 30 to 45 minutes to complete and requires that the individual sit or lie motionless. Small children or children who are difficult to test may need to be sedated for the examination. Because the ABR does not require a volitional response on the part of the individual, it is a very powerful assessment technique to use with individuals who are difficult to test. Problems of the ABR include an inability to discern frequency-specific responses, an overestimation of the hearing loss, and difficulty in interpreting the data when the ABR detects no responses to the auditory stimuli (Niswander, 1987).

Acoustic immitance measures may be used to assess the condition of the eardrum, middle ear functioning, acoustic reflexes, and eustachian tubes (Sobsey & Wolf-Schein, 1991). The procedure involves a small probe tip that is inserted in the ear and emits a low-frequency tone. The tone is transmitted into the middle ear and reflected to a microphone connected to the probe tip. The magnitude of the reflected tone indicates if there is an ear mechanism problem. Because these measures require the passive participation of the individual who is being tested, they may not be useful for difficult-to-test individuals (Niswander, 1987).

Adaptive Devices

The most obvious remedy to a hearing problem is to amplify the sound so it can be heard. There are three types of hearing aids: ones that are worn in the ear, ear level aids, and body style (Niswander, 1987). Body-style aids are typically used with infants and toddlers whose small ears cannot accommodate an ear level aid, individuals with ear malformations, and older children with limited manual dexterity who can more easily use a body aid (Sobsey & Wolf-Schein, 1991). Children with hearing impairments should be fitted with an amplification device as soon as the hearing loss is diagnosed (Niswander, 1987). Most individuals can benefit from amplification, although for some persons the hearing aid will enable the user only to detect environmental sounds and noises.

Cochlear implants are surgically implanted prostheses that have been designed to provide auditory awareness to individuals who are profoundly hearing impaired. The device involves a microphone that detects sound and feeds it to a processor unit that converts the sound to electrical impulses that are directed into the inner ear and stimulate the auditory nerve. The wearer can hear environmental sounds and sometimes speech, although the words are not discernible.

Vibrotactile communication aids provide alternate sensory input through vibrations on the skin. The devices use a microphone to pick up sounds that are delivered to a small vibrator that is attached to the arm or finger of the user (Niswander, 1987). The vibratory signals provide information about the pitch, timing, and intensity of the sounds.

A critical issue for intervention with students who are severely disabled and hearing impaired is to develop communication skills. Manual sign language may be an appropriate form for receptive and expressive communication skill development, although many students do not have the manual dexterity or cognitive ability to become fluent sign-language users. A discussion of alternative communication systems is provided in chapter 10.

When a student is hearing impaired the collaborative team must make an effort to assess the amount of hearing that is present and design strategies to maximize the use of residual hearing. Sound discrimination, localization, and awareness should be taught within functional activities in the natural environment (Sobsey & Wolf-Schein, 1991).

Vision Impairments

Students who are visually impaired experience a restriction in vision of sufficient severity that it interferes with their ability to interpret and use visual input (Scholl, 1986). Definitions of visual impairment are determined by measuring visual acuity in the better eye. Visual acuity is measured by using an eye chart and determining the distance at which the individual can read letters that a person without visual impairment can read at 20 feet. A visual acuity of 20/20 means that the person has no impairment. A visual acuity with a denominator that is higher, for example 20/200, indicates an ability to read letters at 20 feet that a person without a visual impairment can read at 200 feet. A visual acuity in both eyes of 20/200 or less with the best visual correction is considered legal blindness. A visual impairment is visual acuity of 20/70 to 20/200. A restriction in the visual field may also be defined as legal blindness when a visual field is determined to be less than 20 degrees in diameter (Hollins, 1989) as compared to a normal visual field of 120 to 150 degrees on each axis (Jose, 1983).

The leading causes of blindness among individuals who are under age 20 are congenital cataracts (clouding of the lens), optic nerve atrophy (degeneration of the optic nerve), and retinopathy of prematurity (damage to the retina due to high concentrations of oxygen used to treat premature infants with respiratory distress) (Ward, 1986). The prevalence of visual impairments among students with other disabilities is much higher than students without disabilities (Scholl, 1986; Sobsey & Wolf-Schein, 1991). The diagnosis and assessment of a visual impairment involves a physiological examination of the eye and an evaluation of the functional use of vision. These assessment activities are conducted by a vision or eye specialist, ophthalmologist, or optometrist.

Vision Assessment

The following behaviors may cause a teacher to suspect that a student has a visual impairment: moving clumsily in the environment;

I. Presence and nature of the visual response

a. Pupillary reaction: __present __absent __R __L
b. Muscle imbalance: __present __absent __R __L
c. Blink reflex: __present __absent __R __L
d. Visual field loss: __present __absent __R __L
e. Peripheral field loss: __present __absent __R __L
f. Visual field preference: __present __absent __R __L
g. Eye preference: __present __absent __R __L

II. Reaction to visual stimuli

a. Inappropriate visual behaviors: __present __absent
b. Tracking ability: __present __absent
   __light __objects: __vertical
   __circular __horizontal __oblique
c. Reaches for toys: __present __absent
   __in front of him __to his right
   __to his left __above eye level
   __below eye level
d. Shifts attention: __present __absent
   __both sides __one side __R __L
e. Scanning ability: __present __absent

III. Distance and size of objects and pictures

a. Locates dropped toy: __present __absent __distance
   __peg or candy
   __inch-cubed blocks __shape chips
b. Small toy observed: __present __absent __distance

Figure 12–7
Functional Vision Checklist

From "Functional Vision Screening for Severely Handicapped Children" by B. Langley & R. E. Dubose, 1989, in *Dimensions: Visually Impaired Persons with Multiple Disabilities,* Selected papers from the *Journal of Visual Impairment and Blindness,* pp. 47–51. Reprinted with the permission of the American Foundation for the Blind.

holding the head down or to the side when moving; shuffling the feet when walking; bumping into objects; finger flicking in front of the eyes; bringing objects to the mouth for exploration; locating objects on sound cues; responding to objects that are shiny or certain colors; overreaching or underreaching when picking up objects; squinting or closing one eye when looking at objects; poking, pressing, or rubbing the eyes; losing interest or avoiding visually demanding tasks; becoming quiet when sounds are presented; and not making eye contact with conversation partners. An informal test for functional vision can be per-

c. Large toy observed: __present __absent __distance
d. Objects matched: __present __absent __distance
__large toys __distance
__small toys __distance

IV. Integration of visual and cognitive processing
a. Visual pursuit: __present __absent
b. Causality: __present __absent
c. Object permanence: __present __absent
d. Object concept: __present __absent
e. Means-ends: __present __absent

V. Integration of visual and motor processing
a. Approach:
1. pegs: __visual __tactual reach: __O __U
2. stacking cone: __visual __tactual reach: __O __U
3. puzzles: __visual __tactual reach: __O __U
4. pounding bench: __visual __tactual reach: __O __U
5. beads: __visual __tactual reach: __O __U

b. Matching:
1. colored blocks:
__matches __does not match __near distance __far distance
2. shapes:
__matches __does not match __near distance __far distance
3. pictures:
__matches __does not match __near distance __far distance

Figure 12–7, *continued*

formed by the teacher to determine if further diagnostic assessment should be conducted. Langley and Dubose (1989) provide a checklist (see Figure 12–7) to record information on the student's visual response, reaction to stimuli, the distance and size of objects the student responds to most consistently, the ability to integrate cognitive and visual information, and the integration of visual and motor processing.

A visual response is assessed by examining the student's pupillary reaction, muscle balance, visual field, blink reflex, and eye preference. Pupillary response is assessed by directing a penlight into the student's eyes and observing whether the pupils constrict and then dilate when the light is removed. The light is flashed into the center of the student's eyes to see if the light is reflected in the middle of each pupil. If a deviation is present, it may indicate muscle imbalance. Light perception is assessed by passing a hand across the student's eyes to elicit a blinking response and by flashing the penlight at points above, below, to the left and to the right of the student's face to see if he responds to the light and to determine the range of the visual field. The evaluator then sits behind the student and slowly brings the light into the student's visual field while noting the point at which the student turns to look at it. Eye preference can be assessed by holding up a motivating toy and then alternately covering the student's eyes. If one eye is not functional, the student will indicate distress when the functional eye is covered.

The student is observed to determine if any atypical visual behaviors are present, such as eye poking or light filtering with the fingers. Toys or other motivating objects can be used to assess if the student can track, shift visual attention from one object to another, and scan an array of objects. Objects of various sizes can be used to note the distance and size of the object that the student will attend to. The evaluator can ask a student to match sets of duplicate toys (large and small) that are placed at varying distances to assess the distance that is optimal for vision.

The integration of vision, cognitive, and motor skills is assessed by observing the student interacting with objects. Sensorimotor skills (cognitive skills from birth to 24 months) are assessed to determine the student's developmental level. If there is evidence that a student is at a very early sensorimotor stage of cognitive development, the vision difficulty may be related to cognition rather than the integrity of the sensory system.

Visual pursuit can be assessed by seeing if the child will watch small objects as they are poured from a container. The cognitive skill of understanding causality can be assessed by scribbling on a large paper and offering the marker to the student. The cognitive skill of object permanence can be assessed by putting a motivating object in a container or hiding it under a cloth and watching the student to see if he searches for the object. Means-end ability may be assessed by activating an object (e.g., wind-up toy), letting it wind down, and then watching the student to see if he attempts to reactivate the toy. Visual and motor processing can be assessed in the young child by using a pounding bench or stacking cones and observing if the child underreaches or overreaches as he attempts to place objects in the appropriate place. The ability to match color and configuration can be assessed using shapes or colored blocks at various distances, although for many students more motivating materials may be needed to elicit a response.

Vision Correction

Correction of a visual disorder can be done for some students with visual impairments through surgery or the use of corrective lenses. The presence of multiple disabilities should never be used as an excuse for denying a student visual correction (Cress et al., 1981). If eyeglasses are recommended for a student with severe disabilities, the collaborative team may need to develop strategies that will support the student (e.g., reinforcement procedures, shaping) as he becomes adjusted to wearing them. In addition to correcting vision, the team should design strategies and adaptations that will assist the student with visual impairments to maximize the use of his or her residual vision.

Some students with visual impairments can discriminate more easily when illumination is provided. The appropriate level of illumination should be determined by the collaborative team. Students who are learning functional reading skills or survival sign interpretation can be taught to look for other clues that are easier to discriminate. For example, most exit signs are illuminated and have red lettering. Work surfaces for the student with visual impairments should support the forearm so the student can explore with his hands without strain. Some students may need to have visual distractions eliminated as they focus on tasks. Highly reflective work surfaces should be avoided and contrasts should be provided when possible. Persons who are working or interacting with the student with visual impairments should avoid standing in front of a window or an open door so that glare is reduced. Copiers can be used to enlarge printed materials, and tactile clues can be added to items to assist the student in discrimination.

Visual stimulation, a popular method that is thought to enhance residual vision skills, involves the noncontingent presentation of visual stimuli such as blinking lights and fluorescent objects (Barraga, 1970). There is no published literature to support the effectiveness of this method for teaching students functional vision use.

One method for enhancing the use of residual vision is to provide systematic instruction in the use of visual skills. Research has demonstrated that structured vision training can be an effective vision enhancement method (Goetz & Gee, 1987; Mosk & Bucher, 1984; Utley, Duncan, Strain, & Scanlon, 1983). Goetz and Gee (1987) have described a method for instructing functional vision in the context of a functional, community-based curriculum.

Functional Vision Training

There are two components involved in functional context vision training (Goetz & Gee, 1987). The first involves teaching visual attention behaviors within tasks that require visual attention for successful performance. For example, the student must visually scan a vending machine to find the coin slot and successfully make a purchase. The second component is to use the systematic instructional procedures of repeated prompting or continuous correction to prompt the student until visual attention occurs.

Five steps are used to develop a functional vision program. The first step is to determine the targeted visual skill. Some of the skills that may be appropriate to target include orienting to the presence of a stimulus, visual fixation, accommodative convergence, gaze shift, tracking, scanning, and peripheral vision (Goetz & Gee, 1987). The second step is to select the skill contexts that require visual behavior for accurate task performance. The skills that are selected for functional vision training must be functional, age-appropriate, and motivational for the learner.

The third step is to design the instructional program for teaching the vision skill. In order to decide upon a criterion for determining if a student's skill performance is correct or incorrect, the teacher must identify the critical moment that the vision behavior must occur in the task and the duration or accuracy of the visual skill that is needed to perform the task correctly. For example, a student may need to visually scan a box of crackers to find the open tab, but then may not need to visually fixate while opening the box.

When the critical moment is identified, the teaching strategies that will be used to ensure that the student performs the visual behavior are selected. The prompting techniques that are chosen will depend on the abilities of the student being taught and the nature of the target skill and skill context. Prompting techniques that have been used with students learning visual behaviors include the use of physical and tactile cues, auditory cues, additional visual cues such as shining a light on an item involved in the task, and interrupting the task until the student performs the visual behavior that is required (Utley, Goetz, Gee, Baldwin, & Sailor, 1981).

Goetz and Gee (1987) also recommend the use of continuous-loop training procedures, which involves repeating trials until a correct response is achieved so the student understands that successful task performance is contingent on the use of visual skills. Continuous-loop training or repeated prompting should not be used if the student reacts negatively to the procedures or if their use in community settings is not practical or calls undue negative attention to the learner.

The fourth step of designing a functional vision program is to select the instructional strategies that will be used to teach the functional skill. Once the student is performing the visual skill at the critical moment, a systematic instructional program should be used to ensure competence in performing the functional task. The final step of the functional vision program is to implement and monitor the program that has been designed in steps one through four.

Orientation and Mobility Skills

Students with visual impairments have to be taught how to move safely and purposefully in their environment. These skills are called orientation and mobility skills (Hill, 1986; Welsh & Blasch, 1980). The traditional approach to teaching these skills is based on a developmental model (Hill, 1986) in which individuals are assessed to determine if they understand the concepts that are designated as prerequisites to independent travel skills. Once those concepts are established, training in traveling with a sighted guide, using self-protection techniques, basic cane skills, specific cane techniques, and traveling in outdoor environments is provided (Hill & Ponder, 1976).

A functional approach to orientation and mobility has been implemented for individuals with severe and multiple disabilities (Gee, Harrell, & Rosenberg, 1987; Joffee & Rikhye, 1991). In a functional approach, travel training is taught without requiring prerequisite skills. The purpose of the functional approach is to give students with severe disabilities the opportunity to travel independently or semi-independently in the environments that naturally call for orientation and mobility skills (Gee, Harrell, & Rosenberg, 1987). Skills that may be taught in a functional orientation and mobility program are presented in Table 12–2.

Implementing a functional orientation and mobility program is a process with six phases (see Figure 12–8). The first phase involves a thorough review of assessment information (motor, hearing, and vision skills) and observations of the student when there are natural cues for the performance of the targeted skills. Planned observations can only occur after the orientation and mobility skills that will be assessed are targeted and natural contexts in which the skill is necessary have been identified. For example, the orientation skills of using landmarks and sound localization could be assessed when the student approaches the cafeteria and, hearing the sounds of the cafeteria, turns toward the ramp and reaches for the handrail.

When the performance observations in natural contexts have been completed, the team can select the routes that will be used for instruction. There are several factors that should be considered. The routes of travel that are selected should be ones the student encounters on a regular basis, occur when there is an appropriate amount of supervision for instruction, lead to a desirable activity, and be an appropriate length for the practice and use of the skills that are targeted (Gee, Harrell, & Rosenberg, 1987).

After the routes are selected for instruction, a task analysis is completed. It should include information on every change in direction, landmarks, cane use, or changes in the hand or

Table 12–2
Mobility Skills and Purpose (the sequence is modified from Hill & Ponder, 1976)

Skill	Purpose
Sighted guide	To travel safely and efficiently with a sighted person within different environments and under varying conditions
Basic	
Reversing	
Transferring	
Narrow passages	
Accept & refuse aid	
Stairways	
Doorways	
Seating	
Self-protection	To enable the student to travel efficiently and independently, primarily in familiar indoor environments, affording the student maximum protection without the use of a mobility aid
Upper hand & forearm	
Lower hand & forearm	
Trailing	
Traversing open doorways	
Direction taking	
Search patterns	
Dropped objects	
Basic cane skills	To enable the student to travel safely, efficiently, and independently in familiar and unfamiliar environments
Walking with a guide	
Transferring sides with a guide	
Doorways with a guide	
Accept or refuse aid	
Placement of the cane	To enable the student to position his or her cane so that it is easily accessible and will not interfere with others
Diagonal technique	To enable the student to travel independently, primarily in a familiar indoor environment with some degree of protection
Changing hands	
Objects/Obstacles	
Doorways	
Trailing	Cane is held at a diagonal across and in front of the student and pushed forward ahead of the student
Stairways	
Cane manipulation	

From "Teaching Orientation and Mobility Skills Within and Across Natural Opportunities for Travel" by K. Gee, R. Harrell & R. Rosenberg, in L. Goetz, D. Guess & K. Stremel-Campbell (Eds.), *Innovative Program Design for Individuals with Dual Sensory Impairments* (pp. 127-157), 1987, Baltimore: Paul H. Brookes Publishing Co., P.O. Box 10624, Baltimore, Maryland 21285-0624. Reprinted by permission.

foot (Gee, Harrell, & Rosenberg, 1987). Once the route has been task-analyzed, the student is asked to travel the route and the present level of performance is observed. Baseline information is used to determine where instruction will be necessary, where adaptations should be used, and the instructional techniques that may be appropriate.

Table 12–2, *continued*

Skill	Purpose
Touch technique	To enable the student to detect drop-offs and objects in the vertical plane in familiar or unfamiliar environments
Basic	
Trailing	
Changing from diagonal to touch technique	
Examine objects	
Outdoors/residential	Enter and exit cars
Car familiarization	
Outdoor travel	
Shorelining	To establish and maintain a desired line of travel and to locate a specific object perpendicular to his line of travel
Sidewalk recovery	
Touch & slide	To detect textual changes, subtle drop-offs, etc.
Touch & drag	For use on curbs, expansion joints, elevated walkways, and platforms
Residential street crossings	
Outdoors/commercial	
Street crossing at traffic light	
Pedestrian traffic control	
Soliciting aid	
Buses	
Primary commercial facilities	
Escalators, elevators	
Revolving doors	
Airports, etc.	

The fourth phase of designing an orientation and mobility program is called the "context instruction" phase (Gee, Harrell, & Rosenberg, 1987). The student is assisted to travel the routes with the instructor calling attention to the tactile, auditory, and situational cues. The student is assisted with making turns, holding the cane, and the other movements necessary to complete the route. Gee, Harrell, and Rosenberg (1987) suggest that the "context instruction" phase should occur for 5 to 10 days and that a second baseline should be conducted then on the student's performance. The rationale for this phase is that

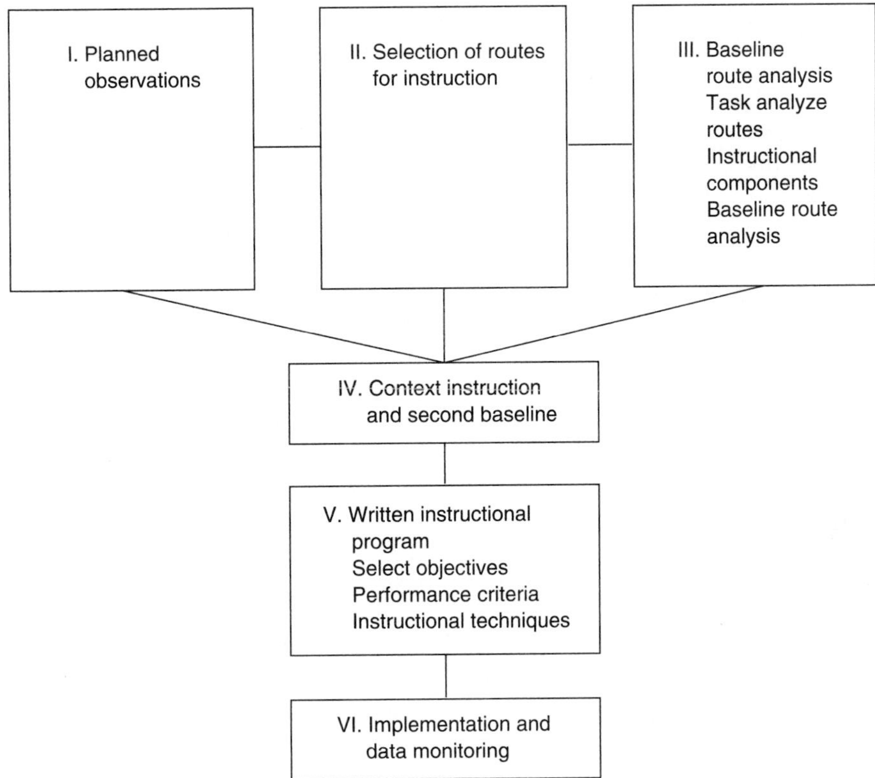

Figure 12–8

Model for the Development of O&M Instruction

From "Teaching Orientation and Mobility Skills Within and Across Natural Opportunities for Travel" by K. Gee, R. Harrell, & R. Rosenberg, in L. Goetz, D. Guess, & K. Stremel-Campbell (Eds.), *Innovative Program Design for Individuals with Dual Sensory Impairments* (pp. 127–157), 1987, Baltimore: Paul H. Brookes Publishing Co., P.O. Box 10624, Baltimore, Maryland 21285-0624. Reprinted by permission.

many students with severe disabilities may have never experienced the expectation of traveling a route independently. Once an expectation for moving through the environment is established, the student may demonstrate acquisition of some of the skills or be more likely to attempt to travel the route.

Information from the second baseline is used to select the instructional objectives and design the instructional program. Gee, Harrell, and Rosenberg (1987) advise that instruction should begin on the motor skills (turning, cane use) involved in traveling the route rather than route memory. Modifications on equipment, such as a marshmallow tip cane (Wurzberger, 1980) or diagonal cane extension (Morse, 1980), and adaptations that make route travel easier (such as printed cards to use for requesting assistance) should be considered to ensure that the student can travel as independently as possible. Once the instructional program is designed, implementation and evaluation of the student's progress should be made through ongoing data collection.

Some students can use Electronic Travel Aids (ETAs) to assist them with moving in the environment (Warren, Horn, & Hill, 1987). These devices emit signals to detect obstacles and objects in the environment and transmit the information to the user through auditory or tactile feedback.

Dual Sensory Impairments

Students with severe disabilities who have both hearing and vision impairments have educational needs that present significant challenges for teachers (Fredericks & Baldwin, 1987). Instructional modifications and adaptations can be made by the collaborative team to support the learner with dual sensory impairments. The first task in developing specific instructional strategies is to assess the extent of the hearing and vision impairment. Most individuals with dual sensory impairments have some functional vision and hearing skills (Fredericks & Baldwin, 1987). The instructional strategies that may be used include enhancing auditory and visual stimuli, using tactile teaching, and targeting visual and auditory skill development within meaningful activities (Downing & Eichinger, 1990). These are techniques that can be used within the functional curriculum that is currently provided to students with severe disabilities. There is no reason to specialize the instruction of an individual with dual sensory impairments in a way that results in segregated programming or segregated placement (Downing & Eichinger, 1991).

Enhancing visual and auditory stimuli is done through the modification of materials and their presentation so that students with dual sensory impairments can use their residual hearing and/or visual skills. Adaptations that may be used include enlarging pictures, reducing glare, illumination, presenting stimuli within the student's visual field, using enhanced auditory cues, or positioning the student so that the stimuli are closer. The teacher can also stress the use of tactile cues to guide the student through activities. Presenting real objects as tactile prompts to conduct an activity will assist the student with dual sensory impairments to transfer the skill to natural contexts. Natural auditory and visual stimuli should also be used to teach the student to attend to stimuli as he or she completes activity routines. For example, when teaching a student with dual sensory impairments to do laundry, listening for the water flow should be encouraged as a check on the completion of loading the washer, and the slam of the dryer door could serve as an auditory cue that a dryer-loading task sequence has been completed.

Another approach that has been used with students with dual sensory impairments is the movement-based approach as described by Jan Van Dijk (Writer, 1987). This approach is based on the provision of motor experiences that provide the student with reference points to organize the world and enable the student to communicate and build relationships with others (Writer, 1987). The teacher moves with the students and does activities with them rather than to them. It is through the process of these reciprocal movement actions that learning takes place.

Conclusion

In this chapter, the special concerns associated with students who have multiple impairments were presented. It was stressed that collaborative teaming is essential to developing an appropriate program for students with motor or sensory impairments. It is critical that the collaborative team work together in assessing the sensory and motor capabilities of the student and design interventions that are appropriate for the home, school, and community. The educator is not expected to be well-versed in the techniques of specialized disciplines such as physical therapy or audiology, but is expected to know what questions to ask and how to use the knowledge provided by other disciplines and the family to support the student with multiple impairments.

Questions for Reflection

1. How would the presence of sensory or motor impairments affect the inclusion of a student in general education classes? in community-based instruction? in supported employment?
2. What unique concerns might a family have about the education of their child with a sensory impairment?
3. Many people believe that students who are deaf should be educated in segregated environments where their peers and teachers understand sign language and will be able to communicate with them. How would you respond to parents who asked you if you believed that a segregated environment would be a more appropriate placement for their child?
4. Sometimes students with sensory impairments exhibit challenging behavior that has a relationship to the inability to see or hear. Why might this occur?
5. Students with motor impairments often need specialized equipment for positioning. How can teachers in inclusive programs minimize the disruption that may be caused by taking the student in and out of equipment?
6. Make a list of activities that take place in an elementary classroom. Look at that list and then think of adaptations that might be made to accommodate the needs of a student who is hearing or visually impaired.

References

Albano, M., Cox, B., York, J., & York, R. (1981). Educational teams for students with severe and multiple handicaps. In R. York, W. K. Schofield, D. J. Donder, D. L. Ryndak, & B. Reguly (Eds.), *Organizing and implementing services for students with severe and multiple handicaps* (pp. 24–34). Springfield, IL: Illinois State Board of Education.

Arendt, R. E., MacLean, W. E., & Baumeister, A. A. (1988). Critique of sensory integration therapy and its application in mental retardation. *American Journal on Mental Retardation, 92*, 401–411.

Ayres, A. J. (1979). *Sensory integration and the child.* Los Angeles: Western Psychological Services.

Ball, T. S., McCrady, R. E., & Hart, A. D. (1975). Automated reinforcement of head posture in two cerebral palsied retarded children. *Perceptual and Motor Skills, 40*, 619–622.

Barraga, N. (1970). *Teacher's guide for the development of visual learning abilities and utilization of low vision.* New York: American Printing House for the Blind.

Bobath, K. (1980). *A neurophysiological basis for the treatment of cerebral palsy.* London: William Heinemann Medical Books.

Campbell, P. H. (1987a). Integrated programming for students with multiple handicaps. In L. Goetz, D. Guess, & K. Stremel-Campbell (Eds.), *Innovative program design for individuals with dual sensory impairments* (pp. 159–188). Baltimore: Paul H. Brookes.

Campbell, P. H. (1987b). Programming for students with dysfunction in posture and movement. In M. E. Snell (Ed.), *Systematic instruction of persons with severe handicaps* (pp. 188–212). Columbus, OH: Merrill.

Campbell, P. H. (1989). Dysfunction in posture and movement in individuals with profound disabilities: Issues and practices. In F. Brown & D. Lehr (Eds.), *Persons with profound disabilities: Issues and practices* (pp. 163–189). Baltimore: Paul H. Brookes.

Cicirello, N., Hyltm, J., Reed, P., & Hall, S. (1989). *Teaching nontherapists to do positioning and handling in educational settings.* Portland, OR: Child Development and

Rehabilitation Center Publications, Oregon Health Sciences University.

Cress, P., Spellman, C., DeBriere, T., Sizemore, A., Northam, J., & Johnson, J. (1981). Vision screening for persons with severe handicaps. *Journal of the Association for Persons with Severe Handicaps, 6,* 41–49.

Cusick, B. (1991). Therapeutic management of sensorimotor and physical disabilities. In J. Bigge (Ed.), *Teaching individuals with physical and multiple disabilities* (pp. 16–49). New York: Merrill/Macmillan.

Downing, J., & Eichinger, J. (1990). Instructional strategies for learners with dual sensory impairments in integrated settings. *Journal of the Association for Persons with Severe Handicaps, 15,* 98–105.

Dunn, W. (1991). The sensorimotor systems: A framework for assessment and intervention. In F. P. Orelove & D. Sobsey, *Educating children with multiple disabilities: A transdisciplinary approach* (2nd ed.) (pp. 33–78). Baltimore: Paul H. Brookes.

Filler, J., & Kasari, C. (1981). Acquisition, maintenance, and generalization of parent taught skills with two severely handicapped infants. *Journal of the Association for Persons with Severe Handicaps, 6,* 30–38.

Finnie, N. R. (1974). *Handling the young cerebral palsied child at home* (2nd ed.). New York: E. P. Dutton.

Fraser, B. A., Hensinger, R. N., Phelps, J. A., & Jacques, K. (1987). Seating systems. In B. A. Fraser, R. N. Hensinger, & J. A. Phelps, *A professional's guide: Physical management of multiple handicaps* (pp. 107–136). Baltimore: Paul H. Brookes.

Fredericks, H. D., & Baldwin, V. L. (1987). Individuals with sensory impairments: Who are they? How are they educated?. In L.Goetz, D. Guess, & K. Stremel-Campbell (Eds.), *Innovative program design for individuals with dual sensory impairments* (pp. 3–12). Baltimore: Paul H. Brookes.

Gee, K., Harrell, R., & Rosenberg, R. (1987). Teaching orientation and mobility skills within and across natural opportunities for travel. In L. Goetz, D. Guess, & K. Stremel-Campbell (Eds.), *Innovative program design for individuals with dual sensory impairments* (pp. 127–157) Baltimore: Paul H. Brookes.

Goetz, L., & Gee, K. (1987). Functional vision programming. In L. Goetz, D. Guess, & K. Stremel-Campbell (Eds.), *Innovative program design for individuals with dual sensory impairments* (pp. 77–97). Baltimore: Paul H. Brookes.

Grove, D. N., & Dalke, B. A. (1976). Contingent feedback for training children to propel their wheelchairs. *Physical Therapy, 56,* 815–820.

Hill, E. W. (1986). Orientation and mobility. In G. T. Scholl (Ed.), *Foundations of education for blind and visually handicapped children and youth* (pp. 315–340). New York: American Printing House for the Blind.

Hill, E., & Ponder, P. (1976). *Orientation and mobility techniques: A guide for the practitioner.* New York: American Printing House for the Blind.

Hollins, M. (1989). *Understanding blindness.* Hillsdale, NJ: Lawrence Erlbaum.

Horn, E. M. (1991). Basic motor skills instruction for children with neuromotor delays: A critical review. *Journal of Special Education, 25,* 168–197.

Horn, E. M., & Warren, S. F. (1987). Facilitating the acquisition of sensorimotor behavior with a microcomputer mediated teaching system: An experimental analysis. *Journal of the Association for Persons with Severe Handicaps, 12,* 205–215.

Hulme, J., Poor, R., Schulein, M., & Pezzino, J. (1983). Perceived behavioral changes observed with adaptive seating devices and training programs for multihandicapped, developmentally disabled individuals. *Physical Therapy, 63,* 204–208.

Kohn, J., Enders, S., Preston, J., & Motloch, W. (1983). Provision of assistive equipment for handicapped persons. *Archives of Physical Medicine and Rehabilitation, 64,* 378–381.

Joffee, E., & Rikhye, C. H. (1991). Orientation and mobility for students with severe visual and multiple impairments: A new perspective. *Journal of Visual Impairment and Blindness,* 211–216.

Jose, R. T. (1983). *Understanding low vision.* New York: American Printing House for the Blind.

Langley, B., & Dubose, R. E. (1989). Functional vision screening for severely handicapped children. In *Dimensions: Visually impaired persons with multiple disabilities* (pp. 47–51). Selected papers from the *Journal of Visual Impairment and Blindness.* New York: American Foundation for the Blind.

Lee, J. M., Mahler, T. J., & Westling, D. L. (1985). Reducing occurrences of an ATNR. *American Journal of Mental Deficiency, 89,* 617–621.

Leiper, C., Miller, A., Lang, J., & Herman, R. (1981). Sensory feedback for head control in cerebral palsy. *Physical Therapy, 61,* 512–518.

Morse, K. A. (1980). Modifications of the long cane for use by a multiply impaired child. *Journal of Visual Impairment and Blindness, 74,* 15–18.

Mosk, M., & Bucher, B. (1984). Prompting and stimulus shaping procedures for teaching visual motor skills to retarded children. *Journal of the Association for Persons with Severe Handicaps, 17,* 23–34.

Niswander, P. S. (1987). Audiometric assessment and management. In L. Goetz, D. Guess, & K. Stremel-Campbell (Eds.), *Innovative program design for individuals with dual sensory impairments* (pp. 99–126). Baltimore: Paul H. Brookes.

Orelove, F. P., & Sobsey, D. (1991). Designing transdisciplinary services. In F. P. Orelove & D. Sobsey, *Educating children with multiple disabilities: A transdisciplinary approach* (2nd ed.) (pp. 1–31). Baltimore: Paul H. Brookes.

Rainforth, B., & York, J. (1991). Handling and positioning. In F. P. Orelove & D. Sobsey, *Educating children with multiple disabilities: A transdisciplinary approach* (2nd ed.) (pp. 79–117). Baltimore: Paul H. Brookes.

Rainforth, B., York, J., & Macdonald, C. (1992). *Collaborative teams for students with severe disabilities: Integrating therapy and educational services.* Baltimore: Paul H. Brookes.

Richman, J. S., & Kazlowski, N. L. (1977). Operant training of head control and beginning language development for a severely developmentally disabled child. *Journal of Behavior Therapy and Experimental Psychiatry, 8,* 437–440.

Scholl, G. T. (1986). What does it mean to be blind? Definitions, terminology, and prevalence. In G. T. Scholl (Ed.), *Foundations of education for blind and visually handicapped children and youth* (pp. 23–33).

Skrotzky, K., Gallenstein, J. S., & Osternig, L. R. (1978). Effects of electromyographic feedback training on motor control in spastic cerebral palsy. *Physical Therapy, 58,* 547–552.

Sobsey, D., & Wolf-Schein, E. G. (1991). Sensory impairments. In F. P. Orelove & D. Sobsey, *Educating children with multiple disabilities: A transdisciplinary approach* (2nd ed.) (pp. 119–153). Baltimore: Paul H. Brookes.

Stern, F. M., & Gorga, D. (1988). Neurodevelopmental treatment (NDT): Therapeutic intervention and its efficacy. *Infants and Young Children, 1,* 22–32.

Utley, B., Duncan, D., Strain, P., & Scanlon, K. (1983). Effects of contingent and noncontingent vision stimulation on visual fixation in multiply handicapped children. *Journal of the Association for Persons with Severe Handicaps, 8,* 29–42.

Utley, B., Goetz, L., Gee, K., Baldwin, M., & Sailor, W. (1981). *Vision assessment and program manual for severely handicapped and/or deaf-blind students.* (ERIC Document Reproduction Service No. ED 250 840). Reston, VA: Council for Exceptional Children.

Ward, M. E. (1986). The visual system. In G. T. Scholl (Ed.), *Foundations of education for blind and visually handicapped children and youth* (pp. 36–64). New York: American Foundation for the Blind.

Warren, S. F., Horn, E. H., & Hill, E. W. (1987). Some innovative educational applications of advanced technologies. In L. Goetz, D. Guess, & K. Stremel-Campbell (Eds.), *Innovative program design for individuals with dual sensory impairments* (pp. 283–309). Baltimore: Paul H. Brookes.

Welsh, R. D., & Blasch, B. (Eds.). (1980). *Foundation of orientation and mobility.* New York: American Foundation for the Blind.

Wurzberger, P. (1980). Wurzburger Mobility Aids. 3960 Cottonwood Drive, Concord, CA 94519.

CHAPTER 13

Providing Support for Health and Medical Needs

Chapter Overview

In this chapter, guidelines are provided for managing students' health and medical needs. The chapter gives general guidelines for classroom hygiene practices, dental care, seizure management, skin care, postural drainage, range of motion, medication, and eating difficulties. Procedures for caring for students with tracheostomies, ileostomies and colostomies, and catheters are also provided. The chapter concludes with a discussion of infectious diseases, including HIV.

The provision of support to students with health-care needs is a prominent issue for teachers of students with severe disabilities (Lehr & Noonan, 1989; Mulligan-Ault, Guess, Struth, & Thompson). As more children who are medically fragile survive the neonatal period and enter the school system, public schools have seen an increase in the number of students with severe disabilities who have health-care needs.

The health-care needs of students with severe disabilities have expanded the role of the special educator. In many school programs, special educators are providing services that have been traditionally viewed as nursing care. Mulligan-Ault et al. (1988) surveyed all of the teachers of students with severe and multiple handicaps in Kansas to determine status of the provision of health services to those students. They found that in over 75% of the classrooms, teachers were monitoring seizures, providing emergency seizure care, engaging in teeth and gum care, and administering medication. In over 50% of the classrooms, teachers were involved in the prevention of skin breakdowns and establishing bowel habits. In 25 to 50% of the classrooms, teachers were involved in the treatment of skin breakdowns, diet monitoring and supplementation, postural drainage (assisting the student in clearing secretions from the lungs), handling and positioning, CPR, shunt care, and percussion (cupping and vibrating the chest to loosen bronchial secretions).

Because there are not clear administrative policies or legal guidelines for the implementation of health-care procedures in the classroom in most states (Walker, 1989: Wood, Walker, & Gardner, 1986), the delineation of the appropriate role of the classroom teacher is not clear. Despite the ambiguity of legal and policy guidelines, practicing teachers of students with severe disabilities report that they are comfortable performing a variety of health-care procedures and feel that the performance of those procedures is within the scope of their role as classroom teacher (Mulligan-Ault et al., 1988; Thompson & Guess, 1989).

A transdisciplinary approach to the provision of health-care services appears to be the most practical way to meet the needs individuals (Sobsey & Cox, 1991). The delegation of all health-care services to nursing personnel might lead to the inappropriate clustering of students with medical needs in one classroom or school and to the performance of procedures based on the schedule of the health-service provider rather than on student needs (Sobsey & Cox, 1991). Through a transdisciplinary approach, practices and services can be individually tailored to the student's needs. Health-care plans can be developed by the collaborative team with specific procedures outlined for each student. Classroom personnel can be trained by the nurse or parent on how to implement needed health-care procedures. The collaborative team should include at minimum the parent, the school nurse, and the classroom teacher. The team may also be expanded to include the physician, additional teachers, therapists, and other personnel who have daily contact with the student. Issues the team should address include not only the health-care procedure or medication administration procedure, but also a plan for in-service training of care providers, case coordination responsibilities, and procedures to be used in an emergency.

In this chapter, the health-care procedures that teachers of students with severe disabilities should be familiar with are discussed. The first section of the chapter includes guidelines for practices that we describe as therapeutic management. These are low-technology procedures that may be required by students on a daily basis. Subsequent sections offer information on nutrition and feeding, medication, special concerns, and infectious disease. The information offered in this chapter is not meant to be a "how-to" manual for the implementation of specialized procedures, but is meant to provide basic knowledge for the teacher who may need to seek more detailed information in collaboration with the team before these procedures are carried out in the classroom.

Therapeutic Management

The instruction of students with severe disabilities requires intimate contact between the teacher and the student. Often students with severe disabilities require positioning and handling by the teacher for instruction and self-care practices. Teachers may have responsibilities that include toileting assistance and diapering, food preparation, and oral hygiene assistance. Some students with severe disabilities may have no health concerns; others may exhibit the normal range of student illnesses (e.g., colds or flu), and some may have infectious diseases (e.g., HIV, herpes, cytomegalovirus). It is for these reasons that good hygiene practice in the classroom is of particular importance.

Universal Precautions

The Centers for Disease Control recommends that universal blood and body fluid precautions be implemented in classrooms to prevent the transmission of infections and to decrease risk to care providers and students (Haynie, Porter, & Palfrey, 1989). The concept of universal precautions implies that all students should be assumed to be infectious for HIV and other blood-borne pathogens (U.S. Dept. of Health and Human Services, 1989). Staff should wear disposable gloves whenever the direct care of a student involves contact with blood, body fluids, urine, feces, and respiratory infections. A gown or apron should be used if the splattering of body fluids is possible.

Used gloves should be disposed of in a sealed plastic bag that is placed in a second plastic bag and then thrown in the garbage. When spills of body fluids are cleaned up, the teacher should wear gloves and mop up the spill with paper towels or other absorbent material (Haynie, Porter, & Palfrey, 1989). After the spill is mopped and the area is cleaned, a solution of 1/4 cup of bleach to one gallon of water should be used to disinfect the area (U.S. Department of Health and Human Services, 1989). Paper towels and gloves should then be double bagged as described above and placed in the garbage. If clothing, bedding, or towels become contaminated with body fluids or blood, they should be washed in hot water and detergent for at least 25 minutes (Haynie, Porter, & Palfrey, 1989).

In addition to observing the cautions listed above, classroom personnel must provide an environment that is as clean as possible and minimizes infection transmission risk. Play surfaces and toys should be washed and then disinfected with bleach solution each day. Trash should be disposed of in plastic bags that are tied and disposed of daily. Soiled clothing and diapers should be placed in sealed plastic bags until they are laundered.

Hand-Washing

One of the most important hygiene practices for all personnel who are intimately involved with students is to use appropriate hand-washing procedures. Proper hand-washing is critical to prevent the spread of infection, and must occur prior to and after physical contact with a student, after using the toilet, and after contact with items that may carry infection, such as mouthed objects, tissues, or eating utensils. Hands must be washed whether gloves are worn or not and after gloves are removed.

Before washing hands, all textured jewelry on the hands or wrists should be removed and kept off until the contact with the student is completed and hands are rewashed. Hands should be washed with running warm water and soap in a sink that is not used for food preparation. If no running water is available (e.g., on the playground), a towelette or aerosol soap may be used, although running water is preferred to carry contaminants away. Hands should be washed with adequate soap (liquid is preferred), and all skin surfaces at least to the midpoint of the lower arm should be scrubbed. Hands should be rinsed, then dried with a paper towel. A clean paper towel should be used to turn off the faucets. Paper towels should be disposed of in a lined, covered trash receptacle.

Incontinence and Toileting

Toileting and assisting students with incontinent wear can be a high-risk procedure for contamination of the child, support person, and the environment (Taylor & Taylor, 1989). Staff members must wash their hands and put on gloves prior to assisting students in these activities.

Changing a student's incontinent wear must occur only in a designated area on a changing surface with a disposable covering. Once changing has occurred, the soiled diaper should be placed in a sealed bag and disposed of in a covered trash can. The changing surface must be washed and disinfected after each student. Both the adult and the student must wash their hands before returning to the classroom.

Privacy When staff members change a student who is soiled, they must be very cautious that the student's privacy is protected. Some schools (and community sites) provide a rest room that is separated from the general men's and women's rest room for individuals who need attendant care when toileting. If that is not available, arrangements may be made to use a private rest room in another location in the school, such as the office or the clinic. Another option for ensuring privacy is to make an "occupied" sign that may be hung on the outside of the rest-room door when the privacy of the student is compromised if other students are present in the bathroom. For example, if the student is in high school and incontinent it would be very stigmatizing for the student (and uncomfortable for his peers) to be changed in the general rest room. The collaborative team should examine the needs of the student and the options that are available. The student must be provided with a changing area that is both safe and private. If one is not available, the collaborative team should work with school personnel to make sure that arrangements are made to provide an appropriate changing area. The team should resist the temptation to make do with temporary or makeshift accommodations (e.g., a mat on the floor or a cardboard screen).

Safety Issues Adults must be aware of students' safety and should assure that all of the needed materials (washcloth, incontinent wear, plastic bags) are gathered before placing a student on a changing surface. When assisting a student to the changing surface, the adult must use the appropriate lifting techniques. A student must never be left alone on the changing surface for any amount of time. Students who are capable should be encouraged to assist with the change as much as possible.

Staff who assist students with toileting should also use universal precautions if it is likely that they will have contact with body fluids. If a student needs assistance only with clothing and fasteners, gloves are not necessary. If the student must be assisted with menstrual care, wiping, or is being toilet trained, the adult should wear gloves. Hand-washing in a sink that is not used for food preparation must occur before and after assisting students in the bathroom.

Positioning and Transfer Many students require adapted toilets to accommodate their physical disabilities. Proper positioning on the toilet is critical to safety and aids in elimination. There are three ways that a student in a wheelchair can be transferred to a toilet: forward, sideways, and backward (Bigge, 1991). A forward transfer is made by pushing the wheelchair to the toilet so that the front wheels rest against the base of the toilet. The student's feet are placed on the floor and the student slides onto the toilet facing the back. A backward transfer can occur when the back of the wheelchair is detachable. The wheelchair is pushed against the toilet so that the rear wheels touch the base. When the chair wheels are locked, the back is detached and the student slides backward onto the toilet. To transfer sideways, the wheelchair is placed at the side of the toilet. The chair is locked and the arm rest on the toilet side is removed. The student then places one hand on the toilet seat and one hand on the wheelchair back and swings his or her body onto the toilet seat.

Few students with multiple disabilities are able to assist in a transfer from wheelchair to toilet and will need to be assisted by the adult. To assist the student who can bear weight in a standing position, the adult should place the wheelchair in front of the toilet and assist the student in standing while holding on to the toilet handrails and pivoting his or her body to the toilet seat. Other students will need to be lifted from the wheelchair and transferred to the toilet.

Dental Care

Students should be provided with opportunities to brush their teeth after every meal at school. Some students will be learning to brush their teeth independently; others may need complete assistance. The procedure should occur in the most normalized fashion possible (i.e., at the sink and in front of a mirror), although students who are unable to sit or stand at the sink will require different procedures (Graff et al., 1990).

To assist the student who cannot brush his or her teeth at a sink, the student can be in a

Graduated guidance is an effective approach in teaching a student to brush teeth.

supine or side-lying position with a towel or basin under the chin. If the student can sit on the floor, the adult can sit behind the student and straddle the student's head with the adult's thighs while supporting the student's face with one hand and brushing his or her teeth with the other. If the student can sit at the sink in a wheelchair or chair, the adult can stand or sit behind the student and assist by supporting the student's chin with one hand and brushing with the other.

After the teeth have been brushed, the student's mouth should be rinsed with water. Flossing should occur at least once a day and may also be included as part of the dental hygiene routine at school. The adult should wear gloves when assisting students with toothbrushing and flossing.

Classroom personnel may notice that a student's gums appear sore or swollen or that they bleed during toothbrushing. If this or any other unusual condition is noted, the family and health-care provider must be notified. Special procedures may be indicated for students with oral problems.

Seizure Management

The prevalence of epilepsy ranges from .5 to 2% in the general population (Yousef, 1985), with as many as 31% of persons with severe disabilities experiencing seizure disorders (Richardson, Koller, & Katz, 1981). Epilepsy is defined as two or more seizures that occur in the absence of fever, acute disease, or physical injury to the brain (Prensky & Palkes, 1982). A seizure is erratic electrical activity in the brain that affects a part of or the whole body and may involve a loss of consciousness (Scipien, Chard, Howe, & Barnard, 1990).

Seizure Classification Seizures are classified as either partial or generalized. Partial seizures are limited to a small area of the cerebral cortex; generalized seizures result from a widespread, diffuse electrical discharge in the central portion of the brain spreading to the cortex and brain stem and affecting other systems of the body (Scipien et al., 1990). The diagnosis of epilepsy is made after the documentation of recurrent seizures. The electroencephalogram (EEG) and Computerized Axial Tomography (CAT scan) may be used to assist in the diagnosis of a seizure disorder.

Tonic-clonic seizures are generalized seizures and occur most commonly. The onset of a tonic-clonic seizure is sudden and may be preceded by an aura (unusual visual or sensory sensation) or a change in appearance or behavior that warns of the impending seizure. During the first phase of the seizure, the tonic phase, the individual falls to the ground and becomes rigid, breathing does not occur, and the person may begin to turn blue (cyanosis). The tonic phase may last from 20 to 40 seconds or longer and is followed by the clonic phase, in which there is shaking of the extremities and generalized twitching. The entire seizure is usually less than 5 minutes long. When the seizure ends, the student may need to sleep, may seem lethargic, and may have a headache, fever, or hypertension. The individual may involuntarily urinate or defecate during the seizure and may awaken distressed and embarrassed.

Absence seizures are generalized seizures that are characterized by a brief (5 to 30 seconds) loss of consciousness. The individual usually resumes activity without awareness that the seizure has occurred. Other generalized seizures include myoclonic seizures (repetitive contractions of a muscle), clonic seizures, tonic seizures, and atonic seizures (drop attacks).

Partial seizures may be simple (focal) partial seizures, complex partial seizures, or partial seizures that evolve to secondarily generalized seizures. Simple partial seizures may involve repetitive twitching of the mouth or fingers, dilation of the pupils, or excessive sweating. A focal seizure typically lasts less than 30 seconds and usually involves only one part of the body. Partial complex seizures (also referred to as temporal lobe or psychomotor seizures) may begin with an aura that can be accompanied by strange smells and/or tastes and hallucinations. After the aura, the student may lose consciousness or may engage in stereotyped motor behaviors such as lip smacking, chewing, or picking at clothes. The seizure lasts from 5 to 15 minutes.

Medication Individuals with seizure disorders are treated with medication that may reduce or inhibit seizure activity. Sometimes total suppression of the seizures cannot occur without medicating the individual so much that daily activity is inhibited. Most students who have seizure disorders receive medication several times a day and will be receiving medication during school hours. It is vital that medication be administered according to the physician's instructions and that complete dosages be given. Because mixing a medication with food or crushing a tablet or capsule can change the dosage or absorption rate of the medication, strategies used to administer the medication should be approved by the physician or pharmacist. Additional considerations regarding medication administration and storage are discussed later in this chapter. The medications that are commonly used to treat epilepsy are listed in Table 13–1.

It is possible for seizures to be evoked by environmental stimuli, such as loud sounds, flashing lights, or extreme temperature changes, or conditions within the student, such as fatigue, stress, and missed meals or fluids. Through careful observation of the student, these events can be noted and avoided in an effort to prevent the seizure activity.

Responding to a Seizure If a seizure occurs, the adult should remain calm and stay with the student. The student should be placed on his or her side with a soft object under the head. The area around the student should be cleared of furniture and objects. The adult may loosen student's tight clothing and should *not* place anything in the student's mouth. (Objects placed in the mouth could injure the student or obstruct the airway.) The adult should observe the student carefully and take note of the length of the seizure, color of the student's skin, breathing pattern during the seizure, and movement of the body. Once the seizure is over, the adult should interact with the student to ascertain his or her level of awareness or confusion. The student should be checked for incontinence and injuries and then given an opportunity to rest. The length of the seizure and what happened during the seizure should be documented in writing. In addition, the parent or physician may request that staff

Table 13–1
Some Commonly Used Anticonvulsant Drugs

Drug	Seizures Typically Treated	Untoward Reactions/Side Effects
Carbamazepine *Tegretol*	Complex partial Tonic-Clonic	• Confusion, incoordination, speech disturbances, rash, blood abnormalities, frequent urination, loss of appetite, impaired liver function, changes in blood pressure. • Educational impairment often less severe than with other drugs, but blood and liver problems may be serious. Sore throat, loss of appetite, or easy bruising may be early signs of serious problems.
Dextroamphetamine *Dexedrine*	Absence Sleep	• Dry mouth, diarrhea, loss of appetite, headache, hyperactivity, increased blood pressure, irritability, aggression, psychotic episodes. • May increase the frequency of some types of seizures.
Diazepam *Valium*	Myoclonic	• Drowsiness, fatigue, lethargy, coordination problems, depression, constipation, weight gain.
Ethosuximide *Zarontin*	Absence	• Gastric irritation, drowsiness, coordination problems, dizziness, irritability, hyperactivity, impaired concentration, insomnia, blurred vision, blood abnormalities, rash, hair loss, vaginal bleeding. • May increase aggressive behavior.
Mephobarbital *Mebaral*	Tonic-Clonic	• Lethargy, dizziness, irritability, nausea, diarrhea, blood abnormalities, rash. • Often used if phenobarbital causes hyperactivity.

From "Integrating Health Care and Educational Programs" by D. Sobsey and A. W. Cox, 1991, in F. P. Orelove & D. Sobsey, *Educating Children with Multiple Disabilities: A Transdisciplinary Approach* (2nd ed.) (pp. 155–185), Baltimore: Paul H. Brookes Publishing Co., P.O. Box 10624, Baltimore, Maryland 21285-0624. Reprinted by permission.

record other observations (e.g., lethargy, skin color, body temperature). A sample seizure record form is provided in Figure 13–1.

When a seizure occurs, the student does not require any medical help unless he or she stops breathing (begin mouth-to-mouth resuscitation), the seizure lasts longer than 5 minutes, he or she is injured during the course of the seizure, or if this is the first known seizure he or she has experienced. Another concern is if the seizure is followed by additional seizures that are so frequent that they appear to be constant. This condition, status epilepticus, requires emergency medical intervention and

Table 13–1, *continued*

Drug	Seizures Typically Treated	Untoward Reactions/Side Effects
Methsuximide *Celontin*	Absence	• Blood abnormalities, liver damage, nausea, diarrhea, vomiting, loss of appetite, drowsiness, coordination and balance problems, confusion, headache, insomnia, rash.
Phenobarbital *Luminal*	Tonic-Clonic	• Hyperactivity, sedation, impaired learning, dizziness, rash, nausea, diarrhea, blood abnormalities, loss of calcium, bone weakness.
Phenytoin *Dilantin*	Tonic-Clonic	• Overgrowth of gums, coarsening of facial features, drowsiness, impaired coordination, loss of calcium, bone weakness, slurred speech, nausea, diarrhea, vomiting, difficulty swallowing, rash, increased facial and body hair, joint pain, liver damage, blood abnormalities. • May worsen partial seizures.
Primidone *Mysoline*	Complex partial	• Folic acid anemia, sedation, impaired learning, rash, nausea, drowsiness, hyperactivity, dizziness, coordination problems.
Valproic Acid *Depakene*	Myoclonic Tonic-Clonic	• Nausea, vomiting, indigestion, lethargy, liver damage, eye damage, dizziness, coordination problems, tremor, loss of hair, hyperactivity, aggression, weakness. • Irritation of mouth and throat are likely if capsules are not swallowed whole.

is treated through emergency anticonvulsant therapy that is usually given intravenously. The staff will become familiar with what is normal for each student and when medical assistance should be requested.

Sensitizing Others The occurrence of a seizure may be embarrassing to the student with disabilities and frightening or confusing to peers and adults. The collaborative team should discuss procedures that can be used to minimize the impact that seizures may have on others in the school and community. The teacher or parent may wish to inform other students and faculty that the student may have a seizure and provide information on how to react if it occurs. The school may also want to bring in a person from the local epilepsy foundation to educate the student body about seizure disorders. If a seizure occurs when peers are not prepared, they will most likely react with concern for the student. The teacher should reassure them that the student will recover and that there is no imminent danger. If the student is

•• SEIZURE RECORD ••

Student's Name: ______________________ Date: ______________
Time (of occurrence): ______________________ Classroom: ______________

ANTECEDENTS

Student's location: ______________________
Student's activity: ______________________
Warning signs ☐No Yes☐ *If "Yes," describe:* ______________________

SEIZURE BEHAVIOR

Duration (*If approximate, state it*): ______________________

			Parts of Body Involved:
Did student's body stiffen?	☐ No	☐ Yes	
Did student's body shake?	☐ No	☐ Yes	Arms ☐ Left Right ☐
Did the student fall?	☐ No	☐ Yes	Legs ☐ Left Right ☐
Any apparent injury?	☐ No	☐ Yes	Other: ______________

Describe: ______________________

Did the student appear to become unaware of the environment? ☐ No ☐ Yes
Was there a change in color of the student's lips, nailbeds, etc.? ☐ No ☐ Yes

Describe: ______________________

Did student wet or soil? Urine: ☐ No ☐ Yes Feces: ☐ No ☐ Yes
Did student have difficulty breathing?
Before: ☐ No ☐ Yes During: ☐ No ☐ Yes After: ☐ No ☐ Yes

Other/*Describe:* ______________________

SUBSEQUENCES

Describe first aid given: ______________________

Describe student's activity after seizure: ______________________

Notifications: ☐ None required ☐Parents ☐Physician
☐Other (Specify): ______________________

Reported By: ______________________ Date/Time Filed: ______________

Figure 13–1
A Behavioral Seizure Observation Record

From *Educating Children with Multiple Disabilities: A Transdisciplinary Approach* (2nd ed.) (p. 207) by F. P. Orelove & D. Sobsey, 1991, Baltimore: Paul H. Brookes Publishing Co., P.O. Box 10624, Baltimore, Maryland 21285-0624. Reprinted with permission.

likely to be confused, embarrassed, or incontinent when the seizure ends, the teacher should explain that to the peers and redirect their attention to their activity.

Skin Conditions

Monitoring the skin condition of students with severe disabilities is a concern for staff.

Unhealthy skin and skin breakdowns (pressure sores) can occur if the skin is not kept clean and dry, if nutrition is inadequate, if activity is minimal, and if there is continuous pressure on parts of the body. Students with multiple disabilities may be at increased risk for the development of pressure sores because of their lack of activity, difficulty in repositioning themselves, and incontinence.

Staff should monitor students' skin to ensure that sores do not develop and that the skin is kept clean and dry. Pressure sores begin with redness that disappears when the pressure is relieved. If the pressure is not relieved, the skin becomes reddened, hardened, and warmer than the surrounding skin, then develops a sore, which may present drainage. If untreated, the sore will continue to deepen. To prevent pressure sores, the student should be checked for redness of the skin in areas that experience pressure as a result of positioning or prosthetic and orthotic equipment. When red areas are noted, the skin must be monitored to see if the redness will disappear (in 20 minutes). If it persists, a health-care provider should be notified.

Staff should also make sure that students are provided with adequate nutrition, hydration, and activity. Students who are at risk for the development of pressure sores should be repositioned every 20 minutes. If a pressure sore is being treated, the staff must conscientiously follow the treatment regimen. Any change in skin condition should be reported immediately to a health-care provider.

Postural Drainage

Some students with severe disabilities experience chronic bronchial and lung problems that result in pooling of secretions in the lungs and bronchi. If the student lacks the muscle control or coordination necessary to effectively cough and clear fluid from the lungs, the physician may recommend postural drainage.

Adults who will perform postural drainage must be trained by a health-care provider or parent. The procedure should occur well before (an hour and a half) a meal and should never be done following a meal. The student can be placed on the adult's lap or on a padded incline board. The student is encouraged to breathe deeply. The adult strikes one side of the student's chest with a cupped hand (percussion) for 1 to 2 minutes, then the opposite side of the chest for 1 to 2 minutes. After cupping, the student is encouraged to breathe deeply while the adult vibrates the chest wall. Percussion is performed over the anterior upper and lower lobes, lateral lobes, and posterior lower and upper lobes of the lungs (Scipien et al., 1990). The trainer should demonstrate the proper sites for percussion.

After the postural drainage procedure is completed (20 to 30 minutes), the student should be allowed to rest. Mucus that the student coughs up should be disposed of in a lined garbage container. If the student coughs up yellow, green, or blood-tinged mucus, the health-care provider should be notified. If the student vomits during the procedural drainage procedure, care must be taken to remove the vomitus without allowing it to be pulled into the trachea or lungs (Graff et al., 1990).

Passive Range of Motion

Passive joint range of motion exercises are performed to prevent joint deformities, aid in the normalization of muscle tone, and prevent shortening of the muscles. It is termed a "passive" procedure because the adult performs the movement rather than the student. These exercises do not strengthen the muscles but are used to maintain joint mobility.

The movements listed in Figure 13–2 are typically performed in passive joint range of motion.

The physician, nursing supervisor, or physical therapist should instruct classroom personnel on the movements to perform and the number of times each day the procedure should be done. Ideally, the adult should seek functional contexts in which to perform the movement (Graff et al., 1990). For example, elbow flexion and extension may be provided in a switch toy activity by flexing and extend-

BODY PART	TYPE OF MOVEMENT	
Neck	**Flexion:**	Chin is brought to rest on chest.
	Extension:	Head is returned to erect position.
	Hyperextension:	Head is bent back as far as possible.
	Lateral flexion:	Head is tilted as far as possible toward each shoulder.
	Rotation:	Head is turned as far as possible to the right and to the left.
Shoulder	**Flexion:**	Arm is raised from side position forward to a position above head.
	Extension:	Arm is returned to position at side of body.
	Hyperextension:	Arm is moved behind the body, keeping elbow straight.
	Abduction:	Arm is raised to side to a position above head with palm away from the head.
	Adduction:	Arm is lowered sideways and across the body as far as possible.
	Internal rotation:	With elbow flexed, shoulder is rotated by moving the arm until thumb is turned inward and toward the back.
	External rotation:	With elbow flexed, the arm is moved until thumb is upward and lateral to the head.
	Circumduction:	Arm is moved in a full circle.
Elbow	**Flexion:**	Elbow is bent so that the lower arm moves toward its shoulder joint and the hand is level with the shoulder.
	Extension:	Elbow is straightened by lowering the hand.
	Hyperextension:	Lower arm is bent back as far as possible.
Forearm	**Supination:**	Lower arm and hand are turned so that palm is up.
	Pronation:	Lower arm is turned so palm is down.
Wrist	**Flexion:**	Palm is moved toward inner aspect of forearm.
	Extension:	Fingers are moved so that fingers, hands, and forearm are level.
	Hyperextension:	The back of the hand is brought back as far as possible.
	Abduction:	Wrist is bent toward the thumb.
	Adduction:	Wrist is bent toward the fifth finger.

Figure 13–2
Range of Joint Motion Exercises
From *Health Care for Students with Disabilities* (pp. 144–147) by J. C. Graff, M. M. Ault, D. Guess, M. Taylor, & B. Thompson, 1990, Baltimore: Paul H. Brookes Publishing Co., P.O. Box 10624, Baltimore, Maryland 21285-0624. Reprinted by permission.

BODY PART	TYPE OF MOVEMENT	
Finger	**Extension:**	Fingers are straightened.
	Hyperextension:	Fingers are bent back as far as possible.
	Abduction:	Fingers are spread apart.
	Adduction:	Fingers are brought together.
Thumb	**Flexion:**	Thumb is moved across palm of hand.
	Extension:	Thumb is moved straight away from hand.
	Opposition:	Thumb is touched to each finger of the same hand.
Hip	**Flexion:**	Leg is moved forward and up.
	Extension:	Leg is moved back beside other leg.
	Hyperextension:	Leg is moved behind body.
	Abduction:	Leg is moved laterally away from body.
	Adduction:	Leg is moved back toward center of body and beyond if possible.
	Internal rotation:	Foot and leg are turned toward other leg.
	External rotation:	Foot and leg are turned away from other leg.
	Circumduction:	Leg is moved in a circle.
Knee	**Flexion:**	Heel is brought toward back of thigh.
	Extension:	Leg is returned to floor.
Ankle	**Dorsal flexion:**	Foot is moved so that toes are pointed upward.
	Plantar flexion:	Foot is moved so that toes are pointed downward.
Foot	**Inversion:**	Sole of foot is turned in toward middle of the body.
	Eversion:	Sole of foot is turned out away from middle of the body.
Toes	**Flexion:**	Toes are curled downward.
	Extension:	Toes are straightened.
	Abduction:	Toes are spread apart.
	Adduction:	Toes are brought together.

Figure 13–2, *continued*

ing the student's elbow so that he or she can press a switch attached to an age-appropriate, battery-operated toy. Professionals with a medical orientation may not be able to readily identify functional contexts for the performance of passive range of motion. In medical settings, these procedures constitute an activity in themselves. The teacher may have to provide a rationale for the purpose of embedding procedures within functional activities and collaborate with medical team members to determine the appropriate procedures to be used.

It is critical that the staff person who provides the passive range of motion exercises understand the appropriate techniques for performing the exercises and the appropriate range of movement for each joint. If muscle resistance is encountered or if the adult attempts to force stretching, the student may experience pain and injury. The student should be relaxed and properly positioned before range of motion exercises are performed.

Medication

Students with severe disabilities are more likely than any other population in school to need medication administered during school hours. The most common types of routine medication are anticonvulsants for seizure management, psychotropic medication for treating undesirable behavior, stimulants for hyperactivity or depression, and muscle relaxants (Sobsey & Cox, 1991). The prevalence of students with severe disabilities who may be receiving medication ranges from 15% for students labeled trainable mentally disabled (Gadow & Kalachnik, 1981) to 53% of students labeled profoundly mentally disabled (Fox & Westling, 1986). Anticonvulsants and tranquilizers account for the majority of medications prescribed to students with severe disabilities (Fox & Westling, 1986). Thus, teachers must become familiar with methods for administering medication and monitoring its effects.

Anticonvulsants Some commonly prescribed anticonvulsant medications are phenobarbital, Dilantin, Depakene, and Tegretol. The type of medication prescribed is determined by the seizure classification and the medical history of the individual. Reactions may occur from high levels of the drug in the blood, side effects of the medication, or idiosyncratic reactions (Gadow, 1982). The side effects of anticonvulsants may include confusion, dizziness, irritability, impaired learning, drowsiness, and impaired coordination.

Pyschotropics Psychotropic medications include stimulants, major tranquilizers, and minor tranquilizers; such drugs may be prescribed for the management of hyperactivity or extreme maladaptive behavior, as a sedative, or as a muscle relaxant. The side effects of psychotropic medication can include reduction of activity, drowsiness, impairment of attention, skin reactions, nausea, and dry mouth. Other very alarming side effects include four disorders that involve the motor area of the brain called the extrapyramidal tract: parkinsonian syndrome, akathisia, acute dystonic reactions, and tardive dyskinesia (Gadow, 1987). In parkinsonian syndrome, the medication user appears depressed, has decreased spontaneous movement, and may walk with a shuffling gait. Akathisia is characterized by motor restlessness. Acute dystonic reactions include the symptoms of facial grimacing, a fixed upward gaze, and an unnatural twisting of the neck. Tardive dyskinesia involves involuntary, repetitive movements such as smacking the lips, tongue movement, movements of the arms, and jerky body movement.

Medication Administration Because medication administration is critical to the student's medical management and can involve serious side effects, the teacher plays an important role in providing information to the student's family and health-care providers. Before medication is administered by school personnel, the information listed in Figure 13–3 should be obtained from the physician.

Some system of ongoing communication should also be established so that the physician is aware of any changes in the student's behavior that may be related to the medication and the dosages that the student is receiving in the classroom. The collaborative team should discuss how information will be relayed to the student's health-care provider. For some stu-

Figure 13–3
Information Needed to Administer Medication

1. Medication needed, dosage level, and schedule
2. Purpose of medication
3. Method of administration
4. Precautions about administration (e.g., only after meals or with water)
5. Physician who prescribed the medication
6. Side effects and interaction effects associated with the medication
7. Medication storage information
8. Emergency contact person and phone number

dents, the teacher may wish to provide the information to the family, who will communicate directly to the physician. In other situations, the teacher or school nurse may be in direct contact with the health-care provider.

It is desirable for medical personnel to administer medications, but when a school nurse is not available for this function, classroom personnel may have to take on the responsibility. Because medication may be in pill, capsule, suppository, or liquid form, teachers and aids should be trained in the appropriate procedures to be used. The precautions for medication administration listed in Figure 13–4 should be noted by school personnel who are involved in medication administration.

Procedures for handling and storing medications in the classroom are also a concern. Some medications need refrigeration and should be kept cold at all times. This may mean that the medication will need to be stored in a cooler when taken off campus with the student. Classroom personnel should also pay close attention to medication expiration dates. If a medication has expired it should not be used. Some medications should be stored in a locked cabinet. The collaborative team should discuss ways to ensure that medications are stored safely and are not vulnerable to theft or misuse.

Nutrition and Feeding

Nutrition

The nutritional status of students is a growing concern among educators. Many students have inadequate diets that are not nutritionally complete. Students with severe and multiple disabilities are at increased risk of nutritional problems. They may need special diets to address their unique nutritional status, may require assistance with eating to ensure that an adequate amount of food is safely consumed, and may need to be monitored for growth and weight gain.

The collaborative team should develop individual nutrition and feeding plans for students whose nutritional status is a concern. Areas of concern may be the student's medication and its effects on the student's physical status, oral-motor skills, medical conditions that may affect the absorption of nutrients or eating ability, and eating skills or habits.

Many students with severe disabilities may be receiving medications that interfere with the absorption of nutrients; some drugs may cause nausea or decrease appetite. The collaborative team should review the student's medications for nutritional impact and develop

Figure 13–4
Precautions for Medication Administration

1. The caregiver must wash hands before medication administration.
2. Student should be in a relaxed position and calm when receiving medication.
3. Medication can be placed in the student's mouth by spoon, dropper, plastic syringe, or by placing a tablet on the tongue.
4. If the student refuses to take the medication or vomits after administration, the caregiver should wait 20-30 minutes and try again.
5. Missed dosages should be recorded and reported to the health care provider or caregiver.
6. The caregiver should maintain a record of medication administration including the dosage given, the time it was administered, and concerns that the caregiver or health-care provider should be aware of.

procedures to assure that malnutrition does not occur.

Several medical conditions may also impact a student's nutritional status. A student who has Prader-Willi syndrome, which is associated with insatiable appetite, will be on a strict diet and must have food intake monitored. A student with a cleft palate may have difficulty with managing food orally and can be at risk for malnutrition because eating is a difficult activity. A student with cerebral palsy may have oral-motor skill difficulties that result in decreased food intake and may be at risk for nutritional problems.

The diet for students who are at risk or have nutritional problems must be monitored by the collaborative team; the basic school lunch will not be adequate for many students. Some will require diets that provide increased caloric intake. The goal for these students is to add calories, not bulk, to the diet. It is possible that increased calories can result from providing more snacks and several small meals or the assistance needed to ensure adequate intake. For other students, the meal may have to be enriched with an additive (e.g., dry milk, instant breakfast, vegetable oils, dry infant cereal, cheese, peanut butter) to provide increased calories.

Team members may also be concerned about the fluid intake of students. Students who are on medication or who have oral-motor difficulties may not have adequate fluid intake; team members should offer many opportunities for them to drink and provide diets that are high in water content (e.g., fruit and vegetables). One method for offering liquids throughout the day may be to provide a straw bottle (the kind used by athletes) that is always accessible and filled with water or a preferred drink. If there is a concern about a student's fluid intake, the collaborative team should define the minimal desired intake (based on weight and medical conditions) and develop a tracking system to monitor the student.

The consistency of the diet is a concern for students with oral motor difficulties. Students who are unable to chew need to be provided a blended diet and students who are beginning to bite may need to be provided with finger foods and a chopped diet. The consistency of the meal may also be changed to assist the student with oral motor problems in managing food. Blended foods and liquids may be thickened, using cereal, wheat germ, or vegetable flakes, to assist a student who cannot handle thin consistency. Thicker foods and liquids provide more sensory cues and may help the student coordinate oral motor movements. If the student has very weak tongue and pharynx movements, thick liquids and foods may be more difficult to handle and thinning liquids and foods may be warranted. Any changes in food consistency should be part of the overall feeding plan and discussed by the collaborative team. Regardless of the diet, the presentation of a meal should be appetizing (e.g., do not mix foods together) and students should be offered choices. Forcing a student to consume foods that are not appealing is not an appropriate practice. The goal of supporting students who have difficulty with nutritional intake is to make meals pleasant and desirable events.

Eating Skills

Students with severe disabilities may have motor difficulties or sensory integration problems that impact their ability to eat. Some of the difficulties that students encounter are described in this section. Diagnosis of feeding problems and the development of a feeding program should be done by the occupational therapist or speech therapist in collaboration with the team.

A *jaw thrust* describes an exaggerated up-down extension of the jaw (Morris & Klein, 1987). Students who exhibit an extensor motor pattern or have oral hypersensitivity may exhibit a jaw thrust. Treatment may include: (a) reducing the sensory distractions in the feeding environment, (b) providing a better sitting posture, and (c) assisting with jaw closure by providing jaw stability support (Morris & Klein, 1987). Jaw stability support (see Figure 13–5) may be provided by the feeder who is to the side or behind the student by placing the middle finger under the jaw, index finger on the chin, and thumb at the temporomandibular (jaw) joint (Morris & Klein, 1987). If the feeder is in front of the student, she can place the middle finger under the jaw, the index finger at the temporomandibular joint, and the thumb on the chin or below the lower lip (Morris & Klein, 1987).

Jaw clenching describes the movement of the jaw into a tightly clenched position. This may be caused by low tone in the trunk and a poor sitting position, an overstimulating environment, or oral hypersensitivity. Some treatment options include positioning the student appropriately, reducing hypersensitivity by providing firm pressure to the teeth, face, and gums, and using sensory stimulation procedures to normalize the student's response to sensory stimulation.

Jaw retraction describes the retraction of the jaw in a backward direction. This may be related to poor sitting posture, an overstimulating environment, or a motor pattern of hyperextension. Options for intervention include providing a better sitting posture and reducing distracting sensory stimulation in the feeding environment. *Jaw instability* describes the loose

Figure 13–5
Hand Placement for Providing Jaw Stability
From *Pre-feeding Skills* by Marsha Dunn Klein and Suzanne Evans Morrison, copyright © 1987 by Therapy Skill Builders, a division of Communication Skill Builderes, Inc., PO Box 420050, Tuscon, AZ 85773. Reprinted with permission.

movement of the jaw due to lack of muscle tone and joint control. It may be related to hypotonicity and developmental delays or deviations of the oral musculature. Treatment options include activities to build tone in the trunk, stimulation to the muscles that open and close the jaw, and the use of jaw support techniques.

Lack of *lip closure* occurs when there is low muscle tone in the lips, causing food and saliva to drip from the mouth. To increase muscle tone and facilitate lip closure, the adult may pat the lips or stroke around the lips, using a firm, circular motion. Providing jaw stability support may also facilitate lip closure.

A *tonic bite reflex* describes a sudden bite when the teeth are stimulated by touching them with a finger or a spoon. The tonic bite may be related to an overstimulating environment, oral hypersensitivity, or poor sitting posture. Options for intervention include providing better sitting posture, reducing the stimulation of the feeding environment, and reducing the hypersensitivity that occurs when a finger or a spoon is introduced in the mouth. To reduce hypersensitivity, the adult should wear gloves and begin by sliding her index finger into the student's mouth and applying firm deep pressure to the outer surface of the upper and lower gums (Morris & Klein, 1987). Biting can occur during feeding. A coated spoon or rubber spoon can be used to reduce the hypersensitivity to the spoon. If the student bites on the spoon while it is in his mouth, the adult should wait for the student to release. Pulling on the spoon will only increase the strength of the bite. The adult can move the student's head into alignment with the body or rock gently to reduce the muscle tension in the body to assist the student with the release of the spoon.

Tongue retraction describes the movement of the tongue back into the oral cavity. This may occur with students who have low or high tone, neck hyperextension, or cleft of the hard palate. Proper positioning, including the maintenance of the head in a chin-tucked position, will assist in decreasing tongue retraction. *Tongue protrusion* is the movement of the tongue beyond the border of the gums. A tongue thrust is the forceful protrusion of the tongue from the mouth. Students with low tone may exhibit tongue protrusion. Tongue thrust is typically associated with extensor patterns of movement. Intervention options include appropriate positioning of the student, normalizing tone before positioning for eating, providing a different consistency of food so that tongue protrusion is not needed to move it backward, providing jaw support, presenting the food horizontally at the bottom lip so that the upper lip and a suck are used rather than the tongue, and placing the spoon on the middle of the tongue while pressing evenly downward with a vibratory movement (Morris & Klein, 1987).

If the student's muscle tone is high, *lip retraction* (lips pulled back tightly across mouth) and *pursing* (lips pulled in and puckered to counteract retraction) can occur. Reducing the hypertonicity, working for better sitting posture, and providing a relaxing environment should assist the student to relax the lips.

Some students may exhibit problems with the feeding process that are related to their postural tone, developmental delay, and reflex development. Students who have difficulty with a suckle pattern should be positioned carefully, provided with a quiet mealtime environment, and be given opportunities to suck at different times during the day. The student who does not use mature oral movement patterns when eating soft foods can be provided with jaw control and gentle pressure on the tongue with the spoon as it is placed in the mouth. If a student does not use mature oral movement patterns during cup drinking, the feeder can provide jaw control and provide thickened liquids to drink that are easier to handle. The student who chokes and gags during the meal should be assessed to determine if a hyperactive gag is present. If so, the occupational therapist can design a program to help the student develop a more normalized gag reflex. The student may be gagging to communicate that he doesn't like the food that is being offered or that he wants the meal to end. If the behavior is being used for attention and control, the adult should carefully examine the antecedents, consequences, and setting events that occur with the behavior. An intervention plan should be designed to reduce the behavior that relates to the function of the behavior (see chapter 11) rather than the topography. If the student is using the behavior to communicate dislike of a particular food, the adult should ensure that choices are provided. If the student is using the behavior to signal that he is finished eating, the adult may teach the student an alternative way to signal "finished" or may need to systematically teach the student to tolerate more food.

Some students will vomit food or liquid during or after a meal. This may be caused by difficulty with digestion that results in refluxing of the stomach contents into the esophagus. Some students are able to tolerate only small quantities of food and when that point is surpassed, vomiting occurs. If vomiting is occurring, the teacher should refer the student to the physician to explore medical treatment alternatives. The student should be placed in a stander or over a wedge for 30 to 60 minutes after a meal to assist with the digestion. Another option is to provide small meals at shorter intervals in the day.

Positioning Appropriate positioning is vital to mealtime success for students who have eating difficulties. It is most desirable for the student to be upright, provided with adequate trunk stability, with head in an upright and chin-tucked position, and with hips and knees flexed. Good support should be provided for the student, including support under the feet. The most appropriate position is based on the individual student's medical and orthopedic needs and should be determined by the collaborative team. The person who is feeding the student must also be concerned about his or her position. The feeder should be seated with his or her face at the student's eye level, and should also assume a position that allows freedom of movement so that assisting the student will not call for stretching or straining.

Tube Feeding

When students are not able to eat a sufficient amount or are not able to take nourishment orally, tube feeding may be used. In this method, nourishment is provided through a nasogastric (nose to stomach) tube or gastrostomy (stomach) tube.

Tube feedings are fairly simple procedures and may be managed by any person on the team who has received training from a health-care provider. Such training should cover procedures to be used, the student's special health-care needs, and how to implement an established emergency plan. It is desirable to conduct tube feedings at mealtimes and snack times with other students. Some students who are tube-fed receive oral feedings as well. Oral feedings are conducted with guidance of the medical professional or therapist who has designated the procedures to be used.

Students who are tube-fed are generally placed in an upright position during the tube feeding and for one hour after the feeding. To avoid stomach cramping, the formula should be allowed to reach room temperature before it is used. Unused formula should be refrigerated to prevent bacteria growth.

Nasogastric Tube Feeding A nasogastric tube (see Figure 13–6) is a tube that is inserted through the nose, down the esophagus, and into the stomach. Its use is usually a temporary measure to provide nourishment to the student. Students with nasogastric tubes may be provided with nourishment through the bolus method, the intermittent gravity drip method, or the continuous drip method. The bolus method involves a large amount of fluid or formula that is allowed to flow through the tube in several minutes. The intermittent gravity drip method involves dripping the formula slowly from a hanging container for a 20- to 30-minute period. Students who cannot tolerate a rapid presentation of formula may use a continuous drip method, in which the formula is allowed to drip slowly over a 16- to 24-hour period. Infusion pumps that control the presentation of the formula may be used to provide continuous drip feeding. The general procedure to be used for nasogastric tube feeding is provided in Figure 13–7. A health-care provider should train responsible personnel in the procedures to be used and how to implement an established emergency plan.

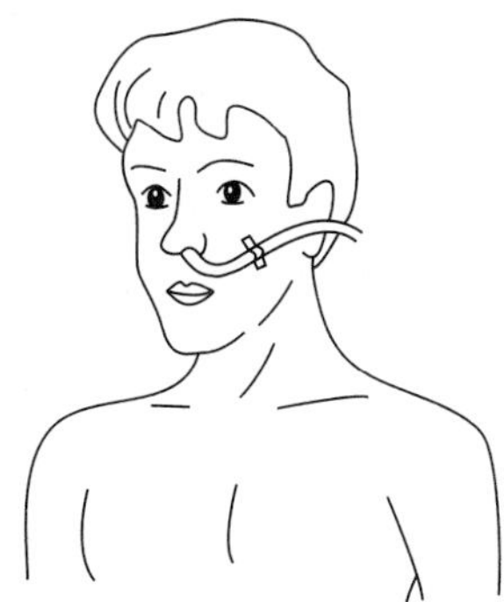

Figure 13–6
Student with Nasogastric Tube

Gastrostomy Tube Feeding A gastrostomy is a surgical opening into the stomach through the surface of the abdomen. A tube is used to maintain the opening and to administer food and fluids directly to the stomach (see Figure

1. Wash hands.
2. Assemble equipment and formula that is room temperature.
3. Position the student.
4. Check the placement of the NG tube by opening the tube, placing a syringe to the end of the tube, and pushing in 5–10 cc of air into the tube. If the tube is properly placed, a whooshing sound of air can be heard through a stethoscope placed over the mid-left abdomen.
5. Remove cap from end of tube and insert syringe for bolus feeding.
6. If using slow drip method or continuous feeding by pump, pour formula into bag and allow to run to tip. Clamp. Hang bag or place in pump. Insert tip of tube into NG tube opening. Open clamp of feeding tube and adjust flow rate.
7. Pour formula into syringe and allow to flow in by gravity. Flow can be regulated by raising or lowering the syringe. Recommended placement height is 6 inches above student's head level.
8. Follow formula with water if recommended.

Figure 13–7
Procedure for Nasogastric Tube Feeding

Developed from *Children Assisted by Medical Technology in Educational Settings: Guidelines for Care* by M. Haynie, S. M. Porter, & J. S. Palfrey, 1989, Boston: The Children's Hospital, Project School Care.

13–8). The gastrostomy tube is held in place by a bubble of air or a mushroom tip inside the stomach. The gastrostomy tube extends 8 to 12 inches and has a small removable plug inserted in the end of the tube to keep the stomach contents from flowing out. Some students may have a skin-level tube called a button, which protrudes only slightly beyond the abdominal wall and provides increased mobility and comfort. Feeding procedures for the button are almost identical to those for the gastrostomy tube, which are described in Figure 13–9.

Students with gastrostomy tubes may be fed using the bolus, intermittent drip, or continuous drip method. Individual procedures and an emergency plan should be described by the health-care provider who is familiar with the student. Problems that may occur with the gastrostomy site are redness, tenderness, and bleeding. If these signs are present, they should be reported to the health-care provider or parent. It is also possible for the gastrostomy tube to come out. If that occurs, a sterile, dry dressing should be placed over the site and the health-care provider or parent should be notified immediately. The student is in no imminent danger, although the opening could close in a few hours if another tube is not inserted.

Figure 13–8
Student with Gastrostomy Tube

Special Concerns

Tracheostomy

A tracheostomy is a surgical opening in the trachea to permit the movement of air into the lungs. Tracheostomies may be performed on students who have an obstruction in the upper airway, respiratory distress, or central nervous system disorders that affect the strength and effectiveness of respiratory movements. A tube of plastic or silastic material is placed in the opening and is held in place by cloth ties (see Figure 13–10). The tracheostomy bypasses the normal wetting and filtering actions of the upper airway and creates a need to humidify the air that enters the tracheostomy opening (Wong, 1993). Students may have a special tracheostomy mask that provides humidified air directly to the opening, may be attached to a mechanical ventilator, or may need a room humidifier placed near them.

Classroom personnel must be trained to provide tracheostomy care to the student. It is important that all staff members have knowledge of the procedures to be used so that regardless of who is present, someone will be able to respond in emergency situations. A suction machine is used for cleaning the trachea of secretions that build up in the tracheostomy tube, and it must be ready for immediate use at all times; if the equipment is not operable or present, the student should not attend school until a suction machine is provided. A backup method for suctioning (manual or battery

1. Wash hands.
2. Assemble equipment and formula that is room temperature.
3. Position the child.
4. Remove cap or plug from G-tube and insert a syringe. Draw back plunger to remove any liquid that may be left in the stomach. If instructed, return contents to stomach. If amount of stomach contents is a concern, the feeding may need to be delayed.
5. Clamp the G-tube, remove the plunger from the syringe.
6. Reinsert the syringe, hold at recommended height, unclamp tube, and allow bubbles to escape.
7. If feeding by slow drip or infusion pump, keep tube clamped and prepare formula bag. Allow formula to run to end of feeding tube tip and clamp. Hang bag and insert feeding tube tip into G-tube tip. Unclamp the G-tube. Open clamp of feeding tube and allow to flow. Adjust rate of flow.
8. Pour formula into syringe and allow to flow in by gravity.
9. When feeding is complete, pour in the recommended amount of water to flush the tube.

Figure 13–9
Procedure for Gastrostomy Feeding
Developed from *Children Assisted by Medical Technology in Educational Settings: Guidelines for Care* by M. Haynie, S. M. Porter, & J. S. Palfrey, 1989, Boston: The Children's Hospital, Project School Care.

operated) should also be available to be used during all school activities (e.g., on the playground) and during transport.

Suctioning is used to clear the trachea of excessive secretions and mucus plugs. The warning signs that indicate a student needs suctioning are restlessness, difficulty breathing, a frightened look, or the sound or presence of bubbles of mucus in the tracheostomy tube (Graff et al., 1990). The procedures used for suctioning are listed in Figure 13–11.

In addition to suctioning, school personnel may also be concerned with cleaning the inner cannula of the tracheostomy, monitoring the skin condition around the stoma, and changing tracheostomy ties and tube. Some tracheostomy tubes are constructed with an inner cannula that can be removed for cleaning. The person removing the inner cannula must wear gloves when conducting the procedure. The inner cannula is then soaked in hydrogen peroxide to loosen the secretions and the tube is cleaned, using a brush or pipe cleaners. The inner cannula is rinsed with water or a saline solution before being replaced in the tracheostomy tube (Graff et al., 1990).

The skin around the stoma must be kept clean and dry. The skin can be cleansed using hydrogen peroxide and water to remove dried or crusted secretions. A dressing may be placed around the tube to soak up excessive secretions. The tracheostomy ties may need to be changed as they become soiled. When changing the ties, the new ties are first threaded and secured before the old ties are cut and removed. Routine replacement of ties should be done at home, although the school must be prepared to conduct the procedure if needed.

It is possible that the tracheostomy tube may need to be changed at school. If the tube comes out, school personnel must be prepared to replace it with a new one. To change a tube, the student is placed on his back with a roll under his neck so that access to the tracheosto-

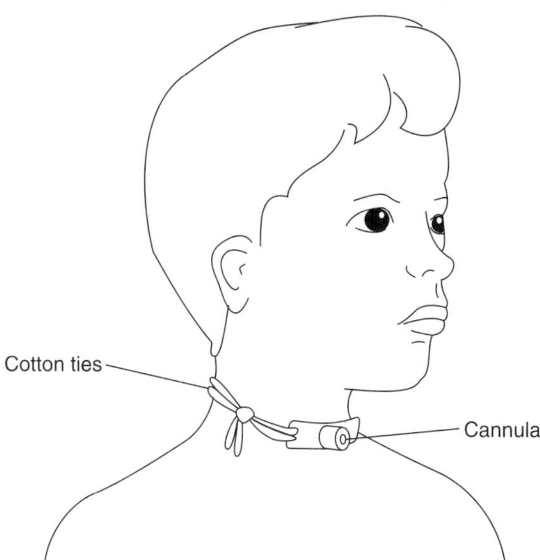

Figure 13–10
Position of the Tracheostomy Tube

my area is easy. The tracheostomy ties are cut and the tube is removed, then the new tube is inserted in the stoma.

Whenever school personnel are involved in tracheostomy care, they must wash their hands and clean the equipment that is used thoroughly. Spare tubes should be kept in their sealed packages to ensure sterility. Suctioning equipment and other supplies should be checked and replenished daily so that any emergency can be handled immediately.

If the tracheostomy tube becomes blocked, classroom personnel must be poised to take immediate action because the student will be unable to breathe. Suctioning may be used to try to remove the blockage, but if that fails the tracheostomy tube should be removed and a new one inserted. If the student does not begin breathing, CPR procedures for individuals with tracheostomies should be performed (mouth and nose are covered and the rescuer breathes into the stoma). Other difficulties that classroom personnel should respond to are respiratory distress, respiratory infections, and skin infections. Concerns about these conditions must be reported to the designated health-care provider.

Ileostomy and Colostomy

An ileostomy or colostomy redirects the flow of feces in individuals who have obstructions or blockages in the intestines that restrict passage of the intestinal contents. A surgical opening is made and a portion of the intestine is pulled out and secured to the abdomen (stoma). A pouch or plastic bag is placed over the stoma for the collection of fecal material (see Figure 13–12). In an ileostomy, the stoma is created from a portion of the small intestine (ileum). In a colostomy, the stoma is created from the colon.

If the student has an ileostomy, the consistency of the stool is liquid or pasty and contains digestive enzymes that can be very irritating to the skin (Graff et al., 1990). The student wears a drainable pouch that collects the fecal materials as it flows. The pouch must be drained frequently during the day; this is done by placing the student over the toilet and opening the pouch, allowing the material to flow into the toilet. For students who are unable to sit on the toilet or young children, the pouch can be drained into a receptacle that is later dumped into the toilet. The pouch may also have to be opened periodically to release accumulated gas. The student's health-care provider should train the classroom staff in procedures to be used and the signs and symptoms of possible complications.

A student with a colostomy may have a drainable pouch or may have a regulated elimination cycle and formed feces. Those students may have a covering over the stoma instead of a drainable bag or may wear a pouch that is not drainable.

1. Wash hands.
2. Assemble needed equipment included a suction backup device.
3. Position student.
4. Open suction catheter or kit without touching the inside of the package to maintain sterility.
5. Fill container with saline solution if recommended.
6. Put gloves on hands. Use dominant hand for handling suction catheter only. Use nondominant hand for manipulating switches, etc.
7. Hold the end of the suction catheter with dominant hand and connect to suction machine tubing.
8. Turn machine on and adjust to prescribed vacuum setting.
9. Encourage the student to cough and take a deep breath. If recommended, place several drops of saline into trach with nondominant hand.
10. Hold suction catheter 2–3 inches from tip and insert tip into saline to test that the suction is functioning.
11. Grasp the catheter connection with nondominant hand and cover vent hole to suction small amount of saline through catheter.
12. Take thumb off vent hole and gently insert catheter into trach 1/2 cm. Cover vent hole with thumb and withdraw the catheter.
13. Rotate the catheter gently when withdrawing to reach all of the secretions in the tube. Insertion and withdrawal should be completed within 10 seconds.
14. Allow the student to breathe between suctioning passes.
15. When suctioning is complete, suction saline through catheter to rinse catheter and tubing. Remove gloves and wash hands. Discard used catheter in appropriate receptacle.

Figure 13–11
Procedure for Tracheal Suctioning
Developed from *Children Assisted by Medical Technology in Educational Settings: Guidelines for Care* by M. Haynie, S. M. Porter, & J. S. Palfrey, 1989, Boston: The Children's Hospital, Project School Care.

Classroom personnel must know the procedures for draining and changing a student's ileostomy or colostomy bag. General procedures are described in Figure 13–13. In addition, classroom staff must be alert to the warning signs that may signal medical problems. Color changes in the stoma (from pink to a dusky or black color), irritation of the skin surrounding the stoma, difficulty with elimination, diarrhea, or excessive gas must be reported to the parent or health-care provider (Graff et al., 1990).

Catheterization

Students with defects of the spinal cord (e.g., spina bifida) may not be able to voluntarily control bladder functioning and may not have a sense of bladder fullness. Clean intermittent catheterization (CIC) is a technique to empty the bladder through the use of a catheter. Students with the cognitive and motor ability may be learning to catheterize themselves; other students will be dependent on adults for the catheterization procedures.

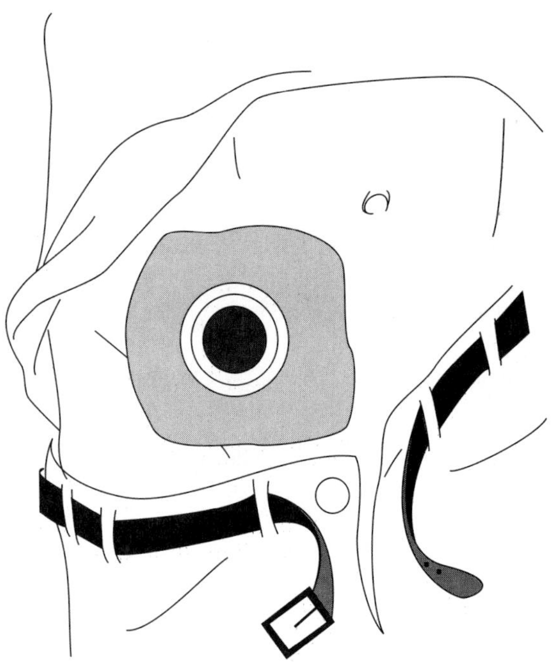

Figure 13–12
Student with Ileostomy Bag

CIC is performed every 3 to 4 hours. The procedure must be conducted in a location that ensures the student's privacy. The catheterization procedures should be specified by the urologist who has determined that CIC be used. Classroom personnel should be trained in the procedures for positioning, cleansing the area, inserting the catheter, draining the bladder, removing the catheter, and cleaning the equipment by the health-care provider or parent.

The adult assisting with CIC must have clean hands and should be wearing gloves. The student may be positioned in a sitting, standing, or reclining position. If the student is a male, the staff person cleanses the penis, using soapy cotton balls and washing toward the base of the penis. The catheter is lubricated and inserted into the urethral opening until there is a flow of urine. When the bladder is emptied, the catheter is removed, then is washed, rinsed, and dried before being stored for use again.

The female student may be catheterized in a sitting or reclining position. If possible, the student may sit on the toilet with legs straddled. The staff person separates the labia and cleanses the area with soapy cotton balls, washing in a direction from the top of the labia toward the rectum. The catheter is then inserted into the urethra until the urine flow begins. When the bladder is empty, the catheter is removed. If the catheter is to be reused, it is washed and dried.

Infectious Disease

Teachers of students with severe disabilities must be concerned, as all teachers are, with the spread of infectious disease in the classroom. Infectious diseases that are commonly encountered in group care settings are listed in Table 13–2. Students with severe disabilities may have increased vulnerability to infection if they have other medical conditions or reduced resistance to infection. In addition, the risk of infection spread is heightened when students are incontinent and mouth their hands or objects. School personnel should be aware that hand-washing is the single most effective method for the prevention of communicable disease in the classroom.

HIV/AIDS

Human Immunodeficiency Virus (HIV) ia a communicable disease that is a growing concern among many educators. HIV is transmitted through sexual contact, exposure to blood, and from mother to child perinatally. Acquired Immune Deficiency Syndrome (AIDS) is diag-

1. Assemble equipment.
2. Wash hands and put on gloves.
3. Empty contents of the bag the student is wearing.
4. Carefully remove the used bag by pushing the skin away from the bag instead of pulling the bag from the skin.
5. Wash the stoma, using a clean cloth or gauze. Cover the stoma and wash the skin around the stoma, using a different cloth or fresh gauze.
6. Inspect the skin for redness, color discoloration, rash, or blistering.
7. Pat skin dry and place skin barrier on skin around stoma.
8. Peel off backing from adhesive or apply adhesive to bag.
9. Remove gauze from stoma and discard. Center new bag over stoma.
10. Firmly press bag to skin barrier.
11. Remove gloves and wash hands.

Figure 13–13
Procedure to Change a Colostomy or Ileostomy Bag
Developed from *Children Assisted by Medical Technology in Educational Settings: Guidelines for Care* by M. Haynie, S. M. Porter, & J. S. Palfrey, 1989, Boston: The Children's Hospital, Project School Care.

nosed when the HIV infection becomes symptomatic. At the early stage of HIV infection, the infected person may show no symptoms.

HIV has affected children and adolescents in increasing numbers. Children may be at risk for HIV infection through perinatal transmission from an infected mother or blood transfusions or blood products received through 1985 (Lewis & Thomson, 1989). Adolescents may be at risk for HIV infection through sexual activity and shared needles during drug use.

Special educators are likely to encounter students with AIDS because of the symptomatology of the disease. Clinical manifestations of AIDS in children include parotitis (inflammation of a salivary gland), generalized lymphadenopathy (persistent swelling of the lymph nodes), recurrent bacterial infections, neurologic disease, and developmental abnormalities (Wong, 1993). Children with AIDS who attend child-care and public school programs are more at risk for being infected with a potentially fatal infection from other children than they are for transmitting the HIV infection to others. The decision about placement of a child in a group-care or classroom situation must be made collaboratively by the family and the medical team. Students with HIV or AIDS have the same needs and rights as other students, including the right to attend school and interact with peers. Although HIV/AIDS is an infectious disease, it cannot be easily transmitted in the school setting. Because HIV is a progressive infection, the student with AIDS will have periods of acute episodes of viral and bacterial infection. During those periods services to students may need to be provided in the home or hospital setting.

Students may not be excluded from public school solely on the basis of their HIV status, and the family is within their legal rights to not notify a school of a student's HIV status. Thus,

Table 13–2
Infectious Diseases in Group Settings

Disease	Mode of Transmission	Causative Agent
Upper respiratory infection*	Respiratory	V
Streptococcal sore throat*	Respiratory	B
Otitis media (ear infection)	Respiratory	V or B
Haemophilus influenzae type b	Respiratory	B
Meningitis	Respiratory	V or B
Tuberculosis	Respiratory	B
Hepatitis A*	Oral-fecal	V
Hepatitis B	Body fluid	V
Hepatitis non-A, non-B	Body fluid	V
Shigella diarrhea*	Oral-fecal	B
Salmonella diarrhea*	Oral-fecal	B
Giardia diarrhea*	Oral-fecal	O
Viral gastroenteritis*	Oral-fecal	V
Impetigo	Direct	B
Ringworm	Direct	F
Scabies*	Direct	O
Herpes simplex (cold sore)	Direct	V
Cytomegalovirus (CMV) infection*	Multiple	V
Chickenpox*	Multiple	V
Head lice*	Direct	O
Pinworms	Oral-fecal	O
Acquired immunodeficiency syndrome (AIDS)	Body fluid	V
Conjunctivitis (pinkeye)	Direct	V or B
Mumps	Respiratory	V
Croup	Respiratory	V
Whooping cough	Respiratory	B
Measles	Respiratory	V
German measles	Respiratory	V
Roseola	Direct	V

V = Virus; B = bacteria; F = fungus; O = other.
*Frequent occurrence in group settings for children.

From *Communicable Disease and Young Children in Group Settings* (p. 37) by J. M. Taylor & W. S. Taylor, 1989, Boston: Little, Brown and Company. Reprinted with the permission of PRO-ED Inc.

the safest route is to use universal precautions with the assumption that the HIV status of students in the classroom may not be known. When the HIV status is known, school personnel must protect the student's right to confidentiality. Only staff who have daily and intimate contact with the student may benefit from knowledge of the student's HIV status. An appropriate action would be to request a notification release from the family so that the appropriate personnel can be informed about the student's condition. The most important reason for knowing about a student's HIV status is to be able to fully meet the needs of the student and the family.

Conclusion

The collaborative team is an essential component of providing an appropriate program to students with health-care needs. The school nurse or health-care provider will not be able to provide direct service to every student with health-care concerns. There are simply not enough health-care personnel in the school systems, and direct service delivery may not be necessary for the majority of students. Students with severe disabilities who have health-care needs should have those needs met as a routine function in their lives. Classroom personnel should treat activities such as administering medications, tube feedings, catheterization, and so forth as uneventful routines. Further, they should use principles of partial participation and activity-based instruction to embed skill instruction in those activities.

In order for classroom personnel to shoulder responsibility for health-care procedures, the collaborative team must thoroughly discuss the implications of those procedures and provide adequate training to the persons responsible for them. Sobsey and Cox (1991) recommend that the team develop a school health-care plan as part of the Individual Education Plan. The plan should list: (1) the health-care procedures that are required, (2) the personnel who will carry out the procedures, (3) a plan for backup if the designated personnel are unavailable, (4) the training needed to carry out the procedure, (5) documentation methods, (6) special precautions, (7) supervision responsibility, (8) equipment and supplies that may be needed, and (9) whom to contact with questions about the procedures.

Before health-care procedures can be performed in the classroom, training must be provided to the responsible classroom personnel. Often this training is best provided by the student's family in collaboration with the school health-care provider. It is very important for all classroom personnel who are in continuous contact with students who have health-care needs to be trained in cardiopulmonary resuscitation (CPR), which should only be performed by individuals who are trained. If all classroom personnel are not trained, they must be aware of the nearest CPR-trained person to contact in an emergency.

In this chapter, we have emphasized the importance of carrying out health-care procedures as routine activities that are part of the student's instructional day. The importance of documentation cannot be minimized. The classroom teacher is responsible for documenting what procedures occur and reporting information of interest to the student's family. Information that is critical to the student's continued health and well-being may include the amount of food consumed, seizure activity, when medications were administered, the amounts of elimination, and other information that is related to the student's health status. A record-keeping system should be developed that will ensure that this information is collected and sent home with the student.

Questions for Reflection

1. If one of your students had a special health-care concern or need, what steps would you

want to take to ensure that you were providing an appropriate program?

2. What resources are available in your community that may provide information on different health-care and medical needs?
3. What concerns do you feel that families may have when enrolling their son or daughter with medical or health-care needs in public school?
4. Medical conditions exist within the general school population (e.g., asthma, seizure disorders, hemophilia). How are medical conditions complicated by the presence of mental disabilities and communication problems in students with severe disabilities?
5. How does the presence of health and medical needs affect a student's participation in community-based instruction and inclusion?
6. How might the presence of a contagious condition (e.g., cytomegalovirus or herpes) affect a student's participation in community-based instruction and inclusion?

References

Bigge, J. L. (1991). *Teaching individuals with physical and multiple disabilities.* New York: Macmillan.

Fox, L., & Westling, D. L. (1986). The prevalence of students who are profoundly mentally handicapped receiving medication in a school district. *Education and Training of the Mentally Retarded, 21,* 205–210.

Gadow, K. D. (1982). *Children on medication: A primer for school personnel.* Reston, VA: Council for Exceptional Children.

Gadow, K. D., & Kalachnik, J. (1981). Prevalence and pattern of drug treatment for behavior and seizure disorder of TMR students. *American Journal of Mental Deficiency, 85,* 588–595.

Graff, J. C., Ault, M. M., Guess, D., Taylor, M., & Thompson, B. (1990). *Health care for students with disabilities.* Baltimore: Paul H. Brookes.

Haynie, M., Porter, S. M., & Palfrey, J. S. (1989). *Children assisted by medical technology in educational settings: Guidelines for care.* Boston: The Children's Hospital, Project School Care.

Lehr, D. H., & Noonan, M. J. (1989). Issues in the education of students with complex health care needs. In F. Brown & D. H. Lehr (Eds.), *Persons with profound disabilities* (pp. 139–160). Baltimore: Paul H. Brookes.

Lewis, K. D., & Thomson, H. B. (1989). Infants, children, & adolescents. In J. H. Flaskerud (Ed.), *AIDS/HIV infection: A reference guide for nursing professionals* (pp. 111–127). Philadelphia: W. B. Saunders.

Morris, S. E., & Klein, M. D. (1987). *Pre-feeding skills.* Tucson, AZ: Communication Skill Builders.

Mulligan-Ault, M., Guess, D., Struth, L., & Thompson, B. (1988). The implementation of health-related procedures in classrooms for students with severe multiple impairments. *Journal of the Association for Persons with Severe Handicaps, 13,* 100–109.

Prensky, A. L., & Palkes, H. S. (1982). *Care of the neurologically handicapped child.* New York: Oxford University Press.

Richardson, S. A., Koller, H., & Katz, M. (1981). A functional classification of seizures and distribution in the mentally retarded population. *American Journal of Mental Deficiency, 85,* 457–466.

Scipien, G. M., Chard, M. A., Howe, J., & Barnard, M. U. (1990). *Pediatric nursing care.* St. Louis, MO: C. V. Mosby.

Sobsey, D., & Cox, A. W. (1991). Integrating health care and educational programs. In F. P. Orelove & D. Sobsey, *Educating children with multiple disabilities: A transdisciplinary approach* (2nd ed.) (pp. 155–185). Baltimore: Paul H. Brookes.

Taylor, J. M., & Taylor, W. S. (1989). *Communicable disease and young children in group settings.* Boston: Little, Brown.

Thompson, B., & Guess, D. (1989). Students who experience the most profound disabilities. In F. Brown & D. H. Lehr (Eds.), *Persons with profound disabilities* (pp. 3–41). Baltimore: Paul H. Brookes.

U.S. Department of Health and Human Services (February 1989). *Guidelines for prevention of transmission of human immunodeficiency virus and hepatitis B virus to health-care and public safety workers.* Atlanta, GA: Centers for Disease Control.

Walker, D. K. (1989). Public education: New commitments and consequences. In R. K. Stein (Ed.), *Caring for children with chronic illness* (pp. 41–60). New York: Springer.

Wong, D. L. (1993). *Essentials of pediatric nursing.* St. Louis, MO: Mosby.

Wood, S., Walker, D. K., & Gardner, J. (1986). School health practices for children with complex medical needs: A national survey of guidelines. *Journal of School Health, 56,* 215–217.

Yousef, M. J. (1985). Medical and educational aspects of epilepsy: A review. *DPH Journal, 8,* 3–15.

CHAPTER 14

Teaching Self-Care and Daily Living Skills

Chapter Overview

An important area of instruction for many students with severe disabilities is self-care, or daily living skills. This chapter includes detailed procedures for teaching several of these skills, including eating skills, toileting skills, learning to dress, and personal grooming skills.

Many personal skills are required of all individuals to improve their physical well-being and/or their acceptability by others in society. These self-care or daily living skills are important instructional objectives for individuals with severe disabilities, especially if they have not acquired the skills to a degree corresponding with their chronological age. Individuals who cannot feed themselves appropriately, use the toilet, dress themselves, or perform personal grooming tasks often need to be taught those skills in order to be accepted by many members of society (Lent, 1975; Westling & Murden, 1977). Since a primary objective is to foster inclusion of people with severe disabilities into society, attention to these needs is often of paramount importance.

The reasons that these types of skills may not have been learned by an age when most people demonstrate them might include limited fine motor development, physical or sensory disabilities, reduced social awareness, inadequate learning opportunities, limited cognitive development, and, most likely, a combination of these conditions (Van Etten, Arkell, & Van Etten, 1980). If such important skills are not present in the skill repertoire of the individual, there is generally a need to provide instruction so they can be learned. In this chapter, attention is given to procedures for teaching self-feeding and related mealtime behaviors, appropriate use of the toilet, and self-dressing and self-grooming skills. Before addressing these areas, however, a few general comments are warranted.

General Considerations

Beginning at about the time of the emergence of the normalization principle in the 1960s, a great deal of effort was placed on the use of applied behavior analysis techniques to teach individuals with severe disabilities how to care for their bodily needs (Osarchuk, 1973; Westling & Murden, 1977). Most of the studies that were conducted involved individuals confined to residential institutions who had been deprived of many basic freedoms and life opportunities. If these persons had been afforded opportunities to grow up in their own homes, in a society that accepted and cared for them, and had attended schools in their own neighborhoods starting at a young age, they may not have gone for so many years without instruction in basic skills. This is pointed out for an important reason: many school-age individuals with severe disabilities today who have had the experience of a good home life and early intervention may have less need for instruction in traditional "self-help" areas than was the case 30 years ago. Today, although many individuals with severe disabilities require instruction in personal skills such as described in this chapter, many do not. Individual determination of need in this area and collaboration with parents, therefore, is very important.

Appropriate Instructional Procedures

Our knowledge about instruction in this area is based on work that was done many years ago. It is important to realize that some of the methods that were used then, although effective in achieving results, are generally not appropriate today because our values and our beliefs about what constitutes appropriate practices have changed over the years. Thus we will not suggest many of the "rapid" training methods that were used years ago to teach new skills to persons who had gone for many years without them. Instead we will offer sound instructional procedures, based on the earlier methods, but without the violations of basic dignity that existed when training was first conducted.

Skill Generalization

Because most personal-care skills of individuals with and without disabilities develop within specific environments (the home) with a limited scope of products, generalization of skills in this area has not often been given much consideration. However, it is important that the teacher and the other professionals involved in teaching these skills be aware of the need for generalization. Critical to this area, of course, is the ability of the student to carry out skills where they are needed. It is not sufficient for students to learn to eat correctly at school only to have to be fed by parents at home, or be able to use the toilet in the school bathroom but not in different parts of the community. Teachers need to make sure that the situations and conditions under which they are teaching correspond to those at home and elsewhere to the extent this is possible. It may also be necessary that parents or caregivers have the opportunity to observe successful methods used in school in order to carry through with them in the home and the community.

When and Where to Teach Personal Skills

As implied above, self-care skills should be taught in natural environments (Freagon & Rotatori, 1982). However, if this is not possible, the teacher should provide instruction in these areas at the most natural times (bathroom time, lunch time, going out for P.E., and so on) and in the most natural locations available during the school day.

The teacher must keep in mind, however, that much of what is being taught (using the toilet, getting dressed and undressed, managing menstrual needs) is a very private matter. When this type of instruction is taking place, the teacher must respect the right of privacy for the student. Instruction should not take place in front of other individuals or in any way that is demeaning. Also, ideally, the person providing the instruction should be of the same sex as the person receiving instruction.

It is very important to involve many members of the collaborative team when developing daily living skills objectives and when teaching them. Because the type of care a person provides for himself or herself is often determined by family practices, it is most important that parents participate fully in identifying instructional goals in this area. Additionally, because of the motor skills required in most self-care activities, a physical or occupational therapist should provide input about how the student can best achieve certain objectives. Likewise, the speech therapist can provide important information about the student's oral-muscular ability as related to eating. The school nurse or another health-care professional can provide key input about many hygiene needs of students with severe disabilities. Thus, as can be seen, collaboration with team members in this particular instructional domain will be critical to achieving success.

With these preliminary considerations in mind, we turn our attention now to specific areas of self-care learning.

Eating, Self-Feeding and Other Mealtime Skills

There are few needs more basic to life functioning than eating. If we are to live, we must be able to adequately eat appropriate foods to sustain the body and allow it to function as it should. If there were no other reasons besides this, teaching adequate eating skills to individuals with severe disabilities would be important. However, there are additional concerns, because in the lives of most people, eating is an important social function as well as a means to keep healthy and stay alive. Mealtimes are often times for relaxation, for conversation, and for relationships to be nourished just as the body is nourished.

The history of how many people with severe disabilities have eaten or been fed in the past is a sad one. Confined to the back wards of institutions, individuals were fed or fed themselves without any concern for personal dignity or the manner of food consumption. Greater attention was given to how expeditiously food could be transferred from the outside of a person's body to the inside, with virtually no consideration for the quality of the food, the acceptability of the eating behavior, or the enjoyment of the experience. Feedings through stomach tubes (fistulas) were done because they were considered to be cost beneficial, even though they were often not a physical necessity. Feeding a person pureed food while he or she was lying down, or "bird feeding" (holding a person's chin up and pouring the pureed food down the throat) were also quick methods, even though the food often ended up in the lungs instead of the stomach. These tragic incidents have been referred to as "quiet little murders" (Perske, Clifton, McLean, & Stein, 1977). Additionally, because of the nature of the environment, limited time, insufficient food, and inadequate training, when individuals fed themselves, their self-feeding behavior was often characterized by a variety of socially unacceptable behaviors such as stealing food, eating with their hands, eating directly from plates or bowls, and eating food off the floor (Barton, Guess, Garcia, & Baer, 1970).

Fortunately, with the advent of the normalization principle and the development of effective instructional procedures based on principles of applied behavior analysis, over the years we have witnessed dramatic improvements in the mealtime skills of persons with severe disabilities (Perske et al., 1977; Snell & Farlow, 1993; Westling & Murden, 1977). We have also come to expect that participation in eating meals by persons with severe disabilities should have no less quality than participation by those without disabilities. Perske and his colleagues (1977) described the ideal mealtime as having the following characteristics:

- Feeling of comradeship and belonging.
- Relaxing and being less defensive.
- Communicating in many ways, with voice, eyes, body, taste, smell, and touch.
- Laughing and feeling joyful.

- Being accepted exactly as you are and being glad you are *you.*
- Making choices.
- Having all the time you need.
- Heightening all the senses.
- Feeling full, satisfied, and relaxed.
- Taking in nutrition for growth and good health.

In order for persons with severe disabilities to be able to more fully participate and enjoy the type of mealtime experiences that Perske et al. suggested, it is helpful if they can develop certain skills, some relatively basic and others more advanced. Banerdt and Bricker (1978) provided a detailed sequence important for eating, including developing skills related to head, trunk, limb, and sitting control; establishing manual dexterity; and establishing specific eating skills (see Figure 14-1).

In the following sections, strategies and tactics for teaching appropriate mealtime skills are described.

Finger-Feeding

The first step in learning to eat independently is using one's fingers to bring food to the mouth. Normally children start feeding themselves with their hands before they learn to use utensils, typically at the age of about 7 or 8 months. As with other skills, however, this may be delayed in children with severe disabilities. If so, it is a skill that should be taught prior to more advanced mealtime skills because the ability to bring the hand to the mouth facilitates drinking independently from a cup, feeding oneself with a spoon, and using other utensils.

The best time to work on teaching finger-feeding is at the beginning of the meal when the child is likely to be hungry and thus motivated to self-feed (Snell & Farlow, 1993). Using foods that the child likes will also increase his or her interest in picking up the food. In order to get the child to practice the required hand-to-mouth movement, foods that have appeal and will stick to the fingers such as peanut butter, applesauce, cake batter, or whipped cream might be put on the child's hands (Bigge, 1991). As the child acquires grasping skills, foods that are easy to hold, such as pieces of banana, hot dogs, chicken sticks, or cheese strips can be used.

Quite often providing the child with many opportunities to eat finger foods is sufficient to improve the skill. (Teachers and care providers must understand, however, that this is not a neat process and a great deal of messiness will occur as the child increases his or her proficiency.) If, however, opportunity alone does not result in acquisition or improvement of finger-feeding, a task analysis should be developed that includes the following steps:

- Reaching to locate the food.
- Grasping the food.
- Lifting the food from the table to the mouth.
- Putting the food into the mouth.
- Chewing and swallowing the food.

To teach the steps of the task analysis, the teacher may use an approach such as partial and full physical assistance within a least-to-most instructional plan, or use graduated guidance. These and other skill acquisition procedures referred to in this chapter are fully discussed in chapter 6.

Drinking from a Cup

Children normally learn to drink from a cup held by a care provider at about one year of age. Soon after this, the typical child is able to hold the cup and drink alone albeit with some amount of spilling. Children with severe disabilities should be taught to drink

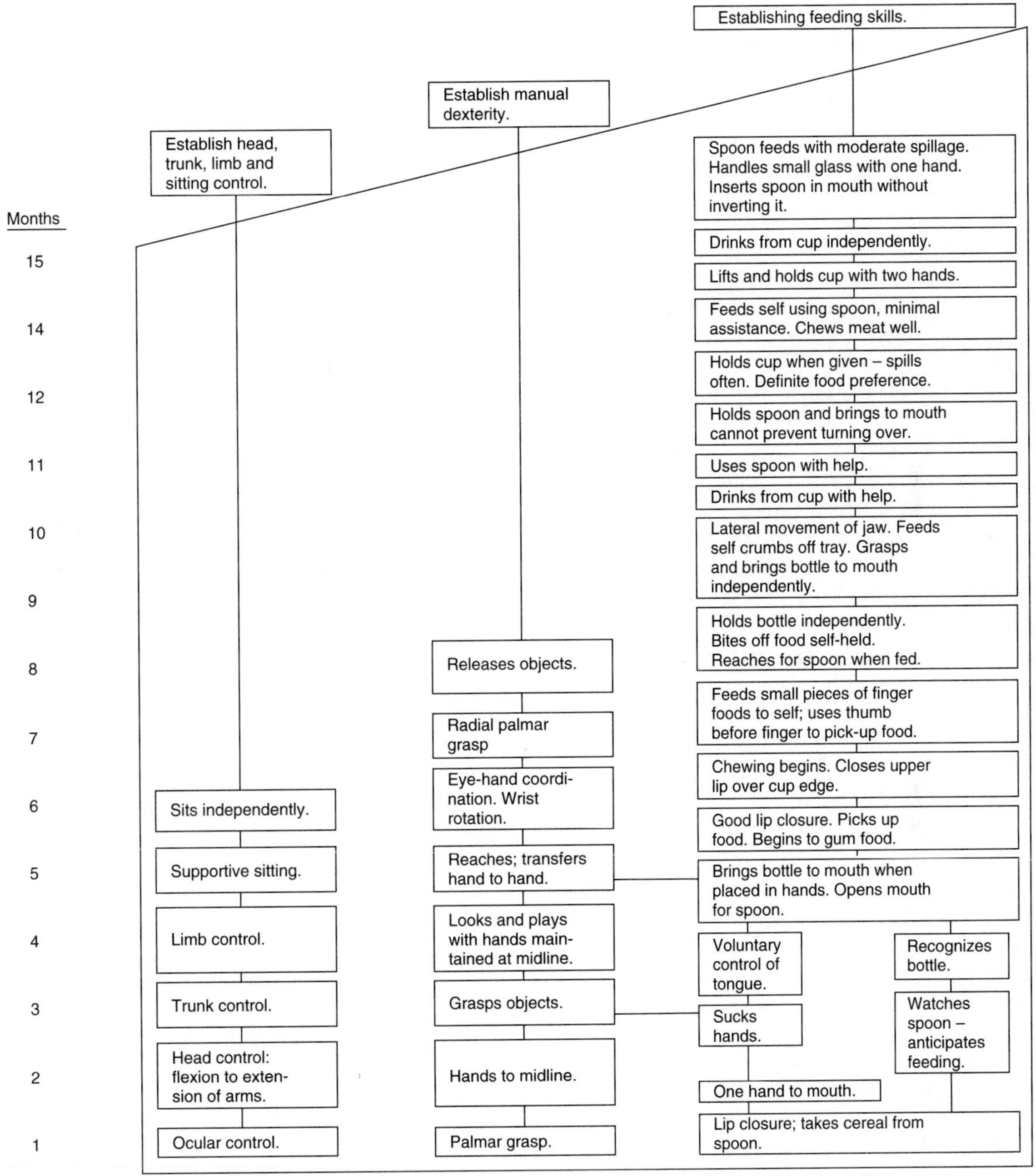

Figure 14–1
Training Lattice for Establishing Independent Feeding Skills

From "A Training Program for Selected Self-Feeding Skills for the Motorically Impaired" by B. Banerdt & D. Bricker, 1978, *AAESPH Review*, 3, p. 224. Copyright 1978 by The Association for Persons with Severe Handicaps. Reprinted by permission.

from a cup held by another and then from a self-held cup if they are motorically capable of doing so.

A flexible plastic cup with a small rim is relatively easy to drink from because it does not impede lip closure. Additionally, because of its flexibility, the teacher can bend it to make it fit the child's lips. If the child has a difficult time tilting his or her head backward, a section of the top of the cup can be cut away so the cup can be tilted farther backward without bumping against the child's nose or forehead. Spouted cups that encourage abnormal sucking, brittle plastic cups that might break, and cups that are too large or difficult to handle should not be used.

The cup should be placed gently on the child's lips (not teeth) and tilted gradually in order to allow the child to take in a small amount of the liquid. While the child is swallowing, the cup should be tilted back but not removed from the lips. The liquid should not be poured into the mouth. Liquids thickened with yogurt, applesauce, or baby cereal are often easier for the child to handle than regular juice (Alexander, 1991; Orelove & Sobsey, 1991).

When the child can take liquids from a cup held by another with ease, he or she often starts reaching for or touching the cup held by the teacher or care provider to ask for a drink. This behavior should always be reinforced and never discouraged. If it does not occur independently, the child's hands should be guided to prompt the behavior. As with all early self-feeding behaviors, a stable, well-supported seating condition will make it easier for the child to grasp and manipulate the cup. Since the behavior consists of one continuous action, a task analysis would not be required. For purposes of data collection, teachers may simply count how many sips of liquid the child takes in a certain period of time. Graduated guidance can be helpful in teaching the skill.

Learning to Eat with a Spoon

Being able to feed oneself with a spoon represents an important first step toward becoming an independent eater. The individual who acquires this skill will have a sound basis for developing more advanced mealtime skills. Many students with disabilities acquire this skill like others, that is, they learn it in an incidental manner in the home. Other individuals do not acquire the skill and need to be directly instructed in order to learn it. If a child or an older student does not eat with a spoon, but has sufficient motor skills and coordination to finger-feed and to grasp and release objects, it should be possible to teach the individual how to eat with the spoon. Several studies have demonstrated that individuals with severe disabilities can learn to eat with a spoon given appropriate instruction (Albin, 1977; Azrin & Armstrong, 1973; Berkowitz, Sherry, & Davis, 1971; Christian, Hollomon, & Lanier, 1973; Groves & Carroccio, 1971; Leibowitz & Holcer, 1974; Lemke & Mitchell, 1972; Miller, Patton, & Henton, 1971; O'Brien & Azrin, 1972; O'Brien, Bugle, & Azrin, 1972; Song & Ghandi, 1974; Zeiler & Jervey, 1968).

Eating correctly with a spoon consists of using the spoon to move the appropriate food (not finger food) from the bowl or plate, with the spoon held right side up, by the handle, in one hand, without spilling any food except back into the container that it came from (O'Brien & Azrin, 1972; O'Brien, Bugle, & Azrin, 1972). Incorrect behaviors include various deviations such as using hands to eat non-finger foods, putting too much food on the spoon, spilling food outside of the bowl or plate, or holding the spoon incorrectly.

As correct self-feeding behavior is observed, one sees a relatively smooth process of picking up and then holding the spoon, lowering it to the plate or bowl, scooping food, lifting it from the container to the mouth, inserting it into the mouth, removing the food with the lips, lowering the spoon to the food again, and repeating the process in a rhythmic, paced manner. These movements constitute a task analysis of spoon-feeding behavior and the teacher may observe and record correct and incorrect performance of each step. The teacher may use a skill acquisition training procedure such as least-to-most assistance or graduated guidance.

Praising the student for correct responding and giving other appropriate social attention may ultimately eliminate any incorrect responses. If incorrect spoon-feeding behaviors persist, such as excessive spilling or eating with hands when a spoon should be used, they can generally be reduced through a brief (15 to 30 second) time-out from the opportunity to eat. Since food is a natural, unconditioned reinforcer, most individuals have a strong desire to eat. When incorrect behaviors occur, the teacher might say no and then briefly remove the food or pull the learner's chair away from the table. This has generally been shown to be effective in reducing inappropriate behaviors when teaching self-feeding skills (Albin, 1977; Azrin & Armstrong, 1973, Barton et al., 1970; Christian et al., 1973; Martin, McDonald, & Omichinski, 1971; O'Brien et al., 1972).

Learning to Use Other Utensils

Students who have learned to use a spoon competently should be taught and encouraged to use other utensils, primarily forks and knives (for both cutting and spreading), as well as napkins (Azrin & Armstrong, 1973; O'Brien & Azrin, 1972; O'Brien et al., 1972; Nelson, Cone, & Hanson, 1975). The skill acquisition instructional processes for teaching these skills are similar to teaching the student to eat with a spoon. However, two additional tactics can be used.

First, the teacher should teach one new skill at a time (e.g., teach the student how to use a napkin, then a fork, then a knife). When a new utensil is being taught, it should be used initially with only one food item that requires the use of the particular utensil. The new skill should be worked on at the beginning of the meal if not throughout. Since the student will have already learned to use a spoon, there may be a tendency for him or her to hold the fork or knife incorrectly (i.e., like a spoon). Therefore, the teacher should provide direct instruction on the proper ways to hold utensils for different purposes. Figure 14–2 shows some of these grips. Posting pictures or photographs of correct ways to grip utensils such as those shown in Figure 14–2 may be helpful (Nelson et al., 1975). While using a spoon is relatively simple, other forms of utensil use are increasingly complex. The teacher should progress from easier to more difficult skills. The suggested order after spoon use is: napkin use, fork use, use of a knife for spreading, and use of a knife for cutting.

Second, after each utensil has been learned, the teacher needs to teach the student which utensils to use for specific needs. The student should learn to discriminate which foods require a spoon as opposed to a fork and vice versa, and which foods can be eaten with the fingers. The student must also learn that the knife may be used for cutting, spreading butter or condiments, and pushing food onto the fork, but cannot be used to scoop or spear food. Since by this time students should know *how* to use the utensil, the teacher should be able to focus on prompting and reinforcing the student's correct discrimination to select and use a particular utensil.

Decreasing Inappropriate Mealtime Behaviors

For various reasons, students with severe disabilities may display inappropriate mealtime

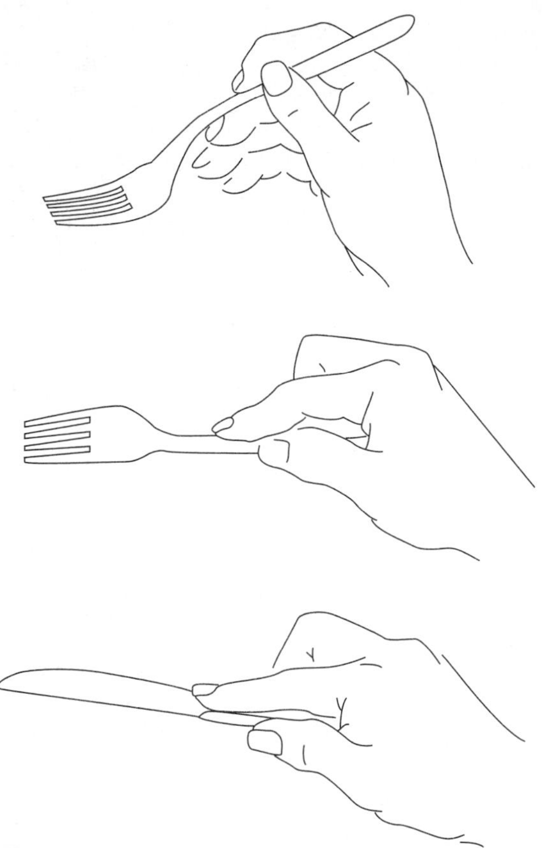

Figure 14–2

Correct Utensil Use: Eating Grip (top), Cutting Grip (center), Spreading Grip (bottom)

From "Training Correct Utensil Use in Retarded Children: Modeling vs. Physical Guidance" by G. L. Nelson, J. D. Cone, & C. R. Hanson, 1975, *American Journal of Mental Deficiency, 80,* p. 115. Copyright 1975 by the American Association on Mental Retardation. Reprinted by permission.

behaviors. Over the years many have been well documented, but they have mostly been reported among individuals residing in residential institutions. It may be hypothesized that if a person grows up in his or her natural home, has had the experience of an early intervention program, and has had the opportunity to model the behavior of children eating appropriately, undesirable mealtime behaviors may be less likely to occur. Nevertheless, teachers of students with severe disabilities may expect to encounter some undesirable activities during meals and should try to reduce them if they appear to be clearly inappropriate and call unfavorable attention to the student.

Some undesirable behaviors may be considered relatively mild, such as eating foods with hands (not including finger foods), eating too fast or taking bites that are too large, chewing with mouth open, eating with face too close to the plate, spilling food or drinks, using the wrong utensil, playing with food (with or without utensils), holding the utensil incorrectly, putting a napkin on wrong, or not wiping mouth with a napkin when necessary. Others are more serious, such as throwing food or utensils, stealing food from another's plate, eating food directly off the plate (without using hands or utensils), eating food that has fallen on the table or on the floor, smearing food, screaming and pushing the table away, and hitting others (Barton et al., 1970; Henriksen & Doughty, 1972; O'Brien & Azrin, 1972; O'Brien et al., 1972).

Sometimes inappropriate behavior occurs because the student has not learned more appropriate behavior. For example, eating with hands is likely to decrease when a student learns to eat correctly using a spoon or other utensil (O'Brien et al., 1972). In other cases, the behavior may occur because of some situation in the environment that prompts the behavior. This may include sitting near someone the student does not like, not having enough food to eat, having undesirable food, or being extremely hungry at the beginning of the meal. Functional assessment of the conditions and communicative intent surrounding the behavior and modifications of instructional practices may result in a decrease in the behavior (see chapter 11).

It is likely that many of these behaviors, when they exist, have been inadvertently reinforced over the years and thus continue to occur. For example, stealing food or eating food in some inappropriate fashion might be reinforced by the food itself. In such cases, a brief removal and time-out from the food (by taking the food away for 15 to 30 seconds), coupled with a reprimand ("No!") each time the behavior occurs and then redirecting the student to engage in more appropriate eating behavior may be sufficient to decrease the undesirable behavior. If not, a longer time-out may be necessary (Barton et al., 1970).

Teaching Other Appropriate Mealtime Behaviors

Beyond specific eating skills, there are other mealtime behaviors that may be important for instruction depending on a student's current and future needs. As mentioned previously, discussing possible needs with a student's parents and other members of the professional team may unveil important instructional targets. One such target might be the need to increase the variety of foods eaten. Sometimes individuals show a strong preference for one particular food or a few food items and will not eat others. In order to increase the variety of foods eaten, the teacher may require that the learner eat a small amount of nonpreferred food before being reinforced with preferred food. Gradually, the nonpreferred food could be increased and the reward of preferred food decreased until it simply becomes dessert. If this approach fails, the preferred food could be presented simultaneously with the nonpreferred food (in the same bowl and on the same spoon) so that the two would need to be taken together. Gradually the proportion of preferred food could be reduced and ultimately offered only as dessert (Leibowitz & Holcer, 1974).

Another instructional target may be to learn the behaviors required for eating family-style. These include setting your place at the table, sitting down and putting your napkin on your lap, serving food to yourself from a bowl on the table, passing a bowl of food to another, and clearing away plates and utensils after the meal (Wilson, Reid, Phillips, & Burgio, 1984). If this is the way the student normally eats at home, these may be important skills to teach.

During planning, parents and professionals should consider the above areas of mealtime instruction and perhaps others. Since conversations typically occur during meals, attention should be given to working on communication skills. Fine motor development is another area that can be incorporated into mealtime activities. Finally, consideration should be given to generalization of dining skills to other foods, meals, and locations, and with different people. To the extent that skill generalization will be important, instructional plans need to be developed for it to occur.

General Suggestions for Improving Eating

In addition to the specific tactics described in the above sections, there are several additional things teachers can do to improve eating and mealtime skills of students with severe disabilities (Westling & Murden, 1977), including:

- During the initial acquisition stages of a skill that requires physical guidance, such as learning to eat with a spoon, the learner may have more success if the same person, the teacher or an assistant, always provides the training. Changing the instructor at this point may result in more mistakes (Henriksen & Doughty, 1967; Zeiler & Jervey, 1968). Changes in instructors should be made gradually as the student is progressing (Christian et al., 1973).

- Although it is desirable for the student to ultimately eat in a normal integrated environment, some have suggested that initial skills may develop faster without the distractions of the typical school cafeteria. It has been proposed that initial instruction should occur in a quiet area; then, when skills are adequately developed, the student should eat in the cafeteria with the other students (Albin, 1977; Groves & Carroccio, 1971; O'Brien & Azrin, 1972; Orelove & Sobsey, 1991). In order to avoid total isolation during the skills-acquisition stage, however, the student may learn to eat with peers in the classroom, may go to the cafeteria when it is less crowded, or may go to the cafeteria for part of the meal.
- Students' skills increase if they are provided with many opportunities to learn and practice. Having several chances to practice eating and receive instruction during the day is sometimes preferable to having only one or two opportunities (Azrin & Armstrong, 1973). Further, it should be noted that because providing instruction on how to eat without real food being present is not natural and is not likely to have an effect on the student's eating skills (Nelson et al., 1975), instruction should always be provided during actual eating times (meals and snacks).
- Students acquiring initial skills with different utensils (i.e., using a spoon, a fork, or a knife) probably do better if there is only one food on the plate during instruction, and it should be a food that is highly desirable (Azrin & Armstrong, 1973). Additional foods can be added as the student's skill increases.
- Some materials are easier to handle than others and may facilitate eating when the student is first learning. For example, simply using large-handled spoons and deeper bowls may help the student learning to feed himself or herself (Albin, 1977; Azrin & Armstrong, 1973).
- The standard of neatness may need to be very liberal during early stages of learning but should become gradually stricter as the student progresses. Excessive spilling and other messy behavior should be ultimately eliminated or reduced as much as possible (Azrin & Armstrong, 1973; Groves & Carroccio, 1971; Lemke & Mitchell, 1972).

Learning to Use the Toilet

Like being able to feed oneself, being able to use the toilet independently and to avoid soiling and wetting oneself helps maintain good health and increases the social acceptability of an individual. As with self-feeding, school-age individuals with severe disabilities have different skill levels with regard to toilet use. Some are fully independent and require no additional training; others may need reminders to use the toilet or, if directed to a toilet on a regular basis, are able to use the toilet successfully. Some are able to use the toilet but have difficulty with related skills such as lowering or raising pants, wiping, or washing hands after toilet use. Still others lack the physical ability to use the toilet and need to have bowel and urinary management procedures provided in order to void. Through contact with parents or caregivers and other members of the professional team, the teacher must learn each individual's unique needs related to toileting and provide the appropriate training or the necessary physical management.

Determining Readiness for Toileting

Most children acquire the ability to control their bladders and bowels between 2 and 3 years of age. While it may be expected that many individuals with severe disabilities will learn toileting skills at this age, many do not. For them, sufficient maturity may not occur until they are older. Early studies suggested that the success of training an individual with severe cognitive disabilities to use the toilet was directly related to the individual's mental development and/or chronological age (Osarchuk, 1973). However, these findings are far from conclusive. Factors such as the ability to recognize physical cues, social recognition of the importance of proper toileting behavior, and modeling other children may have more bearing than general developmental level (Snell & Farlow, 1993).

Instead of relying on the individual's chronological or mental age as an indicator of readiness to learn toilet training, other factors may be more indicative of this potential. Three that are very important include:

- Evidence that the individual has a regular pattern of elimination, meaning that he or she voids at relatively predictable times each day instead of randomly.
- Additionally, the ability of the individual to go for at least one or two hours without wetting or having a bowel movement. This, along with the previous criterion, would suggest that he or she has attained an adequate degree of voluntary control.
- Finally, the individual is at least 2 1/2 years old. Attempting to train the child before this age is generally too soon, even for a child without disabilities (Snell & Farlow, 1993).

Other individual characteristics that may help facilitate the training process include ambulation, fine motor ability, receptive language, and good visual ability (Foxx & Azrin, 1973). However, these should not be considered prerequisites to training. More important will be adequate physiological development as indicated by the above conditions. If the parents and teachers have any doubts about physical readiness, a medical examination should precede training.

Teaching Independent Toilet Use

Several tactics based on the principles of applied behavior analysis have been discovered through research to be effective for teaching independent toileting skills to individuals with severe disabilities. These tactics have been widely presented in the research literature (Anderson, 1982; Azrin, Bugle, & O'Brien, 1971; Azrin & Foxx, 1971; Ellis, 1963; Foxx & Azrin, 1973; Giles & Wolf, 1966; Hundziak, Maurer, & Watson, 1965; Kimbrell, Luckey, Barbuto, & Love, 1967; Lancioni, 1980; Mahoney, Van Wagenen, & Meyerson, 1971; Osarchuk, 1973; Smith, 1979; Trott, 1977; Williams & Sloop, 1978). While some of these tactics are no longer considered appropriate because of ethical concerns (for example, using punishment such as overcorrection for accidents, providing increased amounts of liquids to promote the frequency of urination, spending 6 to 8 hours in the bathroom to be near the toilet), others are effective and allow respect for the dignity of the individual to be maintained. These tactics are presented below.

Pretraining Data Collection The first step in toilet training requires that data be collected to determine the learner's pattern of urination and bowel movements. The most likely time that the individual will wet or soil his or her diaper or training pants is obviously the best time for him or her to be placed on the toilet. A relatively simple chart such as the partial interval one presented in Figure 14–3 allows the teacher to record the student's voiding pattern and type of behavior over several days. The more often checks are made to determine when the student is voiding, the more accurate the teacher's knowledge will be about the time to place the student on the toilet. Therefore, as the chart in Figure 14–3 suggests, checks should be made every 15 minutes and an appropriate notation noted (i.e., dry/clean, wet/soiled); if the teacher placed the student on the toilet at some time during this period, whether or not the student urinated or had a bowel movement while on the toilet. Using the chart, the teacher may also note the relation of wetting or bowel movements to drinking or eating by marking on the chart when these behaviors occurred.

During a pretraining baseline period, this data collection should occur without attempts at toileting until a stable pattern of voiding can be identified. In other words, the teacher should learn at what periods of time during the day the student is most likely to wet or have a bowel movement. This may be determined in as few as 3 days, or it may take a week or longer to discern the pattern. This information will then confirm that the learner meets the prerequisites listed above (has a regular pattern of elimination and can go for an hour or more without voiding) and will tell the teacher the best time to put the student on the toilet. It is very important that each time the pants are checked that they be changed if they are wet or soiled. This is not only for the comfort of the student, but so that accurate detection will be noted at the next pants check. When checking and changing the learner, the teacher should be sure that no reinforcement is inadvertently given and that a neutral demeanor is maintained at this time.

Learning to Sit on the Toilet Knowing when the student is most likely to void will imply the best time for him or her to sit on the toilet. (Sometimes it is suggested that males be taught to stand to urinate, but learning to sit for both urinating and having a bowel movement may be easier to teach at first.) If, for example, the chart in Figure 14–3 shows that the student regularly wets between 9:00 and 9:30, this would be an appropriate time for him or her to be seated on the toilet. However, for some students, sitting on the toilet may be aversive because it is a new and strange experience; if the learner will not willingly sit on the toilet for a period of 5 minutes or longer, it will be necessary to gradually shape this behavior by reinforcing him or her with praise and social attention for sitting on the toilet for longer and longer periods of time. At first the individual may need to be supported and reinforced simply for initial sitting. Then, gradually longer periods of sitting (5 seconds, 10 seconds, 15 seconds . . . 1 minute) will be reinforced until the person becomes accustomed to sitting on the toilet. In the most extreme cases, that is when the student resists through screaming and temper tantrums, a more gradual approach of just walking into the bathroom and getting near the toilet may need to be reinforced initially in order to desensitize the student to the environment and the experience. Students should never be held on the toilet while crying or screaming because this indicates the experience is far too aversive. Instead a very gradual pattern of shaping for approaching the toilet should be used. This will take more time but the effect will be more positive.

Learning to Void While on the Toilet Once the student has learned to sit on the toilet, the idea, of course, will be for him or her to void while there, and stay clean and dry when not there. Three tactics will increase the probability of this occurring. The first is for the student to be on the toilet during those times when he or she is most likely to void (based on the data collected prior to training) and remain on the toilet long enough for it to occur. When the student does void while on the toilet, much praise and age-appropriate social reinforcement should be given: "Look what you did!

Toileting/Pants Check Record Baseline: 9/6 - 9/17 Intervention: 9/20

Name: Jacob Locations: gym, classroom, north hall, cafeteria, bathrooms

Time	9/6	9/7	9/8	9/9	9/10	9/13	9/14	9/15	9/16	9/17	9/20	9/21	9/22	9/23	9/24	9/27	9/28	9/30	10/1	10/2
8:30		(WB)					(W)	W+	W+	A		W+		W+		W+	(W)	W+	A	(W)
8:45		D		(W)	(W)	W+	D	D	D	B		D	W+	D	W+	D	D	D	B	D
9:00	(W)	D		D	D	D	D	D	D	S	W+	D+	D	D	D	W+	D	D+	S	D
9:15	D	D	(BW)	D	D	D	D	D	D	E	(B)	D	D	D	D	D	D	D	E	D
9:30	D	D	D	(W)	(W)	D	D	(W)	D	N	D	D+	D	D+	D	D+	D+	D+	N	D+
9:45	P.E.	P.E.	P.E.	P.E.	P.E.	P.E.	P.E.	P.E.	P.E.	T	P.E.	P.E.	P.E.	P.E.	P.E.	P.E.	P.E.	P.E.	T	P.E.
10:00	D+	D	(WB)	(W)	W+	D	D	D	(W?)		D	D+	(W)	D+	W+	W+	WB+	D+		WB+
10:15	D	(WB)	D	D	D	D	D	D	D		D	D	D	D	D	D	D	D		D
10:30	D	D	D	D	W-	D	D	D	D		D	D+	D+	D+	D+	D+	D+	D+		D+
10:45	D	D	D	(W)	D	W+	W+	D	D		(W)	D	(W)	D	(W)	D	D	D		D
11:00	W-	D	D	D	D	D	D	W	D		D	D+	D	D+	D	W+	D+	D+		W+
11:15	D	D	(W)	(W)	D	D	D	D	D+		D	D	D	D	D	D	D	D		D
11:30	D	D	D	D	(W)	D	D	D	D		D	D+	D+	D	D+	D+	D	BW+		D
11:45	L	L	L	L	L	L	L	L	L		L	L	L	L	L	L	L	L		L
12:00	D	D	D	D	D	D+	D	D	D		D	B+	B+	D	D	D	D?	D		D
12:15	(WB)	(W)	D	(WB)	W+	(W)	WB+	D	(WB)		D	D	D	B+	WB+	B+	WB+	D-		WB+
12:30	D	D	(WB)	D	D	D	D	B+	D		(WB)	(W)	D	D	D	D	D+			D
12:45	D	D	D	D	D	(BW)	D	D	D		D+	D	D	D+	D+	D	D			D
1:00	D	D	D	D	D	D	D	D	D		D	D	(WB)	D	D	D+	D+	A		D+
1:15	D	D	D	D	D	D	D	D	D		D	D	D	D	D	(W)	D	B		D
1:30	D	(W)	D	D	D	D	D	D	D		D	D+	D	D+	D	D+	D+	S		W
1:45	D	D	D	D	D	D	D	W	D+		D	D	D	D	W-	D	D	E		D
2:00	(BW)	(W)	D	(W)	D	D-	W	D	D+		D	D-	D+	W+	W+	W+	D+	N		D
2:15	D	D	(B)	(WB)	(W)			(W)					W-		D		W-	T		D
2:30					D															
# Self initiations / # Accidents	1/3	0/5	0/5	0/7	2/4	3/2	2/2	2/3	4/2		2/3	9/1	5/3	9/0	7/1	11/1	9/1	7/0		6/2

Key	Student Initiated	Teacher Assisted	Accidents
D = Dry	W+ = Wet on toilet	W− = Wet on toilet	(W) = Wet
L = Lunch	B+ = BM on toilet	B− = BM on toilet	(B) = BM
	D+ = Self-initiated, no elim.	D− = Teacher-initiated, no elim.	

Figure 14–3

Data Collection Form for Toilet Training

From Snell, M. E. & Farlow, L. J. (1993). Self-care skills. Reprinted with the permission of Macmillan College Publishing Company from *Instruction of Students with Severe Disabilities fourth edition* by Martha Snell.

That's great! You're going to learn to stay clean and dry!"

The second tactic is to continue the pants checking on a regular basis, just as during the pretraining period, and also to reinforce the student each time a check finds the student clean and dry. In order for the student to make the association, the teacher may guide the student's hand to his or her crotch area and deliver praise while the student feels the dryness, for example, "You're dry and clean! I'm very proud! Can you feel that you are dry? Very good!" During training, at those times when the student is found to be soiled or wet, the teacher should change him or her immediately and do so without providing any attention or reinforcement. Additionally, mild disapproval may be stated ("I'm very disappointed that you are wet!") but nothing more. (Previous approaches have recommended that the learner be required to remain in wet or soiled clothing for a period of time to experience the discomfort or be required to clean up himself or herself and the surrounding area, but these tactics are not recommended.)

The third tactic involves the ratio of the time *on* the toilet to the time *off*. The greater the amount of time the student is on the toilet as compared to the time he or she is off, the greater the likelihood that when urination or a bowl movement occurs, it will occur while the student is on the toilet instead of while off of it. Therefore, in a 15-minute period, if the student is on the toilet for 10 minutes and off for 5, all else being equal, he or she is twice as likely to go when on the toilet (and be reinforced for it) rather than when off it. The actual amount of time for being on and off the toilet is dependent on several factors. Although a 10 minute–5 minute ratio may work for many students and teachers, for others it may not. The teacher may not be able to get the student on and off the toilet that often, or the student may show resistance to getting off and on so often. For some students learning to use the toilet quickly may be a major goal; for others it may not be as critical and more time can be taken. The former situation would call for more opportunities to be on the toilet but the latter would not and a schedule such as 10 or 15 minutes on the toilet every hour would be appropriate. Of course, it must be understood that this may decrease the number of on-toilet successes and thus reduce the opportunity for reinforcement, which would lengthen the period of time required for successful learning.

Also related to the speed of acquiring appropriate toileting behavior will be the amount of time each day the teacher and student spend working on this activity. For some, it may be possible to commit only one hour or so of the school day to toilet training. For example, there may be four 10-minute periods of being on the toilet interspersed with four 5-minute periods of being off. After that time, the teacher would not follow the on-off schedule but might place the student on the toilet only when urination or a bowel movement would be most likely to occur. For others, if toileting skills are a high priority and if conditions warrant it, an on-off schedule may be followed throughout the entire school day. Although this is likely to interfere with other normal daily school routines, it is likely to reduce the total amount of time required for the student to learn to use the toilet. The teacher, the parents, and other members of the collaborative team should weigh the positive and negative aspects of more and less intensive toileting schedules before implementing any particular schedule.

During the toilet training period, regardless of the off and on toilet training schedule and the amount of time committed to training, the teacher should continue to collect data as during the pretraining phase, recording the student's condition at each time period when both on and off the toilet. These data will indicate if success is occurring and, if not, during what times the student needs to be placed on the toilet, or perhaps placed for longer periods of time. If the teacher wishes to chart the data, this can be done by placing the total "correct" and "incorrect" occurrences for the day or the training time on a chart (see chapter 8).

Success at toileting will occur when the student voids when on the toilet and not when off the toilet most of the time. Although 100% success is naturally most preferable, it may be expected that accidents will occur. If these start to occur with some frequency, the teacher will need to return to data collection and the toilet training procedure as described above. However, if the accidents are infrequent, the teacher should simply change the student without any fanfare and expect him or her to use the toilet appropriately in the future.

Teaching Skills Associated with Toileting There are several skills that are typically associated with toileting that should be considered for instruction as the student is learning to use the toilet. These skills include walking to the bathroom, lifting or lowering the toilet seat as necessary, lowering outer pants or lifting skirt or dress, lowering underpants, sitting on the toilet, wiping after voiding, standing up, pulling up underwear, pulling up pants or lowering skirt or dress, washing hands with soap and water, drying hands, and returning to the previous location outside of the bathroom. Each or any of these could be included as instructional targets, task analyzed, and taught during toilet training periods, using the skill acquisition methods described in chapter 6.

Whether or not skills such as these are taught simultaneously with toileting skills will depend on factors that should be considered by the teacher and the planning team. The student may be too young or not have acquired adequate motor skills to be expected to learn some of the related tasks. The teacher may be toilet training several students simultaneously and may not have time to teach all related skills to all students learning to use the toilet. Or, in contrast, it may be judged that it is essential for the student to learn all or certain related skills. Regardless, there are two considerations to keep in mind. First, toilet training provides a natural opportunity to teach related skills; but, second, if for whatever reason it is not possible to teach these skills simultaneously, toilet training may still proceed with the teacher fully assisting the student to carry out all of the related behaviors.

Using the Toilet Independently At the time the student with severe disabilities begins to urinate and defecate in the toilet instead of in his or her pants or diapers, a major step has been achieved. The student can then be taken or directed to the bathroom to use the toilet, at the times determined by the previously established schedule. In this way the habit of using the toilet will be strengthened, and along with pressure on the bowel or bladder, the toilet will ultimately gain influence as the stimulus prompting bowel movements or urination to occur.

It will always be necessary to direct some individuals with severe disabilities to the toilet on a regular schedule. For others, the need to use the toilet is communicated by their facial expression or by indicative acts such as touching their genital area or pulling at the crotch of their pants. In cases such as these, the teacher and others must be vigilant and respond appropriately in order to prevent subsequent accidents. The teacher may also attempt to teach the student an alternate form of communicating the need to go to the bathroom, using either verbal language, a manual sign, or a picture or symbol when he or she feels the urge to void.

The greatest degree of toileting independence will have occurred if and when the individual can reliably indicate the need to go to the toilet, or simply goes to the toilet without being told when the need arises. The teacher may prompt this by teaching the student, when possible, to communicate the need to go whenever the student actually goes to the bathroom. One way to do this may be through a constant time delay procedure (see chapter 6).

Using constant time delay, when it is time for the student to go to the bathroom, or when the student's behavior indicates a need to go, the teacher says, "Do you need to go to the bathroom? Say 'bathroom'" (or "sign bathroom," or "point to bathroom"). After several such occurrences, using the principles of time delay, the teacher delays the final prompt. That is, the question is asked and a 4- or 5-second delay occurs before prompting the student to say, sign, or point to the symbol for bathroom. Ultimately the internal sensation experienced by the student results in the communicative act instead of the teacher's question, and at this point the student is able to indicate his or her need as other students do.

Teaching to Use the Toilet in Different Settings Initial toilet training often occurs in one setting, for example, the bathroom in or nearest to the classroom. However, there is a need for the student to learn to use various bathrooms, for example, bathrooms at home, in different parts of the school, in different community settings, and so forth. Success in learning to use different bathrooms depends on the "continuity of treatment" across settings and the participation of the various individuals who provide supervision and support in those settings (Dunlap, Koegel, & Koegel, 1984).

The most likely way to ensure that the student has toileting success in different areas is to arrange coordinated training practices. The intent is that those providing supervision in the various sites will follow essentially the same plan as the teacher in the primary training site. This can occur if (1) there is contact with the supervisors, teachers, or trainers in additional areas to initiate coordination, (2) the student carries written instructions to secondary support persons to help maintain consistency across settings, and (3) there is phone contact or other regular contact between the primary teacher and others to help maintain coordination and consistency (Dunlap et al., 1984). Of course, as the learner gains greater toileting independence, opportunity to practice in a variety of bathrooms helps promote generalization.

General Suggestions for Improving Toileting

The basic procedures for teaching someone to use the toilet should result in toileting success for many students. The following suggestions may add to this success.

- The parents' desire to have their child learn to use the toilet is an important factor; if the parents feel this is an important goal, it will be easier to coordinate efforts between home and school and the child may learn more quickly.
- The teacher should attempt to determine the time pattern that exists between eating and elimination. This physiological relationship will help the teacher to know when the student is most likely to need to be directed to the toilet or when he or she might signal the need to go.
- The most difficult part of learning to use the toilet is going for the first time while sitting on the toilet and without training pants or a diaper on. This presents a completely different sensation to the student than he or she has experienced before. When it does occur, much social reinforcement should be given.

- If a teacher cannot devote an extensive amount of time to toilet training each day, shorter periods can be used. Successful toileting during these periods will help toileting occur more easily after it has been learned in an initial time period.
- Parents who report that their children are bedwetters should be informed that daytime control is typically achieved before nighttime control. If bedwetting continues after day control has been learned, parents may eliminate it by (1) making sure the child uses the toilet before going to bed, (2) withholding caffeine drinks including coffee, tea, and cola during the evening, (3) waking the child before the parents' bedtime to use the bathroom, (4) checking the bed for wetness periodically during the night and if it is wet, awakening the individual, cleaning him or her, changing the bed, and requiring the use of the toilet before he or she returns to bed, and (5) praising and reinforcing the individual after a dry night (Azrin, Sneed, & Foxx, 1974; Mohr & Sharpley, 1988).

Learning to Dress

A third major area of personal self-care is learning to dress and undress oneself. Students with severe disabilities who can manage putting on and taking off articles of clothing at appropriate times during the day have to rely less on others and therefore are more independent. For this reason, the ability to dress and undress oneself is often considered an important objective for students with severe disabilities. Additionally, more advanced, related skills such as buying clothes, selecting clothes for daily wear, and caring for clothing are sometimes considered important objectives for instruction (Wilcox & Bellamy, 1987). Targeting specific skills related to the process of dressing should be given due consideration by parents, teachers, and other members of the team.

Selecting Skills to Teach

When deciding what specific dressing skills should be taught, consideration should be given to three factors: current and future needs, normal dressing sequence, and physical ability.

Current and Future Need It is most important to determine what dressing or undressing skills the student needs in his or her current life to increase independence and decrease dependence on others. For example, if a student's parents say that the morning routine would be less hectic if their child could take off pajamas and put on socks and underwear or a dress or pants and a shirt, it would suggest that these skills should be made primary instructional targets. For others, it may be helpful to learn to put on or take off sweaters and coats so that going out to play or coming in for dinner could be done without the involvement of a parent or caregiver.

Additional thought may need to be given to dressing skills needed for the immediate future. If colder weather is coming, if the student is moving to a different climate, if the student is learning a job that requires different clothing, or if an important social event is on the horizon that requires special dressing, then any of these conditions could imply that certain dressing skills should be learned.

Normal Sequence of Dressing Although not always the most important factor, particularly for older students, members of the collaborative team should be aware of the normal pattern of dressing that occurs among most children who do not have disabilities. Typically, dressing skills begin at about 12 months with cooperative acts such as holding out an arm to have a shirt put on, or a foot to have a sock or shoe put on. From this point the child progresses until by the age of 4 years he or she can pretty well dress and undress with only a little assistance (Orelove & Sobsey, 1991). Table 14–1 provides a sequence of dressing skills as they normally develop. Note that many undressing skills occur before dressing skills. Also, in accordance with general developmental patterns, skills requiring gross motor movements typically precede those requiring fine motor movements. It is not always appropriate to follow a normal developmental dressing sequence, but in some cases it is, particularly with younger individuals who have mastered few or no skills.

Student's Physical Ability Some students will likely not be able to learn independent dressing skills. This will particularly be true for students with the most severe disabilities or those who have both cognitive and physical disabilities. Still, this does not mean that they cannot learn any useful dressing skills or that no effort should be made to teach them some skills. Instead, consideration should be given to teaching skills that will allow them to participate as fully and meaningfully as possible in dressing and undressing processes. An occupational therapist will be able to provide critical assistance in this area. An example of this was reported by Reese and Snell (1991), who taught students with multiple physical and sensory disabilities how to take coats and jackets off and put them on. In performing these skills, the students performed many steps in the task analysis and the teacher assisted with those steps that the students were physically unable to do. The task analyses for the three students are presented in Figure 14–4. Note that the teacher's involvement was individually determined for each task for each student.

Assessing Dressing Ability

An overview assessment of the student's current dressing and undressing abilities can be

Table 14–1
Normal Developmental Sequence of Dressing Skills

Approximate Age	Dressing Skill
12 months	Begins to cooperate by holding out foot for shoe, arm for sleeve
12-18 months	Begins to remove hat, socks and mittens
2 years	Removes unlaced shoes, socks, and pants
2 1/2 years	Removes all clothing Can put on socks, shirt, coat
3 years	Undresses rapidly and well Dresses, except for heavy outer clothing
4 years	Dresses and undresses with little assistance

From *Educating Children with Multiple Disabilities: A Transdisciplinary Approach* (2nd ed.) (p. 391) by F. P. Orelove & D. Sobsey, 1991, Baltimore: Paul H. Brookes Publishing Co., P.O. Box 10624, Baltimore, Maryland 21285-0624. Reprinted by permission.

Lynn
Jacket/Coat Off

1. Take jacket/coat off left shoulder
2. Bend left elbow
3. Take elbow out of sleeve opening
4. Grasp left sleeve with right hand
5. Take left arm out of sleeve
6. Lean forward
7. Bring jacket/coat from behind to right side
8. Shake jacket/coat off right arm
9. Hang jacket/coat on hook

Jacket/Coat On

1. Take jacket/coat off hook
2. Place jacket/coat on your lap, hood/collar next to stomach with inside facing up

*(T) Place left hand into sleeve opening

3. Place right hand into other sleeve opening
4. Lean forward
5. Raise right arm up and over head
6. Pull sides of jacket/coat down

Anne
Jacket/Coat Off

1. Grasp sleeve with preferred hand
2. Bend arm of opposite hand
3. Take arm out of sleeve
4. Grasp remaining sleeve
5. Bend sleeved arm
6. Take arm out of sleeve

Jacket/Coat On

*(T) Place jacket/coat on child's lap, hood/collar next to stomach with inside facing up

1. Place hands in sleeve opening simultaneously
2. Raise arms
3. Flip garment over head
4. Straighten arms

*(T) Pull coat down at sides

Kari
Jacket/Coat Off

1. Grasp right sleeve with left hand
2. Bend right elbow
3. Take right arm out of sleeve
4. Grasp left sleeve with right hand
5. Bend left elbow
6. Take left arm out of sleeve

Jacket/Coat On

*(T) Place jacket/coat on child's lap, hood/collar next to stomach with inside facing up

1. Place hands in sleeve openings at the same time
2. Raise arms
3. Lean forward
4. Flip jacket/coat over head
5. Straighten arms
6. Pull jacket/coat down at sides

Figure 14–4

Task Analyses for Dressing Skills for Students with Cognitive and Physical Disabilities

From "Putting On and Removing Coats and Jackets: The Acquisition and Maintenance of Skills by Children with Severe Multiple Disabilities" by G. M. Reese & M. E. Snell, 1991, *Education and Training in Mental Retardation, 26,* pp. 398–410. Copyright 1991 by the Division on Mental Retardation and Developmental Disabilities, The Council for Exceptional Children. Reprinted by permission.

determined by interviewing parents or caregivers. As an aid to this procedure, adaptive behavior scales or commercial checksheets that itemize different skills can be used (see chapter 5). In addition to the above considerations, this process can help determine dressing skills that might be taught.

Once the dressing skills to be taught have been determined, as with other skills, it is important to assess the student to see what specific abilities he or she has with the articles of clothing to be taught (Snell & Farlow, 1993). As with most other skills that will be taught, the teacher should first conduct a task analysis and then ask the student to perform the task. As the student attempts to do so the teacher records performance on each step, noting whether or not the student can perform the step independently. Three to five days of such observation and recording should indicate to the teacher the exact deficiencies that exist in the student's dressing or undressing ability for specific articles of clothing. After this baseline data has been collected, the teacher may begin instructional activities, continuing to record progress as he or she does so.

Instructional Strategies for Teaching Dressing

After the teacher has conducted the initial assessment, the instructional intervention may start. As the instruction proceeds, the teacher should continue to collect data on the student's performance. If there are several students in need of the same instruction, for example, learning to put on a coat or sweater, group instruction may be provided. Regardless of whether one individual or several are being taught, however, the teacher must select effective instructional strategies. The available literature in the area of teaching dressing skills to persons with severe disabilities has provided various instructional strategies and tactics of great utility (Azrin, Schaeffer, & Wesolowski, 1976; Diorio & Konarski, 1984; Kramer & Whitehurst, 1981; Martin, Kehoe, Bird, Jensen, & Darbyshire, 1971; McKelvey, Sisson, Van Hasselt, & Hersen, 1992; Minge & Ball, 1967; Reese & Snell, 1991; Young, West, Howard, & Whitney, 1986). Several of these strategies are discussed below.

Order of Instruction Dressing skills have been taught to persons with severe disabilities in three different ways: the whole task approach, the forward chaining approach, and the backward (or reverse) chaining approach. All three require teaching the steps listed in the task analysis, but the nature of the instruction is very different. The whole task approach has been recommended previously (see chapter 6) and it is recommended here for most situations as well. This approach requires that at every instructional session, the teacher instruct the student in every step of the task analysis. The steps that the student cannot perform, either independently or with assistance, are performed for the student by the teacher. In this way the student experiences the entire chain of behavior occurring in a natural order.

The forward chaining approach begins in the first instructional session to teach the first step of the task and continues in subsequent sessions to teach only this step until it is learned to some criterion level. Instruction then proceeds to the next step, and then the next, and so on. For example, in a task analysis of putting on pants, the student might learn to put his or her right leg in and then all of the other steps of the task would be performed with direct assistance from the teacher. After the student satisfactorily learns the first step, the instruction is broadened to include the second step of the task as well as the first. This continues until ultimately the student learns all of the steps in the task analysis. Important to note is that each step in the task is taught, one after the other, to a level of satisfactory performance before other steps are taught.

Backward chaining is just the opposite of forward chaining. In the first session, the teacher directly assists in the performance of all the steps in the task analysis for the student, and then requires the student to learn to do the last step. Only after the student can do the last step independently does the teacher require the student to do both the last step and the next to the last step. Once these are learned, the student adds another earlier step in the sequence, and so on and so on. Again using putting on pants as an example, the following procedure would be used:

1. Place the trousers on the student pulled up to hips, have the student pull them up the rest of the way.
2. Place the trousers on the student pulled up to the thighs, have the student pull them up the rest of the way.
3. Place the trousers on the student pulled up to the knees, have the student pull them up the rest of the way.
4. Place both feet in the trousers and allow them to lie around the ankles; have the student pull them up all the way.
5. Place one foot in the trousers, require that the student place the other foot in and pull the pants up around the waist.
6. Have the learner put both feet in the trousers and pull them all the way up around the waist (Mori & Masters, 1980).

Prompting Strategies As discussed in chapter 6, there are various instructional prompting strategies that may be used during skill acquisition. For dressing instruction, two approaches have been dominant: graduated guidance and least-to-most assistance. Just as it is used for teaching self-feeding skills, graduated guidance used to teach self-dressing consists of the teacher's placing his or her hand over the student's hand(s) and guiding the student through the sequence of dressing activity (usually using a whole task approach). As the student shows more independent ability, the teacher gradually reduces the amount of contact, allowing the student more independent movement.

The least-to-most assistance strategy, as discussed in chapter 6, establishes a prompting hierarchy to be employed on each step of the task analysis. A typical example is the following:

1. No assistance
2. Verbal cue only
3. Verbal cue + gesture or pointing
4. Verbal cue + light physical prompt
5. Verbal cue + gentle physical guidance

This would give the student an opportunity on each step to perform with no more assistance than necessary to complete the task.

Instructional Materials Although most instruction on dressing skills naturally calls for the use of the student's regular clothes, for some particularly difficult parts of the dressing process, temporary modifications may be helpful. Realizing, for example, the difficulty associated with various motor movements (putting arms in sleeves, legs in pants) suggests the use of clothing that is one or two sizes too large during early phases of instruction. This would allow the student to get into and out of garments more easily. After success is experienced with these movements, the teacher could then reduce the size of the clothes, in one or two steps, to the student's actual size.

The same principle can be applied to different features of clothing, such as using larger buttons and then gradually reducing their size (Kramer & Whitehurst, 1981). Because students with severe disabilities typically have difficulty with fine motor skills, working with objects that are easier to grasp, such as larger buttons, zippers, laces, clasps, or other clothing components is initially easier than working with smaller items. As students become more skilled at manipulating these larger items, they can be replaced with smaller and smaller ones.

In some cases the parents and professionals (teacher, occupational therapist) may come to agree that the time it would take the student to learn to manipulate certain aspects of clothing, such as shoelaces, would simply be too long. In other cases the physical ability of the student may be inadequate for certain tasks. For example, the student may lack adequate motor skills to tie a shoe or may be getting older and more critical skills may be necessary for functioning in the near future. In these types of situations, a decision may be made to use different clothing materials or different types of clothes. Shoes that have velcro straps instead of laces, for example, may be worn and the student may then have greater success in learning to put them on with no or little assistance.

There are some commercially available devices that have been built to provide practice for dressing skills; they come in various shapes and typically contain buttons, snaps, zippers, and so forth. It is not suggested that these be used because they are not natural. Students might improve their fine motor skills by working on them, but they would not necessarily be able to transfer these skills to actual clothes.

Dressing and Students with More Severe Disabilities

Some students with more severe disabilities or students who have multiple disabilities, as indicated previously, are not able to carry out all of the functions of dressing even if there is adequate time and appropriate instructional practices have been used. In these cases, additional modifications in the dressing process should be provided (Bigge, 1991; Orelove & Sobsey, 1991; Reese & Snell, 1991). An occupational therapist should provide assistance in planning instructional processes and determining the most effective strategies for teaching the student or involving the student through partial participation.

Since many of these individuals are nonambulatory, they should be appropriately positioned for dressing activities—in a sitting position if possible, with their back against the teacher's chest if necessary. The student may also be dressed while lying in a side-lying position with appropriate supports, but generally lying flat on the back will be the most difficult way for the student to participate in the dressing activity.

Partial participation should be encouraged whenever the student can control his or her movements to do so. For this reason, the teacher will need to conduct a task analysis for these students and give them the opportunity to participate, to the extent that they can, on each step of the task. On some steps, they may be able to complete the movement independently; on others, the teacher will have to provide full physical assistance. Nevertheless, it is extremely important that as much participation as possible be encouraged.

Teachers should also look for other ways to construct a dressing task that may make it easier for the student with more severe disabilities. A task analysis need not be constructed in the order in which it typically occurs for nondisabled individuals. It will generally be better to stress satisfactory completion of the function of a task instead of adherence to the common form of the task. For example, Bigge (1991) described an uncommon process for putting on a coat:

> *. . . flipping a coat over one's head is a technique often used by students with coordination or weakness problems. The student lays the garment flat on her lap, the floor or a table. The collar should be near her body with*

the front of the coat on top and the lining showing. The student can then push both arms into the sleeves or push the involved arm in first and the other arm second. Ducking the head forward while extending the arms over the head is next. Finally the coat is slipped into place when the student shrugs her shoulders and pulls down with her arms (Bigge, 1991, p. 387).

Working with parents and occupational therapists, teachers may devise several additional ways to facilitate dressing.

Besides varying the way in which the student may put clothes on, parents may also be advised to purchase clothes for their children with multiple disabilities that will be more comfortable and better meet their unique needs. Bigge (1991) suggests expandable neck openings and stretchable fabrics, large zipper tabs, large buttons that are loosely sewn on, Velcro fastenings, and large hook-and-eye fasteners that are easy to see. Students who wear leg braces may need full-length crotch openings in the inseam that can be fastened with zippers or Velcro. Wide pants legs may also be helpful. An individual who uses full-length crutches may benefit from double-stitched underarm seams. Pantsuits and culottes are often more comfortable and modest for girls and women in wheelchairs than are skirts or dresses. Also for individuals in wheelchairs, a wool cape can provide warmth in cold weather and can also be taken off and put on more easily than a coat or jacket. Table 14–2 provides additional suggestions for modifying clothing for students with multiple severe disabilities.

Teaching Skills Related to Dressing

As with other skills, dressing should be taught as much as possible in relation to other skills, as part of a natural sequence of activities whenever possible, and in the context of teaching other skills. For example, in the discussion on teaching toileting skills it was pointed out that this would be an appropriate opportunity to also teach associated dressing skills. Other times of the day would also provide opportunities, for example, arriving at school in the morning, going out to and coming in from outside play activities, dressing for physical education, changing clothes for different work activities, putting on smocks for art activities, getting ready to go home in the afternoon, and so forth. While teaching dressing skills the teacher can also teach various incidental skills and thus increase the efficacy of instruction. For example, the color, size, and weight of the material might be taught. The concepts of right and left, back and front, top and bottom, and in and out can be taught in an incidental, natural fashion. Students with more advanced abilities may have already learned many of the more basic dressing skills but it may be appropriate to teach them advanced skills. One very important such skill would be appropriate clothing selection. For example, Nutter and Reid (1978) taught women with cognitive disabilities how to select color-coordinated clothes that met community standards of normalcy. They did so by teaching them to match appropriate-colored blouses to selected slacks. This is an important type of skill. Individuals who can dress themselves have even more independence if they select the types of clothes they should wear. Besides color coordination, learning to select clothes for different types of weather, for different occasions, and for different seasons may also be important skills related to dressing.

General Suggestions for Improving Dressing

Some final general suggestions for teaching dressing skills to students with severe disabilities include:

- It will generally be easier to teach undressing before dressing. If appropri-

Table 14–2
Specific Suggestions for Modifying Clothing

Problem of Disability	Suggested Solutions
Difficulty with pullover shirts or sweaters	Use garments of stretchable knits Use elasticized necklines Open seams under arms and at sides Use Velcro dots along seam lines Use large sleeve openings
Difficulty with cardigans, jackets, or front-opening shirts	Use garments of stretchable knits Select styles with fullness in back (add gathers, action pleats, gussets) Use large sleeve openings Use smooth, nonslippery fabrics
Difficulty with pants or pull-on skirts	Sew loops at waistband Use elasticized waistbands
Difficulty with socks	Use tube socks Sew loop tabs at top sides of socks
Crutches	Add fabric patches to underside Line garment Choose knit or stretch fabric Select longer shirt tails Use overblouses or sweaters
Long leg braces or cast	Choose pants legs loose enough to fit over braces/cast Apply long zipper to inside seam

From *Educating Children with Multiple Disabilities: A Transdisciplinary approach* (2nd ed.) (p. 399) by F. P. Orelove & D. Sobsey, 1991, Baltimore: Paul H. Brookes Publishing Co., P.O. Box 10624, Baltimore, Maryland 21285-0624. Reprinted by permission.

ate (that is, if undressing and dressing are both to be taught), the teacher should teach undressing first in order to give the student initial success with the experience.

- The same principle should also be applied to other dressing skills when appropriate. For example, it is easier to teach putting on shoes than putting on socks, pants are easier to put on than shirts, and button shirts are easier than pullover shirts.
- The student may have preferences for wearing certain articles of clothing. If the teacher can learn from the parent what these are, these pieces may be used during instruction to heighten the student's interest and motivation.
- Although teaching should occur at natural times of the day, the more often

instruction is offered, the faster the skill will be learned. For particularly difficult skills, short periods of massed practice instruction may be appropriate.

- For some students, it may be necessary to work on their attention to the task as well as the task itself. This may be done by reinforcing them for looking at the clothes for greater periods of time and then reducing the frequency of reinforcement after adequate attending skills have been developed. The teacher should not, however, attempt to teach attending before teaching dressing, because this would fractionalize the skills too much.
- As with other skills, brief periods of time-out may be sufficient to reduce inappropriate behaviors during dressing instruction periods.
- A well-dressed individual is often reinforced for his or her attire. Students learning to dress should always be naturally reinforced for looking nice after they finish a dressing skill. This reinforcement should occur in the presence of others.
- Teachers should always know what parents are working on and vice versa in the area of dressing. Using the same procedures to practice dressing skills both at home and at school will hasten the learning process.
- Practicing learning skills using different types of clothing of the same form (different types of sweaters) in different locations will increase skill generalization.

Learning Personal Grooming Skills

Personal grooming skills include the things a person does to (or for) his or her body on a regular basis to maintain hygiene and an acceptable standard of personal presentation, such as bathing or showering; washing hands and face; brushing teeth, flossing, and using mouthwash; shaving; using deodorant; washing and drying hair; using rollers or a curling iron; using cologne, perfume, and powder; combing or brushing hair; taking care of menstruation; and using cosmetics (Wilcox & Bellamy, 1987). Some of these activities are very important for hygiene purposes; others are important for self-expression or developing personal appeal. Obviously it is not possible to discuss all of these here. However, basically, the procedures for most are similar to procedures that have been discussed in chapter 6 and throughout this chapter. Assessment must be conducted to determine what skills the person needs and the degree to which they exist. If it is desirable to teach them, a task analysis should be constructed along with a format for data collection. Finally, a systematic means of instruction must be developed.

Two skills that are critical for hygiene purposes but are often neglected are personal dental care and menstrual care for young women. These skills are discussed here in some detail.

Personal Dental Care

Students with severe disabilities, like other people, need to maintain proper oral hygiene. In many cases this is even more significant than in the general population because an individual's disabilities may be indirectly related to inordinate dental problems. Mouth breathing, tooth grinding, finger sucking, and tongue thrusting are common among students with disabilities and may lead to periodontal disease and malocclusion (Batshaw & Perret, 1986). Additional problems may be caused by the buildup of plaque resulting in gum disease, dental decay, and cavities. This is sometimes compounded by the use of drugs to control seizures (e.g., Dilantin) that have a side effect of excessive gum growth, infection, and bleed-

1. *Pick up and hold the toothbrush.* The student should turn on the water and pick up the toothbrush by the handle.
2. *Wet the toothbrush.* The student should continue to hold the toothbrush, placing the bristles under the running water for at least 5 sec. Then, the student should turn off the running water and lay the toothbrush down.
3. *Remove the cap from the toothpaste.* The student should place the tube of toothpaste in his least-preferred hand, unscrew the cap with the thumb and index finger of his preferred hand, and set the cap on the sink.
4. *Apply the toothpaste to the brush.* The student should pick up the toothbrush by the handle, hold the back part of the bristles against the opening of the toothpaste tube, squeeze the tube, move the tube toward the front bristles as toothpaste flows out on top of the bristles, and lay the toothbrush on the sink with the bristles up.
5. *Replace the cap on the toothpaste.* The student should pick up the toothpaste cap with the thumb and index finger of the preferred hand, screw the cap on the toothpaste tube, which is held in the least-preferred hand, lay the tube of toothpaste down, and with the preferred hand pick up the toothbrush by the handle.
6. *Brush the outside surfaces of the teeth.* The student should brush the outside surfaces of the upper and lower teeth on both sides and in the center of the mouth, using either an up and down or back and forth motion, for at least 30 sec.
7. *Brush the biting surfaces of the teeth.* The student should brush the biting surfaces of the upper and lower teeth on both sides and in the center of the mouth, using a back and forth motion, for at least 30 sec.

Figure 14–5
Description of Toothbrushing Skills
From "Training Mentally Retarded Adolescents to Brush Their Teeth" by D. R. Horner & I. Keilitz, 1975, *Journal of Applied Behavior Analysis, 8,* pp. 301–309. Copyright 1975 by the Journal of Applied Behavior Analysis. Reprinted by permission.

ing. The best approach to dealing with such problems is through preventive maintenance, that is, caring for the teeth and gums as well as possible in order to prevent or reduce dental problems (Coffee, 1977).

It has been well demonstrated that many students with severe disabilities can learn to brush their teeth or assist in the process of toothbrushing (Abramson & Wunderlich, 1972; Horner & Keilitz, 1975; Snell, Lewis, & Houghton, 1989). The instructional methods are similar to others used to teach self-care skills, beginning with a task analysis of the process. The task analysis used by Horner and Keilitz (1975) is presented in Figure 14–5.

A graduated guidance or least-to-most assistance method can be used to guide students through each step of the toothbrushing task. Horner and Keilitz used a least-to-most assistance procedure that included (1) no help, (2) verbal instruction, (3) demonstration and verbal instruction, and (4) physical guidance and verbal

8. *Brush the inside surfaces of the teeth.* The student should brush the inside surfaces of the upper and lower teeth on both sides and in the center of the mouth, using a back and forth motion, for at least 30 sec.
9. *Fill the cup with water.* The student should lay the toothbrush down, pick up the cup, place it under the faucet, turn on the water, fill the cup, and turn off the water.
10. *Rinse the mouth.* The student should spit out any excess toothpaste foam, take a sip of water, hold it in the mouth, swish it around in the mouth, and spit it out. If any toothpaste foam should be repeated.
11. *Wipe the mouth.* The student should pull a tissue from the container (or pick up a hand towel) and dry his mouth.
12. *Rinse the toothbrush.* The student should pick up the toothbrush by the handle, turn on the water, and place the bristles under the running water until the bristles are free of toothpaste (any toothpaste not removed by the water may be dislodged by drawing the fingers across the bristles), turn off the water, and lay the toothbrush down.
13. *Rinse the sink.* The student should turn on the water, rub around the inside of the sink with the hand to wash any residue of toothpaste or toothpaste foam down the drain, turn off the water.
14. *Put the equipment away.* The student should put the toothpaste and toothbrush in the proper storage place. (If a glass and hand towel are used, these should be placed in the proper place.)
15. *Discard the disposables.* Any used paper cups and tissues should be placed in a waste receptacle.

Figure 14–5, *continued*

instruction if necessary. Even students who lack the ability to self-conduct many of the steps of toothbrushing can often still participate. Note the task analysis used by Snell et al. (1989) presented in Figure 14–6. Students who had severe physical disabilities were able to participate in dental care by opening the mouth and holding it open, rinsing the mouth, and turning the head back and forth to assist in wiping the mouth.

Whether students with severe disabilities require more or less assistance to effectively brush their teeth, a thorough brushing should occur at least once a day. Additionally, students should learn to floss and to use mouthwash if they are physically able to do so. Some students may lack the fine motor skills required for flossing or may have a tendency to swallow the mouthwash or the toothpaste. In these cases, the teacher should attempt to teach the student as much as possible and do for the student those things that he or she simply cannot do, unless these needs are adequately handled at home.

For students who must have oral hygiene provided for them by another person, several suggestions are noteworthy (Coffee, 1977). If there is a problem with swallowing toothpaste or mouthwash, these products may be omitted

Toothbrushing

Discriminative stimuli (teacher)		Task steps (Student and teacher)
"Brush your teeth."		
Presents toothbrush		1. Open your mouth wide.
Inserts toothbrush		2. Keep it open (5 s).
	Teacher:	a. Brushes outside of upper left teeth, back to front.
		b. Brushes cutting edge of upper left teeth, back to front.
Removes toothbrush		3. Close your mouth (lips touch).
Presents toothbrush		4. Open your mouth wide.
Inserts toothbrush		5. Keep it open (5 s).
	Teacher:	a. Brushes outside of lower left teeth, back to front.
		b. Brushes cutting edge of upper left teeth, back to front.
Removes toothbrush		6. Close your mouth (lips touch).
Presents toothbrush		7. Open your mouth wide.
Inserts toothbrush		8. Keep it open (5 s).
	Teacher:	a. Brushes outside of upper right teeth, back to front.
		b. Brushes cutting edge of upper right teeth, back to front.
Removes toothbrush		9. Close your mouth (lips touch).
Presents toothbrush		10. Open your mouth wide.
Inserts toothbrush		11. Keep it open (5 s).

Figure 14–6
Task Analysis of Toothbrushing
From "Acquisition and Maintenance of Toothbrushing Skills by Students with Cerebral Palsy and Mental Retardation" by M. E. Snell, A. P. Lewis, & A. Houghton, 1989, *Journal of the Association for Persons with Severe Handicaps, 14,* p. 218. Copyright 1989 by The Association for Persons with Severe Handicaps. Reprinted by permission.

and only water used. It is actually more important to adequately brush all of the surfaces of the teeth at least once a day than to use toothpaste. Also, children who have very sensitive teeth or gums may have their teeth thoroughly cleaned with a warm wet washcloth or gauze pad. One thorough cleaning per day is better than several less adequate attempts. Additional suggestions made by Coffee (1977) include the following:

- The five surfaces of each tooth must be cleaned. The side surfaces that cannot be reached by toothbrush must be flossed.
- A soft, nylon-bristled toothbrush is the best to use. Toothbrushes with enlarged or adapted handles may be easier to handle for some students. An occupational therapist should be consulted to assist with this need.
- A systematic brushing pattern should be used to avoid missing any surface areas.
- Brushing should be done with a gentle back-and-forth or circular motion with the bristles held at a slight angle to tooth surfaces.
- Each brushing should be followed with flossing, stretching the floss across fingers or using a floss holder, and cleaning the inside surfaces of each tooth.
- A commercial plaque-disclosing solution should be used to identify areas that have been missed.
- Assistance should be sought from the school nurse or occupational therapist to

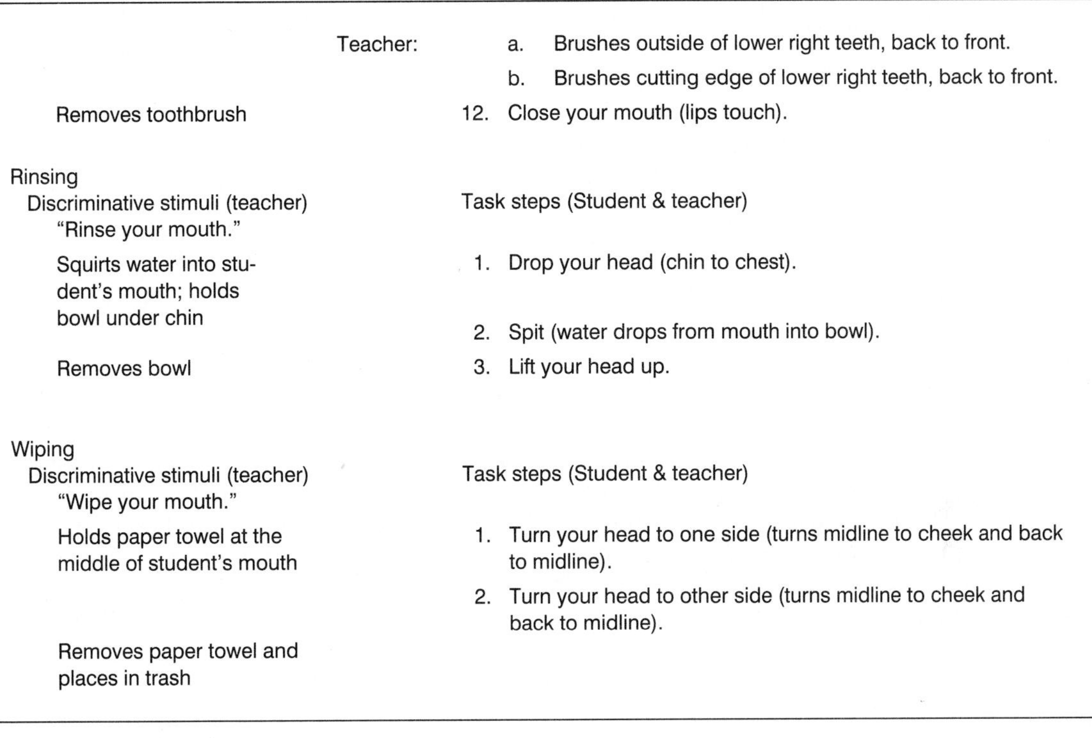

Teacher:	a. Brushes outside of lower right teeth, back to front.
	b. Brushes cutting edge of lower right teeth, back to front.
Removes toothbrush	12. Close your mouth (lips touch).
Rinsing	
Discriminative stimuli (teacher)	Task steps (Student & teacher)
"Rinse your mouth."	
Squirts water into student's mouth; holds bowl under chin	1. Drop your head (chin to chest).
	2. Spit (water drops from mouth into bowl).
Removes bowl	3. Lift your head up.
Wiping	
Discriminative stimuli (teacher)	Task steps (Student & teacher)
"Wipe your mouth."	
Holds paper towel at the middle of student's mouth	1. Turn your head to one side (turns midline to cheek and back to midline).
	2. Turn your head to other side (turns midline to cheek and back to midline).
Removes paper towel and places in trash	

Figure 14–6, *continued*

learn how to get the student to open his or her mouth and hold it open if doing so is normally a problem. Often slight pressure on the jaw can be used to open the mouth and two or three gauze-covered tongue blades can be used to hold the mouth open. In some cases, students may learn to hold the mouth open for short periods of time so that brushing or flossing can occur (Snell et al., 1989).

- The student should be encouraged to look in a mirror to see his or her clean teeth after brushing and should be reinforced for practicing good oral hygiene.

In addition to brushing and flossing, healthful eating habits, fluoridation, and regular dental care can greatly reduce diseases of gums and teeth (Batshaw & Perret, 1986). Snacks should include fresh vegetables and nuts if the student can handle them, and if the local water is not fluoridated, fluoride tablets or fluoridated mouthwash or toothpaste can be used. By the time a child is 2 years old, all of the primary teeth have emerged and regular visits to the dentist should begin.

Menstrual Care

A key need for young women is to learn how to manage their own menstrual care independently. As with other personal care areas, this may be taught at home by parents or caregivers, but there is sometimes a need for it to be included in the school curriculum. Naturally, the teacher should have a high level of communication with the student's home if it is deemed necessary to provide instruction in this area at school. In some cases, the young woman may be primarily instructed at home, and the teacher's role may be to provide advice about instructional procedures.

Two methods may be used to provide instruction and it is suggested that input from parents or caregivers and other team members be solicited regarding the method to be used. This is very important; different individuals have different opinions regarding the appropriateness of each approach (Epps, Prescott, & Horner, 1990). One method is to provide direct instruction to the student both during menses and during role-playing activities in which sanitary napkins and underwear have been stained with red dye, food coloring, or nontoxic theater blood. The second method is to use large adult dolls and miniature clothes, underwear, and napkins to demonstrate appropriate personal care during menses (Epps, Stern, & Horner, 1990; Richman, Ponticas, Page, & Epps, 1986; Richman, Reiss, Bauman, & Bailey, 1984).

The primary objective of both approaches is for the student to recognize that there is a need to respond appropriately when the underwear and/or the sanitary napkin is stained. In the role-playing situation the student is taught to go into the bathroom, check her underwear and pad (if she is wearing one), and if the pad or underwear is stained, to remove them and dispose of them properly, wash hands, obtain clean underwear and another pad, and put them on. Several learning opportunities need to be provided with the student experiencing both the need to change the underwear and/or pad and having no need to make a change, that is, when no stain exists. Of course, training should occur when the student is having her period, but role-playing can also be used to increase the frequency of instruction. When this is done, the instructional process begins with the young woman donning prestained underwear or pad. In both the real situation and the role-playing situation, the student is cued to "check your pants."

Teaching menstrual care through the use of dolls has been shown to be a successful approach in at least one study (Epps, Stern, & Horner, 1990). The advantage of this approach is that several young women can be given the simulated instruction simultaneously, and then self-use of the skill can be carried out at home or in private. Using this approach, the teacher needs to create all of the materials in miniature form and then, as with the above method, teach the students how to respond to the different situations.

Again, regardless of the approach used, it is critical that parental or caregiver permission and cooperation be sought. Of course, for ethical reasons the training should be provided by a professional woman. If the teacher is male, a female counterpart should be sought to provide instruction. If the school nurse is female, she is the ideal individual to provide the training.

General Suggestions for Improving Personal Grooming

When teaching any personal grooming skill, the following general suggestions are recommended.

- This is probably the instructional domain that calls for the most cooperation and interaction with the home. The teacher should know what is considered important and what idiosyncratic features of instruction should be used to coordinate with what is done in the home.
- Many skills in this area bear on the health of an individual and should not be ignored if there is a need for instruction.
- Most people normally engage in grooming activities to be socially accepted as well as to have good health. Teachers and others should make sure a strong dose of

positive, age-appropriate, social reinforcement follows appropriate grooming behavior.

- Students who have had many personal-care skills provided for them in the past may be uncomfortable when initially being taught to take care of these needs themselves. The teacher may need to move gradually but surely in these areas.
- Learning personal-care skills is a private matter, and training should be conducted in private, natural locations and with respect for the needs of the individual.
- Safety should also be a concern when students are learning skills in this area. Toxic material that could be ingested should be avoided, and even nontoxic material, such as mouthwash, should be carefully monitored. The teacher should also be extremely careful about water temperature when teaching washing, bathing, and so forth.

Questions for Reflection

1. In comparison to other skills that might be important for students with severe disabilities to learn, how do self-care skills compare? When might it be appropriate *not* to focus on self-care skills?
2. What other skills (besides eating skills) could be learned during mealtimes?
3. In what type of environment do you like to eat? Do you think persons with severe disabilities would like to learn to eat appropriately in this type of environment?
4. What ethical guidelines should be developed for working with individuals, particularly those who are older, on private activities such as toilet training or menstrual care?
5. What are some natural times and places to teach dressing skills during the day? How about in the regular classroom?
6. How does a person's dressing ability relate to his or her participation in various social activities?
7. In what ways might students without disabilities play important roles when students with severe disabilities are learning self-care skills?
8. Besides the areas discussed in this chapter, what might be some other important areas of personal self-care that should be taught?

References

Abramson, S. E., & Wunderlich, R. A. (1972). Dental hygiene training for retardates: An application of behavioral techniques. *Mental Retardation, 10*(3), 6–8.

Albin, J. B. (1977). Some variables influencing the maintenance of acquired self-feeding behavior in profoundly retarded children. *Mental Retardation, 15*(5), 49–52.

Alexander, R. (1991). Prespeech and prefeeding. In J. L. Bigge *Teaching individuals with physical and multiple disabilities* (pp. 175–198). New York: Macmillan.

Anderson, D. M. (1982). Ten years later: Toilet training in the post-Azrin-and-Foxx era. *Journal of the Association for the Severely Handicapped, 7*(2), 71–79.

Azrin, N. H., & Armstrong, P. M. (1973). The "mini-meal"-A method for teaching eating skills to the profoundly retarded. *Mental Retardation, 11*(1), 9–13.

Azrin, N. H., Bugle, C., & O'Brien, F. (1971). Behavioral engineering: Two apparatuses for toilet training retarded children. *Journal of Applied Behavior Analysis, 4*, 249–253.

Azrin, N. H., & Foxx, R. M. (1971). A rapid method of toilet training the institutionalized retarded. *Journal of Applied Behavior Analysis, 4*, 89–99.

Azrin, N. H., Schaeffer, R. M., & Wesolowski, M. D. (1976). A rapid method of teaching profoundly retarded persons to dress. *Mental Retardation, 14*(6), 29–33.

Azrin, N. H., Sneed, T. J., & Foxx, R. M. (1974). Dry-bed training: Rapid elimination of childhood enuresis. *Behaviour Research and Therapy, 12*, 147–156.

Banerdt, B., & Bricker, D. (1978). A training program for selected self-feeding skills for the motorically impaired. *AAESPH Review, 3,* 222–229.

Barton, E. S., Guess, D., Garcia, E., & Baer, D. (1970). Improvements of retardates' mealtime behaviors by timeout procedures using the multiple baseline technique. *Journal of Applied Behavior Analysis, 3,* 77–84.

Batshaw, M. L., & Perret, Y. M. (1986). *Children with handicaps: A medical primer* (2nd ed.). Baltimore: Paul H. Brookes.

Berkowitz, S., Sherry, P. J., & Davis, B. A. (1971). Teaching self-feeding skills to profound retardates using reinforcement and fading procedures. *Behavior Therapy, 2,* 62–67.

Bigge, J. L. (1991). *Teaching individuals with physical and multiple disabilities.* New York: Macmillan.

Christian, W. P., Hollomon, S. W., & Lanier, C. L. (1973). An attendant operated feeding program. *Mental Retardation, 11*(5), 35–37.

Coffee, L. (1977). Planning daily care for healthy teeth. In R. Perske, A. Clifton, B. M. McLean, & J. I. Stein, (Eds.). *Mealtimes for severely and profoundly handicapped persons: New concepts and attitudes* (pp. 119–122). Baltimore: University Park Press.

Diorio, M. S., & Konarski, E. A. (1984). Evaluation of a method for teaching dressing skills to profoundly mentally retarded persons. *American Journal of Mental Deficiency, 89,* 307–309.

Dunlap, G., Koegel, R. L., & Koegel, L. K. (1984). Continuity of treatment: Toilet training in multiple community settings. *Journal of the Association for Persons with Severe Handicaps, 9,* 134–141.

Ellis, N. R. (1963). Toilet training and the severely defective patient: An S-R reinforcement analysis. *American Journal of Mental Deficiency, 68,* 98–103.

Epps, S., Prescott, A. L., & Horner, R. H. (1990). Social acceptability of menstrual care training methods for young women with developmental disabilities. *Education and Training in Mental Retardation, 25,* 33–44.

Epps, S., Stern, R. J., & Horner, R. H. (1990). Comparison of simulation training on self and using a doll for teaching generalized menstrual care to women with severe mental retardation. *Research in Developmental Disabilities, 11,* 37–66.

Foxx, R. M., & Azrin, N. H. (1973). *Toilet training the retarded.* Champaign, IL: Research Press.

Freagon, S., & Rotatori, A. F. (1982). Comparing natural and artificial environments in training self-care skills to group home residents. *Journal of the Association for the Severely Handicapped, 7*(3), 73–86.

Giles, D. K., & Wolf, M. M. (1966). Toilet training institutionalized severe retardates: An application of behavior modification techniques. *American Journal of Mental Deficiency, 70,* 766–780.

Groves, I. D., & Carroccio, D. F. (1971). A self-feeding program for the severely and profoundly retarded. *Mental Retardation, 9*(3), 10–12.

Henriksen, K., & Doughty, R. (1972). Decelerating undesired mealtime behavior in a group of profoundly retarded boys. *American Journal of Mental Deficiency, 72,* 40–44.

Horner, D. R., & Keilitz, I. (1975). Training mentally retarded adolescents to brush their teeth. *Journal of Applied Behavior Analysis, 8,* 301–309.

Hundziak, M., Maurer, R. A., & Watson, L. S. (1965). Operant conditioning in toilet training severely mentally retarded boys. *American Journal of Mental Deficiency, 70,* 120–124.

Kimbrell, D. L., Luckey, R. E., Barbuto, P. F., & Love, J. G. (1967). Operation dry pants: An intensive habit training program for the severely and profoundly retarded. *Mental Retardation, 5*(2), 32–36.

Kramer, L., & Whitehurst, C. (1981). Effects of button features on self-dressing in young retarded children. *Education and Training of the Mentally Retarded, 16,* 277–283.

Lancioni, G. E. (1980). Teaching independent toileting to profoundly retarded deaf-blind children. *Behavior Therapy, 11,* 234–244.

Leibowitz, M. J., & Holcer, P. (1974). Building and maintaining self-feeding skills in a retarded child. *American Journal of Occupational Therapy, 28,* 545–548.

Lemke, H., & Mitchell, R. D. (1972). Controlling the behavior of a profoundly retarded child. *American Journal of Occupational Therapy, 26,* 261–264.

Lent, J. R. (1975). Teaching daily living skills. In J. M. Kauffman & J. M. Payne (Eds.), *Mental retardation: Introduction and personal perspectives* (pp. 246–274). Columbus, OH: Merrill.

Mahoney, K., Van Wagenen, R. K., & Meyerson, L. (1971). Toilet training of normal and retarded children. *Journal of Applied Behavior Analysis, 4,* 173–181.

Martin, G. L., Kehoe, B., Bird, E., Jensen, V., & Darbyshire, M. (1971). Operant conditioning in the dressing behavior of severely retarded girls. *Mental Retardation, 9*(3), 27–30.

Martin, L., McDonald, S., & Omichinski, M. (1971). An operant analysis of response interactions during meals with severely retarded girls. *American Journal of Mental Deficiency, 76,* 68–75.

McKelvey, J. L., Sisson, L. A., Van Hasselt, V. B., & Hersen, M. (1992). An approach to teaching self dressing to a child with dual sensory impairment. *Teaching Exceptional Children, 25,* 12–15.

Miller, H. R., Patton, M. E., & Henton, K. R. (1971). Behavior modification of a profoundly retarded child: A case report. *Behavior Therapy, 2,* 375–384.

Minge, M. R., & Ball, T. S. (1967). Teaching self-help skills to profoundly retarded patients. *American Journal of Mental Deficiency, 71,* 864–868.

Mohr, C., & Sharpley, C. F. (1988). Multi-modal treatment of nocturnal enuresis. *Education and Training in Mental Retardation, 23,* 70–75.

Mori, A. A., & Masters, L. F. (1980). *Teaching the severely mentally retarded: Adaptive skills training.* Germantown, MD: Aspen Systems Corporation.

Nelson, G. L., Cone, J. D., & Hanson, C. R. (1975). Training correct utensil use in retarded children: Modeling vs. physical guidance. *American Journal of Mental Deficiency, 80,* 114–122.

Nutter, D., & Reid, D. H. (1978). Teaching retarded women a clothing selection skill using community norms. *Journal of Applied Behavior Analysis, 11,* 475–487.

O'Brien, F., & Azrin, N. H. (1972). Developing proper mealtime behaviors of the institutionalized retarded. *Journal of Applied Behavior Analysis, 5,* 389–399.

O'Brien, F., Bugle, C., & Azrin, N. H. (1972). Training and maintaining a retarded child's proper eating. *Journal of Applied Behavior Analysis, 5,* 67–72.

Orelove, F. P., & Sobsey, D. (1991). *Educating children with multiple disabilities: A transdisciplinary approach* (2nd ed.). Baltimore: Paul H. Brookes.

Osarchuk, M. (1973). Operant methods of toilet behavior training the severely and profoundly retarded: A review. *Journal of Special Education, 7,* 423–437.

Perske, R., Clifton, A., McLean, B. M., & Stein, J. I. (Eds.) (1977). *Mealtimes for severely and profoundly handicapped persons: New concepts and attitudes.* Baltimore: University Park Press.

Reese, G. M., & Snell, M. E. (1991). Putting on and removing coats and jackets: The acquisition and maintenance of skills by children with severe multiple disabilities. *Education and Training in Mental Retardation, 26,* 398–410.

Richman, G. S., Ponticas, Y., Page, T. J., & Epps, S. (1986). Simulation procedures for teaching independent menstrual care to mentally retarded persons. *Applied Research in Mental Retardation, 7,* 21–35.

Richman, G. S., Reiss, M. L., Bauman, K. E., & Bailey, J. S. (1984). Teaching menstrual care to mentally retarded women: Acquisition, generalization, and maintenance. *Journal of Applied Behavior Analysis, 17,* 441–451.

Smith, P. S. (1979). A comparison of different methods of toilet training the mentally handicapped. *Behaviour Research and Therapy, 17,* 33–43.

Snell, M. E., & Farlow, L. J. (1993). Self-care skills. In M. E. Snell (Ed.), *Instruction of students with severe disabilities* (4th ed.) (pp. 380–441). New York: Macmillan.

Snell, M. E., Lewis, A. P., & Houghton, A. (1989). Acquisition and maintenance of toothbrushing skills by students with cerebral palsy and mental retardation. *Journal of the Association for Persons with Severe Handicaps, 14,* 216–226.

Sobsey, R. J. (1983). Nutrition of children with severely handicapping conditions. *Journal of the Association for Persons with Severe Handicaps, 8*(4), 14–17.

Sobsey, R., & Orelove, F. P. (1984). Neurophysiological facilitation of eating skills in severely handicapped children. *Journal of the Association for Persons with Severe Handicaps, 9,* 98–110.

Song, A. Y., & Ghandi, R. (1974). An analysis of behavior during the acquisition and maintenance phases of self spoon feeding skills of profound retardates. *Mental Retardation, 12*(1), 25–28.

Trott, M. C. (1977). Applications of Foxx and Azrin toilet training for the retarded in a school program. *Education and Training of the Mentally Retarded, 12,* 336–338.

Utley, B., Holvoet, J., & Barnes, K. (1977). Handling, positioning, and feeding the physically handicapped. In E. Sontag, J. Smith, & N. Certo (Eds.), *Educational programming for the severely and profoundly handicapped* (pp. 279–299). Reston, VA: Division on Mental Retardation, Council for Exceptional Children.

Van Etten, G., Arkell, C., & Van Etten, C. (1980). *The severely and profoundly handicapped: Programs, methods and materials.* St. Louis, MO: C. V. Mosby.

Westling, D. L., & Murden, L. (1977). Self-help skills training: A review of operant studies. *Journal of Special Education, 12,* 253–283.

Wilcox, B., & Bellamy, G. T. (1987). *The activities catalog: An alternative curriculum for youth and adults with severe disabilities.* Baltimore: Paul H. Brookes.

Williams, F. E., & Sloop, E. W. (1978). Success with a shortened Foxx-Azrin toilet training program. *Education and Training of the Mentally Retarded, 13,* 399–402.

Wilson, P. G., Reid, D. H., Phillips, J. F., & Burgio, L. D. (1984). Normalization of institutional mealtimes for profoundly retarded persons: Effects and noneffects of teaching family style dining. *Journal of Applied Behavior Analysis, 17,* 189–201.

Young, K. R., West, R. P., Howard, V. F., & Whitney, R. (1986). Acquisition, fluency training, generalization, and maintenance of dressing skills of two developmentally disabled children. *Education and Treatment of Children, 9*(1), 16–29.

Zeiler, M. S., & Jervey, S. S. (1968). Development of behavior: Self-feeding. *Journal of Consulting and Clinical Psychology, 32*(2), 164–168.

CHAPTER 15

Teaching Leisure and Recreation Skills

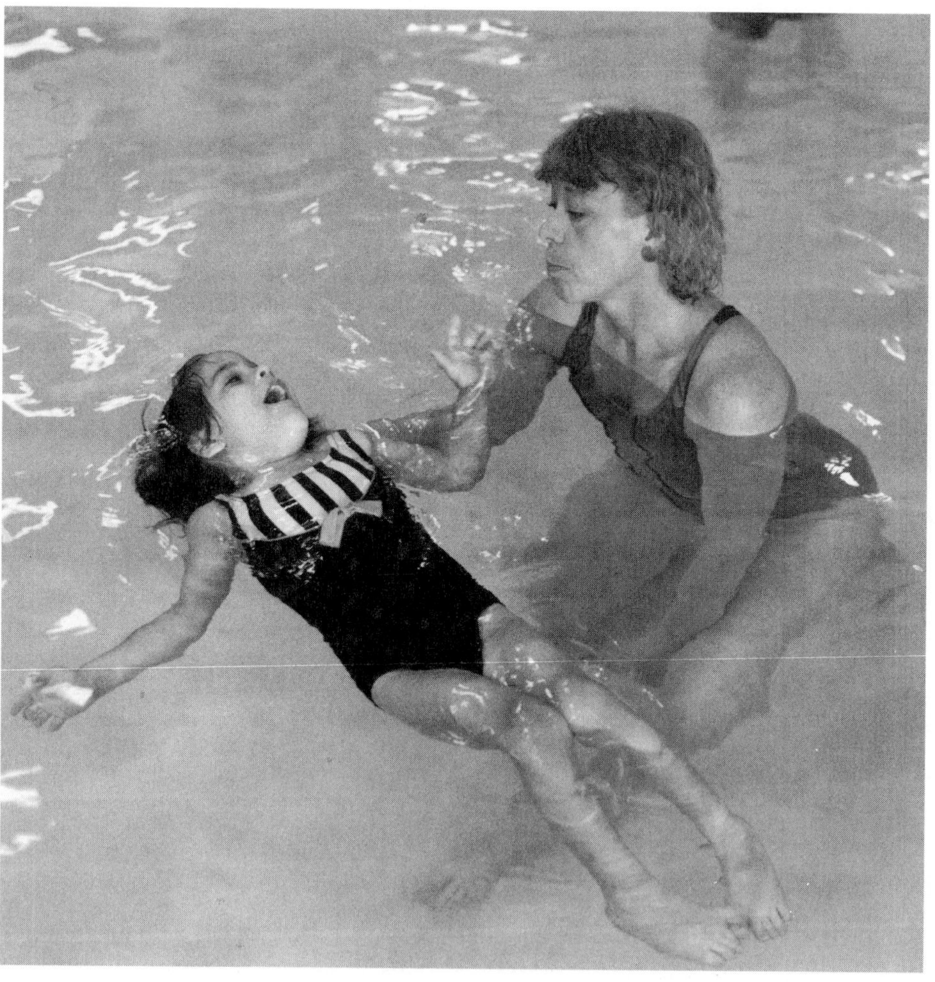

Chapter Overview

In this chapter, the importance of teaching students leisure and recreation skills is discussed. The chapter provides guidelines on how to select and teach leisure skills with an emphasis on facilitating the development of skills that may be used in inclusive environments.

The leisure and recreation curricular domain involves the instruction of skills that students may use for enjoyment and entertainment in their free time. *Leisure* is defined as "freedom from occupation; spare time, unoccupied time"; *recreation* means "refreshment from weariness; any pleasurable interest; amusement." Recreation has been identified as a major curricular domain in addition to community, vocational, and domestic skills.

Instruction of recreation skills is particularly important for students with severe disabilities because of their limited skill repertoires and difficulty in accessing environments and peers. Teachers of students without disabilities do not typically address recreation skill development outside of physical education, library skills, and art and music instruction; they are usually assured that the recreation needs of their students are met outside of school hours or during the more informal parts (e.g., free play, after school) of the day. Unfortunately, an assumption that students with severe disabilities can meet their recreation needs without instruction cannot be made, so a systematic approach to the development of recreation skills must be provided. In this chapter, the importance of recreation as a curricular domain is presented, along with strategies for teaching recreation skills. The chapter provides a detailed discussion on how to select appropriate recreation and leisure activities with an emphasis on choice, age appropriateness, and peer interaction. In addition, the issues surrounding friendship development are discussed.

Recreation Skill Instruction

What would your life be without recreation time? Many of us complain about the fast pace of our society leaving little time to "play." The time for leisure pursuits is highly valued in our society. If you think about your life without leisure time you might describe it as unfulfilling, boring, stressful, and lonely. Most people use recreation time to build friendships with others, relax, keep physically fit, explore interests, and learn new skills, and as a diversion from work time.

People with severe disabilities often have large blocks of time with nothing to do. Because they may be limited in mobility and access to others, they spend a large amount of time waiting for someone to assist them. The time available for leisure pursuits is not an issue; it is usually the lack of opportunities to engage in recreation activities and the lack of recreation skills that are barriers to fulfilling leisure activities.

Recreation skill instruction is important for individuals with severe disabilities for many of the same reasons that it is important to all other persons in society. Recreation is fun, provides opportunities for social affiliation, increases physical fitness, and offers a satisfying way to spend one's free time. In addition, participation in play activities and training in play skills have been related to increases in skills in other domains (Voeltz & Apffel, 1981; Voeltz, Wuerch, & Wilcox, 1982). Many recreational and leisure skill activities create opportunities for persons with severe disabilities and nondisabled peers to practice social interaction and communication behaviors and to develop friendships.

Recreational and leisure activities help eliminate unstructured or "down" time; they provide for constructive use of free time. An increase in play skills has been related to a decrease in negative and inappropriate social behavior (Gaylord-Ross, 1980). Moreover, an increase in the constructive use of leisure time may reduce the need for supervision by others and enhance the independence of individuals with severe disabilities.

In the past, recreational programs for individuals with severe disabilities were segregated and often not responsive to the preferences of the person. For example, a swimming or camp program may have been the only opportunities offered within a community. When segregated recreational programs were the only opportunities offered, there was little focus on the need to teach individuals leisure skills that could be used in a variety of environments or to develop the social support needed to assist individuals with disabilities to participate in leisure activities with nondisabled persons.

In the last decade, the emphasis on inclusion and normalization has changed the approach to teaching recreational skills. The goal of leisure instruction is to assist individuals with severe disabilities in the acquisition of the skills and supports needed to engage in a variety of recreational activities in the community and with nondisabled persons. In addition, there is an emphasis on matching the preferences of the individual to the recreational skills and activities that are selected (Dattilo & Rusch, 1985).

Selecting Recreation Activities

The recreation activities that are selected for instruction must be individually determined, using the same process that is used for developing individualized objectives in the other curricular domains. The definition of *recreation* includes the components of amusement and relaxation, concepts that are individually determined. For example, one individual may enjoy playing basketball; another may prefer collecting baseball cards. Personal preference is a critical feature of determining the recreational skills that are taught. Teachers cannot simply teach skills that match the materials available in their classrooms or assume that a recreational curriculum can be determined for a group of students without individualization.

In addition to personal preference, the teacher should select recreational activities that are chronologically age-appropriate and provide interaction opportunities with nondisabled persons. The activities that are selected should also be ones that can be adapted for active participation by the individual with disabilities and can be used in a variety of environments currently and in the future. The leisure skills curriculum should include leisure activities that have life value in terms of independence and integration. Leisure activities in which the individual can participate without assistance should be a priority as well as activities that promote integration into the community.

The first step in determining recreational activities and skills to be taught is to conduct ecological inventories of the environments where recreation activities occur. The process for conducting ecological inventories is discussed in chapter 5.

The environments and activities that are selected for analysis should be determined by consulting with the family, peers, and siblings, and by analyzing the student's preferences. Since much of leisure time occurs in the home, parents' assessment of preference for their child's leisure activities is often crucial to the success of any leisure education program (Voeltz & Apffel, 1981). Questions that the teacher may want to ask family members are listed in Figure 15–1.

A useful resource in determining recreation activities are nondisabled peers. An open-ended peer interest questionnaire can provide parents, educators, and others with useful information to develop age-appropriate activities. York, Vandercook, and Stave (1990) developed a two-page recreation/leisure questionnaire that can be used or modified for any age group. The questionnaire consists of the following seven open-ended, short-answer questions:

1. What are some of your favorite after-school, evening, and weekend recreation/leisure activities that you do by yourself, with your family, and with your friends?
2. If you use any type of equipment during your leisure time, what do you like to use?
3. What magazines do you like to read or browse through?
4. If you have a favorite music group and rock star, who are they?
5. If you like to play cards or board games, which ones are your favorites?
6. If you have hobbies that you enjoy, what are they?
7. If you could get any two items for your birthday, what would you want?

It is important not to approach the selection of recreation activities for students with severe

1. What does your child do during his or her free time after school?
2. What does your child do during his or her free time on the weekends?
3. What recreation activities does your child do with the family?
4. What recreation activities does your child do with neighbors and friends?
5. What are your child's favorite recreation activities?
6. What are the favorite recreation activities of your family?
7. Are there any special problems that occur for your child during these activities?
8. What are recreation activities that you think your child may want to try?
9. What community recreation activities (e.g., scouts, after-school, little league, etc.) would you like to see your child become involved in?

Figure 15–1
Home Leisure Questions

disabilities in a conventional way. Family members and teachers may have difficulty in thinking beyond the array of activities that have been traditionally offered to individuals with disabilities. Swimming, woodworking, plant care, and bowling are examples of activities that are easily adapted for individuals with disabilities and, as a consequence, they may be the options that are thought of first. Playing pinball (Hill, Wehman, & Horst, 1982; Vandercook, 1991), photography (Giangreco, 1983), and playing darts (Schleien, Wehman, & Kiernan, 1981) are examples of activities that can be done alone or with a group and in a variety of environments that may be appealing to individuals with disabilities and their peers.

A variety of common leisure preferences of students in elementary, middle, and high school are listed in Figure 15–2. This list is not meant to be exhaustive, but was developed to demonstrate the array of options that are available. The activities in the list are categorized by eight major leisure curriculum categories developed by Bender, Brannan, and Verhoven (1984): play and games; sports and physical development; camping and outdoor activities; nature study; hobby activities; craft activities; arts activities; and educational, entertainment, and cultural activities.

Assessing Student Preference

Although we have stressed the importance of using student preference in determining potential leisure activities, it may be difficult to determine preference because of the student's limited communication skills and his or her lack of experience with a variety of activities. A student's initial reaction may be one of apprehension but, after repeated exposure, he or she may find the activity very pleasurable.

Wuerch and Voeltz (1982) have designed an inventory that may be used to determine student leisure preferences. The Student Interest Inventory (see Figure 15–3) is based on the assumptions that an individual's feelings are reflected in outward behaviors and that these outward behaviors are related to his or her interest and enjoyment of activities (Wuerch & Voeltz, 1982). For example, if the student smiles and vocalizes when assisted in playing a computer game, the teacher would determine that the computer game is a preferred activity. Conversely, if the student withdraws or sleeps during an activity, a lack of interest in the activity may be assumed.

It is important to realize that analyzing student behavior to determine preferences can be a little tricky. For example, think about a student who closes his eyes and becomes very relaxed when activating a tape player with a music tape. Should the teacher assume that it is a preferred activity or a boring one? Obviously, more information would be needed to determine preference. The teacher might want to examine the student's response to different types of music as one method of determining the meaning of the response. The teacher might also compare the reaction to the tape player to the student's reaction to known preferred and nonpreferred activities.

What about the student who reacts to all new activities in a manner that appears to signal dislike? Repeated sampling of a variety of activities may be necessary to assist with the initial resistance to something new. Participation in activities should not be forced or coerced; the activity should be offered several times in a gentle and supportive manner to determine if it holds interest for the student.

Student response to activities may also be determined by nonessential components of the activity. For example, a student who has difficulty with auditory stimulation may enjoy playing a hand-held video game if the noise is turned off. A student who has difficulty with close contact with others may not be able to

	Sample Recreation Activities							
	Play and Games	Sports and Physical	Camping and Outdoors	Nature Study	Hobby Activities	Crafts Activities	Art Activities	Educational, Entertainment, Cultural
Elementary	puzzles tag hide and seek card games (UNO, Go Fish) board games (Sorry, Jr. Monopoly)	swimming T ball soccer tumbling	camping day hikes	bird watching shell collecting nature walks pet care	card collecting comic collecting action figures doll collection	T-shirt art ceramics models	painting clay coloring puppet shows musical instruments	reading recreation courses scouts zoo park
Middle School	board games card games video games computer games catch	karate softball basketball jogging swimming	camping hiking canoeing/boating snorkeling	pet care gardening aquariums rocks	stamp collecting coin collections comic collections	bead work leather craft tie dye sewing	musical instruments painting dance drama	listen to music parties shopping sports events
High School	pool/billiards cards darts video games computer games	bowling jogging tennis aerobics	canoeing/boating camping backpacking cooking outdoors	gardening pet care bird watching plant identification astronomy	poster collections button collections jewelry collections records/cd's	candle making stitchery jewelry craft	drawing musical instruments dance mime drama	listen to music attending plays art shows concerts shopping dating sports events

Figure 15–2
Sample Recreation Activities

Student:____________________

Instructions: For each activity, answer each of the questions below by placing the number of the description that best matches the child's behavior in the appropriate box for that activity.	Activity					
	Date					
	Rater					
A. For this child's usual level of interest in play materials, he or she is: 1. Not as interested as usual 2. About as interested as usual 3. More interested than usual						
B. For this child's usual level of physical interaction with materials (pushing control buttons, turning knobs, putting things together, etc.), he or she is: 1. Not as busy as usual 2. About as busy as usual 3. Busier than usual						
C. For this child's usual "affective" behaviors (smiling, signs of enjoyment, etc.), he or she seems to be: 1. Enjoying this less than usual 2. Showing about the same amount of enjoyment as usual 3. Enjoying this more than usual						
D. For this child's usual level of "looking" or "visual regard" of an activity, object, or person, he or she is: 1. Not looking as much as usual 2. Looking as much as usual 3. Looking more often or longer than usual						
E. Compared to this child's usual behavior during a short period of time with minimal supervision, he or she is: 1. Engaging in more negative behavior than usual 2. Engaging in about the same amount of negative behavior as usual 3. Engaging in less negative (or off-task) behavior than usual						
Activity Interest Scores: *Total the numbers in each column*		______	______	______	______	______

Figure 15–3

Student Interest Inventory

From *Longitudinal Leisure Skills for Severely Handicapped Learners: The Ho'onanea Curriculum Component* by B. B. Wuerch & L. M. Voeltz, 1982, Baltimore: Paul H. Brookes Publishing Co., P.O. Box 10624, Baltimore, Maryland 21285-0624. Reprinted by permission.

handle participating in a basketball game, but may do well with "one on one." The person assessing preferences should use information on the student's reaction to stimuli and current behavior patterns to offer variations of activities that match the student's needs. Once preference is determined, the issue of changing student response to components of the activities can be handled through instruction.

A related difficulty to assessing preference is student attachment to objects or activities that are not age-appropriate and are used in a manner that is stereotypic. Teachers may feel that these attachments constitute preference and be reluctant to direct students to other activities. For example, a student may select a tambourine when offered a variety of materials and then use the tambourine to shake in stereotypic manner for a prolonged duration. What we see in that example is not a student selecting a leisure activity but rather a person engaging in stereotypic behavior. Students who engage in such excess behavior should be taught appropriate leisure skills so that the acquisition of a leisure behavior could serve as a replacement for the stereotypic behavior. When selecting options for leisure activities, the teacher may want to analyze the stereotypic behavior to determine the sensory features of the material that the student uses and look for leisure activities that include those sensory components. For example, a student who repeatedly picks at cloth (blankets, towels, upholstery) to separate the fibers may be taught rug hooking, which involves the repeated practice of pulling yarn strands tightly. Another alternative is to shape the stereotypic behavior so that it occurs within normalized conditions. For example, shaking a tambourine is appropriate when it occurs with music and in the context of playing instruments. The teacher may wish to teach the student to demonstrate the behavior in conditions where the behavior is appropriate.

Leisure Activity Goals

When the ecological inventories are completed and preferences are determined, the teacher should select goals for leisure instruction. Ford et al. (1989) identified five major goal areas in the recreation/leisure domain and suggested that students participate in activities in each of the goal areas. Those goal areas are:

1. School and extracurricular activities
2. Activities to do alone: at home and in the neighborhood
3. Activities to do with family and friends: at home and in the neighborhood
4. Activities to do with family and friends: in the community
5. Physical fitness

Teachers should determine potential instructional goals for activities in each of these areas while paying attention to ensuring that the activities selected will require active participation by the student. In addition to increasing students' skill abilities in leisure activities, Dattilo (1992) states that leisure goals should also address choice-making abilities, social interaction skills, and knowledge of leisure options.

School and Extracurricular Activities The school is a rich resource for leisure activities that are planned and informal. Recreational goals should target those existing opportunities to provide students with disabilities opportunities to learn and practice leisure skills with their peers. Leisure activities that may occur in the school include participating in sports, playing musical instruments, taking part in craft and art activities, playing board and card games, reading books and magazines, playing computer games, attending special events and assemblies, and hanging out with friends. In addition, the school may offer organized extracurricular activities such as sports teams, collector clubs, hobby clubs, special interest lessons (e.g., ceramics, ballet, computer), after-school programs, and scout programs.

Activities to Do Alone Leisure activities that the student can perform alone are as important as activities that involve peers. Students with severe disabilities find that there are many times at home when someone cannot interact with them when they would benefit from being able to entertain themselves. In addition, there may be times when an individual prefers to be alone and would benefit from leisure skill instruction to use that time for amusement and relaxation.

Activities that a student may perform alone include reading books and magazines, playing computer or video games, listening to music, working on craft and hobby projects, interacting with and caring for pets, and organizing collections (e.g., arranging baseball cards). Adaptations of equipment (e.g., microswitches, page turners) and activity expectations (e.g, arranging baseball cards involves placing them from a box into card sleeves in random order) allow the student to complete the activity independently.

Activities with Others The teacher should look for a match between leisure activities that can be taught at school and activities that are available in the home and neighborhood. Activities that occur across environments are more desirable instructional targets because the student will have more opportunities to practice the skill. Activities that may occur in the home and neighborhood are usually very similar to those that are available during free time in school; examples include playing card games, playing board games, playing computer and video games, playing ball (basketball, kickball, soccer) or frisbee, listening to music, and using playground or riding (e.g., bikes, wagons) equipment.

Activities in the Community Leisure activities that occur in the community may also be activities that are targeted for community-based instruction. For example, using the public library, eating at a fast-food restaurant, and shopping may be considered by many individuals to be leisure activities in addition to being important community skills. Other community activities might include attending special events and performances and using public parks and recreation facilities. Teachers should look for opportunities to teach skills that have application for community-based instruction as well as matching the leisure opportunities the student has when not in school. If going to the mall is a frequent community leisure experience offered to the student with disabilities, the teacher may want to include instruction in that setting as a component of community-based instruction. Many families may want their child to enjoy community leisure experiences, but are unsure of how to make adaptations or how to provide the supports the student needs to enjoy the experience. The community instructor can be an important resource in assisting families with designing the supports a student may need to more fully participate in those activities.

Activities for Physical Fitness There are many noncompetitive physical fitness activities that may be appropriate leisure activities for students with disabilities. Running in community "fun" runs, aerobics and slimnastics, yoga, dance, skipping rope, walking, riding bicycles, skating, and swimming are just a few activities that may be performed by people of all ages and ability levels. In addition, many of the activities in the recreational/leisure domain involve fitness as a primary component. The crux of the inclusion of physical fitness in leisure skill components for individuals with severe disabilities is the person's active participation. Learning is more effective when people are actively involved in the instructional activity. The ability to participate for individuals with significant physical challenges often relies on the physical adaptation of materials. For example, a student with severe disabilities may need the support of a float or a kickboard to participate in swimming. A student may be able to use a tennis racket if the handle is modified so that it is easier to grasp or is attached to the hand.

Educators and recreators must systematically identify the materials and activities that foster active involvement of individuals with severe disabilities. In cases where independent active participation is not occurring, cooperative participation with a peer can facilitate skill acquisition. Cooperative participation could be used for a soccer game by assigning a peer buddy to assist a student with severe disability in goal-keeping or having the student in a wheelchair throw in foul balls.

It may appear that some students are so limited in physical ability that physical fitness is not an issue. In these cases, the definition of physical fitness should be thought of in a broader sense. A student who has an arm extension response may learn a switch activation program that facilitates maintaining the physical skill of arm extension as well as allowing the student to access a radio or computer for a leisure activity.

Choice-Making Issues

Dattilo (1992) has stressed the importance of including choice-making skills in leisure education programs. Some researchers have used adaptive switches connected to different leisure materials to show that students with multiple disabilities will demonstrate their preferences of activities (Dattilo & Mirenda, 1987; Realon, Favell, & Lowerre, 1990; Wacker, Berg, Wiggins, Muldoon, & Cavanaugh, 1985). For example, the teacher might connect a radio, a video game, and a computer to different switches. He or she can then assess preference by observing the devices the student activates and the amount of time the student is engaged in the activity.

Instructional goals that focus on choice making may include the use of switches or augmentative communication systems for selecting an activity. Other instructional goals related to choice may be for students to make a selection and then follow through with the activity, to make a selection and invite a peer to join, or to plan leisure activities for the

Social interaction with nondisabled peers is an important aspect of leisure activities.

week. Bambara and Ager (1992) were able to teach adults with disabilities to schedule their leisure preferences by choosing picture cards that represented the activities and placing them in a sequenced activity book for each day of the week.

Social Interaction

It is critical to teach students with severe disabilities the skills they need to play with peers if there is an expectation for them to engage in leisure activities with peers. It is important for teachers to include the important skills of initiating play, taking turns, and interacting with peers while they are teaching the student to perform an activity.

Social interaction skill instruction should be embedded in all leisure activities. Behaviors that may be taught include initiating the interaction, using appropriate nonverbal behaviors such as eye contact and body postures in social situations, elaborating on or expanding a social exchange, and terminating a social interaction.

A common approach to teaching social skills within activities is to include them in the task analysis. Gaylord-Ross, Haring, Breen, and Pitts-Conway (1984) taught a student with autism to socially interact with peers in the context of playing a hand-held video game, using a Walkman, and chewing gum. The task analyses for those sequences are shown in Figure 15–4.

Instructional Methods

When the priority activities and goals have been identified by the teacher, the family, and the student, several important decisions remain before instruction can begin. The teacher must decide where the instruction will occur, with whom the activity will occur, and how often instructional sessions will be scheduled.

The nature of the activity influences the decision for the choice of the optimal site for instruction. Instruction should occur in the most natural environment, although many activities can take place in both the school and the home environment. Activities like learning to play a computer game are not as dependent on special environmental cues as are others, such as playing basketball or using a fast-food restaurant. If instruction occurs in an environment other than the environment in which the behavior is expected to be used, generalization procedures should be used in instruction and generalization to the natural environment should be assessed (Ford et al., 1989)

In choosing the optimal instructional site for learning a leisure skill, the opportunity for receiving instruction with peers who are not disabled is a basic part of the decision (Ford et al., 1989). For example, the student could be taught to play a board game in the school's media center with two 8th graders instead of participating in the same activity with a teaching assistant in the special education classroom. It is important for the student to learn from peers and to have an opportunity to get to know others and develop friendships. The attractive atmosphere of the media center with student activity and movement may increase the student's interest in the board game.

The acquisition and generalization of the leisure skill is dependent on how frequently instruction occurs. Activities that are selected should allow for instruction that can occur with enough frequency that the student will make significant gains over the school year (Ford et al., 1989). An instructional goal that targets a leisure activity that only occurs weekly for a student who needs daily, repeated practice to learn will not be mastered and should be replaced with skill instruction in an activity with more opportunities for instruction and practice.

When the instructional goal has been defined, skill instruction can begin. The sys-

Pacman

1. AS approaches NS.[a]
2. AS establishes one m proximity.
3. AS establishes a face-forward orientation.
4. AS says, "HI."
5. AS waits for response.
6. AS says, "Want to play?"
7. AS waits for response. AS finds someone else if NS does not indicate willingness to play. AS then begins sequence at step 1 again.
8. AS turns on game.
9. AS hands game to NS.
10. AS watches NS play.
11. AS receives game from NS.
12. AS reads NS's score.
13. AS turns off game.
14. AS turns game on to reset score to zero.
15. AS plays game.
16. AS reads own score.
17. AS offers game to NS. If NS accepts, play continues in alternating fashion. When NS indicates that she or he is finished, AS takes game back.
18. AS says, "Bye."

Walkman

1. As approaches MS.
2. AS establishes one m proximity.
3. AS establishes face-forward orientation with NS.
4. AS says, "Hi."

Figure 15–4
Task Analyses for Social Skills Training
From "The Training and Generalization of Social Interaction Skills with Autistic Youth" by R. J. Gaylord-Ross, T. G. Haring, C. Breen, & F. Pitts-Conway, 1984, *Journal of Applied Behavior Analysis, 17,* pp. 198–199. Copyright 1984 by the Journal of Applied Behavior Analysis. Reprinted by permission.

tematic procedures that are used to teach all other skills also apply to the instruction of leisure skills. The following are some additional hints for instruction that are specific to leisure skill instruction:

1. Determine the natural cues that are used to prompt a leisure activity. The adult should not say " Jim, play basketball" when the natural cue given to typical peers is "You can have free time now."

5. AS waits for response.
6. AS says (and writesb[b]), "Want to listen?"
7. AS shows radio to NS. If NS is not interested in interacting, AS approaches another student (step 1).
8. AS turns on radio.
9. AS adjusts volume to level 6.
10. AS hands headphones to NS.
11. AS puts on headphones.
12. AS selects rock and roll station.
13. AS remains in proximity to NS until termination of interaction by NS.
14. AS says "Bye."

Gum

1. AS approaches NS.
2. AS establishes one m proximity.
3. AS establishes a face-forward orientation.
4. AS says "HI" to NS.
5. AS waits for a response.
6. AS says (and writes[b]), "What are you doing?"
7. AS waits for a response.
8. AS says (and writes[b]), "Want some gum?" and shows pack of gum.
9. If NS says yes, AS hands pack of gum to NS.
10. NS hands pack back to AS.
11. AS selects a stick of gum and chews it until the end of the interaction.
12. AS remains in one m proximity to NS for at least 30 seconds or until the end of interaction.
13. AS says "Bye" when NS terminates the interaction.

Figure 15–4, *continued*

2. Use the most natural reinforcer possible that matches the activity. It would be inappropriate and stigmatizing to a student to say "Good, you threw the frisbee." A more acceptable form of praise may be "Cool, look how far the frisbee went."
3. Be very cautious about getting in the way of peer interactions. Often an adult is needed to begin a leisure activity but then he or she should retreat into the background as soon as possible. If the adult is in the middle of the interaction, the nondisabled peer does not have the opportunity to engage the student with disabilities in his or her own way.
4. Some students with disabilities may need the support of an adult throughout an activ-

Galaxian

1. AS approaches NS.
2. AS establishes one m proximity.
3. AS establishes face-forward orientation with NS.
4. AS says "Hi."
5. AS waits for a response.
6. AS writes and says, "Want to play?"
7. AS shows message and game to NS.
8. If NS indicates no, AS goes to another student (step 1).
9. AS turns on game.
10. AS hands game to NS.
11. AS looks at game for 10 out of every 15 seconds NS is playing.
12. AS receives game from NS.
13. AS says NS's score.
14. AS turns off game.
15. AS turns on game.
16. AS depresses right directional dial with right hand.
17. AS repeatedly depresses fire button with left hand.
18. AS depresses left directional dial with right hand.
19. AS reads own score at end of game.
20. AS offers game to NS. Steps 11-20 continue if NS indicates interest in playing.
21. AS says "Bye" when NE ends interaction.

[a] AS = student with autism, NS = nonhandicapped student.

[b] Applies only to AS, who would write on a notebook the words he or she was saying and display the notebook to the NS.

Figure 15–4, *continued*

ity with a peer. In those cases, the adult should try to remain in the background and encourage peer interaction by prompting interactive behavior or by interpreting the communication efforts of the student with disabilities to the nondisabled peer.

5. Leisure activities should be fun. The adult who is instructing the student with disabilities should model the affective expressions of joy or pleasure! Setting the stage for having fun should include a relaxed pace of instruction, unobtrusive forms of data collection, positions that the student prefers, and the relaxed interactional style of the instructor.

Partial Participation

The principle of partial participation was introduced in 1982 by Baumgart et al., and is an important idea for helping teachers create and implement effective educational programming for students with severe disabilities. In age-appropriate settings, students with severe disabilities may be unable to participate as fully and effectively as other students involved in an activity, and therefore, adaptations to facilitate active participation must be considered.

The principle of partial participation was proposed to ensure that even those students who are currently unable to acquire the functional skills needed to completely participate in the activities of their lives can still partially participate. As teachers have implemented the concept of partial participation, they have made some errors that should be avoided (Ferguson & Baumgart, 1991).

Partial participation is not defined as presence in an activity. Students should be active participants rather than passive observers. Activities that use partial participation must be community- and family-referenced. Partial participation does not imply that the recreational or leisure activity does not have to be meaningful to the student and responsive to his or her learning needs. Partial participation in functional activities should occur throughout the day in a curriculum that is activity-based and meaningful.

When partial participation is being implemented, the student should not have to do so much of an activity that he or she misses opportunities to move on to other activities. For example, it may seem important for a student to learn to put his own materials away, unless doing so is so physically difficult and time-consuming that he cannot keep up with his peers as they move to another activity. Students with disabilities should be working to increase skill development but should not be forced to perform a skill "all by himself" to the point that it is burdensome or image-damaging.

Ferguson and Baumgart (1991) describe four strategies that explain the core of partial participation.

Strategy 1: Achieving active instead of passive participation. Ferguson and Baumgart (1991) report that using a "practice abilities" logic for instruction will assist students in building skills in the context of activities. The teacher must determine ways to maximize the students' opportunities for practicing the behaviors they currently possess, however small and inconsistent. Although they may not be able to complete a movement independently, they may contribute to a movement or continue a movement that they have been assisted to begin. In addition, active participation may enhance the image of the students with disabilities to nondisabled peers. For example, a student might kick a ball that is placed next to his or her wheelchair to participate in a kickball game, then be pushed by a peer to the bases. A student with disabilities might be assisted to pick up a puzzle piece and encouraged to place the piece in the area where it fits, before a peer fits the piece in its place.

Strategy 2: Use multiple perspectives. Teachers should use family- and community-referenced strategies to build a functional curriculum focused on participation in activities rather than isolated skill development. Instructional assessment should be broadened in scope to include other measures such as a student's enjoyment of an activity or a rating by peers of the student's participation. This means that proficiency at leisure skill performance should not be the teacher's primary concern. Other ways to assess leisure skill outcomes include the length of time a student is engaged in an activity, the affect of the student while engaged, or the evaluation by peers of whether or not the student is having fun.

Strategy 3: Use information from multiple sources for curriculum planning to avoid piecemeal participation. Leisure activities should be a part of an activity-based, functional curriculum that is comprehensive and meaningful to the students.

Strategy 4: Enhance the student's image and achieve interdependence by facilitating participation. Teachers may need to shift instructional choices when the situation suggests that performance gaps will not change or will not need to change. They should offer opportunities for students with severe disabilities to depend on their more able partners to help with parts of the activity that are difficult, time-consuming, or burdensome. For example, in card-playing, a person with limited grasping and reaching ability might use eye gaze to choose the card he wishes his nondisabled partner to discard. The activity is more normalized and thus more enjoyable to all participants when the natural flow of the activity remains constant. This also enhances the self-image of the student with severe disabilities as to his ability to participate in normal, age-appropriate activities.

Adapting Activities

The concept of adaptations is usually related to the design and usage of materials and devices, but it may also be expanded to include adapting skill sequences, adapting rules, using personal assistance to increase participation, modifying the physical and social environment, and choosing or creating materials and devices that meet a student's individual needs (Baumgart et al., 1982).

When determining whether or not to use an adaptation and determining the adaptations that should be used, several factors must be considered (Bishop, Eshilian, & Falvey, 1989):

1. Does the activity have a valid goal? If an activity takes place frequently, several adaptations may be necessary to lead to greater independence. The effort expended to make such adaptations is valid if practice of the skill is provided on a regular basis. Extensive adaptations may not be cost-effective for activities that are performed infrequently.
2. Does the activity require an adaptation for the individual to succeed? There must be a balance between the goal of independence and fostering dependence on the use of adaptations. Students need to use their motor skills as much as possible, but in promoting normalization with nondisabled peers, speed of response and uninterrupted play may be just as important. For example, in playing some computer games with a nondisabled peer, using a microswitch adaptation to compete helps the student display an equal amount of speed and accuracy and normalizes the student with disabilities in the eyes of his peers.
3. What adaptation is most appropriate? There are many types of adaptations. The optimal adaptation allows for greater participation and control over one's environment and compensates for factors that may impede independent performance. The student's current skills, strengths, weaknesses, and motivation should also be taken into account when determining an appropriate adaptation. The usage and maintenance of the adaptation must also be considered. If an adaptation may not be reliable or easily replaced, it may not be appropriate for use.
4. Does the adaptation fit the student? Adaptations that are selected should match the positions that students prefer and the motor movements that are dominant.
5. Is the adaptation safe? The fit and function of any adaptation must be continually evaluated.

In addition, the adaptation should be evaluated for continued need by the student. Adaptations and special equipment are used to enhance physical abilities, but fading the use of the special devices as soon as possible will lead to more normalized appearance and functioning.

A variety of adaptations have been developed by researchers to assist the active involvement of students with disabilities in leisure activities. Some equipment adaptations are using a cable release and tripod to adapt taking pictures with a camera, using a tee so that a student can hit a softball, using enlarged pieces for a table game, and using a microswitch to operate a computer or video game. Activities have also been modified so that students with disabilities may participate, including having others keep score for a student who is bowling, changing the "go fish" card game so that a peer looks for the match and the student with disabilities activates a tape-recorded "go fish" message when prompted, and using a designated runner for a student in a wheelchair who is playing softball.

Adaptations may be made for almost any activity, only limited by creativity, finances, and mechanical ability. Teachers who need assistance in thinking of adaptations may want to consult peers, other professionals in the classroom, or family members for ideas. Often people who are somewhat removed from the situation can see possibilities that the person who is most intimate with the student may miss. Ideas for adaptations can also be found in catalogs from companies that sell assistive devices and patient-care supplies. Companies that sell microswitches are also good resources for ideas and equipment.

Community Recreation Opportunities

The inclusion of individuals with severe disabilities into community recreation programs is a relatively new concept that is not widely practiced. The Americans with Disabilities Act (P.L. 101-336), which prohibits discrimination in employment, transportation, public services, and communication, also forbids discrimination in community recreation programs.

This legislation is helpful in gaining access to recreation programs, but access is not all that is needed. Appropriate supports must be provided if individuals with severe disabilities are going to be successful and benefit from these programs. Schleien, Green, and Heyne (1993) describe three approaches for establishing the inclusion of individuals with disabilities into community recreation programs. The reverse mainstreaming model involves programs that are designed for persons with disabilities but also include nondisabled individuals. The advantage of the reverse mainstreaming model is that programs are basically designed for persons with disabilities and that their needs are assured of being met. The major disadvantage of reverse mainstreaming is that there are a disproportionate number of participants who are disabled, which does not enhance integration or friendship development.

The second model is the integration of an existing program for nondisabled participants. The advantages are that persons with disabilities are included in a natural proportion and that there is potential for development of peer friendships. The main disadvantage is that the staff may not be trained to work with individuals with disabilities.

The third approach is through programs that meet the needs of all persons in the community. These programs are collaboratively designed by persons trained in therapeutic recreation and those who provide general recreation programs. Unfortunately, not many communities have developed such programs and many families are left with trying to achieve the integration of their child into a community recreation program or requesting that programs for individuals with disabilities be expanded to include nondisabled persons.

Hamre-Nietupski et al. (1992) describe the efforts of one community to provide a summer recreation program for elementary-age children that included students with severe disabilities. The development of the program involved: (1) surveying community recreation options, (2) approaching community recreation programs, (3) obtaining funding, (4) publicizing the program, and (5) collaborative planning of activities that met the needs of all students. In-service was provided to the recreation staff that presented the rationale for inclusion, descriptions of the students who would be included, plans for partial participation and adaptations, and ways to facilitate peer interactions. Nondisabled children were also prepared for the inclusion of the students with disabilities through formal presentations that introduced the students and informal modeling throughout the summer program.

Developing Friendships

The development of friendships has not traditionally been included as a goal in a leisure education program for individuals with disabilities. Prior to the current emphasis on inclusion and supports in the community, human service workers did not give much thought to supporting social relationships. It has only been in the most recent years that professionals have directed their attention to promoting friendships among students with severe disabilities and their peers (Haring, 1992). Because the concept of friendship is difficult to define and the promotion of friendships is a new area of interest, little empirical work is available to guide professionals. Most of the published work in this area is comprised of narrative and descriptive information on how specific friendships have been developed and maintained (Forest, 1987; Perske, 1988; Strully & Strully, 1985).

Friendship is important to everyone. Close friends give us the opportunity to meet our needs for intimacy and affection (The G. Allan Roeher Institute, 1990). It seems that all people need at least one special friend to talk with and share their feelings. When intimacy and affection are denied for long periods of time, people develop feelings of frustration and rejection. Close friendships make people feel valued and important.

To understand the importance of friendship, we can examine our own lives. Our friends are the people with whom we share our feelings, thoughts, secrets, and life stories. When we want to celebrate, have fun, or receive support in a crisis, we look for our friends to be there. Now, imagine your life with no friends in it.

Friendships can develop when people have proximity to each other and adequate opportunity to become acquainted (Grenot-Scheyer, Coots, & Falvey, 1989; Rubin, 1980). Most parents take for granted that their children will have friends in their lives. Parents of children with disabilities are unable to count on the natural development of friendships (Forest & Pearpoint, 1992) because many students with severe disabilities do not have the proximity to typically developing peers and may not have the skills needed to initiate and establish relationships. People with disabilities usually have family and human service workers in their lives, but very few friends.

Leisure education is a natural context for the development of friendships. Although professionals cannot program friendships, they can create the opportunities that may foster and support the development of peer relationships (Grenot-Scheyer et al., 1989; Perske, 1988).

Proximity and shared experiences seem to be a foundation for friendship development. Although establishing friendships is not guaranteed in those situations, students cannot build relationships unless they have access to each other. Teachers can provide proximity and shared experiences by planning leisure activities that bring students together on a regular basis. They can also plan activities that encourage students to express their interests and discover their peers' interests. Students with disabilities can be assisted to share their interests through augmentative communication, presentations by a family member, or slides and photographs that depict the student with disabilities in activities he or she enjoys.

Closer friendships may develop when students and peers have opportunities to share activities after school and on weekends. The teacher may have to take an active role in facilitating these events by suggesting that peers exchange phone numbers or by letting family members know about peers who are developing a relationship with their child. Sometimes families will want support in planning parties or recreation activities in which peers can be invited to participate.

Friendship Skills

Stainback, Stainback, and Wilkinson (1992) identified behaviors that may be taught to students who lack friends to encourage others to be supportive and friendly toward them. Some of those behaviors are:

1. Positive interaction style: Students who are positive, attentive, and encouraging to others are more likely to be included by others. Students who like and support others are more likely to be supported by peers (Rubin, 1980). Teachers can assist students with severe disabilities in having a positive interaction style by teaching them interaction skills such as the ability to give "high fives" as a greeting or how to listen to others as they speak. Teachers may want to address interaction issues in designing communication systems by providing a mechanism for the student with disabilities to inquire "How are you?" or "Are you having fun?"
2. Communicating about areas of interest: Friendships are built around areas of compatibility. Students who can communicate about their interests and express interest in learning about other people's favorite activities are more likely to build relationships with others. Teachers should assist students with severe disabilities in expressing their interests to their peers. One way to do this is by programming communication devices or providing communication symbols to reflect a student's interests (e.g., "Do you like race cars?"). Other ways are to find activities that will match the student's interests with peers who share the same interests.
3. Taking the perspective of others: Students who are able to listen to others and show sensitivity to their feelings are more able to contribute to a friendship relationship. It is important for teachers to realize that the student with disabilities must be able to be a sensitive friend to peers. Teachers can interpret the feelings of the nondisabled peer for a student with disabilities who may not pick up on subtle cues (e.g., "Bobby is disappointed. He lost the game") and provide the student with disabilities with the skill or mechanism to share empathy (e.g., say or sign "I'm sorry").
4. Providing support: Students who can provide support and encouragement to others who are in need are better prepared for a reciprocal relationship. One way that peers support one another is by inquiring about important events such as birthdays or the outcome of an exam. Teachers can assist students with disabilities in being supportive

by prompting them to remember friends' birthdays by making cards or by saying "Happy birthday." Communication devices can be programmed with a message that says "How did you do on the test?" or "Is everything OK?"

5. Demonstrating trustworthiness and loyalty: In order to solidify a budding relationship, the student must demonstrate trustworthiness and loyalty to the friend. Teachers should respect the loyalty of one friend to another and not try to artificially force the interaction of a student with disabilities with a variety of peers.
6. Conflict resolution skills: The student must be able to express and defend his or her needs and rights without compromising the needs and rights of peers.

One way to teach friendship skills is to discuss them and then encourage students to think of real-life situations where they can use the skills. The teacher observes the students in social interactions and then discusses their progress in developing the skills. The issues surrounding friendship and friendship skills development can also be infused in a variety of other classes (e.g., social studies, reading) and class activities (e.g., group projects, classroom rules discussions).

In chapter 9, the development of circles of friends was discussed as a way to support the inclusion of students with disabilities with their nondisabled peers. The "circles" strategy is used to build a network of friends who will support the student in developing relationships and becoming integrated in the school community (Forest, 1987).

Friendships with Disabled Peers

Many people enjoy the support of others who share the same circumstances. Support networks of people who share an interest, cause, or the same oppression are abundant in most communities (e.g., political parties, National Organization of Women, NAACP). Adults with disabilities have described friendship with and the support of others with disabilities as very important in their lives (Huemann, 1993).

Although there is a very strong emphasis in this text on teaching students recreation and leisure skills so that they may build relationships with their nondisabled peers and have fun in community environments, there is no intention to exclude the possibility that friendships with peers who have disabilities may also be important. That may seem counter to many of the themes in this text. Note that there is no mention of Special Olympics in this chapter. This was an intentional omission; Special Olympics is viewed by some as a segregated fitness activity that promotes undesirable and undignified images of people with disabilities. Developing a friendship with a peer because he or she shares similar circumstances is an act of choice by the student with severe disabilities rather than a situation that develops because there are no other opportunities.

Connections with other peers with disabilities in informal friendships or in advocacy groups such as People First can offer students with disabilities opportunities to share experiences and problems with someone else who has been there. Huemann (1993) summarizes this issue well:

> *At the end of the day, I feel that as disabled people we must feel good about ourselves and be able to choose our friends, and if we choose to spend most of our time outside of work with disabled people, that should not be considered "an inappropriate model." We must have the ability and the opportunity to choose from a broad group of the people with whom we truly feel most comfortable, which can change over time, the same way nondisabled people choose their friends. (p. 246)*

Conclusion

In the past, students with severe disabilities were offered opportunities for recreation and leisure activities only in segregated programs. In the last decade, there has been an increased emphasis on the inclusion of individuals in the community and with that comes the promise of recreation opportunities with nondisabled peers.

The role of the teacher is not only to prepare the student for integrated recreation activities outside of the school but also to provide opportunities for fulfilling leisure activities with peers during the school day. The teacher must remember that the ultimate goal for all students in the recreation and leisure curriculum are fitness, friendship, and, most of all, fun. The instructor must keep a student-centered focus. The curriculum must be based on the student's interest as well as his or her instructional needs. Age-appropriate environments and inclusive situations with nondisabled peers will facilitate normalization and personal happiness. If students are allowed to choose activities from their own interest inventories and have friends with common interests with whom to participate, the instructor will see more active participation from these students. If the teacher is able to combine all the components for an inclusive recreation/leisure curriculum through adaptations, peer support, and student choices, the ultimate goals of fitness, friendship, and fun will naturally occur.

Questions for Reflection

1. What leisure activities do you most enjoy? Can you think of ways that those activities might be adapted for a person who is physically disabled? Nonverbal?
2. Are activities such as Special Olympics, horseback riding for the disabled, and therapeutic swimming important to leisure instruction? What feedback would you give a family who asked you about their child's participation in those types of activities?
3. In high school, important leisure activities may be dating, hanging out, playing sports, and participating in clubs. How can a secondary teacher ensure that a student with disabilities will be included in those leisure activities?
4. How do you select your friendships? What behaviors may indicate that a student with disabilities wants to be a friend to a peer?
5. Think about your own leisure preferences. How did those preferences develop and change as you grew older? In what ways have your peer relationships influenced your leisure preferences? How can teachers promote a student's awareness of his peers' leisure interests?
6. If you were to include a student with severe disability in a community recreation activity (e.g., a community run or a golf tournament), what preparation should occur before the event? How would you ensure that other participants would accept the individual with disabilities?

References

Bambara, L. M., & Ager, C. (1992). Using self-scheduling to promote self-directed leisure activity in home and community settings. *Journal of the Association for Persons with Severe Handicaps, 17*, 67–76.

Baumgart, D., Brown, L., Pumpian, I., Nisbet, J., Ford, A., Sweet, M., Messina, R., & Schroeder, J. (1982). Principle of partial participation and individualized adaptions in education programs for severely handicapped students. *Journal of The Association for Persons with Severe Handicaps, 7*(2), 17–27.

Bender, M., Brannan, S. A., & Verhoven, P. J. (1984). *Leisure education for the handicapped.* San Diego, CA: College-Hill Press.

Bishop, K. D., Eshilian, L., & Falvey, M. A. (1989). Motor skills. In M. A. Falvey, *Community-based curriculum: Instructional strategies for students with severe handicaps* (2nd ed. (pp. 229–254). Baltimore: Paul H. Brookes.

Dattilo, J. (1992). Recreation and leisure: A review of the literature and recommendations for future directions. In L. H. Meyer, C. A. Peck, & L. Brown (Eds.), *Critical issues in the lives of people with severe disabilities* (pp. 171–193). Baltimore: Paul H. Brookes.

Dattilo, J., & Mirenda, P. (1987). An application of a leisure preference assessment protocol for persons with severe handicaps. *Journal of the Association for Persons with Severe Handicaps, 12,* 306–311.

Dattilo, J., & Rusch, F. (1985). Effects of choice on behavior: Leisure participation for persons with severe handicaps. *Journal of the Association for Persons with Severe Handicaps, 11,* 194–199.

Ferguson, D. L., & Baumgart, D. (1991). Partial participation revisited. *Journal of the Association for Persons with Severe Handicaps, 16,* 218–227.

Ford, A., Davern, L., Meyer, L., Schnorr, R., Black, J., & Dempsey, P. (1989). *The Syracuse Community-Referenced Curriculum Guide for Students with Moderate and Severe Disabilities.* Baltimore: Paul H. Brookes.

Forest, M. (1987). *More education integration.* Downsview, Ontario: G. Allan Roeher Institute.

Forest, M., & Pearpoint, J. (1992). Families, friends, and circles. In J. Nisbet (Ed.), *Natural supports in school, at work, and in the community for people with severe disabilities* (pp. 65–86). Baltimore: Paul H. Brookes.

G. Allan Roeher Institute (1990). *Making friends: Developing relationships between people with a disability and other members of the community.* Downsview, Ontario: The G. Allan Roeher Institute.

Gaylord-Ross, R. (1980). A decision model for the treatment of aberrant behavior in applied settings. In W. Sailor, B. Wilcox, & L. Brown (Eds.), *Methods of instruction for severely handicapped students.* Baltimore: Paul H. Brookes.

Gaylord-Ross, R. J., Haring, T. G., Breen, C., & Pitts-Conway, F. (1984). The training and generalization of social interaction skills with autistic youth. *Journal of Applied Behavior Analysis, 17,* 229–247.

Giangreco, M. (1983). Teaching basic photography skills to a severely handicapped young adult using simulated materials. *Journal of the Association for the Severely Handicapped, 8,* 43–49.

Grenot-Scheyer, M., Coots, J., & Falvey, M. A. (1989). Developing and fostering friendships. In M. A. Falvey, *Community-based curriculum: Instructional strategies for students with severe handicaps* (2nd ed.) (pp. 345–358). Baltimore: Paul H. Brookes.

Hamre-Nietupski, S., Nietupski, J., Krajewski, L., Maravec, J., Riehle, R., McDonald, J., Sensor, K., & Cantine-Stull, P. (1992). Enhancing integration during the summer: Combined educational and community recreation options for students with severe disabilities. *Education and Training in Mental Retardation,* 68–74.

Haring, T. G. (1992). Social relationships. In L. H. Meyer, C. A. Peck, & L. Brown (Eds.), *Critical issues in the lives of people with severe disabilities* (pp. 195–217). Baltimore: Paul H. Brookes.

Hill, J., Wehman, P., & Horst, G. (1982). Toward generalization of appropriate leisure and social behavior in severely handicapped youth: Pinball machine use. *Journal of the Association for the Severely Handicapped, 6*(4), 38–44.

Huemann, J. E. (1993). A disabled woman's reflections: Myths and realities of integration. In J. A. Racino, P. Walker, S. O'Connor, & S. J. Taylor (Eds.), *Housing, support, and community: Choices and strategies for adults with disabilities* (pp. 233–249). Baltimore: Paul H. Brookes.

Perske, R. (1988). *Circles of friends: People with disabilities and their friends enrich the lives of one another.* Nashville, TN: Abingdon Press.

Realon, R., Favell, J. E., & Lowerre, A. (1990). The effects of making choices on engagement levels with persons who are profoundly multiply handicapped. *Education and Training in Mental Retardation,* 299–305.

Rubin, Z. (1980). *Children's friendships.* Cambridge, MA: Harvard University Press.

Schleien, S. J., Green, F. P., & Heyne, L. A. (1993). Integrated community recreation. In M. E. Snell (Ed.), *Instruction of students with severe disabilities* (4th ed.) (pp. 526–555). New York: Macmillan.

Schleien, S. J., Wehman, P., & Kiernan, J. (1981). Teaching leisure skills to severely handicapped adults: An age-appropriate darts game. *Journal of Applied Behavior Analysis, 14,* 513–519.

Stainback, W., Stainback, S., & Wilkinson, A. (1992). Encouraging peer supports and friendships. *Teaching Exceptional Children, 24*(2), 6–11.

Strully, J., & Strully, C. (1985). Friendship and our children. *Journal of the Association for Persons with Severe Handicaps, 10,* 224–227.

Vandercook, T. (1991). Leisure instruction outcomes: Criterion performance, positive interactions, and acceptance by typical high school peers. *Journal of Special Education, 25,* 320–339.

Voeltz, L. M., & Apffel, J. A. (1981). A leisure activities curricular component for severely handicapped youth: Why and how? *Viewpoints in Teaching and Learning, 57*, 82–93.

Voeltz, L. M., Wuerch, B. B., & Wilcox, B. (1982). Leisure and recreation: Preparation for independence, integration, and self-fulfillment. In B. Wilcox & G. T. Bellamy, *High school programs for severely handicapped students.* Baltimore: Paul H. Brookes.

Wacker, D. P., Berg, W., Wiggins, B., Muldoon, M., & Cavanaugh, J. (1985). Evaluation of reinforcer preferences for profoundly handicapped students. *Journal of Applied Behavior Analysis, 18*, 173–178.

Wuerch, B. B., & Voeltz, L. M. (1982). *Longitudinal leisure skills for severely handicapped learners: The Ho'onanea curriculum component.* Baltimore: Paul H. Brookes.

York, J., Vandercook, T., & Stave, K. (1990). Recreational and leisure activities: Determining the favorites for middle school students. *Teaching Exceptional Children*, 10–13.

CHAPTER 16

Teaching Appropriate Academic Skills

Chapter Overview

Many students classified as having a severe disability, particularly those considered to have moderate mental disabilities, can learn basic academic skills. This chapter provides considerations regarding teaching academic skills, describes methods for teaching reading and writing, provides an overview of the whole-language approach, and describes methods for teaching functional arithmetic skills.

Children and adolescents have traditionally attended school to learn academic skills ranging from basic reading to calculus. However, any discussion of academic skills for students with severe disabilities raises several questions. Some of the following are typical.

- To what extent are these students capable of learning traditional academic subjects such as reading, writing, and arithmetic?
- Will these skills be functional for students with severe disabilities? How will they be applied to meeting students' needs?
- Is it appropriate to teach academic skills for reasons other than their functionality?
- When in their school career will students be in most need of learning academic skills? When will they be most capable of learning these skills?
- Where is the most appropriate location for delivering academic instruction? In the special classroom? In the regular classroom?
- What type or form of curriculum will be appropriate?
- What instructional techniques might be successful?

One reason these questions exist is because for many years there was a fundamental assumption that individuals whose measured intelligence fell at or below the level of moderate mental retardation (IQ $\leq$ 55) could not be expected to acquire any skills requiring cognitive abilities. They were referred to as being "trainable mentally retarded," implying that they might be capable of learning some nonacademic skills, but they were not capable of more sophisticated learning (Kirk, 1972).

Another reason people often question teaching academic skills is the need to focus on relevant and functional skills during the school years. Because the relevance of some academic skills is not always apparent, it is perhaps appropriate to question spending valuable instructional time teaching them. However, there are appropriate circumstances for teaching academic skills and there are relevant academic skills that should be taught. Techniques for academic instruction are discussed in this chapter. However, we must first consider some of the issues raised above.

Issues Related to Academic Instruction

Who Can Learn Academic Skills?

Although all students with severe disabilities can learn relevant skills that will increase their opportunities to participate in normal life activities, most of the research on academic learning has demonstrated that individuals within the traditional range of moderate mental disabilities (IQ approximately 40 to 55) have the ability to learn useful academic skills (Baroody & Snyder, 1983; Conners, 1992; Rynders & Horrobin, 1990). Therefore, teachers can generally assume that students functioning at this level of cognitive ability are viable candidates for learning fundamental academic skills.

However, although one's initial thought may be to include only individuals at this level when providing academic instruction, there are two limitations associated with this reasoning. First, the learning potential of individuals should never be underestimated. If there is any question about a person's ability to learn relevant academic skills in some form, it would probably be best to err on the side of attempting instruction rather than discounting potential with no attempt at instruction. Second, as discussed below, there are different levels of academic instruction. If a student is not successful at one level, perhaps he or she will have success at another.

Levels of Academic Curricula

Some authorities have suggested that academic curricula for students with severe disabilities should be multileveled in difficulty (Browder & Snell, 1993; Ford et al., 1989). Depending on various conditions, such as a student's needs, abilities, age, time remaining in school, and student and parent desires, the student may be appropriately placed in an academic curriculum drawn from several options.

The first option would be to place the student in the general academic curriculum provided to students without disabilities. A placement of this nature is most likely to be successful in the earlier school years (K–3) because there is often a wide range of instruction in early education; in addition, the discrepancy between the abilities of students with and without disabilities is relatively narrow (Ford et al., 1989). As the individual with disabilities grows older and the curricular emphasis becomes more abstract, the appropriateness of much of the regular curriculum decreases.

The second alternative is to provide an academic curriculum that is parallel to the general curriculum but emphasizes only selected components of the general curriculum. For example, a student in a reading program might focus on sight-word identification skills, increasing reading fluency, and answering comprehension questions instead of using a dictionary and learning about the card catalog in the library. In arithmetic, students may spend more time on computational skills and solving reasoning problems and little or no time on activities such as decimals and writing Roman numerals. Ford et al. (1989) referred to this as a *regular-adapted or streamlined curriculum.*

The regular-adapted curriculum may be appropriate for many children during the early to middle elementary years, but as students grow older (or for some younger students who are not succeeding with the regular-adapted curriculum), concern must be raised about the extent to which such skills will serve students as they participate in activities in their homes and communities. Skills such as reading, writing, and understanding words in natural environments, handling money, and telling time increase in significance as the student's world grows larger. At that time there is often a need to shift to a *functional or limited academic curriculum* (Browder & Snell, 1993; Ford et al., 1989). In the functional curriculum the instructional targets are based on the student's current and future environmental needs as determined through ecological inventories.

For many students, functional curricular targets may be taught in a more or less traditional academic manner. That is, in a regular classroom setting, students learn to read their unique sets of words, handle money appropriately, and so forth, and later practice these skills in natural environments. For other students, however, instruction on such skills outside of the contexts in which they will ultimately be applied will not be very meaningful. These students will be more likely to benefit from academic instruction when it is *embedded-functional instruction,* that is, when it is presented as they are learning other functional skills in appropriate contexts (Ford et al., 1989). When an embedded-functional curriculum is used, academic prostheses (such as money that has been precounted and placed in a marked envelope for paying for food at a restaurant) is often helpful for the student (Browder & Snell, 1993).

The academic goals and objectives for students in the regular or adapted/streamlined regular curriculum will be determined largely by that curriculum and the special and general educators implementing the curriculum. Discussion of the full scope of these areas is beyond what can be covered here. Instead, the focus of the remaining portions of this chapter will be on teaching functional academic skills.

Defining Functional Academic Instruction

Functional academics are areas of instruction that will best serve the individual in his or her current and future life. When one thinks of the types of academic skills that are actually needed to operate daily and to experience a relatively good quality of life, there are actually very few. Most important, there will be a need to read and understand select words that allow us to do things like order from a menu or catch the right bus; write notes to ourselves to remind us to do some things or to others to convey our thoughts or needs; count out an adequate amount of money to pay for movie tickets and popcorn; or know what time it is so we won't be late for work or miss our favorite TV show.

The ability to do these things and similar activities largely dictates the nature of functional academic instruction. In this chapter, then, instructional methods for teaching basic reading, writing, and comprehension skills, handling money, and telling time are highlighted. An overview of the whole-language approach, popular now among many elementary teachers and teachers of students with mild disabilities, is also presented. Although other areas of academic instruction may be appropriate for some individuals, the areas covered here are generally considered the most critical. Helpful references for teaching other areas are available if the reader requires information in these areas (Choate, Enright, Miller, Poteet, & Rakes, 1992, for curriculum-based assessment and adaptations; Rakes & Choate, 1989, for language arts; Enright, 1989, for basic math; Cain, 1990, for science; Smith & Smith, 1990, for social science).

Beyond Functional Instruction

Should academic instruction be only functional in nature? Are there other purposes for learning academic skills? Of course there are, and these should not be neglected when academic instruction is provided. If we analyze our own reading, writing, and counting behavior, for example, or that of an adolescent or a child, we may note that quite often we apply our skills for our pleasure and enjoyment.

Reading magazines, newspapers, or supermarket tabloids is often done for recreational purposes and being able to do so enhances one's quality of life. Keeping a diary or writing notes and letters to those we care about can be a nice way to spend an afternoon or evening. Keeping score when bowling, golfing, or playing cards allows us to enjoy these games more. A huge number of examples of applying even relatively basic academic skills to various fun activities can be imagined. Although teachers are often concerned (and rightly so) about how particular academic skills will be applied in functional ways, they should also consider how these skills can be used in fun ways.

Location of Academic Instruction

Considering the desirability of including students with severe disabilities in general education classrooms and assuming that many students will be learning academic skills at levels somewhat different from those of their nondisabled classmates, we need to know how to manage instruction in the regular classroom so that all benefit. Although this presents a challenge, general and special educators can work together in many ways to provide a high quality of instruction for all students. Procedures for doing so are presented briefly in the final section of this chapter and were discussed more fully in chapter 9.

Summary of Issues Related to Teaching Academic Skills

It is arguable that the most important skills for individuals with severe disabilities are not academic in nature. It should also be realized that academic instruction, even instruction primarily of a functional nature, is likely to be of benefit to students who are functioning within the moderate range of mental disabilities. However, underestimating the ability of students in special education has more often been a problem than overestimating it. As with other areas of learning, academic instruction should be approached with a view that all students can learn skills to some degree and so the teacher must find the appropriate level for each student. Many parents feel that it is most appropriate for their children to learn academic tasks (Hamre-Nietupski, Nietupski, & Strathe, 1992) and their desires should not be ignored.

Having students with different levels of academic ability in the regular classroom can be a challenge even for skilled teachers. However, the benefits of including children with disabilities in typical classes warrants that the challenge should be accepted and successfully addressed.

Teaching Reading

Teaching reading skills to individuals with moderate mental disabilities can utilize the following approaches:

- Teaching individual sight words.
- Teaching word analysis (phonics) skills.
- Teaching oral reading from books.
- Using commercial programs to teach reading.
- Teaching comprehension skills and reading in applied settings.

Most of the efforts in both practice and research have consisted mainly of the first three approaches (Conners, 1992). The following sections describe the methods that have been used. Before discussing them, however, we must consider the origin and organization of the reading vocabulary that should be targeted for instruction.

Reading Targets

Teaching basic reading skills requires the teacher to identify materials that need to be read. In most cases, when teaching reading to students with moderate mental disabilities, the material should include high-frequency words that the student can learn to identify by sight and read in various important contexts. Many of these may be drawn from basic reading lists, such as those of Fry (1957, 1972) or Dolch (1950). Textbooks on reading instruction will contain such lists.

Although these are "high-frequency" words, they are words that are most often found in basal readers and may not be entirely relevant to the functional or recreational needs of students with disabilities. The teacher should put greater emphasis on teaching words that occur in the students' natural environments. These could include words found on signs and labels, on schedules, in listings such as the Yellow Pages, in stores and other community settings, in directions and recipes, and on forms such as job applications. When conducting an ecological inventory of a student's environments, attention should be given to the words in the environments that will allow the student to operate in that setting. Ford et al. (1989) identified various opportunities for reading and writing in the school, for both functional activities and for pleasure. Several of these opportunities are listed in Table 16–1. Analyses of other environments could yield similar results. For example, in their study, Cuvo and Klatt (1992) identified 30 signs in community settings that later served as instructional targets for the individuals they were teaching.

Differentiating the words to be learned based on the age of the student is also important (Feinberg, 1975). For children, Feinberg suggested that words appropriate for reading instruction could be those that are naturally spoken and heard by children, that is, an extension of their natural language. For those closer to the adult years, however, Feinberg recommended words that would best allow them to operate successfully in community settings, such as *men, woman, ladies, exit, entrance, enter, in, out, stop, push, pull, emergency, danger, walk, don't walk, wait, up, down, bus stop, keep out, keep off,* and *no smoking*. Feinberg (1975) also pointed out that it is important to teach sight words in various contexts in order for the concepts to be learned.

Regardless of the particular source of the words, after they are identified for instruction, they should be arranged and then taught in sets; typically these sets include three to ten words. The grouping of the words should be in some logical order, but there is no definitive rule for doing so. Some teachers group them based on their appearance in different settings (e.g., grocery-store words, words in the bowling alley); in other cases they are grouped as they appear in books that the student will read. What is important is that word groups be identified for instruction.

When the student masters one set by being able to read all of the words correctly, say for three days in a row, the next group of words may be introduced. Although the new words are learned as a group, time should be set aside, perhaps one or two days a week, for students to review all previously learned words. Various teaching methods are discussed below.

Teaching Individual Sight Words

The most common method for teaching sight words is for the teacher to print the target words clearly on plain index cards, using a black felt-tip pen to form block letters, and then show the words, one at a time, to a student or a group of students, having them read one word at a time. During each daily instructional session, the entire group of words is studied. Until a word has been learned, of course, it is modeled by the instructor. After several episodes, the student should be able to

Table 16–1
Reading and Writing Opportunities

School Level	For Pleasure	For Functional Use
Elementary school: reading	Looking at books during free time Checking out books from the library Listening to stories read aloud (by peers, by teacher, by librarian) Participating in structured reading time Reading self-composed stories aloud to class mates Reading books	Following sequence cards for classroom jobs Reviewing daily lunch menu Reviewing daily schedule Managing weekly/monthly calendar Using communication booklet Reading portions of newsletters or "notes" to go home Reading signs, posters, and bulletin boards Following recipe for snack preparation
Elementary school: writing	Writing stories or drawing pictures to illustrate messages Writing cards and letters Constructing photo albums and writing captions Writing journals	Writing name on school projects Writing name on card to check out library book Filling out "emergency cards" and other forms that require name, address, and telephone number Leaving notes or messages for a friend or teacher Signing up for a classroom job
Middle school and high school: reading	Looking at books during free time Checking out books from the library Participating in structured reading program in English class or reading lab	Following sequence cards at job site Following written daily schedule Reading the weekly cafeteria menu and menus in restaurants Managing weekly/monthly calendar Using communication booklet Looking at school newspaper Reading signs, posters, and bulletin boards Following recipe in home economics class Identifying labels on items in store
Middle school and high school: writing	Writing collection of stories Writing cards and letters Constructing photo album or essay with captions Writing journals diaries	Writing name on belongings (papers, books) Writing name on library cards Writing name on sign-up sheets Filling out forms requiring identifying information Leaving notes or messages for friends or teacher Writing events/reminders on personal calendar Writing grocery lists Writing address and phone number down for friend

From *The Syracuse Community-Referenced Curriculum Guide for Students with Moderate and Severe Disabilities* (p. 98) by A. Ford, R. Schnorr, L. Meyer, J. Black, & P. Dempsey, 1989, Baltimore: Paul H. Brookes Publishing Co., P.O. Box 10624, Baltimore, Maryland 21285-0624. Reprinted by permission.

say the word when he or she sees it. Several variations that have been found to improve the effectiveness of this approach are discussed below. You will note the application of several of the skill acquisition procedures discussed in chapter 6.

Constant Time Delay A simple and effective technique for teaching sight words is to apply a constant time delay procedure. Using this method, the teacher presents the word on a flashcard and waits four or five seconds for the student to say the word; if the student does not respond, the teacher models the word for the student to repeat (Gast, Ault, Wolery, Doyle, & Belanger, 1988; Koury & Browder, 1986). To initially help the students learn the words, on the first several trials or the first one or two sessions of instruction, the teacher would have a zero-second delay between showing the word on the card and modeling the word. When showing the word, the teacher might also say "what word?" or "read, please" as a verbal cue along with the written word to get the student to respond. Ultimately, however, it is desirable to eliminate this verbal prompt and allow the written word to serve as the cue for the student to say the word.

Progressive Time Delay The teacher might vary the constant time delay procedure when teaching sight words by starting with a shorter delay period between showing the word and saying it (if the student does not), but then extending the delay by increasing it every session by one or two seconds. Using this method, instead of having a constant time delay of four or five seconds, the teacher would start with a zero delay on the first day (just as with constant time delay), but then have a two-second delay on session two, a four-second delay on session three, six seconds on session four, and so on until reaching an eight- or ten-second delay (Ault, Gast, & Wolery, 1988; Browder, Hines, McCarthy, & Fees, 1984).

The theoretical advantage of the progressive time delay method is that it allows more time for the student to try to read the word. However, it is more cumbersome for the teacher to use, requires more time, and has not been found to be more effective than the constant time delay method (Ault et al., 1988).

System of Least Prompts The principle of providing only as much prompting as is necessary to get the student to read the word is also a viable technique for teaching sight words. Using this method, the teacher begins by developing a series of prompts that are applied in increasing order of assistance if the student does not read the word correctly when shown the card. Using the system of least prompts requires the teacher to show the word to the student and after ensuring that the student is looking, deliver a sequence of prompts such as the following:

1. Teacher says "read this" and then waits four seconds. If the student does not respond correctly (does not respond at all or says the wrong word),
2. Teacher says "read this" and also verbally describes the word (for example, if the word is *milk,* the teacher might say "this is something white that we drink"). If the student still does not respond,
3. The teacher repeats "read this" and shows the student a picture of the item.
4. Finally, if the student does not respond correctly, the teacher says "Read this . . . milk, say milk."

This procedure is intended to get the student to respond correctly with the least amount of assistance required. While it has been shown to be effective, it may not actually be any more effective than constant time delay and will take more time to implement (Gast et al., 1988).

Pairing Pictures with Sight Words The abstract nature of the configuration of words as they are formed by letters linked together can result in difficulty in correct responding by students with mental disabilities. It may be helpful if, when words are initially presented, they are presented on cards or pages paired with pictures of what the words represent. This approach requires the material to be altered by attaching a picture, or drawing one, on the card. The instructional delivery uses one of the methods above (e.g., constant time delay). Ultimately the student may be able to transfer attention from the picture to the word and thus read the word when it is seen without the picture (Barudin & Hourcade, 1990; Dorry & Zeaman, 1973, 1975; Entriken, York, & Brown, 1977; Miller & Miller, 1971; Singh & Solman, 1990). There is one major concern with this method. The transferral of attention by the student from the picture to the word may not always occur. In fact, because the picture is likely to have greater attentional value, transferring attention may be very difficult (Singh & Solman, 1990). Therefore, the teacher might need to devise a *fading procedure* that will ultimately (over several sessions) result in the picture being completely eliminated while the word remains on the card. This change in the stimulus requires that the student shift attention gradually from the picture to the word. Figure 16–1 displays how this process may be applied. Because of the time required to prepare the material (several cards would be required for each word, as shown in Figure 16–1), this approach may not be as efficient as other methods. On the other hand, it may help students who are otherwise having difficulty interpreting the written word.

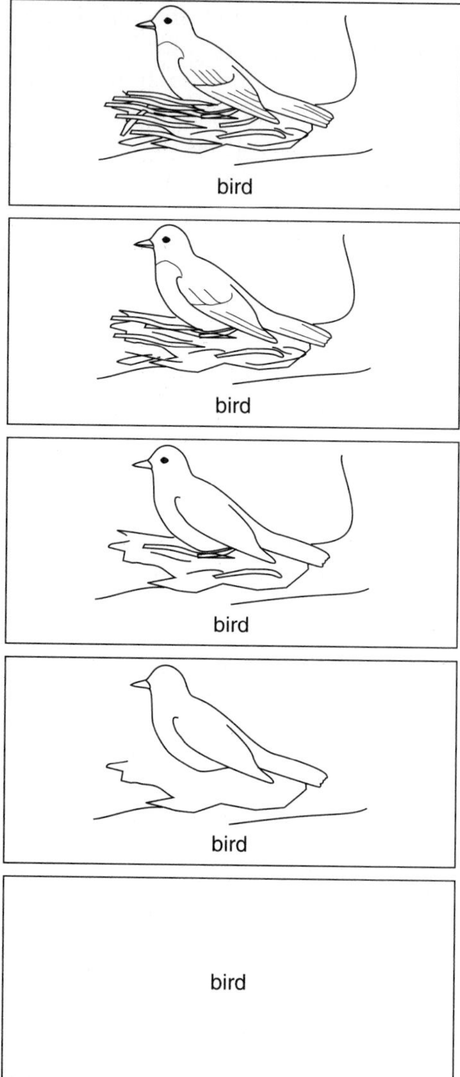

Figure 16–1
Example of Using a Fading Procedure to Teach Sight Words

Embedding Sight Words in Pictures and Figures This approach is very similar to the one described above, but with an important distinction: the word to be learned is *embedded* in the figure that represents it (or there is a figure embedded in the word) instead of simply being paired with it (Miller & Miller, 1968,

1971; Worrall & Singh, 1983). The advantage of this method over the pairing method is that the student does not have to make an overt shift of attention away from the figure and to the word. Because of this, the embedded arrangement tends to be more effective than only pairing the word and the picture (Conners, 1992). Again, however, as with the above method, it is necessary to gradually fade the figure until only the word remains. Figure 16–2 provides an example of this process.

Using Symbols and Pictures Instead of Words It may be possible for some students with mental disabilities to learn to read symbols or pictures even if they cannot actually learn to read sight words. Symbols, line drawings, pictures, or photographs may be placed in sequence in order for the student to "read" a story to someone. They may also be used to provide cues to the student for completing the steps in a particular task (House, Hanley, & Magid, 1980; Roberson, Gravel, Valcante, & Maurer, 1992). In some cases, students may be able to use the symbols or pictures to generate their own sentences.

When pictures or symbols are used in this way, they are not faded out and therefore remain as the symbolic unit that is being interpreted. There are two disadvantages to using this approach. First, only the student and a few other people will know the meaning of the pictures or symbols. Second, the student will not be able to respond to real words when they appear in the natural environment. Of course, the advantage of the approach is that the student who has not been able to learn to read words can still learn to "read."

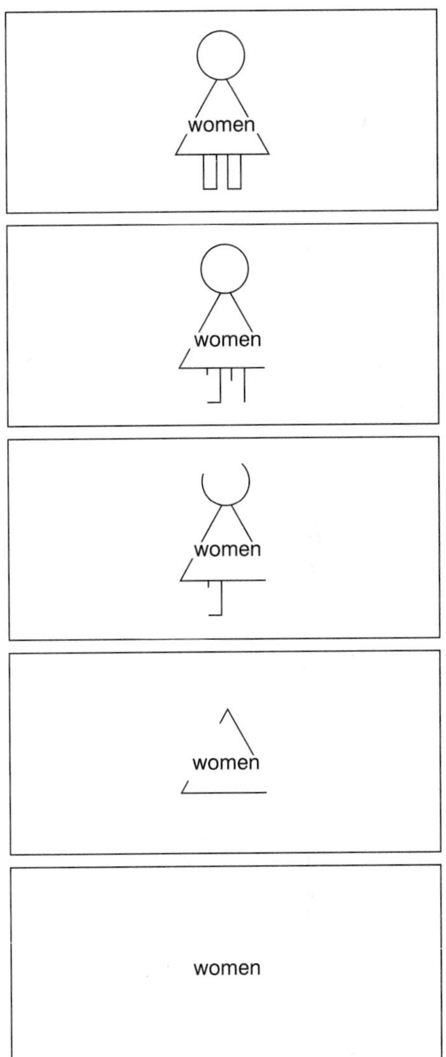

Figure 16–2
Example of Using Embedding and Fading to Teach Sight Words

Teaching Word Analysis (Phonics) Skills

Although most reading instruction for students with moderate mental disabilities has focused on teaching whole words, several efforts have been made to teach students to analyze the sounds of the letters in words and thus be able to "sound out" unknown words without having to rely on visual memorization of the entire word. Students who can accomplish this skill are at an advantage because they then have the potential for deciphering any unknown word that they may encounter in the future (Nietupski, Williams, & York, 1979). It should be realized, however, that this is a high-risk undertaking. Because the time and effort required to teach phonics to a level of generalizable applicability would be substantial, it may be better to spend instructional time teaching individual words.

A preferred strategy would most likely be a combination of approaches in which a functional list of sight words is first taught, perhaps 100 to 200 words, followed by an attempt at teaching word analysis (Conners, 1992). If this process is undertaken, the following methods are likely to be helpful.

Teaching Letter Names and Sounds The first step in the process of teaching phonics skills is generally to teach the names of the letters. This process can be undertaken using a flashcard method or alphabet sets until all letter names are committed to memory. It is not actually necessary for students to know the names of the letters in order to know their sounds, but this is the most conventional way.

The next step is to teach individual letter sounds and letter combinations. The teacher first models the letter sounds for the students and has them repeat them. When students can demonstrate that they can imitate letter sounds, they should then be able to indicate if the sounds they hear are the same or different (Nietupski et al., 1979). These skills (modeling sounds and being able to indicate whether two sounds are the same or different) will be done with both individual letter sounds and with combined letter sounds.

Next, students must learn to hear and combine separate letter sounds into one sound. This may be easier if they first learn to blend together words heard separately (e.g., *dog . . . house, doghouse),* and then syllables heard separately (e.g., *hap . . . py, happy),* and finally letter sounds heard separately (e.g., *b . . . l, bl)* (Hoogeveen & Smeets, 1988).

The process of teaching phonics skills should continue in an orderly fashion by teaching certain letter combinations in sets. Nietupski et al. (1979) used the following sequence:

1. Say single consonant sounds to a preset criterion level. The sounds were taught in this order: Set 1: *b, d, m, t, w;* Set 2: Set 1 plus *c, g, h, n, p;* Set 3: Set 2 plus *f, j, l, r, s;* Set 4: Set 3 plus *k, v, x, y, z.*
2. Say short vowel sounds to criterion.
3. Read vowel-consonant (VC) combinations *(an, up, of).*
4. Read consonant-vowel-consonant combinations *(sat, beg, rip).*

Ford et al. (1989) proposed that the sequence of phonics skills listed in Figure 16–3 be used after a basic sight word vocabulary has been acquired.

Using Games to Teach Phonics Skills At each phase of instruction, Nietupski et al. (1979) reported that the use of various games helped students with moderate mental disabilities learn phonics sounds. The games included "sound bingo" (marking the sounds on cards as they were heard), "chutes and ladders" board games (roll dice, move to the position, say the sound or move back to your original position), "phonics concentration" (find and label pairs of the same sounds), and "word wheels" (form and say new words by spinning the word wheels). This last game is displayed in Figure 16–4.

Using Visual Prompts to Teach Letter Sounds Students who have difficulty remembering the sounds of particular letters may do better if picture cues are embedded on, or used

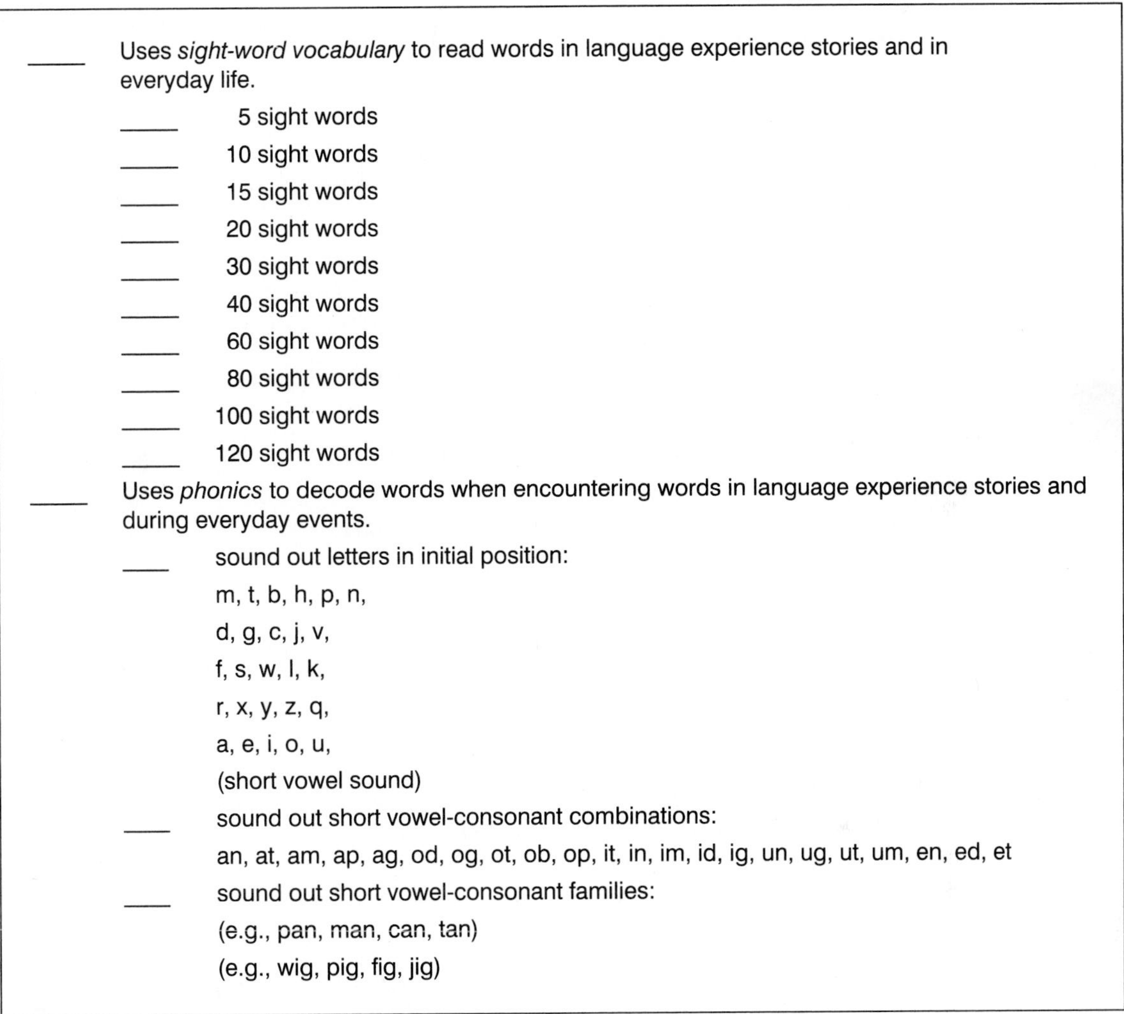

____ Uses *sight-word vocabulary* to read words in language experience stories and in everyday life.

- ____ 5 sight words
- ____ 10 sight words
- ____ 15 sight words
- ____ 20 sight words
- ____ 30 sight words
- ____ 40 sight words
- ____ 60 sight words
- ____ 80 sight words
- ____ 100 sight words
- ____ 120 sight words

____ Uses *phonics* to decode words when encountering words in language experience stories and during everyday events.

____ sound out letters in initial position:
m, t, b, h, p, n,
d, g, c, j, v,
f, s, w, l, k,
r, x, y, z, q,
a, e, i, o, u,
(short vowel sound)

____ sound out short vowel-consonant combinations:
an, at, am, ap, ag, od, og, ot, ob, op, it, in, im, id, ig, un, ug, ut, um, en, ed, et

____ sound out short vowel-consonant families:
(e.g., pan, man, can, tan)
(e.g., wig, pig, fig, jig)

Figure 16–3
Sequence of Reading Skills for Instructing Students with Severe Disabilities
From *The Syracuse Community-Referenced Curriculum Guide for Students with Moderate and Severe Disabilities* (pp. 112–114) by A. Ford, R. Schnorr, L. Meyer, J. Black, & P. Dempsey, 1989, Baltimore: Paul H. Brookes Publishing Co., P.O. Box 10624, Baltimore, Maryland 21285-0624. Reprinted by permission.

to accentuate, particular letters, similar to the procedure used with recognizing sight words. This can be done in one of two ways. One way is to incorporate a picture with a letter that represents the sound the letter makes (Hoogeveen, Smeets, & Van der Houven, 1987). An example of this is incorporating a picture of a snake around the letter *S*, as displayed in Figure 16–5. As with the use of pictorial prompts with words, it is important to gradually fade the prompt so that the student ultimately associates the letter sound with the

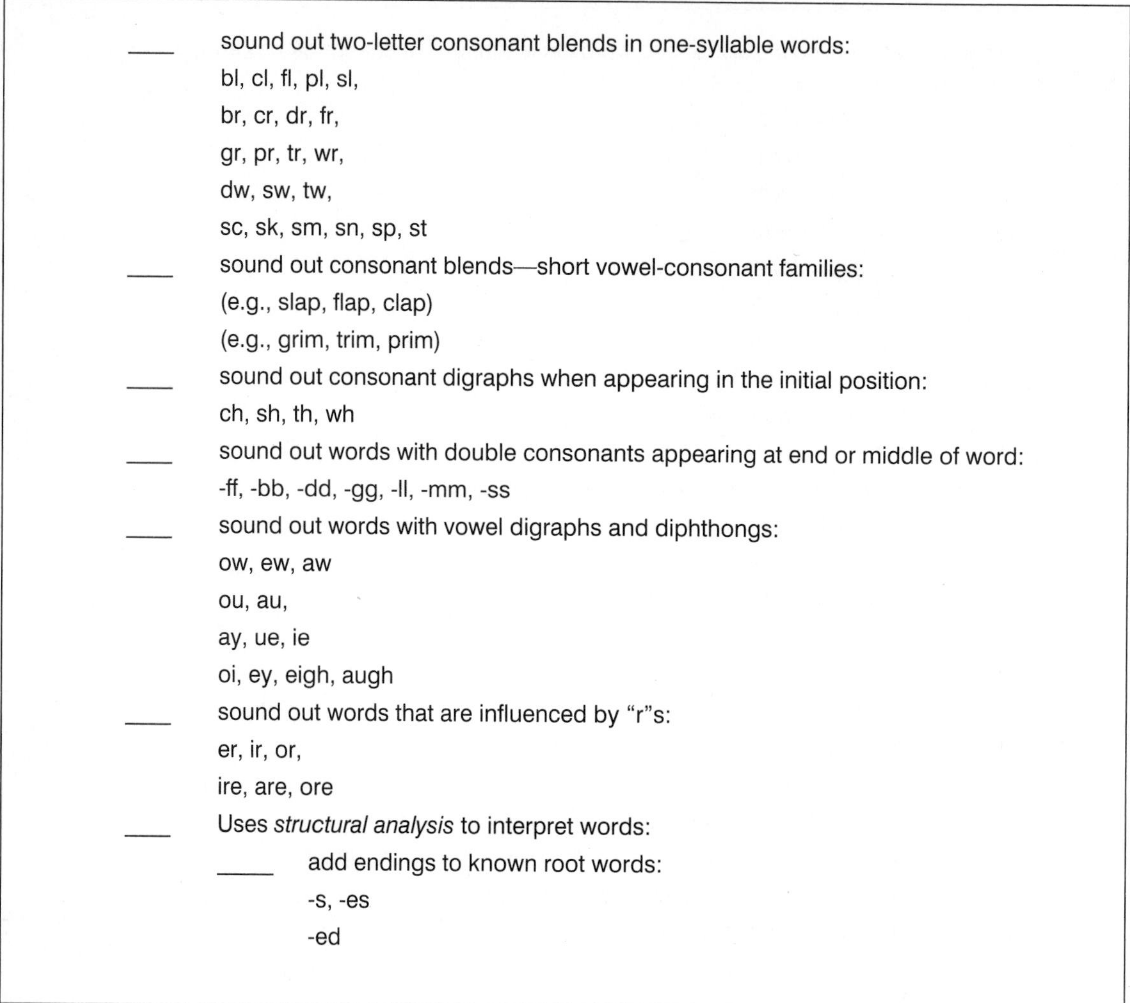

____ sound out two-letter consonant blends in one-syllable words:
bl, cl, fl, pl, sl,
br, cr, dr, fr,
gr, pr, tr, wr,
dw, sw, tw,
sc, sk, sm, sn, sp, st

____ sound out consonant blends—short vowel-consonant families:
(e.g., slap, flap, clap)
(e.g., grim, trim, prim)

____ sound out consonant digraphs when appearing in the initial position:
ch, sh, th, wh

____ sound out words with double consonants appearing at end or middle of word:
-ff, -bb, -dd, -gg, -ll, -mm, -ss

____ sound out words with vowel digraphs and diphthongs:
ow, ew, aw
ou, au,
ay, ue, ie
oi, ey, eigh, augh

____ sound out words that are influenced by "r"s:
er, ir, or,
ire, are, ore

____ Uses *structural analysis* to interpret words:

____ add endings to known root words:
-s, -es
-ed

Figure 16–3, *continued*

actual letter without the prompt (see Figure 16–6). As students learn individual letter sounds, they can be taught to combine them either with or without the continued use of the prompts, but the prompts would eventually need to be eliminated.

A second approach is similar to the first except instead of using a picture to represent the sound of the letter, the picture represents an object whose *initial sound* is the same as the sound of the letter (Hoogeveen, Smeets, & Lancioni, 1989). For example, if the teacher wanted to teach the long *e* sound (ee), a picture of an eel with the letter *e* embedded in it would be presented to the student and he or she would be taught to say "eeeeel." Ultimately the teacher would help the student drop the undesired part of the sound and say "ee" when the picture of the eel with the letter *e* was shown. Finally, the picture would be

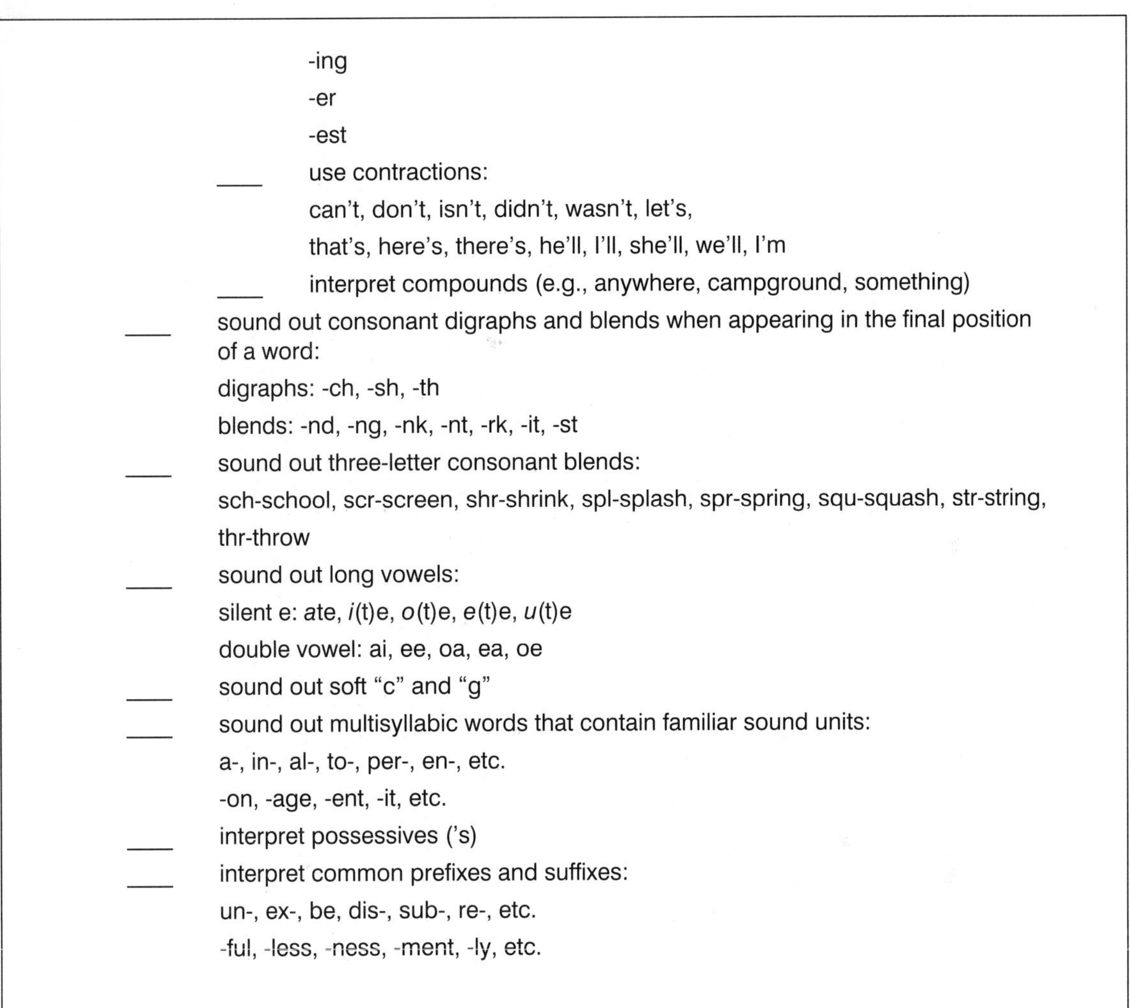
-ing
-er
-est
____ use contractions:
can't, don't, isn't, didn't, wasn't, let's,
that's, here's, there's, he'll, I'll, she'll, we'll, I'm
____ interpret compounds (e.g., anywhere, campground, something)
____ sound out consonant digraphs and blends when appearing in the final position of a word:
digraphs: -ch, -sh, -th
blends: -nd, -ng, -nk, -nt, -rk, -it, -st
____ sound out three-letter consonant blends:
sch-school, scr-screen, shr-shrink, spl-splash, spr-spring, squ-squash, str-string, thr-throw
____ sound out long vowels:
silent e: ate, *i*(t)e, *o*(t)e, *e*(t)e, *u*(t)e
double vowel: ai, ee, oa, ea, oe
____ sound out soft "c" and "g"
____ sound out multisyllabic words that contain familiar sound units:
a-, in-, al-, to-, per-, en-, etc.
-on, -age, -ent, -it, etc.
____ interpret possessives ('s)
____ interpret common prefixes and suffixes:
un-, ex-, be, dis-, sub-, re-, etc.
-ful, -less, -ness, -ment, -ly, etc.

Figure 16–3, *continued*

faded over five or more steps, leaving only the *e*, and the student would say this sound. Individual letter sounds could then be combined to create new words and syllables.

These approaches suggest that with careful planning and program development, some students with moderate mental disabilities can learn letter sounds. However, the procedures are quite elaborate and if letter sounds are not being learned at an adequate rate using these approaches or other methods of skill acquisition (such as time delay or a system of least prompts), time and effort might be better spent on learning more whole words.

Teaching Oral Reading from Books

Oral reading skills allow students to go beyond reading individual whole words or sounding

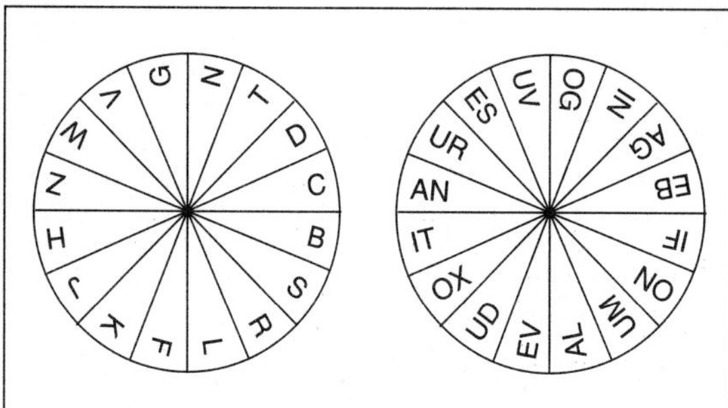

Figure 16–4
A Word Wheel Game
From "Teaching Selected Phonic Word Analysis Skills to TMR Labeled Students" by J. Nietupski, W. Williams, & R. York, 1979, *Teaching Exceptional Children, 11*, p. 80. Copyright 1979 by The Council for Exceptional Children. Reprinted by permission.

Figure 16–5
Example of Using a Picture Around a Letter to Teach the Letter Sound
From "Establishing Letter-Sound Correspondence in Children Classified as Trainable Mentally Retarded" by F. R. Hoogeveen, P. M. Smeets, & J. E. Van der Houven, 1987, *Education and Training in Mental Retardation, 22*(2), p. 80. Copyright 1987 by the Division on Mental Retardation and Developmental Disabilities, The Council for Exceptional Children. Reprinted by permission.

out words by letter sounds to reading entire sentences, paragraphs, or multiword passages from books. In most initial learning processes reported in the literature, these books have been limited to basal readers, but they may also include various magazines, storybooks, or other books that contain vocabulary within the students' learning potential. Most students without disabilities begin reading from books while they are acquiring basic sight words and initial phonics abilities. Students with moderate mental disabilities should also have such initial skills or at least be able to read by sight most of the words in the books to be read.

Oral reading from books should allow the student to improve the speed of reading and also acquire new vocabulary words. It can also serve as a basis for learning to sound out new words. The tactics below have been found helpful in improving the oral reading ability of students with moderate mental disabilities.

Previewing Material Taking time to preview a story or passage before it is read may help students read with fewer errors during oral reading. Previewing consists of discussing the story with the student by talking about the title, looking at and discussing any pictures that may appear in the text, introducing new words and phrases that will appear and talking about their meaning, and answering any questions about the story students may have before they read (Singh & Singh, 1984). This process takes relatively little time and it is one many students enjoy and benefit from. One of the positive byproducts of previewing is that it may involve all students, even those who cannot read the text.

Positive Practice Often when students are reading orally and they miss a word by reading it incorrectly or not reading it at all, the teacher supplies the word and the student continues reading. If, instead of allowing the student to continue immediately, the teacher asks the student to say the word five times while looking at it, on subsequent occasions the student will be less likely to miss the word when it appears again in the story (Singh & Singh, 1988).

Word Analysis Skills As discussed previously, some students will be able to sound out words by looking at the individual letters or letter combinations. If teachers help with this process during oral reading, rather than simply telling the word that has been omitted or read incorrectly, students may be more likely to read the word correctly on subsequent appearances (Singh & Singh, 1985).

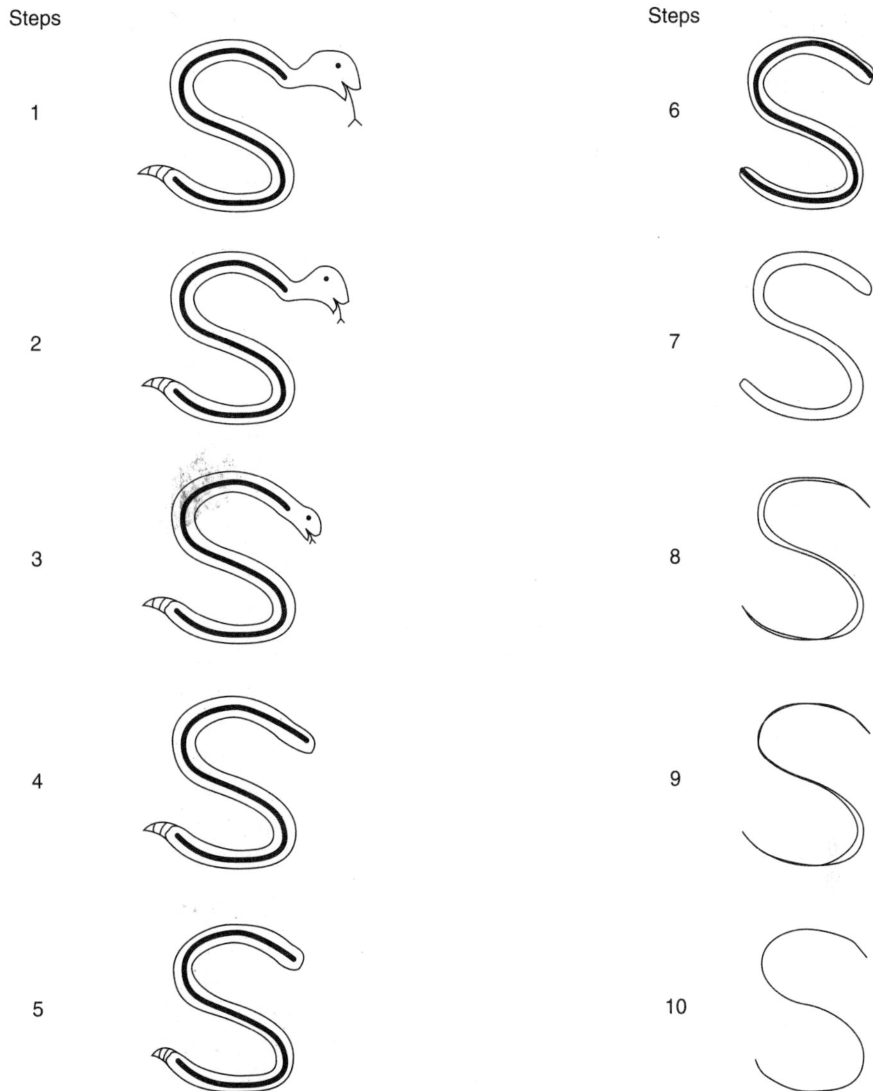

Figure 16–6
The Gradual Transition from the Pictorial Cue Snake to the Letter s (10 Steps)
From "Establishing Letter-Sound Correspondence in Children Classified as Trainable Mentally Retarded" by F. R. Hoogeveen, P. M. Smeets, & J. E. Van der Houven, 1987, *Education and Training in Mental Retardation,* 22(2), p. 82. Copyright 1987 by the Division on Mental Retardation and Developmental Disabilities, The Council for Exceptional Children. Reprinted by permission.

Using Pictures and Context Clues Some oral reading errors may be avoided by teaching students to use available information to figure out the word (Entriken et al., 1977). If a student knows the sound of the first letter of the word, he or she may be able to determine what the word is by looking at pictures in the story or by recalling information provided in the narrative. Considering such information as this may help the student who has basic phonics skills.

Students who can read orally from books have the potential for becoming functional in their reading and being able to read both for need and for pleasure; those who can advance to this level should be given adequate instruction in the reading process. The instructional goals should be to acquire a greater vocabulary, read faster, and make fewer errors at increasingly higher reading levels. Words read correctly and incorrectly are discrete behaviors that can be counted and charted, using procedures described in chapter 8. By keeping such records, the teacher can monitor students' progress.

Using Commercial Programs to Teach Reading

There are two commercially produced instructional programs that have been used successfully to teach reading to students with moderate mental disabilities (Conners, 1992)—the Edmark Reading Program (1972, 1984) and the DISTAR Reading Program (Engelmann & Bruner, 1974).

The DISTAR program uses a direct instruction approach to teach a series of phonics skills that have been carefully sequenced. The student must master each skill before moving on to a new one. The teacher follows an instructional script that includes cues that are to be provided to the students and the error-correction techniques. Students are instructed in small groups and reinforced for correct responses. The instruction is very quickly paced. Although DISTAR was designed primarily for students with mild disabilities with poor reading skills, it has also been used with some success with students with moderate mental disabilities (Bracey, Maggs, & Morath, 1975; Gersten & Maggs, 1982).

The Edmark Program is based on the process of visual discrimination. Students learn first to simply point to an isolated word when it is said by the teacher. They then learn to point to the word as it appears in increasingly complex arrays of words. After target words can be accurately identified, the students learn to say the word as they see it. As they progress, they learn to identify and read more and more sight words. Walsh and Lambert (1979) found the Edmark Program to be more effective than a picture-fading technique for recognition, matching, and identification of words.

Teaching Comprehension Skills and Reading in Applied Settings

It will not be sufficient simply to have students be able to read words individually or in texts. Even the ability to sound out new words does not mean the student will be able to use reading skills in a beneficial way. The utility or pleasure of reading, of course, comes from the ability to gain meaning from what has been read. This may range from knowing that *ball* represents an object that we can toss around to understanding someone's experiences by reading about them in a magazine.

There are several possible ways to develop or improve the reading comprehension skills of students with moderate mental disabilities. One way is to teach them to read certain materials and then act out or follow the directions stated or implied by the reading material. In one study, for example (Brown & Perlmutter, 1971), students learned to read words that indicated the location of a penny in a specially built cabinet (e.g., *in front, behind, on top,* and then respond to the directions by correctly locating the penny. To do this successfully, they had to understand what the words meant. In another study, students were taught to say the names of objects, read the written name, and then demonstrate that they understood that the written word represented an object by touching it when it appeared in an array of objects (Brown et al., 1972).

Acting out written activities could range from following relatively simple directions such as the above to much more complicated ones. The criterion of ultimate functioning should be kept in mind and reading comprehension requiring actions in the natural environment should be a desired goal. Around the school and community, teachers could teach students to respond to signs, notices, and directions such as "please clear your table," "only two garments allowed in the dressing room," and "take a number."

Besides following directions to demonstrate comprehension, students could respond orally to questions about signs, directions, or stories they have just read. Cuvo and Klatt (1992) asked students to read certain community signs that had been learned, and then asked them to "Tell me what you would do if you saw the sign." The signs included "Not an Exit," "Service," "Sorry, We're Closed," "Cashier," "NO SHOES, NO SHIRT, NO SERVICE!" and "Shoplifters will be prosecuted." In situations where it is impractical for students to actually do what the sign is directing, they could instead verbally describe the actions they would take and thereby demonstrate how well they understood the information that the sign was conveying.

Oral responses to questions about stories can also demonstrate comprehension. Teachers can develop their own questions about the content of stories read by students if questions are not supplied as part of the story. These questions should allow the student to demonstrate knowledge of the main facts about the story by answering questions about who, what, when, where, and so forth.

Such questions might also be answered in writing by some students with moderate mental disabilities, which would be another method to teach and evaluate reading comprehension. Domnie and Brown (1977) taught students to write answers to who, what, and where questions by gradually progressing them through several phases of instruction. Students first learned to read up to 90 sight words and then learned to copy 40 potential components that would be necessary to answer the questions. Next, they read the sight words they had learned within the contexts of stories and also read questions about the stories. Finally, they learned to write the answers to the questions about the stories, successfully demonstrating comprehension of what they had read.

Regardless of the approach selected, it is important for the teacher to give students the opportunity to practice and demonstrate that they understand what has been read. There are many students with moderate mental disabilities who are able to read words but do not fully comprehend what they have read or how they should respond to the written signs in the environment. This critical part of reading instruction should not be overlooked if reading is to be a part of a student's curriculum.

There are several locations in which reading skills (both word identification and comprehension) may be learned. Although the classroom is the place where most formal reading instruction will occur, other locations should also be considered, particularly when the reading skills that are being learned are of an applied nature. A good example of this, as already mentioned, would be to identify signs in community settings for students to read. Cuvo and Klatt (1992) did this and then taught the signs, using three different approaches: instruction in the community settings, instruction with the signs appearing on videotape, and traditional instruction with the words from the signs printed on flashcards. They found all approaches to be successful.

Another form of reading application is the use of written directions in individual instructional books to complete daily chores. Browder et al. (1984) developed individual booklets and taught adults with moderate mental disabilities to read the instructions in them to complete various chores in their residence: following recipes, doing the laundry, and using the telephone. The reading instruction occurred in the settings in which the activities were to take place (the kitchen, the laundry room, etc.), and as the students learned to read the words, they learned to follow the directions. Such booklets can be individually developed by the teacher to meet students' needs, and might include some for shopping, some for preparing food, some for following public transportation schedules, and so forth, depending on the needs of the student. Commercial materials may be used to supplement teacher-made materials. The Attainment Company offers materials that combine pictures and words to teach students daily planning, meal selection, shopping, cooking, grooming, and housekeeping. While such stimulus materials could be developed by teachers, and perhaps be made to better meet the individual needs of students, commercial materials may be of assistance.

Summary of Approaches to Teaching Reading Skills

It is apparent from the research literature that students with moderate mental disabilities can learn to read whole words, sometimes use word analysis skills, and comprehend the meaning of what they have read. Students with more severe cognitive disabilities can often learn to "read" pictures that have greater iconic value as symbols than individual letters or whole words. This is not to imply that every student needs to learn reading skills or that reading skills are essential for daily living. However, the fact that many students can learn these skills and that the skills can increase their participation in life activities in both fun and functional ways suggests that reading instruction be considered in the development of individual educational plans.

Teaching Writing

Teaching writing to students with moderate mental disabilities should be considered a parallel learning activity to teaching reading. Words targeted for writing should be some of the same words that the student is learning to read or has already learned, and, as with reading, the writing activities should be both functional and recreational. The mechanics of writing generally are considered to be less cumbersome when letters are formed in manuscript style rather than cursive and the possibility of using typewriters or word processors should also be considered, as this may be easier and more efficient for some students.

Writing Targets

Various potential writing opportunities—both for pleasure and functional purposes—that occur in the school environment are presented in Table 16–1. As can be seen, functional activities tend to require very specific writing targets (such as writing one's name, address, and phone number), whereas pleasurable writing activities allow for more creativity and personal expression (such as writing stories, cards or letters, and journals).

Functional writing should focus on skills that are required in natural environments. For example, at a relatively young age, children must learn to write their name on school papers, even if the papers contain no other written words (for example, pictures or worksheets). During the early school years (K–3) it is not uncommon for children without disabilities to write only their first name or their first name and the initial of their last name. This type of skill, then, would be an appropriate writing target for a student with a moderate mental disability.

As students get older, functional writing calls for writing that will meet key needs in environments other than the classroom. These needs might include notes to remind oneself of certain activities, shopping lists, or travel directions to get from one place to another. The teacher must be knowledgeable about these needs and develop the functional writing skills necessary to meet them. The student must learn to write the content in a format that he or she can read and understand and that is suitable for the event. Consider, for example, writing directions to take a bus from one's home to downtown. It would not be useful for the student to write down words or abbreviations that could not be comprehended independently. Nor would it be sufficient for a student to learn to write directions on a chalkboard but not on a piece of paper that could be folded and put in a pocket. During instruction the teacher must therefore be certain that the student can write what is necessary in an appropriate format, and then read and comprehend it.

Besides writing "functional" information, students with moderate mental disabilities should be taught and encouraged to write for fun or leisure purposes. This has several benefits. It can provide age-appropriate recreational activity, it can help develop or improve social interactions, and it can naturally improve reading and writing skills. At an early age students can learn to express themselves through symbols. For some these symbols may be pictures, for others they may be simple words (e.g., "Mom I love you" or "Happy Father's Day"). As students progress, their personal writing activities may become more extensive and complex. Notes to friends, letters to pen pals, scrap books, journals, and letters to the editor are a few examples of leisure writing activities that can be undertaken by students with moderate mental disabilities. Specific desirable writing activities can be determined through initial assessment when interviewing parents or the student.

Expanding Writing Content

Words targeted for writing instruction, including those for both functional and recreational writing, can be the same words identified for reading, using any of the reading instructional methods described previously. Sight words or words in books that the student has learned or is learning, or a subset of the most important words, can be used to develop word sets that the student can learn to spell and write. As with the reading process, learning to write the words can be based on either the whole-word configuration or through a word-analysis approach, depending on a student's ability.

A most often proposed method for teaching both reading and writing skills to students with moderate mental disabilities is the language experience approach (Ford et al., 1989). This procedure, which is relatively easy to implement, considers reading and writing to be a natural extension of spoken language. The teacher asks each student to tell a brief story or describe a recent event. For example, students may talk about a recent field trip with their class or a recreational outing with their family. As the student tells what happened, the teacher uses a large blank chart paper to write down word for word what is being said. Several sentences are written in this way. The teacher points to and reads the words that have been written, then the student is asked to read them, and the teacher helps him or her when a word is not known. This narrative is practiced until the student can read it and then write it, first copying the words and then writing them from memory. Practice on individual words can also be done by transferring them to flashcards. This has the negative effect of taking the words out of context but the positive effect of allowing the student to learn the words without relying on contextual cues. As a result, the student may learn to read the words in other contexts and use them to write new sentences. Language experience is useful not only for teaching reading and writing skills, but also for improving speaking and language skills. It is desirable because most students may participate at their own level of language, speech, reading, or writing.

Another method for improving writing skills, as well as language and reading skills, is shared writing (Mather & Lachowicz, 1992). Although developed primarily for children with mild disabilities, it may also be useful for individuals with moderate mental disabilities. The process is a relatively simple one in which the teacher and the student (or two or more students without the teacher) work together, taking turns to write the same story. The process begins with the writers identifying a topic that they will write about. Then they take turns writing different elements of the story (words, sentences, or paragraphs). The elements need not be the same for both (or all) writers. For example, the teacher could write a sentence, and the student could write one word. After each writes a portion, the words are read by the teacher and then by the student, with the teacher helping when necessary.

Using the shared writing approach, the teacher can control the vocabulary she wants the student to learn to read and also prompt the student to write new words. Writing errors made by the student may be corrected incidentally when the teacher writes an addition to the story.

Teaching Writing Mechanics

Often students with moderate mental disabilities learn to form letters correctly by first tracing them and then copying them. In order to do this, they must be able to hold a pencil correctly and use the pencil to make controlled marks on paper. If writing exercises are to be realistic, they must be undertaken using words students will need to read and write in their daily lives. In other words, students should not work on letter formations in isolation.

Some letters may be more difficult for students to form than others; some students may have significant difficulties forming any letters. In such cases, a more structured teaching method may be required. Such a method has been described by Vacc and Vacc (1979). These authors suggested the use of specific verbal cues along with visual models to help students form each letter. The verbal cues include five basic directions, all of which begin with the cue to "touch"; for example, touch, pull; touch, cross; touch, slant; touch, slide; and touch, dot. The cues as they are applied to specific letters are presented in Figure 16–7.

Using these cues, Vacc and Vacc suggested nine steps for teaching letter formation. They proposed that for each letter, students practice these steps one at a time before moving on to the next one. The steps include:

1. The teacher presents the letter and says the letter name.
2. The teacher demonstrates writing the letter, using verbal cues while making the letter strokes.
3. The student traces a sandpaper letter, using verbal cues while making the letter.
4. The student writes the letter in sand, using verbal cues while writing.
5. Holding chalk, student writes letter in air, using verbal cues.

Figure 16–7
Verbal Cues for Manuscript Letters
From "Teaching Manuscript Writing to Mentally Retarded Children" by N. N. Vacc & N. A. Vacc, 1979, *Education and Training of the Mentally Retarded* (Dec.), p. 288. Copyright 1979 by the Division on Mental Retardation and Developmental Disabilities, The Council for Exceptional Children. Reprinted by permission.

A	touch slant, touch slant, touch cross
B	touch pull, touch slide around, touch slide around
C	touch slide up and around
D	touch pull, touch slide around
E	touch pull, touch cross, touch cross, touch cross
F	touch pull, touch cross, touch cross
G	touch slide up and around, touch cross
H	touch pull, touch pull, touch cross
I	touch pull
J	touch pull and slide
K	touch pull, touch slant, touch slant
L	touch pull, touch cross
M	touch pull, touch slant, touch slant, touch pull
N	touch pull, touch slant, touch pull
O	touch slide up and all the way around
P	touch pull, touch slide around
Q	touch slide up and all the way around, touch slant
R	touch pull, touch slide around, touch slant
S	touch slide and slide
T	touch pull, touch cross
U	touch pull and slide, touch pull and slide OR touch pull and slide and straight up
V	touch slant, touch slant
W	touch slant, touch slant, touch slant, touch slant
X	touch slant, touch slant
Y	touch slant, touch slant, touch pull
Z	touch cross, touch slant, touch cross

6. Student writes letter on chalkboard, using verbal cues.
7. Holding pencil, student writes letter in air, using verbal cues.
8. Student writes letter on paper, using verbal cues.
9. Student writes letter on paper without using verbal cues.

For many people, learning to write only manuscript letters is sufficient, and this is generally the case for persons with moderate mental disabilities. It is possible to teach many of these students to write using cursive letters, but most likely this would not increase the speed of writing or reduce errors and therefore would not usually be considered a high priority.

In some situations it may be desirable to teach students to use word processors or typewriters. Obviously this would require that the necessary equipment be available and that students be able to learn the basic procedures necessary for operating it, for example, to give the appropriate commands or to put paper in the machine, and so forth. Beyond that, students would need to learn to find and hit the appropriate keys on the keyboard. Calhoun (1985) reported success using typewriters with adolescents with mild mental disabilities. Their typing (which used the "hunt and peck" approach) started out very slowly when compared to writing words with a pencil. However, after only 10 days of practice on the typewriters, their speed got three times faster and became comparable to their rate of handwriting, and they made more strokes correctly and fewer errors per minute when using the typewriter.

Summary of Strategies for Teaching Writing

Teaching writing is a natural extension of teaching reading, which is itself an extension of spoken language. The writing skills the student may develop can be used for functional purposes and for leisure or recreational pursuits. Some or all of the words the student is learning to read will also be targets for developing writing skills. Increased writing opportunities can be developed by increasing reading opportunities and also by using language experience and shared writing methods.

Many students can learn the mechanical skills for forming letters by seeing the teacher form the letters, by tracing over the letters, and by copying the letters. Some students may require more structured input and this may be provided by the teacher giving verbal cues to help the student form letters properly.

Whole Language

Most of the instruction and research in the areas of reading and writing for students with moderate mental disabilities has focused on teaching discrete skills such as those discussed in the previous sections. In fact, many teachers of students without disabilities adhere to the traditional approach of teaching sight words and phonics skills and use basal readers as the basic elements of their reading program. However, in recent years many general educators—as well as a large number of educators of students with mild disabilities—have developed a more holistic philosophy of promoting the learning of language in its various forms, including speaking, listening, reading, and writing. This approach is referred to as whole-language instruction or sometimes literacy instruction. Its primary purpose is to teach reading, writing, and other language arts in a natural fashion within a learning community in which discrete skill instruction is de-emphasized in favor of learning the forms of language in a more natural fashion.

Defining and Describing Whole Language

Arriving at a precise definition or description of whole-language or literacy instruction has been an elusive undertaking. Watson (1989) noted that most whole-language advocates reject a dictionary-type definition because many have their individual views of what it is. More than a set of instructional methods, whole language is considered by most of its proponents a philosophy of learning, a way of thinking, or even a way of life. Altwerger, Edelsky, and Flores (1987) wrote that whole language is based on the following ideas:

> *(a) Language is for making meanings, for accomplishing purposes; (b) written language is language—thus what is true for language in general is true for written language; (c) the cuing system of language (phonology in oral, orthography in written language, morphology, syntax, semantics, pragmatics) are simultaneously present and interacting in any instance of language use; (d) language always occurs in a situation; (e) situations are critical to meaning making. (Altwerger et al., p. 145)*

Altwerger et al. (1987), as well as others, proposed that the primary assumption of the approach is that acquiring reading and writing skills through actual use (as opposed to practicing skill exercises) is the best way to learn these skills. In order to create learning opportunities, whole-language teachers do not teach isolated words or phonics skills or use basal readers or other commercial instructional materials to teach reading and writing. Instead they create classroom environments that are rich in literature appropriate for the age of the learners they have and teach the students to read, write, speak, and listen, using natural literary materials. In an early literacy program (kindergarten through first or second grade), teachers show and share books and pictures with children and read aloud to them. Children are expected to join in and take part through predicting events and participating in problem-solving. They also role-play reading, writing, and publishing and participate in the selection of materials. Teachers serve as managers of the activities, conferring with children, guiding them, and ratifying their success. In later elementary school years, students learn to select reading materials from a wider range, read and write silently, engage in related arts activities, and share outcomes of their experiences with the entire community of learners. Teachers of older students conference with the students, instruct individuals and groups, and reinforce their activities (Holdaway, 1986).

Elements of Whole-Language Instruction

Key elements for providing whole language instruction have been provided by many authorities in the area (Altwerger et al., 1987; Au, Scheu, Kawakami, & Herman, 1990; Bear & Cheney, 1991; Holdaway, 1986; Manning, Manning, Long, & Wolfson, 1987; Watson, 1989). Holdaway (1986) outlined some of the more common aspects of this approach:

- Learning through literacy centers around real texts, whole texts.
- Learning is centered around favorite, highly familiar texts.
- Favorite texts are usually predictable. Rhyme, repetition, and cumulative structure allow for predictability.
- Print is always perceived as an intent to mean something and is the focus of attention when the teacher reads or writes.
- Experiences with print are "precise, rich, and lively." Early reading and writing allows for approximation of correctness, which is expected to improve with experience. The teacher corrects and instructs largely upon request.
- During early years of learning, teacher and students engage in sharing (demonstration and participation). As the student learns, more time is spent in role-playing and performance modes expressed in emergent writing and reading-like behavior during the sharing of books.
- Ultimately the acts of reading and writing are "rapidly characterized in the learner's mind as distinctive, print-oriented and conventionally rule-bound." (Holdaway, 1986, p. 62)

Observing the principles of whole language applied to a classroom setting would likely result in certain practices being pursued. Although there is likely to be some variability, Watson (1989) suggested that the following strategies are commonplace:

- Teachers read to their students or tell them stories every day. This includes not only stories but plays, poems, riddles, and other authentic and appropriate texts.

- Students write their own stories and their ideas, undertake editing and revising, and publish and present their stories to others. They also write poems, notes, letters, newspapers, journals, and other real written material, generally of their own choosing.
- Personal interactions occur regularly. Students have the opportunity to work individually and quietly, but are also encouraged to share their literacy activities with each other. They are dissuaded from relying on the teacher and instead are encouraged to solve their own problems and collaborate with each other.
- Whole-language teachers "plan to plan." They do not formalize instructional curricula until they know their students and learn their interests. They explore a variety of themes, topics, and lessons. Topics are selected only after the interests of the students are known and understood.

Use of Whole Language with Students with Disabilities

Although the whole-language approach has grown substantially in recent years, it has not been fully accepted by all. Some educational authorities have noted that it does not have a solid research base in comparison to other instructional approaches, especially for poor readers (McKenna, Robinson, & Miller, 1990). Stahl and Miller (1989) concluded from their review of available research that whole language was not very effective for teaching reading to students with mild disabilities although it was beneficial in developing early language skills. Furthermore, reports on the use of whole language or literacy instruction with students with more severe disabilities has been extremely limited.

Mirenda (1992) presented a report that noted that children with severe disabilities are often neglected with regard to early literacy experiences. She then described the instructional reading activities of two adults with severe physical disabilities based on the whole-language–literacy instruction model. Larry, a 20-year-old man with severe spastic cerebral palsy, learned to read stories from newspapers and magazines that were rewritten at a first-grade level. He and his mother picked out the stories together and they were rewritten by his instructor. (His favorite topics included serial killers, executions, and natural disasters.) After the stories were rewritten, they were previewed and new or unfamiliar words were explained. Larry then read the story quietly while the instructor followed his eyes. Phonics was worked on within the context of the story. *Yes* and *no* questions were presented to check his comprehension.

The second individual described by Mirenda (1992) was Mary Lou, a 39-year-old woman who also had severe cerebral palsy. In stark contrast to the interest of the first student, this woman's favorite reading was the Bible. She learned to read out loud from a children's Bible written at the second- to third-grade level. Phonics was again worked on within the context of the reading material and rereading was done to build fluency. Additional activities included listening to the Bible being read at home, use of questioning to increase inferential thinking and comprehension, and spelling practice.

Unfortunately there is little to guide teachers of students with cognitive disabilities, particularly students with moderate mental disabilities who wish to attempt whole-language instruction. Nor is there much research at this time to suggest the practice would be effective. However, it is suggested that some practices within the whole-language approach may be effective in some ways for students with moderate or even severe mental disabilities. For example, some students may acquire interest in reading and writing, and this interest may serve as a springboard toward the cognitively more complex skills of understanding written words and comprehending their holistic meanings in context. There is perhaps a greater likelihood that participation in a whole-language environment, such as an inclusive multigrade experiential classroom, provide the student with supportive conditions for developing better oral language and listening skills and personal-social cooperative skills. Certainly a well-developed whole-language learning environment presents the possibility for at least such an outcome if not more. As explained by Holdaway (1986):

> *A rich literature of story, poem, and song is presented for communal sharing. No one is excluded from this community, and the shared literature becomes the basis of a group "culture." Individual differences are met during the sharing session with an appropriate response by each individual, whether publicly, in unison or privately.*

Perhaps in the near future practitioners and researchers will be able to provide more information and greater understanding about the application of the philosophy and principles of whole language to students with disabilities.

Teaching Arithmetic

Like reading and writing, arithmetic is one of the basic areas of academic instruction in schools. And like reading and writing, arithmetic skills can add significantly to the quality of a person's life. Being able to determine if you have enough money to buy a soda and a magazine, and if the store will be open long enough for you to make the purchase, requires fundamental math skills, skills that many individuals with cognitive disabilities can acquire. Teachers must be aware of appropriate goals and objectives for learning arithmetic skills and instructional methods that will help to achieve them.

Arithmetic instruction for students with moderate mental disabilities should focus on at least three areas of learning:

- Acquiring basic concepts and skills
- Applying skills to handling money
- Applying skills to time management

Instruction in each of these areas is discussed below.

Acquiring Basic Concepts and Skills

The application of fundamental arithmetic skills will be improved by an understanding of some basic concepts about numbers and quantities. Although authorities in the past concluded that individuals with moderate mental disabilities have only rote arithmetic skills (for example, the ability to memorize single-digit addition), more recent studies have challenged this conclusion, reporting that these individuals often have the ability to acquire generalized arithmetic concepts (Baroody, 1987, 1988; Baroody & Snyder, 1983; Caycho, Gunn, & Siegal, 1991; Mastropieri, Bakken, & Scruggs, 1991). These concepts tend to be developed by persons with moderate mental disabilities in about the same way as they are developed by nondisabled children, although generally at a later chronological age. Learning these skills to the extent possible in the elementary-school years would help students acquire more applied skills later. Critical concepts and basic skills include the following.

Counting Word Sequence This skill consists of saying numbers in their appropriate order, beginning with one and counting to some target number, for example 100. After memorizing the numbers 1 through 13, students may be able to continue counting, using numerical logic.

Enumeration and Cardinality Students demonstrate this by being able to count a set of objects (using 1:1 correspondence), saying the number of each object as it is counted, and knowing the last number they say in the count represents the number of objects in the set.

Order Irrelevance Principle This concept requires students to realize that the order in which they count the objects in a set does not change the total number.

$N + 1 > N$ Rule The purpose of counting is to be able to compare quantities of objects contained within sets. Students must learn that numbers counted later in a sequence represent greater quantities than numbers counted earlier.

Addition and Subtraction These basic skills are learned initially when students develop methods to determine the sum or difference of two numbers by using a counting strategy. Typically students begin with one number in the problem and, starting with its cardinal value, add to it or subtract from it by counting forward (or backward) the number of times represented by the second number. For example, given the problem 5 + 3, the student might say: "5 and 3 more, that's 5, 6 (that's 1), 7 (that's 2), 8 (that's 3). 5 + 3 is 8." Often students use their fingers or other concrete objects and may also devise their own strategies for adding or subtracting.

The Commutativity Principle Students who understand the commutative nature of numbers realize that the order in which numbers are added together (3 + 2 vs. 2 + 3) does not affect the outcome.

In their study Baroody and Snyder (1983) examined the ability of several adolescents with moderate mental disabilities to perform on various number tasks such as those listed above and found that the students had the ability to perform correctly on several of the tasks. Those that were more difficult included applying the rule that $N + 1$ is greater than N and using the principle of commutativity in addition. Based on their findings, Baroody and Snyder recommended the following:

1. Except for the first several numbers (up to 13), counting should not be taught rotely, but in terms of the structure of the numbers. Rote counting results in errors occurring in the teens and the decades and understanding the rules that govern the order of numbers can help avoid errors. In order for students to learn more advanced skills such as enumeration, the $N + 1 > N$ rule, addition, and estimation, they must master oral counting.
2. The ability to count objects accurately (enumerate) is another important basic skill and one that presents difficulty to some students. Students must be given practice in both counting objects within sets and producing the number of objects requested.
3. Students must learn to compare sets of objects and know which has more and which has fewer. Because students may not realize that the count sequence can be used to compare sets, practice in this skill is important. The process is easier if the student learns what numbers come after other numbers (the N after rule).
4. Some students with moderate mental disabilities have the ability to use unique self-developed strategies to add and subtract accurately. If the teacher discovers that students have such abilities, they should be

encouraged to use them. Various game activities give students the opportunity to develop these types of skills.

Using Concrete Materials Initial instruction on counting, addition, and subtraction will require the use of concrete, manipulative materials. Flexer (1989) and Paddock (1992) stressed the importance of using units (single items) that could be grouped into sets of five and/or ten in order to help develop a mental model for understanding quantities. Flexer proposed the use of 5- and 10-frames such as displayed in Figure 16–8. Recognizing and being able to identify the number of objects as they appear within the frames is intended to help students acquire an image of the number that will become significant and easier to recall than items that appear only as unrelated units. This recognition of the number structures is intended to reduce the need for counting each item when adding or subtracting and to develop the concept of place values (Flexer, 1989).

After students acquire skills in oral counting, enumeration and cardinality, recognizing quantities, and the concepts of greater than and less than, they may use the manipulatives to begin developing concepts of addition and subtraction. Using the frames proposed by Flexer, the addition of two numbers can be taught by using the following steps:

1. Place two 5-frames with different numbers of objects in them side by side.
2. Move objects from one frame to another to fill missing cells.
3. Place the frames together and read the sum.

This procedure is pictured in Figure 16–9. For subtraction, the process would require these steps:

1. Identify the total from which a smaller amount will be subtracted and place this number in a frame.
2. Identify the number to be subtracted and remove it from the first frame and into another one.
3. Read the number of items remaining in the first frame.

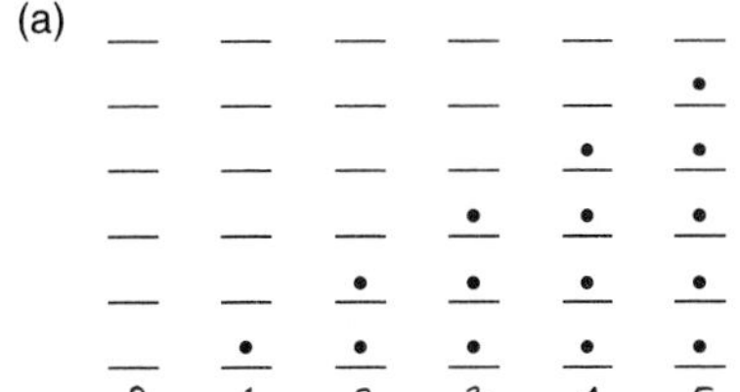

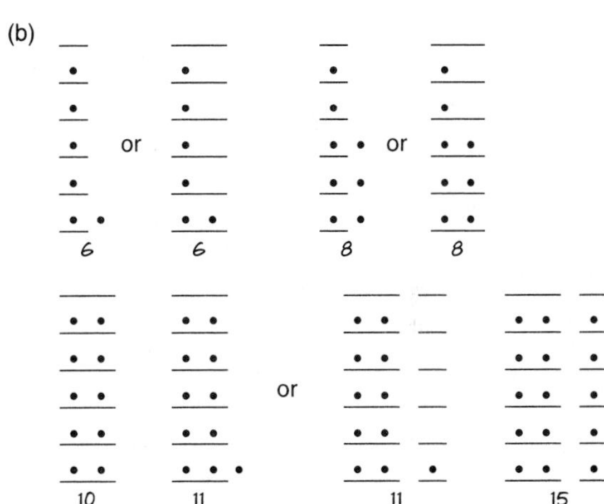

Figure 16–8
Configurations of Numbers with 5- and 10-Frames
From "Conceptualizing Addition" by R. Flexer, 1989, *Teaching Exceptional Children, 21*(4), p. 23. Copyright 1989 by The Council for Exceptional Children. Reprinted by permission.

The development of initial concepts and skills by students with mental disabilities during the early school years may lead to more advanced arithmetic skills such as addition and subtraction with regrouping, multiplying, dividing, estimating, graphing, measuring, and so forth. Students with the ability to learn such skills should be encouraged to do so. They will be best served by a regular or regular-adapted arithmetic curriculum (Ford et al., 1989). If students' progress does not continue at an ade-

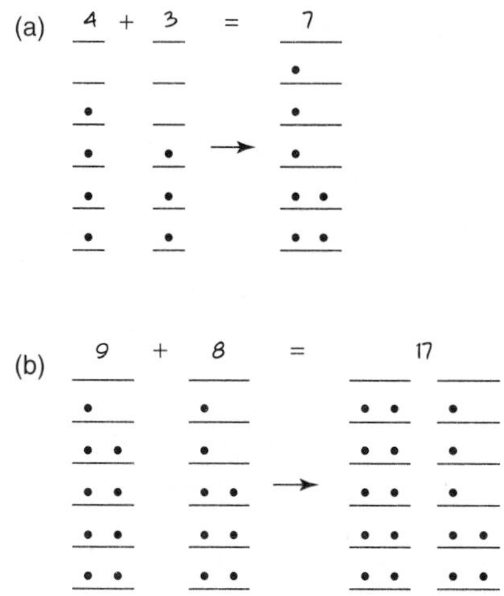

(a) 4 + 3 = 7

(b) 9 + 8 = 17

Figure 16–9
The Addition of Numbers Using 5- and 10-Frames
From "Conceptualizing Addition" by R. Flexer, 1989, *Teaching Exceptional Children, 21*(4), p. 24. Copyright 1989 by The Council for Exceptional Children. Reprinted by permission.

quate pace, however, and as they approach the middle and high school years, instructional efforts should be devoted to more functional math skills, particularly using money and telling time.

Applying Skills to Handling Money

The ability to handle money in order to make a purchase requires three essential skills: identifying the cost of an item or the total cost of several items; determining if one has enough money to purchase the item; and, if so, selecting the necessary amount of money from what is available to pay for the item(s) (Ford et al., 1989). If there is more than one item the individual must be able to add the separate prices and calculate a total cost. The person must also be able to decide if he or she has enough to make the purchase, and this requires an understanding of quantities (in this case of money) being more or less than other quantities. Along with these skills, students must learn the names or identity of different coins and paper currency and their corresponding values. Several studies have demonstrated that students with moderate mental disabilities can learn to develop such skills (Bellamy & Buttars, 1975; Borakove & Cuvo, 1976; Cuvo, Veitch, Trace, & Konke, 1978; Lowe & Cuvo, 1976). The steps typically included in an instructional process are outlined below. These steps were used by Bellamy and Buttars (1975) to teach students with moderate mental disabilities to purchase a single item costing less than one dollar.

- Students learn (or demonstrate the ability) to count to 100 by ones, fives, tens, and twenty-fives.
- Students learn to read all prices on price cards or tags between one cent and one dollar.
- Students learn to identify coins by touching a coin when the teacher says its name.
- Students learn to count out the amount of money as identified on individual price cards.

When students are learning to count coins, the task is easier if they first learn to count all coins of one value and then coins of another value, for example, first learn to count pennies and then to count nickels. After learning to count these coins separately, they should learn to count the two different sets together. When they can do this, they can learn to add a third set of coins (e.g., dimes); after they can do so, this set would be added to the pennies and nickels.

Numberline Strategy A numberline can be a helpful tool for students to determine if they have enough money to purchase an item (Ford et al., 1989; Frank, 1978). The student determines the price of an item and marks that amount on the numberline, then counts the money he or she has and marks that amount on the moneyline. The student then compares the two amounts; if the mark indicating the amount of money the student has is to the right of the mark indicating the cost, the student knows it is possible to make the purchase. Figure 16–10 demonstrates the application of a moneyline strategy.

Ford et al. (1989) recommended that numberline skills be learned sequentially in the following order:

- Learning to purchase items with pennies (items costing 1 to 10 cents).
- Learning to purchase items between 1 and 10 cents, using a dime.
- Using dimes to purchase items up to a dollar.
- Learning to purchase items up to a dollar, using quarters.
- Learning to purchase items up to a dollar, using two quarters and five dimes.
- Learning to purchase items up to a dollar, using nickels.
- Learning to purchase items up to a dollar, using various combinations of coins: quarters + nickels; dimes + nickels; quarters + dimes + nickels.

After students have mastered the use of the numberline with coins, the strategy should be taught using singles, fives, tens, and twenty-dollar bills, following a sequence similar to the one for coins. Ford et al. (1989) stressed the importance of using price tags that correspond to the real cost of real items. They also noted that students must learn to add a little more to the cost for taxable items. When the cost of an item falls between two marks on the numberline, students must learn to estimate where a price falls in order to mark the appropriate spot on the line (e.g., 34 cents).

Using Calculators Many students with moderate mental disabilities are able to learn to use

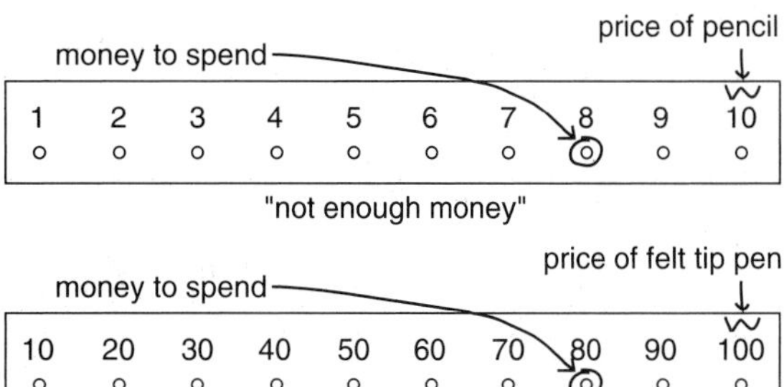

Figure 16–10
Using a Numberline

From *The Syracuse Community-Referenced Curriculum Guide for Students with Moderate and Severe Disabilities* (p. 121) by A. Ford, R. Schnorr, L. Meyer, J. Black, & P. Dempsey, 1989, Baltimore: Paul H. Brookes Publishing Co., P.O. Box 10624, Baltimore, Maryland 21285-0624. Reprinted by permission.

calculators and their use is likely to improve the accuracy and efficiency of the calculations (Horton, 1985; Koller & Mulhern, 1977; Matson & Long, 1986). Calculators might be especially practical when students are learning to purchase multiple items, for example, when shopping in a grocery store or department store (Ford et al., 1989; Matson & Long, 1986). A procedure for using them, based on subtraction, has been described by Ford et al.

- The student determines the money available for spending by counting it.
- This amount is entered on the calculator. (Ford et al. recommend that the decimal point be omitted, for example, entering 100 for one dollar.)
- When an item to be purchased is found, the student presses the minus sign on the calculator.
- The student finds the price of the item and enters it, again disregarding the decimal point.
- The student presses the equals sign.
- After each such entry, the student checks the display on the calculator to determine

if there is enough money remaining to purchase an additional item.

- If the display indicates the amount of money remaining is less than zero (e.g., -78), the student should realize that he or she does not have enough money.

As with the use of the numberline strategy, the use of a calculator should begin with limited amounts of money and relatively few items and increase to more money and more items. Again, teachers should remember that students need to account for taxes. One way to do this is to determine the maximum amount of sales tax that could be applied to the total amount of money the student has to spend, and teach the student to subtract this amount from the total before entering item amounts. A tax table could be written on a card for the student to determine this amount (Ford et al., 1989).

Other Money-Handling Tactics Many students can acquire basic arithmetic skills and learn to use numberlines and calculators to gain greater independence in their lives by making purchases in various community settings. For some students, particularly those with more severe cognitive disabilities, however, the use of these devices may be too difficult. If this is the case, the teacher may be able to teach them to use other money-handling techniques (Ford et al., 1989).

One possibility is to provide students with predetermined amounts of money for certain purchases. The money is placed in an envelope and the student learns to give the envelope to a particular individual at a specific time in order to make a purchase. As students progress in this skill, they may learn to select an appropriate envelope from a group packaged together in a purse or backpack. In this way, they can make a purchase at one location, then select another envelope to make another purchase, and so on. The envelopes should be marked or coded in some fashion to help students make the correct selection and purchase.

Students may also learn to use coin displacement cards or coin books, which are available commercially or may be made by the teacher and can be used in different ways. In one way, pictures or drawings of certain items (for example, a soda or a bus fare) are displayed on the card, along with either indentations in which the required coins may be inserted or true-size pictures of the necessary coins. The student must learn to select from the coins he or she possesses the ones that match the requirement for the purchase. This is a match-to-sample activity and therefore does not require the student to know the name of the coin or the amount it represents. However, students must learn to make a correct match.

If students can read numbers, the cards can be used more generically by having different price amounts affixed to different cards or pages without pictures of particular items. Once again, indentations or pictures of coins would be included. When the student sees or hears the price of a particular item, the card representing that amount is found, and the student selects the coins that match those on the card.

Students may make purchases using single dollar bills (even if they do not know the value of coins or bills) if they can count the single bills and round up, using the *next dollar strategy*. Using this procedure, the student takes an item or items to a cashier along with several dollar bills. The cashier calculates the amount and tells the student what it is. The student adds one additional dollar to the dollar amount that is heard and gives this amount to the cashier. For example, if the student is told the amount is $4.86, then he or she would count out five dollar bills and give them to the cashier, who would then return the change to the student.

Although these strategies do not allow students to be as independent as using numberlines or calculators, they afford the opportunity to participate in activities that call for money-handling. Because of this, they are useful when students have difficulty obtaining more advanced skills.

Applying Skills to Time Management

Being able to tell time allows individuals to identify when certain events occur during the day. This means they can predict when something is going to occur, when it will start, and when it will end, and thus regulate their lives in a corresponding manner. Being able to tell time and to manage one's life accordingly allows a person to have greater independence. For this reason, when possible, it is important for persons with intellectual disabilities to learn how to tell and manage time.

In order to know what time it is, a person must be able to understand the numbers on a clock and what these numbers mean in two dimensions: hours and minutes. Additionally, it is necessary for the person to understand the language of telling time, for example, "ten after," "a quarter till," "nine thirty," and so forth. Although we typically take this skill for granted, learning to tell time is a relatively complicated cognitive task. Even so, many students with moderate mental disabilities can learn to do so given appropriate instruction. Instructional procedures useful for teachers have been described by Ford et al. (1989) and by Smeets, Van Lieshout, Lancioni, and Striefel (1986).

Learning to Tell Time Using a large clock or an accurate facsimile, the teacher should teach students how to tell time by employing an instructional plan such as the following. Sufficient trials should be allotted for each step so that the student can learn the requirement of the step accurately.

- First students learn to read the hour. The teacher removes the minute hand and uses the hour hand (the little hand) to point to different numbers. The students learn to say "It is ____ o'clock."
- After students can read the hour, the teacher replaces the minute hand and leaves it pointing to the 12. The hour hand is moved to point to different numbers. As it points, the students should say, "It is ____ o'clock."
- Next, students learn to read the time at half past the hour. The teacher moves the hour hand half way between various numbers, and moves the minute hand to point to the 6. The students read the time, using different, appropriate statements: "It's 6:30," "It's half past 8," "It's 30 minutes after four," and so forth. Some students may benefit from counting the individual minutes (1 to 30) in order to understand why they are saying "____:30," or "30 minutes after ____."
- After students have mastered the above skill, they should be given several opportunities to read the time at both the hour and the half hour. This is important because they need to learn to discriminate between the two.
- When students can reliably read the time at the hour and the half hour, the quarter hour before and after the hour should be introduced. The minute hand should be placed appropriately and the hour hand should be placed just a little before or a little after the hour depending on the time that is to be read. It is important that the placement of the hands be as accurate as possible in order for correct discrimination and generalization to occur. Once again, students learn to say the time,

using several appropriate phrases: "It's 15 after three," "It's a quarter till 7," "It's 11:15," and so forth.

- Once again, maintenance and discrimination training must be used to practice all of the clock configurations studied thus far: the time on the hour, half past the hour, and a quarter hour before and after the hour.

Most stores, offices, businesses, schools, and other community settings open and close on the hour, the half hour, or at quarter hours. Jobs and recreational events also usually begin and end at such times. If students are successful in learning to tell time to this degree of accuracy, they will have accomplished a significant skill. All of the remaining indications of time can be stated by the student in terms of approximations without indicating the exact number of minutes. For example, students can learn to read a clock that shows between 1 and 8 minutes after the hour by saying, "It is a little after ____." Similarly, they can learn to read clocks and say, "It's almost _____:30," or "It's just past ____:45," and so forth.

Students who can learn to read the time more accurately by referring to the exact number of minutes should continue the sequence in the following order:

- After students can discriminate and read the time on the hour, at the half hour, and 15 minutes before and after the hour, they should be taught 5 and 10 minutes before and after the hour. It will be necessary to position the hands on the clock precisely and allow many practice opportunities.
- Success with the above step requires discrimination instruction that allows the student to practice telling time on the hour; at 5, 10, and 15 past the hour; on the half hour; and 15, 10, 5 minutes before the hour.
- The remaining major time configurations to be identified are 20 and 25 minutes before and after the hour. When these have been learned, discrimination practice should again be instituted because it will continue to be important for the student to learn to vary the verbal statements used to tell time and to hear the variations in order to understand them.

Each progressive step has brought the student closer to being able to read, tell, hear, and understand time with greater degrees of accuracy. With adequate progress to this point, it may be appropriate to teach students to understand minutes and seconds and thus have a more complete understanding of time, clocks, and watches.

It can be expected that students will have various types of difficulties as they learn to tell time. For many individuals with cognitive disabilities, the ability to discriminate is relatively difficult. Smeets et al. (1986) found that when the hour hand was situated between two numbers, the students would often make reference to the incorrect number. For example, 1:15 might be misread as 2:15. They also had difficulty in discriminating before and after, that is, "10 till" was sometimes read as "10 after." But still they found that with adequate instruction, all of their students were able to learn time-telling skills.

Learning to Manage Time Being able to tell time does not necessarily mean that students will use these skills as normally required. Teachers and others should provide ample opportunities for students to practice telling time and responding according to what the time calls for. For example, class schedules may show that physical education begins at 10:15. Individual students can be asked to inform the teacher when the clock says 10:15 so everyone will know when it is time to go to P.E. Ultimately it may be expected that natural environmental contingencies will maintain the skill, but until that happens, emphasis should be placed on telling and managing time. Given adequate ability, students should ultimately learn how to tell and understand time, estimate time needs, predict when something is expected to occur, and solve problems related to the use of time (Ford et al., 1989).

Students with less ability can also acquire some time-management skills even though they cannot read a watch or clock face to tell time. Since using time correctly means that we can tell what time it is and simultaneously know what is to happen at that time, some students can acquire this skill by learning to match the time on the clock with a certain activity that should occur at that time. This can be facilitated through the use of picture cues. This technique requires having a figure representing the activity and a clock face showing the time for the activity appear on the same chart, card, or page. When the student sees that the time on the clock or watch matches the time on the chart, he or she learns to engage in the activity that is also represented on the chart. This task requires the ability to match the real time with that beside the figure and then engage in the activity, which is somewhat less complex than actually being able to read a clock or watch.

If students cannot acquire a skill such as the above, instructional efforts on time management should focus on getting the student to recognize sequences of events in relation to each other and to environmental cues (Ford et al., 1989). For example, students could learn that when others start gathering their belongings, the school day is nearly over and it's almost time to go home. In this way, even though students do not acquire skills for reading or responding to clock time, they learn broad concepts of time and the organization of events in their day.

Whether a student uses a watch or clock to tell time, uses pictures or figures to help, or learns to understand the relation between environmental cues and activities, there are several natural opportunities when these skills may be practiced. A number of these are listed in Table 16–2.

Table 16–2
Time-Management Opportunities

Elementary School	Middle and High School
Responds to bells or other cues for arrival and departure	Responds to bells or other cues for passage between classes
Uses class calendar to determine which day it is, what activities are planned, and so forth	Use personal calendar to keep track of birthdates and other special dates, events that are planned, and so forth
Follows classroom schedule of daily activities	Follows personal schedule of classes for day and week
Uses wall clock and/or watch to manage time throughout day	Uses wall clock and/or watch to manage time throughout day
	Uses timer during home economics class to monitor cooking activities
	Manages time card at job site
	Manages time as needed in community situations (e.g., bus use, arrival, breaktime, and departure from job site)

From *The Syracuse Community-Referenced Curriculum Guide for Students with Moderate and Severe Disabilities* (p. 154) by A. Ford, R. Schnorr, L. Meyer, J. Black, & P. Dempsey, 1989, Baltimore: Paul H. Brookes Publishing Co., P.O. Box 10624, Baltimore, Maryland 21285-0624. Reprinted by permission.

Summary of Strategies for Teaching Arithmetic

During the elementary-school years students with moderate mental disabilities may do well in the acquisition of basic arithmetic skills. To the extent that they can have success learning these skills, instruction should be provided that focuses on basic concepts and uses a variety of concrete instructional materials. As with reading and writing, during the younger years, students with cognitive disabilities are closer to their nondisabled peers in terms of their academic ability than they are later in life. Therefore, instructional time might be best spent teaching arithmetic skills similar to (if not the same as) those being taught to children without disabilities.

Ultimately, however, when the student reaches the middle school years (or sooner for children with more severe disabilities), the focus of instruction must shift to arithmetic skills more directly applicable to everyday life. The primary areas of instruction at this time will be learning to use money and to tell and manage time. The extent of success achieved by students on learning basic arithmetic skills and concepts will likely bear on how well students can learn these more functional skills. However, even if students have not been able to acquire many of the basic arithmetic concepts, they may learn some skills related to handling money and managing time. These should be taught, practiced, and applied in order that the student can become as competent as possible with their use.

Teaching Academics in the Regular Classroom

Inclusion of students with severe disabilities in regular classroom settings is an important goal. Strategies and tactics for doing this have been discussed previously (see chapter 9), and therefore in this section only a brief description of how some of these approaches can be used to teach academic skills will be provided. Because regular classrooms are the primary sites for academic instruction, it makes sense that much academic instruction for students with disabilities should occur in the regular classroom. Many of the instructional goals and strategies discussed in this chapter can be used in regular class settings if special and general educators work together and employ the cooperation of other professionals, teacher aids, and students. Some ways to do this are described below.

Cooperative Learning

Cooperative learning allows several students to work together toward some common goal. Each student uses his or her skills to contribute to the group. Students do not have to have the same level of ability nor do they need to be working on the same skill or objective as long as they are working together to achieve some goal designated by the instructor. This format allows a student with a disability to work on academic skills targeted for him or her while the other students work at their own skill levels (Johnson & Johnson, 1986, 1989; Putnam, Rynders, Johnson, & Johnson, 1989).

There are several ways students with cognitive disabilities can work on academic skills in a regular classroom setting in a cooperative learning arrangement. For example, they might read part of the text containing words they know, write down some key words during an activity, say the beginning and ending time of an experiment, or count objects or add them together.

Parallel Learning Activities

Parallel or alternative learning activities occur in the regular classroom and are related to the primary class activities, but are designed to meet the instructional needs and abilities of students with disabilities. Ford and Davern (1989) provided several examples of such activities. One was of two boys with disabilities in the fourth grade who developed and operated a hot chocolate business along with other class members. The students without disabilities worked on applying the math skills they were learning; the two students with disabilities worked on learning their individually determined skills: one using a calculator and the other matching coins to a number card.

Multilevel Curriculum

In a multilevel curriculum, the area of instruction includes objectives at several different levels (to accommodate students of different abilities) within the same learning exercise (Giangreco & Putnam, 1991). For example, some students might be working on single-digit addition using concrete materials, others might be working on multidigit addition without regrouping, and still others could be working on multidigit addition with regrouping. A multilevel curricular approach could be applied easily within a cooperative learning model.

Curriculum Overlapping

Curriculum overlapping is similar to the multilevel curriculum but the instructional activities do not all have to be within the same instructional domain (Giangreco & Putnam, 1991). The implication is that while for most students in a class the learning activity may be one thing; for others, it may be another. This fits well into the cooperative learning model. For example, some students might practice their writing skills from a model while others are working on writing a play.

Adaptive Instruction

Adaptive instruction is a model in which all students are instructed based on individually determined objectives (Walberg & Wang, 1987). Instruction is based on the determined abilities and needs of each student, and materials and instruction are designed for each student to make individual progress. Students have a voice in determining their learning objectives and assist each other during instruction.

Individual Tutoring

Within the activities of the regular classroom, the student with disabilities may receive individual or small-group instruction from a general education or special education teacher, a paraprofessional, or a peer (Giangreco & Putnam, 1991). This form of instructional activity is most appropriate at the initial acquisition of specific academic skills, for example, when the student is first learning to read a section of a book with new words or carry out a new arithmetic exercise. After the student has shown the ability to perform the task, he or she may practice it in another format in the regular classroom.

Considerations for Delivering Instruction in the Regular Classroom

It is possible for students with disabilities to acquire many skills in the regular classroom, including different types of academic skills.

Success, however, depends largely on the ability of special educators and general educators to work cooperatively (see chapter 9). Both must participate in planning and implementing instruction for all children, those with and without disabilities, if the process is to be effective.

Unfortunately, sometimes students are placed in regular classrooms but are there only physically, not truly participating or learning anything of relevance. Of course this is not much better than being in a segregated environment. The procedures described in general terms above and in more detail in chapter 9 are intended to avoid this outcome. As integration progresses, teachers will find many new and innovative ways to make it work successfully.

Conclusion

The importance of academic skills for individuals with severe disabilities varies. Some, primarily those whose cognitive disabilities are more moderate, will have more success at learning traditional academics than others, particularly those who have more severe or profound mental disabilities. It is important that those who acquire academic skills be able to apply them to daily life. Those whose ability to learn academic skills is more limited need either to learn skills that can be immediately and directly applied or to learn how to operate as successfully as possible without academic skills.

Often it is difficult to determine precisely how much a student might be able to learn. Students may seem to show poor ability because they lack motivation or because they have not been given the opportunity to learn. Additionally, students' learning potential may change over time as they become older and acquire more life experience. Teachers should not assume a person's ability or inability, particularly based on his or her diagnostic label. During the process of initial assessment, the teacher will have plenty of opportunity to determine both needs and abilities. Even beyond this time, the teacher, along with the other members of the planning team, should consider the appropriateness of teaching academic skills and the nature of the skills to be taught.

The most important academic skills will be those that will allow the student to function and enjoy life more in the environments in which he or she participates. The words, sentences, signs, menus, directions, or books the student should learn to read should be determined in this way. So should writing needs and money-handling and time-telling skills. When these determinations are made, fun and leisure should be considered just as should functional and work activities. Traditional academic skills can bring pleasure to life and students should be taught with that in mind.

Questions for Reflection

1. What feelings or concerns might parents of children with moderate mental disabilities have about academic instruction?
2. How could academic instruction affect inclusion in the regular classroom?
3. Describe some important "nonfunctional" academic instructional objectives.
4. What factors should be considered when developing the reading material for a student with moderate mental disabilities?
5. What are some ways in which a student with moderate mental disabilities can participate in a classroom in which whole language is used? What are some "academic" and some "nonacademic" ways?

6. Why do you think more teachers have used a skills-based approach rather than a whole-language approach with students with moderate mental disabilities?
7. How can a person's quality of life be affected by basic arithmetic skills?
8. How do you believe most students with moderate mental disabilities feel about receiving academic instruction?

References

Altwerger, B., Edelsky, C., & Flores, B. M. (1987). Whole language: What's new? *The Reading Teacher, 40,* 144–154.

Au, K., Scheu, J. A., Kawakami, A. J., & Herman, P. A. (1990). Assessment and accountability in whole literacy curriculum. *The Reading Teacher, 43,* 574–578.

Ault, M. J., Gast, D. L., & Wolery, M. (1988). Comparison of progressive and constant time delay procedures in teaching community-sign word reading. *American Journal of Mental Retardation, 93,* 44–56.

Baroody, A. J. (1987). Problem size and mentally retarded children's judgment of commutativity. *American Journal of Mental Deficiency, 91*(4), 439–442.

Baroody, A. J. (1988). Number comparison learning by children classified as mentally retarded. *American Journal on Mental Retardation, 92,* 461–471.

Baroody, A. J., & Snyder, P. M. (1983). A cognitive analysis of basic arithmetic skills of TMR children. *Education and Training of the Mentally Retarded, 18*(4), 253–259.

Barudin, S. I., & Hourcade, J. J. (1990). Relative effectiveness of three methods of reading instruction in developing specific recall and transfer skills in learners with moderate and severe mental retardation. *Education and Training in Mental Retardation, 21,* 286–291.

Bear, D. R., & Cheney, C. O. (1991). Literacy education: An integrated approach for teaching students with handicaps. *Intervention in School and Clinic, 26,* 221–226.

Bellamy, T., & Buttars, K. L. (1975). Teaching trainable level retarded students to count money. *Education and Training of the Mentally Retarded, 10,* 18–26.

Borakove, L. S., & Cuvo, A. J. (1976). Facilitative effects of coin displacement on teaching coin summation to mentally retarded adolescents. *American Journal of Mental Deficiency, 81,* 350–356.

Bracey, S., Maggs, A., & Morath, P. (1975). The effects of a direct phonics approach in teaching reading with six moderately retarded children: Acquisition and mastery learning stages. *Exceptional Child, 22*(2), 83–90.

Browder, D. M., Hines, C., McCarthy, L. J., & Fees, J. (1984). A treatment package for increasing sight word recognition for use in daily living skills. *Education and Training of the Mentally Retarded, 19,* 191–200.

Browder, D. M., & Snell, M. E. (1993). Functional academics. In M. E. Snell (Ed.), *Instruction of students with severe disabilities* (4th ed.) (pp. 442-479). New York: Merrill/Macmillan.

Brown, L., Jones, S., Troccolo, E., Heiser, C., Bellamy, T., & Sontag, E. (1972). Teaching functional reading to young trainable students: Toward longitudinal objectives. *Journal of Special Education, 6,* 51–56.

Brown, L., & Perlmutter, L. (1971). Teaching functional reading to trainable level retarded students. *Education and Training of the Mentally Retarded, 6,* 74–84.

Cain, S. E. (1990). Sciencing: *An involvement approach to elementary science methods.* New York: Macmillan.

Calhoun, M. L. (1985). Typing contrasted with handwriting in language arts instruction for moderately mentally retarded students. *Education and Training of the Mentally Retarded, 20,* 48–52.

Caycho, L., Gunn, P., & Siegal, M. (1991). Counting by children with Down syndrome. *American Journal on Mental Retardation, 95*(5), 575–583.

Choate, J. S., Enright, B. E., Miller, L. J., Poteet, J. A., & Rakes, T. A. (1992). *Curriculum-based assessment and programming* (2nd ed.). Boston: Allyn & Bacon.

Conners, F. A. (1992). Reading instruction for students with moderate mental retardation: Review and analysis of research. *American Journal on Mental Retardation, 96*(6), 577–597.

Cuvo, A. J., & Klatt, K. P. (1992). Effects of community-based, videotape, and flash card instruction of community-referenced sight words on students with mental retardation. *Journal of Applied Behavior Analysis, 25*(2), 499–512.

Cuvo, A. J., Veitch, V. D., Trace, M. W., & Konke, J. L. (1978). Teaching change computation to the mentally retarded. *Behavior Modification, 2,* 531–548.

Dolch, E. W. (1950). *Teaching primary reading* (2nd ed.). Champaign, IL: Garrard Press.

Domnie, M., & Brown, L. (1977). Teaching severely handicapped students reading skills requiring printed answers to who, what and where questions. *Education and Training of the Mentally Retarded, 12*(4), 324–331.

Dorry, G. W., & Zeaman, D. (1973). The use of a fading technique in paired-associate reading vocabulary with retardates. *Mental Retardation, 11*(6), 3–6.

Dorry, G. W., & Zeaman, D. (1975). Teaching a simple reading vocabulary to retarded children: Effectiveness of fading and non-fading procedures. *American Journal of Mental Deficiency, 79,* 711–716.

Edmark Reading Program. (1972, 1984). Seattle: Edmark.

Engelmann, S., & Bruner, E. C. (1974). *DISTAR reading: An instructional system.* Chicago: Scientific Research Associates.

Enright, B. E. (1989). *Basic mathematics: Detecting and correcting special needs.* Boston: Allyn & Bacon.

Entriken, D., York, R., & Brown, L. (1977). Teaching trainable level multiply handicapped students to use picture cues, context cues, and initial consonant sounds to determine the labels of unknown words. *AAESPH Review, 2,* 169–190.

Feinberg, P. (1975). Sight vocabulary for the TMR child and adult: Rationale, development, and application. *Education and Training of the Mentally Retarded, 10*(4), 246–251.

Flexer, R. (1989). Conceptualizing addition. *Teaching Exceptional Children, 21*(4), 21–24.

Ford, A., & Davern, L. (1989). Moving forward with school integration: Strategies for involving students with severe handicaps in the life of the school. In R. Gaylord-Ross (Ed.), *Integration strategies for students with handicaps* (pp. 11–31), Baltimore: Paul H. Brookes.

Ford, A., Schnorr, R., Meyer, L., Davern, L., Black, J., & Dempsey, P. (1989). *The Syracuse community-referenced curriculum guide for students with moderate and severe disabilities.* Baltimore: Paul H. Brookes.

Frank, A. R. (1978). Teaching money skills with a number line. *Teaching Exceptional Children, 10*(2), 46–47.

Fry, E. (1957). Developing a word list for remedial reading. *Elementary English, 33,* 456–458.

Fry, E. (1972). *Reading instruction for classroom and clinic.* New York: McGraw-Hill.

Gast, D. L., Ault, M. J., Wolery, M., Doyle, P. M., & Belanger, S. (1988). Comparison of constant time delay and the system of least prompts in teaching sight word reading to students with moderate retardation. *Education and Training in Mental Retardation, 25,* 117–128.

Gersten, R. M., & Maggs, A. (1982). Teaching the general case to moderately retarded children: Evaluation of a five year project. *Analysis and Intervention in Developmental Disabilities, 2,* 329–343.

Giangreco, M. F., & Putnam, J. W. (1991). Supporting the education of students with severe disabilities in regular education environments. In L. H. Meyer, C. A. Peck, & L. Brown (Eds.), *Critical issues in the lives of people with severe disabilities* (pp. 245–270). Baltimore: Paul H. Brookes.

Hamre-Nietupski, S., Nietupski, J., & Strathe, M. (1992). Functional life skills, academic skills, and friendship/social relationship development: What do parents of students with moderate/severe/profound disabilities value? *Journal of the Association for Persons with Severe Handicaps, 17*(1), 53–58.

Holdaway, D. (1986). The structure of natural learning as a basis for literacy instruction. In M. R. Sampson (Ed.), *The pursuit of literacy: Early reading and writing.* Dubuque, IA: Kendall/Hunt Publishing Co.

Hoogeveen, F. R., & Smeets, P. M. (1988). Establishing phoneme blending in trainable mentally retarded children. *Remedial and Special Education, 9*(2), 46–53.

Hoogeveen, F. R., Smeets, P. M., & Lancioni, G. E. (1989). Teaching moderately retarded children basic reading skills. *Research in Developmental Disabilities, 10,* 1–18.

Hoogeveen, F. R., Smeets, P. M., & Van der Houven, J. E. (1987). Establishing letter-sound correspondence in children classified as trainable mentally retarded. *Education and Training in Mental Retardation, 22*(2), 77–84.

Horton, S. (1985). Computational rates of educable mentally retarded adolescents with and without calculators in comparison to normals. *Education and Training of the Mentally Retarded, 20,* 14–24.

House, B. J., Hanley, M. J., & Magid, D. F. (1980). Logographic reading by TMR adults. *American Journal of Mental Deficiency, 85,* 161–170.

Johnson, D. W., & Johnson, R. T. (1986). Mainstreaming and cooperative learning strategies. *Exceptional Children, 52*(6), 553–561.

Johnson, D. W., & Johnson, R. T. (1989). Cooperative learning and mainstreaming. In R. Gaylord-Ross (Ed.), *Integration strategies for students with handicaps* (pp. 233–248). Baltimore: Paul H. Brookes.

Kirk, S. A. (1972). *Educating exceptional children* (2nd ed.). Boston: Houghton Mifflin.

Koller, E. Z., & Mulhern, T. J. (1977). Use of a pocket calculator to train arithmetic skills with trainable adolescents. *Education and Training of the Mentally Retarded, 12*(4), 332–335.

Koury, M., & Browder, D. M. (1986). The use of delay to teach sight words by peer tutors classified as moderately mentally retarded. *Education and Training of the Mentally Retarded, 21,* 252–258.

Lowe, M. L., & Cuvo, A. J. (1976). Teaching coin summation to the mentally retarded. *Journal of Applied Behavior Analysis, 9,* 483–489.

Manning, M. M., Manning, G. L., Long, R., & Wolfson, B. J. (1987). *Reading and writing in the primary grades: A whole-language view.* Washington, DC: National Education Association.

Mastropieri, M. A., Bakken, J. P., & Scruggs, T. E. (1991). Mathematics instruction for people with mental retardation: A perspective and research synthesis. *Education and Training in Mental Retardation, 26*(2), 115–129

Mather, N., & Lachowicz, B. L. (1992). Shared writing: An instructional approach for reluctant writers. *Teaching Exceptional Children, 25*(1), 26–30.

Matson, J. L., & Long, S. (1986). Teaching computation/shopping skills to mentally retarded adults. *American Journal of Mental Deficiency, 91,* 98–101.

McKenna, M. C., Robinson, R. D., & Miller, J. W. (1990). Whole language: A research agenda for the nineties. *Educational Researcher, 18*(8), 3–6.

Miller, A., & Miller, E. E. (1968). Symbol accentuation: The perceptual transfer of meaning from spoken to printed words. *American Journal of Mental Deficiency, 73,* 200–208.

Miller, A., & Miller, E. E. (1971). Symbol accentuation, single-track functioning, and early reading. *American Journal of Mental Deficiency, 76,* 110–117.

Mirenda, P. (1992). *Literacy instruction for persons with severe disabilities.* Paper presented at the Conference of the Association for Persons with Severe Handicaps. San Francisco.

Nietupski, J., Williams, W., & York, R. (1979). Teaching selected phonic word analysis skills to TMR labeled students. *Teaching Exceptional Children, 11*(4), 140–143.

Paddock, C. (1992). Ice cream stick math. *Teaching Exceptional Children, 24*(2), 50–51.

Putnam, J. W., Rynders, J. E., Johnson, R. T., & Johnson, D. W. (1989). Collaborative skill instruction for promoting positive interactions between mentally handicapped and nonhandicapped children. *Exceptional Children, 55*(6), 550–557.

Rakes, T. A., & Choate, J. S. (1989). *Language arts: Detecting and correcting special needs.* Boston: Allyn & Bacon.

Roberson, W. H., Gravel, J. S., Valcante, G. C., & Maurer, R. G. (1992). Using a picture task analysis to teach students with multiple disabilities. *Teaching Exceptional Children, 24*(4), 12–15.

Rynders, J. E., & Horrobin, J. M. (1990). Always trainable? Never educable? Updating education expectations of children with Down syndrome. *American Journal on Mental Retardation, 95,* 77–83.

Singh, J., & Singh, N. N. (1985). Comparison of word-supply and word-analysis error correction procedures on oral reading by mentally retarded children. *American Journal of Mental Deficiency, 90,* 64–70.

Singh, N. N., & Singh, J. (1984). Antecedent control of oral reading errors and self-corrections by mentally retarded children. *Journal of Applied Behavior Analysis, 17,* 111–119.

Singh, N. N., & Singh, J. (1988). Increasing oral reading proficiency through overcorrection and phonic analysis. *American Journal on Mental Retardation, 93,* 312–319.

Singh, N. N., & Solman, R. T. (1990). A stimulus control analysis of the picture-word problem in children who are mentally retarded: The blocking effect. *Journal of Applied Behavior Analysis, 23,* 525–532.

Smeets, P. M., Van Lieshout, R. W., Lancioni, G. E., & Striefel, S. (1986). Teaching mentally retarded students to tell time. *Analysis and Intervention in Developmental Disabilities, 6,* 221–238.

Smith, L. J., & Smith, D. L. (1990). *Social science: Detecting and correcting special needs.* Boston: Allyn & Bacon.

Stahl, S. A., & Miller, P. D. (1989). Whole language and language experience approaches for beginning reading: A quantitative research synthesis. *Review of Educational Research, 59,* 87–116.

Vacc, N. N., & Vacc, N. A. (1979). Teaching manuscript writing to mentally retarded children. *Education and Training of the Mentally Retarded* (Dec.), 286–291.

Walberg, H. J., & Wang, M. C. (1987). Effective educational practices and provisions for individual differences. In M. C. Wang, M. C. Reynolds, & H. J. Walberg (Eds.), *Handbook of special education: Research and practice* (pp. 113–128). New York: Pergamon.

Walsh, B. F., & Lambert, F. (1979). Errorless discrimination and picture fading as techniques for teaching sight words to TMR students. *American Journal of Mental Deficiency, 83,* 473–479.

Watson, D. J. (1989). Defining and describing whole language. *The Elementary School Journal, 90,* 129–141.

Worrall, N., & Singh, Y. (1983). Teaching TMR children to read using integrated picture cuing. *American Journal of Mental Deficiency, 87,* 422–429.

CHAPTER 17

Teaching Community and Domestic Skills

Chapter Overview

Several considerations about teaching skills for functioning in community and home settings are discussed in this chapter. Specific methods are presented for teaching skills for operating in grocery stores and restaurants, for using vending machines, for teaching pedestrian skills and using public transportation, for preparing food, for completing different household chores, and for using a telephone.

There are many functional life activities that are learned incidentally by most people. Shopping for clothes and groceries, using buses and laundromats, preparing meals, and making phone calls are a few examples. We generally do not take courses or receive formal instruction on how to perform the tasks and subtasks incorporated in these activities, but learn them through less formal experiences. As we learn them, we learn to apply basic skills such as language, reading, writing, arithmetic, and appropriate social behavior. Most of the time we acquire these skills by accompanying and observing parents, siblings, relatives, or friends as they perform the tasks in home and community settings.

For several reasons, however, persons with severe disabilities do not learn skills of this kind to a level commensurate with their age in the same informal ways as many others (Brown et al., 1983). Obviously, cognitive limitations interfere with the ability to attain information, synthesize it, remember it, and use it correctly in appropriate settings. Further, as discussed in chapter 7, generalization of skills is also a problem, meaning that even if students learn skills in one setting, they may have difficulty using them in another. These problems are multiplied by the fact that the tasks are often relatively complex, requiring the student to complete many steps in a functional order. Because of these conditions, direct instruction in nonschool settings is often necessary if students with severe disabilities are going to learn domestic and community skills. Traditional classroom instruction in these areas is insufficient in most cases to ensure that the skills will be used and learned.

Why Teach Community and Domestic Skills?

What we teach individuals with severe disabilities is largely influenced by the normalization principle (Nirje, 1969; Wolfensberger, 1972), and people normally spend a great deal of time functioning in their home and in different community settings (Aveno, 1987; Falvey, 1989; Snell & Browder, 1986). Because many people with severe disabilities do not learn community and domestic skills in an incidental way, there is a need to teach these skills directly and intentionally. Community and domestic skills allow people to function more normally in their world. The more a person can operate in his or her home and community, the greater freedom he or she has. Individuals who lack the ability to travel in their neighborhoods or towns and use their community facilities are destined to have rather dull, routine lives, often limited to remaining at home and in their own yards (Stanfield, 1973). Fortunately, this does not have to be the case. Research has clearly demonstrated that if adequate instruction is provided, many individuals with severe disabilities can learn a wide variety of the functional skills necessary for successful operation in home and community environments (Snell & Browder, 1986; Westling & Floyd, 1990).

General Procedures Related to Teaching Community and Domestic Skills

Several procedural matters that must be considered in order to provide community and domestic instruction are discussed in the next several sections.

Who Should Participate in Community and Domestic Instruction?

Students who are not incidentally acquiring chronological age-appropriate community and domestic skills are usually good candidates for community instruction. Most of the time this group consists of older students in the middle school or high school years, but younger students may also participate if parents and collaborative team members feel it would be beneficial for them to do so. Particularly during the elementary school years, however, it is more desirable for students to spend their time with their peers in typical school activities instead of in nonschool instruction. If elementary-age students are to be taught community skills, the nature and degree of their community instruction should be appropriate for their age. For example, 8-year-olds do not usually shop for groceries, but they may go with older siblings to the movies, and so the necessary skills for this type of community participation could be targeted for instruction.

Partial Participation

Students should not be eliminated from community-based instruction (CBI) because of the severity of their disability, but should have instructional targets identified that will allow them to increase their participation. Everyone has the right to be as active as possible in home and community settings, including people with very severe (i.e., profound) mental disabilities and multiple disabilities. There are many ways to participate partially but meaningfully in community settings (see chapter 6). Although most research on community instruction has ignored the inclusion of these individuals (Snell & Browder, 1986; Westling & Floyd, 1990), there are various ways they may participate in community and domestic activities. Helmstetter (1989) stressed three points about the involvement of individuals with the most severe disabilities in community activities:

- There should be emphasis on partial participation as opposed to no participation at all. For example, a student who cannot perform all of the steps necessary to operate a vending machine may be able to press a button to make a selection.
- Various adaptations to material and equipment may be made to allow for partial participation. For example, a student who might have difficulty changing the television station at home could have all of the remote-control buttons covered except for the one to change the channel. Although the student has poor motor control, he or she can still participate

meaningfully by having better control over channel selection.

- Participation in various community activities can give parents and teachers information about a student's preference for different environments. By watching facial reactions, body tone, and behavioral reactions, an observer can draw inferences about a student's likes and dislikes. This information can then be used to determine in which environments and activities the student would like to participate.

Where to Teach Community and Domestic Skills

Given the learning characteristics of students with severe disabilities, it should be understood that much of the instruction of skills appropriate for application in homes and community settings must be directly instructed in those settings. Students with severe disabilities are taught certain skills in actual settings in order to increase the probability that they will learn and be able to demonstrate those skills in natural contexts and in response to natural cues. School-based instruction on community skills, even in well-designed simulations, generally has not been found to be effective when tests for generalization to community settings have been conducted. The literature has reported successful community-based instruction occurring in restaurants, grocery stores, department stores, banks, and various recreational settings, and in teaching students to use vending machines, automatic banking machines, public transportation, and safe pedestrian skills (Westling & Floyd, 1990). These and similar settings in individual communities are primary settings for instruction.

Likewise, instructional programs have been developed for teaching students to function adequately in their homes. However, teaching students in their actual homes may present more difficulty than does teaching in community settings because of several important distinctions. First, the community settings in which students are taught are open to the public and there are generally few or no limitations on teaching students with severe disabilities in them (Aveno, Renzaglia, & Lively, 1987). On the other hand, parents of students with severe disabilities may not care for the idea of teachers coming into their home to teach domestic skills to their children, even though they may consider the skills important. This issue may be raised in sessions with parents, but teachers should not usually expect that parents will want them to teach in their homes.

Second, even if doing so were possible, it would not necessarily be a good idea to teach individuals in their parents' private homes. Since out-of-school instruction generally takes place in small groups, working in the home of a particular student requires the other students to learn in environments not natural to them. This would likely reduce the effectiveness of instruction because it would not necessarily generalize to their own home.

Third, at the age when it is becoming increasingly important for students to acquire domestic skills—during adolescence—students are usually getting closer to the day when they will move away from their parents' home into a supported apartment setting, a group home, or some other type of shared residence. In this setting, the washing machines, stoves, bathrooms, and so on may be different from those found in the student's current home. Therefore, even if teaching skills at home were possible, they might not generalize well to the individual's postschool residence.

For these reasons, the most logical place to teach domestic skills might be the high school home economics classroom or perhaps the cafeteria, although they are not natural environments. For many students, it is possible to teach these skills when they are participating in regular home economics classes, given the understanding that their instructional goals are different. In this setting, the special educator and the general educator can work together to ensure that students are learning domestic skills as indicated by their individual educational plan.

One alternative to providing domestic instruction in the regular school setting would be to provide training for domestic skills in actual apartments or homes specifically developed for such training (Freagon et al., 1983; Livi & Ford, 1985). Freagon and her colleagues described a home site that was designed to teach domestic skills to students with severe disabilities who were between the ages of 18 and 21. Students learned various chores associated with independent living and took turns staying over on three successive long weekends in order to learn independent living skills. The program served up to 20 students a year and was judged very successful for preparing students for natural home environments.

The setting and learning activities described by Livi and Ford (1985) were similar. An important finding by Livi and Ford, however, was that the skills learned in their nonschool Domestic Training Site (DTS) did not generalize well to the students' own homes until the stimulus conditions within the DTS were modified to be more similar to those found in the homes. Besides this problem with generalization, there are two additional drawbacks to a nonschool site developed explicitly for teaching domestic skills to students with severe disabilities. First, it segregates them from their nondisabled peers. Second, it must be financed by someone, and typically most school districts cannot be expected to fund such a site. Therefore, if there is an appropriate setting in the school such as a home economics classroom, it may be the best place to teach domestic skills. Some teachers have taken their students to their own homes or apartments, but such decisions have to be individually made and sanctioned by the school district.

Determining Target Sites and Skills

Community and domestic sites and related skills should be individually targeted for instruction, using the procedures described in chapter 5. Most important, parents should be interviewed and the entire collaborative team should be involved in determining which settings and which skills are most appropriate for individual students. Although it has been found that persons with severe disabilities participate in a range of home and community activities (Aveno, 1987), teachers should expect a great deal of variability in what students need to learn and where they need to learn it. It should not be assumed that there is a universal set of community and domestic skills that students must learn. Professionals should discuss with parents, the student, and other family members what community sites are important for instruction.

Determining Operational Skills to Be Taught

After determining instructional target sites, the teacher must visit the community and domestic settings where instruction is to take place to conduct an analysis, or ecological inventory, of what skills must be learned in the setting (see chapter 5). The operational skills (those that are basic to the completion of the task) that will be targeted should be specific to the settings in which the skills are taught. The teacher should observe nondisabled individuals in the setting, "walk through" the activity the student is expected to learn, and write the steps down in the appropriate sequence, which should include both operational skills and associated skills (see below) clustered together. Task analyses or functional routines (see chapter 6) should be written as guides for instructional activities (Snell & Browder, 1986).

In at least two cases, a full list of operational skills will not be an appropriate instructional goal. First, as discussed previously, individuals with the most severe disabilities should have learning goals individually determined that will allow them to participate in functional and meaningful ways. Second, young children should have goals that are designed for them based on their chronological age. Usually these do not consist of completing major functions typical of adults, but are roles appropriate for children.

Determining Associated Skills to Be Taught

In addition to the skills required for completing a specific task in a community setting (i.e., operational skills), teachers, parents, and other team members should target related or associated skills for instruction in the setting. Language skills, social skills, physical skills, and academic skills that are a part of the student's instructional needs should be incorporated into skill clusters that are to be taught, thus forming a functional routine. For example, Westling, Floyd, and Carr (1990) focused on both operational skills and social skills when teaching adolescents with moderate and severe mental disabilities to shop in a department store. These skills are listed in Figure 17–1.

Responds appropriately to accidents.
Asks for help when necessary.
Says "thanks" when assistance is provided.
Waits turn at checkout counter.
Greets cashier appropriately.
Says good-bye appropriately.

Figure 17–1
Social Skills Taught as Part of Department Store Shopping
Adapted from "Effect of Single Setting Versus Multiple Setting Training on Learning to Shop in a Department Store" by D. L. Westling, J. Floyd, & D. Carr, 1990, *American Journal on Mental Deficiency, 94,* pp. 616–624. Copyright 1990 by the American Association on Mental Retardation. Reprinted by permission.

Developing Instructional Plans

Each group or cluster of skills to be taught requires an instructional procedure that will result in skill acquisition and generalization. Most instruction in community settings calls for teaching the whole skill sequence during each instructional episode as opposed to teaching isolated skills (Snell & Browder, 1986). As indicated above, the first step in an instructional plan is to develop the task analysis or functional routine, including both operational and associated behaviors (see chapter 6). After the components of the task have been written, the teacher must determine the natural cues that will be present in the environment that the student must learn to attend to in order to complete each part of the task. Additionally, the teacher must determine the instructional prompts that he or she will present when the student does not respond to the natural cues. A system of least prompts or time delay (see chapter 6) will often be effective (Snell & Browder, 1986).

Regardless of the prompting system used, it is most important that the teacher reference the student to the natural cues in the environment in order that these stimuli, and not the prompts provided by the teacher, will ultimately become the cue for the student's behavior (Ford & Mirenda, 1984). For example, using constant time delay, the teacher places the student at a certain location in the setting where the available cues call for a particular action (e.g., being in front of an empty washing machine in a laundromat with a load of dirty clothes should adequately prompt the student to put the clothes in the washing machine). During an initial instructional phase, the teacher points out the student's location and all of the key aspects of the environment and demonstrates what the student is expected to do. On subsequent occasions, once in the environment, the teacher waits a brief period of time before using instructional prompts in order to allow the natural stimuli to have an effect.

Planning for Skill Generalization

Most of the time it will be necessary for the student to learn generalizable community skills, meaning that he or she can apply the skills in different community settings or in a variety of circumstances. Strategies for achieving skill generalization are discussed in chapter 7. Although some researchers have reported students learning to generalize without specific training to do so, most of the time spontaneous generalization does not occur (Westling & Floyd, 1990). This being so, teachers usually need to devise instructional strategies to help achieve generalization. The most effective approach identified to date is the general case method, which is discussed in chapter 7. Its application in teaching community skills consists of identifying all of the specific community settings of a particular type in which the student might need to operate and then training him or her to operate in a sufficient number of the settings that reflect the range of discriminative stimuli and responses necessary to perform in any setting.

While skill generalization is often an important instructional goal, in some cases of instruction for community participation, it may not be. For example, quality of life may be quite good even though an individual learns to use only one bank or check out movies from only one video store. This, in fact, is often the case among individuals who do not have severe disabilities. The assessment and planning procedures discussed in chapters 4 and 5 will help determine how much generalization of community skills is necessary (Westling & Floyd, 1990).

Implementing Instruction in Community Settings

Teaching students in community settings is often considered by teachers to be more interesting and stimulating than teaching in traditional school settings because it is easier for them to see the relevance of the instruction and the direct benefit of students learning relevant skills (Westling & Fleck, 1991). However, providing instruction in nonschool settings requires some special considerations.

Teacher-Student Interactions When teaching in community settings, the style of interaction with students must be somewhat different from that normally used in schools. Most important, the teacher should interact as naturally as possible so that both students and teacher fit normally and unobtrusively into the setting. Verbal directions should be made in conversational tones, reinforcement should be very subtle, and correction of incorrect or inappropriate behavior should not be loud or harsh.

Instruction should follow the written sequence of skills and utilize the instructional tactic or tactics that have been decided upon (e.g., time delay or system of least prompts). Again, for most students, it is important that the teacher work toward ultimately allowing natural environmental cues to control the occurrence of the behaviors and eliminating the delivery of verbal, visual, or physical prompts. When the student no longer requires artificial prompts to complete the skill sequence in the community, the teacher should begin to gradually fade his or her presence. This can be accomplished, for example, by slowly increasing the distance that the teacher is following along behind the student. This type of action is important because the student needs to learn to adequately complete the task without the teacher's presence and, by doing so, become more self-reliant.

Number of Students per Instructional Session Teachers should limit the number of students being instructed in community settings to two or three per session for several reasons. First, of course, objectives for students must be individually determined. It is unlikely that more than a few students will need to learn the same skills in the same setting. Generally, it would be inappropriate to take students to a community setting for instruction if the setting had not been identified through the process assessment and planning as one in which instruction should occur. Students going en masse to community settings simply for the sake of going somewhere off campus are actually taking a field trip, and while field trips have benefits, they should not be confused with providing true community-based instruction.

Second, it is important to limit the number of students in order to avoid negative attention that might be drawn to a large group of students with disabilities. Gathering many individuals with severe disabilities together in one place often results in attitudes of pity and patronization, which is most certainly an undesirable outcome. People working in and using community settings are not likely to arrive at conclusions of individual competence and ability if a large group consisting only of individuals with disabilities comes into the place and proceeds through it in a haphazard fashion. Learning in community settings by individuals without disabilities, which as stated earlier is generally incidental, usually occurs in small natural groups, for example, a parent and a child, an adult and a few children, or a small group of preadolescents or adolescents. A small group in most community settings looks natural, is likely to receive a more natural response, and therefore should be the grouping pattern of choice when teaching students with severe disabilities.

How Often to Provide Instruction The schedule of community instruction should allow the students to be in the settings two or three times per week, at least when the skill is being initially learned. This should provide adequate opportunity for them to learn target skills without forgetting them from one visit to another. After the skill is learned, trips to the community setting might be reduced to a level that is relatively natural for the setting, as long as the frequency of visits is adequate for the skill to be retained by the student. It would never be advisable to visit one type of community setting for a certain period of time, say 6 to 9 weeks, stop the visits, then begin to visit other settings. In other words, sometimes teachers might want to approach community-based instruction using a "units of instruction" or "thematic" approach (i.e., "This six weeks we will be visiting banks because we are doing a unit on banking. During the next six weeks we will visit shoe stores."). This is not how people normally use community settings, nor is it how they learn to use them. Therefore this approach to community-based instruction should give way to more natural schedules of visits.

Using Prosthetic Aids Sometimes students with disabilities can learn to be more independent in community settings by using prosthetic devices that help them accomplish certain skills that otherwise would be too difficult or would take a long time to learn. Many individuals without disabilities also use these types of devices, for example, many people use shopping lists to help them remember what they need to buy at the grocery store.

Certainly these types of devices and others can also be useful for persons with severe disabilities as can others. In chapter 16 number-lines, coin cards, and calculators were described to assist students in making purchases during shopping routines. Figure 17–2 lists some additional devices that may be helpful for some students with disabilities.

Using Simulated Community Settings in Schools

Over the years many teachers have attempted to teach functional community-referenced skills to students with severe disabilities by creating simulations of community settings in their classrooms. For example, teachers might create a "make believe" bus for students to learn to ride or a grocery store for them to shop in. Although the intentions are good, most research does not support the use of simulated settings as effective approaches when used alone (Westling & Floyd, 1990).

If simulations are to be effective, at least two conditions must exist. First, the simulations must contain stimuli very close to that which students must learn to respond to in actual community settings. This may be done by bringing real items into the classroom or using slides projected on the wall to create life-size simulations. If the material does not re-create the cues that exist in the natural environment, it is not very likely to be effective.

The second condition is that training in simulated conditions has a chance of being effective only if it is paired with training in the actual settings. Teachers may find that instruction that is alternated between actual community settings and school-based simulations may

- Written list of items to buy.
- Picture list of items to buy.
- Prewritten messages on card to store employees: "I would like to buy____."
- Clock/watch faces drawn on cards with indications when to come, go, leave, stay, etc.
- Picture list of activities to complete (task analysis) within a setting.
- Card stating learner's name, school, home address, and phone number.
- Prerecorded messages for store employees stating what is desired.
- Money cards showing different amounts required for different purchases.
- Number lines and/or calculators.

Figure 17–2
Devices That Can Help in Community Learning Settings

be an effective instructional practice. Again, though, the importance of the simulation clearly representing the real environment should not be ignored.

In some cases, teachers create simulations of parts of the nonschool environment so that a specific set of skills may be taught and then practiced in the community setting. This can be especially useful if the skill is one a student is having particular difficulty with and/or one that may be improved with massed practice. It can also be useful if the specific part of the community setting environment is one that the student could not use very frequently in the actual community for one reason or another. For example, a grocery store checkout line complete with a cash register and racks of tabloid newspapers may be placed in the classroom to teach the steps required for checking out of the grocery store (McDonnell, Horner, & Williams, 1984). Another example would be creating a simulated Automatic Teller Machine (ATM) to teach the tasks required for taking money out of an account (Shafer, Inge, & Hill, 1986). Obviously, because it is not easy for students to get a great deal of practice in these types of unique settings, well-developed simulations may be useful. Again, however, adequate community training cannot rely solely on simulations; actual community-based site training will always be necessary.

Providing Concurrent Instruction in School

In addition to simulations, other classroom-based instruction might help students achieve in community settings. Verbal instructions as to how to perform in the community settings and role-playing have been shown to contribute to community-based learning (Aeschleman & Schladenhauffen, 1984). Another tactic may be the use of modeling to show students what to do in particular settings. One way to do this is through the use of videotapes of people without disabilities performing the targeted task in the actual community setting, which could then be followed up by role-playing and, of course, by training in the actual community setting (Haring, Kennedy, Adams, & Pitts-Conway, 1987).

Most important, the skills to be learned in the community sometimes require (or are enhanced by) academic skills and when this is the case, instruction in these skills should occur at school. Since such skills and related instructional practices were discussed in the previous chapter, they will not be repeated here.

Evaluating Community Skills

When community skills are identified for instruction, including the desired degree of generalization, the "criterion of ultimate performance" should be determined. For some students, particularly younger students and those with more severe disabilities, total completion of a particular task may not be appropriate or possible. In these cases participation based on chronological age expectations or meaningful partial participation may be the ultimate goal. For many students, however, particularly those who are older, the goal will often be for them to perform the community-based task independently.

Using the data collection procedures described in chapter 8, the teacher should monitor and record the student's performance on a frequent basis. As previously discussed, this will allow the teacher to make necessary adjustments in the instructional process if adequate progress is not being made. When the student reaches the desired criterion, the teacher should reduce the frequency of instruction and instead provide adequate practice so that the skill will be retained.

For students whose performance criterion is complete independence on a task, either in one setting or generalized to several settings, it will be necessary that the skills be tested without the student receiving any assistance or support. For these students, as stated previously, it is very important that the teacher gradually fade all instructional prompts so that the student learns to complete the task alone and without assistance.

Ultimately the teacher should devise a means whereby the student can be unknowingly observed by someone the student does not know. The purpose of this secret observation is not to spy on the student, but to determine if the task can be undertaken without the presence or assistance of the teacher or another support person. This type of assessment should take place in all settings in which independent performance is desired.

Securing Adequate Funds for Community Instruction

One problem that is often related to providing community instruction is the availability of money for learning to ride the bus, buying various items, eating in restaurants, and so forth. When teachers intend to initiate community instruction, they must consider where the money will come from.

Undoubtedly the most legitimate source of money is the school or the school district. The instructional goals the students will be working to achieve are of consequence and will have been identified by parents and members of the planning team as important for students to learn. Schools should have in their budgets adequate funds to support community-based instruction. To offset this cost, teachers and school administrators should realize that many traditional instructional materials are simply inappropriate and money should not be wasted on them.

Unfortunately, there may not be money in the budget for community-based instruction and, even if there is, it may not be enough. Alternative or supplemental funds will sometimes be needed. One source of these funds is through traditional school fund-raising activities (car washes, bake sales), but this is not generally recommended for two reasons. First, it is easy for this type of event to turn into a "help the handicapped" charity event, and this is totally undesirable. Second, it casts community training as some type of extracurricular activity and, of course, this is not what it is.

A more appropriate alternative would be to use the family's money to shop for items that they would need anyway. Another would be to shop for teachers' needs from shopping lists they provide. Similarly, a shopping service could be provided for elderly individuals who have difficulty getting into the community as often as they would like. Of course, all of this would require coordination, but it may be a source of revenue that would provide some important learning experience.

Teaching Community and Domestic Skills in the Most Meaningful Way

When all of the different skills one may need in the community and the home are considered, we realize there is much that can be taught and learned. One way to approach this task is to avoid teaching skills in isolation but instead teach them in a way that is natural and that maximizes the effect of the instruction, that is, to teach related skills together. Teaching skills in this way means we look at them as they would normally occur over a day, a week, or several weeks.

Consider, for example, students who need to learn goals related to shopping, preparing food, cleaning up after a meal, using community transportation, crossing streets safely, and so forth. The teacher may find on the student's educational plan a list of goals to be met in each of these areas, but these goals may be approached in very different ways. The most desirable approach would be for the teacher to instruct the tasks so that they have some relation to each other. First plan the meal, prepare a shopping list, then decide where to shop, and learn about the public transportation that will take you there. The process continues until ultimately the students have had instruction directed at completing each goal, concluding with completing the meal and cleaning up afterward.

This approach is not suggested in order that school will become "fun" or "watered down" for students with severe disabilities, but instead so that environmental cues will have greater meaning and skills will be seen as relevant. If it happens that the experience is also enjoyable, so much the better.

In the following sections, learning to function in different settings and to use different skills will be discussed. It should be kept in mind that in practice, the preferred approach to instruction is one in which the activities are related in a meaningful and functional way.

Community Settings and Activities

Many of the possible settings in which community instruction may occur are listed in Figure 17–3 and some typical tasks that often require instruction in the community at large are suggested in Figure 17–4. Although it is understood that skills and settings must be individually determined, it may be expected that many of the settings listed in Figure 17–3 and the activities in Figure 17–4 will quite often be targets for instruction for students with severe disabilities. Of course, other settings and skills may also be appropriate for instruction depending on the student and the nature of the local community.

Community instruction also presents an important opportunity to teach students social skills. Acquisition and generalization of these skills will increase the acceptance of individuals with severe disabilities in various settings and help them function more appropriately in those settings. Some important skills many students will need to learn are listed in Figure 17–5.

Figure 17–3
Community Settings in Which Instruction May Occur

Grocery stores	Convenience stores
Department stores	Regular restaurants
Fast-food restaurants	Cafeteria restaurants
Public transportation	Vending machines
Pay telephones	Banks
Automatic tellers	Bowling alleys
Miniature golf	Pinball machines
Video games	Movie theaters
Theaters & concerts	Churches, synagogues, temples
Museums	Barber shops/hair salons
Public parks	Recreation centers
Doctors/Dentists	Post office
Public library	Skating rink
Public swimming pool	Club meetings (Scouts)
Sporting events	Friend's house

Crossing the street	Putting on seat belt
Paying for items	Telling time
Preparing shopping lists	

Figure 17–4
General Skills for Community Participation

Although it is not possible to address instructional practices appropriate for all community settings and skills, suggestions for teaching skills for four conditions are presented below: grocery stores, restaurants, vending machines, and pedestrian skills/public transportation. These are discussed because they have a relatively high frequency of use.

Grocery Stores

Many teachers have taught students with severe disabilities to shop in grocery stores and several researchers have documented some effective practices (Aeschleman & Schladenhauffen, 1984; Haring et al., 1987; Horner, Albin, & Ralph, 1986; Matson, 1981; Matson & Long, 1986; McDonnell et al., 1984; Nietupski, Welch, & Wacker, 1983; and Sarber, Halasz, Messmer, Bickett, & Lutzker, 1983). Most students who need to learn grocery shopping skills are adolescents or young adults. Some relevant suggestions for teaching students to shop in grocery stores are presented here.

Students need to prepare a shopping list or have one prepared for them before they enter the store. This list should consist of items desired by the student or parents and required for use in the home. Picture shopping lists that may be homemade or purchased commercially can be used for students who cannot read words. The student must carry an adequate amount of money and needs to know how to use a numberline or a calculator (as described in chapter 16) to determine if he or she has enough money to make the desired purchase.

The task analysis developed by the teacher will guide the student's activity through the store. Many of the previously listed references have task analyses that may serve as models, but the most appropriate one is individually designed. The task analysis calls for the student to enter the store, get a shopping cart, select the appropriate items as indicated by the list, go to the checkout line, pay for the groceries, and carry them out of the store. Details are listed depending on the student's needs. Along with the operational behaviors, the teacher probably needs to focus on social behaviors. This is true in grocery stores as well as in various other community settings. Figure 17–5 lists some of the more common social behaviors that may be important instructional targets; others may be developed by the planning team.

As discussed earlier, the natural cues in the setting need to be referenced by pointing them out to the student during the initial stages of the instructional process and then delaying instructional prompts so that the student learns to respond to the naturally present cues. For example, the shopping baskets at the entrance of the store should ultimately serve as the cue to take a basket and start searching for the first item. As the student enters different parts of the store, other cues can be pointed out.

Students do better if they are taught to shop in a systematic fashion, going up one aisle and down another and from one side of the store to the other. This helps them learn the location of items and ultimately decreases the amount of time required for shopping. Persons with the most severe disabilities may participate in grocery store shopping in several ways. As they go up and down aisles with parents, teachers, or cohorts they may indicate choices

Being wary of strangers	Requesting assistance from store employees
Greeting others appropriately	Ending conversations appropriately
Keeping appropriate distance when speaking	Not asking personal or embarrassing questions
Apologizing for mistakes	Refrain from inappropriate touching of others
Refrain from touching items not to be purchased	Waiting in line for turn
Controlling emotions/temper	Following community rules (e.g., "don't litter")
Sitting quietly when necessary	
Keeping appointments on time	
Earning and saving money	

Figure 17–5
Social Skills Appropriate for the Community

of items by looking at different products and pointing to them or reaching for them. Some individuals may be able to push a cart or drop items into it. When checking out, they may be able to place items on the counter and hand money or a credit card to the cashier (Helmstetter, 1989).

Several classroom activities may help the student improve his or her ability to shop in the grocery store. These include developing shopping lists based on household needs and menus; learning to match the pictures or words on the shopping list to the actual items; learning to read sight words found in grocery stores, particularly on signs that mark specific aisles; practicing money skills, using the calculator or the numberline system; scanning and selecting sale items in newspaper ads and cutting out appropriate coupons; and practicing the social skills that may be targeted for instruction in the grocery store.

Although, as stated, grocery shopping is an activity that is more important for older individuals, the planning team might receive input from parents that a younger child requires some instruction in this activity. When this is the case, the instructional targets need to be made age-appropriate. Typically, younger children "help" their parents as they take a shopping cart, select items, and so forth. It is quite likely that social behavior targets are important instructional objectives for younger children with disabilities, just as they are for young children without disabilities in grocery stores.

Restaurants

Today more than ever many people are routinely eating several meals a week in restaurants, and so these settings should be considered important community locations where individuals with severe disabilities must learn to function. Several studies have been conducted documenting effective instructional practices in restaurants (Marholin, O'Toole, Touchette, Berger, & Doyle, 1979; McDonnell & Ferguson, 1988; Storey, Bates, & Hanson, 1984; Van den Pol, Iwata, Ivancic, Page, Neef, & Whitley 1981).

Restaurants in which students need to learn to operate can vary, suggesting that the required skills will be different depending on the setting. Fast-food restaurants are different from traditional restaurants in which one sits down and orders food, and both are different from cafeteria-style restaurants. The specific type of restaurant in which the student needs to learn to function is best determined by the parent, and perhaps the student, through the planning process. It should be realized, however, that success in one particular type of restaurant does not necessarily mean the individual will know how to function in other types. Again, it will be important for the teacher to visit the particular restaurants in which skills will be taught and conduct task analyses.

In a traditional restaurant, the student must learn to enter, wait to be seated or select a seat (depending on the sign in the entry foyer), interact with a waiter or waitress, look at a menu, make a selection, place an order, eat the meal appropriately, ask for the check, leave a tip, pay the check at the cash register or through the waiter, and leave through an appropriate exit. In a fast-food restaurant, the student must wait in line to place an order, review the menu on the wall over the front counter, order when it is his or her turn, pay for the food, take the tray with the food to the table, eat appropriately, and finish by cleaning off the table and taking the wrappings and the tray to the receptacle. Cafeterias call for the patron to locate the end of the line moving through the food display area, select appropriate items from each food section, place the items carefully on the tray as they are delivered, pay for the items, and take the items to a table.

Some of these skills may be within the ability of students with more severe disabilities. If not, the student may still partially participate. Helmstetter (1989) suggested that students could learn to order by looking at pictures of foods held up by peers or by handing the waiter or counter attendant a picture of the desired food. Of course, there are many eating skills that the individual can work on in restaurants. A person with very severe disabilities may also participate by learning to use the restroom to wash up before eating and by paying the bill when leaving the restaurant.

Perhaps more than in other community settings, the display of appropriate social behavior is necessary in restaurants. Most important, students should learn to interact with hosts or hostesses, waiters and waitresses, meal companions, and other patrons in the restaurant. Students also need to learn suitable table manners, utensil usage, appropriate conversational voice levels, and other skills that will allow them to mix comfortably with other customers in the restaurant.

Instructional procedures for teaching operational and social behaviors for functioning in restaurants are like those described for grocery stores. Again, it is important for the teacher to fade instructional prompts so that the student learns to rely on the natural cues in the setting. Ultimately, for students whose goal is to acquire total independence, the teacher will need to arrange for the student to visit the restaurant independently and follow through on all aspects of the procedure, successfully consuming a meal without assistance.

Several concurrent school-based activities can help students learn to function in restaurants. Money skills are important, particularly in determining what items on a menu can be afforded and selecting the correct amount to pay for them. Reading menus or recognizing key food words can also be useful. For both restaurants and grocery stores, basic information on the nutritional value of different foods can be taught in the context of useful community skills. Many skills can be taught at breakfast time and lunch time in the school cafeteria: table manners, ordering food, carrying trays, paying for food, waiting in line, and others.

Although being able to use basic academic skills is helpful, many students who cannot do so can still learn to function adequately in restaurants by using some alternative skills.

For example, students who cannot read or order verbally from a menu may be able to recognize key words on menus and point to them to indicate what they want. If they cannot discriminate particular words, they may carry pictures of certain favorite foods in small wallet-size picture books or even a prewritten food order, in order to indicate their desired item. Likewise, being able to handle money is desirable but if a student cannot do so he or she may still be able to function with some independence in a restaurant by having predetermined amounts of money placed in an envelope to give the counter attendant, waiter, or cashier when paying for the food.

If it is determined through assessment and planning that restaurant skills are desired learning goals, it is important to consider some unique characteristics of the student. Different students may be at different levels of self-feeding skill acquisition (e.g., properly handling a fork or a knife); some may require some form of assistance when eating. Students who have food allergies, are on special diets, or require their food to be prepared in a certain way should learn what to order and not order in restaurants. Other students may have a tendency to order the same item each time and will need to be prompted to order different items at least on occasion so that he or she can benefit from a more complete experience.

As with grocery stores, most young children do not use restaurants independently but may do so with their parents or with older siblings or friends, and so preadolescent individuals may warrant instruction on appropriate restaurant use. Most of the skills they need are proper eating skills and social skills as opposed to more independent skills such as selecting, ordering, and paying for the food. Instructional targets might include waiting and walking with parents or an accompanying adult, sitting properly, using napkins, utensils, straws, and so forth correctly, occupying self appropriately before the food arrives (often by drawing or coloring with restaurant-supplied material or playing on the restaurant's playground equipment), eating properly, speaking at an appropriate volume, and communicating needs and desires effectively.

Vending Machines

It cannot be said with certainty, but it may be that vending machines are used by more people than stores or restaurants. Certainly there are many of them in most modern environments and they are used to dispense items ranging from food and drink to toys, stamps, and more. It should not be surprising then that several researchers have studied ways to teach the required skills for individuals with severe disabilities to use vending machines (Browder, Snell, & Wildonger, 1988; Nietupski, Clancy, & Christiansen, 1984; Sprague & Horner, 1984). The ability to use at least some vending machines adds convenience to the lives of some persons and perhaps gives them access to items that are not otherwise readily available.

As with other community skills, it is important for the teacher to determine if this particular skill is of current or future importance in the lives of students being taught. In this process, the teacher must also determine the extensiveness and generalizability of skills required. For some individuals there may be a limited opportunity to use vending machines and only one or a few machines must be learned. It may be more important to focus on other community skills with them. For others, however, those who have greater mobility in the community, for example, there may be a need to learn to operate all different types of vending machines. Obviously the level of skills required and the amount and type of instruction will be different for different needs.

The basic process for using a vending machine begins with deciding that there is something in a machine that is desirable and determining that the machine that is needed is present or in the vicinity. (Of course, the order in which these decisions are made is not particularly important.) A process of familiarizing the student with vending machines and what they contain might be undertaken by teachers in an incidental manner around the school and the community. Experience with family members and other students will help the student understand the nature, purpose, and contents of the machines.

When planning instruction, as stated above, the teacher must begin with knowledge of how much generalization is desired. Assuming that the student is to learn to operate any vending machine that might be encountered, the teacher should use the general case method of instruction as described in chapter 7. Using this method, Sprague and Horner (1984) taught their students to use several different vending machines that varied by the types of stimuli presented (types of items displayed, amount of money required, directions) and in the types of responses required (where to insert money, where to press the button, where to retrieve the items). They were able to teach students how to select any food or beverage item that cost between 25 and 75 cents from any appropriate vending machine in their community. Teachers teaching generalized vending machine use should vary the machines they use for instruction in a like fashion to maximize generalization.

When the teacher has determined the types of machines to be learned, the task analysis for each machine will be conducted. Each will include similar steps that require the user to select an appropriate amount of money, insert the money in the machine, press the button or activate the machine in an appropriate manner, obtain the item from the machine, and check to see if there is any change. Individual actions from this list may be isolated and targeted for instruction to allow partial participation for students with the most severe disabilities.

The two most difficult aspects of making a vending machine purchase may be determining what is to be bought and handling money adequately to make the purchase. The first problem may be dealt with by teaching the student to use a prosthetic card or booklet that lists by word or picture the various items contained in the machine. The student could then preview the contents of the machine and point to or circle the item on the card before attempting to make a purchase and then match the identified item with the button or lever on the machine that allows it to be dispensed. The second problem requires that the student identify the price of the item, select the amount of money that is required, and insert it into the machine. Again, this could be facilitated by using a booklet or card that shows various amounts of money (e.g., 50 cents) matched with depictions of the coins that equal the amount. The student would then have to select the coins that match the picture from a pocket, wallet, or purse. The student could also use a numberline to determine if he or she has a sufficient amount of money. Naturally, the more advanced the student's money skills, the less need there would be for using such aids. In addition, the more familiar the student becomes with certain machines, the easier and more automatic it will be to make desired purchases from vending machines.

One thing about vending machines that students who use them must ultimately learn is that they sometimes do not operate correctly. Certainly this is a frustration that many have experienced. When it occurs, teachers should take the opportunity to teach students that they should not continue to put money into the machine and that if there is a nearby proprietor of the machine, this person should be told about the problem.

Public Transportation and Pedestrian Skills

Regardless of the community settings one may use, there will always be a need to travel to get to them. This may require simply walking from a nearby street corner after being dropped off or walking from home, school, or work, or, if the distance is too great for walking, the individual may need to use public transportation such as a city bus. Although young children, both with and without disabilities, are usually accompanied by an older, more competent person when traveling around the community, adolescents are often expected to demonstrate local travel skills independently. Research suggests that some persons with severe disabilities can learn pedestrian skills (Horner, Jones, & Williams, 1985; Marchetti, McCartney, Drain, Hooper, & Dix, 1983; Vogelsberg & Rusch, 1979) and the appropriate use of public transportation, specifically buses (Coon, Vogelsberg, & Williams, 1981; Marchetti, Cecil, Graves, & Marchetti, 1984; Neef, Iwata, & Page, 1978; Sowers, Rusch, & Hudson, 1979; Welch, Nietupski, & Hamre-Nietupski, 1985).

The most critical pedestrian skill requires an individual to cross the street at the appropriate time to avoid traffic. To be safe, the student must learn to cross at different types of intersections and must be 100% correct in his or her attempts. Until the student can do this consistently, supervision is required.

The instructional intersections may be uncontrolled, or they may be controlled by traffic lights, walk-don't walk signs, or stop signs. Traffic conditions may be light or heavy; the direction of the traffic may be one or two ways; and the street may have two lanes or more (Horner et al., 1985). Other variations in the conditions of intersections that exist in local communities must also be identified and incorporated into the training sessions.

When learning to cross, students must learn to attend to the correct stimuli for the particular type of intersection and then make a decision as to whether or not to cross depending on the status of the stimulus. Verbal directions and cues are required initially, but then, as with other learning situations, are faded out by the teacher so that the student learns to attend to the natural cues and does not rely on the teacher's prompting. Students who cannot learn to cross independently can participate by pushing the button for walking if there is one, by watching for the light to change, and then by walking independently or semi-independently or assisting in pushing their wheelchair if they are in one.

After the student has learned to cross the street safely, further walking to a particular location can be learned through practice. The procedure requires that the student learn to identify landmarks that indicate that he or she is progressing satisfactorily along the route. For some students, written directions or a map may be helpful; for others, repeated practice is the best instructional technique. Once again, as the student acquires more independence on the skill, the teacher should fade his or her presence so the student can walk independently.

In addition to learning to walk to certain locations, the independence of students with severe disabilities is increased if they can learn to use public transportation, assuming it is available in an area. The operational skills involved require that the student learn to recognize the bus to be taken by identifying its number or route sign; board the bus; pay the fair, using coins or tokens; take a seat; identify the stop where he or she is to get off and signaling the bus driver to stop if necessary (by pulling the cord); getting off the bus; and proceed by walking. If the student has difficulty in recognizing the bus or the name of the street at which he or she wants to get off, written words, numbers, or picture cues (pictures taken by the teacher as he or she learned the route) may be carried and used as prompts. Whenever bus riding skills are being taught, it is suggested that round trips be used so that the student can learn the way back to the origin as well as the way to the designated target.

As with other community-based learning activities, there are some skills associated with the use of public transportation that students with the most severe disabilities may find difficult. Again, this is no reason to exclude these students from developing key skills in this area. For example, they might learn to purchase a ticket by handing their money to the driver or depositing the money or ticket as they proceed through the turnstile; they may learn to get on and get off the bus or train as independently as they are able; they can find an empty seat; and they can sit appropriately and ride until they are directed to get up and get off at a particular stop.

The training procedures for teaching bus riding skills to most students consists of the instructor accompanying the student to the bus stop and providing the verbal directions and cues necessary for the student to complete each of the steps in the task. As trials progress, the teacher should use time-delay prompting by waiting an adequate amount of time for the student to respond to the natural cues. When the student has achieved criterion by completing all of the steps in the task for several days without cues from the teacher, the teacher (with the parents' and school administrator's permission) should allow the student to take the bus independently. In order to be able to maintain a "safety net," however, the teacher may enlist an ally unknown to the student to see that the trip is safely completed. This person should be aboard the bus when it picks the student up.

Although some studies have shown some effectiveness by creating simulated conditions in classrooms to teach pedestrian skills and bus riding, it is doubtful that this type of training alone would ever be sufficient for the student to learn adequately. At the very least, assessment of the skill needs to occur in actual settings. It is suggested that for the time and effort required to create the simulated conditions in the school, the teacher would make wiser use of time by teaching students in the actual situations. If simulations are to be used, it might be best to use videotapes or slides showing the bus the student is to board, the street sign where he or she is to get off, and traffic signs and conditions signaling whether or not to cross the street. The effectiveness of this procedure may not be worth the effort.

Individuals who learn to walk through their community and use public transportation will have acquired much independence. However, because there is a clear element of danger associated with traveling independently in the community, certain commonsense safety skills are very important. Students must learn to be wary of strangers and not interact with them except to subtly greet them as they proceed. They should be able to recognize police and public safety officers and know that they can get help and protection from them when necessary. They should realize that well-lighted places where there are many people are generally safe and that isolated and dark areas should be avoided. They should always carry identification that includes the names and phone numbers of persons to be contacted in an emergency. In addition, students should learn to practice relevant social skills when traveling through the community. Acting in a way that suggests one is not competent may serve to invite danger.

Domestic Activities

Just as students need to learn to operate independently in community settings, they also need to learn to perform various domestic chores that will allow them to be more independent. The domestic activities that are listed in Figure 17–6 represent daily or weekly activities that are typically required by persons living in their own homes. Of course, once again, it is important to understand that not all individuals with severe disabilities need to learn to perform all of these tasks. Tasks that may be more suitable for those with the most severe disabilities are listed in Figure 17–7. It should also be realized that the importance of specific household tasks may vary from family to family. For some students with severe disabilities, some of the tasks listed in Figure 17–6 and 17–7 may not be considered very important. More significant ones would usually be those that allow the person more freedom. Therefore, instruction of three such sets of skills are discussed below: preparing meals and snacks, performing household chores, and using a telephone.

Preparing Snacks and Meals

Individuals who are able to prepare food or to contribute to any degree in its preparation will be able to use their skill in several ways: to sustain themselves, as a form of leisure activity, as a way to save money (by not needing to dine out all the time), and as a mechanism for appropriate social interaction (Schuster, 1988). Obviously, preparing food plays an important part in a normal life routine. Various studies with individuals with mild, moderate, and severe mental disabilities have reported that these individuals can learn to prepare a variety of foods, including Jello, hot chocolate, hot dogs, baked chicken, roast beef, spaghetti, broiled fish, fried eggs, boiled eggs, toast, cheese toast, boiled vegetables, and various other food items (Schuster, 1988; Browder & Snell, 1993).

The instructional process for teaching food preparation skills is much like other instruction. The teacher must begin with communicating with the parents to determine if cooking or other food preparation skills should be taught and if so, what specific food items the student should learn to prepare. Often parents look upon these skills as being particularly useful, even for preadolescent children, because they allow their children to handle chores that previously the parent had to take care of, for example, fixing a sandwich to take for lunch or preparing a snack after school. Many parents indicate that learning such a functional skill would be helpful to them as well as to their child.

Figure 17–6
Skills Often Required for Domestic Activity

Preparing snacks and meals
Cleaning up after meals
Doing laundry
Straightening & picking up
Cleaning bathroom
Cleaning refrigerator
Using a telephone
Planning appointments
Making beds
Dusting
Responding to fire alarm
Washing car
Abiding by various safety rules

Figure 17–7
Examples of Domestic Skills for Students with the Most Severe Disabilities
Adapted from "Curriculum for School Age Students: The Ecological Model" by E. Helmstetter, 1989, in F. Brown & D. H. Lehrer (Eds.), *Persons with Profound Disabilities: Issues and Practices,* Baltimore: Paul H. Brookes. Used with permission.

Bathroom: Clean mirror, clean counter tops, pick up clothing and place in hamper.

Kitchen: Scrape plates for washing, load into dishwasher, operate dishwasher or do parts of the process, sort and put away clean dishes, prepare or participate in meal preparation.

Bedroom: Make bed or assist, straighten room.

Utility room: Separate clothes for washing, wash clothes or assist in the process, remove clothes from dryer.

General housekeeping: Dust furniture surfaces, vacuum, take out trash.

Depending on the age of the student, it may be desirable for the food preparation process to include meal planning. Students who are older should be given the opportunity not only to learn how to prepare food but also how to decide on the food to be prepared. The meal-planning component should capitalize on the opportunity to teach students about nutrition, food groups, and balanced meals, and allow them to indicate which foods they would like to prepare for particular meals. When planning meals, students may find it more practical to plan entire meals that include an entree, vegetables, bread, salad, drink, and dessert. Such meals could be listed on cards for subsequent use. For example, if students plan to prepare broiled chicken for dinner, they can pull the "broiled chicken" card; all of the necessary food items are listed on it. Some authors have also suggested that using prepackaged frozen foods might be more desirable than "cooking from scratch" because the packages provide all of the parts of a meal in the correct proportions, promote choice making, and allow more independence (Wilcox & Bellamy, 1987). As a follow-up to planning, students can practice grocery shopping skills as they purchase the food at their local grocery store.

Having planned and gathered the necessary food for preparation, the teacher should develop a task analysis for food preparation, whether the task is making sandwiches or cooking a roast. The basic elements of the analysis should include selecting a recipe (if one is to be used), gathering the food items together, gathering the equipment necessary for the preparation (pots, pans, plates, glasses, utensils, etc.), opening the food items, measuring and mixing items as called for by the recipe, turning on the stove or oven, placing food on the stove or in the oven (or in the microwave), stirring the food if required, taking the food off the stove or out of the oven, and serving the food. More detailed cooking task analyses have been provided by Sobsey (1987) for cooking with a microwave, frying, baking, boiling, broiling, making sandwiches, making coffee or tea, and cleaning up after preparing food.

Given that the food to be prepared is relatively simple and involves only a few steps, individuals with severe disabilities may be able to learn the task after several instructional sessions. Many researchers, however, have found that learning occurs more easily and faster if the student can follow a recipe. Although most of the time complete formal recipes are too difficult to read, they can be simplified by using a list of key words and/or drawings to serve as cues for each step in the food preparation task. About half of the studies on teaching food preparation skills used some type of picture recipe cards or books (Schuster, 1988).

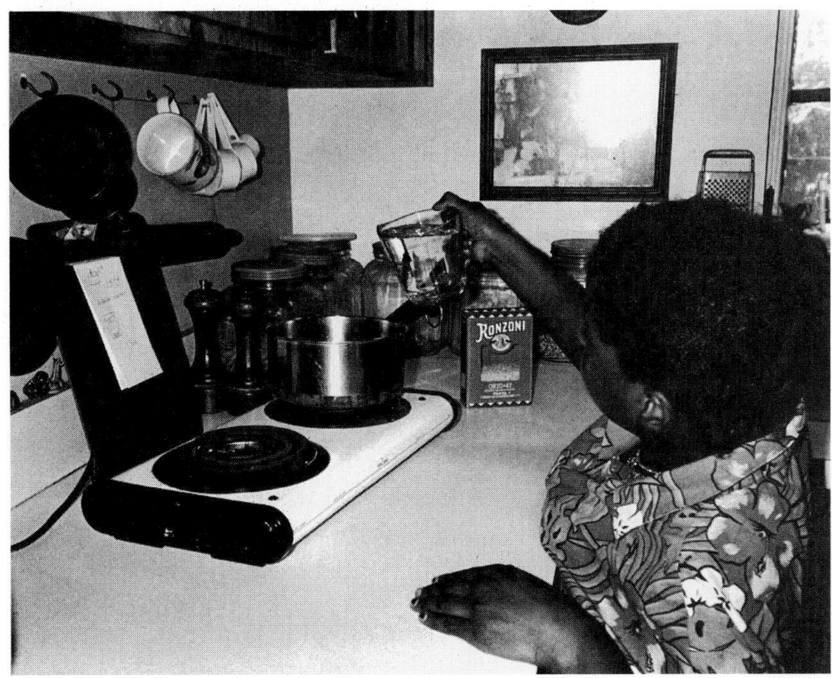

Picture recipes can make independent meal preparation possible.

When picture (or word) recipes are used, the pictures (and/or the words) are arranged so that they serve as a cue to the student as to what must happen next in the preparation sequence. For example, the first card might show a picture of all of the ingredients and necessary equipment sitting on a kitchen table, the second would show the first ingredient being emptied into the first bowl, and so forth. One very practical arrangement is for the cards to be hooked together in a book-like format so that they can be flipped as they are completed, with the newly displayed card providing the cue for the next step. The food item or the meal is complete when the student has progressed through the entire recipe book.

The instructional tactic that seems to be most efficient and effective is the constant time delay procedure (Schuster, 1988; Schuster, Gast, Wolery, & Guiltinan, 1988; Schuster & Griffin, 1991). As described in chapter 6, following the presentation of a stimulus, the instructor waits for a brief period of time (e.g., 5 seconds), then uses a controlling prompt to get the student to perform the behavior if he or she has not already done so. When preparing food, teacher begins by giving a general activity direction, for example "You're probably hungry; why don't you make a sandwich for yourself?" Then the teacher observes to see if the student starts on the sequence as called for by the task analysis. If this is not done within 5 seconds, the teacher gives the controlling prompt for the first step: "Get out the bread and peanut butter and jelly." The completion of each step of the task analysis is considered the cue for the next step. If the student does not initiate the next step in 5 seconds, the teacher then prompts the student, for example, "Open the peanut butter jar and spread some on one piece of bread." After several sessions, the controlling prompt is delayed, and the student learns to initiate the step before being told to do so and ultimately is able to perform all the steps independently. The use of a picture recipe provides the student with a more concrete cue as to what is expected to occur. In other words, instead of the only cue being the completion of the previous step in the task analysis, the student learns to flip the page and be prompted by the picture that indicates the next step. For longer food preparation tasks, this may be helpful.

During food preparation times, the teacher should take advantage of the natural opportunity to teach related skills, including washing hands before cooking and washing dishes, wiping counter tops, and sweeping the floor afterwards.

Performing Household Chores

Living independently or semi-independently means that an individual must assume responsibility for several household chores or share responsibilities with other people. A typical family may have one person whose primary job is to cook, another to clean up afterwards, someone to do the laundry, another to take out the trash, someone else to clean the floors, and so on. In some homes these chores are permanently assigned to individuals and in others the chores might be rotated on a weekly or monthly basis.

As with many activities, household chores are likely to change with the age of the individual. Although young children may have responsibilities such as putting their dirty laundry in the hamper, they most likely would not be required to operate the washer and dryer. Further, chores may be divided based on the preferences of family members. Some may like to do one thing but not another and so cooperative agreements are established so that each person's duty is less burdensome.

It should not be expected that families of individuals with severe disabilities are any different with regard to the need for completing household chores. Additionally, it can be assumed that as the individual grows older and closer to the time of completing school, more instruction is required so that more independence can be developed. Through the assessment and planning process, teachers should ascertain what chores can be learned that would better allow the student to function in the family and, as the student grows older, what should be learned that will help with greater independence as an adult.

As is seen in Figures 17–6 and 17–7, there are a host of household duties that may be required. Additional duties can be found in other sources (Ford et al., 1989; Sobsey, 1987; Wilcox & Bellamy, 1987). Based on interviews with parents, the teacher may determine which household chores should be targeted for instruction. Again, it is important to realize that not all students need to learn all chores. Skills taught in the home economics classroom or elsewhere at school that are not needed or desired at home are soon forgotten, and the instructional time will have been wasted for the student and the teacher.

After the instructional targets have been identified, the teacher must task-analyze them into sequential steps. For many household tasks, this process has already been undertaken and is available in published materials (Sobsey, 1987; Wilcox & Bellamy, 1987) and the teacher may need to make only slight modifications. The instructional procedures for teaching household chores are similar for teaching other skills (see chapter 6). Although the teacher has several approaches to choose from, constant time delay is the one that appears to be easiest to use and results in the fastest learning of household chores such as using a washer and dryer (Miller & Test, 1989).

An important consideration when teaching household chores is the likelihood of the student's being able to perform the chores at home after learning them at school (Livi & Ford, 1985). It would be more desirable for the initial learning to occur at home, but as discussed previously, this may not be possible. On the positive side, however, the teacher typically does not need to plan instruction that results in unlimited generalization because the student is living in only one home (at least for the time being). However, if the skill does not generalize at least to the one location in which it is needed (i.e., the student's home), it will not be practical. Therefore it is critical that the teacher arrange the instructional environment for teaching so that the stimulus conditions during instruction are as similar as possible to those in which the student will need to demonstrate the skill. Close communication between home and teachers can better ensure that similar brooms, mops, detergents, and so forth are being used. Undoubtedly, however, the school will not be able to purchase appliances for the school that are the same as in everyone's home. This being the case, the only way the student will be able to learn to use the models that are in the home is to receive instruction on them. Parents need to understand the basic problem of generalization and why their child may have difficulty at home while performing well in school on household chores.

Using a Telephone

The opportunity to communicate with individuals who are not physically present via the telephone is one we generally take for granted. It allows us to have immediate contact with others and therefore to have greater freedom, independence, happiness, and security. In this world of immediate communications, individuals who do not know how to call others or receive telephone calls are at a disadvantage. It is suggested, therefore, that telephone skills are a very important goal for many individuals with severe disabilities.

Various skills for using the telephone can be divided into four categories: making telephone calls using a standard phone; making phone calls using a pay phone; answering the phone; and engaging in telephone conversation. Each of these four skill areas consists of several subskills, which are listed in Figure 17–8. The skills and subskills listed are based on several reports that have appeared in the literature (Karen, Astin-Smith, & Creasy, 1985; Leff, 1974, 1975; Risley & Cuvo, 1980; Smith & Meyers, 1979).

Teaching students with severe disabilities to use the phone should be preceded by determining which of the skills in Figure 17–8 are most appropriate. For some, it may be most important simply to learn to answer the phone properly. Others may need to learn to use the phone to make contact with another specific individual. For others still, learning to engage appropriately in conversation is the desired goal. Students who are learning to participate in various community activities might need to learn to use a telephone to call businesses to get certain information ("What time does the movie start?") or call a friend to see if he or she wants to go to the movie.

Making Calls from a Standard Phone As with other skills discussed in this chapter, teaching students to use telephones should occur in natural environments and at natural times when possible. For obvious reasons, however, this may not be possible and the use of real phones may be restricted to testing for skill acquisition and generalization. Basic skill training will

Making calls from a standard phone

Identify the number to be called.
Pick up the receiver and listen for a dial tone.
Dial the number, listen for ringing or busy signal.
Engage in greeting, hang up if phone is busy, or leave message if there is an answering machine.

Making calls from a pay phone

Identify the number to be called.
Select the appropriate coins to insert into the pay phone.
Pick up the receiver and continue as above.

Answering the phone

Pick up the phone when it is ringing.
Greet caller and ask for whom the call is if caller does not say.
Determine if the call is for you. If so, engage in conversation.
Determine if another person being called is there, if so, tell the caller to wait one minute and notify the person.
Determine if the person is there; if not, tell caller and volunteer to take message. Write down name and phone number of caller.
Determine if the person has the wrong number. Ask what number was called. Tell person if number is different.

Engaging in telephone conversation (when making a call)

Determine the purpose of the call: to report an emergency, to get information, to give information, to have a conversation.
Tell the person why you are calling:
"This is an emergency..."
"I am calling to find out..."
"I wanted to let you know..."
"I just wanted to chat. Do you have time now?"
Provide details of the message.
End the conversation after purpose is achieved by saying thank you, you're welcome, or nice talking to you, as appropriate.

Engaging in telephone conversation (when receiving a call)

Identify yourself, "Hello, this is..."
Ask why the person is calling: "What can I do for you?" "What are you calling about?" "Why did you call me?"
Provide information as requested, engage in conversation.
Conclude conversation appropriately: "Good-bye." "Thanks for calling." "Call again." "Glad I could help."

Figure 17–8
Skills for Using a Telephone

probably need to occur using phones not connected to the actual system.

Many people maintain a list or a small personal phone book of numbers they frequently call. This commonly used device is also useful for students with severe disabilities. The book can identify by name (or picture) persons or places that are called with some regularity

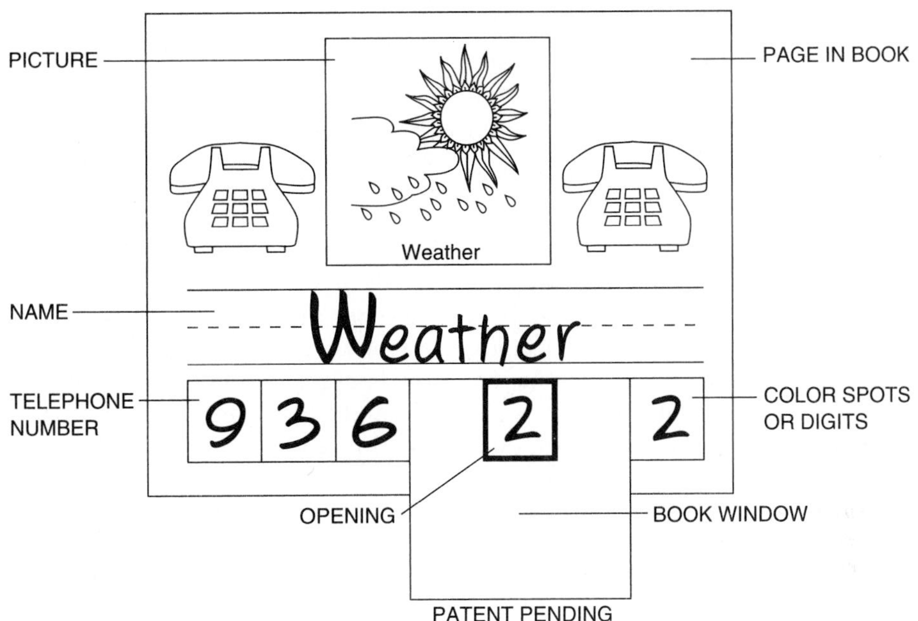

Figure 17–9
Facilitating Telephone Dialing
From "Teaching TMR Children and Adults to Dial the Telephone" by R. B. Leff, 1975, *Mental Retardation, 13,* pp. 9–11. Copyright 1975 by the American Association on Mental Retardation. Reprinted by permission.

(Leff, 1974, 1975). Students who have difficulty transferring recognition of the number in their book to the number to be dialed can learn to block out the numbers, unveiling them one at a time while dialing each number as it appears. This process is depicted in Figure 17–9.

Students who have adequate verbal skills should be able to learn without difficulty how to express an appropriate greeting to the person being called. A more difficult skill, however, may be learning to differentiate between a ring and a busy signal at the other end of the line, and so an adequate amount of practice needs to be devoted to this. Learning how to leave an appropriate message on an answering machine also takes practice, requiring the student to leave his or her name, phone number, and a brief message. Students who cannot accomplish this need to be taught to simply hang up and call at a later time.

Making Calls from a Pay Phone Students who can use a standard telephone should have little difficulty learning to use a pay phone, except that they may have to learn to deal with more distractions when using a phone in a public area. In addition, they need to learn to select the appropriate coin and insert it before dialing. If selecting a coin and inserting it into the slot presents a problem, a coin equivalence card can be used. Students should also be taught how to retrieve the coin if the line is busy or if no one answers, and it is also important for them to learn to wait a specified amount of time before repeating their call or taking some alternative action.

Answering the Phone Although answering the phone may seem a relatively simple task, its difficulty is better understood when we realize, as Figure 17–8 shows, how many variations can occur with regard to the calling party and what he or she wants (Karen et al., 1985). A call to the student per se will be relatively easy to handle, and the student can proceed to engage in conversation. But another type of call will require a series of decisions and may be more difficult. When teaching students to answer the phone, the teacher must present the student with opportunities to practice all variations of possible incoming calls: calls for the student, calls for someone else who is present, calls for someone who is normally at the number called but who is not present, and calls to the wrong number.

Different skills are required depending on the nature of the call. The most important and the one requiring the most instructional time is learning to take a message. If students are expected to learn this, that is, if it is important in their current or future life situation, they need to learn how to write down the name of the caller, the time he or she called, and the phone number. A brief message may also be required, although standard office phone message forms may be used so that the student can simply check the appropriate message. Although such skills are within the ability of many individuals with cognitive disabilities, they require a substantial amount of instruction and practice.

Engaging in Conversation When learning to make phone calls, in addition to learning how to dial numbers, students must learn to identify the purpose of the call and, from that, the type of conversation they will have when the person answers the phone. When calling friends for simple conversation, this is not so important because friends can discuss anything and can call for no particular purpose. However, when calling to get or give specific information, students must know what they are going to say. They also must know how to respond to what is said. The teacher should outline a number of situations for incoming phone calls and also for making calls. Scripts should be developed that allow the teacher and other students to "call in" and to answer calls. There should also be a list of various practice calls to be made to businesses, friends, services, and so forth. Before making practice calls, students should be asked to state why they want to make the call, what they intend to ask or say, and how they will respond to questions that may be asked of them.

One very important area of training is making emergency (911) phone calls. This should be taught to all students who are learning to use the telephone. The skills are relatively straightforward, assuming that the student can recognize an emergency situation. They must dial 911 (or the local emergency number), give their name and address, and state the nature of the emergency. If possible, they should learn to stay on the line until help arrives.

The most effective way for teaching telephone skills is through role-playing. Verbal prompts and models are probably the best type of instructional tactics and may be systematically faded as students' skills increase with practice. Instruction on the use of the phone should occur several times a week. Training telephones, available from most local phone companies, should be used. As skills develop, they should be used in natural settings whenever possible. One way to do this is for teachers to incorporate telephone activities into community-based activities. For example, when students are in the department store, they might call other businesses to see what time they close, and so forth.

Issues Related to Community-Based Instruction

Few people would argue with the need for students with severe disabilities to learn relevant community and domestic skills, but it must be realized that there are some complicated issues related to teaching them, and that these issues and corresponding practices must be considered.

School Administrative Policies

As discussed earlier, providing community-based instruction requires that students be taken off the school campus for their instruction, raising questions about instructional schedules, teaching assignments, liability, transportation, and so on. Clearly, some school administrative policies may make it difficult to take students off campus for instruction and such policies should be studied and modified to the extent possible if nonschool instruction is to occur. In other cases, though, school policy-makers and administrators have already come to realize that providing instruction in actual settings in which skills must be used is an important part of the educational process for students with severe disabilities, and nonschool instruction has become an integral part of school life.

If students are to leave the school grounds for instruction, some authorities have suggested that administrative practices and normal school scheduling procedures be employed to better accommodate this strategy (Baumgart & VanWalleghem, 1986; Hamre-Nietupski, Nietupski, Bates, & Maurer, 1982; Nietupski, Hamre-Nietupski, Houselog, Donder, & Anderson, 1988). Their suggestions have included the following:

- Peers without disabilities and volunteers can be used to assist in instructional activities in community settings.
- Team teaching should be used so that one teacher can accompany students into community settings while another remains in school providing instruction to other students.
- Paraprofessionals can be used effectively both in the school and in nonschool instruction.
- Other professionals providing related services can occasionally accompany students and teachers to nonschool settings to assist in teaching skills and providing therapeutic services in natural settings.
- Heterogeneous groupings of students, including students without disabilities as well as those with less severe and more severe disabilities, will be preferable to homogenous groupings.
- Consultant teachers can help with planning, site identification, scheduling, and some instructional activities.
- Implementation of nonschool instruction can be staggered across students, beginning at different times for different students. Ultimately all students whose educational plan calls for community or domestic instruction will need to be provided this instruction.
- Liability and insurance issues should be reviewed by school administrators to ensure that there is adequate coverage. Since many school districts have provided nonschool instruction for several years now, it is suggested that risk issues do not pose a major barrier to such procedures.
- All school employees engaged in nonschool instruction should be prepared in first aid and know the school's policy for handling emergency situations.

Separating Students With and Without Disabilities

Another important issue concerns the extent to which nonschool instruction away from nondisabled peers should be provided. If a primary goal is to include students with disabilities in the typical school program, then taking them away from school, even to provide valuable instructional experiences, is a form of segregated instruction, a condition that is antithetical to policies of integration and inclusion. Some would argue that community-based instruction may not be desirable because of the segregated condition it may create. Certainly this is an issue that must be considered and corrected to the extent possible.

One method that might be used is to include students without disabilities in community-based instruction. Although this type of instruction might be beneficial to many students, having such a policy within a school would itself create an uncommon situation. More likely is the possibility that students without disabilities might simply accompany those going out of the school for instruction. Ideally, those who go along into the setting would be the student's siblings, friends, and neighbors, in other words, individuals who would normally accompany someone into various community settings. Although this may in some ways prove to be satisfactory, it must be kept in mind that usually some segregation for community instruction is likely to occur and this must be considered a drawback. Hopefully, if this cannot be avoided, skills that are learned will be judged worth the temporary separation.

Relation of Other Instruction to Community Instruction

Additionally, the relationship of community instruction to other aspects of the student's curricular or therapeutic needs must be considered. What should be the relative emphasis on community and domestic instructional targets and learning activities versus academic objectives? How, when, and where should physical therapy, occupational therapy, or communication therapy be provided in order to improve the student's functioning and application of skills in these areas? Will instruction in nonschool settings interfere with the provision of therapy?

Although these questions seem to propose that conflicts exist, in many cases they actually are not major problems. Community-instructional goals, academic goals, and therapeutic needs may often be addressed in multiple environments. Students may practice many academic skills in community settings and then go back to the classroom to work on academic skills that will help them in the community. Likewise, there are many therapeutic goals that can be worked on in natural, nonschool environments. What is important is for parents and professionals to work cooperatively to identify goals and then to determine proportionally how much time should be spent in various environments—the school, the community, and the home—to achieve the goals.

Conclusion

Learning community and domestic skills is necessary for students with severe disabilities and should be included on the educational plans for most students. The most effective site of instruction for these skills is outside of the typical classroom setting, either in community settings, in homelike environments, or in actual homes. Providing out-of-school instruction is uncommon for some teachers and it may take a little while for teachers to become comfortable with the process (Westling & Fleck, 1991), but the effort will be worthwhile.

This instruction should not be mistaken for field trips or in any other way be considered an instructional frill. It provides for many students the opportunity to develop skills that will give them more independence and a better quality of life. Of course, the more the instruction intermeshes with students' needs, the more worthwhile it will be. That is why, as has been stated several times in this chapter, community and domestic instruction must be individually prescribed.

Questions for Reflection

1. What is the relative importance of students with severe disabilities learning skills for use in community and domestic settings?
2. Why should teachers provide training in natural community settings and not simply construct simulations in the classroom? To what degree might simulations be helpful?
3. Give some examples of how school-based instruction can assist in developing functional community and domestic skills.
4. Besides those listed in Figure 17–2, what other aids might be used to assist functioning in community settings?
5. Describe an afternoon of community-based instruction that might incorporate different objectives being learned in different settings.
6. Why might it be better for students to learn to prepare complete sets of foods (snacks or meals) instead of individual items?
7. Besides some of the partial participation activities described in this chapter, what other types of activities might be appropriate for students with the most severe disabilities in different settings?
8. What are some ways that community and domestic instruction can be provided without separating students with severe disabilities from other students?

References

Aeschleman, S. R., & Schladenhauffen, J. (1984). Acquisition, generalization and maintenance of grocery shopping skills by severely mentally retarded adolescents. *Applied Research in Mental Retardation, 5,* 245–258.

Aveno, A. (1987). A survey of activities engaged in and skills most needed by adults in community residences. *Journal of the Association for Persons with Severe Handicaps, 12,* 125–130.

Aveno, A., Renzaglia, A., & Lively, C. (1987). Surveying community training sites to insure that instructional decisions accommodate the site as well as the trainees. *Education and Training in Mental Retardation, 22,* 167–175.

Baumgart, D., & VanWalleghem, J. (1986). Staffing strategies for implementing community based instruction. *Journal of the Association for Persons with Severe Handicaps, 11,* 92–102.

Browder, D. M., & Snell, M. E. (1993). Daily living and community skills. In M. E. Snell (Ed.), Instruction of students with severe *disabilities* (4th ed.). New York: Macmillan.

Browder, D. M., Snell, M. E., & Wildonger, B. A. (1988). Simulation and community-based instruction of vending machines with time delay. *Education and Training in Mental Retardation, 23,* 175–185.

Brown, L., Nisbet, J., Ford, A., Sweet, M., Shiraga, B., & York, J. (1983). The critical need for non-school instruction in programs for severely handicapped students. *Journal of the Association for the Severely Handicapped, 8,* 71–77.

Coon, M. E., Vogelsberg, R. T., & Williams, W. (1981). Effects of classroom public transportation instruction on generalization to the natural environment. *Journal of the Association for the Severely Handicapped, 6,* 46–53.

Falvey, M. A. (1989). *Community-based curriculum: Instructional strategies for students with severe handicaps* (2nd ed.). Baltimore: Paul H. Brookes.

Ford, A., Schnorr, R., Meyer, L., Davern, L., Black, J., & Dempsey, P. (1989). *The Syracuse community-referenced curriculum guide for students with moderate and severe disabilities.* Baltimore: Paul H. Brookes.

Ford, A., & Mirenda, P. (1984). Community instruction: A natural cues and corrections decision model. *Journal of the Association for the Severely Handicapped, 9,* 79–88.

Freagon, S., Wheeler, J., Hill, L., Brankin, G., Costello, D., & Peters, W. M. (1983). A domestic training environment for students who are severely handicapped. *Journal of the Association for the Severely Handicapped, 8,* 49–61.

Hamre-Nietupski, S., Nietupski, J., Bates, P., & Maurer, S. (1982). Implementing a community based education model for moderately/severely handicapped students: Common problems and suggested solutions. *Journal of the Association for the Severely Handicapped, 7*(4), 38–43.

Haring, T., Kennedy, C., Adams, M., & Pitts-Conway, V. (1987). Teaching generalization of purchasing skills across community settings to autistic youth using videotape modeling. *Journal of Applied Behavior Analysis, 20,* 89–96.

Helmstetter, E. (1989). Curriculum for school age students: The ecological model. In F. Brown & D. H. Lehrer (Eds.), *Persons with profound disabilities: Issues and practices.* Baltimore: Paul H. Brookes.

Horner, R. H., Albin, R. W., & Ralph, G. (1986). Generalization with precision: The role of negative teaching examples in the instruction of generalized grocery item selection. *Journal of the Association for Persons with Severe Handicaps, 11,* 300–308.

Horner, R. H., Jones, D. N., & Williams, J. A. (1985). A functional approach to teaching generalized street crossing. *Journal of the Association for Persons with Severe Handicaps, 10,* 71–78.

Karen, R. L., Astin-Smith, S., & Creasy, D. (1985). Teaching telephone answering skills to mentally retarded adults. *American Journal of Mental Deficiency, 89,* 595–609.

Leff, R. B. (1974). Teaching the TMR to dial the telephone. *Mental Retardation, 12*(2), 12–13.

Leff, R. B. (1975). Teaching TMR children and adults to dial the telephone. *Mental Retardation, 13*(3), 9–11.

Livi, J., & Ford, A. (1985). Skill transfer from a domestic training site to the actual homes of three moderately handicapped students. *Education and Training of the Mentally Retarded, 20,* 69–82.

Marchetti, A. G., Cecil, C. E., Graves, J., & Marchetti, D. C. (1984). Public transportation instruction: Comparison of classroom instruction, community instruction, and facility grounds instruction. *Mental Retardation, 22,* 128–136.

Marchetti, A. G., McCartney, J. R., Drain, S., Hooper, M., & Dix, J. (1983). Pedestrian skills training for mentally retarded adults: Comparison of training in two settings. *Mental Retardation, 21,* 107–110.

Marholin, D., O'Toole, K. M., Touchette, P. E., Berger, P. L., & Doyle, D. A. (1979). I'll have a Big Mac, large fries, large coke, and apple pie,. . . or teaching adaptive community skills. *Behavior Therapy, 10,* 249–259.

Matson, J. L. (1981). Use of independence training to teach shopping skills to mildly mentally retarded adults. *American Journal of Mental Deficiency, 86,* 178–183.

Matson, J. L., & Long, S. (1986). Teaching computation/shopping skills to mentally retarded adults. *American Journal of Mental Deficiency, 91,* 98–101.

McDonnell, J. J., & Ferguson, B. (1988). A comparison of general case in vivo and general case simulation plus in vivo training. *Journal of the Association for Persons with Severe Handicaps, 13,* 116–124.

McDonnell, J. J., Horner, R. H., & Williams, J. A. (1984). Comparison of three strategies for teaching generalized grocery purchasing to high school students with severe handicaps. *Journal of the Association for Persons with Severe Handicaps, 9,* 123–133.

Miller, U. C., & Test, D. W. (1989). A comparison of constant time delay and most-to-least prompting in teaching laundry skills to students with moderate retardation. *Education and Training in Mental Retardation, 24,* 341–351.

Neef, N. A., Iwata, B. A., & Page, T. J. (1978). Public transportation training: In vivo vs. classroom instruction. *Journal of Applied Behavior Analysis, 11,* 331–344.

Nietupski, J., Clancy, P., & Christiansen, C. (1984). Acquisition, maintenance, and generalization of vending machine purchasing skills by moderately handicapped students. *Education and Training of the Mentally Retarded, 17,* 91–96.

Nietupski, J., Hamre-Nietupski, S., Houselog, M., Donder, D. J., & Anderson, R. J. (1988). Proactive administrative strategies for implementing community based programs for students with moderate/severe handicaps. *Education and Training in Mental Retardation, 23,* 138–146.

Nietupski, J., Welch, J., & Wacker, D. (1983). Acquisition, maintenance and transfer of grocery item purchasing skills by moderately and severely handicapped students. *Education and Training of the Mentally Retarded, 18,* 279–286.

Nirje, B. (1969). The normalization principle and its human management implications. In R. B. Kugel & W. Wolfensberger (Eds.), *Changing patterns in residential services for the mentally retarded.* Washington, DC: President's Committee on Mental Retardation.

Risley, R. M., & Cuvo, A. J. (1980). Training mentally retarded adults to make emergency phone calls. *Behavior Modification, 4,* 513–516.

Sarber, R. E., Halasz, M. M., Messmer, M. C., Bickett, A. D., & Lutzker, J. R. (1983). Teaching menu planning and grocery shopping skills to a mentally retarded mother. *Mental Retardation, 21,* 101–106.

Shafer, M. S., Inge, K. J., & Hill, J. (1986). Acquisition, generalization and maintenance of automated banking skills. *Education and Training of the Mentally Retarded, 21,* 265–272.

Schuster, J. W. (1988). Cooking instruction for persons labeled mentally retarded: A review of literature. *Education and Training in Mental Retardation, 23,* 43–50.

Schuster, J. W., Gast, D. L., Wolery, M., & Guiltinan, S. (1988). The effectiveness of a constant time delay procedure to teach chained responses to adolescents with mental retardation. *Journal of Applied Behavior Analysis, 21,* 169–178.

Schuster, J. W., & Griffin, A. K. (1991). Using constant time delay to teach recipe following skills. *Education and Training in Mental Retardation, 26,* 411–419.

Smith, M., & Meyers, A. (1979). Telephone-skills training for retarded adults: Group and individual demonstrations with and without verbal instruction. *American Journal of Mental Deficiency, 83,* 581–587.

Snell, M. E., & Browder, D. M. (1986). Community referenced instruction: Research and issues. *Journal of the Association for Persons with Severe Handicaps, 11,* 1–11.

Sobsey, D. (1987). (Ed.) *Ecological inventory exemplars.* Edmonton, Alta: University of Alberta, Department of Educational Psychology.

Sowers, J., Rusch, F. R., & Hudson, C. (1979). Training a severely retarded young adult to ride the city bus to and from work. *AAESPH Review, 4*(1), 15–23.

Sprague, J. R., & Horner, R. H. (1984). The effects of single instance, multiple instance, and general case training on generalized vending machine use by moderately and severely handicapped students. *Journal of Applied Behavior Analysis, 17,* 273–278.

Stanfield, J. S. (1973). Graduation: What happens to the retarded child when he grows up? *Exceptional Children, 39,* 548–552.

Storey, K., Bates, P., & Hanson, H. B. (1984). Acquisition and generalization of coffee purchase skills by adults with severe disabilities. *Journal of the Association for Persons with Severe Handicaps, 9,* 178–185.

Van den Pol, R. A., Iwata, B. A., Ivancic, M. T., Page, T. J., Neef, N. A., & Whitley, P. F. (1981). Teaching the handicapped to eat in public places: Acquisition, generalization and maintenance of restaurant skills. *Journal of Applied Behavior Analysis, 14,* 61–69.

Vogelsberg, R. T., & Rusch, F. R. (1979). Training severely handicapped adolescents to cross partially controlled intersections. *AAESPH Review, 4,* 264–273.

Welch, J., Nietupski, J., & Hamre-Nietupski, S. (1985). Teaching public transportation problem solving skills to young adults with moderate handicaps. *Education and Training of the Mentally Retarded, 20,* 287–295.

Westling, D. L., & Fleck, L. (1991). Teachers' views of community instruction. *Teacher Education and Special Education, 14,* 127–134.

Westling, D. L., & Floyd, J. (1990). Generalization of community skills: How much training is necessary? *Journal of Special Education, 23,* 386–406.

Westling, D. L., Floyd, J., & Carr, D. (1990). Effect of single setting versus multiple setting training on learning to shop in a department store. *American Journal on Mental Deficiency, 94,* 616–624.

Wilcox, B., & Bellamy, G. T. (1987). *The activities catalog: An alternative curriculum for youth and adults with severe disabilities.* Baltimore: Paul H. Brookes.

Wolfensberger, W. (1972). *The principle of normalization in human services.* Toronto: National Institute on Mental Retardation.

PART V

Instructional Considerations for Younger and Older Students

CHAPTER 18 Meeting the Needs of Young Children

CHAPTER 19 Teaching Employment Skills and Planning for Transition

CHAPTER 18

Meeting the Needs of Young Children

Chapter Overview

This chapter describes practices in early childhood special education and procedures that may be used to meet the unique needs of infants, toddlers, and preschoolers and their families. The chapter includes information on assessment practices, developing Individualized Family Support Plans, service delivery arrangements, instructional strategies, and supporting the transitions of young children and their families.

Recent legislation has mandated the provision of services to young children with special needs and their families. In 1986, Public Law 99-457, an amendment to P.L. 94-142, extended all of the rights and protections of P.L. 94-142 to 3- to 5-year-old children with disabilities. Under Public Law 99-457, preschoolers with disabilities have a right to a free appropriate public education, which includes an individualized education program, least restrictive environment, and procedural safeguards. Because nondisabled preschool children do not typically attend public education programs, the provision of preschool programs to children with disabilities may occur in the community. Public Law 99-457 provides for the provision of services in a number of different ways, including contracting with outside agencies and providing programs that vary in intervention location and length of service day (Trohanis, 1989).

Part H of Public Law 99-457 created a discretionary program to assist states in planning and implementing early intervention programs for families and their children who are at risk or disabled from birth up to 3 years of age. Part H funding provided financial assistance to states as they planned and implemented an expanded early intervention program to infants and toddlers. States that chose to participate in Part H were eligible to receive funding over a 5-year period if specific criteria were met each year. States that received fifth-year funding are the states that have made services available to all eligible infants and toddlers in a statewide comprehensive system. The components of the statewide system must include the minimum criteria listed in Figure 18–1.

Historical Development

The roots of the field of early childhood special education can be found in the establishment of kindergarten, nursery school, special education, and compensatory education programs (Peterson, 1987). The establishment of kindergarten and nursery school programs provided the foundation for the concept that young children may benefit from early education, and the special education movement established the rights of children with disabilities to a public education. But it was the compensatory education program that introduced the concept of early intervention through the establishment of Head Start programs (Bricker, 1989; Peterson, 1987).

Head Start, which began in the late 1960s in the social-political climate of the civil rights movement and the War on Poverty, was estab-

1. Definition of developmentally delayed
2. Timetable for serving all in need in the state
3. Comprehensive multidisciplinary evaluation of needs of children and famlies
4. Individualized family service plan and case management services
5. Child find and referral system
6. Public awareness
7. Central directory of services, resources, experts, research and demonstration projects
8. Comprehensive system of personnel development
9. Single line of authority in a lead agency designated or established by the governor for implementation of:
   a. general administration and supervision
   b. identification and coordination of all available resources
   c. assignment of financial responsibility to the appropriate agency
   d. procedures to ensure the provision of services and to resolve intra- and interagency disputes
   e. entry into formal interagency agreements
10. Policy pertaining to contracting or making arrangements with local service providers
11. Procedure for timely reimbursement of funds
12. Procedural safeguards
13. Policies and procedures for personnel standards
14. System for compiling data on the early intervention programs

Figure 18–1
Minimum Components of a Statewide Comprehensive System for the Provision of Appropriate Early Intervention Services to Infants and Toddlers with Special Needs
From "An Introduction to PL 99-457 and the National Policy Agenda for Serving Young Children with Special Needs and Their Families" by P. L. Trohanis, 1989, in J. J. Gallagher, P. L. Trohanis, & R. M. Clifford (Eds.), *Policy Implementation and PL 99-457: Planning for Young Children with Special Needs,* p. 5. Baltimore: Paul H. Brookes Publishing Co., P.O. Box 10624, Baltimore, Maryland 21285-0624. Reprinted by permission.

lished to provide 3- and 4-year-old children who were environmentally at risk with an intervention designed to improve their health and their physical, social, and emotional well-being; improve their mental processes and skills; and establish a climate of expectations that would enhance the child's ability to be successful in school (Bricker, 1989).

Research on the effects of Head Start published as the Westinghouse Study (Cicirelli et al., 1969) dampened the enthusiasm for the program by reporting that summer Head Start gains did not persist in the early grades, full-year programs were more effective in producing lasting cognitive gains, and that parents felt the programs were valuable. Three ideas emerged from the Westinghouse Study analysis that have had an impact on the design of current early intervention efforts. These concepts are that interventions must begin earlier and last longer if they are going to be effective, that intervention should not stop abruptly when the child enters public school, and that support of families should be an area of focus for early intervention programs. Later research documented that a "sleeper effect" could be detected in the later elementary grades where Head Start graduates showed superior academic achievement in comparison to a control group (Zigler & Yale Research Group, 1976).

The expansion of early intervention programs to include children with disabilities was initiated on the basis of improving the outcomes of individuals who could be considered disadvantaged and might later become a burden to society. Parallel to societal concern about the future of disadvantaged children was the civil rights movement, which focused on the provision of equal opportunity to all. The civil rights approach to providing services may be a stronger factor in accounting for the expansion of services to young children with severe disabilities rather than the cost-benefit perspective (Westlake & Kaiser, 1991). Young children with severe disabilities are not likely to have their needs for continued support ameliorated through early intervention. The goals of early intervention programs were to maximize the child's developmental outcomes, prevent the establishment of secondary disabilities, provide support to families, and diminish the costs of institutionalization and other services needed if early intervention had not been provided (Bricker, 1989).

Efficacy Research

Research on the efficacy of early intervention programs for children with severe disabilities is difficult to interpret given the methodological flaws of the majority of studies (Dunst & Rheingrover, 1981). In addition, much of the research on early intervention is also conceptually flawed (Dunst, 1986). In the majority of studies, early intervention is defined globally as an independent variable, and developmental outcome (measured by changes in developmental or intellectual quotient) is used as the primary dependent measure. This approach is problematic in that early intervention is not a well-defined construct and can be comprised of varying levels of support and services. The use of developmental changes in the child as the primary dependent variable neglects to consider the effects of early intervention programs on the family. Dunst (1986) states that early intervention should be conceptualized as "an aggregation of the many types of help, assistance, and services" (p. 122) and suggests that researchers move from the question of "Does early intervention work?" to "What dimensions of early intervention are related to different outcome measures?" (p. 124). This approach to evaluating the efficacy of early intervention programs is based on an ecological or social systems view. From this perspective early intervention programs are viewed as comprising a broad array of supports and services that may affect both the child and the family in a variety of ways. A social systems view of early intervention programs looks beyond the goal of changing a child's developmental status to assisting families in developing the resources and skills they need to support their child's development and participation in normalized life experiences.

Goals of Early Intervention

Bailey and Wolery (1992) have described seven broad goals for early intervention programs:

1. to support families in achieving their own goals;

2. to promote child engagement, independence, and mastery;
3. to promote development in key domains (e.g., motor, cognition, communication, daily living, and social);
4. to build and support children's social competence;
5. to promote the generalized use of skills;
6. to provide and prepare for normalized life experiences;
7. to prevent the emergence of future problems or disabilities.

These goals do not appear to be unique to young children with disabilities; we could say that they apply to all students with severe disabilities. Early intervention programs are unique because the population of concern is very young, which has a significant impact on how interventions are structured. Bailey (1989) presented an analysis of the differences between intervention programs that are designed for infants and toddlers, for preschoolers, and for elementary-school-age children with disabilities that is shown in Table 18–1.

In this chapter the issues concerning the characteristics of young children, the family-centered approach of early childhood special education, and the design of intervention programs for young children are presented. Within each of these areas of concern, strategies for providing appropriate programs to young children with severe disabilities are presented.

Teaching Young Children

A distinguishing feature of early intervention programs is that they typically serve a diverse group of children and families. Unlike Public Law 94-142, Public Law 99-457 does not require that the states report the enrollment of children by categorical labels to the federal government. In addition, it allows for services to be provided to children who have documented developmental delays or who are at risk for developmental delay. This flexibility allows for a noncategorical approach to service delivery. Young children with severe disabilities and their families are usually served by programs that serve children and families with a variety of needs.

The age of the population being served by early intervention programs has a profound impact on the nature of services that are provided. In the early childhood stage of development, young children move from the infancy stage of exhibiting behavior that is restricted, uncoordinated, and primarily reflexive to independently responding to environmental demands as preschoolers. Developmental changes occur in the context of the social environment (Lewis, 1984). Infants learn through interactions with caregivers and the environment that they can act on the world. Developmental changes in cognitive, sensory, and motor development allow them to interact with the environment in increasingly sophisticated ways.

Transactional Approach

Young children with severe disabilities do not spontaneously exhibit the rapid developmental growth that is seen with typically developing children. Thus, the focus of early intervention becomes promoting development within the context of interactions with caregivers and the environment. A transactional perspective (Sameroff & Chandler, 1975) offers a way to approach early intervention that is based on the theory that the individual and the environment are interdependent and constantly interacting. Interventions that are based on a transactional perspective are not concerned only with the attainment of developmental skills; they also view the achievement of developmental milestones in the broader context of the behavior, beliefs, and values of all the players in the system (Sameroff & Fiese, 1990). This is a somewhat different approach from the educational model that is applied for school-age children. In programs for school-age children, educators bring the student to school and teach skills in the context of interactions with peers and the community. In programs for young children, interventionists design ways to support the development of the child in the context of interactions with the caregiver and the environment.

Instructional Activities

The capacity of young children for direct intervention also has an influence on how early intervention programs are designed. In programs for students who are school-age, an effort is made to maintain a high level of active engagement in instruction in an instructional day that can last from 5 to 7 hours. Although active engagement is a goal of early intervention, young children, especially young children who may have medical concerns or multiple disabilities, have very low thresholds for continual engagement. Activities that are designed for young children must be brief and based on the child's interest. As a consequence, the early interventionist must be able to embed instruction in playful or child-motivating activities that can be applied throughout the day by a variety of caregivers. Young children have little to gain from intensive, didactic training sessions that are scheduled by the adult. Instruction must occur when the child is ready and last only as long as the child can tolerate.

Instructional Content

The nature of what is taught to young children is different from what is taught to older individuals with severe disabilities. Instructional goals are more likely to contain very early developmental skills. The focus of infant intervention may be to teach an infant to mediate his behavior states, basic motor movements, and contingent responsiveness. These goals would be taught in reciprocal exchanges that are meaningful to the infant. The goals for young children are developmentally based although an emphasis is placed on teaching the skills in meaningful routines in the same way that we teach older individuals with severe disabilities. A functional curriculum is also a concern of early interventionists. Instructional goals that are developed for young children should center around the types of skills that are functional in a variety of environments and that will lead to greater independence. Skill instruction occurs in routine and meaningful activities rather than in isolated, situation-specific contexts.

Family Support

In addition to providing intervention to young children, the early interventionist is concerned with providing support to families. The expressed focus on supporting families is different from the traditional role educators have assumed for school-age children. In Public Law 99-457 the involvement of families in the development of an Individual Education Plan (IEP) is clearly specified for 3- to 5-year-olds and the development of the Individual Family Service Plan (IFSP) for birth to 2-year-olds. This approach to family involvement goes beyond teaching parents techniques to facilitate the development of the child. It is broadly aimed at providing positive support to caregivers and

Table 18–1

A Comparison of Interventions with Infants, Preschoolers, and Elementary-Age Children with Special Needs

Domain	Infants and Toddlers (0-36 months)	Preschoolers (36-60 months)	Elementary (5-12 years)
I. Characteristics of children			
Population parameters	Noncategorical; developmentally delayed, conditions that typically result in delay, at risk of substantial delay; results in wide range of ability levels and types of handicaps	Noncategorical; wide range of ability levels and handicaps (some states, however, will choose categorical descriptions)	Categorical; more restricted range of ability levels and disability types; formal eligibility criteria
Goals for intervention	Behavior and motor organization, differentiated responses to environmental cues, cause and effect, early communication and social skills, attachment	Cognitive, self-help, social, fine motor, communication, behavior, toy play, gross motor	Reading, spelling, mathematics, appropriate social behavior
Schedule regularity	Low—almost entirely determined by infant	Moderate—some adult determination of schedules, but requires flexibility depending on children's needs and interest	High—preset routine and time allocation for tasks; very little in the way of child-initiated activities
Endurance	Short—interactions typically last less than 2-3 minutes	Moderate—interactions may last 5-15 minutes	Long-interactions may last 30 minutes to 2 hours
Motivation	Must come from inherent appeal of material or activity; based on infant's interest	Begin to follow adult expectations, but high-interest toys and activities are critical	Based on adult expectations for compliance; reliance on self-regulation and response to rules

II. The intervention context			
Context of teaching	Parent-child interactions; feeding, bathing, diapering, and dressing routines; object play	Object play, peer interactions, adult-child interactions, routines	Classroom instruction, written materials
Sites for intervention/services	Homes, day care centers, family day homes, specialized developmental centers, developmental evaluation centers, hospital settings (NICU, pediatrics ward)	Specialized developmental center/classrooms, day care centers, homes, developmental evaluation centers, hospital settings	Elementary schools (regular classroom, resource room, self-contained classroom)
Responsible agencies	Mental health centers, hospital, public health services, private day care, specialized nonprofit agencies, public school	Public school, mental health, Head Start, day care	Public school
Team functioning	Often involves multiple professionals from multiple agencies; considerable role overlap, requiring extensive communication and coordination	Moderate blending of roles, but work in isolation is possible	Differentiated and specific roles, isolation likely
III. Family role			
Mandated family role	Essential and family-focused—IFSP requires documentation of family needs and strengths, a statement of family goals, and the provision of family services, including case management	Very important—IEP provisions pertain, all parents' rights protected, and parent training encouraged when necessary	Important—IEP provisions pertain, all parents' rights protected

From Issues and Directions in Preparing Professionals to Work with Young Handicapped Children and Their Families, by D. B. Bailey, 1989, in J. J. Gallagher, R. M. Clifford, & P. Trohanis (Eds.), *Policy Implementation and P.L. 99-457: Planning for Young Children with Special Needs* (pp. 101–102), Baltimore: Paul H. Brookes Publishing Co., P.O. Box 10624, Baltimore, Maryland 21285-0624. Reprinted by permission.

family members as the critical context for the child's development (Kaiser & Hemmeter, 1989). In a family-centered approach to early intervention, the family's needs and desires determine the provision of resources and services (Dunst, Johanson, Trivette, & Hamby, 1991). Early interventionists work as the agent of the family to strengthen the family's capacity to provide for the child.

Family-Centered Approach

The term *family-centered* is used to describe an approach to early intervention that is consumer-driven and focused on enhancing the competencies of families to support the development of their children (Dunst et al., 1991). In early intervention there has been an evolution of ways to consider families and their roles in the early intervention program (Bricker, 1989). The first stage, professionally controlled, did not consider the family at all in the evaluation of the child or in the design and implementation of the intervention program. In the second stage, family involvement, families were recognized as important to the child's progress, and interventionists made an effort to include them in the IEP process and requested that parents carry out treatment plans in the home. In the third stage, family focused, early interventionists regarded understanding the family as fundamental to the focused approach, the assessment of family needs as they relate to the child were a concern, and IFSP or IEP goals were mutually selected by the family and professionals (Dunst et al., 1991).

The family-centered approach is markedly different from the earlier ways that professionals viewed families. In a family-centered approach, family needs and desires determine what services are provided. The goal of early intervention is to provide the resources and supports that will strengthen the family's capacity to meet their needs (Dunst et al., 1991). The words *empowerment* and *enablement* reflect the spirit of the family-centered approach (McGonigel, 1991). In early intervention, *empowerment* means that families are supported in a way that results in a feeling that they are in control and that positive changes that occur are the result of their strengths and abilities (Dunst, Trivette, & Deal, 1988). *Enablement* is used to describe the process of finding ways for families to use their competencies or to acquire new competencies to meet their needs (Dunst et al., 1988).

A family-centered approach is important for several reasons (Bricker, 1989). First, the family spends more time with the child than the early interventionist. Any intervention that is delivered is far more powerful if the family is involved and interventions that are designed in response to a family-identified need are far more likely to be carried out at home. Second, it is economically more sound to empower the family to find ways to coordinate resources to meet their unique needs than for one agency to try to coordinate and deliver all of the services. Third, families have a legal right to be participants in the design of interventions for their child. Embracing a family-centered approach means that parents will be fully informed and integrally involved in their child's program. Finally, the design of an early intervention program will be far more relevant and appropriate if it is done with an understanding of and respect for the family who is involved.

The adoption of a family-centered approach requires the early interventionist to use a social-systems perspective of the family and understand that the family is a social unit embedded in other social networks (Dunst et al., 1988). The ability of a family to fulfill their role in supporting their child's development involves far more than their relationships with their child or the information they have about the child; it is contingent on the family's role demands, stresses, and supports from other units in their social system (Bronfenbrenner, 1975). Thus, the adoption of a family-centered approach broadens the focus of early intervention from the child to the family. The emphasis of the focus on the family is not to find problems in the family system, but to assist families in identifying their strengths, needs, and sources of support, and to assist them in the achievement of the resources they desire (Dunst et al., 1988).

Inherent in a family-centered approach are new roles for professionals. The early interventionist must be willing to move beyond the traditional role of working only with the child and be able to become a consultant, resource, enabler, mobilizer, mediator, and advocate for the family. Most important, the early interventionist must be able to actively and reflectively listen to families, allowing them to guide the intervention. The roles of the early interventionist in a family-centered approach are described in Figure 18–2.

Individualized Family Service Plan

The configuration of services and supports is formalized in the IFSP process. Although the

Empathetic Listener	The early interventionist must be able to use active and reflective listening in interactions with families.
Teacher/Therapist	The early interventionist must be able to address family and child needs in the design of interventions that will enhance the developmental status of the child and the competence of the family.
Consultant	The early interventionist must be able to provide information and opinions in response to requests made by the family or their social network members.
Resource	The early interventionist must be able to share information about different sources of support and resources with the family.
Enabler	The early interventionist must be able to create opportunities for families to become skilled at obtaining resources and supports they need.
Mobilizer	The early interventionist must be able to link the family with others who can assist in gaining access to needed resources and supports.
Mediator	The early interventionist must be able to mediate the interactions between different agencies and support network members in a manner that promotes cooperation.
Advocate	The early interventionist must be able to provide the family with knowledge of the rights of families and children and how to negotiate with policy-makers.

Figure 18–2
The Roles of the Early Interventionist In a Family-Centered Approach

From *Enabling and Empowering Families: Principles and Guidelines for Practice* by C. J. Dunst, C. M. Trivette, & A. G. Deal, 1988, Cambridge, MA: Brookline Books. Copyright 1988 by Brookline Books, Inc. Reprinted by permission.

IFSP is similar to an IEP in terms of intervention goals for the infant or toddler, it differs significantly in the area of family involvement and concerns, as described in chapter 2.

The process involves far more than the generation of an IFSP. Before an IFSP can be developed, the early intervention professionals and the family must work together to determine the priorities and needs of the family. The principles that underlie the IFSP process have been identified by McGonigel (1991) and are listed in Figure 18–3.

- Infants and toddlers are uniquely dependent on their families for their survival and nurturance. This dependence necessitates a family-centered approach to early intervention.
- States and programs should define "family" in a way that reflects the diversity of family patterns and structures.
- Each family has its own structure, roles, values, beliefs, and coping styles. Respect for and acceptance of this diversity is a cornerstone of family-centered early intervention.
- Early intervention systems and strategies must honor the racial, ethnic, cultural, and socioeconomic diversity of families.
- Respect for family autonomy, independence, and decision making means that families must be able to choose the level and nature of early intervention's involvement in their lives.
- Family/professional collaboration and partnerships are the keys to family-centered early intervention and to successful implementation of the IFSP process.
- An enabling approach to working with families requires that professionals reexamine their traditional roles and practices and develop new practices when necessary—practices that promote mutual respect and partnerships.
- Early intervention services should be flexible, accessible, and responsive to family-identified needs.
- Early intervention services should be provided according to the normalization principle—that is, families should have access to services provided in as normal a fashion and environment as possible and that promote the integration of the child and family within the community.
- No one agency or discipline can meet the diverse and complex needs of infants and toddlers with special needs and their families. Therefore, a team approach to planning and implementing the IFSP is necessary.

Figure 18–3
Principles Underlying the IFSP Process

From Philosophical and Conceptual Framework by M. J. McGonigel, 1991, in M. J. McGonigel, R. K. Kaufman, & B. H. Johnson (Eds.), *Guidelines and Recommended Practices for the Individualized Family Service Plan* (2nd ed.), p. 9, Bethesda, MD: Association for the Care of Children's Health. Reprinted by permission.

Initial Contact The IFSP process begins with the initial contact between the family and the early intervention agency. It is during the initial contact that the family should be introduced to the concept of a family-centered approach. This means that a child's developmental status, family's income level, or some other agency criteria does not drive what services are considered for the family. Early intervention services that are allowed under Part H include family training, counseling, and home visits; special instruction; speech pathology and audiology; occupational therapy; physical therapy; psychological services; service coordination services; medical services for the purpose of diagnosis and evaluation; screening and assessment services; health services needed to help the child benefit from other services; social work services; vision services; assistive technology; and transportation costs. At this stage, the early intervention team should seek to determine family needs and priorities in order to offer services that are family-centered. Some families will come to an early intervention program with prior experience in working with professionals (e.g., in a hospital setting) and may have a clear vision of what they want, while other families may not be aware of the services that are available. It is important at this stage in the IFSP process to inform families of the services that may be available, but to do so in a way that does not communicate that their needs in other areas are not a concern to the early intervention team.

Planning the Assessment After the first contact is made, the family and professionals should plan the assessment process. The early intervention team will want to assess the child, and Part H requires that the child be assessed by a multidisciplinary team composed of persons with training in the appropriate methods and procedures. Another activity to be completed in this stage is identifying family concerns, priorities, and resources. This is an activity that is not familiar to most early interventionists and is one that should be approached with sensitivity and caution.

Part H of P.L. 99-457 does not require that family strengths and needs be formally assessed. Families who participate in early intervention programs are not under an obligation to provide information on aspects of their family life that they do not wish to share. Moreover, the identification of family concerns, priorities, and resources should be based on the family's determination of which aspects are relevant to supporting their child's development (Kaufmann & McGonigel, 1991).

There are formal and informal measures that have been used with families to assist them in identifying their concerns, priorities, and resources. Figures 18–4 and 18–5 present examples of self-assessment scales that can be used as a foundation for the discussion of family needs and sources of support. The use of more formal measures that have been developed for clinical settings and have a pathological orientation are not recommended for early intervention. These types of instruments are highly intrusive and may cause families to feel as if they have problems or deficits (Slentz & Bricker, 1992).

Planning for assessment involves determining what assessments will be conducted, when and where the assessments will take place, and the roles the family wishes to play in assessment activities. The early interventionist may want to ask the family about places they should observe the child, what time of day would be best to assess the child, who might have important information about the child, and what assessments have already been conducted.

Developing the IFSP When the assessment activities have been completed, the team should meet with the family and discuss the results.

Family Support Scale

Carl J. Dunst, Vicki Jenkins, & Carol M. Trivette

Name: ______________________________ Date: ______________

Listed below are people and groups that often times are helpful to members of a family raising a young child. This questionnaire asks you to indicate how helpful each source is to your family.

Please circle the response that best describes how helpful the sources have been to your family during the past 3 to 6 months. If a source of help has not been available to your family during this period of time, circle the NA (Not Available) response.

How helpful has each of the following been to you in terms of raising your child(ren):	Not Available	Not at All Helpful	Sometimes Helpful	Generally Helpful	Very Helpful	Extremely Helpful
1. My parents	NA	1	2	3	4	5
2. My spouse or partner's parents	NA	1	2	3	4	5
3. My relatives/kin	NA	1	2	3	4	5
4. My spouse or partner's relatives/kin	NA	1	2	3	4	5
5. Spouse or partner	NA	1	2	3	4	5
6. My friends	NA	1	2	3	4	5
7. My spouse or partner's friends	NA	1	2	3	4	5

Figure 18–4

One Example of a Self-Assessment Scale: Family Support

From *Enabling and Empowering Families: Principles and Guidelines for Practice* by C.J. Dunst, C.M. Trivette, & A.G. Deal, 1988, Cambridge, MA: Brookline Books. Copyright 1988 by Brookline Books, Inc. Reprinted by permission.

Once the child assessment activities and family concerns and priorities have been identified, the early intervention team, composed of the family, the service coordinator, and other relevant program staff, should identify the outcomes desired from the early intervention. This is accomplished by developing the IFSP.

The IFSP should be viewed as a dynamic document that represents an ongoing process. The form of the written IFSP is not as important as the collaboration and interactions that occur in the process, although there are some required features (see earlier discussion) that the IFSP must include.

The first step in developing the IFSP is to determine the desired outcomes of the early intervention. Outcome statements are not behavioral objectives. In keeping with the family-centered approach, outcome statements should come from the family, be written in the family's language (Kramer, McGonigel, & Kaufman, 1991), and should list the changes the family wants for themselves and their child.

When outcomes have been identified, the team should examine the resources that are available from the family, the early intervention program, and the community to con-

How helpful has each of the following been to you in terms of raising your child(ren):	Not Available	Not at All Helpful	Sometimes Helpful	Generally Helpful	Very Helpful	Extremely Helpful
8. My own children	NA	1	2	3	4	5
9. Other parents	NA	1	2	3	4	5
10. Co-workers	NA	1	2	3	4	5
11. Parent groups	NA	1	2	3	4	5
12. Social groups/clubs	NA	1	2	3	4	5
13. Church members/minister	NA	1	2	3	4	5
14. My family or child's physician	NA	1	2	3	4	5
15. Early childhood intervention program	NA	1	2	3	4	5
16. School/day-care center	NA	1	2	3	4	5
17. Professional helpers (social workers, therapists, teachers, etc.)	NA	1	2	3	4	5
18. Professional agencies (public health, social services, mental health, etc.)	NA	1	2	3	4	5
19. ____________________	NA	1	2	3	4	5
20. ____________________	NA	1	2	3	4	5

Figure 18–4, *continued*

tribute to the achievement of the outcomes (Kramer et al., 1991). It is at this point in the process that knowledge of family strengths and resources is critical. The goal for the professionals on the team is to build on and use family strengths and resources for accomplishing outcomes rather than trying to provide all of the resources that are needed.

The identification of strategies and activities designed to accomplish outcomes is a natural extension of the discussion of strengths and resources (Kramer et al., 1991). When they have been identified, a criteria for the achievement of the outcome and a timeline for evaluation is established. It is important to emphasize that this is not the end of the IFSP process. The IFSP should be reviewed and revised as frequently as needed. Early intervention programs must resist the temptation to ritualize the IFSP process or the document or to establish procedures that may inhibit the intended family-centered philosophy of the process. An example of a completed IFSP is provided in Appendix C.

The Intervention Context

The environments that serve as the context of interventions are quite diverse. Professionals may work in the home, community childcare programs, public school early childhood class-

Family Needs Scale

Carl J. Dunst, Carolyn S. Cooper, Janet C. Weeldreyer, Kathy D. Snyder, & Joyce H. Chase

Name: ______________________ Date: __________

This scale asks you to indicate if you have a need for any type of help or assistance in 41 different areas. Please circle the response that best describes how you feel about needing help in those areas.

To what extent do you feel the need for any of the following types of help or assistance:	Not Applicable	Almost Never	Seldom	Sometimes	Often	Almost Always
1. Having money to buy necessities and pay bills	NA	1	2	3	4	5
2. Budgeting money	NA	1	2	3	4	5
3. Paying for special needs for my child	NA	1	2	3	4	5
4. Saving money for the future	NA	1	2	3	4	5
5. Having clean water to drink	NA	1	2	3	4	5
6. Having food for two meal for my family	NA	1	2	3	4	5
7. Having time to cook healthy meals for my family	NA	1	2	3	4	5
8. Feeding my child	NA	1	2	3	4	5
9. Getting a place to live	NA	1	2	3	4	5
10. Having plumbing, lighting, heat	NA	1	2	3	4	5
11. Getting furniture, clothes, toys	NA	1	2	3	4	5
12. Completing chores, repairs, home improvements	NA	1	2	3	4	5

Figure 18–5

Another Example of a Self-Assessment Scale: Family Needs

From *Enabling and Empowering Families: Principles and Guidelines for Practice* by C.J. Dunst, C.M. Trivette, & A.G. Deal, 1988, Cambridge, MA: Brookline Books.

rooms, developmental centers, and hospitals. Programs that are designed for infants and toddlers are more likely to deliver services in the home, a community childcare program, or a hospital. Programs for 3- to 5-year-olds often use a classroom approach, bringing the children into a center for instruction.

The role of the professional is different in each of these settings. In home-based programs, the professional works directly with the family and supports them in meeting their needs and the developmental needs of their child. In center-based programs, the professional must coordinate instruction of a small group of children for an extended period of time and, in addition, must also find a way to maintain a family focus and support the family in meeting their needs although they may not be involved in the program on a daily basis. A combination of center- and home-based

To what extent do you feel the need for any of the following types of help or assistance:	Not Applicable	Almost Never	Seldom	Sometimes	Often	Almost Always
13. Adapting my house for my child	NA	1	2	3	4	5
14. Getting a job	NA	1	2	3	4	5
15. Having a satisfying job	NA	1	2	3	4	5
16. Planning for future job of my child	NA	1	2	3	4	5
17. Getting where I need to go	NA	1	2	3	4	5
18. Getting in touch with people I need to talk to	NA	1	2	3	4	5
19. Transporting my child	NA	1	2	3	4	5
20. Having special travel equipment for my child	NA	1	2	3	4	5
21. Finding someone to talk to about my child	NA	1	2	3	4	5
22. Having someone to talk to	NA	1	2	3	4	5
23. Having medial and dental care for my family	NA	1	2	3	4	5
24. Having time to take care of myself	NA	1	2	3	4	5
25. Having emergency health care	NA	1	2	3	4	5
26. Finding special dental and medical care for my child	NA	1	2	3	4	5
27. Planning for future health needs	NA	1	2	3	4	5

Figure 18–5, *continued*

approaches is helpful in providing an intensity of services to the child and maintaining the involvement of the family (Bricker, 1989). The role of the professional is also different when he or she provides services in a hospital or community childcare program, where the primary caregivers are typically not the early interventionists. In those settings, the early interventionist functions as a consulting team member, designing interventions collaboratively and providing caregivers with the support and skills they need to support the child's development.

Interagency Collaboration and Teaming

The unique needs of the young child and the varied contexts in which intervention occurs result in a heavy emphasis on collaboration between agencies and professionals. Thus, the early interventionist may need to function as a team member on a multi-agency team and/or a collaborative team. The goals of a multi-agency team may be to assess the needs of families and young children, provide interventions to families and children, assess the array of services available to families and children, and coordi-

To what extent do you feel the need for any of the following types of help or assistance:	Not Applicable	Almost Never	Seldom	Sometimes	Often	Almost Always
28. Managing the daily needs of my child at home	NA	1	2	3	4	5
29. Caring for my child during work hours	NA	1	2	3	4	5
30. Having emergency child care	NA	1	2	3	4	5
31. Getting respite care for my child	NA	1	2	3	4	5
32. Finding care for my chid in the future	NA	1	2	3	4	5
33. Finding a school placement for my child	NA	1	2	3	4	5
34. Getting equipment or therapy for my child	NA	1	2	3	4	5
35. Having time to take my child to appointments	NA	1	2	3	4	5
36. Exploring future educational options for my child	NA	1	2	3	4	5
37. Expanding my education, skills, and interests	NA	1	2	3	4	5
38. Doing things that I enjoy	NA	1	2	3	4	5
39. Doing things with my family	NA	1	2	3	4	5
40. Participation in parent groups or clubs	NA	1	2	3	4	5
41. Traveling/vacationing with my child	NA	1	2	3	4	5

Figure 18–5, *continued*

nate resources to provide programs (Garland & Linder, 1988). The multi-agency team is almost always also multidisciplinary and involves the challenges that emerge when professionals from different backgrounds work together. Teaming across agencies also results in the challenges that surface when agencies that have different organizational structures, missions, and funding sources attempt to collaborate.

The goals of the collaborative team may be to assess the needs of the child and the family, develop and implement an intervention plan for the child and the family, evaluate the effectiveness of interventions, and support the child and the family during transition. In addition, all of these activities must be carried out in the family-centered framework.

To establish effective teams, the philosophy and the principles that underlie the purpose of the team should be a topic of discussion. The key skills that are needed by professionals on early intervention teams are a family-centered philosophical approach, effective communication skills, and skills related to team process and decision making (Bailey, 1991).

Assessment in Early Intervention

Assessment in early intervention programs is used to (1) screen and identify children who may be in need of services; (2) diagnose the nature and extent of developmental delay; (3) develop a program plan; and (4) evaluate the effectiveness of the intervention program. Assessment practices that are used by early interventionists must be sensitive to the unique characteristics and needs of very young children and their families. The complex needs and abilities of young children with severe disabilities require assessment practices that use multiple measures, derive information from multiple contexts, and examine multiple developmental domains (Neisworth & Bagnato, 1988).

Public Law 99-457 and the Individuals with Disabilities Education Act call for the development of an Individualized Family Service Plan (IFSP) and Individual Education Program (IEP) that are based on an assessment of children's current level of development and family strengths and needs. The early interventionist is typically involved in assessing the functioning level and individual instructional needs of a child, assessing family needs and strengths, and monitoring the ongoing progress of the families and children served by the early intervention program.

Curriculum-Based Assessment

Curriculum-based assessment measures are used to determine a child's current abilities, derive instructional goals, and track a child's progress along a continuum of objectives. Curriculum-based assessment measures that may be useful for young children with severe disabilities are the *Carolina Curriculum for Infants and Toddlers with Special Needs* (Johnson-Martin, Jens, Attermeier, & Hacker, 1991); *The Carolina Curriculum for Preschoolers with Special Needs* (Johnson-Martin, Attermeier, & Hacker, 1990); *Assessment, Evaluation, and Programming System (AEPS) Measurement for Birth to Three Years* (Bricker, 1992); *Early Intervention Developmental Profile* (Schafer & Moersch 1981), and the *Hawaii Early Learning Profile* (Furono et al., 1979).

Infant Learning: A Cognitive-Linguistic Intervention Strategy (Dunst, 1981) is an assessment/intervention system that is based on Piagetian theory of cognitive development. The system uses the *Uzgiris-Hunt Infant Psychological Development Scale* to determine the child's abilities in the sensorimotor period of cognitive development and then provides intervention suggestions based on the child's developmental stage. The scale uses a process approach to assessment that examines changes in the child's reaction to stimulus events to determine his or her cognitive stage (Neisworth & Bagnato, 1988). This approach is very flexible and allows the interventionist to use toys and situations that the child will find attractive and motivating.

Judgment-Based Assessment

Judgment-based assessments are clinical judgment devices that collect and quantify clinical observations (Neisworth & Bagnato, 1988). Such assessments offer a way to measure qualitative traits and behaviors such as consolability, temperament, motivation, self-control, and so forth that are important to interventionists but not often measured by traditional assessment devices. The *Carolina Record of Individual*

Behavior (Simeonsson, Huntington, Short, & Ware, 1982), which measures the behavioral style of young children with severe disabilities, is designed to allow parents and professionals to rate their perceptions of the child's social orientation, frustration, activity, reactivity, object orientation, endurance, and stereotypic behavior.

Interactive Assessment

Interactive assessment examines the social interactions of the caregiver and the child. These measures are particularly useful for early interventionists who are providing home-based intervention. Scales that may be used to assess caregiver/child interaction are the *Parent Behavior Progression* (Bromwich, 1981); the *Teaching Skills Inventory* (Rosenberg, Robinson, & Beckman, 1984): and the *Maternal Behavior Rating Scale* (Mahoney, Powell, & Finger, 1986).

Norm-Based Assessment

Norm-based assessments are used to compare a child's developmental skills to a normative group; they describe the child's level of functioning, predict his or her developmental outcome, and place him or her in a diagnostic category (Neisworth & Bagnato, 1988). Norm-based scales allow you to compare a child's developmental level to the average child, but they are not helpful in evaluating progress and will provide little guidance in determining the instructional program for a child with severe disabilities. Norm-based scales that are frequently used by early interventionists are the *Battelle Developmental Inventory* (Newborg, Stock, Wnek, Guidubaldi, & Svinicki, 1988) and the *Bayley Scales of Infant Development* (Bayley, 1969).

Systematic Observation

Early interventionists find that a valuable tool in determining educational goals and evaluating child progress is the use of systematic observation. Although early interventionists deal with very young children and families, an ecological approach to determining intervention targets can be very helpful. The procedures that are used are the same as those used in conducting ecological inventories and constructing a functional curriculum for older students. Moreover, the use of systematic observation to track the developmental progress of children is of paramount importance. There is no other measure that is as dynamic and sensitive to behavior change.

Instructional Programs for Young Children

Instructional programs for young children with severe disabilities should consist of systematic instruction embedded in the context of age-appropriate activities just as we have recommended for the school-age student with severe disabilities. However, for young children, their primary activity is play with a caregiver, toys, or peers. Early childhood educators, who have recognized the importance of play in the programs that they design for infants and young children who are typically developing, believe that the primary vehicle for promoting learning is child-initiated, child-directed, teacher-supported play (Hanline & Fox, 1993). The teacher's role is to arrange the environment to encourage play and to support children as they are playing in a way that promotes skill development. The components of best practices in early childhood education programs are described in *Developmentally Appropriate Practice in Early Childhood Programs*

Serving Children from Birth through Age 8 (Bredekamp, 1991).

Developmentally Appropriate Practice

Developmentally appropriate practice (DAP) is defined as providing interventions that are (1) individually appropriate and (2) age appropriate. Early educators use their knowledge of child development in conjunction with their knowledge of individual children to plan a curriculum that supports the child's development.

A developmentally appropriate curriculum focuses on all areas of a child's development through an integrated approach. The process of learning is emphasized rather than the creation of a product. The activities and materials that are used in the curriculum are concrete and relevant to children's daily lives. The environment is prepared by the teacher to encourage active exploration and interaction with adults, peers, and materials. Teachers facilitate children's learning by asking questions, adding more complex materials, and making suggestions to children as they work with materials or activities. Adults provide children with many opportunities to make choices and time to explore through active involvement. Infants and toddlers are given opportunities to use self-initiated repetition to practice newly acquired skills. Activities for the preschooler include dramatic play materials, wheeled toys, art activities, puzzles, blocks, and simple stories. Worksheets and isolated drill activities are not considered appropriate.

In developmentally appropriate programs, adult-child interactions are characterized by adults responding to children immediately, warmly, and directly. Adults provide varied opportunities for children to participate in two-way communication and respond to children by identifying and elaborating on their feelings, perceptions, interests, and activities. In early childhood special education, the role of the adult is much more intrusive. Young children with severe disabilities often need to be positioned or assisted with movement and to have their communication facilitated or interpreted; they need more intrusive, systematic instructional techniques. The DAP framework is viewed by early educators as a dynamic approach to curriculum development and implementation that will accommodate these more intrusive approaches if they are needed by individual children (Bredekamp & Rosegrant, 1992; Kostelnik, 1992).

Activity-Based Instruction

The concept of activity-based instruction can be applied to young children with severe disabilities in the manner that has been discussed (see chapter 9) for school-age students. Bricker and Cripe (1992) describe an activity-based approach as "a child directed, transactional approach that embeds intervention on children's individual goals and objectives in routine, planned, or child-initiated activities, and uses logically occurring antecedents and consequences to develop functional and generalizable skills" (p. 40). The context for the activity-based approach, which is a play-based environment, is the same as that used for typically developing young children (Hanline & Fox, 1993).

The adoption of an activity-based approach to instruction means that instruction will be delivered from a normalized perspective by providing the same activities to children with disabilities that are provided to typically developing children and using instructional procedures that are only as intrusive as necessary (Bailey & McWilliam, 1990). The implementation of an activity-based approach begins with the identification of functional and generative target skills (Bricker & Cripe, 1992). Although typical early childhood experiences will be used for the context of instruction (e.g., sandbox play, easel painting), the skills that are selected for instruction should be focused on the development of generalized motor, communication, cognitive, self-help, and social skills that will lead to independent functioning. For example, it would be inappropriate to have an instructional goal of painting a picture at the easel. A more appropriate goal would be to grasp a variety of objects. Then the skill of grasping could be instructed when the child attempted to easel paint in addition to a variety of other activities. Once the instructional goals are selected, the early interventionist uses an activity/skill matrix to determine opportunities for embedding skill instruction within activities.

The activities that are selected for instruction can be routine, planned, or child-initiated. Routine activities occur daily in a predictable sequence—washing hands before meals, picking up toys before moving to another activity, and putting on outer clothing before going outside—and offer practical opportunities to use motor, communication, social, and cognitive skills. Planned activities are child-relevant activities that are fun and interesting and also create opportunities for specific skill development. An example of a planned activity might be a cooking activity where the child with disabilities is prompted to reach and grasp, pour ingredients into a bowl, and take turns. Child-initiated activities are ones that children express an interest in or introduce. An example of a child-initiated activity is a child walking to a swing to indicate that he wishes to get on and be pushed. These types of activities should be used by the early interventionist to embed instruction or guided practice on targeted skills.

Figure 18–6 presents an activity/skill matrix for Trina, a preschooler with severe disabilities. Trina's goals include lifting her head up and maintaining it in an upright position, reaching and grasping for objects, initiating social interactions by vocalizing to peers and adults, maintaining attention to an activity, engaging in turn-taking, and indicating preferences by looking at a desired object. In Trina's preschool program she learns these skills in a play-based curriculum with typical peers. Much of Trina's schedule includes large blocks of time where children are free to select activities. Trina is assisted to make an activity selection by an adult or peer. When she begins an activity, the adult follows her lead and embeds systematic instruction within the selected context.

Naturalistic Teaching Procedures

Naturalistic teaching is an approach to instruction that is easily accommodated in a play-based classroom. Naturalistic teaching procedures fall within the framework of DAP in that they are based upon child interest and promote child exploration. Fox and Hanline (1993) describe how naturalistic teaching may be used to teach young children with disabilities cognitive, preacademic, motor, and presymbolic skills in a developmentally appropriate preschool classroom.

The teaching episode begins with child selection of an activity or a toy. If it is difficult to determine what activity the child is interested in, the teacher takes the child to the various centers and observe his or her behavior. Signs of interest may include smiling, relaxation of tone, manipulation of materials, and vocalizing. Another way to provide choices is to offer representational objects of the center (e.g., a block to represent blocks or a plate to represent the dramatic area) or a picture board that displays the activities for selection.

Once the child has made a selection, the teacher should join the child in the play activity and should provide focused attention by (a) modeling the desired target behavior and/or identifying peers who are engaging in the target behavior, (b) verbally labeling the behavior, and (c) looking expectantly at the child. If the child does not respond to the focused attention cues, the teacher should provide a verbal cue in the form of a question (e.g., "Do you want a block?"). If the child does not respond to the question, the teacher provides a mand (instruction) to engage in the behavior (e.g., "Pick up the block"). If the child does not respond correctly to the mand, the teacher provides physical assistance to perform the skill. An example of the naturalistic teaching procedure for teaching a child with severe disabilities to put objects in a container, give an object on request, and manipulate objects with two hands is shown in Figure 18–7.

Environmental Arrangements

Environments for preschoolers, infants, and toddlers are arranged in ways that are safe, nurturing, and will support the development of skills. Young children should not be required to sit at tables and engage only in teacher-selected activities. The environments provided to young children with severe disabilities should be very similar to those provided for typically developing children.

Classrooms for young children are usually large open rooms with activity areas that are defined by low bookcases or storage shelves, which make it easy for an adult to have a view of the entire classroom while providing the children with defined spaces for their activities (Twardosz, Cataldo, & Risley, 1974). The barriers around activity areas should be arranged to allow for ease of movement from one activity to another.

The classroom should be furnished with child-sized furniture, including tables, chairs, and toilets. Appropriate adaptive seating equipment should be available for each child who has specialized seating needs. It is important that adaptive seating or positioning equipment allow the child to access activity areas and to be at the same level as his peers. For example, it is not appropriate to use an adaptive chair that raises the child with disabilities above his peers; the physical separation will hinder social interaction opportunities. In addition to child-sized furniture, the classroom should have a personal storage space for each child.

Displays that are used to decorate the classroom should be relevant to children and reflect an acceptance of diverse cultures and individuals. Wall displays and bulletin boards should be placed where children can see them and should include products from the children. When commercial displays are used (e.g., bulletin-board kits) the teacher should be careful to select those that reflect multicultural values. Some displays reinforce stereotyped images of other cultures (e.g., Native Americans as Indians with tomahawks), abilities (e.g., children with disabilities not participating actively), and sex (e.g., girls playing house and boys building with blocks).

The activity areas that are typically provided in classrooms for young children are arts/craft area, dramatic play area, blocks, fluid play, manipulatives, and reading. In addition, it is important to provide a quiet, comfortable area for children who need a break and an area where parents have a bulletin board or message book for home/school communication. A typical classroom arrangement is shown in Figure 18–8.

Materials should be stored in activity areas so that they are easily accessible to children. They should be stored on open shelves or in clear bins so that they are visible to the children. Storage containers can be labeled with pictures of the items that belong in them to

Skills to Be Taught

Time/Activity	Lift Head	Reach & Grasp	Initiate Social Interactions	Indicate Preferences	Maintain Attention	Turn Taking
9:00-9:10 arrival with Dad	look at teacher or peer	pull out cubby for belongings	vocalize or smile a greeting			
9:10-10:15 center time (choice of blocks, microspheric sociodramatic, macrospheric sociodramatic, quiet area, art/fluid materials)	within chosen activity	with materials of choice	with peer in play	a. in activity selection b. when peers offer objects	time spent in play activity	exchange of toys/materials in play
10:15-10:40 transition to snack/handwashing & toileting/snack	a. standing at sink b. sitting in chair	a. soap b. towel c. spoon d. cup	with peers at snack	when offered drink & snack items		
10:40-11:30 outdoor activities (choice of water play, sand play, sociodramatic, riding toys, climbing)	within chosen activity	with materials of choice	with peers in play	a. in activity selection b. when peers offer objects	time spent in play activity	exchange of toys/materials in play
11:30-12:15 transition to lunch/handwashing & toileting/lunch	a. standing at sink b. sitting in chair	a. soap b. towel c. spoon d. cup	with peers at lunch	when offered drink & meal items		

12:15-12:30 lunch clean-up/toileting/tooth brushing/transition to quiet activity of choice	a. standing at sink b. sitting in chair	a. soap b. towel c. toothbrush d. play material or book	with peers in activity	a. in activity selection b. when peers offer objects	time spent in activity	exchange of toys/materials in activity
12:30-12:45 group storytime/songtime or quiet centers	sitting on rug or sitting at center	materials in center	within group activity	a. in activity selection b. when peers offer objects	time spent in activity	exchange of toys/materials in activity
12:45 nap time or quiet centers (books, fine motor manipulatives)	not addressed unless awake; if awake, goals are addressed as in 9:10-10:15 center time					
1:15 transition to outside with toileting or continue napping	not addressed unless awake; if awake, goals are addressed as described					
1:25 continue napping or outdoor centers	not addressed unless awake; if awake, goals are addressed as in 10:15-10:45 outdoor activities if sleeping, toileting clusters (as indicated at 1:15) occur at 1:50					
2:00 review of the day	sitting on rug		within group activity		time spent in activity	exchange of materials in activity
2:15 depart with child care provider	look at teacher/peer/child care provider	receive home notebook	vocalize or smile a greeting			

Figure 18–6
Activity/Skill Matrix for Trina, a Preschooler with Severe Disabilities

From "Learning Within the Context of Play: Providing Typical Early Childhood Experiences for Children with Severe Disabilities" by M. F. Hanline & L. Fox, 1993, *Journal of the Association for Persons with Severe Handicaps, 18,* pp. 121–129. Copyright 1993 by The Association for Persons with Severe Handicaps. Reprinted by permission.

Target One: Puts object in container	Target Two: Gives object on request	Target Three: Manipulates object with both hands
1. The teacher, Josh, and his peers are playing in the housekeeping area, pretending to cook dinner. Josh is watching a peer place plastic green beans into a pan that is on the stove. The teacher looks at the peer engaging in the target behavior, turns to Josh with an expectant look, and waits for a response. If Josh does not respond in 4 seconds, the teacher provides a comment on the peer's engagement in the target behavior (e.g., "Japre is putting beans in the pan.").	1. The teacher, Josh, and his peers are playing in the block area with blocks and small plastic zoo animals. Josh is seated on the floor along side a pile of blocks. The adult begins to hand blocks one at a time to the peers. They are using the blocks to build an enclosure in which to put the animals. When Josh looks at the teacher handing blocks to his peers, the teacher turns to Josh with an expectant look, and waits for a response. If Josh does not respond in 4 seconds, the teacher provides a comment on her engagement in the target behavior (e.g., "I'm handing blocks to your friends.").	1. The teacher, Josh, and peers are outdoors engaging in water play. The water table is equipped with small plastic dolls, baby bottles, and washcloths. Some of the children are washing the dolls, some are dripping water on their arms with a washcloth, and others are feeding the dolls. Josh is watching a child who is holding her doll with two hands, dipping it in and out of the water. The teacher looks at the peer engaging in the target behavior, turns to Josh with an expectant look, and waits for a response. If Josh does not respond in 4 seconds, the teacher provides a comment on the peer's engagement in the target behavior (e.g., "Kathryn is using her hands to dip her baby doll.").
2. If Josh does not respond to the comment on the peer's engagement in 4 seconds, the teacher provides a verbal cue in the form of **a question** (e.g., "Do you want to take a turn putting beans in the pan?").	2. If Josh does not respond to the comment in 4 seconds, the teacher provides a verbal cue in the form of **a question** (e.g., "Do you want to give Andy a block?").	2. If Josh does not respond to the comment on the peer's engagement in 4 seconds, the teacher provides a verbal cue in the form of **a question** (e.g., "Do you want to dip a baby doll?").
3. If Josh does not respond to the question in 4 seconds, the adult provides **a mand** to engage in the target behavior (e.g., "Josh, take a turn, please. Put the beans in the pan.").	3. If Josh does not respond to the question in 4 seconds, the adult provides **a mand** to engage in the target behavior (e.g., "Josh, take a turn, please. Give Andy a block.").	3. If Josh does not respond to the question in 4 seconds, the adult provides **a mand** to engage in the target behavior (e.g., "Josh, take a turn, please. Use your hands to dip the baby.").
4. If Josh does not respond to the mand in 4 seconds, the adult provides **physical assistance** to engage in the target behavior.	4. If Josh does not respond to the mand in 4 seconds, the adult provides **physical assistance** to engage in the target behavior.	4. If Josh does not respond to the mand in 4 seconds, the adult provides **physical assistance** to engage in the target behavior.
5. The skill is **reinforced** by affirmation of the child's engagement in the target behavior by the adult (e.g., "This is fun! We're putting beans in the pan with Japre.").	5. The skill is **reinforced** by affirmation of the child's engagement in the target behavior by the adult (e.g., "I like playing with blocks with you and your friends.").	5. The skill is **reinforced** by affirmation of the child's engagement in the target behavior by the adult (e.g., "We're dipping the baby. Isn't this fun?").

Figure 18–7
Examples of Naturalistic Teaching Procedure
From A Preliminary Evaluation of Learning Within Developmentally Appropriate Early Childhood Settings by L. Fox & M. F. Hanline, 1993, *Topics in Early Childhood Special Education, 13*, pp. 308-327. Copyright © by PRO-ED, Inc. Reprinted by permission.

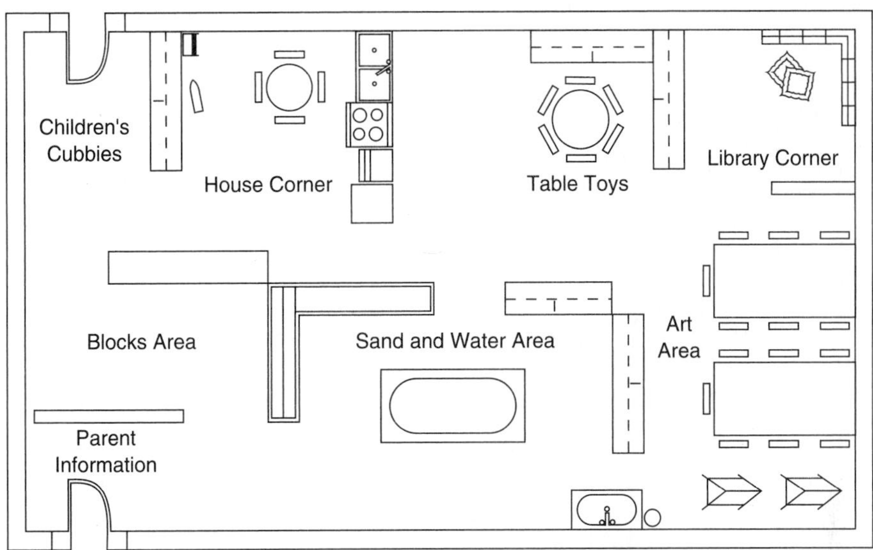

Figure 18–8
Room Arrangement
From Activity-Based Instruction by T. Udell, in J. Peters, C. Bunse, L. Carlson, L. Doede, G. Glasenapp, K. Hayden, C. Lehman, T. P. Templeman, & T. Udell (Eds.), *Supporting Children with Disabilities in Community Programs* (p. 23), 1992, Monmouth, OR: Teaching Research Publications. Copyright 1992 by The Teaching Research Division. Reprinted by permission.

facilitate putting materials away after use. The number of materials that are available in each activity area is of importance. When too few toys are provided, children will have difficulty playing together. Some teachers may feel that providing only one of each toy will teach children to share, but very young children, and especially children who have social development delays, are not ready to share or play cooperatively until they are 4 or 5 years old. It is better to have enough duplicates of each item for the number of children who are expected to play in the activity center. For example, if you expect four children to play in the dramatic play area, you should provide four hats or four shopping baskets.

Blocks Block areas should provide enough blocks so that several children can work together. Bender (1978) suggests that 60 to 80 blocks be provided in a block area that is designed to accommodate several children. In addition to blocks, small people, vehicles, and animals should be provided to facilitate the building of structures and pretend play. The block area is an appropriate activity area for children who are not yet engaging in pretend play. Young children with severe disabilities can engage in "putting in and taking out" play sequences, knocking down structures, and other skills as they are embedded in play activities with peers.

Dramatic Play Dramatic play areas are usually noisy and should be located away from the quiet area or reading area. It should include dress-ups and props for acting out real-life roles, and dolls of different ethnic backgrounds, kitchen equipment, telephone, tea sets, a mirror, and other dramatic play props should be available as well. Teachers often change the content of the dramatic play area to

In the dramatic play center, children can practice many targeted skills.

reflect different community environments, such as a hospital, a restaurant, or an office, that are relevant to the children in the classroom. Although young children with severe disabilities may not yet understand the concept of "dressing up," they can work on embedded skills within play sequences with their peers. For example, a child with severe disabilities may put dishes in and out of the toy sink while practicing the skills of grasp and release and social interactions with a peer.

Arts and Crafts The arts and crafts area typically provides easel painting, cutting and pasting activities, and markers with paper. This area offers children the opportunity to practice fine motor skills and engage in creative construction activities. Children with severe disabilities may need adaptive equipment such as a built-up handle on a paintbrush or material adaptations such as taping the paper to the table to facilitate their engagement in these activities.

Sand and Water Sand and water play are considered fluid play activities and can take place outdoors or indoors. The sand or water table can also be filled with rice or dried beans to vary the experiences offered to children. Other options for fluid play include bathing a doll in a small dishpan, playing with toy boats in water in a small wading pool, and sand play on a cafeteria tray with cookie cutters for imprinting shapes. Fluid play activities are very soothing to some young children; however, other children may have difficulty with containing the fluids. For children who have difficulty with fluid play, offering them a more controlled fluid experience such as pouring water from a pitcher into a bowl or washing a doll in a small pan may be an appropriate first step (Wolfgang & Wolfgang, 1992).

Manipulatives The manipulatives area provides puzzles, counting markers, beads to string, small building blocks such as Legos or Bristle Blocks, lotto, lacing boards, parquetry sets, and pegboards for children's construction play. This area should not be viewed as a preacademic area where "real" teaching occurs, but only as another area where children learn through play and exploration. This is also an appropriate area to house a computer. When properly outfitted with a switch or touch screen, a computer can provide a wealth of exploratory learning experiences for children with severe disabilities. Computer software that encourages the discovery of simple cause-and-effect relationships as well as concept development would be useful in the preschool classroom.

Reading In the reading center, quality children's literature and a comfortable place to read should be provided. Books should be displayed on shelves with their covers clearly visible so that children will be encouraged to explore them. The reading area could also include a puppet theater, Language Master, or tape recorder with books on tape. Children with disabilities may need adaptive equipment to turn pages, hold a book, or activate the tape recorder.

In every activity center, adaptations may have to be made to accommodate children with severe disabilities. Rosenberg, Clark, Filer, Hupp, & Finkler (1992) describe a process where the barriers to active participation are examined and interventions occur to increase the participation of the child with disabilities. The process begins by analyzing how much the child participates and identifying the factors that lead to low participation. Then interventions are designed that (a) increase the child's skills, (b) identify alternative behaviors that can be used, (c) modify the environment, or (d) adapt the activity to circumvent the barrier. For example, a child with physical disabilities who has difficulty using regular blocks can be provided with magnetic blocks on a cookie tray.

Electromechanical switch toys might also be used to increase active participation by children with severe disabilities. The preschool teacher may want to include an activity center of switch toys or integrate them into centers as appropriate. For example, it may be appropriate to have a switch toy of cars on a track in the block center and a switch attached to a "spin art" toy in the arts/crafts center.

Infant Intervention

Many early intervention programs do not provide classroom programs for infants and toddlers, but do provide home-based early intervention in the child's home or childcare setting. In such situations, an activity/skills matrix can still be used to organize the instruction of skills in routine, planned, and child-initiated activities. The design of the activity/skill matrix should occur in collaboration with the caregiver and should be responsive to the caregiver's schedule and time demands. Routine activities in the home are activities such as diapering, feeding, dressing, and bath time. Child-initiated activities are activities such as play interactions or requests for attention. Planned activities could be reading stories, a walk in the stroller, or play time. An activity-skill matrix for Sita, a 12-month-old with severe disabilities, is shown in Figure 18–9.

In some home-based programs the early interventionist works primarily with the child while the caregiver observes and learns techniques that can be used to facilitate the child's development. A recent trend is for interventionists to provide support to the caregiver as the caregiver interacts with the child (Mahoney & Powell, 1988; McCollum & Stayton, 1985). Because the caregiver is with the child more than the interventionist, supporting and guiding the caregiver's interactions with the child may be a more effective practice. Moreover, the quality of the caregiver/infant relationship is critical to the development of the child. Programs that have been designed with a focus on the caregiver/infant relationship are the Transactional Intervention Program (Mahoney & Powell, 1988), the ECO model (McDonald & Gillette, 1986), and the Hanen Program (Hanlonson, 1992).

Inclusion and Young Children

The inclusion of young children with disabilities is important for legal, educational, and moral reasons as described in chapter 9. Much of the research that supports the feasibility and benefits of inclusion programs was conducted with young children (Peck, Furman, & Helmstetter, 1993). Despite the clear rationales for providing inclusive programs and the

	Skills to Be Taught				
Time/Activity	**Stand Independently**	**Objects in Containers**	**Take Turn in Social Game**	**Imitate "Ma" "Ba"**	**Extend Arms to Request**
Play time	by table by shelf	toys away toys in containers	peek-a-boo tickle game	vocal play	to get in lap to be picked up
Feeding				vocal play	to get in high chair
Diapering	before lifting to changing table		tickle game	vocal play	to get down
Bath time	before lifting into tub	toys in/out tub	peek-a-boo bath game tickle game	vocal play	to get out
Dressing	before lifting to changing table		peek-a-boo tickle game	vocal play	to get down
Walk in stroller	before placing in stroller	toys in/out of bag	social games when resting	vocal play	to get in/out of stroller

Figure 18–9
Home Activity/Skill Matrix for Sita

wealth of literature that supports inclusion, programs face professional and bureaucratic barriers that impede implementation (Odom & McEvoy, 1990).

A significant barrier to inclusive programs for preschoolers with disabilities is that schools are not typically serving nondisabled children of the same age. Similar problems exist for the agencies who serve infants and toddlers in early intervention programs. Often they have no access to typically developing children. A solution to the difficulty is for early intervention programs to work with the programs that are serving typically developing children (i.e., childcare centers, Head Start, family day care providers, and play groups).

In programs that have made a commitment to work with other agencies in the provision of inclusive programs, a new set of challenges can emerge. Issues that may need to be addressed include the differences in educational philosophy of early educators and early childhood special educators, lack of experience of early educators in teaching young children with disabilities, and the need to provide related services within the early childhood program. Progress in these areas requires extensive preservice and in-service training as well as administrative support, including state level support of systems change (Odom & McEvoy, 1990).

Some schools provide experiences for interactions with nondisabled peers by using mainstreaming or reverse mainstreaming options. Young children with disabilities may be mainstreamed with kindergarten children or kindergarten children may spend time in the classroom for preschoolers with disabilities. Some school districts operate Head Start programs or early intervention programs for at-risk children and their families that offer opportunities for interaction with age-matched peers.

Providing opportunities for the inclusion of infants and toddlers is even more challenging. Hanline and Hanson (1989) suggest that the inclusion of infants and toddlers with typically developing children can occur by capitalizing on opportunities that are available in the community, which may include playgroups, infant/toddler swimming classes, childcare, family events and festivals, and story hour at the library. In order to implement the inclusion of infants and toddlers with disabilities in those situations, the developmental needs, family needs, and health and safety concerns of the child must be considered. Hanline and Hanson (1989) support a flexible approach to providing inclusive programs with inclusion experiences being designed to meet the individual needs of each child.

Transition Issues

Families with young children who are severely disabled experience transitions that team members can assist them in managing. Predictable transitions may include discharge from the Neonatal Intensive Care Unit (NICU), moving from an early intervention program to a preschool program, and moving from preschool to kindergarten.

Transition planning involves a set of procedures that can be used to assist the family and the child in experiencing a smooth transition. Because transition planning is perceived by families and professionals as an essential service to families in early intervention programs, P.L. 99-547 specifies that each IFSP must document that steps should be taken to support the transition of the 3-year-old child to the preschool program. The steps involved include a discussion with the parents about future placements and other related matters, procedures to prepare the child for changes in service delivery, and, with parental permission, the transmission of information about the child to the receiving program.

Preparing for Transition

There are basic general procedures that most programs use to prepare for transitions, although different programs may use a variety of ways to conduct the procedures (Hains, Fowler, & Chandler, 1988; Hanline, 1993; Hanline & Knowlton, 1988; Lazzari, 1991). The first step in preparing for a transition is to identify the receiving program or agency. The family or the sending program may then initiate a referral to the new program. The family may be prepared for the transition to the new program by learning about the services that may be offered, the procedures that the receiving agency will use to provide services (e.g., IEP meetings), and their legal rights. Prior to the transition, a new evaluation is performed on the child, with family permission, to determine current levels of functioning. When the transition involves an array of program options, the family may be encouraged at this point to visit those programs. The sending program may provide parents with information (e.g., what to look for in a preschool program) to assist the family with site visits.

Typically, the transition will involve a discharge conference (e.g., from the NICU) or eligibility staffing (e.g., into a public school preschool). A staff person from each of the sending and receiving programs should attend these meetings to exchange information and open lines of communication between agencies. Information that will be helpful to the receiving program is provided by the sending agency with parent permission. Once the transition is complete, the sending agency provides a follow-up contact.

Each transition involves a different set of parent concerns and requires variations of the procedures. In the following sections, information relevant to transitions from the NICU, infant and toddler program, and preschool program is provided.

Transition from the NICU

The discharge of the infant with severe disabilities from the NICU to home can be a time of great parental concern and stress. The family's concerns may include adjusting to caring for an infant with specialized medical, physical, and nutritional needs, locating and accessing services in the community, and managing the day-to-day care of the child (Hanline & Deppe, 1990). A supported and planned transition may be helpful in assisting families with the discharge and adjustment to caring for the infant at home.

One way to provide a smooth transition is for the hospital or early intervention service provider to assign a professional who will be a support person for the family when the child is in the NICU and when the child goes home. When the child is in the NICU, this person can help the family understand the roles of the professionals who are involved in the infant's care and assist in gathering the information and supports the family needs in coping with their situation. In planning for the discharge, the support person can assist the family in developing questions that they have about bringing their child home. Many infants leave the NICU already linked with an agency that will provide early intervention services. If that occurs, the support person can prepare the family for the IFSP meeting by explaining the process and purpose. In addition to the IFSP meeting, the support person should attend the preparation sessions on nutritional and medical management of the infant at home with the family (Hanline & Deppe, 1990).

When the discharge has occurred the support person can assist the family in responding to the child's needs (Hanline & Deppe, 1990). The family may have questions about caregiving routines, about their child's developmental status, and about resources and services that are available in the community. Once the family has been successfully linked to an early intervention program, the role of the support person can be diminished.

Transition from the Early Intervention Program to Preschool

The transition from an early intervention program to a preschool program typically occurs when the child is 3 years old. Planning for the transition should occur several months before that day. The first step is to build a transition planning team, which should be composed of the family, the family's service coordinator, professionals who work with the family and the child, and other service providers who have frequent contact with the family. Transition planning usually occurs with the IFSP meeting because Public Law 99-457 mandates that transition concerns are to be addressed in the IFSP.

Transition planning begins by identifying the transition date for the child and the tasks that should be accomplished prior to the transition. Some of the tasks are contacting the receiving program, making the referral, visiting program options, updating the child's evaluation information, preparing the family for developing an IEP, meeting with the receiving program, and transferring information and records to the receiving program.

The transition team should remember that the goal of transition planning is to minimize the difficulties the child and the family experience with the change of service agencies. The team should discuss anticipated problems that could occur with the transition and develop strategies to minimize them. For example, if the child has a gastrostomy feeding tube, the team may wish to offer to train the receiving programs in the proper procedures to use. In addition, the early interventionist may want to conduct an ecological inventory of the preschool classroom to anticipate skill demands that she can begin to prepare the toddler to manage. For example, if children in the preschool classroom are expected to make a choice of an activity before moving to a center, the toddler teacher may want to introduce that procedure in her classroom.

It is permissible for a preschool program to continue to use an IFSP instead of the IEP for 3- to 5-year-olds (if permissible through state guidelines and approved by the family). If that does not occur, families must be prepared for participating in the IEP process. Hanline and Knowlton (1988) offered families a book that describes the referral, IEP, and placement procedures. In addition, they showed families a videotape of a mock IEP meeting and discussed the video with them. Another strategy that may be used to prepare the family for their first IEP meeting is to guide them in determining what goals and services they wish to request for their child. A person from the early intervention program should attend the IEP meeting and eligibility staffing to provide support to the family and to maintain a collaborative relationship with the receiving program.

Transition to Kindergarten

The transition to kindergarten brings a change in the curriculum and, potentially, in the amount of inclusion that can be provided to the child with severe disabilities. In some programs children will be moving from a program for preschoolers with disabilities to a full-inclusion classroom. Other children may be offered opportunities for integration from a special education classroom. Hopefully, the prospect of inclusion will not be a new idea that parents must be prepared for, although for many families this will be the case. Thus, families may need information on why inclusion is important and how inclusive programs are structured.

Several early childhood special educators have written about the need to identify the skills required in kindergarten in order to prepare preschoolers to function independently in those classrooms (Hains, Fowler, Schwartz, Kottwitz, & Rosenkeotter, 1989; McCormick & Kawate, 1982; Vincent et al., 1980). Those skills, which have been called "kindergarten survival skills," include following rules and routines, expressing wants and needs, cooperating with others, complying with directions given by an adult, sharing materials with a peer, socializing with peers, taking turns, interacting verbally with adults and peers, focusing attention on the speaker, and making decisions (Noonan & McCormick, 1993).

For many young children with severe disabilities the mastery of such skills before kindergarten is not realistic. The intent of identifying kindergarten survival skills is for the preschool teacher to gain knowledge about the kindergarten curriculum and to prepare the students for those expectations. Another tactic, which fits with that intent, is to conduct an ecological inventory of the kindergarten program so that appropriate goals can be identified and adaptations planned so that the child with severe disabilities can participate actively in the kindergarten classroom (Fowler, Schwartz, & Atwater, 1991).

A kindergarten classroom can be very different from a preschool classroom. Often the number of children is greater, the school day is more structured, and the program is less flexible. Families should have an opportunity to visit a kindergarten classroom before the transition so that they will be able to anticipate these differences. A visit to a kindergarten classroom will also assist the family in actively participating in the development of the IEP. All of the IEP team will need to understand the demands of the kindergarten classroom before designing the IEP. Both the preschool teacher and the receiving teacher should be present at the IEP meeting so that an exchange of information and collaborative planning can occur.

Conclusion

In this chapter, the rationale for and design of early childhood special education programs for young children with severe disabilities were presented. Many aspects of providing programs for young children are different due to the young age of the child and the need to provide programs in a variety of settings. Most important, early intervention programs embrace the philosophy of a family-centered approach that is supported through early intervention legislation.

Despite the unique features of early intervention programs, the foundation of these programs should be the principle of normalization (Bailey & McWilliam, 1990). Young children with severe disabilities should be provided services in normalized environments and taught using procedures that are least intrusive but result in skill acquisition. Most important, families of children with disabilities should be assisted with determining and obtaining the supports and resources they need in the community to nurture their child's development.

Questions for Reflection

1. Are there features of the Individualized Family Support Plan that, if adopted, could enhance the Individualized Education Plan for students with severe disabilities?
2. What skills are important for the early interventionist to have for working in such close collaboration with families?
3. What are some issues that the collaborative team could face when working with families from diverse cultures?
4. What do you think the benefits and difficulties are when implementing home-based instruction?
5. In what ways might the achievement of inclusion be easier in early childhood programs than in school-age programs?
6. How would *functional instruction* be defined for an infant or toddler?

References

Bailey, D. B. (1989). Issues and directions in preparing professionals to work with young handicapped children and their families. In J. J. Gallagher, R. M. Clifford, & P. Trohanis (Eds.), *Policy implementation and P.L. 99-457: Planning for young children with special needs* (pp. 97–132). Baltimore: Paul H. Brookes.

Bailey, D. B. (1991). Building positive relationships between professionals and families. In M. J. McGonigel, R. K. Kaufmann, & B. H. Johnson (Eds.), *Guidelines and recommended practices for the Individualized Family Service Plan* (2nd ed.) (pp. 29–38). Bethesda, MD: Association for the Care of Children's Health.

Bailey, D. B., & McWilliam, R. A. (1990). Normalizing early intervention. *Topics in Early Childhood Special Education, 10,* 33–47.

Bailey, D. B., & Wolery, M. (1992). *Teaching infants and preschoolers with disabilities* (2nd ed.). New York: Merrill/Macmillan.

Bayley, N. (1969). *Bayley scales of infant development.* New York: Psychological Development.

Bender, J. (1978). Large hollow blocks: Relationship of quantity to block-building behaviors. *Young Children, 34,* 17–23.

Bredekamp, S. (Ed.). (1991). *Developmentally appropriate practice in early childhood programs serving children from birth through age 8.* Washington, DC: National Association for the Education of Young Children.

Bredekamp, S., & Rosegrant, T. (Eds.). (1992). *Reaching potentials: Appropriate curriculum and assessment for young children,* vol. 1. Washington, DC: National Association for the Education of Young Children.

Bricker, D. D. (1989). *Early intervention for at-risk and handicapped infants, toddlers, and preschool children* (2nd ed.). Palo Alto, CA: Vort Corporation.

Bricker, D. D. (1992). *AEPS measurement for birth to three years.* Baltimore: Paul H. Brookes.

Bricker, D. D., & Cripe, J. J. W. (1992). *An activity-based approach to early intervention.* Baltimore: Paul H. Brookes.

Brofenbrenner, U. (1975). Is early intervention effective? In B. Friedlander, G. Sterrit, & G. Kirk (Eds.), *Exceptional infant, vol. 3. Assessment and intervention* (pp. 449–475). New York: Brunner/Mazel.

Bromwich, R. (1981). *Working with parents and infants: An interactional approach.* Baltimore: University Park Press.

Cicirelli, V., Evans, J., & Schiller, J. (1969). *The impact of Head Start: An evaluation of the effects of Head Start on children's cognitive and affective development.* Report to the U.S. Office of Economic Opportunity by Westinghouse Learning Corporation and Ohio University. Washington, DC: Government Printing Office.

Dunst, C. J. (1981). *Infant learning: A cognitive-linguistic intervention strategy.* Allen, TX: DLM/Teaching Resources.

Dunst, C. J. (1986). Overview of the efficacy of early intervention programs. In L. Bickman & D. L. Weatherford (Eds.), *Evaluating early intervention programs for severely handicapped children and their families* (pp. 79–147). Austin, TX: Pro-Ed.

Dunst, C. J., & Rheingrover, R. (1981). An analysis of the efficacy of infant intervention programs with organically handicapped children. *Evaluation and Program Planning, 4,* 287–323.

Dunst, C. J., Johanson, C., Trivette, C. M., & Hamby, D. (1991). Family-oriented early intervention policies and practices: Family centered or not? *Exceptional Children, 58,* 115–126.

Dunst, C. J., Trivette, C., & Deal, A. (1988). *Enabling and empowering families: Principles & guidelines for practice.* Cambridge, MA: Brookline Books.

Fowler, S. A., Schwartz, I., & Atwater, J. (1991). Perspectives on the transition from preschool to kindergarten for children with disabilities and their families. *Exceptional Children, 58,* 136–145.

Fox, L., & Hanline, M.F. (1993). A preliminary evaluation of learning within developmentally appropriate early childhood settings. *Topics in Early Childhood Special Education, 13,* 308–327.

Furono, S., O'Reilly, K., Hosaka, C., Inatsuka, T., Allman, T., & Zeisloft, B. (1979). *Hawaii early learning profile.* Palo Alto, CA: Vort Corp.

Hains, A. H., Fowler, S. A., & Chandler, L. K. (1988). Planning school transitions: Family and professional collaboration. *Journal of the Division for Early Childhood, 12,* 108–115.

Hains, A. H., Fowler, S. A., Schwartz, I. S., Kottwitz, E., & Rosenkoetter, S. (1989). A comparison of preschool and kindergarten expectations for school readiness. *Early Childhood Research Quarterly, 4,* 75–88.

Hanline, M. F. (1988). Making the transition to preschool: Identification of parent needs. *Journal of the Division for Early Childhood, 12,* 98–107.

Hanline, M. F. (1993). Facilitating integrated preschool service delivery transitions for children, families, and professionals. In C. A. Peck, S. L. Odom, & D. D. Bricker (Eds.), *Integrating young children with disabilities into community programs* (pp. 133–146). Baltimore: Paul H. Brookes.

Hanline, M. F., & Deppe, J. (1990). Discharging the premature infant: Family issues and implications for intervention. *Topics in Early Childhood Special Education, 9,* 15–25.

Hanline, M. F., & Fox, L. (1993). Learning within the context of play: Providing typical early childhood experiences for children with severe disabilities. *Journal of the Association for Persons with Severe Handicaps, 18,* 121–129.

Hanline, M. F., & Hanson, M. J. (1989). Integration considerations for infants and toddlers with multiple disabilities. *Journal of the Association for Persons with Severe Handicaps, 14,* 178–183.

Hanline, M. F., & Knowlton, A. (1988). A collaborative model for providing support to parents during their child's transition from infant intervention to preschool special education public school programs. *Journal of the Division for Early Childhood, 12,* 116–125.

Johnson-Martin, N. M., Attermeier, S. M., & Hacker, B. J. (1990). *The Carolina curriculum for preschoolers with special needs.* Baltimore: Paul H. Brookes.

Johnson-Martin, N. M., Jens, K. G., Attermeier, S. M., & Hacker, B. J. (1991). *The Carolina curriculum for infants and toddlers with special needs* (2nd ed.). Baltimore: Paul H. Brookes.

Kaiser, A. P., & Hemmeter, M. L. (1989). Value-based approaches to early intervention. *Topics in Early Childhood Special Education, 8,* 72–86.

Kaufman, R. K., & McGonigel, M. J. (1991). Identifying family concerns, priorities, and resources. In M. J. McGonigel, R. K. Kaufman, & B. H. Johnson (Eds.), *Guidelines and recommended practices for the individualized family service plan* (2nd ed.) (pp. 47–55). Bethesda, MD: Association for the Care of Children's Health.

Kramer, S., McGonigel, M. J., & Kaufman, R. K. (1991). Developing the IFSP: Outcomes, strategies, activities, and services. In M. J. McGonigel, R. K. Kaufman, & B. H. Johnson (Eds.), *Guidelines and recommended practices for the individualized family service plan* (2nd ed.) (pp. 57–66). Bethesda, MD: Association for the Care of Children's Health.

Kostelnik, M. J. (1992). Myths associated with developmentally appropriate programs. *Young Children, 47,* 17–23.

Lazzari, A. M. (1991). *The transition sourcebook: A practical guide for early intervention programs.* Tucson, AZ: Communication Skill Builders.

Lewis, M. (1984). Developmental principles and their implications for at-risk and handicapped infants. In M. Hanson (Ed.), *Atypical infant development* (pp. 3–17). Baltimore: University Park Press.

Mahoney, G., & Powell, A. (1988). Modifying parent-child interaction: Enhancing the development of handicapped children. *Journal of Special Education, 22,* 82–96.

Mahoney, G., Powell, A., & Finger, I. (1986). The maternal behavior rating scale. *Topics in Early Childhood Special Education, 6,* 44–56.

McCollum, J., & Stayton, V. (1985). Infant/parent interaction: Studies and intervention guidelines based on the SIAI model. *Journal of the Division for Early Childhood, 9,* 125–135.

McCormick, L., & Kawate, J. (1982). Kindergarten survival skills: New directions for preschool special education. *Education and Training of the Mentally Retarded, 17,* 247–252.

McDonald, J. D., & Gillette, Y. (1986). Communicating with persons with severe handicaps: Roles of parents and professionals. *Journal of The Association for Persons with Severe Handicaps, 11,* 255–265.

McGonigel, M. J. (1991). Philosophy and conceptual framework. In M. J. McGonigel, R. K. Kaufman, & B. H. Johnson (Eds.), *Guidelines and recommended practices for the individualized family service plan* (2nd ed.) (pp. 7–14). Bethesda, MD: Association for the Care of Children's Health.

McGonigel, M. J., Kaufman, R. K., & Johnson, B. H. (1991). A family-centered process for the individualized family service plan. *Journal of Early Intervention, 15,* 46–56.

Neisworth, J. T., & Bagnato, S. J. (1988). Assessment in early childhood special education. In S. L. Odom & M. B. Karnes (Eds.), *Early intervention for infants and children with handicaps: An empirical base* (pp. 23–49). Baltimore: Paul H. Brookes.

Newborg, J., Stock, J. R., Wnek, L., Guidubaldi, J., & Svinicki, J. (1988). *Battelle developmental inventory.* Allen, TX: DLM Teaching Resources.

Noonan, M. J., & McCormick, L. (1993). *Early intervention in natural environments: Methods and procedures.* Pacific Grove, CA: Brooks/Cole Publishing Co.

Odom, S. L., & McEvoy, M. A. (1990). Mainstreaming at the preschool level: Potential barriers and tasks for the field. *Topics in Early Childhood Special Education, 10,* 48–61.

Peck, C. A., Furman, G. C., & Helmstetter, E. (1993). Integrated early childhood programs: Research on the implementation of change in organizational contexts. In C. A. Peck, S. L. Odom, & D. D. Bricker (Eds.), *Integrating young children with disabilities into community programs* (pp. 187–205). Baltimore: Paul H. Brookes.

Peterson, N. L. (1987). *Early intervention for handicapped and at-risk children.* Denver, CO: Love Publishing.

Rosenberg, S., Clark, M., Filer, J., Hupp, S., & Finkler, D. (1992). Facilitating active learner participation. *Journal of Early Intervention, 16,* 262–274.

Rosenberg, S., Robinson, C., & Beckman, P. (1984). Teaching skills inventory: A measure of parent performance. *Journal of the Division for Early Childhood, 8,* 107–113.

Sameroff, A. J., & Chandler, M. J. (1975). Reproductive risk and the continuum of caretaking casualty. In F. D. Horowitz, M. Hetherington, S. Scarr-Salapatek, & G. Siegel (Eds.), *Review of child development research* (Vol. 4) (pp. 187-244). Chicago: University of Chicago Press.

Sameroff, A. J., & Fiese, B. (1990). Transactional regulation and early intervention. In S. J. Meisels & J. P. Shonkoff (Eds.), *Handbook of early childhood early intervention* (pp. 119–149). Cambridge: Cambridge University Press.

Schafer, D. S., & Moersch, M. S. (Eds.) (1981). *Developmental programming for infants and young children.* Ann Arbor: University of Michigan Press.

Simeonsson, R. J., Huntington, G. S., Short, R. J., & Ware, W. B. (1982). The Carolina record of individual behavior: Characteristics of handicapped infants and children. *Topics in Early Childhood Special Education, 2,* 43–55.

Slentz, K. L., & Bricker, D. (1992). Family-guided assessment for IFSP development: Jumping off the family assessment bandwagon. *Journal of Early Intervention, 16,* 11–19.

Trohanis, P. L. (1989). An introduction to PL 99-457 and the national policy agenda for serving young children with special needs and their families. In R. M. Clifford, J. J. Gallagher, & P. L. Trohanis (Eds.), *Policy implementation & PL 99-457: Planning for young children with special needs* (pp. 1–17). Baltimore: Paul H. Brookes.

Twardosz, S., Cataldo, M. F., & Risley, T. R. (1974). Open environment design for infant and toddler day care. *Journal of Applied Behavior Analysis, 7,* 529–546.

Vincent, L. J., Salisbury, C., Walter, G., Brown, P., Gruenewald, L. J., & Powers, M. (1980). Program evaluation and curriculum development in early childhood special education: Criteria of the next environment. In W. Sailor, B. Wilcox, & L. Brown (Eds.), *Methods of instruction for severely handicapped students* (pp. 303–328). Baltimore: Paul H. Brookes.

Westlake, C. R., & Kaiser, A. P. (1991). Early childhood services for children with severe disabilities: Research, values, policy, and practices. In L. H. Meyer, C. A. Peck, & L. Brown (Eds.), *Critical issues in the lives of people with severe disabilities* (pp. 429–458). Baltimore: Paul H. Brookes.

Wolfgang, C. H., & Wolfgang, M. E. (1992). *School for young children: Developmentally appropriate practices.* Boston: Allyn and Bacon.

Zigler, E., & Yale Research Group. (1976). *Summary of findings from longitudinal evaluations of intervention programs.* New Haven: Yale University Press.

CHAPTER 19

Teaching Employment Skills and Planning for Transition

Chapter Overview

In this chapter, issues associated with the movement of the student with disabilities from high school to the adult world are addressed. The chapter provides information on how to prepare for transition, the development of the transition plan, and the development and implementation of supported employment.

One of the most difficult transitions that students with severe disabilities and their families face is leaving the public school system and entering the adult world. The transition from school to adulthood involves major adjustments for the student with disabilities. Issues of importance are where the individual will live and work and how access to peers for friendship and leisure opportunities will be provided. In addition, the student's family will be leaving a public school system that offers services on an entitlement basis and entering an adult service system that operates on the basis of eligibility. This means that employment and living opportunities are not guaranteed for every individual and that families face many unknowns when they plan for their child's future.

Transition planning is a process that was designed to prepare for the inevitable exit of the student from the public school program. In transition planning, the school, the family, and the community work together to anticipate and prepare for adulthood activities. Aspects that are considered in this planning process are the student's employment and financial independence, living arrangements, mobility, peer and community relationships, and self-esteem (Wehman, 1992).

The importance of transition services was legislatively recognized when Public Law 94-142 was reauthorized and expanded under PL 101-476, the Individuals with Disabilities Education Act (IDEA), in 1990. In IDEA, transition services must be included in the student's individualized education program, with the first transition document written no later than the student's 16th birthday. In the area of severe disabilities, the learning characteristics of the student and the need for more intensive forms of support require that planning occur when the student is much younger. For many students with severe disabilities, thinking about transition should occur in the middle-school years with documentation of transition goals and activities by age 14. Transition services are addressed in IDEA in the following way:

> *Transition services means a coordinated set of activities for a student, designed within an outcome-oriented process, which promotes movement from school to postschool activities, including postsecondary education, vocational training, integrated employment, including supported employment, continuing adult education, adult services, independent living or community participation. The coordinated set of activities shall be based upon the individual student's needs taking into account the student's preferences and interests and shall*

include instruction, community experiences, development employment, and other postschool adult living objectives and, when appropriate, acquisition of daily living skills and functional vocational evaluation. (PL 101-476, 20 U.S.C. 1401 [a][19])

Transition programs can be effective only if they are connected to community. Planning for adult employment, living, and recreation cannot occur without working in partnership with the businesses and agencies that provide those services. Thus, schools and teachers may be placed in the unfamiliar role of connecting with the business community and developing collaborative relationships with other agencies. Moreover, any planning that involves a student's future requires the direct involvement of the family and the student.

When planning a student's transition, these principles should guide the nature of the planning process and program (Steere, Pancsofar, Wood, & Hecimovic, 1990). A first priority must be to include students and their families as equal and collaborative partners. The decisions of where an individual should work and live cannot be made without the full involvement of the family and recognition of the preferences of the student. Transition planning should not be regarded as an additional aspect of an appropriate program, but should serve to direct curricular efforts. Students with severe disabilities must be provided with a program that results in the acquisition of functional, community-referenced skills. The emphasis of transition planning should be aimed at preparing supports for the student, rather than focusing on preparing the student to meet the eligibility criteria of existing situations. This emphasis requires that the planning team work collaboratively in an ongoing partnership with adult service and funding agencies. Finally, a major goal of the team should be to ensure that each student graduates into paid community employment. Transition planning efforts should result in employment experiences that allow each student to attain an improved quality of life.

Halpern (1993) has proposed that teams consider broad dimensions when attempting to develop a variety of life goals for students in transition. He has identified the life domains of physical and material well-being, performance of adult roles, and personal fulfillment as areas

Physical and Material Well-Being

- physical and mental health
- food, clothing, and lodging
- financial security
- safety from harm

Performance of Adult Roles

- mobility and community access
- vocation, career, employment
- leisure and recreation
- personal relationships and social networks
- educational attainment
- spiritual fulfillment
- citizenship (e.g., voting)
- social responsibility (e.g., doesn't break laws)

Personal Fulfillment

- happiness
- satisfaction
- sense of general well-being

Figure 19–1
Quality-of-Life Domains
From Quality of Life as a Conceptual Framework for Evaluating Transition Outcomes by A. Halpern, 1993, *Exceptional Children, 59,* 486–498. Copyright © 1993 by The Council for Exceptional Children. Reprinted with permission.

of concern when considering outcomes for students in transition. These quality-of-life domains, presented in Figure 19–1, can be used to structure and evaluate a student's transition program.

For example, the domain of physical and material well-being includes the basic outcomes of physical and mental health; food, clothing, and lodging; financial security; and safety from harm. These outcomes should be viewed by the transition program as basic entitlements and the "minimal conditions" that should be met (Halpern, 1993, p. 490). The outcomes in the domain of performance of adult roles include a variety of opportunities that should be considered by the transition program to ensure that all aspects of an individual's life are addressed. Finally, the domain of personal fulfillment should be examined as an essential outcome in both the planning and the evaluation of a transition program.

In this chapter, the process for developing an individualized transition plan is described with a particular focus on providing employment opportunities for students with severe disabilities. The development of a longitudinal vocational program is described, and strategies for developing, placing, and maintaining students with disabilities in supported employment are provided.

Developing an Individualized Transition Plan

Preparing for the transition of students with severe disabilities takes place long before a transition plan is formally developed. The entire focus of the curriculum should be to prepare the student for living and working in the community. By the time a formal transition plan is considered, there should be documentation of the achievement of a variety of skills that will relate to the student's transition to adulthood. In addition, there should be a rich knowledge base of the supports that may be needed by the student. The transition plan will build upon the skills of the individual, but will extend the discussion of the student's instructional needs to his or her support after graduation.

A major focus of transition planning is to determine options for regular employment of the student with disabilities, although employment is not the only option available to students graduating from secondary schools. The transition team may want to consider the placement of the student in a community college or vocational technical program for further training. In addition to employment, the transition team will want to address the supports that are needed to meet the student's financial, recreation, medical, case coordination, mobility, advocacy, housing, social, and personal care needs (Wehman, Moon, Everson, Wood, & Barcus, 1988).

Identifying Transition Goals

Transition goals should relate to the desired adult outcomes for the student. Because outcomes and transition goals are discussed in the formal transition planning meeting, the family, the student, and relevant school personnel should prepare carefully for that meeting. Prior to discussing outcomes, community options should be explored and discussed with the family and the student. Students and their families will have a difficult time discussing community living options if they have not visited such facilities or do not have knowledge of their features. Similarly, a discussion of supported work options may be difficult for a family that does not understand how supported work is structured. Long before a transition plan is developed, school personnel must begin sharing information with families about postschool opportunities and options. Hopefully, this can occur over the years as the student's instructional program becomes more community-based and supported employment opportunities are explored. The transition planning meeting should not be the first time that a parent is asked to think about the child's future as an adult.

Preparing families for postschool options requires that school personnel gather information on what is available in their community and how other communities meet the needs of adults with severe disabilities. This information is essential not only for transition planning but also to build an ecological, functional curriculum for each student. All instructional activities should have a direct link to situations in the community.

In the elementary and middle-school years, preparation for transition will involve the instruction of basic domestic, community, leisure, and vocational skills that are age-appropriate and related to life in the community. For example, students in middle school may be taught the domestic skills of making a snack or doing yard work and the vocational skills of mopping floors or busing tables in the cafeteria. In high school, the skills targeted become much more specific to situations that are viable postschool options for the student with severe disabilities. Vocational skills may be related to a specific job, such as performing food-stocking tasks at a grocery store; a community skill may be to deposit a paycheck into a bank account.

The outcomes for transition are not based solely on the expertise and judgment of school personnel, but should be based on the student's preference and family desires. For some families, discussing postschool outcomes can be an overwhelming process. Often they are dealing not only with the issue of a child who now needs options for community working and living, but may also be confronting the emotional issues related to a child's transition to adulthood. Personal futures planning (described in chapter 4) is a process that can help families and school personnel approach identifying outcomes in a systematic and positive fashion. School personnel may want to schedule a personal futures planning session in advance of a transition planning meeting.

Another method for assisting families in preparation for the transition planning meeting is to provide them with a checklist of postschool options that they may want to consider for their child. A checklist may be developed by interviewing adult service providers and adults with disabilities in the community, listing the options that have been developed for school graduates in the past. It may also be helpful to examine the options that nondisabled persons utilize after high school. The vision of what may be possible should not be obscured by what has been traditionally provided to individuals with disabilities.

Probably the most meaningful way to administer a checklist of this type is to review it with the family, offering explanations for what the options are, and then giving the family time to discuss and select options in private. A strong caution is warranted about the use of checklists. They can be helpful in that an array of options are available to be considered, but also may be restrictive in that the items on the checklist may guide the decision making rather than the student's unique situation. When developing the checklist, be sure to include an open-end question that allows the family or student to write in an option that may not have been thought of by the checklist designer.

Conducting the Transition Planning Meeting

Transition planning meetings are often conducted in conjunction with an Individual

Education Program meeting. Persons who should attend a transition planning meeting are the student, the family, and school personnel who are primarily involved with the student. When the student is in the last two years of schooling, representatives of adult service agencies should join the team (Wehman, 1992).

The ITP meeting should begin with a discussion of what the student and the family want for the student after graduation. It is important that the professionals on the team allow the family to express their desires openly. School personnel can then discuss the outcomes that they feel are appropriate for the student and the support services that may be needed to accomplish those outcomes. Once long-term outcomes are identified in the areas of vocational and residential options, short-term goals can be developed by the ITP team. This process mirrors the IEP process in that transition outcomes (e.g., supported employment) are the long-term goals and transition goals (e.g., provide the student with at least three types of employment opportunities) are the short-term objectives. The difference is that in the ITP the transition goals are not usually skill acquisition goals that the student must achieve, but rather support goals that the team must implement. When transition goals are written on the ITP, a completion date, the service agencies that will work toward the goal, and the person responsible for seeing that the goal is achieved should also be listed (Wehman, 1992). A sample ITP is provided in Appendix B.

Vocational Preparation

A primary area of emphasis for students in secondary programs is vocational training. Only in recent years has the employment of students with severe disabilities been a realistic expectation. This change in expected outcomes has developed through the provision of longitudinal vocational training in the school system and opportunities for supported employment. Before such opportunities for real work in the community were available, students with severe disabilities were often relegated to adult activity programs or sheltered workshops, or sat at home after graduation from high school.

Traditional practice in vocational education for students with severe disabilities was to provide training in a variety of work skills (e.g., sorting, assembling, packaging) to prepare for eventual vocational training. The rationale was that students should learn to sort objects or complete simple assembly projects to develop the prerequisite skills needed for employment. But because the skills that were taught had little or no relationship to jobs in the community, this type of prevocational training did not increase a student's employability. Students with severe disabilities must be taught functional skills in settings and with materials that will be used by the student. For example, students who live in a community where there are potential jobs in a hospital and in several shopping malls should not be trained to do assembly tasks. The most efficient method of instruction is to use the community environment and the tasks that are involved in the job for training.

Vocational Instruction

The thrust of vocational programs for students with severe disabilities is to prepare them for eventual work placement in the community. Sowers and Powers (1991, p. 3) have identified the critical components of successful vocational programs as:

1. Identify and train for jobs and tasks that reflect the local community job market.

2. Train work-related skills that are critical to job success.
3. Train students in community settings.
4. Use systematic instructional procedures to train students.
5. Identify adaptive strategies that will increase student independence.
6. Reconceptualize staff roles and organizational structures.
7. Involve parents in the vocational preparation of their children.
8. Establish paid employment for students before they leave school.
9. Coordinate and collaborate with adult service programs.

Preparation for living and working in the community can begin as early as preschool and elementary school. For example, in the preschool classroom, students with severe disabilities can be taught that there are activity periods and then cleanup periods and that individuals are responsible for putting away their belongings and materials. These are skills that are used by all workers and are important to adult functioning.

In the elementary school, teachers can begin to prepare students for work by assigning them classroom chores or school jobs. Students may be responsible for classroom pet or plant care, assisting in the office or cafeteria, working in the media center, and doing tasks assigned by the teacher (e.g., stacking chairs, passing out books, collecting lunch money). At this time community-based instruction also begins with students learning individualized objectives that enhance independence and participation in relevant community environments (see chapter 18).

In the middle school, preparation for work in the community receives more attention. Teachers should assess the school to determine potential work sites that are relevant to jobs in the community. For example, filing and photocopying, which may be skills required in jobs that are potential supported employment placements, are tasks that are done in the school in multiple environments (e.g., office, media center, department office) and could be used for work-skill instruction. Other jobs may be found in the media center, the computer room, the attendance office, the cafeteria, and the office. Examples of relevant tasks are delivering messages, computer entry, cleaning, answering phones, and sorting mail. In the middle school, the emphasis of the vocational program should include assessing the work opportunities in the community, assessing student job preferences, determining adaptations that may be needed to perform tasks, and teaching job skills (Sowers & Powers, 1991).

In high school a large portion of the instruction should occur in community environments and employment sites. Some authors have recommended that by high school half the day should be spent in vocational training (Hutchins & Renzaglia, 1990). Once the high school student is eligible, the curriculum should also consist of paid employment experiences in the community. The goal for a high school vocational program is to provide students with experiences in a range of employment situations so that they graduate with several paid work experiences on their résumé.

The thrust of the high school curriculum should not be only vocational placement. The transition team should consider community living and leisure activities and design the curriculum to provide functional skill instruction that will result in those outcomes. For example, a supported living placement in an apartment with a personal care attendant may be a goal for a particular student. In preparation, skill instruction in simple meal preparation, cleaning, laundering clothes, emergency procedures, and operating home appliances may be appropriate. In addition, the student may receive instruction in community recreation activities, extending invitations to peers, and using community transportation. All of these skills may be important to a student's postschool living experiences.

A major component of the high school vocational program is to provide students with disabilities with community work experience. Before job matching can occur, evaluation of both student needs and employment opportunities must take place (Hutchins & Renzaglia, 1990).

The evaluation of employment opportunities can be conducted by talking to the city or county employment agency, visiting businesses in the community, and/or surveying businesses in the community to establish what employment opportunities exist. From those contacts, the employment specialist or teacher can generate a task pool of potential jobs that may be appropriate for the supported employment of individuals with severe disabilities. A sample task pool is provided in Table 19–1.

Table 19–1
Generic Task Pool for Students with Physical/Multiple Disabilities

Tasks	Examples/Descriptions
Typing	Type membership cards at banks, associations, clubs, libraries. Type file folder labels. Type addresses on mailing labels or envelopes.
Computer Data Entry	Input customer, patient, client information for businesses and medical offices, and billing, inventory information for same. Input mailing list information for associations and commercial businesses.
Word Processing	Word process memos and letters. This occurs in almost any office. It requires ability to read cursive writing.
Filing	Place papers in individual file folders, placing folders in file drawers, and retrieving files. Complexity varies depending on file system.
Phone Answering	In small, informal offices one person may answer phone and then tell co-workers they have a call. Larger and more formal offices will include putting callers on hold and transferring calls. Typically will require taking messages (usually written, but potentially recording messages).
Photocopying	Few businesses are without a photocopy machine. The type of copying done varies among companies. Some only need copies of single page documents; others need large documents and books or manuals. In most cases the person who photocopies is also responsible for collating (if it is not done by the machine) and stapling.
Collating/Stapling	Companies that perform a large amount of photocopying or have materials printed elsewhere may hire persons to collate and staple. Examples include print shops, direct mail businesses, associations.

From *Vocational Preparation and Employment of Students with Physical and Multiple Disabilities* (p. 30) by J. Sowers and L. Powers, 1991, Baltimore: Paul H. Brookes Publishing Co., P.O. Box 10624, Baltimore, Maryland 21285-0624. Reprinted by permission.

Table 19–1, *continued*

Tasks	Examples/Descriptions
Mail Preparation	Includes folding letters, stuffing envelopes, placing labels and stamps on envelopes, running a postage meter machine.
Packaging	Packaging products in manufacturing or distribution businesses. Type of product and packaging process will vary greatly.
Unpackage/Price	Most stores require merchandise received from distributors to be unpackaged (in some cases repackaged for sale) and a price tag or label placed on it. Pricing may be done by hand or with price gun. May also include placing the items on shelves.
Delivery	Deliver food for a restaurant, items from central supply or pharmacy to floors in hospital, fax messages that come in on central machine, documents from one office to other offices (e.g., legal documents from law office to courthouse).
Assembly/Light	Electronics assembly is a common type of light manufacturing task. There are hundreds of other products assembled in large and small businesses in most communities.
Light Cleaning	Most offices desire some light clean-up and straightening in addition to the more heavy cleaning done by a janitorial service. For example, banks need to have someone straighten up the !obby a couple of times a day.
Microfilming	Microfilming is becoming less prevalent due to the advent of computers. However, some businesses still employ microfilming for recordkeeping. Some banks microfilm checks. Hospitals and government offices also typically maintain microfilm records.

Once a task pool is developed, some jobs can be eliminated because they are not a match to the student's capabilities. The task pool that is developed should be viewed as a dynamic list that will need to be updated as the local job market changes.

Once a task pool is identified, student needs should be assessed to determine a match between individual students and particular jobs. Factors that should be included in the assessment of student needs are the student's and the family's preferences, task- and work-related skills, and supervision needs in a potential placement.

Community Work Experience

To provide high school students with community work experience, the secondary teacher should identify sites that match the task pool that was generated. The purpose in doing this is to develop a list of work experience sites that are willing to serve as employment training sites and offer opportunities for students to gain experience in tasks that relate to jobs in the community. Often the employment teacher will want to use one community site to train a group of students because it is easier to supervise them and transport them. When that model is used, the employment teacher should try to ensure that the students are well dispersed in the site and have opportunities to learn several tasks (Sowers & Powers, 1991). The rotation of students in various employment training sites is part of the student assessment process. The goal in providing such rotations is to assess student preferences and work behavior in order to discern the employment situations that offer the best match to individual students.

Before placing a student, the Fair Labor Standards Act (FLSA) Section 14 compliance specialist in the regional U.S. Department of Labor, Wage, and Hour Division office should be contacted to determine if the student should be paid in the work placement (Moon, Kiernan, & Halloran, 1990). For a student to not be paid as a worker, the following six criteria must be met (U.S. Department of Labor, 1962):

1. the training, even though it includes actual operation of the facilities of the employer, is similar to that given in a vocational school;
2. the training is for the benefit of the trainees or students;
3. the trainees do not displace regular employees but rather work under their close observation;
4. the employer who provides the training derives no immediate advantage from the activities of the trainees, and on occasion the employer's operations may actually be impeded;
5. the trainees or students are not necessarily entitled to a job at the conclusion of the training period; and
6. the employer and the trainees understand that the trainees or students are not entitled to wages for the time spent in training.

If these criteria are not met, there is an employment relationship, and the student must be paid minimum wage even if the work experience is part of the IEP or transition plan.

Instructional Strategies

The instruction of vocational skills is broader than teaching students with severe disabilities to perform work tasks. Work-related skills such as punching in on the time clock, gathering materials, and social behavior such as greeting coworkers and interacting on breaks are instructional issues in addition to work-task skills.

The use of a task analysis is fundamental to the instruction of work tasks. In task analysis the job is broken down into meaningful and measurable steps, and instruction begins once an initial task analytic assessment has been conducted (see chapter 5). Other instructional methods that may be used to teach students work-related skills and social behaviors have been described by Buckley, Mank, and Sandow (1990) and are presented in Table 19–2. Strategies that teachers have used for skill acquisition and generalization in other domains apply to achievement of work tasks and work-related behavior (Storey, Sandow, & Rhodes, 1990).

There are instructional issues that should receive careful attention when teaching students work skills. The use of reinforcers should be carefully approached with particular attention paid to using natural reinforcers and a reinforcement schedule that does not inhibit work progress. For example, the use of praise for each work step may call undue attention to the employee and may serve to reduce his or her productivity. An alternative strategy may be to use exchangeable reinforcers such as checks on a card or tokens that can be exchanged at break time for a tangible reinforcer or to solicit feedback. Another issue is the fading of the instructor as quickly

Table 19–2

Direct Service Strategy Definitions, Procedures, and Decision Rules

Support Strategy	Procedures	Decision Rules
Task analysis—Analysis of the stimulus and response requirements of each step in a task across the range of variability that occurs in the specific conditions in which the task is performed.	• Establish efficient task design. • Identify task-related stimulus for each response. • Articulate steps in terms of employer criteria. • Identify all conditions/variations. • Identify errors that occur. • Identify variations in criteria.	• Complete after job analysis. • Use in response to documented performance problems. • Analyze errors and error patterns to provide efficient assistance. • Criteria for mastery must be based on performance according to employer criteria across all relevant conditions encountered.
Self-management—The use of systems that enable the user to gain control of environmental events and/or work behaviors. Self-management is further defined by the particular component emphasized, antecedent cue regulation, self-monitoring, or self-recruited feedback.	• Define the performance requirement, i.e., some specific form of initiation, monitoring or feedback. • Select and teach a system that emphasizes the appropriate component. • Use standard instructional procedures (task analysis, assistance, reinforcement and error correction) to document that the user knows how to manipulate the system.	• Determine when to initiate by analyzing dependence and/or trainer presence. • System must be individualized for the target worker and job site. • Systems should be as unobtrusive as possible. • Systems should be easy for target worker, employment training specialist and employer to operate, maintain, and adapt over time. • Decisions regarding fading or withdrawing the system depend on obtrusiveness of the system, time involved in use, and worker and employer preference.
Productivity programming—Rate increase programs help target workers perform units of work according to time criteria specific to the task and work rate. Pacing programs help target workers identify varying environmental conditions that require different performance rates.	• Identify rate requirements for each task (beginning in job analysis). • Identify the frequency with which the pace changes. • Document the rate(s) at which the worker is able to perform. • Set incentives for increases in rate. • Select/identify cues for differences in pace. • Teach workers to respond to pacing cues.	• Rate issues depend on a system for identifying employer standards across varying production demands. • Task modification may increase productivity. • Self-managed systems can help workers increase rates of production and/or identify environmental cues requiring changes in pacing. • Criteria need to be validated for the job site according to the actual conditions the target worker encounters. • Production criteria change should therefore be assessed over time.
Community-referenced behavior management — Functional analysis to determine the relationship between difficult behavior (or classes of behavior) and events in the person's environment in order to	• Observe and assess the individual in as many natural settings as possible. • Identify a range of stimulus conditions within and across environments. • Develop and test hypotheses regarding stimulus control factors.	• Functional analysis should be used when extinction procedures are not successful. • Many individuals with challenging behaviors have little experience in employment settings. More natural stimuli may control more appropriate responses and obviate the need for intervention.

apply an intervention that meets the unique demands of the individual, job site, and behavior under analysis.	• Design a model for desired and excess responses. • Continue to analyze the behavior and presence or absence of various stimuli.	• Support must be adequate for individuals with challenging behaviors. • Criteria need to based on individual dignity, safety, security, and job site standards.
Social skill training—The development of specific behaviors that occur in the context of interactions that take place in specific work sites.	• Identify specific activities and events and the social interactions involved. • Assess target worker participation and performance in these events. • Analyze targeted skills across the range of variation encountered in the work place. • Select performance alternatives. • Model the skill and allow the target worker to practice. • Shape, reinforce, and fade assistance.	• Target workers' preference in selecting activities and performance alternatives is critical. • Task analyses and/or self-management can be of assistance to the target worker and the trainer. • Social competence refers to perceived adherence to cultural rules. Co-worker orientation and support can be invaluable.
Communication training—Development of the modality or type of system used, the form or rules, and the content of the "language" (Stremel-Campbell & Matthews, 1987).	• Identify job-related communication requirements. • Designate a communication modality or system. • Ensure that critical communication requirements are covered. • Add work-related and social content as needed. • Test for ease of use. • Train the worker, co-worker, and employer to operate the system.	• Existing and highly technical systems may not enable the worker to communicate with co-workers, employers and the public. • Systems and content should be introduced as needed. • Systems should be easy for the target worker, employment training specialist, co-workers, and employer to use, maintain, and adapt over time. • Due to skill and/or experiential deficits, some workers with no apparent communication disorders may need communication training.
Mobility training—Enabling a target worker to gain access to areas that are critical for worker performance and socialization in and around the work place.	• Identify environments in which the individual has optimum mobility. • Identify the amount and range of mobility required for the job. • Match mobility strategies to demands of the job. • Identify discrepancies and make modifications. • Teach the target worker, co-workers, and the employer to optimize mobility.	• Job match is the first issue. • The person must learn to enjoy full access to work and social opportunities. • Shaping and sensitization may help some individuals overcome reticence. • Due to skill and/or experiential deficits, some individuals with no apparent mobility impairments may need mobility training. • Co-worker orientation and training can help target workers feel welcome in new settings.

From Developing and Implementing Support Strategies by J. Buckley, D. Mank, & D. Sandow, 1990, in F. R. Rusch (Ed.), *Supported Employment: Models, Methods, and Issues* (pp. 131–144), Sycamore, IL: Sycamore. Copyright © 1990 By Sycamore Publishing Co. Reprinted by permission of Brooks/Cole Publishing Company, Pacific Grove, CA 93950.

as possible. The teacher's presence must be systematically faded so that the employee is able to rely on the cues of the workplace rather than on the instructor (Chadsey-Rusch, 1990).

Many students with severe disabilities will need the support of adaptations to perform job tasks. Sowers and Powers (1991) have identified six major ways to approach adapting a job or task to meet the needs of the student (Sowers & Powers, 1991).

1. Redesign the task to eliminate the difficult steps;
2. Provide the individual with disabilities with an alternative way to perform the task or task component;
3. Rearrange the environment to eliminate barriers or to increase worker productivity;
4. Reposition equipment to a position that enhances worker performance;
5. Teach the worker to use environmental cues (e.g., picture prompts, tape-recorded instructions) to assist them through the task; and
6. Provide an assistive device that allows the worker to manipulate materials or operate equipment needed in the task.

Sowers and Powers (1991) have provided processes that can be used to approach job design systematically. The first step is to task analyze the job, then identify the steps that the worker may have difficulty with, using the job design analysis form shown in Figure 19–2. When the areas of difficulty have been identified, design modifications and adaptations are selected (see example in Figure 19–3). After design changes have been made, a new task analysis is constructed that includes task modifications, and the individual is trained to perform the task.

Supported Employment

The goal of a vocational program for students with disabilities should be to place the students in real jobs before graduation so that there will not be a gap in services (Sowers & Powers, 1991). This means that the school program will be involved in the placement of students in supported employment situations. In the following sections, the models of supported employment and strategies for job development and job placement are described.

The Importance of Supported Employment

Supported employment, which provides paid work to individuals with severe disabilities who may need support or supervision, was designed to meet the needs of persons who have not been traditionally eligible for rehabilitation services and who may need ongoing support because of the severity of their disability. In Figure 19–4, supported employment is described.

The supported employment model was developed in response to the inadequacy of the traditional approach to employment services. In the past, the options available to persons with disabilities were competitive employment, sheltered workshops, and work activity programs. The traditional model was conceptualized as a continuum with individuals moving from sheltered work situations to jobs in the community as their skill level increased. In reality, few persons with severe disabilities ever moved beyond the sheltered situations. In addition, sheltered work situations provided very low wages and limited contact with nondisabled persons.

Supported employment is valued over other work programs (e.g., sheltered workshops,

JOB DESIGN ANALYSIS FORM

Task *Preparing to enter data* Staff *Steve*

Site *Acme Insurance* New Employee *Beth*

Step	Physical difficulties	Discrimination difficulties
Obtain disk from disk holder.	Holder located on high shelf. Beth cannot reach.	20 disks in holder. Coding of disks complicated. Beth will have difficulty identifying the one to use.
Remove disk from sleeve.		
Insert disk into drive.		
Push switch in back of computer to turn on.	Switch is located in back of machine. Beth will not be able to reach it.	

Figure 19–2
Job Design Analysis Form

From *Vocational Preparation and Employment of Students with Physical and Multiple Disabilities* (p. 123) by J. Sowers & L. Powers, 1991, Baltimore: Paul H. Brookes Publishing Co., P.O. Box 10624, Baltimore, Maryland 21285-0624. Reprinted by permission.

DESIGN STRATEGY IDEAS

Task Preparing to enter data

Worker Beth

Difficult step Push switch to turn on computer

Site Acme Insurance

Strategy type	Specific design strategy ideas
Eliminate step	Have someone else turn on computer for her.
Alternative response strategy	
Rearranging environment	Have table on which computer is placed pulled away from wall so Beth could move her chair behind it and turn it on.
Repositioning equipment	
Environmental cues	
Assistive devices–special	Buy and install switch that fits on side of computer—available at all computer stores.
Assistive devices–generic	Buy a power cord—plug into computer and place on the floor.
Assistive devices–constructed	

Figure 19–3
Design Strategy Ideas

From *Vocational Preparation and Employment of Students with Physical and Multiple Disabilities* (p. 126) by J. Sowers & L. Powers, 1991, Baltimore: Paul H. Brookes Publishing Co., P.O. Box 10624, Baltimore, Maryland 21285-0624. Reprinted by permission.

Supported employment means competitive work in an integrated work setting with ongoing support services.

Supported employment may be provided to individuals with severe disabilities who traditionally have been unable to perform competitive work or who have performed competitive work only intermittently.

Competitive work means work that is performed on a full-time or part-time basis as determined in an individualized written rehabilitation program for which the individual is compensated consistent with the Fair Labor Standards Act.

Integrated work settings are job sites where most employees are not disabled and where the individual with severe disabilities interacts on a regular basis with other employees who are not disabled.

If an individual with severe disabilities is placed in a work setting as a member of a group of individuals with disabilities, there should be no more than eight individuals with disabilities in that group.

Ongoing support services are specified in the individualized written rehabilitation plan and are the services needed to support and maintain the individual in employment.

Ongoing support services must include at a minimum twice-monthly monitoring at the work site of the individual unless off-site monitoring is determined to be more appropriate. Off-site monitoring must consist of at least two meetings with the supported individual and contact with the employer each month.

Figure 19–4
What Is Supported Employment?

work activity programs) because it offers workers with disabilities the support they need to work in the community in real jobs with nondisabled coworkers. In the evaluation of supported work programs, supported employees have stated that they prefer their jobs to sheltered work programs and value their relationship with their job coach. They have stated that job coaches assist them not only to learn the job, but also to learn appropriate behavior and to advocate for themselves in situations other than work (Test, Hinson, Solow, & Keul, 1993). They also experience increase of wages (Thompson, Powers, & Houchard, 1992; Tines, Rusch, McCaughrin, & Conley, 1990).

Supported Work Models

There are several models for supported work placements. A common aspect of all of them is that individuals are supported by a job coach who ensures that the job will be completed and provides training to individuals with disabilities until they are able to do the job independently. In addition to training, the job

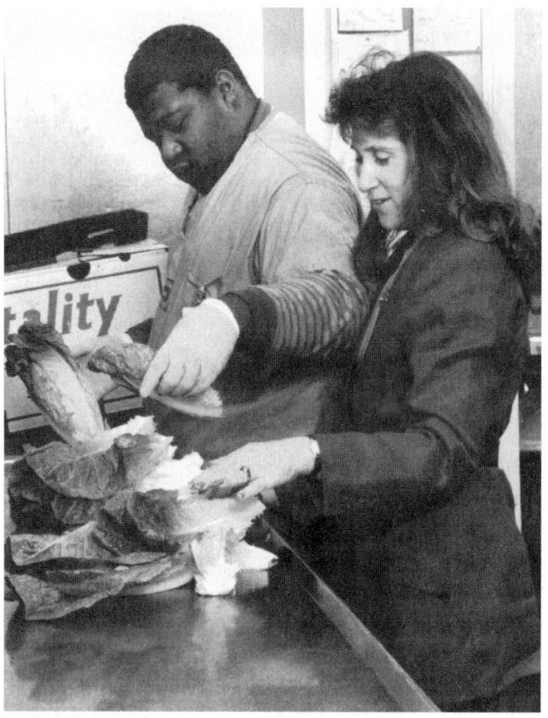

The job coach provides training and support to the employee with disabilities.

coach provides follow-along support to ensure that the worker with disabilities is able to maintain the employment position.

The individual placement model provides the most opportunity for integration in the work environment. In this model, workers with disabilities are individually placed in community settings, and job training is provided until the job can be performed satisfactorily by the employee. Unfortunately, the support needs of persons with severe disabilities can make the cost of individual placement prohibitive for most agencies. Workers with severe disabilities are often employed in one of the group placement models discussed below.

Enclaves and work crews are two common models of group employment placement. In an enclave, a small group of individuals with disabilities are placed together in a business setting and earn wages based on productivity or on the completion of a product. A supervisor, who is typically an employee of the business or employment services agency, provides training and support. An example of an enclave might be a group of workers who are employed by a large hotel to clean guest rooms. Work crews are groups of workers who travel to various locations to perform contract services. An example of a work crew might be a group of workers who provide landscaping and lawn maintenance services to several businesses.

There are several concerns about the use of enclaves and work crews for supported employment. The disadvantages of these models are that the workers usually make less than minimum wage, are isolated from nondisabled workers and the general public, and may be limited from potential job independence (Johnson & Rusch, 1990; Moon, Inge, Wehman, Brooke, & Barcus, 1990; Rusch, Johnson, & Hughes, 1990). A mobile work crew is the model that is least likely to support interactions with nondisabled workers (Rusch, Johnson, & Hughes, 1990).

Group placements are more appropriate when workers with disabilities work side by side with other workers and perform the same job duties. Workers with disabilities should be dispersed in the work setting rather than all performing the same job tasks in close proximity to each other. In group placements workers with disabilities should be employed by the business and receive regular wages. This may be different from the traditional enclave approach where the supported employment agency contracts with the business and pays the employees subminimum wages (Moon, Inge, Wehman, Brooke, & Barcus, 1990). Group placements should also make an effort to minimize the number of workers with disabilities. A group placement of 10 persons with disabilities into a business that employs 20 other persons will be a much different experience from the placement of 5 persons with disabilities into a setting that employs 50 other persons. A group work placement may be an appropriate first job situation for a young or inexperienced worker or a worker who has been unsuccessful at other placements, although it is very important that workers are trained and advanced to an individual job placement (Moon, Inge, Wehman, Brooke, & Barcus, 1990).

Another type of group placement model is the entrepreneurial model, in which a business hires workers with and without disabilities to create a product or provide a service. This model is similar to a sheltered work situation, although workers without disabilities may be present. The entrepreneurial model may be limited in its ability to assist workers with disabilities in gaining employment in the community.

Natural Supports

The model of supported employment that relies on a job coach to provide services to a worker with disabilities does present some problems. It is an expensive model that may call attention to the worker's disability (Nisbet & Hagner, 1988). It is also possible that the presence of the job coach might influence other workers' perceptions of the employee with disabilities as well as influencing the behavior of the worker with disabilities.

Early efforts at obtaining job placements involved marketing the benefits of supported employment to potential employers and assuring them of their minimal involvement. This practice may restrict the inclusion and participation of workers with disabilities. In recent years, business management has begun to recognize the need to support all workers. Job developers and job coaches should identify and use those resources for individuals with severe disabilities. This calls for a new framework of support that involves the teaching of supported employment techniques (precise instruction, supervision, job analysis, and self-management strategies) to supervisors and coworkers. Employment specialists and job coaches could provide assistance to company training programs and use existing assistance programs to provide needed job supports (Rhodes, Sandow, Mank, Buckley, & Albin, 1991).

Nisbet & Hagner (1988) suggest that before placement of a worker with disabilities, work environments should be examined to determine the natural supports and social interactions that are available so that supported employment efforts can build on what is already in place. One option for providing support and supervision to workers may be to use coworkers rather than the job coach.

Nisbet and Hagner (1988) propose several models that could be used as alternative, natural support options. One is to have a vocational agency provide the initial job development, analysis, and training of the worker with disabilities. Once the worker is placed and trained, a coworker assumes the role of mentor. The mentor may assist the worker in solving problems, answering questions, or acting as a liaison between the employer and the worker's residence. A training stipend could be provided to the mentor, although it may not be necessary.

Another option might be to train coworkers to train and support an employee with disabilities. The vocational service agency provides a consultant who trains the coworkers. The amount of instructional and support time provided by the coworkers is documented and reimbursed by the vocational service agency.

In job sharing, two persons are hired for one position. The worker with the disability may receive 25% of the wage and the coworker 75%. The vocational agency pays the coworker an additional 25% as a training stipend.

Finally, in the attendant option, the worker with disabilities hires an attendant who provides personal care services and vocational assistance and receives a training stipend from the vocational agency. Another option is for the person with disabilities to pay the attendant and then deduct it from his or her social security as an impairment-related expense.

Job Development

Developing potential employment situations for individuals with disabilities can be a very challenging task. Not many businesses understand the value of employing such persons or understand their capacity to contribute to the workplace. In addition, most jobs are structured in ways that present barriers to people who have severe disabilities.

Job development is the process of identifying employment situations in the community that may be appropriate for individuals with disabilities. The job-development process goes beyond locating available positions; it typically involves the restructuring of jobs so that individuals with disabilities can be accommodated in the workplace.

The first step in job development is to analyze the labor market of the community to determine what jobs may be available. The purpose of such an analysis is to find out who the major employers are in the community, the number of workers they hire, and the type of work performed. In addition, the job developer should determine if a particular industry or employer anticipates growth in the near future. Once the job developer has a feel for the community job market, individual employers can be contacted to determine if they have opportunities for workers in supported employment.

The most effective methods of contacting employers and developing jobs is to make cold calls to initiate a contact, interview employers, use brochures to explain the supported employment service agency, and to follow up on initial contacts (Culver, Spencer, & Gliner, 1990). Presentations to community groups and advisory boards are strategies that build awareness of the goals of supported employment but rarely result in actual job placements.

Before contacting a potential employer, the job developer must be prepared to sell the concept of hiring a supported worker (Nietupski, Verstegen, & Hamre-Nietupski, 1992). Job developers should be familiar with the business so that they can identify the areas in which supported employment can be of benefit. It should be pointed out that supported employment may save money for the business through reduced turnover, hiring, training, and supervision costs. In addition, it may contribute to a positive corporate image. Research on individual businesses can be done through corporate publications, trade publications, the chamber of commerce, job service agencies, the community newspaper, and observation of retail establishments. Job developers must also prepare a presentation to help potential employers understand the services that are provided.

When the job developer has conducted research on a business and has developed a presentation tailored to the employer, an initial contact—a phone call, a personal visit, or a letter—should be made to share information on the supported employment service, mention possible benefits to the business, and ask for an appointment (Nietupski et al., 1992). Suggestions for successful initial contacts are presented in Figure 19–5.

In preparation for the initial appointment with a potential employer, job developers may wish to consider using different forms of media and materials to introduce, describe, or illustrate their services (Nietupski et al., 1992). Tools that may be used by job developers are described in Figure 19–6.

Figure 19–5
Suggestions for Successful Initial Contacts
From "Incorporating Sales and Business Practices into Job Development in Supported Employment" by J. Nietupski, D. Verstegen, & S. Hamre-Nietupski, 1992, *Education and Training in Mental Retardation, 27*, 207–218. Copyright 1992 by the Division on Mental Retardation and Developmental Disabilities, The Council for Exceptional Children. Reprinted by permission.

1. Be prepared—script/practice your message.
2. Define your service and key benefits.
3. Refer to your letter if one was sent.
4. Offer two appointment dates rather than asking a yes/no question (e.g., "Could we meet to discuss this?").
5. Have your calendar ready to select a different date/time if necessary.
6. Request a brief appointment (e.g., 25 minutes) and stick to it when you do meet.
7. Call/drop in at a less busy time (e.g., mid AM/PM in food service, generally not just prior to lunch break or closing time; typically not Friday PM).
8. Don't do all the talking. Ask for the appointment and wait for the employer to respond.
9. Remember your goal: to get an appointment.
10. Avoid human service jargon.
11. Speak as naturally as possible.
12. Be brief.

The goal of the first appointment is to determine if the employer will hire a supported employee. The meeting consists of three parts: the introduction, questions about areas of need, and arranging a subsequent meeting (Nietupski et al., 1992). In the introduction, the job developer should define the services of the agency, present the benefits of the services, and indicate that the purpose of this meeting is to determine if supported employment may be a benefit to the employer.

After the introduction, the job developer should determine the employer's areas of need and ways in which supported employment could benefit the business by asking such questions as: What are your hiring and training processes? In what areas are you experiencing high turnover? Would it be of benefit if someone could provide the training and supervision to new hires? Would it benefit your business if we could reduce the turnover or increase attendance?

In the last part of the meeting, the job developer should request a tour of the facility and ask how hiring decisions are made. The meeting should end with a request for a follow-up appointment when the job developer will make a presentation on how supported employment could meet the needs of the employer and to secure a yes/no hiring decision (Nietupski et al., 1992).

In the follow-up meeting, the job developer should first state that the purpose of the meeting is to present his or her findings relevant to the company's personnel needs and to receive a yes/no hiring decision (Nietupski et al., 1992). Then he or she should review the benefits to the company of hiring a supported employee and ask for verification from the employer that these are benefits. Once the

Business cards

1. Your name and title printed, not handwritten or typed.
2. Uncluttered
3. Phone number and FAX number if available.

Introductory letters

1. One page in length.
2. Three paragraph format: a) description of service; b) key benefits; c) indication that you will call to set an appointment.
3. Original (not photocopy) letter and actual signature.
4. Tailor letter to a given business by emphasizing benefits for that type of business. Have several forms in computer files.
5. Use business terms, not human service jargon.
6. Use emphatic verbs (e.g., "We reduce your turnover." not "We may assist you in possible reducing turnover.").

Follow-up letters

1. Can be used as appointment reminders or as a thank you following appointments.
2. Brief, to the point.

Brochures

1. Highlight benefits.
2. Brief—key points bulleted, minimal text.
3. Quality layout, paper and printing. A poor brochure is worse than none at all.
4. Phone numbers to call for more information.

Figure 19–6
Tools for Use in Job Development
From "Incorporating Sales and Business Practices into Job Development in Supported Employment" by J. Nietupski, D. Verstegen, & S. Hamre-Nietupski, 1992, *Education and Training in Mental Retardation, 27,* 207–218. Copyright 1992 by the Division on Mental Retardation and Developmental Disabilities, The Council for Exceptional Children. Reprinted by permission.

benefits are acknowledged, the duties for the supported employee should be reviewed and trial closed: "If someone were to . . . , would this solve your problem of . . . ?" Following an acknowledgment of the need, the job developer can describe the candidate for the job, emphasizing the match of the candidate for the position, and try to get the employer to acknowledge the match. Then the job developer should ask for the decision. "We agree that someone needs to . . . and Bill Smith looks like a good candidate for this position. Why don't we go ahead and get him started next week?"

The employment specialist or job coach, who must be able to perform the job and orga-

5. Testimonial statements from employers regarding their experience with supported employment.
6. Business terminology.

Fact sheets

1. May be substituted for brochure.
2. Defines/describes service and benefits.
3. Lists businesses using the service, contact persons and phone numbers.
4. Describe the positions filled.
5. May include testimonial statements.

Testimonial letters

1. Letters from respected/recognized company officers.
2. Brief letter citing specific benefits/positive experiences.
3. Not just "blue sky"—honest indication of concerns, and how agency worked to address concerns.
4. Use variety of types of businesses (e.g., manufacturing, financial institutions, retail, food service, health care).

Video tapes

1. Brief—5–10 minutes.
2. Highlight 2–3 benefits.
3. Combination of client action sections and employer interviews.
4. Quality sound and lighting.
5. Call to action (e.g., "For more information...").

Figure 19–6, *continued*

nize the routine, should work at least one day before introducing the worker in the supported employment setting. The job coach should keep a record of the job duties that are required and the approximate time needed to perform each task. Guidelines for job duty analysis have been developed by Moon, Inge, Wehman, Brooke, & Barcus (1990) and are presented in Figure 19–7.

Once the job coach is familiar with the job and has conducted a job duty analysis, a schedule for training can be determined and the supported worker can begin in the position. Some strategies to ease the anxiety of the first day of work might be for the job coach to meet all of the coworkers and supervisors prior to the first day, tour the workplace, and participate in the company orientation. The job coach should provide an orientation for the worker with disabilities on the first day, introduce him or her to coworkers, and provide reinforcement frequently as he or she adjusts to the new situation (Moon, Inge, Wehman, Brooke, & Barcus, 1990).

Identify only those job skills that can be observed and measured.

Include only those observable skills a worker must perform in order to master the job task.

Break each job task into the sequential steps required to successfully perform the task.

Include all necessary machinery and tools.

Concentrate on the job task that is being analyzed rather than the worker who will master it (By focusing on the task, those skills that are essential to successful completion of the job task can be easily identified.)

Talk with co-workers to learn tricks of the trade.

Field test the job task analysis by observing a co-worker completing the task.

Determine the most efficient procedure to complete a task.

Be concerned with reducing unnecessary worker movement when completing the task.

Have the final job task analysis approved by the employer/supervisor.

Give the employer a copy for his or her records.

Figure 19–7
Guidelines for Job Duty Analysis
From *Helping Persons with Severe Mental Retardation Get and Keep Employment* (p. 105) by M. S. Moon, K. J. Inge, P. Wehman, V. Brooke, & J. M. Barcus, 1990, Baltimore: Paul H. Brookes Publishing Co., P.O. Box 10624, Baltimore, Maryland 21285-0624. Reprinted by permission.

Situational Assessment

The determination of a good match between a supported employee and a job can be a difficult process. Individuals with severe disabilities should not be placed in whatever position is available with no regard for their preferences and needs. Job satisfaction is linked to control over the tasks to be done, the ability to work as part of a team, contact with coworkers, equitable pay, and the ability to perform tasks of complexity sufficient to hold one's interest. Potential placement of a person with severe disabilities should be evaluated to ensure that the job matches the worker's interest and abilities (Moseley, 1988).

On-the-job evaluation or situational assessment (Moon, Inge, Wehman, Brooke, & Barcus, 1990) can be used by employment specialists to understand worker preferences and skills in an actual job placement. A situational assessment should be conducted to find a match between a worker and a job. Before situational assessments are conducted, potential job matches should be identified based on information from the family and the worker and knowledge of the worker's abilities and interests.

To recruit sites for situational assessment, the employment specialist should make a request to set up an assessment program. Once permission is gained to use the site for a situational assessment, the employment specialist should make an appointment to meet with the department supervisor to work out scheduling, job duties, regulations, and job standards. The employment specialist will then want to identify several jobs in the site and conduct task analyses, after which individuals may be scheduled to go to the site for the situational assessment.

The situational assessment screening form is filled out by the parent or a teacher familiar with the individual. At the job site, as the student is guided through the job task, relevant information on his or her ability to complete the job tasks and cope with the work environment is entered on the form. A sample of a completed situational assessment form is provided in Figure 19–8.

Social Interaction

One of the most frequent reasons individuals with disabilities are unable to maintain employment is that they display socially inappropriate behavior (Chadsey-Rusch, 1990). The importance of fitting in in the workplace cannot be minimized, although it is an area that is frequently neglected. Workers with disabilities must be assisted in developing the social skills needed to become a part of the social network in their employment setting.

Social skills can be defined as goal-oriented, rule-governed learned behaviors that are situation-specific and vary according to social context; they involve both observable and nonobservable cognitive and affective elements that assist in eliciting positive or neutral responses from others (Chadsey-Rusch, 1992). For example, social skills include an awareness of the rules about what is an appropriate topic of conversation and the duration of a conversation. In some settings, shouting a greeting to a coworker fits in the social context, but shouting a greeting in the work context of a library or a hotel may not be appropriate.

People use social skills to meet their affection, attention, and affiliation needs while modifying and adapting their expression to fit different settings, cultural expectations, and situations. In order to understand the social skills needed by individual workers, the job coach must consider the perceptions or judgments of significant others in work settings, the perceptions and social goals of the individual, and the performance of the behaviors within specific contexts.

Supported employment situations may actually serve as a barrier to promoting social interactions between employees with disabilities and their coworkers. Employees with disabilities are more likely to interact with employment specialists and receive instruction and compliments than other workers (Ferguson, McDonnell, & Drew, 1993; Parent, Kregel, Metzler, & Twardzik, 1992; Storey, Rhodes, Sandow, Loewinger, & Petherbridge, 1991). In a study that compared workers with disabilities to workers without disabilities, researchers found that workers without disabilities initiated three times as many contacts with coworkers (Ferguson et al., 1993). Researchers have also determined that teasing and joking is a form of social interaction frequently used by nondisabled workers and rarely used by workers with disabilities (Chadsey-Rusch & Gonzalez, 1988; Ferguson et al., 1993). In addition, the frequency of job coach interactions was negatively correlated with workers initiating social interactions with coworkers (Ferguson et al., 1993).

Job coaches must attend to the development of social relationships between the supported employee and coworkers; this task could include skills such as requesting assistance, greeting coworkers, social amenities, responding to criticism, offering help, and asking and responding to questions. In addition, the work-

Figure 19–8
Situational Assessment

Consumer: Mary **Employment specialist:** Norton **Date:** September

Directions: Indicate the response for each item in the appropriate category based on information gathered from the consumer's parents, teacher, and observations during the situational assessments. For each item, describe the behavior, characteristic, or activity. When applicable, include the frequency of its occurrence and the environment where it occurs (antecedent, consequences, location, people).

	Parent: mother	Teacher: Mrs. B.	Dietary—Situational Assessment I	Supply—Situational Assessment II	Laundry—Situational Assessment III
Strength: lifting and carrying • Poor (<10 lbs.) • Fair (10–20 lbs.) • Average (30–40 lbs.) • Strong (>50 lbs.)	10–15 lbs., not very strong	Poor, has a hard time carrying items over 10 lbs.	10 lbs. only, had a hard time pushing supply cart	Poor, needed assistance over 10 lbs.	No problems since items in laundry not over 10 lbs.
Endurance • Works <2 hours • Works <2–3 hours • Works 3–4 hours • Works <4 hours	<2 hours	<2 hours in school	Worked 1 hour and said she was tired	Worked 2 hours before asking for a break	Worked 3 hours before asking for a break
Orienting • Small area only • One room • Several rooms • Building wide • Building and grounds	Several rooms	School wide	Small room only, could not find way from dish area to carts	Only room only, could not find way from trash area to supply	Not observed
Physical mobility • Sit/stand in one area • Fair ambulation • Stairs/minor obstacles • Physical abilities	Fair ambulation, falls often over own feet	Same as parent comment.	Poor mobility that affected ability to use hands when walking	Unsteady gait, tripped over curb leaving building	Not a problem in the laundry area

Independent work rate (No prompts) • Slow pace • Steady/average pace • Above average/ sometimes fast • Continual fast pace	Slow pace	Slow pace	Slow! Asked for verbal praise (e.g., "Am I doing a good job?")	Slow	Steady/average pace, had some trouble starring around room
Appearance • Unkempt/poor-hygiene • Unkempt/clean • Neat/clean but clothing unmatched • Neat/clean and clothing matched	Always likes to look nice	Neat/clean clothing matched	Very neat!	Same	Same
Communication • Uses sounds/ gestures • Uses key words/ signs • Speaks unclearly • Communicates clearly, intelligible to strangers	Communicates clearly	No problem	Intelligible to strangers	Same	Same
Social interactions • Rarely interacts appropriately • Polite, responses appropriate • Initiates social interactions infrequently	Very polite, sometimes shy with strangers	Sometimes interacts inappropriately (e.g., tickles, hugs)	Polite, responses were appropriate	Initiated too frequently, yelling to co-workers across room	Polite, initiated interactions

Figure 19–8, *continued*

	Parent: mother	Teacher: Mrs. B.	Dietary—Situational Assessment I	Supply—Situational Assessment II	Laundry—Situational Assessment III
Social interactions *(continued)* • Initiates social interactions frequently					
Attention to task/perseverance • Frequent prompts required • Intermittent prompts/high supervision • Intermittent prompts/low supervision • Infrequent prompts/low supervision	Needs a lot of supervision to continue working	Frequent prompts are always needed to keep Mary on task	Frequent prompts required	Frequent prompts required	Responded to gesture prompts to keep working
Independent sequencing of job duties • Cannot perform tasks in sequence • Performs two to three tasks in sequence • Performs four to six tasks in sequence • Performs seven or more tasks in sequence	Cannot do at home	Can sequence two to three tasks after skill training	Needed prompt to sequence tasks	Waited for instructions to move to next task	Sequenced two to three tasks (e.g., stacked folded laundry and moving on to next item to fold)
Initiative/motivation • Always seeks work • Sometimes volunteers	Sometimes volunteers to do work at home	Sometimes volunteers for work in the class	Usually waited for directions	Waited for directions	Sometimes volunteers (i.e., "What do I do now?")

• Waits for directions • Avoids next task					
Adapting to change • Adapts to change • Adapts to change with some difficulty • Adapts to change with great difficulty • Rigid routine required	Adapts with great difficulty, she will cry easily if things are not consistent	Same as parent comment	Not observed	Seemed to need a rigid schedule	Not observed
Reinforcement needs • Frequently required • Daily • Weekly • Paycheck sufficient	Frequent	Frequent! Asks often for praise of work completed	Frequent verbal praise to encourage through difficult tasks	Seemed dependent on verbal praise and prompts	Seemed to need verbal praise after each item folded
Level of Support • Very supportive of work • Supportive of work with reservations • Negative about work	Very supportive	Parents very supportive but overprotective	Not applicable	Not applicable	Not applicable
Discrimination skills • Cannot distinguish between work supplies • Distinguishes between work supplies with an external cue • Distinguishes between work supplies	Fair, Mary can distinguish between simple items (e.g., Comet vs. Windex)	Can be trained to easily distinguish between work supplies	Made gross discrimination of work supplies (i.e., mop, bucket, rags)	Could not distinguish size of trash bags	No problem in this area

Figure 19–8, *continued*

	Parent: mother	Teacher: Mrs. B.	Dietary—Situational Assessment I	Supply—Situational Assessment II	Laundry—Situational Assessment III
Time awareness • Unaware of time and clock function • Identifies breaks/lunch • Can tell time to the hour • Can tell time in hours and minutes	Tells time to the hour	Same	Same	Same	Same
Functional reading • None • Sight words/symbols • Simple reading • Fluent reading	Some words by sight (e.g., women, exit, Coke)	Same	Found women's restroom by the sign	Not observed	Not observed
Functional math • None • Simple counting • Simple addition/subtraction • Computational skills	Simple counting to 10	Same	Observed counting to 4 when putting shelves on cart	Not observed	Not observed
Independent street crossing • None • Two lane street (with or without light) • four lane street (with or without light)	2 lane street only	Same	Would only cross in outlined pedestrian crosswalk	Not observed	Looked both ways when crossing 2 lane street

Handling criticism/stress • Resistive/argumentative • Withdraws into silence • Accepts criticism/ does not change	Cries when frustrated	Does not accept criticism readily, cries under stress	No problems	Withdrew into silence when corrected	Responded by saying, "I was going to do that!"
Acts/speaks aggressively • Hourly • Daily • Weekly • Monthly • Never	Never	Never	Not observed during 4-hour assessment	Not observed	Not observed
Travel skills • Requires bus training • Uses bus independently (with or without transfers) • Able to make own travel arrangements	None... willing to learn	None	None	None	None
Work experiences • Employment site • Job tasks performed • Dates, hours, wages	Situational job sites through school	Food bank, clothing rack, nursing home laundry			
Physical limitations • Impairment • Medications • Medical restrictions	Seizure medication, cerebral palsy, and scoliosis. The seizures are under control. Mary also has severe visual limitations and must wear glasses. Perceptual problems are also evident when she attempts to perform tasks.				

Figure 19–8, *continued*

	Parent: mother	Teacher: Mrs. B.	Dietary—Situational Assessment I	Supply—Situational Assessment II	Laundry—Situational Assessment III
Responding to survival words • Street signs • Restrooms • Danger, stop	Yes, she recognizes all of these	Same	Recognized signs for the restroom	Same	Recognized the exit sign
Hurtful to self/others • Banging head, pulling hair • Biting, scratching • Hitting, pinching	Never!	No	Not observed	Not observed	Not observed
Destructive to property • Breaks, burns, tears things	Never!	No	Not observed	Not observed	Not observed
Disruptive behavior that interferes with activities of others • Yelling, screaming • Clinging • Laughing/crying for no reason • Interrupting	Sometimes cries for no apparent reason	Same as parent comment	Some inappropriate laughter, but this did not interfere	Cried several times when corrected	Not observed
Unusual or repetitive behavior/habits • Pacing • Rocking • Twirling fingers • Twitching	None	None	Not observed	Not observed	Not observed
Behavior that is socially offensive to others • Talking too loudly	Sometimes talks too loudly and will hug	Same as parent comment	Not observed	Talked too loudly to get co-worker's	Not observed

• Burping, picking nose, • Touching, hugging	and touch inappropriately			attention five times in 4-hour period	
Withdrawal or inattentive behavior • Keeping away from people • Expressing unusual fears • Showing little interest in activities	She will hide when she is angry	She will get very quiet and withdraw after she has cried and been angry	Not observed	Pulled away from the trainer for 5 minutes after corrected, would not talk	Not observed
Uncooperative or noncompliant behavior • Refusing to attend school/work • Refusing to follow rules/requests • Acting defiant/pouting	Will pout and act defiant if corrected	Same as parent comment	Not observed	Pouted when criticized and told to return to work, did return immediately on verbal prompt	Not observed
Leisure skills/interests	Card games, TV, teen magazines, social clubs with mom	Loves to talk! Likes to dress-up and use make-up; this has been used as reinforcer	Not observed	Not observed	Not observed
Chores or responsibilities	Cleans up room (i.e., hangs up clothes, makes bed)	Delivers notes to the office on a regular basis for the teacher	Not applicable	Not applicable	Not applicable
Activities, foods, and items that are reinforcing	Bowling, going out for pizza, candy, popcorn, make-up, audiotapes	Same comments as parent	Used break as a reinforcer for working, soda given	Coke	Coke

Figure 19–8, *continued*

	Parent: mother	Teacher: Mrs. B.	Dietary—Situational Assessment I	Supply—Situational Assessment II	Laundry—Situational Assessment III
Money skills • Discriminates between coins • Makes minor purchases • Makes major purchases • Amount of spending money given to consumer • Willingness of family to give consumer money from paycheck	Makes minor purchases (i.e., soda, candy, make-up) by herself	Makes minor purchases using <2 dollars	Used the vending machine independently	Did not show any skills during lunch	Same as I
Asking for assistance • Peers • Co-workers • Acquaintances • Persons in authority	Will ask for help if she needs it	Often asks for help even if she does not need it	Asked for help even when it was not needed	Same as I	No problems observed

Other:
Mary had a lot of difficulty moving and doing fine motor skills at the same time. For example, in the dietary department she could not bend over and put the shelves on the cart at the same time. When she tried she often would lose her balance and fall forward. It seems that a stationary position would be most appropriate for her.

From *Helping Persons with Severe Mental Retardation Get and Keep Employment* (pp. 80–89) by M. S. Moon, K. J. Inge, P. Wehman, V. Brooke, & J. M. Marcus, 1990, Baltimore: Paul H. Brookes Publishing Co., P.O. Box 10624, Baltimore, Maryland 21285-0624. Reprinted by permission.

er may need to be taught when the use of these skills is appropriate and when it is not. For example, teasing and joking may be common during break time or in the photocopying room, but are not appropriate in another setting.

In addition to learning appropriate social skills for the work setting, the job coach should look for opportunities to assist the worker with disabilities in developing social relationships with coworkers. Coworkers who are not familiar with interacting with individuals with disabilities may need to be provided with information on the interests of the individual with disabilities or ways to involve the supported worker in after-work social occasions.

The importance of developing social skills has implications for school vocational programs. While the importance of teaching students work and community skills in preparation for postschool life is obvious, the importance of instruction in developing social relationships may not be as apparent. Teachers should provide students with ample opportunities to have contact with nondisabled students and to develop interests and friendships with peers. These relationships will provide the student with disabilities many opportunities to learn and practice social skills.

Evaluating Employment Outcomes

The measure of success in a traditional vocational program was whether the individual with disabilities was able to perform a task in a sheltered work situation. In current vocational programs, the goals of employment have become much more broad. To evaluate the success of vocational programs, factors beyond worker productivity should be examined.

Some individual outcomes that may be assessed include the performance of the job task and the economic benefits derived from the supported work situation. Employment specialists should be interested not only in the frequency, rate, and duration of job tasks but also in the level of engagement of the worker, the efficiency with which tasks are completed, and the ability to meet job performance standards (Gaylord-Ross & Chadsey-Rusch, 1991). In assessing economic benefits, the employment specialist can assess the wages earned and examine the number of hours worked, the duration of the employment, and the reduced public support needed by the worker.

A major area of interest in the movement to place workers in real jobs in the community is the integration of the worker in the employment setting. The level of integration may be measured by the direct observation of social interactions between the worker and his or her peers, the worker's participation in social activities with coworkers, and the assessment of the worker's satisfaction with his or her integration in the workplace.

Another area of interest in determining the outcomes of an employment program should be the satisfaction of the consumer. Interviews, observations, and case histories may be used to document the satisfaction of the supported worker with the vocational program.

Measurement procedures are used by teachers and service providers to assess if programs are meeting their service goals and if individuals are benefiting from interventions. The assessment of outcomes for vocational programs must be broadly based; the goals for employment are not just to achieve a work placement but to assist persons with disabilities in achieving the quality of life outcomes that are provided through employment.

Conclusion

In this chapter the importance of transition planning and vocational training was discussed. The chapter was primarily focused on the transition of students with disabilities into employment. It is important to note that the process of transition also involves outcomes in community access, leisure, relationships, spiritual fulfillment, participation in the community, and a sense of well-being. Most of these issues have been addressed in other chapters because the transition process does not involve a separate set of strategies for instructing students with disabilities. Rather, transition planning is a process for anticipating the needs of the student in the adult world and preparing for that eventual outcome.

Questions for Reflection

1. What may be a family's greatest worries as their son or daughter with severe disabilities approaches graduation from high school?
2. Will planning for transition assist families in resolving their worries or might it heighten their anxiety?
3. In what ways can students with disabilities participate in the transition plan?
4. How will changes in society's acceptance of persons with disabilities impact postschool outcomes for students with severe disabilities?
5. How can the outcomes of personal fulfillment and satisfaction be measured for a student with severe disabilities?
6. Who in the family and community should participate in transition planning? Why?

References

Buckley, J., Mank, D., & Sandow, D. (1990). Developing and implementing support strategies. In F. R. Rusch (Ed.), *Supported employment:. Models, methods, and issues* (pp. 131–144). Sycamore, IL: Sycamore.

Chadsey-Rusch, J. (1990). Social interactions of secondary-aged students with severe handicaps: Implications for facilitating the transition from school to work. *Journal of the Association for Persons with Severe Handicaps, 15,* 69–78.

Chadsey-Rusch, J. (1992). Toward defining and measuring social skills in employment settings. *American Journal on Mental Retardation, 96,* 405–418.

Chadsey-Rusch, J., & Gonzalez, P. (1988). Social ecology of the workplace: Employer's perceptions versus direct observation. *Research in Developmental Disabilities, 9,* 229–245.

Culver, J. B., Spencer, K. C., & Gliner, J. A. (1990). Prediction of supported employment placements by job developers. *Education and Training in Mental Retardation, 25,* 237–242.

Ferguson, B., McDonnell, J., & Drew, C. (1993). Type and frequency of social interaction among workers with and without mental retardation. *American Journal on Mental Retardation, 97,* 530–540.

Gaylord-Ross, R., & Chadsey-Rusch, J. (1991). Measurement of work-related outcomes for students with severe disabilities. *Journal of Special Education, 25,* 291–304.

Halpern, A. (1993). Quality of life as a conceptual framework for evaluating transition outcomes. *Exceptional Children, 59,* 486–498.

Hutchins, M. P., & Renzaglia, A. M. (1990). Developing a longitudinal vocational training program. In F. R. Rusch (Ed.), *Supported employment: Models, methods, and issues* (pp. 365–380). Sycamore, IL: Sycamore.

Individuals with Disabilities Education Act of 1990, Public Law 101-476. (October 30, 1990). Title 20, U. S. C. 1400-1485: *U. S. Statutes at Large, 104,* 1103–1151.

Johnson, J. R., & Rusch, F. R. (1990). Analysis of hours of direct training provided by employment specialists to supported employees. *American Journal on Mental Retardation, 94,* 674–682.

Nietupski, J., Verstegen, D., & Hamre-Nietupski, S. (1992). Incorporating sales and business practices into job development in supported employment. *Education and Training in Mental Retardation, 27,* 207–218.

Nisbet, J., & Hagner, D. (1988). Natural supports in the workplace: A reexamination of supported employment. *Journal of the Association for Persons with Severe Handicaps, 13,* 260–267.

Parent, W. S., Kregel, J., Metzler, H. M. D., & Twardzik, G. (1992). Social integration in the workplace: An analysis of the interaction activities of workers with mental retardation and their coworkers. *Education and Training in Mental Retardation, 27,* 28–38.

Moon, M. S., Inge, K. J., Wehman, P., Brooke, V., & Barcus, J. M. (1990). *Helping persons with severe mental retardation get and keep employment.* Baltimore: Paul H. Brookes.

Moon, M. S., Kiernan, W., & Halloran, W. (1990). School-based vocational programs and labor laws: A 1990 update. *Journal of the Association for Persons with Severe Handicaps, 15,* 177–185.

Moseley, C. R. (1988). Job satisfaction research: Implications for supported employment. *Journal of the Association for Persons with Severe Handicaps, 13,* 211–219.

Rhodes, L., Sandow, D., Mank, D., Buckley, J., & Albin, J. (1991). Expanding the role of employers in supported employment. *Journal of the Association for Persons with Severe Handicaps, 16,* 213–217.

Rusch, F. R., Johnson, J. R., & Hughes, C. (1990). Analysis of co-worker involvement in relation to level of disability versus placement approach among supported employees. *Journal of the Association for Persons with Severe Handicaps, 15,* 32–39.

Sowers, J., & Powers, L. (1991). *Vocational preparation and employment of students with physical and multiple disabilities.* Baltimore: Paul H. Brookes.

Steere, D., Pancsofar, E., Wood, R., & Hecimovic, A. (1990). *The principles of shared responsibility.* Hartford, CT: Institute of Human Resources.

Storey, K., Rhodes, L., Sandow, D., Loewinger, H., & Petherbridge, R. (1991). Direct observation of social interactions in a supported employment setting. *Education and Training in Mental Retardation, 26,* 53–63.

Storey, K., Sandow, D., & Rhodes, L. (1990). Service delivery issues in supported employment. *Education and Training in Mental Retardation, 25,* 325–332.

Test, D. W., Hinson, K. B., Solow, J., & Keul, P. (1993). Job satisfaction of persons in supported employment. *Education and Training in Mental Retardation, 28,* 38–46.

Thompson, L., Powers, G., & Houchard, B. (1992). The wage effects of supported employment. *Journal of the Association for Persons with Severe Handicaps, 17,* 87–94.

Tines, J., Rusch, F. R., McCaughrin, W., & Conley, R. W. (1990). Benefit-cost analysis of supported employment in Illinois: A statewide evaluation. *American Journal on Mental Retardation, 95,* 44–54.

United States Department of Labor (1962). *Field operations handbook* (6/21/62-10b10-10b11). Washington, DC: United States Department of Labor. Author.

Wehman, P. (1992). *Life beyond the classroom: Transition strategies for young people with disabilities.* Baltimore: Paul H. Brookes.

Wehman, P., Moon, M. S., Everson, J. M., Wood, M., & Barcus, M. (1988). *Transition from school to work: New challenges for youth with severe disabilities.* Baltimore: Paul H. Brookes.

PART VI

Trends and Issues

CHAPTER 20 Trends and Issues in the Education of Students with Severe Disabilities

CHAPTER 20

Trends and Issues in the Education of Students with Severe Disabilities

Chapter Overview

This final chapter discusses various trends in society, in reform in general education and special education, and in the field of services for people with disabilities that will have a bearing on how services will be provided in the future. Implications are discussed for the role of teachers.

The philosophy, strategies, and tactics presented throughout this text are intended to provide practitioners with state-of-the-art information about providing instruction for students with severe disabilities. Critical to the successful functioning of a professional in this area, however, is the recognition that this is a very dynamic field. Today's knowledge will not be sufficient for tomorrow. One should not approach the task of educating individuals with severe disabilities without at least a fundamental understanding of the big picture, of where we are going as a society and as a profession. Therefore, in concluding this text, we present an overview of some relevant trends in society and schools, and how persons with severe disabilities are interacting and coming to be viewed and treated in these contexts. No one can state exactly what the future holds, but by examining current apparent trends, we should have a fairly good idea of where we are headed. After some discussion of current trends and issues, we conclude by stating some implications for teachers.

Societal Issues

In the last quarter of the 20th century, dramatic changes have taken place in modern society and in the worldwide community. Many of you have witnessed changes in the most fundamental ways in which societies operate, changes that have occurred both in the United States and in other parts of the world. They have occurred because it has been the will of the majority of people to have more democratic forms of government, broader rights for citizens, and more participation in local and global activities. When those in power have resisted democratization and have continued policies of autocracy and exclusion, they have been shunned and shamed by the world majority. Changes in the former Eastern bloc countries, South Africa, and in Central and South American countries are but a few of the headline producers that most of us have witnessed.

In the United States, one of the most notable changes that has taken place in the last half of the 20th century is the broader inclusion of people with diverse characteristics into the mainstream of society. Since the midpoint of the century, we have witnessed a broad social movement that legitimized the inclusion and participation of people who were once outside the traditional majority of society. Notably, people of color (African-American, Hispanic-American, Asian-American, Native American, and others), women, gays and lesbians, and people with disabilities have sought legal protections and social sanctions that would allow them to enjoy the fruits of society as much as the more traditional beneficiaries. Their efforts have not been in vain. They have resulted not only in their greater inclusion but in an expectation that no one in modern Western society should be excluded from its bounty because of personal characteristics as long as these characteristics do not infringe upon the rights of others. Obviously, people with severe disabilities have been a part of this movement and have benefited from it. The Americans with Disabilities Act and the Individuals with Disabilities Education Act are but two relatively recent manifestations of this change in the social structure of our society.

Of course, not all changes in our society or in others occur smoothly or completely, and much of our social development has been a mixture of success and failure. Although many in our society have enjoyed tremendous personal gains, others are uneducated or undereducated, unemployed or underemployed, hobbled by addictive substances, homeless, and/or disenfranchised from mainstream society in various other ways. While all people may enjoy the same fundamental rights, in reality, many cannot exercise those rights.

What does all of this mean in terms of providing an education for students with severe disabilities? It means a great deal. Because the education we can provide for students with disabilities will be no better than the education we can provide for all students, and because society dictates the quality of public school education, educational professionals must be aware of current and future conditions and their implications. As citizens, more so than as professionals, we must exercise our democratic responsibilities if persons with disabilities are to be considered full members of society. At the very least, all who are responsible for teaching and providing professional services to persons with severe disabilities must be aware of the good and the bad that has occurred and that can occur again in society. Education and other services for people with disabilities have never existed in a social vacuum. It is important to recognize that as the general values of our society go, so goes the nature of services for persons with severe disabilities. When our society tolerated slavery, it also tolerated the inhumane treatment of people with disabilities. When society valued the care and rehabilitation of those who were injured and suffered following major wars, it also valued services for children with disabilities. When society came to recognize that separate education was not equal education for minority children, it soon came to realize that separate education was also not appropriate for children with disabilities.

These parallel occurrences, which can be documented over and over again, teach us three lessons. First, inclusion of people with disabilities is part of a larger social pattern. If we want society to include people with severe disabilities, it must also include others who have often been excluded. Second, by and large, society has never moved away from inclusion once it has started to move toward it. Although the amount of time required to achieve inclusion may be long, the majority of society does not move backwards once it has begun its move forward. And, finally, even though sociolegal progress has occurred, *de facto* it has been limited or nonexistent for many.

This last point means that not all in the mainstream have welcomed the changes that have occurred, neither for people of various ethnic and minority backgrounds nor for people with disabilities. We have heard individual and collective voices raised in anger and speaking in opposition about many of the changes that have occurred. We have sometimes seen efforts by those in power to undermine many of the gains that have been made. We must also note that not all those of minority status have benefited from the changes that have taken place. There are still many outside the mainstream, many who have simply not been included. Witness the Los Angeles riots of April 1992. The rioters had nothing to lose because they had gained none of what many of us have and take for granted.

Notwithstanding this, however, it cannot be denied that we live in a more inclusive and heterogeneous world than existed just 20 years ago. Regardless of the lack of progress that exists on several fronts and the contention of many that these changes are unhealthy and undesirable, most likely society will not revert to its earlier form. This is why the inclusion of people with severe disabilities in the community and in regular schools and classrooms cannot be viewed as simply another special education administrative arrangement that exists on a continuum of services. It is not. It is part of a larger paradigm shift that is evidenced by society and its various constituencies questioning its historical values, assumptions, and approaches about how people with disabilities are to be considered and how they are to be treated (Skrtic, 1991). Ultimately, we can anticipate that although there will continue to be those who believe segregation and isolation is the preferred practice for people with severe disabilities, greater inclusion and participation as well as understanding and acceptance will permeate the lives of these individuals. This will not necessarily occur because it makes these individuals learn more or function more independently (although it will certainly bear on these outcomes), but because it will be perceived by a society as the right thing to do in an era of diverse inclusion. Professionals must understand this and they must be aware that special education as perceived and practiced in the past will be different in the future.

Educational Reform

Since the early 1980s public school education reform efforts have been proposed or initiated at local, state, and national levels. These reforms have been instituted because of the real and perceived shortcomings of public school education in many areas. Large numbers of individuals are not being successful in school, are dropping out, are finding themselves without skills, and often are getting in trouble with the law. In many states, individuals who have not succeeded in school are crowding into limited prison spaces because of their lack of academic and social skills.

In 1981, then U.S. Secretary of Education Terrel Bell created the National Commission on Excellence in Education. Two years later the commission published what would come to be the most noted document of the 1980s educational reform movement in the United States, *A Nation at Risk.* This publication stated that the United States was doing a very poor job of educating its students (a "rising tide of mediocrity") and that public school reform was necessary if we were to remain a world leader in the global community. Various other "educational reform" publications emerged shortly thereafter, most drawing similar conclusions and making various recommendations (Boyer, 1983; Goodlad, 1984; Sizer, 1984).

The result of these concerns was that many public school systems instituted changes in their basic operational and instructional procedures. Some important changes in many schools and school districts included the following (Sailor, Gee, & Karasoff, 1993):

- "School accountability" required that schools begin publicly reporting the level of progress being made by their students through the use of standardized tests. This process was intended to provide the public with a barometer of educational quality.
- Curriculum changes often occurred with a particular emphasis on basic academic skills. In the new curricula there was also a call for the development of critical

thinking and real-life problem-solving abilities and the study of literature in its original forms. Many states and school districts developed core curricula intended to be mastered by all students.

- "Effective schools research" emerged that reported that various factors in schools could be related to the success of the students in those schools. Effective classroom instructional strategies were also studied and proposed for use by teachers. (See below.)
- Restructuring occurred to allow individual schools to more readily control their own resources to deal with students "at risk," that is, the students most likely to fail or drop out. The most important aspect of school restructuring was giving schools more authority to implement the types of changes necessary for them to serve their communities and allow more resources for these students to be directed at the general educational program.

Effective Schools

As the educational reform movement was making headway in the 1980s, many of its tenets resulted from an area of study referred to as "effective schools" research (Bickel & Bickel, 1986; Lezotte, 1989; Purkey & Smith, 1983; U.S. Department of Education, 1986). Subsequently, many schools and school districts started efforts to implement the results of the effective schools research, making fundamental changes in the ways that they operated (Lezotte, 1989).

Effective schools research was initiated by the work of Ron Edmonds (Edmonds, 1982; Edmonds & Fredericksen, 1979) and focused on an examination of factors within schools that differentiated schools that were more successful from those that were less successful in terms of student academic success. Edmonds was particularly interested in looking at inner-city schools that served primarily lower socioeconomic status students.

Edmonds's interest originated because of an earlier study by some prominent sociologists (Coleman et al., 1966). The Coleman report suggested that schools could not be enough of an influence to offset the deleterious conditions that existed in students' homes and communities. Coleman and his colleagues proposed that schools could only be effective if they were "independent of the child's immediate social environment" (Coleman et al., 1966, p. 325). Edmonds's research suggested another point of view: that some schools that were serving low socioeconomic status, high-risk students were doing an effective job with these students and thus there must be something happening within the schools that was causing this (Lezotte, 1989). One important difference between Coleman's and Edmonds's approaches was that Coleman examined broad measures of school achievement based on standardized test scores whereas Edmonds and other researchers of effective schools looked at the achievement of basic skills as they were focused on within individual school curricula. In his review, Lezotte (1989) defined an effective school as follows:

> *an effective school can be defined as one that can, in outcome terms reflective of its teaching for learning mission, demonstrate the joint presence of quality (acceptably high levels of achievement) and equity (no differences in the achievement among the major subsets of the student population). (p.29)*

These schools were identified by comparing them in many ways with schools that were similar in all respects except student achievement. From the research, five factors emerged as being responsible for effectiveness (Bickel &

Bickel, 1986; Lezotte, 1989; U.S. Department of Education, 1986):

1. There was strong leadership provided by the school's principal for academic instruction.
2. A schoolwide focus on basic academic skills instruction and academic achievement existed.
3. Throughout the school there was an orderly, safe climate conducive to teaching and learning.
4. Teachers shared an expectation that all students would obtain at least minimum mastery of basic skills.
5. Pupil measures of achievement were used as the basis for program evaluation.

Perhaps the most significant factor to come from the effective schools research was the notion that positive expectancy can lead to positive results. If schools are organized to reflect factors such as the five listed above, the outcome can usually be good, even for students considered to be at high risk for failure. Making such organizational changes, however, requires sustained effort in several areas. Based on studies intended to make schools more effective, Lezotte (1989) recommended the following principles:

1. The single school (as opposed to entire school districts) should be the focus for the planned change.
2. Teachers and others must be an integral part of the school improvement process. Principals cannot do it alone.
3. School improvement cannot be viewed as a single event occurrence but must be seen as a continuing process.
4. Improving schools must have a choice in what they want to do to improve and how they want to do it. They must have control over the processes of change.

Effective Instruction

As some scholars focused on school-level factors that had positive results on student learning, others looked at classroom organizational and teaching variables (Bickel & Bickel, 1986). Rosenshine (1983) found research to support six instructional strategies important for effective classrooms:

1. The teacher must review and check previous work and reteach it if necessary.
2. Following this the teacher must clearly present new material.
3. The teacher must allow for adequate practice and check students' work for understanding.
4. Feedback and correction must be provided to the student and material retaught if necessary.
5. The student must be allowed independent practice, and
6. There should be periodic reviews (weekly and monthly) of the material.

Other noted factors that have improved student learning in classrooms have been the use of detailed and redundant instruction and explanation of new concepts, ample opportunities for guided practice and student participation, consistent checking for understanding, using teacher questioning and review of homework, movement by the teacher among students during practice, and organizing instructional activities in a way that uses instructional time effectively. Additionally, research indicates that students who are at the greatest risk of not achieving academic success must master material at a relatively high success rate (90% to 100%) before moving on to new material (Berliner, 1984; Rosenshine, 1983).

While these tactics have undoubtedly resulted in success on several measures of student outcome, there has been recent criticism of teachers who rely too heavily on teacher-directed instruction (Blanton, 1992; Englert, Tarrant, & Mariage, 1992; Pugach, 1992). These and other authorities have proposed the need for less teacher directiveness in the classroom and more student participation. Englert et al. (1992) offered a summary of higher-order, student-participant classroom characteristics, which are listed in Figure 20–1.

Meaningful Contexts

Makes learning meaningful and purposeful (emphasizes sense-making) by providing authentic purposes (tasks) and audiences

Engages all student in holistic activities related to the learning task (e.g., students get to read and write whole texts and solve problems) even though students may vary in ability levels

Presents strategies in their natural contexts rather than solely in isolation (e.g., student uses strategies in problems or in texts rather than in isolation)

Supports students until students can engage in the entire cognitive process independently (e.g., through the use of tutors, invented spellings, calculators, writing/reading buddies, etc.), but all students are engaged in the entire process

Classroom Dialogues

Models how to perform a task using **think-alouds** that provide insight into the inner thing of the mature problem-solver

Models use of skill or strategy in context

Models metacognitive or regulatory self-statements to help students self-instruct, self-monitor, and self-evaluate (e.g., What am I supposed to do? Do I understand? How am I doing?) and talks about self as a learner

Provides guided practice (application) by asking students to **think-aloud** when using skills or strategies

Engages students in talk about their own thinking and cognitive processes (e.g., "What strategies did you use when...?" "What were you thinking when...?")

Shares the cognitive work and dialogue with students. Together, teacher and students jointly perform the task of problem solving

Provides frequent occasions for student-to-student discussion during problem-solving. Classroom discourse sounds more like a conversation than recitation

Conveys attitude that students in group have expertise and can be informants for each other and the teacher

Encourages students in group to turn to each other for answers and help. Conveys attitude and opportunities for students to teach, monitor, and assist each other

Asks students to dialogue with one another and collaborate on problem-solving tasks

Provides occasions for students to self-monitor and self-evaluate

Figure 20–1
Classroom Conditions for Promoting Higher-Order Learning

Adapted from "Defining and Redefining Instructional Practice in Special Education: Perspectives on Good Teaching" by C. S. Englert, K. L. Tarrant, & T. V. Mariage, 1992, *Teacher Education and Special Education, 15,* pp. 62–86.

One area of classroom effectiveness worthy of note is how students should be grouped for instruction. Bickel and Bickel (1986) stated that research suggests that various grouping patterns should be used for different instructional purposes and that static groupings should be avoided. Also to be avoided is the homogeneous grouping of students by ability in a way that results in students with less ability being relegated to groups that receive less content, lower cognitive demands, less instructional time, and a lower quality of teacher enthusiasm and peer interaction. One strategy that encourages participation and cooperation and

Responsive Instruction

Embeds instruction in new procedures or strategies at the point where students experience confusion; Adjusts lessons on a moment-to-moment basis

Provides instruction at a level where students are challenged to acquire new strategies

Accepts and incorporates student's ideas, examples and experiences into the lesson content

Provides students with alternatives and opportunities to engage in decision-making

Continually ties new information to that which the student already knows (before, during, and after the lesson)

Displays willingness to "**roam around the known**" (e.g., talks about concepts and ideas that student knows) rather than focuses exclusively on quick, correct answers

When students err, teacher makes bridges between what students know and what they need to know (e.g., new knowledge is anchored to the familiar)

Responds to errors or mistakes as opportunities for the construction of new knowledge and meanings; thus, teachers respond to errors by starting with familiar or known content (e.g., students' own ideas), then transforming that knowledge into more conceptually correct assumptions

Classroom Community

Engages students in collaborative problem-solving activities and uses cooperative learning strategies

Establishes environment that emphasizes student's membership in the community, including occasions when students share ideas, and publish their ideas and thinking in various ways (e.g., author's chair, literature response groups)

Allows students to negotiate the meaning of text and ideas rather than assume that the teacher or text is the ultimate arbiter of the meaning or correctness (e.g., asks questions that do not have a single correct answer)

Asks students to explain their thinking

Publicizes students' ideas, e.g., written publications, author's chair, etc.

Figure 20–1, *continued*

has been shown to have a positive effect on student learning is cooperative learning arrangements.

Finally, it has been determined that the number of students in one class can be an important factor related to student progress. A class of 20 students has been found to be superior in terms of student progress to a class of 40, given certain conditions. The teacher must take advantage of the smaller class size to implement the effective classroom strategies that were presented above. Use of ineffective instructional strategies with smaller classes will not do a great deal to improve students' performance.

Special Education and the Reform Movement

Unfortunately, students with disabilities and the educational system used to serve them were not adequately addressed in the educational reform documents of the 1980s (Pugach & Sapon-Shevin, 1987). Nevertheless, there are several implications of school reform, effective schools research, and effective instruction research that may have a bearing on the organization and delivery of special education services for students with severe disabilities. Perhaps the most important is the call for schools to control their own organization and improve instructional grouping and activities at the classroom level. This means that a school may be internally restructured to better meet the diverse needs of all of its students, including those who are at risk for failure as well as those formally identified as having mild or severe disabilities. The school reform movement may thus provide a window of opportunity for making substantial changes in the way students with severe disabilities are educated (Lipsky & Gartner, 1989; Sailor, 1989; Sailor et al., 1989; Sailor et al., 1993).

To better understand what types of changes are needed and what might occur, we must understand the problems associated with the current system, which have been summarized by several authors (Lipsky & Gartner, 1989; Reynolds, Wang, & Walberg, 1987; Sailor, 1989; Sailor et al., 1989; Skrtic, 1991; Wills, 1986). The most often identified problems are the following:

- The majority of school systems continue to provide segregated programs for students with severe disabilities either in special schools or completely separate special classrooms in regular schools. This violates the principle of least restrictive environment and denies the benefits of integrated learning and social opportunities between students with and without severe disabilities.
- The delivery of special education and related services is fragmented, with teachers and therapists pulling students out of programs and providing services without knowledge of what others are doing. The student's needs are not considered holistically.
- Having a disability is largely viewed as a pathological condition; persons with disabilities are "victims" who face "endless problems"; and in special education a person's disability is considered the major (if not only) dimension of his or her personality.
- The primary focus of intervention is "fixing" the deficits of students with severe disabilities. This often means attempting to teach developmental milestones instead of functional skills that will be of use in everyday life. There is a lack of individualization of instructional objectives and strategies.
- Parents of students with disabilities are often considered as either being disabled

themselves or as lacking the necessary knowledge to contribute to their child's learning and development. They are often thought of as antagonists to the system instead of as consumers of its services.

- Significant resources must be committed to identifying and distinguishing between students who do have disabilities (particularly mild disabilities) and those who do not. Many times these distinctions are artificial and vary from one location to another and one time to another. Categorical distinctions are often necessitated by funding formulas that allocate money to schools based on the number of students in particular categories.
- Research has not supported the efficacy of pull-out special education programs for students with mild disabilities. In other words, students in separate programs generally do not learn more as a result of being in those programs. Assumptions about improving learning opportunities by clustering students in homogeneous groups have never been supported.
- Besides special education categories, there are several other categorical programs that also require resources for the purpose of identification and funding, for example, limited English proficiency programs, Chapter 1 programs for students with reading problems, dropout prevention programs, and so on. For these programs, as with traditional special education programs, students must be identified, be determined to be eligible, and be served in smaller numbers in locations outside of the regular classroom. The result is that the programs are expensive and draw money and resources away from general education. As society discovers new problems, new "special" programs are put in place within schools to deal with the problems.
- Students with mild disabilities placed in special classes are not challenged with more difficult academic material or required to demonstrate higher-order cognitive skills.
- The dichotomy between students with and without disabilities not only is often considered to be arbitrary, it results in some of the nonidentified students who have academic or behavioral difficulties getting no extra support or assistance to help them in areas of need.
- Students with disabilities, especially those with more severe disabilities, are not given opportunities to make choices or have control over various aspects of their lives. Their daily lives are often totally directed by other persons.

How can problems such as these be addressed through educational reform? Perhaps not all of them can be, or at least not fully. However, it should be apparent that some changes are needed in the way special education has traditionally been delivered. As schools, school districts, and states initiate reforms, they should not overlook the shortcomings of the delivery of services to students with disabilities. Three proposals that have been made to restructure special education for students with severe disabilities as part of the educational reform movement are presented below.

Regular Education Initiative One promising alternative to current practices that has received much attention in recent years is the Regular Education Initiative (REI) (Wang, Reynolds, & Walberg, 1987), which is a plan intended to meet the needs of students with disabilities as well as other at-risk students. It calls for all students to be served in a regular classroom without regard to category, disability, or the need for special services. In this setting, any student with a special need would be served without meeting any categorical criteria or being pulled out for services. Reynolds et al. (1987) stated that the program would have two parts:

> *The first part of the initiative involves the joining of demonstrably effective practices from special, compensatory, and general education to establish a general education system that is more inclusive and that better serves all students, particularly those who require greater than usual educational support. The second part of the initiative calls for the federal government to collaborate with a number of states and local school districts in encouraging and supporting experimental trials of integrated forms of education for students who are currently segregated for service in separate special, remedial, and compensatory education programs. (Reynolds et al., 1987, p. 394)*

In their proposal, Reynolds and his colleagues called for "waivers for performance." This would allow the school districts participating in the REI to receive funding as is available under current categorical models. However, instead of being required to pull the students out of regular classroom, schools and districts could serve students in these settings as long as they could demonstrate through student performance data that the students were learning adequately.

Under the REI, special educators and other specialists would become in-class support personnel to the regular class teachers. Instead of students being pulled out, services would be provided in the regular class. Most importantly, categorical labeling could be eliminated and services could be provided based on individual needs of students instead of category. No student would have to be formally identified, yet all students who needed extra services could be served in the regular classroom. Also of significance is the idea that the classroom teacher would not simply turn the student over to the special education teacher for services. The teachers would work together to provide an appropriate education for the student. In effect, this would reduce the dichotomy between "regular" and "special" education.

The REI has not been without its critics (Hallahan et al., 1988; Kauffman, 1989), whose concerns are that students will not be adequately supported in regular classes, that funding sources may be eliminated for students with disabilities, and that some students may be "dumped" into regular classes without receiving an appropriate education there. These are legitimate concerns that would have to be addressed as educational reforms are made in the direction of the REI. Nevertheless, the concept appears to hold promise for dealing with many of the problems listed above associated with pull-out programs.

Merging Special and Regular Education Another, perhaps more "radical," proposal has been to eliminate the dual programs of "regular" and "special" education altogether and have one general education system that serves all students. In making this argument, Stainback and Stainback (1984, 1987) offered different points to support their position. They suggested that there are not two distinct groups of students, "regular" and "special," but that all individuals fall on a continuum of ability. Any dichotomy that exists is arbitrary. They further pointed out that in the current categories of special students there are as many differences between students in a given category as there are between students in different categories.

The Stainbacks argued that the individualization of educational goals and objectives should be applied to all students, not just to those who are in special education. They also pointed out that there are not separate sets of instructional methods for students with and without disabilities, that sound instruction is equally appropriate for all students, and that all students should receive high-quality instruction. They noted, however, that some methods may need to be tailored to meet individual needs.

In their proposal, Stainback and Stainback (1984) discussed many of the problems in the current system that are listed above: the expense associated with the classification of students, the inappropriateness of classifying students based on only one feature (i.e., their primary disability), the lack of cooperation among professionals, the lack of a relationship between categorical designation and actual service needs, reduced curricular options, and the perpetuation of the concept of deviance by the current dual system.

If special education and general education were to merge, Stainback and Stainback (1984) stated that there would be several implications. First of all, of course, teachers would have to be prepared to work with students who have a range of abilities. However, not all teachers would need to know all subject matter or instructional areas. These authors proposed that teachers would specialize in content areas, as they often do now, but that the content areas would be broadened to include how to teach skills such as self-care and community living as well as reading and social studies. Teachers could then serve as resource consultants to each other. "The main difference between what is currently practiced and what would be needed in a merged system is the reorganization of personnel preparation and assignment according to instructional categories rather than by categories of students" (Stainback & Stainback, 1984, p. 107).

As with the REI, merging general and special education would also deal with several of the problems listed above. As noted by the Stainbacks, it would reduce much of the current emphasis on classifying students, pulling them out of regular classes, and placing them in different categorical programs. Students would receive special assistance as it was needed instead of based on their categorical designation. Any special grouping required for unique instructional needs could be done more fluidly, changing as the needs and interests of students change. Funding would be based on service needs rather than categorical placements.

A brief comparison of the important features of the current dual system and the proposed unified system is presented in Table 20–1. The Stainbacks' primary intention was to propose a system that would provide services without stigma. They wrote:

> *While labels have created a wellspring of pity and sympathy that has resulted in strong federal and state support for special education . . . no student should have to be categorized, labeled, and pitied in order to receive a free and appropriate education. (Stainback & Stainback, 1984, p. 108)*

The Comprehensive Local School Plan A third plan to revise special education service delivery within the reform of general education has been proposed by Wayne Sailor and his colleagues and is referred to as the Comprehensive Local School or CLS (Sailor, 1989; Sailor et al., 1989). The CLS was proposed to offer an appropriate education to students with severe disabilities in least restrictive environments based on students' ages and needs. Sailor et al. (1989) proposed that the CLS should serve students in "specialized instructional units" and that the placement of students would sometimes be in the regular classroom and at other times be in other instructional settings based on what the student needed to be

Table 20–1
Comparison of Dual and Unified Systems

	Concern	Dual System	Unified System
1.	Student characteristics	Dichotomizes student into special and regular	Recognizes continuum among all students of intellectual, physical, and psychological characteristics
2.	Individualization	Stresses individualization for students labeled special	Stresses individualization for all students
3.	Instructional strategies	Seeks to use special strategies for special students	Selects from range of available strategies according to each student's learning needs
4.	Type of educational services	Eligibility generally based on category affiliation	Eligibility based on each student's individual learning needs
5.	Diagnostics	Large expenditures on identification of categorical affiliation	Emphasis on identifying the specific instructional needs of all students
6.	Professional relationships	Establishes artificial barriers among educators that promote competition and alienation	Promotes cooperation through sharing resources, expertise, and advocacy responsibilities
7.	Curriculum	Options available to each student are limited by categorical affiliation	All options available to every student as needed
8.	Focus	Student must fit regular education program or be referred to special education	Regular education program is adjusted to meet all student's needs

From "A Rationale for the Merger of Special and Regular Education" by W. Stainback & S. Stainback, 1984, *Exceptional Children, 51,* pp. 102–111. Copyright 1984 by The Council for Exceptional Children. Reprinted with permission.

learning at a particular time in life. "The educational program model that applies to students with severe disabilities at the comprehensive local school is referred to as integrated, community intensive instruction" (Sailor et al., 1989). The CLS was defined as the following:

> *If the local school is defined as the school the student would attend if he or she had no disabilities, then the comprehensive local school is that age-appropriate school nearest to the local school (if other than the local school) that meets the needs of all prospective students in the region. (Sailor, 1989)*

The CLS would have several characteristics that would set it apart from most current educational programs for students with severe disabilities. First, it would be age-appropriate. There would not be students too young or too old for schools in comparison to the other students. Transportation to and from the school would be integrated to the extent possible and would not require students with severe disabilities to travel great distances. Also, to the extent that special classes were used, they would be physically located among other classrooms serving students without disabilities of the same age and there would be well-developed procedures to assure interactions between students with and without disabilities especially when the latter group was not enrolled in regular classes. No CLS would enroll more students with disabilities than would be proportionally appropriate. Only about 10% of the school population would be expected to have disabilities with only about 1% of the total having severe disabilities. Thus in a school of 500 there would be 50 children with disabilities and five of them would have more severe disabilities.

Most important, the CLS would promote the inclusion of students with severe disabilities in all school activities in which nondisabled students participate: social, recreational, administrative, ceremonies, field trips, and so on. The critical idea is that students would not be excluded based on having a disability.

Sailor and his colleagues proposed that the appropriateness of the specific educational environment would vary with the age of the student. They included five stages in their "multiphasic" model.

Phase 1: Mainstreaming. In this phase, preschool- and kindergarten-age children with disabilities would be fully integrated in regular preschool and kindergarten placements and special services and therapies would be offered directly in these programs. In order to serve students with disabilities at this age, it was proposed that school districts contract with private preschool service providers. "No matter how severely or multiply disabled a child is, there is no aspect of his or her educational needs that cannot be met in a private day care or preschool context" (Sailor, 1989, p. 63). Major objectives during this phase and the next would be the development of social and communicative skills.

Phase 2: Integration. From about the first to the fourth or fifth grade, the curricular emphasis for children with severe disabilities often includes functional life skills as the regular school curriculum tends to become more academic in content. At this time "the goal for students with severe disabilities is partial or total participation in all nonacademic activities that characterize their age group. The degree of exposure to academic skills, of course, varies with the level of severity of the intellectual disability of the student" (Sailor, 1989, p. 65). At this age, some nonregular class instruction within the CLS would be expected, although the student's school home base would be the regular classroom and the regular class teacher would have primary responsibility for the student with severe disabilities.

Phase 3: Community-intensive instruction. At about the time the student with severe disabilities begins middle school or junior high school, under the CLS model, instruction begins to be directed more toward functional community-living skills. The most important characteristic of this phase is the increase in the amount of time students spend away from school sites and in the community. The student also is introduced to the concept of work and often begins performing jobs around the school site. At the age of 14, an Individual Transition Plan (ITP) is developed for the student to direct further vocational training activities and identify other transition needs such as community mobility, recreational activities, and domestic living skills.

Phase 4: Transition. The phase of transition begins at about the ninth grade and continues to graduation or until the student leaves the public school. The CLS model calls for the student to experience two or more community jobs per year where he or she will learn a job to an appropriate criterion level. Very important during this phase is developing a linkage with adult service agencies that will provide support to the individual after high school. Of course, family involvement in planning for the postschool years is very important during this phase.

Phase 5: Integrated work and community living. At this phase the individual with severe disabilities is no longer actually attending the CLS but has moved into the community where an appropriate independent or semi-independent home, such as a cooperative apartment, has been arranged and where the person is employed in a community setting. Continued support at this level will be provided by adult service agencies.

As with the other reform-oriented models discussed previously, the CLS as proposed by Sailor and his colleagues represents a significant departure from many current practices. In all of the models, emphasis is placed on providing maximum service in the context of minimum (or no) segregation. Special education thus becomes more supportive education and is clearly intended to be identified more as a service than as a place. And as the educational reform movement makes progress toward improving the quality of general education, many in the field of special education are arguing that changes such as are called for by these models should be incorporated into the movement.

Changes for Persons with Severe Disabilities

The reforms called for in special education and related services are not being proposed only because we are in an era of educational reform. There is a broader, more significant reason. To understand this reason, we should once again consider the general trends in the world and in our society. People want to be included. People want to be empowered. People want to have equal access and equal opportunity. People want to bring an end to class distinctions that have allowed some to have privileges but not others. And most evident among these people are those with disabilities.

This social movement has clear implications for the way services are delivered. Individuals with disabilities do not want keepers, they want service providers to deliver useful services to them without denigration or segregation. They want "rights without labels" (Reynolds et al., 1987). In other words, they want to be a part of society. This desire is reflected in several assertions.

Self-Determination

One important recent development by individuals with disabilities and their advocates is the need and the right for self-determination, the right to make personal choices. The opportunity to make choices is highly valued in our society, and people with disabilities, including those with severe disabilities, want the opportunity to have personal choices in their lives. Self-determination is most likely an "innate, organismic" need of an individual to pursue those activities that he or she desires (Wehmeyer, 1992). Our choices determine our actions.

Many if not most educational programs and other services for people with severe disabilities appear to limit choices and self-determination (Bannerman, Sheldon, Sherman, & Harchik, 1990). Others' choices determine what people with disabilities must do and people with the most severe disabilities are apparently those with the fewest opportunities for self-made choices. Houghton, Bronicki, and Guess (1987) found that teachers and other adults working with students with the most severe disabilities responded at very low rates to student-initiated expressions of choice or preference. Self-determination is much more likely to lead to self-actualization and the realization of one's potential (Bannerman et al., 1990; Wehmeyer, 1992). If a person does not perceive that he or she is in control, learned helplessness is likely to develop. This can lead to depression, lack of motivation, problems with self-concept, external locus of control, and emotional problems and will affect how well people learn, how they deal with new challenges, and how they handle stress. Motivation can be extinguished by environments that are overly controlling.

For these reasons, as individuals with severe disabilities move closer to achieving the goal of being in society, a most fundamental aspect of this movement must be the opportunity to make choices. Educational programs must promote choice-making activity, moving toward ever more important decisions about one's life. For individuals, even those with the most severe disabilities, we need to learn to recognize behavioral patterns that express preferences and dislikes. We should cease doing those things that we believe are "best" for the individual when there is evidence that they are not desired by the individual. Instead we must attempt to understand the communicative efforts of students and build independence and control into their daily lives. Given a choice in the matter, students are likely to be more active (Bannerman et al., 1990). Choice-making should be present in the school and out of the school. It should especially be fostered during adulthood when it is most natural for people to have greater control over their own lives. Therefore, teachers and other service personnel should teach key people, such as family members, that independence must be accepted and encouraged.

Self-Advocacy

A second important trend, one that coincides naturally with self-determination and choice-making, is advocating for one's rights and the rights of other individuals with disabilities. This trend has become very apparent in recent years with the speaking and writing of people with cognitive disabilities on their own behalf (Edwards, 1982; Sutherland, 1981; Martinez, 1990; Williams & Schoultz, 1982) and the development of programs to encourage self-advocacy (Gardner, 1980; Zirpoli, 1989).

Seeing individuals with severe disabilities as full members of society will mean seeing them as active members of society. One of the most important ways in which individuals become participants is to advocate on their own behalf. In the past, there has always been an assumption that individuals with severe disabilities would benefit within society as long as there were those who would help them benefit. Of course, this was true and it continues to be true. However, we are witnessing a strong movement characterized by people with mild to severe disabilities speaking out on their own behalf, advocating for themselves, lobbying lawmakers and policy makers, and demanding, as have others, their rights to be included, to be members, to be beneficiaries of our diverse social fabric. Martinez (1990) expressed quite well why individuals with disabilities want to become self-advocates.

> *I couldn't accept that my mom would watch over me, that they were going to watch over me, that they knew best for me. I couldn't accept that any more. I tried to fight it but it was too strong, and it got stronger and stronger. I'm not saying that mom didn't love me, but I couldn't live the negative. I knew I had to be on my own, to fall down on my face if I had to (and I have, plenty, and yes, I've been hurt), but I knew I would get up and start over again, and I've done that. (Martinez, 1990, p. 6)*

Effective self-advocacy requires that individuals know their civil rights and their responsibilities as citizens. Individuals must learn to listen, develop self-confidence and be assertive, and be leaders in order to be empowered. They must realize that their strength can be increased through organization and mutual support. Although teachers and other professionals can provide support to such groups, they cannot and should not be the group leaders. Instead they should teach people how to make good decisions, but not make them for them; help people identify their own values, but not try to impose values upon them; and advise them of the importance of setting goals, but not set the goals for them (DeMerit et al., 1989). Various resources are available to assist people with disabilities and their parents, friends, advocates, and teachers to develop self-advocacy groups (Crawley et al., 1988; DeMerit et al., 1989; Eddy, Cohen, & Rinck, 1989; Edwards, 1982; Gardner, 1980; People First, 1985; Williams & Schoultz, 1982; Zirpoli, 1989).

Unfortunately, even as this movement is gaining force, just as people are beginning to acquire self-assertiveness, barriers of ignorance and misunderstanding continue to stand. In a recent study, Menchetti and Monroe (1993) found that over 80% of the states have laws that inhibit, or potentially inhibit, the voting rights of people with cognitive disabilities. Further, to add insult to injury, many of the states continue to use demeaning language in their voting laws. "Twelve states (24%) used terms such as 'idiot,' 'insane,' or 'unsound mind' to refer to persons with disabilities in the voting laws. In most cases the language was found in the state constitution" (Menchetti & Monroe, 1993, p. 10). Obviously, there remains a great deal of work for self-advocates with disabilities.

An important responsibility of professionals and families as they engage in planning educational programs for students is to encourage independence and self-sufficiency to the greatest degree possible. It is only logical that the more a person can present his or her own case to society, the better will be that person's quality of life.

Quality of Life

In the late 1960s and early 1970s, the major philosophical underpinning of programs for individuals with severe disabilities was the normalization principle. This philosophy called for persons with cognitive disabilities to have opportunities to experience life in normal ways and be instructed to do so as normally as possible (Nirje, 1969; Wolfensberger, 1972). More recently, quality of life has become a major theme directing services, activities, and life arrangements for persons with severe disabilities (Dennis, Williams, Giangreco, & Cloninger, 1993; Halpern, 1993; Shalock, 1990).

Several definitions of *quality of life* have been proposed, but none has totally captured the spirit of the movement. Likewise, there does not seem to be any way to objectively measure quality of life as there is to measure the learning of a specific task or completion of a specific objective. Nevertheless, striving toward improving the quality of life of persons with disabilities has become important for many family members, advocates, and professionals. These individuals have come to recognize some of the important components interwoven into the concept. They include the following:

- There is satisfaction with one's life and a sense of contentment (Taylor & Bogdan, 1990).
- There is overall life satisfaction, happiness, contentment, or success (Stark & Goldsbury, 1990).
- One's lifestyle is self-satisfying (Karan, Lambour, & Greenspan, 1990).

Quite central to the quality of life concept are the two previously discussed themes of self-determination and self-advocacy. If the quality of a person's life is determinable only in a way that the individual can define, then that person must have the opportunity to select the life he or she desires (self-determination) and have the personal and sociopolitical power to defend it (self-advocacy). People with disabilities often have the rights to their selected life activities usurped by professionals in the name of appropriate instruction and habilitation. They often have no say in decisions about learning goals or how the goals will be taught; they have no experience in making choices or decisions; and they must adhere to rigid schedules arbitrarily determined to satisfy the managerial needs of the service system (Bannerman et al., 1990).

Some would argue that people with severe disabilities would not know how to make appropriate choices, that the quality of life they select would be undesirable, and that professionals must direct them toward a better quality of life. Others would say that choices must be made for the individual until that person can have enough experiences to understand the implications of certain choices and learn the consequences of his or her behavior. Finally, some would say that if a person with a severe disability is allowed to make too many choices about life and its quality, important independent living skills or other functional skills may not be learned.

Nevertheless, as Bannerman et al. (1990) pointed out, there are several good reasons why personal freedoms should be allowed and even encouraged. First, federal legislation guarantees that persons with disabilities have the same fundamental rights as other persons. Second, choice-making experience will allow individuals to live in communities where choice-making is expected. And finally, research has shown that the individuals with cognitive disabilities prefer to be in situations in which they have had an opportunity to make a choice, that the choices rarely prove to be detrimental to the individuals, and that, in fact, when persons with disabilities have a choice, they often respond more positively than if conditions are imposed upon them without concern for their opinion or, worse, against their desires.

Quality of life may be understood by the influence of three spheres: individual values and needs, culturally specific values and needs, and common human values and needs. The relation of these spheres is displayed in Figure 20-2.

Too often people with severe disabilities are thought of in regard to their first set of needs, which are usually limited to those associated with having a disability. For example, it may be thought that in order to improve a person's quality of life, it is important that he or she learn to take care of personal needs, learn to communicate, learn to work at a job, and so on. Although all of these things may be important, to the individual other opportunities may be equally important, such as eating too many french fries and enjoying a milk shake or staying up late at night or going to church or the movies. Everyone has values and needs such

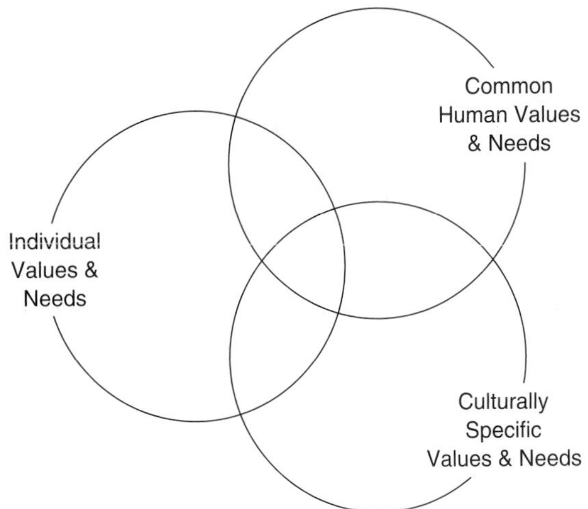

Figure 20–2
Optimal Framework for Subjective Quality-of-Life Values and Needs

From "Quality of Life as Context for Planning and Evaluation of Services for People with Disabilities" by R. E. Dennis, W. Williams, M. F. Giangreco, & C. J. Cloninger, 1993, *Exceptional Children, 59,* p. 501.

as these that may or may not be shared by others. When there is a good quality of life, these values and needs are satisfied.

Cultural values and wishes must also be recognized and respected if there is to be quality in one's life. In our society, if we are nothing else, we are very heterogeneous. African Americans, Latinos, Native Americans, and Asian Americans as well as European Americans all have cultural backgrounds that help define who they are. When we consider quality of life, we must respect and recognize the influences of individuals' cultures, accept them, and encourage them.

Finally, we should note that all humans share at least a core set of values and needs. We all need to interact with others in mutually beneficial ways. At times we will depend on others, but at other times we will be interdependent, sometimes requiring support, sometimes providing it. People with severe disabilities will clearly need some form of support throughout their lives. But that is true for most people. What is often the unfortunate circumstance is that people with disabilities are too often seen as only being capable of receiving support, of being the consumer of care and not a care provider. To have a full quality of life a person must be seen as having some unique strengths and be able to contribute these strengths to others through healthy relationships.

Implications for Teachers

All of what has been presented in this chapter has great significance for professionals and professionals-to-be. Becoming a teacher or another service provider for individuals with severe disabilities today and in the near future calls for a very different type of professional, one not only with specific instructional skills, but also with certain attitudes (Fox & Williams, 1992). It is suggested that the attitude a person must have is at least as important as the skills. In these final sections, some of the more important attitudinal implications are discussed.

World Changes and Individual Differences

Teachers and other professionals serving individuals with severe disabilities must recognize the changes that have occurred in the world. As discussed in the first part of this chapter, it must be understood that we can no longer recognize some to have inherently fewer opportunities because of their individual conditions. We still hear professionals, not to mention members of the general public, referring to individuals with disabilities in demeaning language. It is not that this is a conscious activity; more often, it is habit. This, however, only makes it worse. It is a habit that is very undesirable.

Those entering the teaching profession need to realize that they have an opportunity to develop their own habits, which should include showing respect for individuals regardless of the nature or extent of their disabilities and understanding that having a disability, even a severe disability, does not define or categorize a person in any way other than a very superficial one. Any person will have various strengths and the good teacher will search for those strengths.

Educational Change and Special Education

It is difficult to predict what the future holds for the structure of educational services for students with disabilities. As Stainback and Stainback (1984) suggested, the fields of general and special education may ultimately merge and all teachers will be able to serve students with a variety of characteristics. Or the Regular Education Initiative may be universally implemented and all children may be educated in the regular classroom setting. In this case the special education teacher may become more of a support specialist working on an interdisciplinary team supporting general educators as they serve as the primary instructors.

What is most assured is that the trend toward including students with severe disabilities will continue, albeit the form of continuation will vary in different parts of society. Special education teachers must become a part of the process of educational change and promote quality inclusive education for students with disabilities. This is an important function and attitude. It proposes that as well as providing instruction, teachers must serve as advocates. When schools discuss the movement toward implementing effective school and effective classroom practices, the special educator should step forward to ensure that students with disabilities are included as plans are developed. Too often, in fact, nearly always, they have not been.

Choice-Making and Self-Determination

If we are to respect individual differences and develop restructured educational programs that will include students with severe disabilities, professionals must also work to promote choice-making or decision-making and self-determination. This will not be easy. These are skills that students may not have ever had the opportunity to develop. Furthermore, teachers will have to attend closely to student behaviors if they are going to be able to interpret nonverbal intentions of students. Individual choices or activities of self-determination may be manifested by nonverbal behaviors indicating preferences or by the degree of participation in activities. Some students may be able to self-advocate by providing input on working toward particular objectives, receiving certain services, or planning certain activities. The personal futures planning systems discussed in chapter 4 could be used to encourage this.

Of course no one is completely autonomous or self-determining. We all take direction from some source and this is even more true for children and adolescents. There is no way someone can operate in a world without some structure and restrictions. However, we must carefully assess the nature and degree of restrictions that are imposed and whenever possible not be controlling. Certainly we should not wait until adolescence or adulthood to promote self-determination. Choice-making should be built into the educational routine. However, during adolescence, it is more important than at any earlier time for students to begin to have more opportunity for choices and self-expression.

Students who have not had experiences in learning to make choices must be given instruction in how to do so. Making choices and decisions means learning to identify alternatives, recognizing the consequence of making a particular choice, and finding the means and the resources necessary to act on a choice. In order to attain their goals, students must learn to set realistic and achievable goals, and then develop the ways to reach their goals. Organizational skills such as using weekly and daily calendars for time planning and management will be helpful. Teachers should encourage, expect, and reinforce independence and choice-making. They should provide feedback to students on how well they are doing with the choices that have been made. However, the feedback should be noncontrolling and honest, and negative feedback should be nonevaluative.

Self-Management

Self-management is the application of behavior change processes by oneself to modify or maintain one's own behavior. The process may include self-monitoring, self-evaluation, self-reinforcement, and self-instruction. Self-instruction can help students to generalize newly learned skills and provides students with verbal mediators that can be transported to and used in different settings. Picture prompts may be helpful for some students to self-manage when they cannot adequately verbalize their prompts.

As with making independent choices and decisions, students should be encouraged and taught to manage their own behavior. Teachers and others must be careful to not be overly directive, nor should they rely heavily on teacher-delivered external reinforcers. Instead they should attempt to teach students to self-manage to the extent they are capable of learning to do so. Self-management is the ability to monitor, evaluate, and control one's own behavior. It has resulted in improved competence for persons with cognitive disabilities in areas such as vocational skills, daily living skills, social skills, and academic performance. It will also help students improve their self-esteem and their motivation (Hughes, Korinek, & Gorman, 1991).

Self-Advocacy Movements

Individuals with disabilities today are very likely to become involved in self-advocacy movements and it is suggested here that this will be a very positive experience. By the nature of their construction, self-advocacy groups are maintained by individuals with disabilities, otherwise they would not be individuals advocating for themselves. There is a role for teachers, parents, and other professionals, however, which is simply to support the group in ways that the group members feel are helpful, but not attempt to take over or direct group members as to what they should do. This will be very difficult for many. Traditionally, teachers have been taught to be directive and to "take charge" so that their students receive what is considered best for them. When supporting self-advocacy groups, however, it must be remembered who is in the group and who is not. And those in the group should be expected to determine its activities, positions, and so forth.

Quality of Life

Finally, and most important, professionals should maintain strong attitudes that they will promote a high quality of life for people with severe disabilities. We should all have a great deal of collective shame about the way society has manipulated and treated individuals with disabilities in the past. They have been dehumanized, placed in warehouses, and relegated to a quality of living that virtually no one would accept by choice. At the very least, our assessment, planning, and instruction should be devoted to the notion that a better quality of life should result.

But what does this mean? As discussed earlier, there is no clear definition of this concept. Its application, however, must be reflected both in the process and in the product. Too often we have done certain things, undertaken certain interventions that may have been considered inappropriate and defended them on the basis that "in the long run" the effect would be positive. What we do to promote a high quality of life should apply to the present, just as much as it does the future.

Conclusion

As we consider the social context in which we operate, we can come to realize the significance of educational practices. Years ago, becoming a special education teacher meant learning to do certain activities, learning to apply behavior management principles, and working in a world apart from general education. That is not the condition today. Besides providing instruction, teachers must be ready to participate, to get involved, to be advocates, to be cheerleaders and boosters for self-advocacy groups, to monitor and ensure an adequate quality of life, and to do so in an ever changing world.

The stigma of having a disability is rapidly passing in our society and a new world of opportunity is opening for a group of people who have often been denied access to it. The professionals who are directly involved in assisting people through this new doorway of opportunity may have one of the greatest responsibilities in today's world. They are encouraged to pursue this responsibility vigorously and to enjoy the chance they have to do so.

Questions for Reflection

1. What factors in our society have led to more persons being more integrated into society than ever before in history?
2. In the school reform movements of the 1980s, why was special education largely ignored?
3. Can you identify any of the aspects of "effective schools" or "effective classrooms" that are appropriate for the instruction of students with severe disabilities?
4. Do you believe that changes made in special education are slower than those made in general education? Why or why not?
5. What do you see as the advantages or disadvantages of the merger of special education and general education?
6. What are some important areas in which individuals with severe disabilities should be given more control over their lives?
7. How would you feel about being involved in a "self-advocacy" program for students with severe disabilities? What role would you have?
8. What do you feel is the greatest distinction about being a professional in special education today as compared to 25 years ago?

References

Bannerman, D. J., Sheldon, J. B., Sherman, J. A., & Harchik, A. E. (1990). Balancing the right to habilitation with the right to personal liberties: The rights of people with developments disabilities to eat too many doughnuts and take a nap. *Journal of Applied Behavior Analysis, 23,* 79–89.

Bickel, W. E., & Bickel, D. D. (1986). Effective schools, classrooms, and instruction: Implications for special education. *Exceptional Children, 52,* 489–500.

Boyer, E. L. (1983). *High school: A report on secondary education in America.* New York: Harper & Row.

Berliner, D. C. (1984). The half full glass: A review of research on teaching. In P. L. Hosford (Ed.), *Using what we know about teaching* (pp. 51-77). Alexandria, VA: Association for Supervision and Curriculum Development.

Blanton, L. P. (1992). Preservice education: Essential knowledge for the effective special education teacher. *Teacher Education and Special Education, 15,* 87–96.

Coleman, J. S., Campbell, E. Q., Hobson, C. J., McPartland, J., Mood, A. M., Weinfeld, F. D., & York, R. L. (1966). *Equality of educational opportunity.* Washington, DC: National Center for Educational Statistics, U.S. Office of Education.

Crawley, B., Mills, J., Wertheimer, A., Williams, P., & Billis, J. (1988). *Learning about self-advocacy series.* London, England: Campaign for Valued Futures for People Who Have Learning Difficulties.

DeMerit, K. S., Halter, P. L., Jauron, G., Jirovetz, L., & Krueger, M. (1989). *Charting a bold course: A self-advocacy curriculum.* Green Bay, WI: Brown County Citizen Advocacy Program/Brown Association for Retarded Citizens.

Dennis, R. E., Williams, W., Giangreco, M. F., & Cloninger, C. J. (1993). Quality of life as context for planning and evaluation of services for people with disabilities. *Exceptional Children, 59,* 499–512.

Eddy, B. A., Cohen, G. J., & Rinck, C. (1989). *How to be an effective board member: Manual for self-advocates, manual for facilitators.* University of Missouri-Kansas City: Institute for Human Development.

Edmonds, R. (1982). Programs of school improvement: An overview. *Educational Leadership, 40*(3), 4–11.

Edmonds, R. R., & Fredericksen, J. R. (1979). *Search for effective schools: The identification and analysis of city schools that are instructionally effective for poor children.* ED 179 396.

Edwards, J. P. (1982). *We are people first: Our handicaps are secondary.* Portland, OR: Ednick, Inc.

Englert, C. S., Tarrant, K. L., & Mariage, T. V. (1992). Defining and redefining instructional practice in special education: Perspectives on good teaching. *Teacher Education and Special Education, 15,* 62–86.

Fox, L., & Williams, D. G. (1992). Preparing teachers of students with severe disabilities. *Teacher Education and Special Education, 15,* 97–107.

Gardner, N. (1980). *The self-advocacy workbook.* University of Kansas: Kansas Center for Mental Retardation and Human Development UAF.

Goodlad, J. I. (1984). *A place called school: Prospects for the future.* New York: McGraw-Hill.

Hallahan, D. P., Keller, C. E., McKinney, J. D., Lloyd, J. W., & Bryan, T. (1988). Examining the research base of the regular education initiative: Efficacy studies and the adaptive environments learning model. *Journal of Learning Disabilities, 21*(1), 29–35, 55.

Halpern, A. S. (1993). Quality of life as a conceptual framework for evaluating transition outcomes. *Exceptional Children, 59,* 486–498.

Houghton, J., Bronicki, G. J. B., & Guess, D. (1987). Opportunities to express preferences and make choices among students with severe disabilities in classroom settings. *Journal of the Association for Persons with Severe Handicaps, 12,* 18–27.

Hughes, C. A., Korinek, L., & Gorman, J. (1991). Self-management for students with mental retardation in public school settings: A research review. *Education and Training in Mental Retardation, 26,* 271–291.

Karan, O. C., Lambour, G., & Greenspan, S. (1990). Persons in transition. In R. L. Shalock (Ed.), *Quality of life: Perspectives and issues* (pp. 85-92). Washington, DC: American Association on Mental Retardation.

Kauffman, J. M. (1989). The regular education initiative as Reagan-Bush education policy: A trickle-down theory of education of the hard to teach. *Journal of Special Education, 23,* 256–278.

Lezotte, L. W. (1989). School improvement based on the effective schools research. In D. K. Lipsky & A. Gartner (Eds.), *Beyond separate education: Quality education for all* (pp. 25–37). Baltimore: Paul H. Brookes.

Lipsky, D. K., & Gartner, A. (Eds.). (1989). *Beyond separate education: Quality education for all.* Baltimore: Paul H. Brookes.

Martinez, C. (1990). A dream for myself. In R. L. Shalock (Ed.), *Quality of life: Perspectives and issues* (pp. 3–7). Washington, DC: American Association on Mental Retardation.

Menchetti, B. M., & Monroe, M. (1993). *A national voting rights survey: Identifying potential barriers and accommodations for Americans with disabilities.* Tallahassee, FL: Department of Special Education, Florida State University.

National Commission on Excellence in Education, (1983). *A nation at risk.* Washington, DC: U.S. Department of Education.

Nirje, B. (1969). The normalization principle and its human management implications. In R. B. Kugel & W. Wolfensberger (Eds.), *Changing patterns in residential services for the mentally retarded.* Washington, DC: President's Committee on Mental Retardation.

People First of Washington. (1985). *Speaking up and speaking out: An international self-advocacy movement.* Portland, OR: Ednick Communications.

Pugach, M. C. (1992). Uncharted territory: Research on the socialization of special education teachers. *Teacher Education and Special Education, 15,* 133–147.

Pugach, M., & Sapon-Shevin, M. (1987). New agendas for special education policy: What the national reports haven't said. *Exceptional Children, 53,* 295–299.

Purkey, S. C., & Smith, M. S. (1983). Effective schools: A review. *Elementary School Journal, 83,* 427–452.

Reynolds, M. C., Wang, M. C., & Walberg, H. J. (1987). The necessary restructuring of special and general education. *Exceptional Children, 53,* 391–398.

Rosenshine, B. V. (1983). Teaching functions in instructional programs. *Elementary School Journal, 83,* 335–352.

Sailor, W. (1989). The educational, social, and vocational integration of students with the most severe disabilities. In D. K. Lipsky & A. Gartner (Eds.), *Beyond separate education: Quality education for all* (pp. 53–74). Baltimore: Paul H. Brookes.

Sailor, W., Anderson, J., Halvorson, A., Doering, K. F., Filler, J., & Goetz, L. (1989). *The comprehensive local school: Regular education for all students with disabilities.* Baltimore: Paul H. Brookes.

Sailor, W., Gee, K., & Karasoff, P. (1993). Full inclusion and school restructuring. In M. E. Snell (Ed.), *Instruction of students with severe disabilities* (4th ed.) (pp. 1–30). New York: Merrill/Macmillan.

Shalock, R. L. (Ed.). (1990). *Quality of life: Perspectives and issues.* Washington, DC: American Association on Mental Retardation.

Sizer, T. R. (1984). *Horace's compromise: The dilemma of the American high school.* Boston: Houghton Mifflin.

Skrtic, T. M. (1991). *Behind special education: A critical analysis of professional culture and school organization.* Denver, CO: Love Publishing Company.

Stainback, W., & Stainback, S. (1984). A rationale for the merger of special and regular education. *Exceptional Children, 51,* 102–111.

Stainback, S., & Stainback, W. (1987). Facilitating merger through personnel preparation. *Teacher Education and Special Education, 10,* 185–190.

Stark, J. A., & Goldsbury, T. (1990). Quality of life from childhood to adulthood. In R. L. Shalock (Ed.), *Quality of life: Perspectives and issues* (pp. 71–83). Washington, DC: American Association on Mental Retardation.

Sutherland, A. T. (1981). *Disabled we stand.* Bloomington: Indiana University Press.

Taylor, S. J., & Bogdan, R. (1990). Quality of life and the individual's perspective. In R. L. Shalock (Ed.), *Quality of life: Perspectives and issues* (pp. 27–40). Washington, DC: American Association on Mental Retardation.

U.S. Department of Education. (1986). *What works: Research about teaching and learning.* Washington, DC: U.S. Department of Education.

Wehmeyer, M. (1992). Self-determination and the education of students with mental retardation. *Education and Training in Mental Retardation, 27,* 302–314.

Williams, P., & Schoultz, B. (1982). *We can speak for ourselves: Self-advocacy by mentally handicapped people.* Bloomington: Indiana University Press.

Wills, M. (1986). Educating children with learning problems: A shared responsibility. *Exceptional Children, 52,* 411–416.

Wolfensberger, W. (1972). *The principle of normalization in human services.* Toronto, Canada: National Institute on Mental Retardation.

Zirpoli, T. J. (1989). Partners in policymaking: Empowering people. *Journal of the Association for Persons with Severe Handicaps, 14,* 163–167.

APPENDIX A

Individual Education Plan

PERFORMANCE OR SUBJECT AREA:
Recreation/Leisure

PRESENT LEVEL:
Andy will participate in a leisure activity with an adult for 1 – 5 mins.

ANNUAL GOAL:
Andy will participate in a self-selected leisure activity with a peer

Educational Planning Date 9/01/94
Student Name Andrew Miller
Grade 3rd D.O.B. 7/16/86
Teacher G. Pappas

SHORT-TERM INSTRUCTIONAL OBJECTIVES	EVALUATION OF SHORT-TERM INSTRUCTIONAL OBJECTIVES			
	Criterion for Mastery	Evaluation Procedures and Schedule	Interim Results/Date*	Final Results/Date
1. Andy will choose a leisure activity from an array of four activity cards	75% of	weekly frequency counts		
offered by a peer.	opportunities			
2. Andy will participate in a leisure activity by taking turns with a peer	75% of	weekly duration recording		
for 5 minutes.	opportunities			

*Please post prior to change of teacher

Distribution: White - District
Yellow - School
Pink - Cumulative Folder

PERFORMANCE OR SUBJECT AREA:
Socialization

PRESENT LEVEL:
Andy will respond briefly to peer initiations by smiling and reaching out.

ANNUAL GOAL:
Andy will improve his ability to initiate and maintain interactions with peers

Educational Planning Date 9/01/94

Student Name Andrew Miller

Grade 3rd D.O.B. 7/16/86

Teacher G. Pappas

SHORT-TERM INSTRUCTIONAL OBJECTIVES	EVALUATION OF SHORT-TERM INSTRUCTIONAL OBJECTIVES			
	Criterion for Mastery	Evaluation Procedures and Schedule	Interim Results/Date*	Final Results/Date
1. Andy will initiate an interaction with a peer by touching him or her on the hand	75% of	weekly frequency count		
or by giving him or her an object.	opportunities			
2. Andy will increase his engagement in peer interactions to 50% above	50% above baseline,	weekly duration recording		
baseline level.	3 sessions			

*Please post prior to change of teacher

Distribution: White - District
Yellow - School
Pink - Cumulative Folder

PERFORMANCE OR SUBJECT AREA:
Communication

PRESENT LEVEL:
Andy communicates by pulling others to objects and directed eye gaze.

ANNUAL GOAL:
Andy will use pictures and natural gestures to communicate.

Educational Planning Date 9/01/94

Student Name Andrew Miller

Grade 3rd D.O.B. 7/16/86

Teacher G. Pappas

SHORT-TERM INSTRUCTIONAL OBJECTIVES	EVALUATION OF SHORT-TERM INSTRUCTIONAL OBJECTIVES			
	Criterion for Mastery	Evaluation Procedures and Schedule	Interim Results/Date*	Final Results/Date
1. Andy will point to a picture to indicate a request for an object or activity.	75% of	weekly frequency counts		
	opportunities			
2. Andy will use a natural gesture to indicate yes/no (head shake) and	75% of	weekly frequency counts		
greetings (waving).	opportunities			

*Please post prior to change of teacher

Distribution: White - District
Yellow - School
Pink - Cumulative Folder

PERFORMANCE OR SUBJECT AREA:
Personal Management

PRESENT LEVEL:
Andy will toilet and undress with adult physical prompts.

ANNUAL GOAL:
Andy will independently toilet and undress.

Educational Planning Date 9/01/94

Student Name Andrew Miller

Grade 3rd D.O.B. 7/16/86

Teacher G. Pappas

SHORT-TERM INSTRUCTIONAL OBJECTIVES	EVALUATION OF SHORT-TERM INSTRUCTIONAL OBJECTIVES			
	Criterion for Mastery	Evaluation Procedures and Schedule	Interim Results/Date*	Final Results/Date
1. Andy will pull his pants up and down independently when changing clothes	100% of	weekly frequency counts		
and toileting.	opportunities	(home and school)		
2. Andy will self-initiate using the bathroom and complete a toileting sequence with	75% of	weekly frequency counts		
no adult assistance.	opportunities	(home and school)		

*Please post prior to change of teacher

Distribution: White - District
Yellow - School
Pink - Cumulative Folder

PERFORMANCE OR SUBJECT AREA:
School

PRESENT LEVEL:
Andy will participate in classroom routines with physical and verbal prompts.

ANNUAL GOAL:
Andy will independently participate in classroom routines

Educational Planning Date 9/01/94

Student Name Andrew Miller

Grade 3rd D.O.B. 7/16/86

Teacher G. Pappas

SHORT-TERM INSTRUCTIONAL OBJECTIVES	EVALUATION OF SHORT-TERM INSTRUCTIONAL OBJECTIVES			
	Criterion for Mastery	Evaluation Procedures and Schedule	Interim Results/Date*	Final Results/Date
1. Andy will take out/put away materials independently on teacher's verbal cue	80% of	daily frequency count		
to the class.	opportunities,			
	3 consecutive days			
2. Andy will line up at the door independently on teacher's verbal cue to the class.	80% of	daily frequency count		
	opportunities			
	3 consecutive days			
3. Andy will put folder in the basket when period ends.	80% of	daily frequency count		
	opportunities			
	3 consecutive days			

*Please post prior to change of teacher

Distribution: White - District
Yellow - School
Pink - Cumulative Folder

APPENDIX B

Individualized Transition Program

This form was developed in 1986–87 for a particular student. It is offered here as an example of the scope of an individualized transition plan using terminology common to the field at that time. General application of its specific content for other individuals was not intended, nor should it be inferred. From *The Comprehensive Local School: Regular Education for All Students with Disabilities* by W. Sailor, J. L. Anderson, A. T. Halvorsen, K. Doering, J. Filler, & L. Goetz, 1989, Baltimore: Paul H. Brookes. Reprinted with permission of the authors.

Initial Cover Sheet Date: 5/15/87
Revised Date: 5/94
NAME: Joseph A. Smith **ADDRESS:** 123 Oak Lane, Central City, CA
BIRTHDATE: 5/10/75 **SOCIAL SECURITY #:** 123-45-6789 **TELEPHONE:** 555-5505
PARENT/GUARDIAN: John & Mary Smith **ADDRESS:** —same—
TELEPHONE: —same— **PLANNED GRADUATION DATE:** June, 1995

	ITP Date/Student Age	
Initial:	5/87	12
Annual Review:	6/88	13
	6/89	14
	5/90	15
	6/91	16
	6/92	17
	5/93	18
	5/94	19

MEDICAL ISSUES/INFORMATION:

Joe takes Tegretol for seizures two times a day, monitored by parents. Joe gets bronchial infections very easily, needs to be monitored for signs of recurrence. Joe wears glasses and does not see well without them; he is very meticulous in the care of his own glasses.

PHYSICAL/HEALTH PROBLEMS:

Joe is toilet trained with reminders when to go; he occasionally has an accident. Once reminded, he completes his self care independently.

COMMUNICATION SKILLS:

Verbal skills: Does not use verbal communication.
Adapted system: Uses a few signs with familiar persons, e.g., bathroom, eat, come, etc. Joe effectively uses small (1") black & white line drawings in his communication book and daily schedule. He is learning to request assistance from unfamiliar service personnel in grocery and department stores.

Participating members of transition team:

	Name	Position	Agency	Telephone
1.	John & Mary Smith	Parents		555-5055
2.	Joe Smith	Student		
3.	Carol Jones	Teacher	Central High School	555-1212
4.	Sara Mason	Transition Specialist	" " "	"
5.	Bob Doe	Principal	" " "	"
6.	George Thomas	Case Manager	Central Region	555-7643
7.	Phyllis Young	Vocational Coordinator	Project Opportunity	555-3201
8.	Kathy James	Speech & Language Specialist	Central High School	555-2000
9.				
10.				

(*continued*)

INDIVIDUALIZED TRANSITION PROGRAM (*continued*)

Student: Joe Smith **Anticipated Graduation Date:** June, 1995

Issues to be addressed:

Each of the following areas should be discussed at each transition meeting. Goals and objectives should be developed where appropriate. Please check each area in which a goal has been written.

	Date								
Area:	5/87	6/88	6/89	5/90	6/91	6/92	5/93	5/94	
1. Employment Options: • previous work experience • current job(s)/support needs • future options for employment • expressed preferences	X	X	X	X	X	X	X	X	
2. Residential Options: • previous/current living situation • future options/expressed preferences					X		X	X	
3. Financial Issues: • benefits/unearned income • earned income • insurance • other	X				X		X	X	
4. Recreation Options: • previous experiences • current support needs • future options/expressed preferences	X	X	X	X	X	X	X	X	
5. Community Access: • current skills and support needs • future options/expressed preferences	X	X	X	X	X	X	X	X	
6. Transportation: • current skills/support needs • future options/expressed preferences	X			X		X	X	X	
7. Family/Friends/Advocates						X	X	X	
8. Other: Guardianships				X	X				

INDIVIDUALIZED TRANSITION PROGRAM (*continued*)

DATE: 5/94

Student: Joe Smith **Age:** 19 **Domain:** Vocational

Goal: Joe will be employed at an integrated job site for at least 15 hours per week with pay and with transition of supervision to an adult agency by June, 1995.

Objective: 1. Joe will start his job by October, 1994.
2. Joe will increase length of work period before taking breaks.

	Activities to achieve objectives:	Timeline	Date completed
Parent/ Student Actions	Parents		
	1. Provide school staff with information about Joe's job preferences.	6/94	
	Parents & Joe		
	2. Visit the adult agency that has agreed to supervise Joe's integrated work and community access.	10/94	
	3. Attend ITP meeting.	11/94	
School Personnel Actions	1. Develop job near Joe's home, based on job skills profile and expressed preferences.	10/94	
	2. Provide training and adaptives on job site to increase skills and endurance.	11/94	
	3. Schedule ITP meeting after Joe starts work.	11/94	
	4. Schedule visit to job site for adult service provider.	1/95	
	5. Cooperate in transferring supervision of job to adult agency personnel.	6/95	
Adult Service Representative Actions	DD Case Manager		
	1. Initiate intake procedures with adult agency.	11/94	
	2. Provide funding for adult services.	by agreed transition date	
	3. Attend ITP meeting.	11/94	
	Adult Service Provider		
	1. Visit Joe's job site.	1/95	
	2. Complete intake process.	1/95	
	3. Attend ITP meeting.	11/94	
	4. Cooperate with school personnel in transferring supervision of job site.	6/95	

INDIVIDUALIZED TRANSITION PROGRAM (*continued*)

DATE: 5/94

Student: Joe Smith **Age:** 19 **Domain:** Residential

Goal: Joe will live in an independent or semi-independent setting with support as needed.

Objective: Joe will move from his parents' home into his own apartment or home by June, 1995.

	Activities to achieve objectives:	Timeline	Date completed
Parents/ Student Actions	1. Joe and his parents will visit one to three small residential options and meet the staff.	1/95	
	2. Joe and his parents will select which place to live in.	5/95	
	3. Joe will move into his selected living option.	6/95	
School Personnel Actions	1. Continue instruction with adaptives as appropriate in self-care, housekeeping, meal preparation, and budgeting.	ongoing for school year	
	2. Visit residential options with Joe's parents as requested.	1/95	
	3. Communicate information regarding Joe's skills to residential staff as appropriate.	5/95	
Adult Service Representative Actions	DD Case Manager		
	1. Provide information on residential options currently available.	12/94	
	2. Schedule visits for Joe and his parents.	1/95	
	3. Initiate intake into selected living option.	5/95	
	4. Arrange for funding of program.	5/95	
	Residential Service Provider (once identified)		
	1. Visit and observe Joe in his own home.	5/95	
	2. Carryover use of adapted systems to assure Joe's continued maximum participation in self-care and housekeeping activities.	6/95 and on-going	
	3. Provide opportunities and support for Joe to access natural community environments.		

INDIVIDUALIZED TRANSITION PROGRAM (*continued*)

DATE: 5/94

Student: Joe Smith **Age:** 19 **Domain:** Financial

Goal: Overall financial status for Joe will be determined after employment, to clarify benefits.

Objective: 1. Using SSI formula, based on Joe's income, any changes in fiscal or other benefits will be determined.
2. A budget will be developed based on Joe's income, with parent input, reflecting money to spend and money to save each month.

	Activities to achieve objectives:	Timeline	Date completed
Parent/ Student Actions	Parents 1. Open a bank account with Joe. 2. Share financial information with school personnel, adult agency and SSI as appropriate to assist in reporting Joe's income monthly.	 11/94 11/94 and on-going	
School Personnel Actions	1. Meet with parents to calculate Joe's monthly income and any effect it will have on SSI benefits. 2. Provide instruction to Joe in handling money and paying while he performs banking and shopping activities. 3. Assist Joe to develop and follow a budget of money to spend and money to save each pay period.	12/94 throughout the school year for school year	
Adult Service Representative Actions	DD Case Manager 1. Provide any new information regarding SSI benefits to parents. Adult Service Provider 1. Follow through to assist Joe to keep track of his income for reporting to SSI. 2. Continue to assist Joe with budgeting and handling money in natural environments.	 11/94 Following transition and on-going Ongoing	

INDIVIDUALIZED TRANSITION PROGRAM (*continued*)

DATE: 5/94

Student: Joe Smith **Age:** 19 **Domain:** Recreation

Goal: Joe will participate in integrated community leisure activities at least three times per week.

Objective: 1. Joe will have the opportunity to select and attend a movie at least one time per week.
2. Joe will go to the library and select materials to use one time per week.
3. Joe will have the opportunity to select a leisure activity and invite a friend to participate with him one time per week.

	Activities to achieve objectives:	Timeline	Date completed
Parent/ Student Actions	Parents		
	1. Assist Joe to read the Movie Section in the newspaper each Friday and select one to see.	ongoing	
	2. Assist Joe to mark a calendar and provide reminders when library material is due.	ongoing	
	3. Assist Joe to determine a leisure activity which he would like to do with a friend or family member.	weekly/ ongoing	
	4. Provide transportation to the movies or other activity on Saturday when necessary.	ongoing	
School Personnel Actions	1. Develop adaptives to assist Joe to remember when library materials are due.	94-95 school year	
	2. Develop an adapted activities choice list to assist Joe in deciding how to spend his free time.	10/94	
	3. Provide instruction in community leisure activities of Joe's choice.	94-95 school year	
Adult Service Representative Actions	Residential Service Provider (when identified)		
	1. Visit home to learn support systems parents provide to Joe for leisure activities.	ongoing	
	2. Provide opportunities and transportation to Joe for community leisure activities with friends.	ongoing	
	3. Communicate with Adult Service Provider to identify preferred age-appropriate leisure activities for normalized break and community access times.	ongoing	
	Adult Service Provider		
	1. Collaborate with parents and careprovider to identify preferred age-appropriate leisure activities for community access times.	ongoing	

INDIVIDUALIZED TRANSITION PROGRAM (*continued*)

DATE: 5/94

Student: Joe Smith **Age:** 19 **Domain:** Community Access

Goal: Joe will participate in an array of personal shopping and other activities in various community environments.

Objective: Joe will shop for his toiletries and lunch items at least twice a week.

	Activities to achieve objectives:	Timeline	Date completed
Parent/ Student Actions	Parents 1. Assist Joe to develop a list of needed items weekly. 2. Assist Joe to use purchased items to make lunch each work day.	ongoing ongoing	
School Personnel Actions	1. Develop adaptations and partial participation strategies for * a picture shopping list * paying for items * a communication system in natural environments 2. Provide instruction to Joe on adapted systems while shopping. 3. Share information with parents and adult service providers and residential service providers regarding use of adapted systems.	10/94 and ongoing for 94-95 school year ongoing	
Adult Service Representative Actions	DD Case Manager 1. Provide funding for program of instruction in accessing community environments. Adult Service Provider 1. Provide opportunities and instruction in weekly leisure, banking, and personal shopping activities before and after work. 2. Coordinate with Joe's home regarding activities in which he participates. Residential Service Provider (when identified) 1. Carry over support systems and adaptations for community access activities.	6/95 following transition ongoing ongoing	

INDIVIDUALIZED TRANSITION PROGRAM (*continued*)

DATE: 5/94

Student: Joe Smith **Age:** 19 **Domain:** Transportation

Goal: Joe will schedule and use transportation to get to work, shopping, and leisure activities.

Objective: Joe will receive ongoing training in use of public transportation.

	Activities to achieve objectives:	Timeline	Date completed
Parent/ Student Actions	Parents 1. Provide transportation to activities where Joe cannot use public transportation. 2. Joe will be expected to ask parents to schedule transportation for him when he invites a friend to do something for weekly activities.	ongoing as needed	
School Personnel Actions	1. Continue training Joe to use public transportation from his home to work, to a specific shopping area, and to preferred leisure activities. 2. Provide instruction in street crossing and mobility skills to and from the bus stop and while shopping.	94-95 school year 94-95 school year	
Adult Service Representative Actions	DD Center Case Manager 1. Arrange for funding to assist with transportation costs to work and to shopping and leisure activities. Adult Service Provider 1. Continue with mobility training from home to work and other community environments. Residential Service Provider (when identified) 1. Follow through with mobility training and provision of transportation for Joe.	6/95 following transition and ongoing ongoing	

INDIVIDUALIZED TRANSITION PROGRAM (*continued*)

DATE: 5/94

Student: Joe Smith **Age:** 19 **Domain:** Family and Friends

Goal: Joe will maintain social contacts with friends in adulthood.

Objective: 1. Joe will contact a friend one time per week, with assistance, to schedule a social activity.
2. Joe will participate in social activities with co-workers as appropriate.

	Activities to achieve objectives:	Timeline	Date completed
Parent/ Student Actions	Parents		
	1. Help Joe to determine what friend to contact each week.	ongoing	
	2. Contact friend by phone or assist Joe to make direct contact and invite a friend to an activity each week.	ongoing	
	3. Assist Joe to mark a calendar with any social activities from work to which he is invited.	ongoing	
	4. Assist Joe to arrange transportation to any special social event, e.g., with co-worker.	ongoing	
School Personnel Actions	1. Develop a personal address book of friends with Joe.	10/94	
	2. Provide ongoing instruction to Joe in using his liesure choice list and his phone book to select a preferred activity to do with a friend or family member.	94-95 school year	
Adult Service Representative Actions	Residential Service Provider (when identified)		
	1. Carry over use of adapted systems and materials.	ongoing	
	2. Carry over support for planning and participating in leisure activities with friends.	ongoing	

APPENDIX C

Individualized Family Service Plan

From *Guidelines and Recommended Practices for the Individualized Family Service Plan* by B. H. Johnson, M. J. McGonigel, & R. K. Kaufman (Eds.), 1989, Chapel Hill, NC: National Early Childhood Technical Assistance System.

Family Name: Griffin

Child's Name: Benjamin Griffin

Address: 127 Aspen Lane
Mountain

Birthdate: 1/5/90

Phone: 729-0631

Referral Date: 6/1/90

Coordinator: Pat White, MD

By Whom: NICU

Assessment: 5/90 and 6/90

IFSP Team and Signatures:

Leslie Griffin 6/7/90
Parent or Guardian **Date**

Michael Griffin 6-7-90
Parent or Guardian **Date**

Pat White MD

Neal Sold MD

Kylie Talbot, LPT

Adrienne Wales, OTR

Amanda Grey, M.S.

Timothy Johns

Early Intervention Services (Frequency and Intensity)

Family Information and Support -- with each visit to the NICU, as specified in the activities.

PT and OT Evaluation and Monitoring -- twice weekly during Ben's hospitalization.

After Discharge:

Physical therapy once a week;
Occupational therapy once a week;
Once a week home visits from the early intervention specialist.

Other Services

None

Transition Plan Attached: ______ Yes __X__ Not Applicable

Child's Name: Benjamin Griffin

Date: 6/7/90

Family Members/Social Supports:

Name	Relationship
Leslie	mother
Michael	father
Caroline	sister
Heather	neighbor

Child's Present Levels of Development:

Ben is alert and reponds preferentially to his mother. He is becoming more able to tolerate being touched and to comfort himself. (For more information, see Assessment Report).

Domain	Age Level	Age Range
Cognitive	2-3 months	0-3 months
Fine Motor	2-3 months	0-3 months
Gross Motor	2-3 months	0-4 months
Language	1-2 months	0-3 months
Self-Help	0-1 month	0-1 month
Social/Emotional	0-2 months	1-2 months
Vision	within normal limits	
Hearing	within normal limits	

Child's Health Status:

Ben's health is stabilizing. He is responding well to a reduction of his oxygen levels, and plans are being made to discharge Ben in about a month if his good progress continues.

Other Agencies Involved:

Agency	Contact Person	Phone
Mountain Early Intervention Program	Kathleen Sanford	891-7026
Pulmonary Clinic	Dale Peavy	787-9576
Mountain Medical Supply, Inc.	Alice Strickland	891-2514

Child's Name: Benjamin Griffin

Date: 6/7/90

Outcome #1

Leslie wants to be more secure in her ability to care for Ben at home.

Identified By: Leslie

Family Concerns, Priorities, and Resources for This Outcome:

Although I have formal training in child development and an older child, I worry that I don't know enough about Ben's needs to take care of him at home. I am sure that Michael and I can read professional literature to learn by ourselves, and we can learn from the medical team at the hospital and from the experiences of the other parents. We have many friends who have volunteered to help us in any way they can, but I'm not sure what to ask them for. What I really need is to be confident that when Ben comes home, I'll know what to do. (Leslie)

Service/Action	Dates and Evaluations		
	Begin	Review	End
1. Leslie will spend some time during each visit to the nursery holding and feeding Ben.	6/9/90	7/8/90	#7 7/8/90
2. Ben's neonatalogist and his primary nurse will help Leslie recognize and read Ben's cues and find ways to soothe and comfort him.	6/9/90	7/8/90	#7 7/8/90
3. Ben's primary nurse and the other unit nurses will help Leslie assume as much of Ben's care as she wants to while he is in the nursery.	6/9/90	7/8/90	#7 7/8/90
4. Leslie and Michael are attending the NICU parent-to-parent support group and will continue after Ben is discharged, as long as they want to go. They plan to bring up their fears about taking Ben home at the next meeting. The Griffins will ask the other families about ways these families have used their friends for support and assistance.	Already Begun	Continuing	#7

Child's Name: Benjamin Griffin

Date: 6/7/90

Service/Action	Dates and Evaluations		
	Begin	Review	End
5. The medical team and the hospital infant development specialist will give the Griffins resource materials about the needs and behaviors of preemies.	6/9/90	7/8/90	7/8/90

Criteria/Timeline:

These activities will begin immediately and continue throughout Ben's hospitalization. Leslie will determine whether or not her need has been met, in consultation with Dr. White.

Child's Name: Benjamin Griffin

Date: 6/7/90

Outcome #2

The Griffins want help learning to take care of Ben's medical needs and finding resources in their community before Ben comes home from the hospital.

Identified By: Leslie and Michael

Family Concerns, Priorities, and Resources for This Outcome:

We need help and support to bring Ben home. We want someone to help us translate what we've learned at the hospital into routines we can use to take care of Ben at home. We have a neighbor, Heather, who has volunteered to help me with Ben. We want to learn how to teach Heather the medical care procedures for Ben. (Leslie)

I can't spend as much time at the hospital as Leslie can, but I want to be part of Ben's care. (Michael)

Service/Action	**Dates and Evaluations**		
	Begin	**Review**	**End**
1. Timothy Johns, the discharge nurse, will go with the Griffins to the pulmonary clinic once a week to help them learn how to use and maintain Ben's oxygen equipment and apnea monitor, including recognizing danger signs.	6/12/90	7/12/90	#7 7/1/90
2. Before Ben is discharged, the Griffins will demonstrate to Timothy their ability to use and maintain Ben's equipment.	6/12/90	7/12/90	7/12/90
3. Timothy will make a list of local vendors and service companies for Ben's medical equipment. Michael will contact these companies and arrange for Ben's needs.	6/15/90	7/8/90	#7 6/22/90
4. Michael will take Ben to the pulmonary clinic once a month to have his levels monitored.	After discharge		

Child's Name: Benjamin Griffin

Date: 6/7/90

Service/Action	Dates and Evaluations		
	Begin	Review	End
5. Pat White, the Griffin's pediatrician and case coordinator, will visit the Griffin's home to help Leslie teach her friend, Heather, Ben's care procedures. Timothy will look for resource materials to help.	2 weeks before discharge	8/15/90	#7 8/30/90

Criteria/Timeline:

The Griffins will determine if their expressed need has been met, in consultation with Timothy Johns, the discharge nurse.

Child's Name: Benjamin Griffin

Date: 6/7/90

Outcome #3

Benjamin needs to develop better feeding skills and increase his motor development.

Identified By: Adrienne Wales, OTR, and supported by Leslie and Michael.

Family Concerns, Priorities, and Resources for This Outcome:

I have the time and a car to drive to the hospital to meet with the therapist before Ben comes home, and to take Ben to weekly sessions with the therapist after he does. I want to learn techniques to use at home, and I want someone to come regularly to our house to be sure all is going well. I'd like these visits to be scheduled when I can arrange for someone to take care of our daughter Caroline. (Leslie)

Service/Action	Dates and Evaluations		
	Begin	Review	End
1. Adrienne will visit Ben twice a week during the next four weeks to evaluate and monitor his fine motor development and feeding skills.	6/8/90	7/8/90	#7 7/8/90
2. Adrienne and Ben's primary nurse will show Leslie and Michael how to feed Ben and will help them hold and feed Ben during each visit to the nursery.	6/15/90	7/8/90	#7 7/1/90
3. Adrienne will begin therapy with Ben as soon as he is medically able.	Open		#7 7/1/90
4. Adrienne will work with the neonatologist and Dr. White to develop a feeding program for Ben to help him develop a smooth, coordinated suck and swallow.	6/15/90	7/15/90	#7 7/15/90
5. After discharge, Leslie will bring Ben to the hospital every Tuesday for occupational therapy.	After Discharge	Four weeks after initiation	#7 10/9/90

Child's Name: Benjamin Griffin

Date: 6/7/90

Service/Action	Dates and Evaluations		
	Begin	Review	End
6. During these weekly sessions, Adrienne will show Leslie how to help Ben learn how to use his hands bilaterally and to increase his hand to mouth play.	After discharge	10/1/90	#7 10/9/90
7. Amanda Grey, the infant specialist in the Griffin's community early intervention program, will visit Leslie and Ben once a week to help Leslie carry out Ben's OT activities at home.	After discharge	10/1/90	#5 10/9/90

Criteria/Timeline:

Each activity will begin as specified. Leslie will determine if she is satisfied with Ben's therapy and with the early intervention home visits. Adrienne will monitor Ben's progress by continual clinical observations and through a formal re-assessment using a standardized measure three months after therapy begins.

Child's Name: Benjamin Griffin
Date: 6/7/90

Outcome #4:

Benjamin needs better feeding skills and he needs to improve his motor development.

Identified By: Kylie Talbot, LPT, and supported by Michael and Leslie.

Family Concerns, Priorities, and Resources for This Outcome:

I have the time and a car to drive to the hospital to meet with the therapist before Ben comes home, and to take Ben to weekly sessions with the therapist after he does. I want to learn techniques to use at home, and I want someone to come to our house regularly, to be sure all is going well. I'd like these visits to be scheduled when I can arrange for someone to take care of our daughter Caroline. (Leslie)

Service/Action	Dates and Evaluations		
	Begin	**Review**	**End**
1. Kylie will visit Ben twice a week during the next four weeks to evaluate and monitor his gross motor development.	6/8/90	7/8/90	#7 7/8/90
2. Kylie will begin therapy with Ben as soon as he is medically able.	Open		#7 7/14/90
3. After discharge, Leslie will bring Ben to the hospital every Tuesday for physical therapy with Kylie.	After discharge	Four weeks after discharge	#5 10/9/90
4. Amanda, the infant specialist from the Griffin's community early intervention program, will come to the session with Leslie and Ben once every month to watch Kylie demonstrate the things she wants Leslie to do at home.	After discharge	10/1/90	#5 10/9/90
5. Leslie will carry out Ben's physical therapy activities at home as shown by Kylie.	After discharge	10/1/90	#5 10/9/90

Child's Name: Benjamin Griffin

Date: 6/7/90

Service/Action	Dates and Evaluations		
	Begin	Review	End
6. During her weekly home visit after Ben's discharge, Amanda will monitor Leslie's use of the techniques Kylie has shown Leslie.	After discharge	10/1/90	#5 10/9/90

Criteria/Timeline:

The activities will be implemented as specified above. Leslie will determine her satisfaction with Ben's therapy. Kylie will monitor Ben's progress by continuous clinical observations and through formal re-assessment using a standardized measure every four months.

Child's Name: Benjamin Griffin

Date: 10/9/90

Outcome # **Revision of Outcomes #3-4:**

Outcomes stay the same, but activities and strategies are changing.

Identified By: Leslie

Family Concerns, Priorities, and Resources for This Outcome:

After Ben was discharged and I was responsible for most of his care, my needs have definitely changed. I don't want to spend my time and energy making two separate trips each week to the hospital. Instead, I want to spend more time with Caroline. I'd like Amanda to take over Ben's therapy activities once a week, so I need another visit from Amanda each week. (Leslie)

I now feel more comfortable handling Ben. I also have more time now to take over some of Ben's care from Leslie, including working on therapy. (Michael)

Service/Action	Dates and Evaluations		
	Begin	Review	End
1. Adrienne and Kylie will work together on Ben's OT and PT. They will see Ben together once a week for four weeks, then they will alternate, each seeing Ben every other week.	10/14/90	12/15/90	
2. Adrienne and Kylie have developed the following therapy goals jointly:	10/14/90	12/15/90	
a. Ben will tolerate a prone position for play for 10 minutes, while supporting himself with his arms and manipulating a toy.			
b. Ben will manipulate a toy using both hands at midline.			
c. During feeding, Ben will sit erect, supported, with his head at midline and his chin tucked.			

Child's Name: Benjamin Griffin

Date: 10/9/90

Service/Action	Dates and Evaluations		
	Begin	Review	End
3. Leslie will continue to carry out Ben's program at home, but Michael will now do weekends, and Amanda will visit an extra day each week to be in charge one day.	10/14/90	12/15/90	

Criteria/Timeline:

Ben's progress on the OT/PT joint goals will be clinically evaluated jointly by Adrienne and Kylie. Leslie will decide in eight weeks if she feels the new system is working for her.

Evaluation Rating Scale*

Ratings	Criteria
1	Situation changed or worsened; No longer a need, goal, or project
2	Situation unchanged; Still a need, goal, or project
3	Implementation begun; Still a need, goal, or project
4	Outcome partially attained or accomplished
5	Outcome accomplished or attained, but not to the family's satisfaction
6	Outcome mostly accomplished or attained to the family's satisfaction
7	Outcome completely accomplished or attained to the family's satisfaction

* Source: Deal, A. G., Dunst, C. J., Trivette, C. M. (1989). A flexible and functional approach to the Individualized Family Support Plan. *Infants and Young Children*, *1*(4).

Child's Name: Benjamin Griffin

Date: 10/9/90

DATE	NOTES/COMMENTS
6/7/90	The Griffin's IFSP is being developed by an interagency team consisting of the Griffins, their hospital team, the infant specialist from their local early intervention program, and their pediatrician, who will serve as their care coordinator. Benjamin has been making steady progress, and tentative plans are being made to discharge him home in four weeks. This IFSP is being written as his discharge plan.
10/9/90	Leslie and Michael are unhappy with some aspects of their IFSP, and Dr. White has asked the other members of the IFSP team to meet with the Griffins and her to make some revisions. Outcomes 3-4, which relate to OT and PT for Benjamin, have been very problematic for Leslie. Having two separate appointments each week on different days means four hours of commuting to the hospital. Leslie is beginning to hate the drive and dislikes leaving Caroline with her neighbor so often. The team discussed options to eliminate this problem. Kylie and Adrienne have agreed to work together in the future, thereby requiring only one visit a week. To meet hospital review board requirements, OT and PT outcomes will be written separately, but therapy will be provided jointly. Initially, Adrienne and Kylie will see Ben together. After they have had a chance to learn each other's activities with Ben, they will alternate, each seeing Ben every other week. Leslie also feels swamped by the demands of carrying out Ben's therapy at home, given all the time she must spend caring for him. She would like some time to spend with Caroline or spend alone and has asked that Amanda come to the house twice a week rather than once a week. Amanda will take over Ben's home therapy during that extra day. Leslie has decided that she now wants to be co-care coordinator with Pat White.

NAME INDEX

Abramson, S. E., 410
Abt Associates, 3
Adams, M., 491, 494
Aeschleman, S. R., 491, 494
Ager, C., 428
Agran, M., 14
Albano, M., 326
Alberto, P. A., 145, 161, 189, 198
Albin, J. B., 391, 394, 569
Albin, R. W., 172, 178, 184, 186–187, 188, 304, 310, 494
Alexander, R., 390
Allaire, J., 277
Alpert, C. L., 278
Altwerger, B., 464–465
Alvarez, R., 266
Alwell, M., 288, 289
American Psychiatric Association, 8
Anderson, D. M., 395
Anderson, J., 226
Anderson, R. J., 509
Apffel, J. A., 420, 421
Arendt, R. E., 337
Arkell, C., 385
Armstrong, P. M., 390, 391, 394
Astin-Smith, S., 505, 507–508
Attermeier, S. M., 533
Atwater, J., 547
Au, K., 465
Ault, M. J., 50, 144, 150, 159, 166, 449–450
Ault, M. M., 365–366
Aveno, A., 24, 483, 485, 486
Ayres, A. J., 337
Ayres, B., 23, 232
Azrin, N. H., 390, 391, 392, 394, 395, 401, 404
Baer, Donald M., 171, 172, 173, 174, 175, 240, 387
Bagnato, S. J., 533, 534
Bailey, D. B., 63–64, 97, 519–520, 522–523, 532–533, 535, 548
Bailey, J. S., 32, 414
Baker, B. L., 66
Baker, D., 3
Bakken, J. P., 467
Baldwin, M., 345–346
Baldwin, V. L., 11, 76, 338, 350
Ball, T. S., 338, 404
Balla, D. A., 115
Bambara, L. M., 428
Banerdt, B., 388, 389
Bannerman, D. J., 604, 605, 606–607
Barbuto, P. F., 395
Barcus, J. M., 568–569, 573, 574, 576–584
Barcus, M., 555
Barnard, M. U., 359
Baroody, A. J., 444, 467, 468
Barraga, N., 345
Barton, E. S., 387, 391, 392, 393
Barudin, S. I., 450
Baskir, A., 278
Bates, E., 266, 267
Bates, P., 24, 495, 509
Batshaw, M. L., 16, 409, 413
Battle, C. W., 274, 290
Bauer, A. M., 66
Baum, D., 17
Bauman, K. E., 414
Baumeister, A. A., 299, 337
Baumeister, A. B., 299
Baumgart, D., 20, 143–144, 161, 248, 431–433, 509
Bayley, N., 534
Bear, D. R., 465
Beckman, P., 534
Beckman, P. J., 97
Beckman-Brindley, S., 51
Belanger, S., 449–450
Bellamy, G. T., 24, 172, 178, 184, 186–187, 401, 409, 502, 504
Bellamy, T., 470
Bellamy, T. G., 118, 119, 123, 125
Bender, J., 541
Bender, M., 422
Berg, B. O., 16, 17
Berg, W., 427
Berger, P. L., 495
Berkowitz, S., 390
Berliner, D. C., 595
Bickel, D. D., 594–595, 597
Bickel, W. E., 594–595, 597
Bickett, A. D., 494
Bigge, J. L., 15, 16, 17, 18, 74, 134, 136, 358, 388, 406–407
Biklen, D., 228, 280
Biklen, S. K., 50
Billingsley, F. F., 113, 114, 131–132, 133, 150, 155–156, 171, 181–184, 192, 269
Binkoff, J. A., 299
Bird, E., 404
Bishop, K. D., 433
Black, J., 124, 448, 453–455, 471–472, 473, 475
Blackman, J. A., 11, 17, 18
Blanton, L. P., 595–596
Blasch, B., 346
Bleck, E. E., 11, 16, 18
Bobath, K., 337
Bogdan, R. C., 50, 606

Boomer, L. W., 77–78, 79, 80
Borakove, L. S., 470
Borthwick, S. A., 297
Borthwick-Duffy, S. A., 15
Bourland, G., 300
Boyer, E. L., 593
Bracey, S., 458
Bramman, H., 232
Brannan, S. A., 422
Brantley, J. C., 87
Bredekamp, S., 534–535
Breen, C., 236, 428, 429–431
Brennan, J., 236–237, 250
Breuning, S., 17
Bricker, D. D., 60, 65, 72, 97, 224, 284, 388, 389, 517, 518, 519, 524, 527, 531, 533, 535–536
Brimer, R. W., 3
Brinker, R. P., 14, 22, 226
Bristol, M. M., 97
Bromwich, R., 534
Bronfenbrenner, U., 525–526
Bronicki, G. J. B., 604
Brooke, V., 568–569, 573, 574, 576–584
Brotherson, M. J., 98
Browder, D. M., 22, 23–24, 51, 112, 114, 130, 131, 133, 135, 198, 209, 444, 445, 449, 460, 483, 484, 487, 497, 501
Brown, C. W., 96
Brown, F., 143, 198, 240
Brown, Lou, 3, 12, 24, 33–34, 59, 91, 92, 126, 174, 177, 227, 228–229, 233–234, 254, 450, 458–459, 483
Bruininks, R. H., 115
Bruner, E. C., 458
Bucher, B., 345
Buckley, J., 561, 562–563, 569
Bugle, C., 390, 395
Burgess, D., 192
Burgio, L. D., 393
Burney, J. P., 214
Buttars, K. L., 470

Cain, D., 268, 278
Cain, S. E., 445
Calculator, S. N., 280, 291
Calhoun, M. L., 463–464
Campbell, D. T., 49
Campbell, P. H., 58, 59, 60, 62, 91, 328, 329, 330, 334, 338
Carlson, F., 275
Carlson, J. I., 314
Caro, P., 20, 21, 51, 74
Carpenter, R., 269
Carpignano, J., 134, 136
Carr, D., 487
Carr, E. G., 21, 271, 299–300, 301, 302, 303, 314
Carroccio, D. F., 390, 394
Carter, C. H., 11
Cataldo, M. F., 299, 537
Caughey, E., 248
Cavanaugh, J., 427
Caycho, L., 467
Cecil, C. E., 499
Certo, N., 34
Chadsey-Rusch, J., 51, 564, 575, 585
Chandler, L. K., 174, 175, 176, 177, 178, 179, 545
Chandler, M. J., 520–521
Chapman, R., 278
Chard, M. A., 359
Cheney, C. O., 465
Choate, J. S., 445
Christian, W. P., 390, 391, 393
Christiansen, C., 497
Cicchetti, D. V., 115
Cicirelli, V., 518
Cicirello, N., 332, 335
Clancy, P., 161, 497
Clark, C. R., 275
Clark, M., 543
Clarke, S., 311, 312
Clifton, A., 387–388
Cloninger, C. J., 104, 107, 120, 141, 239, 606, 607
Close, D., 24
Coffee, L., 409–410, 411–413
Coggins, T., 269
Cohen, C., 277
Cohen, G. J., 606
Cole, D. A., 67, 236
Coleman, J. S., 594
Cone, J. D., 115, 117–118, 391, 392
Conley, R. W., 567
Conners, F. A., 444, 446, 451, 452, 458
Connis, R. T., 24
Cooley, E., 67
Coon, M. E., 499
Coots, J., 435
Corrigan, C., 228
Council for Exceptional Children, 47
Courtnage, L., 63
Cox, A. W., 355, 361–362, 367, 381
Cox, B., 326
Crapps, J., 14
Crawley, B., 606
Creasy, D., 505, 507–508
Cress, P., 344
Crimmins, D. B., 305
Cripe, J. J. W., 535–536
Crossley, Rosemary, 280
Cruickshank, W., 32
Cullari, S., 17
Culver, J. B., 570
Curry, P. A. S., 18, 19
Cusick, B., 326
Cuvo, A. J., 447, 459, 470, 505

Dalke, B. A., 338
Dalldorf, J., 299
Darbyshire, M., 404
Dattilo, J., 23, 420, 425, 427
Davern, L., 124, 237, 246–248, 477
Davies, C. D., 275
Davies, C. O., 275
Davis, B. A., 390
Davis, R. R., 14
Davis, V., 17
Deal, A., 68, 524, 525, 528–529, 530–532
Deer, M., 14
Deitz, S. M., 300
Demchak, M. A., 15, 150, 166, 299
DeMerit, K. S., 605–606
Dempsey, P., 124, 448, 453–455, 471–472, 473, 475
Dennis, R. E., 133, 274, 606, 607
Deno, S., 136
Deppe, J., 546
Devany, J., 298

Dever, R. B., 118, 119, 121–122, 126, 127, 160
Diorio, M. S., 404
Dix, J., 499
Doherty, J. E., 274
Dolch, E. W., 447
Domnie, M., 459
Donaldson, J., 226
Donder, D. J., 235–236, 509
Donnellan, A. M., 50, 172, 269, 271, 300, 301, 302, 307–308, 309, 314–315, 316
Dorry, G. W., 450
Dorsey, M. F., 304
Doss, S., 51
Doughty, R., 392, 393
Downing, J., 12, 269, 350
Doyle, D. A., 495
Doyle, P. M., 50, 144, 150, 153, 449–450
Drain, S., 499
Drew, C., 16, 575
Dubose, R. E., 342–343
Duncan, D., 345
Dunlap, G., 171, 172, 240, 311, 312, 314, 400
Dunn, Lloyd, 33, 51
Dunn, W., 60, 62, 63, 64, 74, 254, 326, 327, 328, 337
Dunst, C. J., 68, 70, 519, 524, 525, 528–529, 530–532, 533
Durand, V. M., 21, 51, 299, 302, 305

Eddy, B. A., 606
Edelsky, C., 464–465
Edmark Reading Program, 458
Edmonds, R. R., 594
Education, U. S. Department of, 11, 51, 144, 594–595
Education of the Handicapped, 87
Edwards, G. L., 162
Edwards, J. P., 605, 606
Eichinger, J., 12, 34, 48–49, 250, 350
Eichner, S. J., 226
Ellis, L. L., 14
Ellis, N. R., 12, 145, 395
Enders, S., 335
Engelman, S., 458
Englert, C. S., 596–597
Enright, B. E., 445
Entriken, D., 450, 457
Epilepsy Foundation of America, 16, 17
Epps, S., 414
Erfanian, N., 300
Eshilian, L., 433
Evans, I. M., 143, 297–298, 299, 300, 301, 304, 316–317, 318–319
Everson, J. M., 94, 555
Eyman, R. K., 15, 297

Falor, I., 266
Falvey, M. A., 174, 177, 433, 435, 483
Farlow, L. J., 22, 197, 214, 387, 388, 395, 397
Farmer-Dougan, V., 162
Fassbender, L. L., 269, 300, 309, 314–315
Favell, J. E., 427
Featherstone, H., 98
Fees, J., 449
Feinberg, P., 447
Feise, B., 521
Ferguson, B., 178, 495, 575
Ferguson, D. L., 20, 143–144, 161, 248, 252–253, 432–433
Filer, J., 543
Filler, J., 338
Finger, I., 534
Finkler, D., 543
Finnie, Nancy R., 331, 332, 333, 334
Fleck, L., 488, 510
Flexer, R., 469, 470
Flores, B. M., 464–465
Floyd, J., 23–24, 51, 172, 174–175, 177, 178, 210, 484, 485, 487, 488, 490
Fodor-Davis, J., 14
Ford, A., 34, 118, 119, 121–122, 124–125, 133, 134, 135, 136, 137, 150, 160, 163, 237, 246–248, 425, 428, 444, 445, 447, 448, 452, 453–455, 461, 469, 470, 471–472, 473, 475, 477, 486, 487, 504, 505
Forest, M., 103, 104, 105, 226, 228, 237, 238, 435, 437
Forsyth, S., 330
Foster, R., 115
Foster, W., 14, 22–23
Fowler, S. A., 174, 235, 545, 547
Fox, L., 13, 17, 73, 171, 172, 175, 178, 218–219, 367, 534, 535, 536, 538–539, 540, 608
Fox, T. J., 34, 48, 49, 232, 233, 244, 245
Fox, W. L., 34, 48, 49, 228
Foxx, R. M., 315, 395, 401
Frank, A. R., 470
Fraser, B. A., 337
Freagon, S., 386, 486
Fredericks, H. B. D., 34
Fredericks, H. D., 11, 338, 350
Fredericks, H. D. B., 76
Fredericksen, J. R., 594
Frith, G., 77–78
Fritz, M. F., 231
Fry, E., 447
Fuchs, D., 197
Fuchs, L. S., 197
Furman, G. C., 543
Furono, S., 533

G. Allan Roeher Institute, The, 435
Gadow, K. D., 367
Gallenstein, J. S., 338
Garcia, E., 387
Gardner, J., 355
Gardner, N., 605, 606
Gartner, A., 50, 598
Gast, D. L., 50, 150, 151, 298, 449–450, 503
Gaylord-Ross, R., 14, 226, 227, 236, 299, 420, 428, 429–431, 585
Gee, K., 50, 288, 345–347, 348–349, 593–594
Gerry, M. H., 46, 48
Gersten, R. M., 458
Ghandi, R., 390
Giangreco, M. F., 50, 104, 106, 107, 118, 120, 133, 141, 239, 253, 422, 477, 606, 607
Giles, D. K., 395
Gillette, Y., 282, 543
Gliner, J. A., 570

Goetz, L., 50, 226, 281, 288, 289, 301, 345–346
Gold, M., 24
Goldberg, I., 32
Goldsbury, T., 606
Golinkoff, R., 266
Gonzalez, P., 575
Goodlad, J. I., 593
Gordon, N. J., 68
Gorga, D., 338
Gorman, J., 610
Grace, C., 217
Graff, J. C., 358, 364, 365–366, 375, 376, 377
Graham, N., 50
Gravel, J. S., 451
Graves, J., 499
Green, F. P., 434
Green, J. D., 275
Greenspan, S., 606
Grenot-Scheyer, M., 435
Griffin, A. K., 503
Grigg, N. C., 214
Grossman, H. J., 4, 5
Grove, D. N., 338
Groves, I. D., 390, 394
Gruenewald, L., 92
Guess, D., 67, 145, 198, 239, 240, 241, 266, 282–284, 290, 299, 301, 355, 365–366, 387, 604
Guidubaldi, J., 534
Guiltinan, S., 503
Gunn, P., 467
Guralnick, M. J., 50
Gustason, G., 274

Hacker, B. J., 533
Hagner, D., 569
Hains, A. H., 545, 547
Halasz, M. M., 494
Hall, S., 332
Hallahan, D. P., 600
Halle, J. W., 15, 21, 281–282, 284–285, 291, 299
Halloran, W., 561
Halpern, A. S., 93, 554–555, 606
Halvorsen, A., 226
Hamby, D., 524
Hamre-Nietupski, S., 23, 24, 34, 161, 231, 232, 435, 446, 499, 509, 570–572
Hanley, M. J., 451
Hanline, M. F., 50, 218–219, 534, 535, 536, 538–539, 540, 545, 546, 547
Hanson, C. R., 391, 392
Hanson, H. B., 495
Hanson, M. J., 50, 545
Harchik, A. E., 604, 605
Harding, C., 266
Hardman, M. L., 16, 34, 45, 51, 93, 94, 95, 224
Haring, N. G., 3, 13, 34, 171, 172, 181–184, 198, 214
Haring, T. G., 22, 51, 236, 428, 429–431, 435, 491, 494
Harootunian, B., 228
Harrell, R., 346–347, 348–349
Harris, J., 299
Hart, A. D., 338
Hart, B., 284–285
Hawkins, N., 67
Hayes, S. C., 300
Haynie, M., 356–357, 373, 375, 377, 379
Health and Human Services, U. S. Department of, 355
Healy, A., 15
Heber, R., 4
Hecimovic, A., 554
Heise-Neff, C., 248
Helmstetter, E., 51, 239, 240, 241, 299, 484–485, 495, 496, 502, 543
Hemmeter, M. L., 521, 524
Hendrickson, J. M., 235
Henrikson, K., 392, 393
Hensinger, R. N., 337
Henton, K. R., 390
Herman, P. A., 465
Herman, R., 338
Hersen, M., 404
Heyne, L. A., 434
Hill, B. K., 115
Hill, E. W., 346, 350
Hill, J. W., 24–25, 422, 491
Hines, C., 449
Hinson, K. B., 567
Holcer, P., 390, 393
Holdaway, D., 465, 467
Hollins, M., 341
Hollomon, S. W., 390
Holvoet, J., 239, 240
Hoogeveen, F. R., 452, 453, 454, 456, 457
Hooper, M., 499
Horn, E. H., 350
Horn, E. M., 337, 338
Horner, D. R., 410–411
Horner, R. H., 13, 14, 22, 34, 51, 171, 172, 178, 184, 188, 297, 304, 310, 414, 491, 494, 497, 498, 499
Horrobin, J. M., 134, 444
Horst, G., 422
Horton, S., 471
Horton, W. A., 19
Houchard, B., 567
Houghton, A., 410, 412–413
Houghton, J., 604
Houk, C. S., 78, 79
Hourcade, J. J., 450
House, B. J., 451
Houselog, M., 509
Howard, V. F., 404
Howe, J., 359
Hudson, C., 499
Huemann, J. E., 437
Hughes, C. A., 14, 24, 568, 610
Hughes, G. G., 235
Hulme, J., 335
Hundziak, M., 395
Hunt, P., 226, 288, 289
Huntington, G. S., 533–534
Hupp, S., 543
Hurlbut, B. I., 275
Hutchins, M. P., 558, 559
Hyltm, J., 332

Iacono, T., 20, 21, 51, 74, 265, 274, 280
Inge, K. J., 491, 568–569, 573, 574, 576–584
Irvin, L. K., 51, 67, 68, 71–72

Irvine, B., 67
Ivancic, M. T., 162, 495
Iverson, V. S., 104, 107, 120, 141, 239
Iwata, B. A., 162, 275, 304, 305, 308, 311, 495, 499

Jacobson, J. W., 15
Jacques, K., 337
Janicki, M. P., 15
Janney, R., 214–217, 218
Jeanchild, L., 252
Jens, K. G., 533
Jensen, V., 404
Jervey, S. S., 390, 393
Joffee, E., 346
Johanson, C., 524
Johnson, D. W., 65, 249, 250, 476
Johnson, F., 92
Johnson, J. R., 51, 568
Johnson, R. T., 65, 249, 250, 476
Johnson-Martin, N. M., 533
Jones, D. N., 178, 499
Jones, R. L., 86
Jorgensen, J., 92
Jose, R. T., 341
Juniper, L., 252
Justen, J. E., 3

Kaczmarek, L. A., 291, 292
Kaiser, A. P., 50, 282, 284–285, 519, 521, 524
Kalachnik, J., 367
Kampschroer, E. F., 92
Karan, O. C., 606
Karasoff, P., 593–594
Karen, R. L., 505, 507–508
Kasari, C., 338
Katz, M., 359
Kauffman, J. M., 600
Kaufmann, R. K., 527, 528–529, 530–532
Kawakami, A. J., 465
Kawate, J., 547
Kayser, J. E., 155–156
Kazlowski, N. L., 338
Keetz, A., 284–285
Kehoe, B., 404
Keilitz, I., 410–411
Kemp, D. C., 271
Kennedy, C., 491, 494
Kennedy, C. H., 14, 22
Keogh, W. J., 278
Kern-Dunlap, L., 311, 312
Kerr, M. M., 226
Keul, P., 567
Kiernan, J., 422
Kiernan, W., 561
Kimbrell, D. L., 395
Kirk, S. A., 443
Kishi, G., 236–237, 250
Klatt, K. P., 447, 459
Klein, M. D., 370, 371
Klein, N. K., 241
Knapczyx, D. R., 235
Knoblock, P., 228
Knowlton, A., 545, 547
Knowlton, S., 299
Koegel, L. K., 400
Koegel, R. L., 171, 172, 240, 400
Koehler, F., 24
Kohl, F. L., 235–236
Kohler, F. W., 235
Kohn, J., 335
Koller, E. Z., 471
Koller, H., 359
Konarski, E. A., 404
Konke, J. L., 470
Koorland, M. A., 72, 76, 77, 112
Korinek, L., 610
Kottwitz, E., 547
Koury, M., 449
Kramer, L., 404, 405
Kramer, S., 528–529
Krasner, L., 300
Krauss, M. W., 96, 97
Kregel, J., 24, 575

Labor, U. S. Department of, 561
Lachowicz, B. L., 462
Lacy, L., 239, 240
Lambert, F., 458
Lambour, G., 606
Lancioni, G. E., 235–236, 395, 454, 473
Lang, J., 338
Lang, L., 290
Langer, S. N., 302
Langley, B., 342–343
Langone, J., 14
Lanier, C. L., 390
Lau, M. M., 304
LaVigna, G. W., 51, 314–315
Lazzari, A. M., 545
Lee, J. M., 338
Lee, M., 236
Leff, R. B., 505, 506–507
Lehr, D. H., 89, 130–131, 355
Leibowitz, M. J., 390, 393
Leiper, C., 338
Leland, H., 115, 117
Lemke, H., 390, 394
Lennox, D. B., 15, 51, 300, 304, 305
Lent, J. R., 385
Levin, L., 271
Lewis, A. P., 410, 412–413
Lewis, K. D., 379
Lewis, M., 520
Lezotte, L. W., 594–595
Liberty, K. A., 174, 178, 181–184, 214
Lindgren, A., 273
Lindsey, J. D., 77–78
Lindsley, Ogden, 198
Lipsky, D. K., 50, 598
Lively, C., 485
Livi, J., 486, 505
Lloyd, L. L., 274
Locke, P., 273, 275
Loewinger, H., 575
Long, R., 465
Long, S., 471, 494
Love, J. G., 395
Lowe, M. L., 470
Lowerre, A., 427
Loyd, B., 214
Lubeck, R. C., 174
Luckey, R. E., 395
Lundervold, D., 300
Lusthaus, E., 103, 226, 228, 237, 238
Lutzker, J. R., 494
Lyle, C., 99, 319
Lynch, V. W., 192

Lyon, G., 60, 62
Lyon, S., 59, 60, 62, 66, 67, 254

MacDonald, C., 228, 284, 325
Macdonald, C., 34, 57, 60, 113, 117, 254
MacDonald, J. D., 282
MacDonald, R. F., 302
MacLean, W. E., 337
Madden, N. A., 250
Maggs, A., 458
Magid, D. F., 451
Mahler, T. J., 338
Mahoney, G., 534, 543
Mahoney, K., 395
Maisto, A. A., 299
Maisto, C. R., 299
Mank, D., 561, 562–563, 569
Manning, G. L., 465
Manning, M. M., 465
Marchant, J., 94
Marchetti, A. G., 499
Marchetti, D. C., 499
Marholin, D., 495
Mariage, T. V., 596–597
Markwardt, F. C., 136
Marshall, A. M., 284–285
Martin, G. L., 404
Martin, L., 391
Martinez, C., 605
Maruyama, G., 250
Mason, S. A., 162
Masters, L. F., 405
Mastropieri, M. A., 467
Mather, N., 462
Matlock, B. L., 192
Matson, J. L., 471, 494
Maurer, R. A., 395
Maurer, R. G., 451
Maurer, S., 24, 509
McCarthy, L. J., 449
McCartney, J. R., 499
McCaughrin, W., 567
McCollum, J., 543
McConnachie, G., 271
McCormick, L., 96, 547
McCrady, R. E., 338
McDonald, A., 280
McDonald, J. D., 543
McDonald, S., 391
McDonnell, A. P., 45, 224
McDonnell, J. J., 34, 51, 93, 94, 95, 172, 178, 184, 186–187, 491, 494, 495, 575
McEvoy, M. A., 543–544
McGee, G. G., 162
McGonigel, M. J., 524, 526, 527, 528–529, 530–532
McKelvey, J. L., 404
McKenna, M. C., 466
McKenzie, R. G., 78, 79
McLean, B. M., 387–388
McLean, J., 280
McNerney, C., 269, 290–291
McQuarter, R. J., 236, 284–285, 287–288
McWhorter, C. M., 46, 48
McWilliam, R. A., 535, 548
Meisels, S. J., 217
Menchetti, B. M., 606
Mercer, C. D., 12, 145
Mesaros, R. A., 269, 300, 309
Messina, R., 59, 254
Messmer, M. C., 494
Metzler, H. M. D., 575
Meyer, C. A., 217
Meyer, G., 252
Meyer, L., 34, 48–49, 124, 236, 448, 453–455, 471–472, 473, 475
Meyer, L. H., 3, 34, 67, 214–217, 218, 239, 297–298, 299, 300, 301, 304, 316–317, 318–319
Meyer, L. M., 236
Meyers, A., 505
Meyers, C. E., 297
Meyerson, L., 395
Miller, A., 338, 450
Miller, E. E., 450
Miller, H. R., 390
Miller, J., 277, 278
Miller, J. W., 466
Miller, L. J., 445
Miller, P. D., 466
Miller, U. C., 504–505
Miltenberger, R. G., 15, 51, 300, 304, 305
Minge, M. R., 404
Mirenda, P. L., 20, 21, 50, 51, 74, 150, 160, 163, 172, 265, 269, 275, 280, 300, 309, 427, 466, 487
Mitchell, B., 232
Mitchell, R. D., 390, 394
Moersch, M. S., 533
Mohr, C., 401
Monroe, M., 606
Moon, M. S., 94, 555, 561, 568–569, 573, 574, 576–584
Moore, S., 14
Morath, P., 458
Mori, A. A., 405
Morris, S. E., 370, 371
Morse, K. A., 349
Moseley, C. R., 574
Moses, L. G., 235–236
Mosk, M., 345
Motloch, W., 335
Mount, B., 99–103, 319
Muldoon, M., 427
Mulhern, T. J., 471
Mulligan, M., 239, 240
Mulligan-Ault, M., 355
Murden, L., 385, 387, 393–394
Musselwhite, C., 272
Mustonen, T., 273, 275, 276–277, 278

Nagel, D. A., 18
National Association of State Directors of Special Education, 47, 87
Neef, N. A., 495, 499
Neel, R. S., 113, 114, 131–132, 133, 155–156, 269
Negri-Shoultz, N., 314–315
Neisworth, J. T., 533, 534
Nelson, G. L., 391, 392, 394
Newborg, J., 534
Newsom, C. D., 299
Newton, J. S., 14, 22
Nietupski, J., 23, 24, 34, 59, 161, 232, 235–236, 254, 446, 451–452, 456, 494, 497, 499, 509, 570–572

Nihira, K., 115
Nirje, B., 33, 225, 483, 606
Nisbet, J., 569
Niswander, P. S., 339, 340, 341
Noonan, M. J., 96, 133, 355, 547
Novak, C. G., 235
Nutter, D., 407

O'Brien, F., 390, 391, 392, 394, 395
O'Brien, J., 99, 319
O'Brien, S., 51
Odom, S. L., 235, 543–544
Omichinski, M., 391
O'Neill, R. E., 304, 308, 310, 314
Orelove, F. P., 58, 59, 60, 61, 64, 65, 72, 74, 75, 77, 325, 363, 390, 394, 402, 406, 408
Osarchuk, M., 385, 395
Osnes, P. G., 179–181
Osternig, L. R., 338
Ostrosky, M. M., 282
O'Toole, K. M., 495
Owen, V., 143

Pace, G. M., 162
Paddock, C., 469
Page, T. J., 162, 414, 495, 499
Palfrey, J. S., 356–357, 373, 375, 377, 379
Palkes, H. S., 359
Palumbo, L. W., 300, 303
Pancsofar, E., 554
Parent, W. S., 24–25, 575
Park-Lee, S., 34, 48–49
Patton, M. E., 390
Paul, R., 10
Paulson, F. L., 217
Paulson, P. R., 217
Pearpoint, J., 435
Peck, C. A., 3, 14, 45, 51, 226, 227, 269, 270, 543
People First of Washington, 606
Perlmutter, L., 458
Perret, Y. M., 16, 409, 413
Perske, R., 387–388, 435
Petersen, D. L., 14
Peterson, L., 24
Peterson, N. L., 517
Petherbridge, R., 575
Pezzino, J., 335
Pezzoli, M., 226
Pfetzing, D., 274
Phelps, J. A., 337
Phillips, J. F., 393
Pitts-Conway, F., 428, 429–431
Pitts-Conway, V., 236, 491, 494
Pletcher, L. L., 68
Ponder, P., 346
Ponticas, Y., 414
Poor, R., 335
Porter, S. M., 356–357, 373, 375, 377, 379
Poteet, J. A., 445
Powell, A., 534, 543
Powers, G., 567
Powers, L., 557–558, 559–561, 564, 565, 566
Preis, A., 66, 67
Prensky, A. L., 359
Prescott, A. L., 414
Preston, J., 335
Prizant, B. M., 266, 267, 268, 269, 271
Pugach, M. C., 595–596, 598
Purkey, S. C., 594
Putnam, J. W., 50, 236, 250, 476, 477

Quick, D., 228

Rainforth, B., 34, 57, 60, 62, 63, 65, 113, 117, 133, 134, 254, 284, 325, 329–330, 331, 332, 334, 335, 336
Rakes, T. A., 445
Ralph, G., 178, 494
Realon, R., 427
Reardon, M. M., 304
Reed, P., 332
Reese, G. M., 402, 403, 404, 406
Reichle, J., 51, 272, 273, 274, 278, 279, 280
Reid, D. H., 393, 407
Reiss, M. L., 414
Reiss, S., 15
Renzaglia, A. M., 485, 558, 559
Repp, A., 51
Reynolds, C. J., 14
Reynolds, M. C., 598, 599–600
Rheingrover, R., 519
Rhodes, L., 561, 569, 575
Richardson, S. A., 359
Richman, G. S., 414
Richman, J. S., 338
Rikhye, C. H., 346
Rimoin, D. L., 19
Rinck, C., 606
Rincover, A., 298, 300
Risley, R. M., 505
Risley, T. R., 162, 284–285, 537
Robbins, F. R., 311, 312
Roberson, W. H., 451
Robinson, C., 534
Robinson, R. D., 466
Robinson, S., 300, 303, 314
Roeher Institute, The, 435
Rogers, E. S., 14
Rogers-Warren, A. K., 284–285, 287–288
Rollings, J. P., 299
Romer, L. T., 150
Romski, M. A., 272, 275
Rosenberg, R., 346–347, 348–349
Rosenberg, S., 534, 543
Rosenkoetter, S., 547
Rosenshine, B. V., 595
Rotatori, A. F., 385
Rowland, C., 274
Rubin, Z., 435, 436
Rude, H. A., 235
Rusch, F. R., 14, 24, 51, 420, 499, 567, 568
Rutter, M., 10
Rynders, J. E., 134, 250, 444, 476

Sailor, Wayne, 3, 34, 46, 50, 145, 198, 226, 229, 236, 281, 288, 289, 345–346, 593–594, 598, 601–604
St. Louis, K., 272
Salend, S. J., 14
Salisbury, C. L., 34, 227
Sameroff, A. J., 520, 521
Sandow, D., 561, 562–563, 569, 575

Sapon-Shevin, M., 598
Sarber, R. E., 494
Sasso, G. M., 235
Savage, M., 232
Scanlon, K., 345
Schaeffer, R. M., 404
Schafer, D. S., 533
Scheu, J. A., 465
Schladenhauffen, J., 491, 494
Schleien, S. J., 422, 434
Schnorr, R., 124, 448, 453–455, 471–472, 473, 475
Schoen, S. A., 150, 159
Scholl, G. T., 341
Schor, D. P., 10
Schoultz, B., 605, 606
Schroeder, C. S., 299
Schroeder, S. R., 299
Schubert, D., 280
Schulein, M., 335
Schuler, A. L., 269, 270, 301
Schussler, N., 239
Schuster, J. W., 501, 502, 503
Schwartz, I. S., 547
Schwarz, P., 92
Schweigert, P., 274
Scipien, G. M., 359, 364
Scruggs, T. E., 467
Sears, C. J., 59, 60, 64
Sevcik, R. A., 272, 275
Shafer, M. S., 24, 491
Shalock, R. L., 606
Shane, H., 277, 278
Sharpley, C. F., 401
Shea, T. M., 66
Sheldon, J. B., 604, 605
Shellhaas, M., 115
Sherman, J. A., 604, 605
Sherry, P. J., 390
Shevin, M., 241
Shores, E. F., 217
Shores, R. E., 235
Short, R. J., 533–534
Siegal, M., 467
Siegel-Causey, E., 133, 241, 266, 269, 282–284
Sigafoos, J., 271, 279
Silverman, F. H., 275, 278
Simeonsson, R. J., 533–534
Singer, G. H. S., 51, 67, 68, 71–72
Singh, J., 456
Singh, N. N., 450, 456
Singh, Y., 450–451
Sisson, L. A., 404
Sizer, T. R., 593
Skelly, M., 274
Skinner, B. F., 300
Skrotsky, K., 338
Skrtic, T. M., 593, 598
Slavin, R. E., 250
Slentz, K. L., 97, 527
Sloop, E. W., 395
Smeets, P. M., 452, 453, 454, 456, 457, 473
Smiley, L., 266
Smith, B., 299
Smith, D. L., 445
Smith, L. J., 445
Smith, M., 505
Smith, M. S., 594
Smith, P. S., 395
Smith, S. W., 86, 98, 107
Smithdas, R., 11
Smith-Davis, J., 63
Sneed, T. J., 401
Snell, M. E., 12, 20, 21, 22, 23–24, 34, 42, 51, 74, 135, 145, 151, 197, 198, 214, 225, 226, 330, 387, 388, 395, 397, 402, 403, 404, 406, 410, 411, 412–413, 444, 445, 483, 484, 487, 497, 501
Snyder, P. M., 444, 467, 468
Sobsey, D., 58, 59, 60, 61, 64, 65, 72, 74, 75, 77, 325, 338, 339, 340, 341, 355, 361–362, 363, 367, 381, 390, 394, 402, 406, 408, 502, 504
Solbrack, M., 273
Solman, R. T., 450
Solnick, J. V., 300
Solow, J., 567
Song, A. Y., 390
Sowers, J., 24, 499, 557–558, 559–561, 564, 565, 566
Sparrow, S. S., 115
Spencer, K. C., 570
Spengler, P., 300
Spradlin, J. E., 284–285
Sprague, J. R., 13, 172, 178, 184, 304, 310, 497, 498
Stahl, S. A., 466
Stainback, S., 73, 223, 226, 228, 232, 237, 436, 600–601, 602, 608–609
Stainback, W., 73, 223, 226, 228, 232, 237, 436, 600–601, 602, 608–609
Stanfield, J. S., 483–484
Stanley, J. C., 49
Stark, J. A., 606
Stave, K., 421
Stayton, V., 543
Steele, D. M., 217
Steere, D., 554
Stein, J. I., 387–388
Stern, F. M., 338
Stern, R. J., 414
Sternat, J., 59, 60, 254
Sternberg, L., 269, 290–291
Stettner-Eaton, B. A., 235–236
Stillman, R. D., 274, 290
Stock, J. R., 534
Stokes, T. F., 171, 172, 173, 174, 175, 179–181, 240
Storey, K., 304, 310, 495, 561, 575
Strain, P. S., 34, 226, 235, 345
Strathe, M., 446
Strickland, B. B., 87
Striefel, S., 473
Strully, C., 14, 22, 226, 435
Strully, J., 14, 22, 226, 435
Struth, L., 355
Sullivan, C. A. C., 14, 22–23
Sutherland, A. T., 605
Svinicki, J., 534
Swain, S., 14
Swanson, H. L., 235

Tarrant, K. L., 596–597
Tawney, J. W., 50
Taylor, J. C., 314
Taylor, J. M., 357, 380
Taylor, M., 365–366
Taylor, S. J., 606
Taylor, W. S., 357, 380

Test, D. W., 504–505, 567
Theimer, K., 269, 270
Thompson, B., 290, 355, 365–366
Thompson, L., 567
Thomson, H. B., 379
Thorpe, M. E., 226
Thousand, J. S., 34, 48, 49, 228, 232
Thvedt, J. E., 155–156
Tines, J., 567
Touchette, P. E., 302, 306, 495
Trace, M. W., 470
Tremblay, A., 235
Trivette, C. M., 68, 524, 525, 528–529, 530–532
Trohanis, P. L., 517, 518
Trott, M. C., 395
Troutman, A. C., 145, 161, 189, 198
Tu, J. B., 17
Turnbull, A. P., 67, 87
Turnbull, H. R., 67, 299
Twardosz, S., 537
Twardzik, G., 575

Udell, T., 541
Udvari-Solner, A., 92
Ullmann, L. P., 300
Uptmor, E., 290
Utley, B., 345–346

Vacc, N. A., 462–463
Vacc, N. N., 462–463
Valcante, G. C., 451
Van den Pol, R. A., 495
Vandercook, T., 103, 104, 105, 228, 236, 237, 248, 421, 422
Vanderheiden, C. G., 274
Van der Houven, J. E., 453, 456, 457
Van Dijk, J., 11, 290, 350
Van Etten, C., 385
Van Etten, G., 385
Van Hasselt, V. B., 404
Van Lieshout, R. W., 473
Van Wagenen, R. K., 395
VanWalleghem, J., 509
Veerhusen, K., 161
Veitch, V. D., 470
Veltum, L., 304
Verhoven, P. J., 422
Verstegen, D., 570–572
Villa, R. A., 228, 232
Vincent, L. J., 34, 547
Vitello, S. J., 14, 22–23
Voeltz, L. M., 227, 236–237, 250, 420, 421, 422, 423–424
Vogelsberg, R. T., 499
Vogelsberg, T., 274
Volkmar, F. R., 8
Vollmer, T. R., 305

Wacker, D. P., 427, 494
Walberg, H. J., 477, 598, 599–600
Walker, D. K., 355
Walker, R., 94
Walker, V., 268, 278
Walls, R. T., 155–156
Walsh, B. F., 458
Wang, M. C., 477, 598, 599–600
Ward, M. E., 341
Ware, W. B., 533–534
Warren, S. F., 284–285, 285–286, 287–288, 338, 350
Watson, D. J., 464, 465–466
Watson, L. S., 395
Weatherman, R. F., 115
Weed, K. A., 143
Weeks, M., 299
Wehman, P., 24–25, 93, 94, 95, 422, 553, 555, 557, 568–569, 573, 574, 576–584
Wehmeyer, M., 604
Welch, J., 494, 499
Welsh, R. D., 346
Wesolowski, M. D., 404
West, M., 24
West, R. P., 404
Westlake, C. R., 50, 519
Westling, D. L., 12, 17, 23–24, 51, 72, 73, 76, 77, 112, 172, 174–175, 177, 178, 210, 338, 367, 385, 387, 393–394, 484, 485, 487, 488, 490, 510
Wetherby, A. M., 266, 267, 268, 269, 271, 278
White, O. R., 172, 173, 174–175, 176, 177, 178, 181–184, 198, 209, 210, 214, 305
Whitehurst, C., 404, 405
Whitley, P. F., 495
Whitman, T. L., 13
Whitney, R., 404
Whitten, T., 73
Wiggins, B., 427
Wilcox, B., 13, 34, 51, 94, 118, 119, 123, 125, 172, 178, 184, 186–187, 401, 409, 420, 502, 504
Wildonger, B. A., 497
Wilkinson, A., 436
Will, M., 93
Willard, C., 269, 270
Williams, D. G., 73, 608
Williams, F. E., 395
Williams, J. A., 178, 491, 499
Williams, P., 605, 606
Williams, R., 20, 21, 51, 74
Williams, W., 34, 48, 49, 51, 228, 232, 233, 244, 245, 274, 451–452, 456, 499, 606, 607
Wills, M., 598
Wilson, P. G., 393
Winterling, V., 314
Winton, P. J., 97
Wnek, L., 534
Wolery, M., 50, 144, 145, 147, 148, 152, 156, 157, 158, 162, 163–164, 165–166, 298, 449–450, 503, 519–520
Wolf, M. M., 395
Wolfensberger, W., 33, 483, 606
Wolff, S., 228
Wolfgang, C. H., 542
Wolfgang, M. E., 542
Wolf-Schein, E. G., 338, 339, 340, 341
Wolfson, B. J., 465
Wolraich, M., 17, 19
Wong, D. L., 374, 379
Wong, S. E., 304
Wood, M., 555
Wood, R., 554
Wood, S., 355
Wood, W., 24–25, 94
Woodcock, R. W., 115, 275
Worrall, N., 450–451
Writer, J., 290, 291, 350
Wuerch, B. B., 420, 422, 423–424

Wunderlich, R. A., 410
Wurzberger, P., 349

Yale Research Group, 519
Yoder, P. J., 284–286
Yonclass, D., 268, 278
York, J., 34, 57, 60, 103, 104, 105, 113, 117, 228, 237, 248, 254, 271, 279, 284, 325, 326, 329–330, 331, 332, 334, 335, 336, 421
York, R., 34, 326, 450, 451–452, 456
Young, K. R., 404
Yousef, M. J., 358

Zane, T., 155–156
Zarcone, J. R., 305
Zawolkow, E., 274
Zeaman, D., 450
Zeiler, M. S., 390, 393
Zigler, E., 519
Zingo, J., 252
Zirpoli, T. J., 605, 606
Zwernik, K., 99–103, 319

SUBJECT INDEX

AAMD Adaptive Behavior Scales, 115
AAMR. *See* American Association on Mental Retardation (AAMR)
A-B-C analysis, 129, 305–306. *See also* Antecedents, behavioral
ABR. *See* Auditory Brainstem Response (ABR)
Absence seizures, 17, 360
Academic skills instruction, 443–446. *See also* Reading skills
  assessment, 134–137
  basic arithmetic concepts, 467–470
  money handling, 470–473, 494, 495, 497, 498, 507
  in regular classroom, 476–478
  time management, 473–475
  whole language approach, 464–467
  writing, 460–464, 466
Acquired Immune Deficiency Syndrome (AIDS). *See* HIV/AIDS
Activities, leisure. *See* Leisure and recreation skills
Activities Catalog, The, 119, 123
Activity-based instruction, 252, 521, 535–536, 538–539
Activity compatibility plans, 244, 245–247
Adaptations
  and community skills instruction, 484–485, 490
  for dressing skills, 405–406
  in early childhood instruction, 537, 543
  and employment skills, 564
  for leisure activities, 433–434
  for sensory impairments, 340–341, 350
Adaptive behavior
  alternatives, 319
  defined, 116
Adaptive behavior scales, 113–118
Adaptive instruction model, 477
Addition, 468, 469
Aggression, 299
Alcoholism, 17
Alternative communication systems, 272–273
  aided, 274–278, 280
  gestural, 273–274
  mode selection, 278–280
American Association on Mental Retardation (AAMR), Diagnostic and Classification System, 4, 5–9
American Sign Language, 274
Americans with Disabilities Act (ADA) (P. L. 101–336), 47–48, 434, 592
Amer-Ind, 274
Ameslan, 274
Anecdotal recording, 129
Anger, in parents, 69, 71
Annual goals, in Individual Educational Plans, 88–90
Antecedent prompt and fade, 158
Antecedent prompt and test, 157–158
Antecedents, behavioral, 145, 302, 308. *See also* Cues; Prompts; Stimuli
  A-B-C analysis, 129, 305–306
  and generalization, 176–178
  strategies for change, 313–314
Anticonvulsant medications, 367
Applied settings, for teaching reading, 458–460
ARC. *See* Association for Retarded Citizens (ARC)
Arithmetic skills, 476
  basic concepts, 467–470
  money handling, 470–473, 494, 495, 497, 498, 507
  time management, 473–475
Arts and crafts, 423, 542
Assessment, 36, 38, 59. *See also* Direct measurement; Evaluation
  academic skills, 134–137
  Activities Catalog, 119, 123
  adaptive behavior scales, 113–118
  behavior categories for, 141–142
  Choosing Options and Accommodations for Children, 118–120, 125
  and communication skills, 132–134, 268–272
  Community Living Skills, 119, 121
  of community skills, 491–492
  for curriculum types, 135–137
  direct observation, 128–132, 305–308, 309–310
  of dressing skills, 402–404
  in early intervention, 533–534
  ecological, 125–128, 271–272, 421–422
  and family plan, 527, 528–532
  of hearing loss, 339–340
  indirect, 214–218, 304–305
  of motor skills, 132–134
  and parent interviews, 112–113
  portfolio, 217–219
  of problem behaviors, 303–305

Assessment, *continued*
direct observation, 305–308, 309–310
hypothesis development and testing, 308, 311–312
of recreational preference, 422–425
of related skills, 132–134
for supported employment, 574–575
example, 576–584
Syracuse Community-Referenced Curriculum Guide, 119, 121–122, 124–125
and transdisciplinary team model, 60–62
of vision, 341–344
Assessment, Evaluation, and Programming System (AEPS) Measurement for Birth to Three Years, 533
Assistance method, to inhibit preempting, 282
Associated skills. *See* Related skills
Association for Persons with Severe Handicaps, The (TASH), 3, 45
Association for Retarded Citizens (ARC), 94
Asymmetrical Tonic Neck Reflex (ATNR), 328–329
Ataxia, 16
Athetosis, 16, 331, 333–334
Atrioventricular canal, 17
Attainment Company, 460
Attendant option, in employment, 570
Atypical postures, 329–330
Atypical sensorimotor response, 327–328
Audiologists, 76
Auditory Brainstem Response (ABR), 340
Auditory system, 326. *See also* Hearing impairments
Augmentative communication systems, 272–273
aided, 274–278
gestural, 273–274
mode selection, 278–280
Autism, 6, 8–11, 280
Aversive consequences, 301
Awareness training, as school inclusion strategy, 229–231

Backward chaining approach, for dressing, 404–405
Baseline data, 130, 208
Battelle Developmental Inventory, 534
Bayley Scales of Infant Development, 534
Bedwetting, 401
Behavioral maintenance. *See* Maintenance
Behavioral objectives. *See* Objectives
Behavioral programming approach, for motor disabilities, 338
Behavioral regulation, as communication function, 267–268
Behavioral Seizure Observation Record, 363
Behaviors, types of, 131–132, 141–142, 198–199. *See also* Problem behaviors; Skills, teaching
Bell, Terrel, 593
Best practices, 33–38, 42–43, 51–52
in assessment, 36, 38
for community-based instruction, 39–40, 42
in curriculum and instruction, 39, 41
for early intervention and preschool, 37–38, 39
empirical research for, 49–51
and legal mandates, 45–48
professional consensus regarding, 48–49
and related services, 40–41, 43
for school placement, 38, 40
for social integration, 41–42, 44
social values as basis for, 43–45
Bird feeding, 387
Blissymbols, 275
Blocks, 541
Body mechanics, 331–332. *See also* Motor disabilities
Brain injury, 10
Brief contingent restraint, 317
Brown, Lou, 33–34
Bus riding skills, 500

Calculators, use of, 471–472, 495
Camping, 423
Carbamazepine, 361
Cardinality, 468
Cardiovascular disorders, 17–18
Carolina Curriculum for Infants and Toddlers with Special Needs, 533
Carolina Record of Individual Behavior, 533–534
Catheterization, 377–378
CAT scan. *See* Computerized Axial Tomography (CAT scan)
Celontin. *See* Methsuximide
Center-based programs, for early childhood education, 530–531
Centers for Disease Control, 356
Central Auditory Disorders, hearing loss, 339
Cerebral palsy, 15–16, 369
Challenging behavior. *See* Problem behaviors
Chapter 1 programs, 599
Choice-making, 241, 604–605, 606–607, 609
to inhibit preempting, 282
leisure, 427–428
Choosing Options and Accommodations for Children (COACH)
and assessment, 118–120, 125
and Individual Educational Plans, 104–107
CIC. *See* Clean intermittent catheterization (CIC)
"Circle of friends" process, 238
Civil rights, 44–45, 47–48
Classroom health care, 355–356
catheterization, 377–378
dental, 358–359

feeding, 370–374, 375
handwashing, 357
HIV/AIDS, 378–381
ileostomy and colostomy, 376–377, 379
incontinence and toileting, 357–358
and Individual Education Plan, 381
medication, 367–368
nutrition, 368–370
passive range of motion, 364–367
postural drainage, 364
seizure management, 359–364
skin conditions, 363–364
tracheostomy, 374–376, 377
universal precautions, 356–357
Classrooms. *See also* Inclusive education
early childhood, 537, 541–543, 547–548
effective, 595–598
Clean intermittent catheterization (CIC), 377
Cleft palate, 369
Clinical/medical models, 59
CLS. *See* Comprehensive Local School (CLS)
COACH. *See* Choosing Options and Accommodations for Children (COACH)
Coactive movement level, in Van Dijk method, 290
Cognitive development, and autism, 10–11
Coleman report, 594
Collaboration, 57–58, 64–65, 80–81, 325–326, 505. *See also* Transdisciplinary teams
and classroom health care, 356, 381
and daily living skills, 386–387
and early childhood instruction, 531, 532
and instructional programming for multiple disabilities, 337
interagency, 531–533
interdisciplinary team model, 59–60, 61
multidisciplinary team model, 58–59, 61
with paraprofessionals, 77–80
parent-teacher, 65–69
offering help to parents, 69–72
and positioning, 334–335
and school inclusion, 231–233
between teachers and other professionals, 72–77
Colostomy, 376–377, 379
Commercial reading programs, 458
Communication, teacher-parent, 68–72
Communication boards, 275–276
Communication books, 275
Communication disorders specialists, 74
Communication functions observation tool, 307–309
Communication Intention Inventory, 269
Communication Interview, 269, 270
Communication Programming Inventory, 269
Communication skills, 272–273, 510
aided systems, 274–278, 280
assessment, 132–134, 268–272
conversational training, 289–290
designing instructional strategies, 284
development, 265–268
facilitated communication, 280
functionally equivalent, 317–318
generalization, 291–292
gestural systems, 273–274
and inclusive education, 226
instructional interaction styles, 281–282
interrupted chain strategy, 288–289
naturalistic teaching procedures, 284–288, 291
and nonsymbolic learners, 282–284
selection of alternative/augmentative communication system, 278–280
sign language, 273–274, 285
and telephone use, 507
Van Dijk method, 290–291
Communicative temptations, 269, 271
Community-based instruction, 39–40, 42, 488–490, 509–510. *See also* Community skills instruction; Natural settings
grocery stores, 494–495
and inclusion, 252
partial participation in, 484–485
pedestrian skills, 499–500
public transportation skills, 499–500
restaurants, 495–497
settings listed, 493
simulated settings in schools, 490–491
vending machines, 497–499
Community-intensive instruction, and Comprehensive Local School plan, 603
Community involvement, as school inclusion strategy, 233
Community leisure/recreation activities, 426, 434–435
Community living, and Comprehensive Local School plan, 603–604
Community Living Skills (assessment tool), 119, 121
Community skills instruction, 483–487, 492–493, 494. *See also* Community-based instruction; Domestic skills instruction
and Comprehensive Local School Plan, 603
concurrent in-school instruction, 491
developing instructional plans, 487–488
evaluating skills, 491–492

Community skills instruction, *continued*
funding for, 492
and generalization, 488, 498
learning potential for, 23–24
Community work experience, for older students, 560–561
Commutativity principle, 468–469
Compensatory education, 517
Complex-chained behavior, 131, 141–142, 198, 205, 209
Complex partial seizures, 17
Comprehensive Local School (CLS), and educational reform, 601–604
Computerized Axial Tomography (CAT scan), 359
Concrete materials, in arithmetic instruction, 469–470
Concurrent school/community instruction, 491
Conductive hearing loss, 339
Conflict resolution skills, 437
Congenital heart disease, 17
Consequences. *See* A-B-C analysis; Reinforcement
Constant time delay, 151–152, 449, 503
Consultation therapy model, 63
Context clues, and oral reading, 457–458
Contingencies. *See* Reinforcement
Continuous assessment, 197. *See also* Direct measurement
indirect measurement, 214–217
portfolio, 217–219
Continuous-ongoing behaviors, 131, 141–142, 198
Controlling prompts, 164, 503
Controlling stimuli, defined, 150–151
Conversational skill training, 289–290
Cooperative learning, 249–250, 251–252, 476
Core team, 65
Cornelia de Lange syndrome, 19, 299
Correction procedures, 163–164
Counting word sequence, 467–468
CPR, for individuals with tracheostomies, 376
Crafts, 423
Criterion of ultimate functioning, 34
and community skills, 491–492
and reading instruction, 459
Critical effect, 132
Cues, 132, 148, 151, 160–161, 240–241. *See also* Antecedents, behavioral; Prompts; Stimuli
attending to, 12–13
for community and domestic skills, 487–488, 494, 504
verbal, 316
for writing, 462–463
Cultural activities, 423
Cultural values, and quality of life, 608
Cumulative programming, 188
Current performance levels, in Individual Educational Plans, 88
Curriculum
and best practices, 39
levels for academic skills instruction, 444–445
multilevel, 477
overlapping, 477
reform in, 593–594
types of, 135–137
Curriculum-based assessment, in early intervention, 533
Curriculum infusion, as school inclusion strategy, 231, 232
Curriculum overlapping strategy, 477
Cytomegalic inclusion disease, 19, 356

Daily living skills, 485–487. *See also* Domestic skills instruction
developing objectives, 386–387
dressing, 401–402, 406–409
assessment, 402–404
instructional strategies for, 404–406
grooming, 409–415
dental care, 409–413
menstrual care, 413–414
learning potential for, 22–23
mealtime, 387–388, 393–394
toileting, 394–401
determining readiness, 394–395
pretraining data collection, 395–396, 397
steps in training, 396, 398–400
Daily log, 69, 215
DAP. *See* Developmentally appropriate practice (DAP)
Data collection and recording, 112. *See also* Assessment; Observation
baseline, 130, 208
duration measures, 204
for evaluating community skills, 491
event recording, 199–200
during generalization, 209–210
graphing, 210–214
incident records, 215, 217, 218
during instruction, 208–209
latency measuring, 203–204
momentary time sampling, 202
partial interval recording, 200–202
rate measures, 200
task analytic recording, 205–208
whole interval recording, 204–205
Deaf-blind students. *See* Dual sensory impairments
Decision rules
for generalization strategies, 181–184
for selecting communication modes, 278–280
Deferred imitation level, in Van Dijk method, 290
Deficit-remediation model, 59–60
Deinstitutionalization, 23, 33
Delay, time, 151–153, 281, 286–287, 449
and error correction, 163–164

Dental care, 358–359, 409–413
Depakene. *See* Valproic Acid
Design strategy ideas, for vocational preparation, 566
Developing nurturance strategy, 282–284
Developmentally appropriate practice (DAP), 535
Developmentally Appropriate Practice in Early Childhood Programs Serving from Birth through Age 8, 534–535
Dextroamphetamine (Dexedrine), 361
Diazepam, 361
Differential reinforcement, 146, 314–315
Differential Reinforcement of Alternative behavior (DRA), 315
Differential Reinforcement of Incompatible behavior (DRI), 315
Differential Reinforcement of Low rates of behavior (DRL), 315
Differential Reinforcement of Other behavior (DRO), 314–315
Dilantin. *See* Phenytoin
Dimensions, attention to, 12–13
Diplegia, 16
Directions, verbal, 146, 151
Direct measurement, 197–202, 491
  data collection, 208–210
  duration measures, 204
  graphing, 210–214
  of latency, 203–204
  momentary time sampling, 202–203
  task analytic recording, 205–208
Direct observation, 128–132, 199. *See also* Data collection and recording
  of problem behavior, 305–308, 309–310
Direct service strategy, 62, 562–563
Discrepancy analysis, 127–128
Discrete behaviors, 199
Discriminative stimuli, 145–146
Distal antecedents, 308
DISTAR Reading Program, 458
Distributed practice, 190, 240
Domestic skills instruction, 484–488, 492–493. *See also* Daily living skills
  food preparation, 501–504
  household chores, 504–505
  telephone use, 505–508
Domestic Training Site (DTS), 486
Down syndrome, 17, 19
DRA. *See* Differential Reinforcement of Alternative behavior (DRA)
Dramatic play, 541–542
Dressing skills, 401–402, 407–409
  assessment of, 402–404
  instructional strategies for, 404–406
  and students with more severe disabilities, 406–407
DRI. *See* Differential Reinforcement of Incompatible behavior (DRI)
Drinking from a cup, 388, 390
DRL. *See* Differential Reinforcement of Low rates of behavior (DRL)
DRO. *See* Differential Reinforcement of Other behavior (DRO)
Drugs. *See* Medication
Dual diagnosis, 15
Dual sensory impairments, 11–12, 350
Duration measures, 204
Duration of services, in Individual Educational Plans, 92
Dynamic positioning, 334
Dyskinesia, 16

Early childhood instruction, 517–519, 534–535. *See also* Early intervention; Individual Family Service Plans (IFSPs); Special education
  activity-based, 521, 535–536, 538–539
  age groups compared, 522–523
  developmentally appropriate practice, 535
  environments, 529–531, 537, 541–543, 547–548
  family-centered approach, 521, 524–529
    Family Needs Scale, 530–532
  and inclusion, 543–545
  naturalistic teaching procedures, 536, 537, 540
  transactional approach, 520–521
  transition, 545–548
Early intervention, 18, 37–38, 39, 529–530. *See also* Early childhood instruction
  assessment, 533–534
  efficacy, 519
  goals of, 519–520
  infant, 95–97, 543, 545
  in motor problems, 329
  teaming, 531–533
Early Intervention Developmental Profile, 533
Eating problems and skills, 18, 370–372, 387–390, 393–394. *See also* Nutrition
  and appropriate mealtime behaviors, 391–393
  tube feeding, 372–374, 375
  using utensils, 390–391
Ecological inventories, 125–128
  and communication, 271–272, 278–280
  and recreational activities, 421–422
Ecological strategies, for behavior problems, 313
Edmark Reading Program, 458
Edmonds, Ron, 594
Educational philosophies and reform, 31–33, 593–595. *See also* Best practices; Inclusive education; *specific legislation*
  effective schools and classrooms, 594–598
  merging special and regular education, 600–601, 602

Educational philosophies and reform, *continued*
special education, 598–604, 608–609
Comprehensive Local School Plan, 601–604
Education for All Handicapped Children Act (P. L. 94–142), 32, 46, 59, 86, 87, 553. *See also* Individual Educational Plans
and early childhood, 517, 520
and inclusive education, 224
Education of the Handicapped Act Amendments of 1986 (P. L. 99–457), 46–47, 95–97, 517, 520, 521. *See also* Individual Family Service Plans
and assessment, 527, 533
and transition, 545, 546
EEG. *See* Electroencephalogram (EEG)
Effective classrooms, 595–598
Effective schools, 594–595
Electroencephalogram (EEG), 359
Electronic devices, use of, 278
Electronic mail, 69
Electronic Travel Aids (ETAs), 350
Elementary school, and vocational preparation, 558
Eliminative approach, to problem behavior, 300–301
Embedded-functional curriculum, 136–137, 248, 445
Embedded sight words, 450–451
Empirical research, as basis for best practices, 49–51
Employment skills, 557, 561–564. *See also* Supported employment
community work experience, 560–561
evaluating employment outcomes, 585
job design, 564, 565–566
potential for, 24–25
vocational preparation, 557–560
Empowerment, 524
Enablement, 524
Enclaves work model, 568–569
Encoding, 277
Enhancing sensitivity strategy, 282–284
Entertainment. *See* Leisure and recreation skills
Entrepreneurial work model, 569
Enumeration, 468
Environments
for early childhood instruction, 529–531, 537, 541–543, 547–548
and school inclusion, 234
Epilepsy, 16–17, 359
Error correction procedures, 163–164
ETAs. *See* Electronic Travel Aids (ETAs)
Ethnographic research, 50
Ethosuximide, 361
Evaluation. *See also* Assessment; Direct measurement
of community skills, 491–492
of employment outcomes, 585
Individual Educational Plans, 92–93
of paraprofessionals, 79–80
Event recording, 199–200
Exemplars, multiple, 173, 174–175, 177, 178, 180, 240
Expectations, appropriate, 144
Extensive support, 6
External validity, 50
Extracurricular activities, 425–426

Facilitated communication, 280
Facilitating interactions, as school inclusion strategy, 233–237
Fading
and employment skills instruction, 561, 564
and reading instruction, 450
Fair Labor Standards Act (FLSA), 561
Family-centered approach, 273. *See also* Individualized Family Service Plans; Parents
early childhood instruction, 521, 524–529
Family Needs Scale, 530–532
as school inclusion strategy, 233
Family Prioritization Interview, 106
FAOF. *See* Functional Analysis Observation Form (FAOF)
Fax machines, 69
Feedback, 144
Feeding. *See* Eating problems and skills
Finger-feeding, 388
Fingerspelling, 274
First aid, 509
5- and 10- frames, 469, 470
Fixed interval, 190
Fixed ratio, 190
FLSA. *See* Fair Labor Standards Act (FLSA)
Fluency criterion approach, 174
Food and drink, as reinforcers, 162
Food preparation, instructional process for, 501–504
Forward chaining approach, for dressing, 404–405
Friendships, 14, 22, 226, 236–238, 435–437. *See also* Peers; Social skills
Functional Analysis Observation Form (FAOF), 308, 310
Functional approach, and eliminative approach distinguished, 300–303. *See also* Problem behaviors
Functional curriculum, 444–445
Functionally equivalent communication skills, 317–318
Functional routines, 131–132, 141–142, 198, 205, 209
Functional skills, 135
and generalization, 174, 176, 180
and inclusive education, 239–240, 248
writing, 460–461
Functional vision checklist, 342
Functional Vision Training, 345–346
Funds, for community instruction, 492

Games, 423, 452, 456
Gastroesophageal (GE) reflux, 18
Gastrostomy tube feeding, 373–374, 375
General case approach, 174–175, 177, 178, 184–189
General case programming approach, 178
General education curriculum, 135–136
General education curriculum, adapted, 136
General educators, collaboration with, 73
Generalization, 13, 90, 171–172, 179–181
  of communication skills, 291–292
  of community and domestic skills, 488, 498, 505
  of daily living skills, 386, 505
  data collection during, 189, 198, 209–210
  decision rules, 181–184
  general case approach, 174–175, 177, 178, 184–189
  and leisure skills, 428
  strategy effectiveness, 175–179
  teaching strategies for, 172–175
  writing instructional programs for, 191–193
Genetic scare, 32
Gestural communication, 273–274
Gestural prompts, 147–148
Goals. *See* Objectives
Graduated guidance, 158
  for dressing skills, 405
  for toothbrushing, 410
Grand mal seizures. *See* Tonic-clonic seizures
Graphs, 210–214
Greer by Greer v. Rome City School District, 224, 225
Grocery stores, as instructional settings, 494–495
Grooming skills, 409, 414–415
  dental care, 409–413
  menstrual care, 413–414
Group experimental designs, 49–50
Group placement, in employment, 568–569
Growth impairments, 19
Guidance, 146–147
  graduated, 158, 405, 410
Gustatory system, 326

Handicapped Infants and Toddlers Program (P. L. 99–457), 95, 96, 97
Hand-washing, 357
Hawaii Early Learning Profile, 533
Head Start, 517–519, 544–545
Health and Human Services, U.S. Department of, 356
Health care. *See* Classroom health care
Hearing impairments, 339–341, 350
Hemiplegia, 16
Herpes, 356
Heterogeneous groupings, 34, 509
Higher-order learning, classroom conditions for promoting, 596–597
High school, and vocational preparation, 558–561
Hills and valleys, in assessment, 116, 118
History, of early childhood special education, 517–519
HIV/AIDS, 356, 378–381
Hobbies, 423
Holistic treatment, 12
Holland v. Sacramento City School District, 224, 225
Home-based programs, 530–531
Homogeneous groupings, 34, 509
Household chores, 504–505
Human Immunodeficiency Virus (HIV). *See* HIV/AIDS
Hydrocephaly, 19
Hyperactive gag, 372
Hypertonia, 328
Hypotheses development and testing, about problem behavior, 308, 311–312
Hypotonia, 328

ICS. *See* Individualized Curriculum Sequencing Model (ICS)
IDEA. *See* Individuals with Disabilities Education Act (IDEA)
Idiosyncratic behaviors, 267
IEP. *See* Individual Educational Plans (IEPs)
IFSP. *See* Individual Family Service Plans (IFSPs)
Ileostomy, 376–377, 379
Illocutionary stage, 266–267
Imitation, 146
Immediate consequences, 319
Inadequate portions method, to inhibit preempting, 282
Inappropriate social behavior, 299–300. *See also* Problem behaviors
Incidental learning, 13
Incidental teaching procedure, 288
Incident record, as indirect measurement, 215, 217, 218
Inclusive education, 223–225, 238–239
  benefits of, 225–228
  case studies, 254–257
  and Comprehensive Local School plan, 603
  and Head Start, 544–545
  implementing, 250–252
  and individualized instruction, 241–244
  individualized support, 252–254
  instructional arrangement principles for, 239–241
  model for, 228–229
  and peer interaction, 248–250
  regular classroom instructional arrangements, 244–248
  and social patterns, 592–593
  and young children, 543–545
Incontinence, 357–358
Increasing opportunities strategy, 282–284

Indirect assessment, 214–218, 304–305
Indiscriminable contingencies, 173, 176, 178, 180
Individual Educational Plans (IEPs), 46, 85–86, 521, 615–620
annual evaluation, 92–93
and assessment, 36
and Choosing Options and Accommodations for Children, 104–107
and classroom health care, 381
current performance levels, 88
goals and objectives, 88–90
and inclusive settings, 226, 228
and Individual Family Service Plans, 95–96
initiation and duration of services, 91–92
parental involvement in, 66–67
placement, 90–91
and related services, 41, 90
requirements for, 87–88
and transition, 93, 547–548
Individual Education Program (IEP), 533
Individual Family Service Plans (IFSPs), 41, 46, 85, 95–97, 107, 631–645
and assessment, 36, 527, 528–532, 533
and family involvement, 67, 521, 525–529
and transition, 545, 546, 547
Individualized Curriculum Sequencing Model (ICS), 239
Individualized support, 253–254
Individual placement model, 568
Individual student planning teams, 232–233, 244, 246–247
Individuals with Disabilities Education Act (IDEA) (P. L. 101–476), 47, 87, 93, 533. *See also* Individual Family Service Plans
and inclusion, 224, 225, 592
transition services, 553–554
Individual Transition Plans (ITPs), 36, 85, 93–95, 555–557, 621–630
and Choosing Options and Accommodations for Children, 107
and Comprehensive Local School plan, 603
Individual tutoring, 477
Infant Learning: A Cognitive-Linguistic Intervention Strategy, 533
Infants and toddlers, 95–97, 543, 545. *See also* Early intervention
Infectious disease, in classroom, 378–381
Initial contacts
and Individual Family Service Plan, 527
for supported employment, 571
Initiation of services, and Individual Educational Plans, 91
Institutionalization, 32
Instructional activities. *See* Activity-based instruction
Instructional arrangements. *See* Inclusive education
Instructional materials. *See* Materials
Instructional objectives. *See* Objectives
Instructional plans. *See* Plans
Instructional programming, for multiple disabilities, 337–338, 346–350
Instructional strategies. *See also* Academic skills instruction; Early childhood instruction; Prompts; Reading skills; Reinforcement
communication skills, 281–291
conversational skill training, 289–290
interrupted chaining, 288–289
naturalistic procedures, 284–288, 291
Van Dijk method, 290–291
for daily living skills, 404–406
for employment skills, 561–564
for generalization, 172–175, 179–180
effectiveness of, 175–179
good general practices, 144–145
for leisure skills, 428–431
naturalistic teaching method, 284–288, 291, 536, 537, 540
for skill maintenance, 189–191
Instructional universe, and general case approach, 184–185
Insurance issues, 509
Integrated programming, for multiple disabilities instruction, 338
Integrated therapy approach, 62
Integrated work, and Comprehensive Local School plan, 603–604
Integration, 223, 603. *See also* Inclusive education
Intelligence quotient (IQ), 4–6, 16, 25
Intentional communication, 266–268
Interaction style, in communication skills instruction, 281–282
Interactive assessment, in early intervention, 534
Interactive style, of futures planning, 100
Interdisciplinary team model, 59–60, 61
Intermittent reinforcement, schedules of, 190
Intermittent support, 6
Internal validity, 49–50
Interrupted chain strategy, 288–289
Interval recording
partial, 200–202
whole, 204–205
Intervention. *See* Early intervention; Problem behaviors
Introduce natural maintaining contingencies approach, 173, 176, 178

IQ. *See* Intelligence quotient
ITP. *See* Individual Transition Plans (ITPs)

Jaw clenching, 370
Jaw instability, 370–371
Jaw retraction, 370
Jaw thrust, 370
Job coaches, 569, 573, 575
Job Design Analysis Form, 565
Job development, in supported employment, 570–573
Job sharing, 569
Joint attention, as communication function, 267–268
Journals, 69
Judgment-based assessment, in early intervention, 533–534
Juvenile rheumatoid arthritis, 19

Kindergarten, 517, 547–548

Labor, U.S. Department of, 561
Language experience approach, 461–462
Language skills. *See also* Communication skills; Reading skills
  and autism, 10
  potential for, 20–21
  writing, 461–464, 466, 494
Large-group lesson approach, 252
Latency measuring, 203–204
Law of effect, 161
Learned behaviors, 146
Learning characteristics, of severely disabled people, 12–14
Learning potential, of severely disabled people, 19–25
Least restrictive environment (LRE), 46
Least-to-most assistance
  for dressing skills, 405
  for toothbrushing, 410–411
Legal mandates. *See also specific laws*
  as bases for best practices, 45–48
  for inclusive education, 224–225
Leisure, defined, 419
Leisure and recreation skills
  activities, 419–422, 425–427, 433–434, 438
  assessing preference, 422–425
  choice-making, 427–428
  community opportunities, 426, 434–435
  instructional methods, 428–431
  learning potential for, 23
  partial participation, 431–433
  social interaction and friendships, 428, 429–431, 435–437
Lesch Nyhan syndrome, 299
Liability, 509
Lifestyle understanding
  and assessment of problem behaviors, 303–304
  and behavior intervention plans, 319–320
Limited academic curriculum, 444–445
Limited English proficiency programs, 599
Limited support, 6
Lip closure, 371
Lip retraction, 371
Literacy instruction. *See* Reading skills
Location, of academic instruction, 446
Long-term prevention strategies, 319
Low tone child, carrying of, 334
Luminal. *See* Phenobarbital

Mainstreaming, 223. *See also* Inclusive education
  and Comprehensive Local School plan, 603
  and early childhood instruction, 544–545
  reverse, 434, 544–545
Maintenance, 171, 189–193
Maladaptive behaviors, 180
Managing time, 473–476
Mand-model procedure, 287–288
Manipulatives, and early childhood instruction, 542
Manual blocking, 316
MAPS. *See* McGill Action Planning System (MAPS)
Materials, 34, 36
  for arithmetic instruction, 469–470
  for community skills, 484–485, 490
  for dressing skills, 405–406
  early childhood, 537, 543
  modifying, 158–160
Maternal Behavior Rating Scale, 534
McGill Action Planning System (MAPS), 103–104
Mealtime skills. *See* Eating problems and skills
Mebaral. *See* Mephobarbital
Mediate generalization approach, 174
Medication, 367–368
  seizure, 17, 360, 361, 362, 367
Memory, 13
Menstrual care, 413–414
Mental disabilities. *See also* Academic skills instruction
  categories of, 4–6
  and cerebral palsy, 16
  support systems for, 6–9
  and vocational skills, 25
Mental illness, 15
Mentor, in natural support employment model, 569
Mephobarbital, 361
Methsuximide, 362
Middle school, and vocational preparation, 558
Milieu teaching procedures (naturalistic), 284–288, 291, 536, 537, 540
Minorities, and discrimination, 33
Mixed cerebral palsy, 16
Mixed hearing loss, 339
Mixed prompts, 150
Mobility skills, for visually impaired, 346–350

Model prompts, 149
Momentary time sampling, 202
Money skills, 470–473, 494
 and pay phones, 507
 in restaurants, 495–497
 and vending machines, 498
Monitoring therapy model, 62–63
Monoplegia, 16
Morphology, 274
Most-to-least prompting, 156–157, 289–290
Motion, passive range of, 364–367
Motivation Assessment Scale, 305
Motor disabilities. *See also* Motor system; Positioning and handling students
 and diet, 369–370
 and feeding, 370–374
 instructional programming, 337–338
 skills assessment, 132–134, 136
Motor system
 movement, 329–330, 332–333
 muscle tone, 327, 328
 posture, 329–330
 primitive reflexes, 328–329
Multi-agency teams, and early childhood instruction, 531–532
Multicomponent behaviors, 198–199, 205–208, 209
Multicultural antibias curriculum, 230–231, 537
Multidisciplinary team model, 58–59, 61
Multilevel curriculum strategy, 477
Multiple baseline design, 50
Multiple disabilities, 12. *See also* Motor disabilities; Positioning and handling students
 assessment for curriculum, 136
 and collaborative teaming, 325–326
 and dressing, 406–407
 dual sensory, 11–12, 350
 instructional programming for, 337–338
 and sensory systems, 326–328
Multiple exemplars, 174–175, 177, 178, 180, 240
Muscle tone. *See* Motor system; Positioning and handling students
Myelomeningocele, 19
Mysoline. *See* Primidone

N + 1 > N Rule, 468
Nasogastric tube feeding, 372–373
National Commission on Excellence in Education, 593
Nation at Risk, A, 593
Natural cues, 132, 148, 151, 160–161, 240–241. *See also* Antecedents, behavioral; Cues; Prompts; Stimuli
 for community and domestic skills, 487–488, 494, 504
Natural gestures level, in Van Dijk method, 290–291
Naturalistic observation, 50
Naturalistic teaching procedures, 284–288, 291
 for early childhood, 536, 537, 540
Natural reinforcers, 132, 173, 176, 178, 180, 240–241
Natural settings, training in, 34, 174, 177, 178, 241, 458–459. *See also* Community-based instruction
Natural supports employment model, 569–570
Nature study, 423
NDT. *See* Neurodevelopmental Treatment (NDT)
Neonatal Intensive Care Unit (NICU), 545, 546
Network of support, and futures planning, 102–103
Neurodevelopmental Treatment (NDT), 337–338
New skills. *See* Skills, teaching
Next dollar strategy, 472
NICU. *See* Neonatal Intensive Care Unit (NICU)
Nondisabled peers, 226–228, 509, 510. *See also* Peers
Nonrepresentational reference level, in Van Dijk method, 290
Nonsymbolic communication, 282–284
Normalization, 23, 33, 385, 387–388, 483–484
Norm-based assessment, in early intervention, 534
Numberline system, 470–471, 495
Nursery school, 517
Nurturance level, in Van Dijk method, 290
Nutrition, 368–370. *See also* Eating problems and skills

Oberti v. Board of Education of Clementon School District, 224–225
Objectives, 39
 for community and domestic skills, 486, 497, 504
 for daily living skills, 386–387
 and ecological inventories, 126
 functional, 174, 176, 180, 248
 and instructional plan writing, 164–165
 for leisure instruction, 425–428
 for regular classrooms, 247–248
 selecting, 141–144
 short-term, 88–90
Observation. *See also* Data collection and recording
 baseline, 130, 208
 direct, 128–132, 199, 305–308, 309–310
Observational learning, 13, 146
Occupational therapy, 73–74, 510
Olfactory system, 326
Operant learning, 145–146
Operational skills, for community and domestic instruction, 486–487
Oral reading, 455–458
Order irrelevance principle, teaching arithmetic, 468
Orientation and mobility skills, for visually impaired, 346–350

Out of reach method, to inhibit preempting, 282
Overgeneralization, 188
Overlearning skills, 189–190

Parallel learning activities, 477
Paraplegia, 16
Paraprofessionals, collaboration with, 77–80
Parent Behavior Progression, 534
Parents, 36, 38, 65–67. *See also* Family-centered approach
  and inclusive education, 233
  and student assessment, 112–113
  support for, 67–72
Partial interval recording, 200–202
Partial participation, 143–144, 248
  in community skills instruction, 484–485
  in leisure skills, 431–433
Partial seizures, 359, 360
Passive range of motion, in classroom, 364–367
Pay phones, 507
Peabody Individual Achievement Test-Revised, 136
Pedestrian skills, 499–500
Peer instruction approach, 252
Peer-mediated interventions, 235
Peer partners, 289
Peers, 226–228. *See also* Inclusive education; Social skills
  and community skills, 496, 508
  and cooperative learning, 249–250, 251–252
  and friendships, 14, 22, 226, 236–238, 435–437
  and leisure skills, 428, 429–431, 435–437
  and partial participation, 248
  programs involving, 235–238, 289
  strategies for facilitating interactions with, 233–238
People First, 437
Percussion, 364
Perlocutionary stage, 266, 267
Personal futures plans, 36, 99–103
Personal profile, in futures planning, 100
Personal-social characteristics, of severely disabled persons, 14–15
Pervasive support, 6
Phenobarbital, 362
Phenytoin, 362
Philosophy. *See* Educational philosophies and reform
Phonics. *See* Word analysis skills
Physical characteristics, of severely disabled people, 15–19
Physical cues, 316
Physical disabilities, 15–18. *See also* Motor disabilities; Positioning and handling students
Physical fitness activities, 423, 426–427
Physical prompts, 149–150
Physical therapy, 73–74, 134, 510
Physicians, collaboration with, 76–77
Picsyms, 275
Pictorial prompts, 148–149
Pictures, and oral reading, 457–458
Placement, school, 38, 40, 90–91
Plans, 36, 38, 85–87. *See also* Individual Educational Plans; Individual Family Service Plans
  alternative approaches to, 97–99
  Choosing Options and Accommodations for Children, 104–107
  for community and domestic skills instruction, 487–488
  family involvement, 66–67, 103, 106, 233
  for generalization and maintenance, 191–193
  McGill Action Planning System, 103–104
  personal futures, 36, 99–103
  transdisciplinary team, 60–62, 86–87
  transition, 36, 85, 93–95, 107, 555–557, 603
  writing of, 164–165
Portfolios, assessment, 217–219
Positioning and handling students, 333–337
  body mechanics, 331–332
  facilitating posture and movement, 329–330, 332–333
  during feeding, 372
  transfer, 358
Positive practice, and oral reading, 456
Postural drainage, 364
Posture. *See* Positioning and handling students
Prader-Willi syndrome, 369
Preempting, 281–282
Preschool, 37–38, 39, 546–547. *See also* Early intervention; Infants and toddlers
Pressure sores, 364
Prevention strategies, in behavior intervention plans, 318–319
Previewing material, and oral reading, 456
Primidone, 362
Primitive reflexes, 328–329
Privacy
  and daily living skills, 386
  during toileting, 357–358
Probe testing, general case approach, 187–189, 198, 209–210
Problem behaviors, 297–298
  direct observation assessment, 305–308, 309–310
  functional and nonfunctional approaches contrasted, 300–303
  and functionally equivalent communication skills, 317–318
  hypothesis development and testing, 308, 311–312
  indirect assessment, 304–305
  intervention planning, 318–320
  intervention strategies, 313–317
  lifestyle understanding, 303–304, 319–320
  types of, 298–300

Professional collaboration. *See* Collaboration
Professional consensus, as basis for best practices, 48–49
Profound mental disabilities, and adaptive behavior scales, 118
Program common stimuli approach, 173–174, 177–178
Progressive time delay, 152–153, 164, 449
Project SHaRE (Source of Help Received and Exchanged), 68
Prompts. *See also* Antecedents, behavioral; Cues; Stimuli
  antecedent prompt and fade, 158
  antecedent prompt and test, 157–158
  and communication skills, 284–289
  and community and domestic skills, 487–488
  for dental care, 410–411
  for dressing skills, 405
  and error correction, 163–164
  and food preparation, 503
  graduated guidance, 158, 405, 410
  most-to-least, 156–157, 289–290
  and reading instruction, 449–450, 452–455
  system of least, 153–156, 449–450
  target and control stimuli contrasted, 150–151
  and time delay procedures, 151–153, 163–164, 281, 286–287, 449, 503
  types of, 147–150
Proprioceptive system, 326
Prosthetic devices, 316, 490. *See also* Adaptations
Psychotropics, 367
Public access law, 48
Public Law 94–142. *See* Education for All Handicapped Children Act; Individual Educational Plans
Public Law 99–457. *See* Education of the Handicapped Act Amendments of 1986; Individual Family Service Plans
Public Law 101–336 (Americans with Disabilities Act), 47–48, 434, 592
Public Law 101–476. *See* Individuals with Disabilities Education Act
Public schools. *See* Schools
Public transportation skills, 499–500
Pull-out model, 59
Punishment procedures, for problem behavior, 316–317
Pursing, 371
Pyramid Scales, 115

Quadriplegia, 16
Qualitative research, 50
Quality of life, 554–555, 606–608, 610

Radiation, 17
Rafael Oberti v. Board of Education of Clementon New Jersey, 224–225
Rate measures, 200
Reading areas, in early childhood classrooms, 542–543
Reading skills, 448, 458–460
  for community settings, 494–499
  individual sight words, 447, 448–451
  oral reading from books, 455–458
  targets, 446–447
  whole language approach, 464–467
  word analysis, 451–455, 456
Rebus symbols, 275
Recording. *See* Data collection and recording
Recreation, defined, 419. *See also* Leisure and recreation skills
Reform. *See* Educational philosophies and reform
Regular-adapted curriculum, 248, 444
Regular education
  academic skills instruction in, 476–478
  instructional arrangements for inclusion, 244–248
  placement, 38, 40, 90–91
  special education merged with, 600–601, 602
Regular Education Initiative, 599–600, 609
Reinforcement, 161–163
  differential, 146, 314–315
  in employment skills instruction, 561
  and generalization, 173, 176, 178, 180, 184
  intermittent, 190
  natural, 132, 173, 176, 178, 180, 240–241
  and problem behaviors, 301, 314–317, 319
Related services, 40–41, 43, 90–91
Related skills
  assessment of, 132–134
  in community and domestic skills instruction, 487
  and toilet training, 399
Relevant behavior, 180
Relevant stimulus, in general case approach, 185–187
Residential programs, 94
Resonance level, in Van Dijk method, 290
Respiratory disorders, 18
Respite care, 67
Response exemplars. *See* Exemplars, multiple
Response interruption procedures, 316
Response prompts. *See* Prompts
Response variation, in general case approach, 185–187

Restaurants, as instructional settings, 495–497
Reverse mainstreaming, 434, 544–545
Rigid cerebral palsy, 16
Role-playing, in telephone use, 508
Role release, 62–63
Routines. *See* Functional routines
Rubella, 10, 11, 19

Sabotage method, to inhibit preempting, 281
Safety issues, during toileting, 358
Sand and water play, 542
Scales of Independent Behavior, 115
Scanning, 277
Scatter plot method, 305–308
Schedule
  of community instruction, 489
  of student activities, 214–215, 216
School administrators, 76
School nurses, 75
School psychologists, 75
School reform movement. *See* Educational philosophies and reform
Schools. *See also* Inclusive education
  accountability of, 593
  community-based instruction policies, 509
  community skills instruction in, 484–485, 490–491, 495, 496–497
  effective, 594–595
  and leisure skills instruction, 425–426
  nursery, 517
  placement in, 38, 40, 90–91
Scoliosis, 19
Segregation of severely disabled students, in community-based instruction, 509–510
Seizures, 145
  classification of, 16–17, 359–360
  classroom management of, 359–364
  medication, 17, 360, 361, 362, 367
Self-advocacy, 605–607, 610
Self-care. *See* Daily living skills
Self-determination, 604–605, 606–607, 609
Self-injurious behaviors, 298–299
Self-regulation, 13–14, 609–610
Self-stimulation, 11
Sensorineural hearing loss, 339
Sensory impairments, 338–339
  dual, 350
  hearing, 339–341, 350
  vision, 341–346
    orientation and mobility skills, 346–350
Sensory integration, for multiple disabilities programming, 337
Sensory systems, 326–328
Sequenced functional skills curriculum, 135–136
Sequencing experiences strategy, 282–284
Sequencing teaching examples, in general case approach, 188–189
Sequential modification approach, 172–173
Setting event strategies, 313
Severe disabilities, defined, 3
Severely disabled people, 3–4
  behavioral characteristics of, 3
  learning characteristics of, 12–14
  learning potential of, 19–25
  personal-social characteristics of, 14–15
  physical characteristics of, 15–19
  societal issues regarding, 591–592, 604–610
Sexual relations, 14
Shared writing approach, 462
Sheltered work. *See* Supported employment
Short-term objectives, Individual Educational Plans, 88–90
Short-term prevention procedures, 318–319
Sight words, teaching, 447, 448–451
Sign language, 273–274, 285
Simple-discrete behaviors, 131, 141–142, 198
SIOS. *See* Social Interaction Observation System (SIOS)
Skill clustering, 239, 240, 243–244
Skill generalization. *See* Generalization
Skills, teaching, 144–145, 165–167, 171–172. *See also* Generalization; Prompts; *specific skills*
  error correction, 163–164
  instructional programs, 164–165
  learning paradigm, 145–147
  and learning potential, 20–25
  maintenance, 171, 189–193
  modifying stimulus materials, 158–160
  natural cues, 160–161, 240–241, 494, 504
  objectives, 141–144
  and reinforcement, 132, 146, 161–163, 184, 190, 561
Skill synthesis, 13
Skin conditions, classroom care of, 363–364
Sleeper effect, Head Start, 519
Social integration, 41–42, 44. *See also* Inclusive education; Peers; Social skills
Social interaction, as communication function, 267–268
Social Interaction Observation System (SIOS), 236, 250
Social skills, 428, 487. *See also* Peers
  appropriate for the community, 495–497
  learning potential for, 21–22
  and supported employment, 575, 577–578, 585
  task analyses for, 429–431
  and telephone use, 508

Social values, as bases for best practices, 43–45
Social workers, 74–75
Societal issues. *See* Educational philosophies and reform
Somatosensory system, 326
Spasticity, 15, 333
Special education, 598–599, 608–609. *See also* Early childhood instruction; Early intervention
  characteristics of, 35–36
  Comprehensive Local School Plan, 601–604
  contemporary best practices, 33–35
  placement in, 91
  Regular Education Initiative, 599–600
  regular education merged with, 600–601, 602
Special educators. *See also* Teachers
  and collaboration, 72–73
  inclusion role of, 253–254
Special Friends program, 236–237
Special Olympics, 437
Special schools, placement in, 91
Speech/language therapists, 74
Speech pathologists, 74
Spina bifida, 19
Sports, 423, 426–427
Static positioning, 334
Stereotypic behaviors, 298, 425
Stimuli, 12–13, 145–146. *See also* Antecedents, behavioral; Cues; Prompts
  and generalization, 173–174, 177–178, 180–182, 184, 185–187, 210
  shaping and fading, 159–160
  target and controlling contrasted, 150–151
Streamlined curriculum, 444
Student Interest Inventory, 422, 424
Student schedule, as indirect measurement, 214–215, 216
Subtraction, 468, 469
Supervision, of paraprofessionals, 78–79
Supported employment, 24–25, 94, 564, 567
  job development, 570–573
  situational assessment, 574–575
    example, 576–584
  and social skills, 575, 577–578, 585
  work models, 567–570
Support personnel, and individualized support, 253–254
Support systems, 6–9, 67–68
  futures planning, 102–103
Support team, 65
Symbols
  in aided systems, 274–278
  and reading instruction, 450–451, 453–455, 457–458
Symmetrical Tonic Neck Reflex (STNR), 328–329
Syntax, 274
Syphilis, 19
Syracuse Community-Referenced Curriculum Guide, The, 119, 121–122, 124–125
System of least prompts, 153–156, 449–450

Tactile defensiveness, 327
Tangible-Reinforcer Operant-Conditioning Audiometry (TROCA), 340
Target sites, 486
Target skills. *See* Objectives
Target stimuli, defined, 150–151
TASH. *See* Association for Persons with Severe Handicaps, The (TASH)
Task analyses, 126, 131, 205–208
  for community skills, 494, 496
  for employment skills, 561, 562
  for social skills, 428, 429–431
Task direction, and time delay, 151–153
Task pool, for vocational preparation, 559–560
Teacher mediation, as school inclusion strategy, 234
Teacher modeling, as school inclusion strategy, 231
Teachers
  attitudes of, 31, 35
  collaborating with other professionals, 72–77
  collaborating with parents, 65–69
    offering help to parents, 69–72
  implications of societal issues for, 608–610
  special educators, 72–73, 253–254
  transdisciplinary team role of, 60, 62
Teacher-student interactions, in community instruction, 488–489
Teaching Skills Inventory, 534
Teams. *See* Collaboration; Transdisciplinary teams
Team teaching, 509
Tegretol. *See* Carbamazepine
Telephone use, 505–508
Testing. *See* Assessment
Therapeutic management. *See* Classroom health care
Thinner schedule of reinforcement, 161
Time, telling, 473–474
Time delay, 151–153, 286–287, 503
  and error correction, 163–164
  to inhibit preempting, 281
  and reading instruction, 449
Time management, 473–476
Time-out, 317
Toileting, 357–358
Toilet training, 394–399, 400–401
  associated skills, 399
  independent toilet use, 399–400
  pretraining data collection, 395–396, 397
Tongue protrusion, 371
Tongue retraction, 371
Tonic bite reflex, 371

Tonic-clonic seizures, 16–17, 359–360
Tonic Labyrinthine Reflex (TLR), 328–329
Toothbrushing, 358–359, 409–413
Toxoplasmosis, 19
Toys, and early childhood instruction, 543
Tracheal suctioning procedure, 377
Tracheostomy, 374–376, 377
Train and hope approach, 172, 175–176, 178
Train in the natural setting approach, 174, 177, 178
Train loosely approach, 173, 177, 178
Train sufficient exemplars approach, 173, 177, 178
Train to generalize approach, 174, 176
Transactional approach, to teaching young children, 520–521
Transdisciplinary approach, to health-care services, 355–356
Transdisciplinary teams, 60–65, 91
  professional, 72–77
  professional/paraprofessional, 77–80
Transition, 36, 85, 93–95, 107
  and Comprehensive Local School plan, 603
  for families with young children, 545–548
  from school to employment, 553–557
Travel training, for visually impaired, 346–350
TROCA. *See* Tangible-Reinforcer Operant-Conditioning Audiometry (TROCA)
Tube feeding, 372–374, 375
Typewriters, use of, 463–464

Universal precautions, 356–357
Usher's syndrome, 11
Utilizing movement strategy, 282–284
Uzgiris-Hunt Infant Psychological Development Scale, 533

Valium. *See* Diazepam
Valproic Acid, 362
Valued life outcomes, 104
Van Dijk method, 290–291
Variable interval, 190
Variable ratio, 190
Vending machines, 497–499
Verbal cues, 316
Verbal directions, 146, 151
Verbal prompts, 148
Verbal reprimand, 316
Verbal skills. *See* Communication skills
Vestibular system, 326, 327
Vineland Adaptive Behavior Scales, 115
Vision impairments
  assessment, 341–344
  correction, 344–345
  and dual impairments, 350
  functional training, 345–346
  orientation and mobility skills, 346–350
Vision specialists, 75–76
Visual prompts, and word analysis, 452–455
Visual Reinforcer Auditory (VRA), 339–340
Visual stimulation, 345
Visual system, 326
Vocational rehabilitation, 95
Vocational skills. *See* Employment skills
VRA. *See* Visual Reinforcer Auditory (VRA)

Wait training, 164
Whole interval recording, 204–205
Whole language instruction, 464–467
Whole task approach, for dressing, 404
Word analysis skills, 451–455, 456
Word processors, 463
Word wheels, 452, 456
Work crews, work model, 568–569
Work models, supported, 567–569
Writing skills instruction, 461–464, 466, 494

Zarontin. *See* Ethosuximide
Zero degree inference strategy, 34